Individual and Society

Sociological Social Psychology

Unlike other texts for undergraduate sociological social psychology courses, this text presents the three distinct traditions (or "faces") in sociological social psychology (symbolic interactionism, social structure and personality, and group processes and structures) and emphasizes the different theoretical frameworks within which social psychological analyses are conducted within each research tradition. With this approach, the authors make clear the link between the "face" of sociological social psychology, theory, and methodology. Thus, students gain an appreciably better understanding of the field of sociological social psychology; how and why social psychologists trained in sociology ask particular kinds of questions; the types of research they are involved in; and how their findings have been, or can be, applied to contemporary societal patterns and problems. Great writing makes this approach successful and interesting for students, resulting in a richer, more powerful course experience. In addition, a website offers instructors high quality support material, written by the authors.

Lizabeth A. Crawford, PhD, is an Associate Professor of Sociology in the Department of Sociology and Social Work at Bradley University.

Katherine B. Novak, PhD, is a Professor of Sociology and Chair of the Department of Sociology and Criminology at Butler University.

Kimberly

TITLES OF RELATED INTEREST FROM ROUTLEDGE

The Senses in Self, Society, and Culture
A Sociology of the Senses
By Phillip Vannini, Dennis Waskul, Simon Gottschalk

Sticky Reputations
The Politics of Collective Memory in Midcentury America
Edited by Gary Fine

Sex/Gender
Biology in a Social World
By Anne Fausto-Sterling

Identity Problems in the Facebook Era
By Daniel Trottier

Individual and Society

Sociological Social Psychology

Lizabeth A. Crawford &
Katherine B. Novak

Routledge
Taylor & Francis Group

NEW YORK AND LONDON

First published 2014
by Routledge
711 Third Avenue, New York, NY 10017

and by Routledge
2 Park Square, Milton Park, Abingdon, Oxon OX14 4RN

Routledge is an imprint of the Taylor & Francis Group, an informa business

Library of Congress Cataloging-in-Publication Data
Crawford, Lizabeth.
   Individual and society : sociological social psychology / Lizabeth Crawford, Katherine Novak.
      pages cm
   1. Social psychology.   2. Social psychology—Research.   I. Novak, Katherine B.
II. Title.
   HM1033.C73   2014
   302—dc23
   2013024955

ISBN: 978-0-415-88986-5 (hbk)
ISBN: 978-0-415-88987-2 (pbk)
ISBN: 978-1-315-85652-0 (ebk)

Typeset in Stone Serif
by Apex CoVantage, LLC

Printed and bound by Courier in Westford, MA

To my family
LC

To Mark, Anna, Matthew and Oscar
KN

BRIEF TABLE OF CONTENTS

DETAILED TABLE OF CONTENTS

PREFACE

Social psychology is a subfield of study that bridges psychology, with its focus on individual perception and behavior, and sociology, with its emphasis on linking individual thought and action to broader social structures. Almost all of the social psychological literature is research based. Thus, the field of social psychology has been defined largely by the research studies it has generated.

Most social psychology textbooks are psychological in orientation and do not discuss research by sociological social psychologists. Of those social psychology textbooks that are sociological in orientation, most focus solely on symbolic interactionism (one type of sociological social psychology) and the qualitative research conducted within this tradition. There are some other, more comprehensive, social psychology textbooks written by sociologists. However, these books either have a strong psychological bent or are topical in orientation and minimize the distinctions between different theoretical frameworks within sociological social psychology and the kinds of studies they have generated. They emphasize breadth over depth of coverage.

WHAT MAKES THIS BOOK UNIQUE

This book is broad in its scope and has been designed to reflect the diverse nature of research within sociological social psychology. At the same time, it emphasizes depth of understanding. To this end, each chapter includes detailed examples and illustrations of the concepts, theories, methodologies, and types of social psychological research covered.

There are three distinct research traditions (or "faces") of social psychology within contemporary sociology—symbolic interactionism, social structure and personality (House 1977), and group processes and structures (Berger 1992; Harrod, Welch, and Kushkowski 2009).

Symbolic Interactionism (SI): Social psychological research conducted within the symbolic interactionist tradition focuses on face-to-face interactions in natural settings and on the ways in which meanings are socially constructed.

Social Structure and Personality (SSP): This variant of sociological social psychology focuses on the link between the statuses people occupy (e.g., their gender, race/ethnicity, and social class) and their opportunities, aspirations, feelings, beliefs, and behaviors.

Group Processes and Structures (GPS): Studies within this research tradition focus on perception and behavior in small group encounters and on relations between groups. Because these studies are sociological in orientation, they emphasize the effects of societal characteristics on the nature and content of people's interactions in group settings.

Unlike other textbooks on sociological social psychology that recognize these distinctions, we have organized the initial set of chapters by research tradition (the faces of sociological social psychology), rather than by topic, and emphasize the different theoretical frameworks within which social psychological analyses are conducted within each orientation. We also make clear the link between the face of sociological social psychology, theory, and methodology.

Qualitative research (favored by symbolic interactionists) and quantitative research (used by sociological social psychologists working within SSP and GPS) serve very different purposes. We provide a more detailed discussion of the difference between these two kinds of research than other textbooks and identify when and why particular methods are used by sociological social psychologists. Here, and throughout the rest of the book, we give examples of both classic and contemporary studies from within each of the three faces of sociological social psychology so that students gain a full understanding of the diverse nature of research in the field. Throughout the text, we illustrate how different theoretical perspectives have guided research within sociological social psychology and emphasize the strong empirical basis of this field of study.

As we describe the different faces of sociological social psychology and the research they have generated, we emphasize core sociological ideas and their applications. At various points in each chapter, we ask students to step back from the academic discussion to consider how particular theoretical perspectives and concepts within a given face of sociological social psychology apply to their personal experiences or to the lives of others.

Once students have learned about the three faces of sociological social psychology, the breadth of the research they have generated, and how they can be applied to everyday situations, we discuss the utility of integrating research from across traditions when studying particular topics. We view this as toward the end, rather than as the starting point, of the learning process. By beginning with the foundations of each of the three research orientations or faces, and their unique foci, this book is structured to provide students with an in-depth and thorough understanding of the field of sociological social psychology; how and why social psychologists trained in sociology ask particular kinds of questions; the types of research they are involved in; and how their findings have been, or can be, applied to contemporary societal patterns and problems.

Although this book does not focus on psychological social psychology, we discuss some classic studies within this tradition that are relevant to the topics and issues addressed by sociological social psychologists. Moreover, by making clear the distinction between sociological and psychological social psychology in our introductory chapter, we show how the research questions asked, and answered, by social psychologists working within all three research orientations within sociological social psychology (SI, SSP, and GPS) reflect the key themes of their home discipline.

In general, the book's chapters are cumulative in their organization, such that theoretical frameworks, concepts, and methods that appear early on in the text are revisited and applied in the later chapters. In teaching our social psychology courses, we have found that this integrated approach to knowledge building works well, especially when it comes to the discussion of theories and research findings that are complex or in opposition to common ways of viewing the world.

FEATURES

This book has a number of features that can be used either in or outside of the classroom to enhance students' understanding of research within sociological social psychology and how it pertains to people's everyday lives. At various points within each chapter there are individual and group exercises that facilitate the application of social psychological perspectives, methodologies, and research findings. In many chapters, we also present news articles that discuss, or illustrate, the concepts and studies covered.

In addition, throughout the book, we have embedded standard measures of key social psychological concepts for students to complete within the text. Benchmark scores from one or more studies within the literature are included, with which students can compare their own results.

Providing samples of commonly used measures is a strategy we have found to be effective in cultivating student interest in the field and in increasing their understanding of the relevance of social psychological research to their lives. The measures presented in the book include the Twenty Statements Test (Kuhn and McPartland 1954), the Public Self-Consciousness Scale (Fenigstein, Scheier, and Buss 1975), the Rosenberg Self-Esteem Scale (Rosenberg 1965), the Embarrassability Scale (Modigliani 1966), the Passionate Love Scale (Hatfield and Sprecher 1986), and the Color-Blind Racial Attitudes Scale (Neville et al. 2000), as well as measures of perspective taking (Davis 1980), social support (Turner and Turner 2005), relationship commitment (Sprecher 1988), attitudes toward divorce (Amato and Rogers 1999), and delinquency (Harris 2009).

Finally, each chapter ends with a set of questions for review and reflection, designed to help students to synthesize, apply, and critically evaluate the material presented in the chapter. These questions are relatively broad in focus and are thus appropriate for group discussion, as well as for exam preparation.

GOALS OF THE BOOK

Because sociological social psychology focuses on social relationships and why people think and act as they do, it is inherently interesting. The goal of this book is to introduce students to this field of study and to the wealth of information about social life it provides. In acknowledgment of the diversity of the field, its methods, and applications, this book is also designed to:

- familiarize students with the three faces of sociological social psychology and the kinds of research they have generated;

- illustrate the utility of applying multiple perspectives, and methods, to particular topics;

- introduce students to the social psychological literature pertaining to a number of topics of interest to sociologists;

- facilitate students' abilities to apply social psychological perspectives and findings to various issues and social problems; and

- provide students with the tools needed to analyze their own experiences from a sociological perspective.

Students, when the semester is over, and you have finished this book and your social psychology course, you might go back and think about this last statement. How has your perspective changed over the course of the semester? What have you gained from learning about sociological social psychology?

As you begin reading this book, you will see the relevance of sociological social psychology to yourself and the people with whom you share your life. As human beings, we balance multiple levels of expectations (self, others, societal) and plan patterns of action within this context. Sociological social psychology provides us with frameworks for identifying and understanding the nature of these expectations and their consequences. Thus, there is no field of study more relevant to our day-to-day experiences. Together, the three faces of sociological social psychology yield substantial insight into the nature of human social behavior at both a general and a personal level.

ACKNOWLEDGMENTS

We undertook the creation of this textbook out of a desire to present students with the knowledge and tools they need to more fully understand the social world in which they live. We wanted to develop a textbook that emphasizes theory, methods, and their applications. We owe a special thanks to the graduate faculty in sociology at Indiana University, Bloomington, for the excellent training we received in sociology there and for exposing us to a broad array of perspectives and methodological approaches.

Thanks to the editorial, production, and marketing staff at Routledge for all their help in the preparation of this book. With special thanks to Steve Rutter, for his guidance and support; to Margaret Moore, for her help with obtaining copyright permissions; and to Phyllis Goldenberg, who provided excellent editorial feedback.

We thank both Courtney Wickland and Yolanda Pennock, whose help with the creation of figures for the book was invaluable. We also want to thank the reviewers:

Leslie Irvine	University of Colorado, Boulder
Jessica Garcia	Michigan State University
Tiffiny Guidry	University of Alabama
Dominic Little	California State University, Northridge
Aya Kimura Ida	California State University, Sacramento
Linda Belgrave	University of Miami
David Marple	Loyola Marymount University
Eunice Bakanic	College of Charleston
Sarah Horsfall	Texas Wesleyan University
Medora W. Barnes	John Carroll University
Tiffani Everett	University of Georgia
Jennifer Dunn	Texas Tech University
Jill Kiecolt	Virginia Tech
Thomas Kersen	Jackson State University
Chien-Juh Gu	Western Michigan University
DeeAnn Judge	North Carolina State University
Devereaux Kennedy	Grand Valley State University

who read the text in its earlier versions for their insightful critiques and comments.

Finally, we would like to thank our families, friends, and colleagues. We are grateful for their continuous support as we moved from the inception of this book to its completion.

PART I

Theoretical Perspectives and Research
Methods in Sociological Social
Psychology

CHAPTER 1

What Is Sociological Social Psychology?

The following letters are from a recent Annie's Mailbox, a "life advice" column published daily in newspapers across the country.

Dear Annie: *I am fed up. Every time my family gets together, the women spend the entire time working while the men sit around and watch TV. I am so angry about this sexism that I am ready to stop attending these functions. I don't believe that women who work full-time jobs should be expected to slave away in the kitchen doing prep and cleanup, while the men show up, eat a delicious meal, and then relax on the couch. I've voiced my objections to my mother and sister, but while they agree with me, they do nothing to back up my request for help from my father and brother. My brother-in-law will give us a hand, but his son plays on the computer. What advice do you have for me other than to stop participating?*
—"On Strike"

Dear "On Strike": *If you want the menfolk to help out, you have to insist on it, since they obviously aren't considerate enough to do it voluntarily. Hand your nephew the silverware, and tell him to set the table. Give your brother the plates. Enlist your brother-in-law as an ally. Ask him to inform the guys that they will be clearing the table and putting leftovers away. Tell him it is good training for his son. Your mother and sister may still choose to do most of the work, but it's a start.*

What Do You Think?

- How do "On Strike's" family get-togethers compare with yours?
- Do you think "On Strike's" family is the same or different from most families in the United States? Explain.
- How do women and men learn what their roles are (what's expected of them) in family get-togethers?
- What advice would you give "On Strike"?

This book is an introduction to the field of social psychology from a sociological perspective. Social psychologists would say that the notion that men do not help with cooking and cleaning because they are inconsiderate is overly simplistic. Moreover, they would suggest that Annie's advice is not likely to be effective on a long-term basis. We will discuss the reasons for this in a later chapter. The point we want to make here is that the letter from "on Strike" presents the kind of social issue that social psychologists address in their research. Social psychological studies often provide substantial insights into the causes of common problems by placing them within the context of the larger society.

People rarely regard a particular individual's problems as a reflection of broader societal patterns. They are not trained to do so. This is why we need social psychology.

WHAT IS SOCIAL PSYCHOLOGY?

Social psychology is a field of study that focuses on understanding two kinds of phenomena: (1) the feelings, thoughts, and behaviors of individuals and (2) the relationship of these feelings, thoughts, and behaviors to the social context in which they occur. It is a field that bridges two disciplines: sociology and psychology.

Box 1.1　Have You Ever Wondered?

Social psychologists trained as sociologists ask the following kinds of questions. The chapter in which we provide an answer, based on a review of the relevant research literature, is indicated in parentheses after each question.

1. Should high school students have jobs? Do teenagers who work have different characteristics and experiences than teens without jobs? (Chapter 1)
2. Why don't college students talk more in class? (Chapter 3)
3. Most people don't like housework, so why do women do more of it than men do? (Chapter 4)
4. As a college student, you have probably worked on a number of group projects. Why do men talk more than women in these situations? (Chapter 5)
5. Whether people go to college is not necessarily related to how smart they are. What social factors make some high school students more likely than others to go on to college? (Chapters 4 and 6)
6. Have you ever done something that made you feel really guilty? When do people experience guilt, and how does this emotion influence our behaviors? (Chapter 8)
7. Do you know someone who partied a lot in high school? Why do some adolescents drink alcohol, use drugs, or skip school? (Chapters 1 and 9)
8. What causes stress? (Chapters 4 and 10)
9. Why does racial prejudice increase when the economy is bad? (Chapter 12)
10. What can people do to change the way society operates? (Chapter 13)

Note: The Sociological Abstracts, an electronic database with abstracts (summaries) of articles published in all national and some international sociology journals, is an excellent source of information on these and other topics of interest to social psychologists who are also sociologists. You should be able to access this database through your school's library.

Psychology focuses on the characteristics and behaviors of individuals. Social psychologists trained in psychology study individuals in group settings when trying to understand social behavior. Social psychologists trained in sociology also study individuals in groups, but they locate these groups within the context of the larger society. This shapes the kind of questions they ask about people and their social experiences (see Box 1.1). Sociologists, in general, focus on the ways that society influences our perceptions and behaviors.

SOCIOLOGICAL SOCIAL PSYCHOLOGY AND SOCIOLOGY

Don't worry if you haven't had a class in sociology. We cover what you need to know in the next page or so. We give a brief overview of the focus of the discipline of sociology and define some important concepts before we talk more in depth about sociological social psychology.

The Sociological Perspective

The **sociological perspective** is a way of viewing the world that places people's experiences within their social and historical context. Sociologists believe that forces outside of the individual (e.g., common patterns of thought and behavior within a given society) play a much larger role than idiosyncratic individual characteristics (e.g., personality) do in shaping behavior. The French sociologist Emile Durkheim (1895) called these broader societal patterns social facts. **Social facts** are properties of the collective environment that are not dependent upon the perceptions or behaviors of any one individual. Nonetheless, they shape people's behaviors. Social norms and stratification are important social facts in every society.

Social Norms

Social norms tell individuals how to behave, or not to behave, in specific situations. For example, social norms concerning appropriate style of dress within a society are not dependent on any one person's action, but they affect what people wear on any given day. Look around you. The students on your campus probably dress in somewhat unique ways. Some wear jeans and sweatshirts, whereas others prefer somewhat more formal attire, but probably not too formal. No one wears a ball gown or tuxedo to class. No one appears in public in underwear or naked. We don't even see these as options.

Social Stratification

Social stratification is another social fact that shapes people's lives in important ways. The concept of social stratification is based on the work of Karl Marx and others who have focused on conflict between different groups within society. Sociologists use the term **social stratification** to refer to the rank ordering of groups from low to high in terms of their access to important societal resources such as money, power, and prestige. Social stratification affects people's opportunities, perceptions, and behaviors. Contemporary sociologists are especially interested in the causes and consequences of social stratification.

The important dimensions of stratification in the United States and most other societies are social class, race and ethnicity, and gender. **Social class** reflects individuals' access to resources, including money and power. Social class is typically measured as **socioeconomic status**, or SES, using indicators of education, occupational prestige, and income.

A **race** is a group perceived as genetically distinct. We use the term *perceived* because race is not really a biological construct.

You might be thinking, but racial groups differ in visible physical characteristics (e.g., skin color, hair texture, and eye shape). How can you say that race is not biologically based when this is the case?

The answer is that these physical characteristics are not what defines race or makes it important within a society. What constitutes different racial groups, and the salience of race in people's lives, changes across social and historical contexts. Thus, who is considered a member of a particular racial group, and what this means, is socially rather than biologically determined (Bobo et al. 2012). Because they are socially constructed, definitions of race have changed substantially in the United States over time.

Take a Break

Go to the following Pubic Broadcasting Service (PBS) website for a timeline (Go Deeper: Race Timeline) showing changes in definitions of race in the United States: http://www.pbs.org/race/000_About/002_03_b-godeeper.htm. [Search Terms: PBS and explore the evolution of an idea]

Whereas race reflects perceived biological differences, ethnicity is rooted in perceived cultural differences. An **ethnic group** is a category of individuals perceived as distinct due to cultural characteristics, including customs, language, and a shared heritage.

Gender refers to how males and females are perceived within a given society. This is in contrast to **sex**, which refers to biological differences between males and females. Note that even though sex is biologically based, what criteria (e.g., genitalia) are used to establish sex and an individual's placement into the sex category male or female is socially determined (West and Zimmerman 1987).

Similarly, gender is a social construction because what it means to be male or female is tied to a particular cultural and historical context. The characteristics people associate with being male or female, and men's and women's respective duties and responsibilities (e.g., work outside of the home or housework), vary significantly across societies and over time within a given society.

Sociological social psychologists have argued that it is also useful to think of gender as an interactional accomplishment or production. When people act in a social encounter in a manner that is consistent with the societal expectations placed upon members of their sex category, they are **doing gender** (West and Zimmerman 1987).

The Individual in Society: Constraint and Agency

Sociologists are interested in the effects of inequalities associated with class, race/ethnicity, and gender on a variety of outcomes (behaviors, attitudes, and opportunities). They are also interested in the factors that perpetuate systems of stratification in any given society. This does not, however, mean that sociologists overlook the individual. Although sociologists emphasize **constraint** by studying how society shapes people's perceptions, feelings, and behaviors, they also recognize the dependence of society on individuals. It is only through social interaction that existing societal patterns are reproduced, and it is through social interaction that individuals reshape society (Giddens 1984).

People can and sometimes do act in unique and creative ways. Individuals' capacity to resist broader social forces and to act in a self-directed manner is called **agency**. Within any social setting, people make choices, which have the potential to shape the perceptions and behaviors of others (Blumer 1969). For instance, what happens when you decide to ask a question in class? First the professor comments, and then another student comments, and maybe another and another. As the interaction unfolds, the focus of the conversation is likely to change as one of many potential topics becomes the focal point of people's attention. The direction the conversation takes, and how the material being discussed is perceived, may reflect the unique characteristics or interests of the individuals present in the encounter.

MICRO VERSUS MACRO LEVELS OF ANALYSIS

A **unit of analysis** refers to what a researcher studies. A unit of analysis can be either **micro** (small) or **macro** (large). In micro-level studies, the unit of analysis is the individual. Psychologists often study how micro-level attributes (e.g., personality characteristics such as openness or conscientiousness) affect people's emotions and behaviors. Sociologists, on the other hand, conduct macro-level analyses that focus on aspects of society that exist above and beyond the individual, at the collective or aggregate level. The units of analysis in macro-level studies include the group, the county, the city, the state, the country, or the world. For example, sociologists have studied the relationship between divorce rates and suicide rates at the county, state, and societal level.

THE DIFFERENT FACES OF SOCIAL PSYCHOLOGY

In his classic 1977 article, the sociologist James House identifies what he refers to as the three "faces" of social psychology: psychological social psychology, symbolic interactionism, and social structure and personality. The latter two orientations are part of **sociological social psychology**.

Most social psychologists agree that House's description still holds true. However, since House published his article, a fourth face of social psychology has emerged: group processes and structures. This fourth face of social psychology encompasses research conducted mainly by sociologists (Berger 1992; Harrod, Welch, and Kushhowski 2009).

Each face of sociological social psychology highlights a different aspect of the relationship between individuals and society. Together, they help us understand a broad range of social phenomena and the thoughts and behaviors of others. They also serve as lenses through which we can view our own experiences. Thus, learning about the three faces of sociological social psychology and their applications should give you a new perspective on your life.

The different faces of social psychology are summarized in Figure 1.1. Note that the first face, **psychological social psychology (PSP)**, is included here only for comparative purposes because it deals only with individuals and is not part of

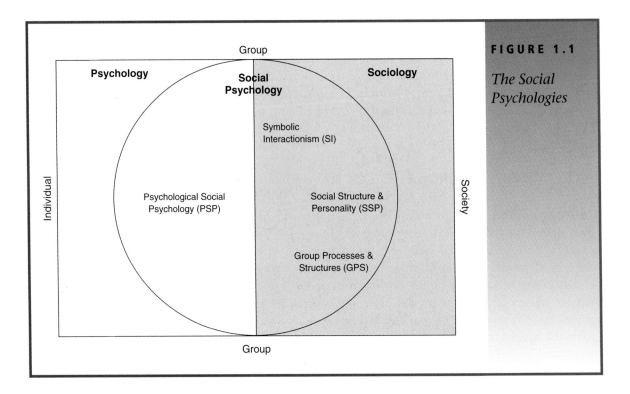

FIGURE 1.1

The Social Psychologies

sociological social psychology. Following are the three faces of sociological social psychology, and each will be covered in more depth in Chapters 3–5.

Psychological Social Psychology (PSP)

Social psychologists trained in psychology study individuals and work at the micro level. They use laboratory experiments to test the effectiveness of techniques designed to increase compliance, to identify the characteristics of effective group leaders, and to study how the presence of others influences people's behaviors. In general, these analyses emphasize individuals' perceptions of and reactions to immediate social situations.

Research on the Bystander Effect

Studies of the bystander effect provide an excellent example of research within psychological social psychology. As recounted by Cialdini (1988), the impetus behind this research was an incident that occurred in New York City in 1964. A woman, Kitty Genovese, was returning home from work late at night when she was attacked outside her apartment. Many neighbors heard her screams and observed the assault through their windows. When the attacker became aware that there were witnesses, he ran away. Despite what they had just observed, no one called the police. The assailant returned and killed Kitty Genovese.

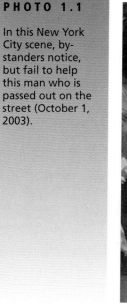

PHOTO 1.1

In this New York City scene, bystanders notice, but fail to help this man who is passed out on the street (October 1, 2003).

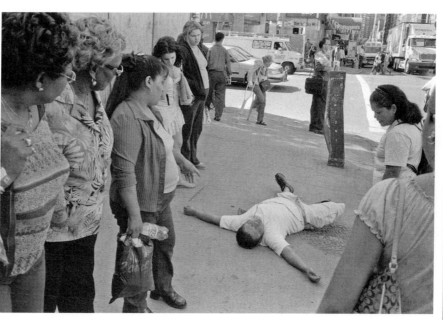

The general perception at the time of the incident was that people in urban areas do not care about their fellow human beings. Kitty Genovese's murder was considered evidence of this apathy. Two social psychologists trained in psychology, John Darley and Bibb Latané, were skeptical. They suspected that there was something about the situation—not urban apathy—that caused this event. In order to assess their view scientifically, they created a fake emergency in their laboratory. Then they observed the responses of subjects, who were led to believe that the situation was authentic (Cialdini 1988).

The results of their experiment, as well as those of a number of subsequent studies, suggest that the likelihood that a victim of an accident or an emergency will receive assistance decreases as the number of observers increases. Often help is offered, but it takes longer for witnesses to respond when others are present. When they are alone, most people will readily help someone in need of assistance. But when multiple people are present, the responsibility for helping is borne by all of them, which makes it relatively easy for each witness to do nothing and assume that others will take over. This process, called **diffusion of responsibility** may result in nobody helping or a substantial delay before assistance is given (Darley and Latané 1968a).

It is also likely that people have difficulty defining emergency situations, given their novelty. Is this really an emergency? Is offering help appropriate?

What do we do when we are not sure how to act? We look at others to see what they are doing. The problem is that the other people present are looking at us to see how we are responding (or, in the case of the Kitty Genovese incident, not responding). This results in a spiral of nonintervention. When people are confused and unsure of what to do in an emergency, they take others' inactivity as evidence that the situation does not call for any direct action. So, even if people are highly concerned about the victim, they may fail to act because others' inaction reinforces their perception that the situation does not require intervention (Darley and Latané 1968b).

What to Do in an Emergency

So, what should you do if you are a victim? You are in a public setting, you need help, and no one stops. According to the psychologist Robert Cialdini, you should do two things: (1) define the situation as an emergency by yelling, "Help! This is an emergency!" and (2) select a particular person and request his or her assistance. It is, as Cialdini notes, very difficult for someone to refuse this kind of request. Once one person responds, the cycle is broken. As a result, others passing by will be much more likely to stop and offer to help you (Cialdini 1988).

The next three orientations or research traditions belong to sociological social psychology.

Symbolic Interactionism (SI)

Working within **Symbolic interactionism** (SI), sociological social psychologists study face-to-face interactions in natural settings and focus on the meanings constructed among individuals through their social interactions. Symbolic interactionists emphasize agency over constraint by documenting how people create their realities (including their perceptions, beliefs, and plans of action) through their relationships with others. SI research is often similar in method to the ethnographic studies anthropologists have traditionally conducted in cultures outside of the United States. SI analyses are highly detailed and give one a sense of what it is like to be a member of a particular group.

Research on Teenagers Working in Coffee Shops

A study by Yasmine Besen (2006) illustrates research within the SI face of sociological social psychology. Besen's study focuses on the experiences of affluent suburban teenagers (ages 16–19) working in two coffee shops. Although lower-level service jobs are often regarded as undesirable, Besen found that the teenagers she studied viewed their work as a positive experience. In general, the teens she observed used the coffee shop as a sort of social hub.

Of course, basic societal rules governing the business of purchasing coffee (e.g., waiting in line, exchanging pleasantries) were in play in the coffee shops where Besen observed the teen workers' behaviors. However, as they interacted with one

PHOTO 1.2

Teenagers and young adults enjoy working in environments where they can connect with others and express themselves in unique ways.

another over time, these employees and their customers constructed norms pertaining to other social relations within the coffee shops. Where customers sat and how much attention they were likely to get from the staff reflected these group norms. Romantic partners and good friends usually sat next to the bar that separates the coffee preparation and seating areas. They often talked extensively with employees in front of and behind the counter, and they sometimes helped out with simple tasks. Less-intimate friends typically sat in the lounge area, where employees would stop by for short conversations while they were working. More casual acquaintances stood by the bar and consumed their drinks while talking to employees for briefer periods. Through all of these interactions, information was exchanged and outside social activities were coordinated.

Besen's one- to two-hour interviews with college students (all 19 or younger) working in the coffee shops revealed additional social functions of their work experience. Many reported that the coffee shop was a place where they were free to express their individuality. Their alternative styles of dress and accessories, which were likely to generate criticism at home and in other settings, were readily accepted by customers and fellow employees. Participants also indicated that the coffee shop provided a space where they could socialize and meet new people without being observed by parents and other authority figures.

Although job-related tasks such as making drinks and cleaning equipment were highly scripted, participants reported substantial latitude in other areas. For many of the study participants, the selection of music and scheduling of shifts (often done so they could work with friends) were important positive aspects of the job. Most of the workers' direct supervisors were similar in age and were regarded as friends rather than adversaries. Instead of being perceived as coercive, work was viewed as a place where employees could hang out with friends they may not otherwise have time to see, given their busy schedules.

Besen contrasts her findings with the results of research studies that characterize all lower-level service jobs as exploitive because of their low pay and repetitive nature. These analyses failed to look at the work experience from the perspectives of affluent, suburban teenagers, like the individuals Besen studied. For many of the teens Besen encountered, money was not a motivating factor: they worked for social reasons.

You might be wondering whether Besen's findings apply to other teenagers who work. They may not. SI research focuses on understanding the unique experiences of a particular group of individuals, not on documenting patterns that apply across individuals and social settings. Certainly, the experiences of less-affluent teens and adults who work in coffee shops and other low-tier service jobs (individuals often exploited given their economic need and lack of alternatives) are different from those of Besen's study participants. Nonetheless, as Besen notes, it is important to acknowledge the experiences and motivations of the individuals in her analysis. As she points out, entering their world makes it clear that situations that appear to be negative and exploitive to sociologists and other social scientists may actually be experienced as worthwhile and enjoyable by some of their participants.

What Do You Think?

With a partner or a small group, create a list of 10 or so questions that you can use to interview one or more fellow students who have part-time jobs. You might start by asking interviewees *why* they are working (what their motivation is), what they do, and whether they feel they are fairly paid. After you finish your interviews, compare your findings with those of your classmates. How do your results compare with Besen's findings?

Social Structure and Personality (SSP)

Social structure and personality is more oriented toward the study of (macro) societal patterns than the SI perspective. SSP researchers focus on the effects of **statuses** (structural positions), such as social class, gender, and race/ethnicity. They study how these statuses affect individuals' thoughts, beliefs, aspirations, emotions, and patterns of social interaction. Their studies are quantitative in orientation and almost always involve the analysis of survey data. Thus, unlike the research done by SI researchers, SSP studies require some number crunching.

Research on the Consequences of Teenage Employment

The literature on the consequences of adolescent employment provides a good example of research within the SSP tradition. Because there are numerous studies on this topic, we summarize the results of a series of articles rather than a single study. This is the approach we took when reviewing the voluminous psychological literature on the bystander effect.

   As shown in Table 1.1, more than one-quarter of young people aged 16–19 are employed. Whereas slightly more females than males within this age range work for pay, the percentage of White teenagers who are in the labor force is almost double that of African Americans. Much of this difference may be due to social class

TABLE 1.1	GENDER (%)		RACE/ETHNICITY (%)		
Percent of Youth Employed by Gender and by Race/Ethnicity, 2010	AGE	MALE	FEMALE	WHITE	AFRICAN AMERICAN	LATINO
	16–19	25	27	29	15	21
	20-24	61	59	64	50	59

Note: Adapted from the 2011 Current Population Survey, Bureau of Labor Statistics.

differences across race. In general, African American and Latino families are less well off financially than White families, and teenagers from low-income families are less likely to have jobs than teenagers from affluent families (Sum, Khatiwada, and Palma 2011).

Those concerned about teens working emphasize the potentially negative social, academic, and psychological consequences of early employment. Although the literature is somewhat mixed, working while in high school does not appear to be especially harmful.

There is a consensus among researchers that employment during adolescence increases teens' autonomy in relation to parents and exposes them to new people and lifestyles. On the negative side, this exposure can lead to increases in drinking, marijuana use, and smoking (Johnson 2004; Longest and Shanahan 2007). The risk for substance use associated with working is strongest among White adolescents (Johnson 2004).

The newfound independence associated with youth employment has been linked to increases in school absenteeism. However, work intensity (the number of hours worked per week) does not affect the amount of time high school students spend on homework or the grades they earn (Schoenhals, Tienda, and Schneider 1998). Working more than 20 hours per week may increase adolescents' likelihood of dropping out of school (Lee and Staff 2007; Warren and Lee 2003), but this relatively weak relationship exists only among students who are already at moderate risk for dropout. Students at high risk for dropping out of high school due to their family situations or for academic reasons are likely to do so whether or not they work for pay. Similarly, students at low risk for dropping out because of their family and academic backgrounds rarely do so, employed or not (Lee and Staff 2007).

Researchers report that working appears to increase adolescents' optimism about the future. Students who work steadily throughout high school are more confident than individuals who work less regularly that they will have a good family life, good friends, respect from others, and a job they like that pays well (Cunnien, MartinRogers, and Mortimer 2009). There may be some validity to these students' assessments, as work habits and skills acquired during adolescence have been linked to financial well-being in adulthood (Painter 2010).

All jobs are not, however, equally valuable. In particular, stressful work experiences that offer few opportunities for skill development have been shown to cause depressive moods in adolescent males, who are taught to value achievement. Adolescent females, on the other hand, seem to be especially vulnerable to difficulties in balancing work and school responsibilities and to work situations where they feel that they are being held accountable for things that are beyond their control. However, the emotional states of adolescents are not affected by work-related factors important to adults, such as pay, opportunities for advancement, and job security (Shanahan et al. 1991).

Does this sound familiar? Perhaps teens, in general, tend to be more concerned with the social aspects of their jobs, much like the coffee shop workers in Besen's

SI analysis described earlier. This comparison, between the participants in the survey research described in the preceding paragraphs and the teens Besen studied, shows us a clear difference between the research goals of SI and SSP. Besen's SI study provides a detailed account of the experiences of a particular subset of individuals (wealthy suburban teenagers working in coffee shops). SSP researchers aim to obtain information that is generalizable (applicable to all individuals in society who occupy a particular social category—e.g., teenagers who work for pay) because their goal is to identify and explain broader patterns of perception and behavior. Their analyses, however, provide notably less detailed descriptions of people's experiences than those within the SI tradition.

Group Processes and Structures (GPS)

Sociologists who work within the **group processes and structures (GPS)** tradition focus on the effects of power on the exchange of resources, on relations between groups, and on the effects of social stratification on perception and behavior in group encounters. Much of their research focuses on small, task-oriented groups. GPS research is unique from a sociological standpoint because it often involves the use of experiments. (SSP research usually involves surveys, whereas SI research relies primarily on direct observation.)

Within the GPS tradition, researchers use controlled laboratory experiments to study how status characteristics influence group interactions. **Status characteristics** are attributes (e.g., being male or being a racial or ethnic minority) that affect the way people are perceived and treated. In this society, being male and White is generally associated with worthiness and competence. Women and racial/ethnic minorities are not viewed as favorably. Social psychologists do not believe that men are superior to women or that Whites are superior to other racial/ethnic groups. In fact, they absolutely reject these notions. However, people in this society tend to hold these views because they are consistent with the existing power structure and patterns of inequality at the macro level (Correll and Ridgeway 2006).

Research on Gender Bias

The example used here to illustrate GPS research focuses on gender, a status characteristic, and its effects on group members' behaviors. Research suggests that gender differences in influence, participation, evaluations, and expected rewards (all of which favor men in mixed-sex groups) are due to differences in the relative status of males and females within the larger society (Wagner and Berger 1997).

In their classic study on gender and influence, M.D. Pugh and Ralph Wahrman (1983) evaluated the effectiveness of strategies designed to eliminate this type of bias. In their experiment, opposite-sex pairs of college student volunteers completed the Contrast Sensitivity task. This task required participants to determine whether visual representations of a series of geometric shapes were predominantly black or predominantly white in color. The task was designed to be highly ambiguous, so there were no obviously right or wrong answers.

On 25 out of 40 trials (where each trial was a slide showing the geometric shapes), subjects were told that their partner gave a different answer from their own. For example, subjects who said the geometric shapes were predominantly black were told that their partners said that the shapes were predominantly white. Thus, every subject's responses were ostensibly challenged by his or her partner at a standard rate (no matter what answers the partner, who was in a different room, actually gave). On each trial during which a challenge occurred, subjects could either change their answer to match that of their partner or stay with their initial response.

In the first (nonintervention, baseline) condition, 44 subjects completed the Contrast Sensitivity task. As is typical, the women in mixed-sex pairs were more likely than men to change their answers to match those of their partner. On average, the women in the baseline condition deferred to men 7 out of 25 times, whereas the men deferred to women 5 out of 25 times.

Pugh and Wahrman (1983) tested the effectiveness of three interventions designed to reduce this gender difference.

> ***Intervention 1:*** Before they viewed any of the slides with the geometric shapes, the 44 subjects who received the first intervention were told by the experimenter that there were no gender differences in performance on the Contrast Sensitivity task. Despite this intervention, the results were similar to those obtained in the baseline condition: women yielded to their partner more frequently than men did. Telling subjects that men and women are equally competent at the experimental task did not reduce gender differences in susceptibility to influence.
>
> ***Intervention 2:*** The 46 subjects who received the second intervention completed a preliminary task (finding hidden objects in a picture) and were told that it required abilities similar to the Contrast Sensitivity task. The preliminary task was easy enough that everyone (both men and women) exhibited superior performance. After they finished the preliminary task, the subjects completed the Contrast Sensitivity task. Showing subjects that women and men were equally competent at a task similar to the experimental task failed to reduce gender differences susceptibility to influence. Women were as likely to give in to their male partners on the Contrast Sensitivity task as they were in the baseline condition.
>
> ***Intervention 3:*** The 40 subjects who received the third intervention completed the preliminary (hidden objects) task, which was now rigged so that the woman in each mixed-sex pair always performed better than her male partner. After this, the subjects completed the Contrast Sensitivity task. This intervention worked. Showing subjects that women were better than men at a task similar to the experimental (Contrast Sensitivity) task eliminated gender differences in the frequency with which subjects yielded to their opposite-sex partners.

Pugh and Wahrman's (1983) study suggests that the perception that women are less competent than men was the reason that women were more susceptible than men to their partners' influence. This widespread, albeit often unconscious, belief affected subjects' behaviors unless they had firsthand evidence that women were likely to outperform men on the task at hand. When women were perceived as more competent then men due to their performance on the preliminary task (Intervention 3), gender differences in influence disappeared.

It is important to note that showing subjects that men and women were equally competent at the experimental task (Intervention 2) was not enough to eliminate preconceived notions about gender and ability. To reduce gender bias in mixed-sex pairs, women had to be perceived as better than men (Pugh and Wahrman 1983).

You might be saying, "Well, yes, but this was in 1983. Surely things have changed since then when it comes to gender and perceived competence." They have somewhat, but numerous experiments suggest that the type of gender bias documented by Pugh and Wahrman (1983) still exists. They also suggest that this bias is due to the way society is organized and not the characteristics or intentions of individuals. We discuss these studies, as well as research on race/ethnicity and small-group dynamics, in greater detail in Chapter 5.

The point we want to make here is that Pugh and Wahrman (1983) found a way to reduce gender bias in mixed-sex pairs. This is important because it shows that it is possible to alter the effects of inequality at the macro level on people's interactions within small-group settings. Patterns of inequality at the societal level persist only insofar as they are reinforced through face-to-face interactions. Therefore, disrupting the micro-level social processes through which inequalities between groups (e.g., men and women) are reproduced may also help to create a more egalitarian society. Research within the GPS tradition is geared toward facilitating this type of social change. Can we say the same about the first set of studies we discussed, on the bystander effect (pages 09–10)?

Experiments in GPS Versus Experiments in PSP

Both of the relevant literatures (on the bystander effect and on gender, performance expectations, and influence in task-oriented groups) are based on laboratory experiments and yield results that are presumed to generalize to real-world encounters. Beyond the similarity in research method (experiment), these literatures are very different.

Q: Do you see the difference between these two examples? They very clearly illustrate the difference between psychological social psychology and sociological social psychology.

A: Research on the bystander effect, conducted by social psychologists trained in psychology, focuses on the impact of the immediate situation (the number of witnesses to an emergency) on people's behavior. Research on gender, perceived competence, and social influence conducted within the GPS tradition focuses on the effects of the immediate situation (group composition and the nature of the task at hand) and broader societal beliefs about the abilities of males and females. These societal beliefs transcend the immediate settings in which social interaction occurs but nonetheless influence people's behaviors. Understanding the effects of these broader societal patterns on group encounters is critical from the perspective of the GPS researcher. Social psychologists trained in psychology rarely consider how these kinds of macro, societal characteristics influence individuals' perceptions and behaviors.

COMPARING THE SOCIAL PSYCHOLOGIES

All three of the sociological faces of social psychology take macro-level societal factors into consideration to one degree or another. Thus, although sociological social psychologists are less macro in their orientation that other sociologists, they are more macro in orientation than psychologists.

These distinctions become clearer when you think about the differences between sociology and psychology, and among the four social psychologies, in terms of a continuum, as in Figure 1.2. Micro-level studies are at the far left end, and macro-level studies at the far right.

Locating the Social Psychologies on the Micro-Macro Continuum

On the far left of the continuum, we have psychology, with its micro focus (its emphasis on individual perception, emotion, and behavior).

1. PSP looks at individuals within group settings and at the effects of situational factors on individuals' thought and behavior (e.g., research on the bystander effect). Because the unit of analysis in these studies is the individual, PSP is also at the left end of the continuum.

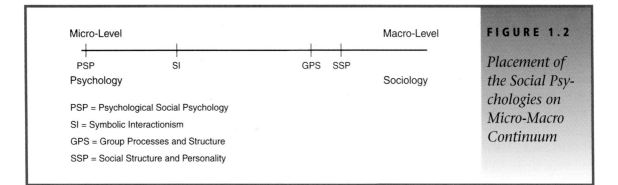

Micro-Level   Macro-Level

PSP   SI   GPS   SSP
Psychology   Sociology

PSP = Psychological Social Psychology
SI = Symbolic Interactionism
GPS = Group Processes and Structure
SSP = Social Structure and Personality

FIGURE 1.2

Placement of the Social Psychologies on Micro-Macro Continuum

The next three traditions on the continuum are all within sociological social psychology.

2. Research within the SI tradition also focuses on social interaction at the micro level. SI researchers believe that reality is socially constructed in that meanings are created and reproduced within the context of individuals' face-to-face interactions. For example, college students continually negotiate and renegotiate what it means to be a student as they interact with peers, teachers, office staff, and other individuals on their campus. Thus, whereas social psychologists trained in psychology focus on individual perception and behavior, SI researchers emphasize the meanings that emerge within social encounters. SI researchers such as Besen (teens working in coffee shops) note how these emergent meanings are shaped by the social context within which the interaction occurs. Often, meanings are also shaped by the characteristics of the actors in relation to other groups within society. As a result, symbolic interactionism is more macro than psychological social psychology. Thus, SI is toward, but not at, the left end of Figure 1.2.

3. Research within the GPS tradition, the newest face of sociological social psychology, is toward the right end of the micro-macro continuum. GPS researchers focus on group differences (typically with gender or race serving as the unit of analysis), on performance expectations, and on task-related outcomes. They do not, however, examine differences in perception or performance within status categories (e.g., among women or among men, among racial/ethnic minorities or among Whites).

4. Research within the SSP tradition is also toward the right end of this continuum. The unit of analysis in these studies is the group (e.g., employed vs. unemployed youth) and more often than not socioeconomic class, gender, or race/ethnicity. This type of research is considered SSP because many of the outcomes examined occur within the individual (e.g., confidence in the future and depression, as in the studies on adolescent employment). However, unlike psychological research, the focus of SSP is on the differences in outcomes between, but not within, groups.

SSP is the most macro of the three faces of sociological social psychology because of its emphasis on the effects of statuses (e.g., employment status, class, race/ethnicity, and gender) on perception and behavior across social contexts. Much of the research within the GPS tradition is similar in orientation to studies in SSP. However, GPS research often focuses on micro-level interactions in the lab, working under the assumption that these interactions mirror patterns within the larger society. Thus, the GPS perspective is slightly closer to the center of our continuum.

General **sociology** is at the far right end of the continuum because of its macro orientation. Studies in sociology emphasize aggregate patterns and tend not to delve into the minds (thoughts, motivations, concerns, and emotions) of individuals.

APPLICATION: STUDYING THE SOCIAL EXPERIENCES OF IMMIGRANTS

Immigration is a highly contentious subject these days as communities change because of an increase in their foreign-born population. In recent years, the percentage of U.S. residents born in China and India has increased substantially (Walters and Trevelyan 2011). However, Mexican Americans are still the largest immigrant group in the United States, making up almost a third of our foreign-born population (Acosta and de la Cruz 2011).

Sociological social psychologists are especially interested in learning about the social experiences of immigrants. What kinds of issues would you want to know about if you were going to study immigrants?

In the following sections, we illustrate the types of questions about immigrants' lives that have been addressed within sociological social psychology. As with any topic, the kinds of questions social psychologists ask about immigrants and their experiences, and what they discover, are shaped by the face of social psychology within which they are working.

Studies by SI Researchers

Focusing on micro-level social processes, SI researchers have studied members of particular immigrant groups and their unique social experiences and relationships.

PHOTO 1.3

Demonstrators protest Arizona's controversial immigration law, SB1070. The most contentious part of the law is the requirement that police determine the immigration status of individuals arrested or detained if they suspect they are not in the country legally (Phoenix, Arizona. May 29, 2010).

They have addressed the following research questions using data based on observations of immigrants' behaviors in natural settings or detailed interviews with members of one or more immigrant groups. How do male immigrants from Latin America struggling to find work maintain positive views of themselves (Purser 2009)? How do Soviet Jewish and Vietnamese refugees respond to intergenerational conflicts within their families (Gold 1989), and how do members of particular immigrant groups (e.g., Lebanese Americans or Indian Americans) integrate racial/ethnic and religious identities (Ajrouch and Kusow 2007; Kurien 2005)?

For example, Kurien (2005) discusses how second-generation Indian American college students (students whose parents were born in India) negotiated understandings of what it means to be Indian American and Hindu through their interactions during meetings of a Hindu student organization. The organization was known for its militant nationalist stance in support of the synthesis of Hinduism and Indian culture.

In general, males from elite families whose Hindu identity was highly prominent embraced this nationalist stance. Other group members, who reported that they joined the organization mainly to learn about their heritage, exhibited a very different orientation. Given their lack of knowledge about Hinduism, the Hindu identity was less salient and emotionally laden for these students, and prior events involving racial discrimination or attacks on their religion were less likely to be framed as identity relevant. Thus, they had a much more moderate view of what it meant to be Hindu than the more extremist faction and were dissatisfied with the direction the Hindu student organization was taking.

The experiences of the Indian American students Kurien studied illustrate the often-contentious nature of identity negotiation within the context of competing personal histories and motivations. Documenting the social processes through which group members construct identities is a common theme within the SI literature.

What Do You Think?

What groups do you identify with? Make a list. What makes these groups important sources of identity for you? Save your responses. We come back to this topic in a later chapter.

Studies by SSP Researchers

Studies within social structure and personality often compare the perceptions, feelings, and behaviors of individuals in different social categories (e.g., men and women, different classes, or different racial/ethnic groups). Immigrant status (immigrant vs. native born) is a social category, and research on immigration within SSP has focused on differences in the social experiences of immigrants and individuals born in the United States. Because the focus of research in SSP is on patterns of perception and behavior at the group level (e.g., immigrant, native born), most of these studies have involved the analysis of survey data.

SSP research on immigration has addressed the following research questions. Why are immigrants often viewed negatively by native-born Whites (Berg 2009)? Why are immigrants at lower risk for depression than ethnic minorities born in the United States (Mossakowski 2007), and why do immigrant youths exhibit lower levels of delinquency than their American-born counterparts?

Delinquency is the label applied to deviant behaviors enacted by adolescents (youths aged 12–18). **Deviant behavior**, which may or may not be illegal, refers to actions that violate prevailing social norms. We focus here on the effect of immigrant status on delinquency because a number of recent studies within SSP have examined this relationship.

Studies within SSP suggest that immigrant youths exhibit low levels of delinquency in part because they have stronger family bonds, more positive feelings about their family relationships, more attentive parents, fewer friends who engage in deviant behavior, and a greater commitment to education than adolescents from nonimmigrant families (Bui 2009; Dinovitzer, Hagan, and Levi 2009; DiPietro and McGloin 2012). Note that these latter analyses focus on how the social experiences and behaviors of immigrant youths differ from those of their native-born counterparts but not on differences in the social experiences and behaviors of the immigrants themselves.

Studies by GPS Researchers

As noted earlier, GPS researchers use experiments to study how status characteristics influence the social interactions that occur in small, task-oriented groups. Immigrant is a status characteristic, like race/ethnicity or gender. Thus, one might ask how immigrants are perceived and treated in small group encounters. What do group members expect from, and how do they evaluate the task performance of, individuals who are immigrants versus those who are native born?

Immigrant status has received little attention from GPS researchers who study interaction in task groups. This is because it is not likely to yield a distinct pattern of results. GPS researchers argue that all status characteristics operate the same way. Thus, immigrant status should affect performance expectations, evaluations, and behavior in the same manner as race/ethnicity and gender, which are the status characteristics most frequently studied.

APPLYING MULTIPLE PERSPECTIVES

There are some instances when a subject of general interest to sociological social psychologists has not been examined within all of the three research orientations. This is because the different faces of social psychology focus on very different aspects of human social behavior.

In other cases, there are studies within all three faces of sociological social psychology that address a particular topic. We demonstrate this in the second part of the book, where we discuss the research literature on a variety of topics of interest to sociological social psychologists. It is through the integration of the information these studies have generated that social psychologists have significantly enhanced our understanding of the human experience and the various facets of social life.

CHAPTER SUMMARY

Social psychology, a highly diverse field of study that bridges sociology and psychology, has four distinct research orientations, or faces. The main features of each of the four faces

TABLE 1.2 *The Four Faces of Social Psychology*	**1. Psychological social psychology**	
	Emphasis	the effects of the immediate social situation on group members' perception and behavior
	Unit of analysis	micro level; the individual
	Primary method of data collection	laboratory experiment
	examples	the bystander effect
	Sociological social psychology	
	2. Symbolic interactionism	
	Emphasis	the social construction of meaning; the negotiation of group norms; the uniqueness of social experiences
	Unit of analysis	micro level; the individual or face-to-face social interaction
	Primary method of data collection	observation in natural settings
	examples	adolescents employed in coffee shops; racial and religious identity among second-generation Indian American college students
	3. Social structure and personality	
	Emphasis	the relationship of status characteristics to perception, emotion, and behavior
	Unit of analysis	macro level; the group (typically social class, gender, or race/ethnicity)
	Primary method of data collection	survey
	examples	consequences of youth employment; immigrant status and delinquency
	4. Group processes and structures	
	Emphasis	the effects of status characteristics on interaction in small, task-oriented groups
	Unit of analysis	macro level; the group (typically gender or race/ethnicity)
	Primary method of data collection	laboratory experiment
	examples	gender and susceptibility to influence in mixed-sex pairs

of social psychology are summarized in Table 1.2. As depicted here, these orientations can be distinguished by their unit of analysis and their underlying assumptions about the nature of social reality. The four faces of social psychology are also distinguished by what researchers seek to learn about human social behavior and how research is generally conducted. Despite their distinctiveness, the three sociological social psychologies share a common theme: namely, that the groups to which people belong are part of a larger society. These three different orientations and the research they have generated provide substantial insight into the nature of human social behavior.

Key Points to Know

- **Social psychology focuses on understanding the nature and causes of social behavior and has its roots in both the discipline of psychology and the discipline of sociology.**

- **Sociological social psychologists ask different questions than social psychologists trained as psychologists.** Psychological social psychologists focus on individuals within groups and how the immediate setting affects their perception and behavior. Sociological social psychologists also examine individuals in groups, but they locate these groups within the context of the larger society.

- **The sociological perspective is a way of viewing the world that places individuals within a broad historical and social context in order to understand their perceptions and behaviors.** Sociological social psychologists study the social processes through which people create society and the ways that society influences people's thoughts, feelings, and behaviors.

- **Research studies can be classified based upon their unit of analysis.** Micro-level analyses focus on the individual or interactions between individuals. Macro-level analyses focus on aspects of societies that exist above and beyond the individual level. Macro analyses examine aggregate or structural units such as the group, the county, the city, the state, the country, or the world. General sociology is at the macro level. Sociological social psychology is more micro in focus than general sociology, but not as micro in its focus as psychological social psychology.

- **There are four faces of social psychology: psychological social psychology (PSP), symbolic interactionism (SI), social structure and personality (SSP), and group processes and structures (GPS).** The latter three fall within the realm of sociological social psychology and are the focus of this textbook.

- **The social psychologies differ in terms of their unit of analysis (placement on the micro-macro continuum), in terms of their**

focus (the questions asked), and in terms of their primary method of data collection and analysis. The selection of topic, research questions, and methodology are shaped by the face of social psychology within which a researcher is working. This is the focus of the first part of this textbook.

- **Research from within the three sociological social psychologies has been combined to increase our understanding of particular topics.** This is the focus of the second part of the book.

Terms and Concepts for Review

Agency	Social class
Constraint	Social facts
Delinquency	Social norms
Deviant behavior	Social psychology
Diffusion of responsibility	Social stratification
Doing gender	Social structure and personality (SSP)
Ethnic group	Socioeconomic status (SES)
Group processes and structures (GPS)	Sociological perspective
Gender	Sociological social
Macro-level analysis	psychology
Micro-level analysis	Sociology
Psychological social psychology (PSP)	Status
psychology	Status characteristics
Race	Symbolic interactionism (SI)
Sex	Unit of analysis

Questions for Review and Reflection

1. Although there are some similarities in the behaviors of students and professors in all colleges and universities, every college class has its own tone. What is considered acceptable in one class (e.g., coming in a few minutes late or talking to a peer) in another course may generate a negative response from the professor or from other students. Describe the kinds of interactions that occur in each of the classes you are enrolled in this semester. How might each of your professors respond to a deviant behavior, such as someone speaking loudly on a cell phone during class? Would their responses be identical? How would the other students in the class react? Which face of sociological social psychology would lead you to consider the unique nature of the interactions between students and between students and the professor in each of your current classes?

2. Is working for pay good for high school students? What does the research literature on this topic say? Do you think these patterns extend to college students? Why or why not?

Questions for Review and Reflection (*Continued*)

3. How can laboratory experiments be used to study the effects of statuses like gender on people's behavior? Are the results of these studies generalizable to everyday social encounters? Why do you take this position? (Note: We discuss this issue in the following chapter.)

4. Choose two of the three faces of sociological social psychology and discuss how a researcher working within each orientation would approach the topic of college student drinking. For each face, develop at least one research question and discuss how relevant information might be gathered.

CHAPTER 2

Research Methods in Sociological Social Psychology

Center Tries to Treat Web Addicts FALL CITY, Wash. (AP)—Ben Alexander spent nearly every waking minute playing the video game "World of Warcraft." As a result, he flunked out of the University of Iowa.

Mr. Alexander, 19, needed help to break an addiction that he called as destructive as alcohol or drugs. He found it in Fall City, where what claims to be the first residential treatment center for Internet addiction in the United States just opened its doors.

The center, called ReSTART, opened in July, and for $14,000 it offers a 45-day program intended to help people wean themselves from pathological computer use.

"We've been doing this for years on an outpatient basis," said Hilarie Cash, a therapist and executive director of the center. "Up until now, we had no place to send them."

Internet addiction is not recognized as a separate disorder by the American Psychiatric Association, and treatment is not generally covered by insurance. But there are many such treatment centers in China, South Korea, and Taiwan, where Internet addiction is taken very seriously, and many psychiatric experts say it is clear that Internet addiction is real and harmful.

Whether such programs work in the long run remains to be seen.

The five-acre center in Fall City, about 30 miles east of Seattle, can handle up to six patients at a time. Mr. Alexander is so far the only patient of the program, which uses a cold-turkey approach. He spends his days in counseling and psychotherapy sessions, doing household chores, working on the grounds, going on outings, exercising, and baking cookies.

Cosette Dawna Rae, a psychotherapist, has owned the bucolic retreat center since 1994, and was searching for a new use for it when she teamed up with Ms. Cash. Ms. Cash, co-author of the book *Video Games and Your Kids,* started dealing with Internet addiction in 1994, with a patient she said was so consumed by video games that his marriage ended and he lost two jobs.

Associated Press. 2009. "Center tries to treat addicts." *New York Times*, September 6, p. A18.

What Do You Think?

■ Do you consider Internet addiction a true addiction in the same sense that cigarettes, drugs, alcohol, and gambling are addictions? Explain why or why not.

■ On a scale of 1 to 10 (10 being the highest), how addicted would you say you are to each of the following: Internet, cell phones, tablets, TV, video games, e-readers? Compare your scores with a partner or small group.

■ Do you think U.S. society as a whole is addicted to electronic technology? Explain.

Internet addiction is certainly an issue of interest to social psychologists, but is it really a serious problem? Yes, it is, according to Kimberly Young, clinical psychologist and founder of the Center for Internet Addiction Recovery in Bradford, Pennsylvania. She argues that college students are especially vulnerable to Internet addiction because most schools provide unlimited Internet access; students are relatively free from parental control, often for the first time; and they are encouraged to use Internet resources by school administrators and faculty (Young 2004). Drawing on her earlier research (Young 1998), she states that over half of all college students suffer from poor grades due to excessive Internet use.

Young's findings must be interpreted with caution. Only 496 college students participated in the original sample on which her study was based. And who were they? The participants were volunteers who found out about the study through advertisements placed in national and international newspapers and fliers posted on local college campuses. Some of the volunteers had learned about her study through postings on electronic support groups geared toward Internet addiction (e.g., the Webaholics Support Group) and on searches for "Internet addiction" on popular search engines such as Yahoo (Young 1998). The small number of participants, and how they came to volunteer for the study, make it highly questionable that Young's results extend to college students in general. Unfortunately, many of the studies about the prevalence of Internet addiction are less than adequate. As a result, we do not really know how problematic Internet overuse is among students or the general population (Byun et al. 2009; Widyanto and Griffiths 2006). A number of case studies within the literature depict the dire consequences of Internet addiction, but how widespread these kinds of experiences are has yet to be determined.

Social psychological studies almost always involve the collection and analysis of data. It is therefore important that you understand the research process. Having some training in research methods will enable you to evaluate claims made about Internet addiction and any other social phenomenon.

THE RESEARCH PROCESS

As illustrated in Chapter 1, not all faces of sociological social psychology address every subject. Rather, each face, or orientation, tends to direct the researcher's attention to particular topics and also shapes the type of questions the researcher asks about the topic under investigation. The type of questions asked, in turn, leads researchers to select a particular method of data collection, presumably the one best suited to study the aspect of human social behavior they are focusing on. Although it is overly simplistic to say that each face of social psychology has its own method, because the methods of data collection used within each face of social psychology do vary, there is a strong association between face and methodology. That is, within each face of social psychology there is a dominant (albeit not exclusive) method of data collection that researchers working within that orientation typically use to gather the information they need to conduct their study.

Social psychologists working in Social Structure and Personality (SSP) or in the Group Processes and Structures (GPS) face of social psychology are interested in how people's characteristics affect specific outcomes. For example, they might study whether the characteristic of employment or gender affects outcomes such as grades or susceptibility to influence. These kinds of issues are best addressed using quantitative methods. **Quantitative research** involves the analysis of numerical data and focuses on identifying causal relationships.

Symbolic interactionists are interested in social processes, such as how people construct meanings through their interactions with others. They might study, for example, how teens working in coffee shops come to define their work experiences as desirable. Symbolic interactionists are also interested in how social norms emerge and are reproduced through everyday social interactions. These kinds of issues are best addressed using qualitative methods. **Qualitative research** involves the observation and analysis of participants' social interactions in natural settings or the analysis of detailed personal accounts of participants' social experiences.

These two types of research are described in the following sections. We emphasize differences in their underlying logic, goals, focus, results, strengths, and limitations.

QUANTITATIVE RESEARCH METHODS

Social psychologists use quantitative methods to test theories about the way the social world works. A **theory** is a set of cause-and-effect statements that can be tested with data.

The Deductive Method and Testing Theories

Often social psychologists start out with a theory about how groups within society differ in terms of their social experiences, which they test through observation. The researchers examine their results and, if they are consistent with the theory, the theory has been supported. If the results are inconsistent with the theory, then the theory is not supported, spurring more research to see if the theory should be rejected completely or reformulated. Sometimes theories are expanded or modified to account for inconsistent research findings.

This research process emphasizes the establishment of causal relationships and is similar to that which exists within the natural sciences. It is rooted in deductive reasoning. **Deductive reasoning** entails going from the general to the specific. Knowing that your friend likes action films, you might deduce that she will like *The Bourne Legacy,* one of the series of high-action spy thrillers starring Matt Damon. Within the context of a research study, deductive reasoning involves going from the general (theory) to specific observations (data). The quantitative research process is depicted in Figure 2.1.

Independent and Dependent Variables

In order to test a theory, social psychologists must formulate one or more hypotheses. A **hypothesis** specifies a relationship between variables. A **variable** is something with attributes that vary. Annual income, for instance, is a variable with scores (attributes) ranging from 0 (no income) to a very large amount. (Sometimes researchers measure income using categories, with the highest category being $100,000 or more.)

Quantitative social psychological studies have at least one independent variable and one dependent variable. An **independent variable** is the presumed cause, and the **dependent variable** is the presumed outcome. For example, social psychologists have theorized that income (cause) affects psychological well-being (the outcome) because food, shelter, and health care, all of which can be costly, are basic human needs. Not having the resources to meet these basic needs leads to stress. Moreover, the leisure activities and the varied material possessions associated with wealth can make life more comfortable and enjoyable (Kahneman and Deaton 2010), especially when one compares his or her circumstances to those of others (Singer 1981).

A quantitative researcher might look specifically at the relationship between income and happiness. In this case, the hypothesis would be "As income (the independent variable) increases, happiness (the dependent variable) increases."

Often, researchers will go one step further and indicate how each variable in their hypothesis will be measured. Specifying how a variable will be measured is a process referred to as **operationalization**. An **operational definition** indicates precisely how a particular variable will be measured (quantified) in a given study.

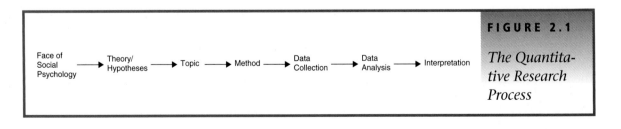

Face of Social Psychology → Theory/Hypotheses → Topic → Method → Data Collection → Data Analysis → Interpretation

FIGURE 2.1

The Quantitative Research Process

For example, in our income-happiness example, a hypothesis with operationally defined variables might state, "As annual income increases, the likelihood of respondents reporting that they are 'very happy' increases." The General Social Survey (GSS), which is administered biannually by the National Opinion Research Center at the University of Chicago, includes questions that can be used to measure both of these variables, and we constructed our operational definitions with this in mind. The relationship between income and happiness among GSS respondents from 2010 is presented in Table 2.1.

Consistent with these results, numerous studies show that income is positively associated with happiness (Diener et al. 1993; Easterlin 2001). That is, as scores on income increase, scores on happiness tend to increase as well. Although many of these analyses were conducted by psychologists or economists, they clearly focus on the relationship between social structure and personality and are thus of interest to sociological social psychologists. It is important to note that the boundaries between the different faces of social psychology, and between sociology and other disciplines, are not always clearly delineated. As we note in the chapters focusing on particular topics, some research literatures reflect studies from within two or all three of the sociological social psychologies. There are also some academic literatures, like studies on the psychological consequences of income, that span disciplines.

One study on the psychological effects of income (Kahneman and Deaton 2010) has garnered a lot of media attention. The study's authors, a psychologist and an economist, found that income has a fairly strong effect on emotional well-being, a concept that encompasses happiness. Emotional well-being was operationally defined (measured) in this study as whether respondents had experienced during the previous day (the day before the phone interview) positive affect (feelings of

TABLE 2.1		TOTAL FAMILY INCOME			
Level of	HAPPINESS[a]	<$24,999	$25,000–$49,999	$50,000–$109,999	$110,000+
General					
Happiness by	Very happy (%)	19.3	21.0	31.6	35.7
Total Family	Pretty happy (%)	56.2	64.1	57.1	58.9
Income, U.S.	Not too happy (%)	24.5	14.9	11.3	5.4
Adults in 2010	n	591	416	557	241

[a]Happiness is measured in the GSS by asking respondents the following question: "Taken all together, how would you say things are these days. Would you say that you are very happy, pretty happy, or not too happy?"

Note: Smith, Tom W., Peter V. Marsden, and Michael Hout. 2011. General Social Surveys, 1972–2010 [machine-readable data file] / Sponsored by National Science Foundation.—NORC ed.—Chicago, IL: National Opinion Research Center [producer]; Storrs, CT: The Roper Center for Public Opinion Research, University of Connecticut [distributor].

enjoyment, happiness, and smiling or laughter), negative affect (sadness and worry), anger, and stress. As the researchers had predicted, increases in income were associated with increases in positive affect and decreases in negative affect, anger, and stress—but only to a point. Increases in income above $75,000 per year did not affect either positive or negative emotions.

Interestingly, income was positively related to a fifth dependent variable, life satisfaction. Participants were asked to rate their life satisfaction with scores ranging from 0 (least satisfied) to 10 (most satisfied). Unlike the impact of income on emotional well-being (with the $75,000 ceiling effect), life satisfaction did not level out at any particular income value. This suggests that increases in annual income increase life satisfaction even among individuals at the very top of the income scale.

Apparently the old adage "Money can't buy happiness" isn't true. Although money may not buy happiness, people who make lots of money report that they are happier than those who earn less.

Indices

Researchers frequently measure their variables using a series of items, rather than a single question. For example, delinquency, discussed in relation to immigrant status in Chapter 1, is commonly measured by asking adolescents a set of questions concerning how frequently they have engaged in various behaviors (e.g., vandalism, theft, and lying to parents). Their responses to these items are then added up to create an overall delinquency score.

This type of measure is called an **index**. Sociological social psychologists often use the terms "index" and "scale" interchangeably. They use indices to measure variables that are complex or multidimensional and thus difficult to assess with just one question. In an index, each question is presumed to measure the same underlying construct (e.g., delinquency).

Although measures of delinquency vary in content across studies, a commonly used delinquency index is presented in Box 2.1. The **mean** score is the average for the national sample of students in grades 7–12 who completed these items (calculated by adding up students' scores and dividing by the number of students

---

Box 2.1   Measuring Delinquency

The following delinquency items are included in the National Longitudinal Study of Adolescent Health (Add Health), a nationally representative study designed to examine the influence of the social context on adolescent health, achievement, and risk behaviors. Adolescents were first interviewed in grades 7–12 during the 1994–1995 academic year and have participated in follow-up interviews, the most recent occurring in 2008 when they were 24–32 years old. A number of researchers have used this set of questions (from the 1994–1995 data) and the other available measures from the Add Health study to better understand why adolescents engage in delinquent behavior.

QUESTION	RESPONSE OPTIONS			
	NEVER (0)	1 OR 2 TIMES (1)	3 OR 4 TIMES (2)	5 OR MORE TIMES (3)
In the past 12 months, how often did you:				
. . . paint graffiti or signs on someone else's property or in a public place?	0	1	2	3
. . . deliberately damage property that didn't belong to you?	0	1	2	3
. . . lie to your parents or guardians about where you had been or whom you were with?	0	1	2	3
. . . take something from a store without paying for it?	0	1	2	3
. . . run away from home?	0	1	2	3
. . . drive a car without its owners permission?	0	1	2	3
. . . steal something worth more than $50?	0	1	2	3
. . . go into a house or building to steal something?	0	1	2	3
. . . sell marijuana or other drugs?	0	1	2	3
. . . steal something worth less than $50?	0	1	2	3
. . . act loud, rowdy, or unruly in a public place?	0	1	2	3
. . . get into a serious physical fight?	0	1	2	3
. . . hurt someone badly enough to need bandages or care from a doctor or nurse?	0	1	2	3
. . . use or threaten to use a weapon to get something from someone?	0	1	2	3
. . . take part in a fight where a group of your friends was against another group?	0	1	2	3
TOTAL SCORE _____				

Mean = 4.28	Standard Deviation = 5.19	Range: 0–45

n = 6,503

Note: This presentation uses data from Add Health, a program project directed by Kathleen Mullan Harris and designed by J. Richard Udry, Peter S. Bearman, and Kathleen Mullan Harris at the University of North Carolina at Chapel Hill and funded by grant P01-HD31921 from the Eunice Kennedy Shriver National Institute of Child Health and Human Development, with cooperative funding from 23 other federal agencies and foundations.

who answered the questions). This serves as a baseline with which individuals delinquency scores can be compared. The **standard deviation** tells us how much variation there is in scores on the measure and is used in the calculation of statistical tests. The **range** includes the lowest and highest possible scores on the delinquency index. A lowercase **n** is used to designate the number of individuals in the study sample. It is common to include this information when discussing scores on an index.

Since you are in college, the concept of delinquency probably does not apply to your age group. (You are likely to be a little too old.) However, it might be interesting to see how you score on this measure with regard to the behaviors you engaged in when you were in high school. Go ahead and answer these questions. Add up your numerical responses to see how your score compares to the mean score for the national sample of middle and high school students.

Hold on to your delinquency score. We refer back to this exercise in Chapter 9 on deviance and social control.

Surveys

All of the studies discussed in the previous section were based on the analysis of survey data. **Surveys** are a method of collecting information by asking a structured set of questions in a predetermined order. They are used to measure the behaviors and psychological states of large numbers of people and are frequently the method of choice for social psychologists working within the social structure and personality (SSP) tradition. Surveys are conducted in person (verbally, during a face-to-face interview), through the mail or e-mail, or over the telephone.

The fact that Kahneman and Deaton's study on income and well-being was based on a phone survey conducted by Gallup gives us a high level of confidence in their results. Gallup is a well-regarded organization known for its rigorous survey design and sampling procedures. The survey that provided the data for Kahneman and Deaton's analysis was administered over the phone to a random sample of over 450,000 U.S. adults.

The survey with the delinquency items (Box 2.1) was administered using face-to-face interviews. It was designed and carried out by researchers at the University of North Carolina Population Center. The adolescents who participated in the study were selected randomly from schools across the United States.

Representative Sampling and Generalizability

A **sample** is the subset of the population the researcher wants to study. The term **population** refers to all of the individuals in the category or group of interest (e.g., U.S. residents, students at a given school, or members of a particular group).

It is often too costly and time-consuming to give a survey to everyone in a population and it is not necessary. If, for example, you want to know whether income and happiness are related among U.S. adults, you need not interview everyone 18 or older living in this country. Instead, you can take a sample of, say, 450,000 (or even a 1,000) U.S. adults. If your sample is selected in the appropriate manner, it will be representative of the U.S. population. Then, you can generalize from your study to U.S. adults with a high degree of confidence. Study results are generalizable when they can be applied beyond those individuals who served as subjects to other people in similar settings or to the population at large.

It is important to note that sample size is not the survey researcher's sole concern. How the sample is selected is equally, if not more, important than the number of individuals who complete the survey. Good samples are representative samples because they contain individuals from all of the various groups within the population from which they are drawn. Representative samples yield results that are generalizable.

The best way for social psychologists to get a **representative sample** is (1) to draw cases (individuals) from a population using a random procedure (called **random sampling**) and (2) to make sure that the individuals they select complete the survey. The percentage of individuals selected into a sample who complete the survey is referred to as a **response rate**. Although it is unlikely that everyone a researcher contacts will agree to participate in the study, ideally the response rate will be above 80%. Response rates lower than 80% yield potentially biased samples because the people who agree to complete a survey are likely to have different characteristics from the individuals who refuse to do so. When a sample is biased, the results of the survey are not generalizable to the population of interest.

Biased Sampling

Person-on-the-street interviews yield biased samples, even if the researcher approaches people at random at the selected location (e.g., by stopping every third person). The problem is twofold: (1) Who is on a particular street at a particular time itself is not random. That is, the people present in that place at that time are likely to have some characteristics that distinguish them from individuals who are not there. (2) The people who agree to answer the researcher's questions probably have different characteristics from those who just keep on walking.

Similarly, handing out surveys in college classes yields nonrepresentative samples unless the classes are selected at random, which is rarely the case. Both of these examples illustrate what is referred to as a **convenience sampling**. Although convenience sampling is less time-consuming and costly than more rigorous, random sampling strategies (also referred to as probability sampling), it does not provide the researcher with data that can be generalized to a broader population.

The issue of sample representativeness, and its implications for the generalizability of a study's findings, is important. It is an issue that people not trained as social scientists often overlook. As mentioned at the beginning of this chapter, the literature on Internet addiction is suspect because the samples upon which these studies are based are not representative of the population (college students) that the researchers want to know about. Convenience sampling is especially problematic when the purpose of a study is to estimate something, like the pervasiveness of Internet addition.

Secondary Data Analysis

Social psychologists often use data from the General Social Survey (GSS) because it is based on representative samples and yields results that are generalizable to the U.S. adult population. Analyzing the results of surveys like the GSS that have been designed and administered by others is relatively common in sociological social psychology. Doing this is advantageous because the implementation of the techniques that yield representative (generalizable) samples is both lengthy and expensive, beyond what most researchers can afford unless they have a large grant from the government, a foundation, or some other organization. Studies based on survey data collected by someone else are referred to as **secondary data analyses**.

The Inter-university Consortium for Political and Social Research (ICPSR) at the University of Michigan houses an online archive of large-scale surveys funded by federal grant moneys. These surveys are available for secondary data analysis. If your school is a member of the ICPSR, you should be able to access the majority of the datasets in their archive. Some ICPSR datasets are also available to the public free of charge, whereas others may be purchased for a fee.

Many of the surveys in the ICPSR are lengthy, taking more than an hour to complete, and were administered using face-to-face interviews. Interviews used in quantitative research tend to be highly structured. That is, respondents answer a fixed set of questions in a fixed order. Although they are costly, face-to-face interviews yield higher response rates than other types of surveys, such as mail or e-mail and telephone surveys. It is harder to kick someone out of your house than it is to discard a questionnaire received in the mail, delete an e-mail, or hang up the phone. It is also more difficult to stop a survey once you have started if you are facing the interviewer. Thus, personal interviews can be longer than other types of surveys.

What Do You Think?

Go to the ICPSR website and browse its data bank at http://www.icpsr.umich.edu/icpsrweb/landing.jsp.

Choose a survey on a topic that interests you, and find out how it was conducted. Look at the list of questions that were given to respondents. You'll find the questions listed in the study codebook, a list of the survey variables and how they are scored. The codebook for most surveys in the ICPSR data bank can be accessed online. When you click on the title of a survey, the link to the survey codebook will appear under "Documentation." Write two research questions that you think would be interesting to explore, using the data in the study. Compare your research questions with a partner or small group. Note: You can complete this exercise even if your school is not a member of the ICPSR. Most study descriptions and codebooks are available to the public.

Experiments

Experiments allow for the collection of data in controlled settings. It is possible to conduct an experiment outside of the laboratory; these studies are referred to as field experiments. However, most experimental research takes place in a laboratory setting because it gives the researcher more control over the conditions the subjects experience.

In social psychological experiments, researchers often stage a social encounter and measure subjects' responses. The studies on the bystander effect, discussed in Chapter 1, provide a good illustration of social psychological experiments within the psychological face of social psychology. Although this text does not focus on psychological social psychology, understanding the kind of research that psychologists do makes it easier to understand the nature and purpose of sociological experiments conducted within the group processes and structures tradition. It also helps explain why some sociological social psychologists (in SSP) favor the use of surveys over experiments.

Experimental Design

Subjects in an experiment are usually unaware of the true purpose of the study because this information might affect their behavior. For instance, knowing that an experiment is about helping might make people more likely to do so. **Debriefing** occurs at the end of an experiment, when the researcher reveals the true nature of the study to the participants and addresses any negative feelings or concerns that may have been caused by the experience.

Experiments are an effective way for determining whether an independent and dependent variable are causally related. The two defining characteristics of an **experiment** are the use of **random assignment** and the manipulation of the independent variable by the researcher. In an experiment, there must be two or more groups of subjects. Who is in which group is determined at random. (This can be done by flipping a coin or through some other random procedure.) The researcher exposes each group to a different level of the independent variable (e.g., the number of witnesses to an emergency), and then the researcher measures the dependent variable (e.g., helping behavior).

If scores on the dependent variable vary between groups at the end of the experiment, then the researcher concludes that the independent variable has an effect on that outcome. The researcher can make this type of statement because other causal variables (such as personality characteristics and prior experiences that may affect people's willingness to help a stranger) are equally distributed across groups when the assignment to those groups is random. If there are differences in scores on the dependent variable at the end of the study, these differences must be due to the independent variable because everything else was held constant. In the case of the experiments on the bystander effect, discussed in the previous chapter, we know that differences in helping behavior between groups had to be due to the number of witnesses present and no other personal or situational characteristic.

Zimbardo's Stanford Prison Experiment

Zimbardo's (1974) classic prison study provides an excellent example of the benefits of conducting a true experiment. It is common for prison guards to abuse inmates. Zimbardo wanted to know whether this abuse of inmates is due to the guards' personalities (people with sadistic tendencies may be more likely than other individuals to become prison guards) or to the structure of the prison environment (anyone who enters into the role of guard is at risk for engaging in this type of behavior). This is a difficult question to answer because researchers cannot readily separate environmental from personality effects in the real world.

 Q: Would you say that you're even tempered? Why are you this way? Is this an innate disposition (something you were born with)? Or did you acquire this characteristic through interactions with family members, friends, and teammates?

A: It's hard to know for sure, although sociological social psychologists favor the latter explanation for reasons that we discuss in detail in Chapter 6 on socialization. In either case, this is the kind of question (personality or environment?) Zimbardo's study was designed to address.

In order to determine whether personality or environment is the cause of guard aggression in prisons, Zimbardo created a mock prison in the basement of the psychology building at Stanford University. He randomly assigned 24 college-age male volunteers to the roles of prisoner or guard. The random assignment was critical to the design of this study. If Zimbardo had allowed his subjects to choose their role (prisoner or guard), he would have been unable to disentangle the effects on their behavior of the subjects' characteristics (including personality) from that of the guard role itself. That is, he would have had a situation that replicates what we see in real life: people with certain personality characteristics may choose to become prison guards.

The experiment was scheduled to last for two weeks, but Zimbardo had to end it early because the guards' behaviors quickly got out of hand. The guards were instructed to do whatever it took, short of physical violence, to keep the prisoners in line. Soon after the experiment began, the guards began using a variety of abusive techniques to assert their authority and maintain control over the prisoners. They put prisoners who failed to comply with their requests in solitary confinement, removed the blankets from prisoners' beds, and had specific prisoners engage in embarrassing and strenuous behaviors. They used these strategies to force the prisoners to follow their orders, even when the orders themselves were designed to do no more than humiliate the prisoners and to remind them who was in power.

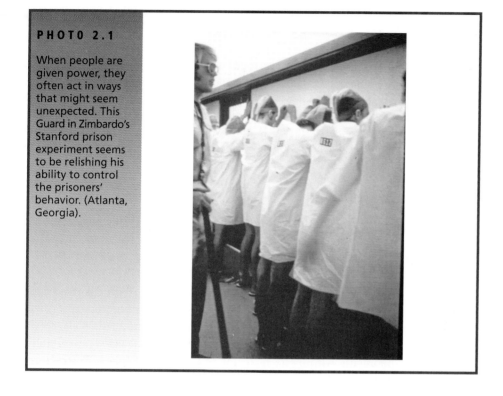

PHOTO 2.1

When people are given power, they often act in ways that might seem unexpected. This Guard in Zimbardo's Stanford prison experiment seems to be relishing his ability to control the prisoners' behavior. (Atlanta, Georgia).

In just six days, Zimbardo had his answer. He observed a group of "normal" college males become cruel and sadistic as they acted out the guard role. Similarly, the prisoners (also "normal" college males) behaved much like inmates in real-world prisons. They showed declines in self-esteem, withdrawal, apathy, and, in at least one case, uncontrolled rage. Thus, Zimbardo's study provides strong evidence that the negative behaviors exhibited by guards in prison settings are likely to be caused not by the personalities of the individuals who become prison guards but by the structure of the social environment. That structure of the environment includes the nature of the roles involved and their interrelationship—namely, the power differential between guards and prisoners.

Many people were both shocked and upset when tapes of American soldiers torturing prisoners at Abu Ghraib surfaced on the Internet during the Iraq War. The military's stance has been that the abuse of prisoners at Abu Ghraib was a reflection of a few bad soldiers and nothing more. Zimbardo disagrees. He has argued that the abuse of prisoners by their guards is a structural (systemic) problem, one not likely to be alleviated unless this is recognized (Zimbardo 2004). Zimbardo and others who take this more structural approach are not excusing the behaviors of the individual soldiers who engaged in the abuse, but they are recognizing the structural forces that make these behaviors likely occurrences.

> **Take a Break**
>
> You can see a brief interview (about four minutes) with Zimbardo about the contemporary applications of his Stanford Prison Experiment using the following weblink: http://www.bbc.co.uk/news/world-us-canada-14564182.
>
> If you're interested, you can find additional information about this study at Zimbardo's Stanford Prison Experiment website: http://www.prisonexp.org/.

Experiments in Sociology

Although Zimbardo is a psychologist, his findings are inherently sociological in that they show the effects of power on social interaction. However, unlike research done by social psychologists trained in sociology, Zimbardo's study focuses on the effects of the immediate social situation (the mock prison setting and the subjects' roles in this context) on subjects' behaviors. As noted in Chapter 1, the same is true of the study on the bystander effect, where the cause of students' nonintervention was shown to be the presence of others in the study setting.

Experimental sociology is more macro in its focus. Like Zimbardo's prison study, sociological experiments within the realm of the group processes and structures (GPS) tradition assess the effects of power on group dynamics. However, they focus on power that stems not from the immediate situation but from the structure of society and the statuses people occupy (e.g., their gender, race/ethnicity, and social class). These status characteristics are associated with ability within this society (men > women, White > minority, high class > low class).

THE EFFECTS OF STATUS: EDUCATION

Sociologist James C. Moore (1968) was one of the first social psychologists to test the effects of a dimension of status (education) on task performance in the laboratory. This topic is the focus of a large body of research within the group processes and structures (GPS) tradition. The subjects in Moore's study were 85 females from a local community college. The first independent variable was status (low or high). The low-status subjects were told that a woman attending Stanford University (a more prestigious school) would serve as their partner in the study. The high-status subjects were told that their partner would be a female from a local high school, which was less prestigious than the community college they were attending.

The second independent variable was task instructions. Half the subjects were told that individuals in the high-status condition perform better than low-status individuals on the experimental task they would soon be completing. For the women in the low-status condition (subjects who were told that their partner was from Stanford University), the experimenter read the following statement: "Another of the interesting things we have found is that Stanford students consistently do much better than Stanford Community College students." For the women in the high-status condition (subjects who were told that their partner was from a California high school), the statement read was, "Another of the interesting things we have found is that Stanford Community College students consistently do much better than California high school students." The other half of the subjects (the control) were not told anything about the relevance of the partner's school to task performance.

With the two independent variables, each with two levels, there were four different conditions (groups) in the experiment. The assignment of subjects to each of the four conditions was done randomly. The four groups are depicted in Figure 2.2.

Subjects completed the Contrast Sensitivity Task described in Chapter 1. The experimental task required subjects to indicate whether the rectangular grids displayed in a series of slides were predominantly black or white in color.

Each subject was ostensibly matched with a partner and placed alone into a booth. Subjects were then asked to indicate whether each of the series of slides was predominantly black or white by pressing the appropriate (black or white) button on the control panel. In each case, they were given bogus feedback. They were told that their partner's choice was either consistent with, or opposite of, their own. In reality, there were no partners, and the feedback was predetermined so that on 28 out of 40 trials (slides), subjects would believe that their partner gave the opposite answer. (Twelve trials were also included during which the alleged partner gave the same response as the subject in order to make the experimental task seem more authentic.) The dependent variable was the number of times out of 28 they stayed with their original response rather than changing it to match that of their partner.

Drawing on prior research on the effects of status characteristics on behavior, Moore derived the following hypotheses. (See Figure 2.2 for the visual representation of the four experimental groups.)

FIGURE 2.2

The Four Conditions (Groups) in Moore's (1968) Experiment on Status and Social Influence

	Low Status	High Status
Subjects Told Status Relevant to Task	Group 1	Group 2
Subjects Given No Information About Status	Group 3	Group 4

1. The women in Group 2 will stay with their responses more frequently than the women in Group 1 (who will be more likely to change their responses to match those of their alleged partners). This comparison is important because it tests the proposition that status differences in susceptibility to influence are due to differences in perceived ability.

2. The women in Group 4 will stay with their responses more frequently than the women in Group 3, even though neither group was given instructions suggesting that education would be relevant to the experimental task. This comparison is important because it indicates whether education is associated with ability (and thus susceptibility to influence) in a situation where there is no explicit link between status and ability.

3. Since their members are of similar status, there will be no difference in the frequency with which subjects stay with their original task responses in Group 1 versus Group 3 (both comprised of low-status participants) or in Group 2 versus Group 4 (both comprised of high-status participants).

The data confirmed all three predictions. Status (level of education relative to one's partner) affected students' susceptibility to influence. High-status subjects yielded to their partner less often than low-status subjects, even in the absence of information linking their status to the task outcome (groups 3 and 4). This suggests that status characteristics (in this case education, a characteristic related to social class) are associated with task abilities, even when there is no reason to believe that they will be related to task outcomes (i.e., in situations where no explicit link between status and ability is made). From a methodological standpoint, Moore's study was significant in that the researcher was successful in inducing status-based performance expectations in a controlled laboratory setting.

As mentioned in Chapter 1, it is rare for social psychologists trained in sociology to use experiments as a method of data collection, even when the purpose of the research is to determine whether variables are causally related. You might be wondering why. Experiments allow researchers to actively control the experiences of their participants rather than simply record participants' self-reported characteristics and experiences. Experiments are an active approach; surveys are a more passive approach. So wouldn't experiments be preferable?

Remember, the two defining characteristics of an experiment are the random assignment of individuals to groups (each of which receives a different level of the independent variable) and the manipulation of the independent variable by the experimenter. The three independent (causal) variables most important to social psychologists working within the SSP tradition are economic class or socioeconomic status, race/ethnicity, and gender. Can you manipulate and randomly assign people to different levels of these variables? Could you, for example, randomly make someone either male or female? Can you, as a researcher, manipulate subjects' social-class background or their race/ethnicity? It isn't possible. This is why SSP researchers, who focus on the effects of these independent variables, typically use surveys as a method of data collection.

Social psychologists working within the GPS tradition are in a unique position. Because they are interested in interactions within small groups, they can control the social settings within which behavior is studied. By manipulating the composition of the groups under investigation (e.g., the education, gender, or race/ethnicity of the participants), they can observe the effects of these statuses on variables such as the susceptibility to influence.

Evaluating Quantitative Research

When evaluating empirical research (studies based on the analysis of data), social psychologists use three criteria: validity, generalizability, and reliability. These criteria must be met for a study to be considered scientific.

1. **Validity** refers to the accuracy of a study's findings. Has the researcher over-looked anything, or do the study results encompass everything of relevance to the topic under investigation? When a study addresses all that it should and thus yields an accurate assessment of its subject matter, it is considered valid.

2. **Generalizability**, described earlier in the section on sampling, refers to the extent that a study's findings apply to a larger population. For a study to yield generalizable results, the sample must be representative of the population of interest. For example, a researcher who wants to study the causes of college students' drinking cannot give her survey to primarily freshman, which might happen if it is administered in introductory-level classes. Freshmen differ from sophomores, juniors, and seniors in many ways, and this is reflected in their drinking habits. Freshmen are less likely to be drinkers than more advanced students. However, when freshmen do drink, they tend to drink more irresponsibly than upperclassmen. Thus, a predominantly freshman sample will lead the researcher to erroneous conclusions about the drinking behaviors of college students in general. Freshmen may differ from more advanced students in other behaviors or in their attitudes and beliefs, which may also influence the study results.

3. **Reliability** reflects the degree to which other researchers can duplicate a study's findings. Reliability is typically high when there is consistency in measurement and interpretation across studies on a particular topic. Reliability may also be affected by the researcher's sample. Samples that vary in composition across studies (e.g., college freshmen versus college undergrad-uates) tend to yield different patterns of results and may reduce the reliability of a set of research findings.

The Strengths and Weaknesses of Surveys and Experiments

When evaluating surveys and experiments, it is conventional to talk about two types of validity. The first, **internal validity**, pertains to the establishment of causal relationships, which is the purpose of most quantitative research. A study is internally valid when it is clear that an independent variable *causes* a dependent variable. The second, **external validity**, pertains to the degree to which study results are generalizable to other individuals in other settings.

ESTABLISHING CAUSALITY AND INTERNAL VALIDITY

The first step in establishing a **causal relationship** (when an independent variable causes a dependent variable) is to determine whether the independent and dependent variable are correlated. A **correlation** exists when an increase in scores on the independent variable is associated with either an increase or a decrease in scores on the dependent variable.

- A **positive relationship** exists when both variables increase together (e.g., the relationship between income and happiness).

- A **negative relationship** exists when one variable increases as the other decreases (e.g., the relationship between income and negative affect).

Establishing whether two variables are correlated using standard statistical techniques is straightforward and rarely a problem for researchers, regardless of their choice of method (survey or experiment). However, in order to conclude that a correlation between two variables reflects a causal relationship, two other issues must be addressed.

Time Order

The researcher must be sure that the independent variable *preceded* the dependent variable in time. Does income really cause happiness, or could happiness cause income? Perhaps people who are happy work harder and more readily establish work relationships that translate into gains in salary.

Cross-sectional data are data collected at one point in time. Working with cross-sectional data sometimes makes it difficult to determine whether the independent variable (income, in the latter example) really came first. Social psychologists who use cross-sectional survey data often run into this problem, which is referred to as *reverse causality*. This is a limitation of Kahneman and Deaton's (2010) study, discussed earlier, which showed a positive relationship between income and happiness. Based on their data, which were collected at one point in time, we don't know for sure whether income came before or after happiness. Thus, although their research findings suggest that money makes people happy, this conclusion is tentative.

Social psychologists who feel that time order, or reverse causality, is especially problematic given the nature of their variables may address this issue by using **longitudinal data**. That is, they collect data from the same respondents at two or more points in time, or they use an already available dataset that is longitudinal in design.

Many SSP studies of delinquency are longitudinal in design. Researchers collect data from students when they are in middle school (e.g., grade 8) and then conduct follow-up surveys at grades 10 and 12. This enables social psychologists to determine the time order of the variables of interest. Do poor quality parent-child relationships, for example, lead to delinquency? Or do kids who become delinquent distance themselves from their parents, thereby decreasing the quality of their relationship? The analysis of data from longitudinal surveys suggests that it's parent-child relationships that affect delinquency (Bui 2009), although this effect may decrease in magnitude over time (Crawford and Novak 2002).

Sometimes using longitudinal data is not necessary because the variables themselves make clear the direction of the relationship. If women are more depressed then men (and they are, a pattern we discuss in Chapter 10), the researcher knows that gender must come first, because depression cannot affect gender.

Time order is not considered to be highly problematic in survey research because it is often clear which variable came first, as in the case of the effect of gender on depression. And, when this is not the case (e.g., does poor quality parent-child relationships cause delinquency or does delinquency cause poor quality parent-child relationships?), longitudinal data may be used. Time order is never a problem in experimental studies because the researcher manipulates the independent variable and then measures the dependent variable.

Spurious Relationships

However, it is important to note that a correlation between an independent and a dependent variable, and evidence that the independent variable came first, are not themselves evidence of a causal relationship. If there is a third variable that causes both the independent and dependent variables the independent and dependent will be correlated even when there is no causal link between them. This is called a **spurious relationship**. Spurious relationships are deceptive and can lead researchers to conclude that one variable causes another when this is not really the case. For example, there is a positive correlation between height and the amount of alcohol people consume. Does this mean that being tall makes people want to drink more? This is not likely. This is a spurious relationship produced by gender. Males tend to be taller than women, and men tend to drink more than women. Thus, when we take gender into consideration, the relationship between height and levels of alcohol consumption disappears. This means that the correlation between height and alcohol was a spurious relationship produced by gender.

Researchers who work with survey data must be wary of spurious relationships. The best way to address this issue is to control for as many likely spurious variables as possible when running statistical analyses. (Gender, race/ethnicity, and social class are usually regarded as likely spurious variables because they affect so many different things.) Controlling for spurious variables can be done easily in a standard statistical program, such as SPSS (Statistical Package for the Social Sciences). When a variable is controlled, the reported effect of the independent variable on the dependent variable is at a constant level of that (control) variable. For example, if income is positively correlated with happiness when gender is controlled (i.e., held constant), this means that the income-happiness relationship persists among men and among women. In the height-drinking example, controlling for gender made the relationship disappear because it was spurious. Among men, height and drinking are unrelated. There is also no relationship between these variables among women.

Spurious relationships are not a problem when working with data collected from an experiment because the random assignment of subjects to the different groups controls for all potential sources of spuriousness (gender, race/ethnicity, social class, and everything else) by equally distributing these variables across groups. Thus, experiments are always high in internal validity. On the other hand, Spurious relationships, and hence internal validity, are potentially problematic in causally oriented research that is not experimental in design, including surveys.

What Do You Think?

- Jim, the father of two young children, sees a television commercial sponsored by a realtor association. The commercial states that kids who live in houses do better in school than those who live in other kinds of residences (e.g., apartments). As a result, Jim begins thinking seriously about buying a house. What might you say to Jim about the basis of his decision to purchase a home?
- The local newspaper publishes the results of a study showing that there are more pedestrian traffic fatalities at intersections with crosswalks than there are at intersections without crosswalks. Based upon this finding, the reporter suggests that crosswalks are a waste of money. Is this conclusion reasonable? Give an alternative interpretation for the study results.
- Jordan, a high school senior, finds that her friends who play a musical instrument have better grades than those who have never had music lessons. She's never played a musical instrument but is considering starting lessons because she needs to improve her grades so that she can get into the college of her choice. Are music lessons an effective use of her time? Explain.

GENERALIZABILITY AND EXTERNAL VALIDITY

External validity is the main strength of survey research, provided that a representative sample is used. It is, however, a potential weakness of experimental studies. When conducting laboratory experiments, social psychologists, who are typically college professors, often use students in their classes as subjects (convenience samples). These individuals are not representative of the general population and may have characteristics that distinguish them from other groups within the larger society. For example, they tend to be from affluent families and in many schools they are predominantly White. Also, they may differ significantly from other students attending their particular college or university. You can guess that students enrolled in sociology courses may have different demographic characteristics and social attitudes from students taking courses in disciplines like business or engineering. Moreover, the laboratory itself is an artificial setting that may yield patterns of behavior different from those that occur in everyday life.

Experimental sociologists working in the group processes and structures tradition do not feel that these are serious issues. In fact, they would say that there is no reason to believe that the processes they are studying (e.g., the effect of gender or education on susceptibility to influence) are not generalizable across individuals and settings. There is no reason to believe that group dynamics in the lab, and the effects of status characteristics such as gender and race on the interactions that occur within that environment, would be any different elsewhere.

Whether this is the case is open to question. Because experiments use nonrepresentative samples, most sociological social psychologists consider generalizability to be a limitation of this type of research.

SUMMING IT UP: INTERNAL AND EXTERNAL VALIDITY

More generally, there are two important points to remember when evaluating quantitative research. They are that

- the strength of experiments (causality or internal validity) is the weakness of surveys, and

- the strength of surveys (generalizability or external validity) is the weakness of experiments.

RELIABILITY

Reliability is rarely considered to be problematic when data are gathered using either an experiment or a survey, provided that the study design is reasonable. This means that the sample is appropriate to the topic under investigation and the researcher has used sound measures of key variables. Social psychologists often use measures that have been developed and tested by others in previous research to increase the reliability of their findings.

QUALITATIVE RESEARCH METHODS

Given their interest in how meanings are constructed through interaction and the unique experiences of specific groups, symbolic interactionists almost always use qualitative methods. (Note: We discuss some exceptions to this general practice in Chapter 3, on the symbolic interactionist face of social psychology.)

The Inductive Method and Grounded Theory

The qualitative research process is inductive in nature. **Inductive reasoning** involves going from the specific to the general. Think about how you learn what a new acquaintance is like. Coming to the conclusion that someone you've recently met is an individual you would like to have as a friend (or not) requires inductive reasoning. As your experiences with this person accumulate, you draw conclusions about his or her character.

Qualitative research is inductive in that it goes from specific (observations and data) to the general (theory). Rather than testing preexisting theories about the way society works or the social realities of the members of a particular group, qualitative researchers *develop* theories to explain the observations they make in the field (the places where people live and routinely interact). This process of going from specific data to general theory is called **grounded theory** (Glaser and Strauss 1967). The qualitative research process through which sociological social psychologists develop theories about various social phenomena is displayed in Figure 2.3.

Sociological social psychologists who do qualitative research (typically symbolic interactionists) try to limit the impact of any preconceived notions they have about the group or process under investigation. The goal of their studies is to achieve **methodological empathy** (Blumer 1969), which requires researchers to view the world through the eyes of the participants. For example, adolescents tend to evaluate people and behaviors differently than adults do. Thus, it is important for researchers studying adolescents to understand what things mean to them. This became clear to the researcher in one study of middle school girls when she discovered that popular females were not well liked by their peers. (Most adults define someone as popular when they are well liked.) Within the girls' peer groups, however, popularity meant visibility, and the most popular girls were those who were the most well-known, usually because they were cheerleaders (Eder 1985). This kind of gap in perception is common, even with adult subjects. Thus, symbolic interactionists stress the importance of getting inside the minds of study participants. Data must be interpreted from their perspective, not the perspective of the researcher.

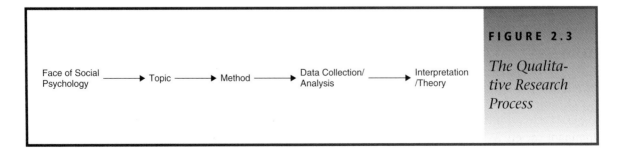

FIGURE 2.3

The Qualitative Research Process

Face of Social Psychology ⟶ Topic ⟶ Method ⟶ Data Collection/Analysis ⟶ Interpretation/Theory

Qualitative researchers aim to provide a detailed account of how the participants interpret relationships, situations, and events. Besen's research on teens working in coffee shops (Chapter 1) is a good illustration of this kind of study. In qualitative research, the thoughts, feelings, and behaviors of the individuals studied are not reduced to numerical patterns, as they are in quantitative research.

Given the depth of their analyses, qualitative studies tend to be based on relatively small samples (usually no more than 50 individuals). Participants are often obtained by using a procedure called **snowball sampling**. Researchers using this technique go into the field, establish a relationship with one or more key informants, who introduce them to the people they know, who introduce them to others, and so forth. (Thus, the sample grows in size like a snowball.) This sampling strategy may be employed when it is difficult to gain access to a group or it is not appropriate to simultaneously introduce oneself to group members in a public setting. Besen obtained her study participants (teens working in coffee shops) through the use of snowball sampling.

Whether or not a particular individual is selected as a subject is ultimately shaped by the characteristics and social ties of the people that the researcher initially established relationships with in the field. Thus, snowball sampling typically does not yield a representative sample of the population under investigation. The fact that the sample is not representative is not a significant concern in this context because the researcher's focus is on understanding the unique experiences of the individuals being studied.

Participant Observation

Social psychologists who are qualitative in orientation often use participant observation as a method of data collection. **Participant observation** is a methodology that involves interacting with the individuals under study and observing their behaviors in their natural environment, often over a lengthy period of time.

As noted in Chapter 1, social psychological studies based on participant observation are similar to the analyses that anthropologists have historically conducted in cultures outside of the United States. This type of research is also called **ethnographic research** or field research. Unlike anthropologists, social psychologists who use participant observation typically study groups and, more specifically, subcultures within the United States.

A **subculture** is a group of individuals with values and norms that differ from those of the mainstream or dominant culture. The use of the term "dominant" implies a power differential. Subcultures, especially those studied by sociologists, are often groups that lack access to important societal resources (i.e., money, political power, and social prestige).

The second-generation Indian American college students Kurien (2005) studied (pages 21) clearly fit the definition of a subculture in that they are distinct from the dominant society in terms of their race/ethnicity, heritage, and religion. As Kurien

PHOTO 2.2

These young males belong to the punk rock subculture, which emphasizes freedom of expression and questions the legitimacy of conventional institutions and authorities (Atlanta, Georgia).

points out, these individuals are frequently marginalized; they are often perceived and treated as inferior by members of the dominant group (Whites). This marginalization was, in fact, the primary reason the more extremist members of the Hindu group gave for their participation in the organization.

The teenagers working in coffee shops studied by Besen (2006) can also be considered a subculture. They were from similar backgrounds. They dressed in ways that were often viewed negatively by individuals who had power over them (e.g., parents), and they had social identities and group norms that were distinct from those existing within the larger culture.

What Do You Think?

Look around you. How would you define or describe the dominant culture in your school? Identify as many subcultures as you can. (Remember that a subculture is a group of individuals with values and norms that differ from those of the mainstream or dominant culture.) Think about whether you belong to any subcultures within your school. How would you describe these groups?

Covert Participant Observation

In **covert participant observation**, subjects do not know that their behaviors are being observed and analyzed by the researcher. The main rationale for conducting a covert study is that the research topic is sensitive, and therefore potential partici-pants may not act naturally or reveal information about their lives if they know they are being observed.

Laud Humphreys's (1970) classic study of homosexual encounters between men in public restrooms, called "tearooms," is an excellent example of this type of research and illustrates why a researcher might feel the need to go under cover. Would people be willing to talk about this kind of activity if the researcher had approached them, declared the purpose of his study, and asked for an interview?

Given the sensitivity of the behavior investigated, Humphreys's study generated substantial debate about the ethical issues associated with covert participant obser-vation. When gathering his data, Humphreys played the role of a "watchqueen," a voyeur who participated in the restroom encounters as a lookout to make sure those participating in the sexual activity weren't interrupted or discovered. From this position, he could observe and gather information about "tearoom" behavior. Hum-phreys later disclosed his role to some of the men he had observed and interviewed them about their daily lives. However, in other cases, Humphreys wrote down the license plate numbers of participants so he could find out where they lived and inter-view them at a later date. So as not to be recognized, he waited a year before going to their homes in disguise. Then he told the men that he was conducting an anonymous public health survey so that they would be willing to talk to him (Humphreys 1970).

Because of increasing concerns about the rights of research subjects, covert research is much less common today than it was in the past. (We discuss ethical issues in research, and concerns about Humphreys's study in particular, toward the end of the chapter.) Instead, researchers interested in studying sensitive topics like sexual behavior often use **covert nonparticipant observation** in public or semi-public settings. In one covert nonparticipant observational study of adult (X-rated) bookstores (McCleary and Tewskbury 2010), the researchers found that almost one fifth of the store patrons were female, confirming the notion that such bookstores are not geared only to men. In studies where the researchers do not interact with their subjects, the researchers do not know their subjects' identities. This anonymity significantly minimizes the level of risk associated with participation in the study. However, the downside of this strategy is that researchers cannot obtain the depth of information accessible to the participant observer.

Overt Participant Observation

Most contemporary participant observational analyses are overt in nature. In **overt participant observation**, the researcher openly identifies himself or herself as a researcher. Both Besen (teens working in coffee shops) and Kurien (Indian American students belonging to a Hindu student organization) used overt participant observa-tion as their method of data collection.

Given the focus of the symbolic interactionist face of sociological social psychol-ogy within which these researchers were working, this methodology was a logical choice. SI researchers are concerned with face-to-face interactions at the micro level. They want to know how individuals actively construct their social realities in natural settings. Rather than focusing on a concrete outcome, such as an attitude or a behavioral pattern, symbolic interactionists focus on the processes through which individuals derive their attitudes toward themselves and others and construct social norms that govern their future actions.

For example, in her study of teenagers working in coffee shops, Besen emphasizes the normative structure of the workplace (constructed by the teens and largely unknown to outsiders) and the ways that customers' relationships to the employees present shaped their level of privilege pertaining to seating, attention, and conversation. Similarly, Kurien focuses on the interactional processes through which second-generation Indian American college students negotiated their own racial and religious identities. In both cases, the researcher developed a theory to explain her findings that challenges preconceived notions about the group under study. Besen questions the idea that work in the coffee shop is a bad job that is merely exploitive. Kurien points to the importance of considering religion, as well as race/ethnicity, when considering the formation of immigrant identities.

Overt participant observation often involves either informal or formal interviews with the individuals being studied. (Note that covert participation precludes any formal interviewing, as such a request would make the participants suspicious and could potentially blow the researcher's cover.) The researcher may probe for details and for additional information during the course of the interview. As new information is revealed, the interviewer may also alter the focus of the interview and ask additional questions.

In-Depth Interviews

In-depth, interviews can also serve as a stand-alone methodology, the researcher's sole source of data. It may be difficult or impossible for a researcher to observe firsthand interactions of relevance to the topic of interest. For example, symbolic interactionists interested in college students' experiences cannot observe all of their behaviors, on campus and elsewhere. In such situations, they use in-depth interviews instead of participant observation to collect their data. Sociologist Allison Hurst (2007) used in-depth interviews as a stand-alone method in her study of the experiences of working-class college students. Because she was interested in their prior home lives, participant observation was not an option.

Hurst argues that getting a college education can be a double-edged sword for students from working-class backgrounds. Their education allows them to become socially mobile, but at a cost. For many individuals, that cost is their abandoning family members and old friends, whom they regard as reminders of a painful past.

Hurst placed the 21 students she interviewed into one of two categories (Renegade or Loyalist) based on their feelings about family members, old friends, and their working-class roots. Renegades admired members of the middle class and felt intimidated and embarrassed about their working-class background. Loyalists, on the other hand, were proud of their working-class roots and were distrustful of their classmates from more affluent families. While Renegades wanted to distance themselves from family members and anyone else associated with their past, Loyalists wanted to better themselves so that they could help family members who were struggling. These individuals identified with their community and did not view being a student as an important part of their identity. For Loyalists, higher education was a way to fight oppression rather than an avenue for social mobility and entry into the middle class.

Not surprisingly, Hurst found that race often intersected with class to influence the narratives students constructed about their past and current selves. Renegades who were racial/ethnic minorities felt that social mobility would negate the impact of their (dark) skin color, and they were willing to do whatever it took to become members of the establishment. On the other hand, Loyalists who were members of racial/ethnic minority groups indicated a resistance to social mobility because they perceived that moving up in the stratification hierarchy would mean leaving behind their cultural heritage. Rather than becoming a member of the dominant group, their goal was to graduate and get a job that would enable them to give back to their community.

One characteristic that influenced students' interpretations of their experiences (and whether they adopted a Renegade or Loyalist stance) was the degree to which they understood the nature of the U.S. class structure. Renegades focused on individuals' personal characteristics and blamed poor people (including their family members and friends) for their situation. Loyalists were more sociological in their thinking. They recognized the structural roots of poverty, the interconnectedness of poverty and race, and the ways that poverty is reproduced across generations, irrespective of an individual's personal characteristics.

From a methodological standpoint, it is important to note that Hurst did not begin her study with the expectation of distinguishing between two groups of students, based on their views of class, race, and the value of social mobility. Rather, these categories emerged out of her data.

Evaluating Qualitative Research Methods

It is difficult to assess qualitative studies in relation to the criteria used to evaluate quantitative research because their purpose is so different. Qualitative research is not causal in orientation, so the concept of internal validity has no relevance. Moreover, because symbolic interactionists view every group as unique, generalizability (external validity) and reliability are considered less important than they are in quantitative studies.

Bearing this in mind, we compare the strengths and weaknesses of qualitative and quantitative research, using the three criteria for evaluating empirical research described earlier. Considering the relative strengths and weaknesses of these two methodological orientations should make their different foci even clearer.

The Strengths and Weaknesses of Qualitative and Quantitative Research

In general, the strength of qualitative studies is their validity. These analyses (e.g., Besen's article on teens working in coffee shops; Kurien's analysis of Indian American college students; and Hurst's research on college, class, and social mobility) are so highly detailed that is likely that the researcher has captured all relevant aspects of the experiences of the study participants. Relative to qualitative research, quantitative research is narrow in focus; it is conducted to test one or more specific hypotheses. Therefore, quantitative research may overlook important aspects of the topic or group being studied.

Qualitative researchers, especially those who use covert participant observation, may also have access to information about sensitive issues (e.g., sexual behavior or illegal drug use) that people are unwilling to discuss in a formal interview or on a survey form. In overt participant observation, researchers spend a substantial amount of time interacting with the subjects in order to gain their trust. Thus, subjects may reveal information in these studies that would otherwise be difficult to access, which enhances the validity of their results.

However, generalizability is often problematic in participant observational studies or in studies based on in-depth interviews. Such studies may not be generalizable because researchers interact with and interview only select individuals who may not be representative of the group being studied. The issue of sampling may also undermine a study's reliability because another researcher with a different sample may obtain different results.

In addition, the subjectivity of qualitative studies can make reliability problematic. Qualitative research requires social psychologists to enter into the minds of their subjects and provide detailed accounts of the meanings the subjects give their experiences. As a result, these studies require a fair amount of subjective interpretation on the part of the researcher, which may make the results difficult to replicate.

Generalizability and reliability are higher in quantitative research for two reasons: (1) these studies are based on larger (often representative) samples, and (2) the interpretation of the findings is more objective. Two variables either are or are not correlated, and this result either supports or does not support the theory being tested.   For all of these reasons, quantitative research is sometimes considered more methodologically rigorous and scientific than qualitative research.

Social psychologists who are qualitative in orientation are often frustrated when the value of their studies is questioned simply because their results may not be generalizable to some larger population or easily replicated. These researchers feel that, given their subject matter, it is impossible for social psychologists to employ quantitative research methodologies comparable to the natural sciences (i.e., laboratory experiments) or surveys and get meaningful findings. From their perspective, doing so is not realistic, or even desirable. Human social behavior is simply too complex to expect results from one setting or group to generalize to others. Who are these individuals? They are symbolic interactionists, who study face-to-face interactions and the social construction of meaning in everyday social encounters.

What Do You Think?

■ Turn back to pages Box 1.1 in Chapter 1, and take another look at the list of 10 questions that sociological social psychologists ask. For each of these questions, think about how a sociological social psychologist might research the question. You might work with a partner or small group.
1. Is the question best explored through qualitative or quantitative research? What methodology (experiment, survey, covert or overt participant, or in-depth interview) would the researcher be most likely to use? Why?
2. How would the researcher choose the participants? How big a sample would be needed?
3. Does the research involve a cause-effect relationship? Explain why or why not.
■ Now choose one research question from the list in Box 1.1. Write a brief summary of how you would go about researching that question. Write at least two paragraphs.

USING MULTIPLE METHODS

Because each research methodology has particular strengths and weaknesses, social psychologists often use multiple methods to validate their findings. For example, suppose that the results of a survey on college students' study habits indicate that many students study for hours on weekends. Then the researchers might go to the school's library for four hours every Saturday and use naturalistic observation (covert nonparticipant observation) to record the number of students present and their behaviors. The researchers would then compare these results to the results of their survey to determine whether they suggest a similar pattern. The use of multiple methods to validate a study's findings is called **triangulation**.

Researchers also combine methods of data collection when they feel that this is the best way to obtain important information about the topic they are interested in. Karp and Yoels's (1976) classic study on student participation in college classes (still relevant today) illustrates the use of multiple methods of data collection. As symbolic interactionists, they were interested in the social construction of meanings within the college classroom. However, it would not be appropriate to use participant observation within this context. Thus, they employed a two-pronged methodological approach that combined nonparticipant observation and a survey so that they could effectively access the information they were seeking.

Some of the studies presented in subsequent chapters use multiple methods of data collection. In particular, we discuss Karp and Yoels's analysis of classroom participation in greater detail in the next chapter, which focuses on the symbolic interactionist face of sociological social psychology.

Finally, as you now know, sociological social psychologists tend to favor one method over others because of the focus of the face of social psychology in which they are working (face → research question → methodology). Thus, we gain the greatest insight in the nature of human social behavior by combining knowledge gained from research involving the use of different methodologies within each of the faces of social psychology.

The Research Cycle

Research within sociological social psychology is reciprocal, or cyclical, in nature. The research cycle in sociological social psychology is depicted in Figure 2.4.

- Quantitative research, which involves deductive reasoning, is used to test theories. Inductive logic is used to modify existing theories that have been tested but have not been supported by the data, which sometimes happens (as indicated by the return arrow from data to theory revision in Figure 2.4). Once the revision is complete, the theory may be retested in another study.

- Qualitative research, which is inductive in nature, is used to create new theories. These theories might also be tested in subsequent studies (the return arrow from theory to data in Figure 2.4).

Thus, researchers may begin at either of the two points in the research cycle. They may start with an already-established theory, as in the case of quantitative researchers in SSP or GPS, or they may start with the collection of data, as in the case of qualitative researchers in SI. It is through this cycle, in which theories are developed, tested, and modified, that knowledge within sociological social psychology is generated.

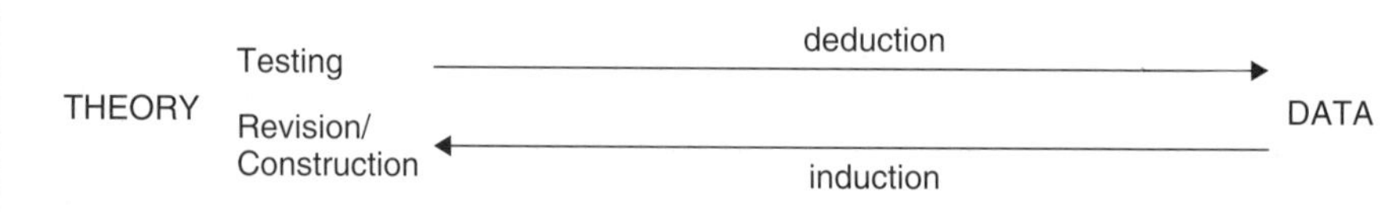

THEORY — Testing / Revision/Construction — deduction → DATA — induction

FIGURE 2.4

The Research Cycle in Sociological Social Psychology

ETHICAL ISSUES IN RESEARCH

Whatever the topic under investigation or the methodology used, researchers must make sure that they do not violate the rights of their subjects. Box 2.2 summarizes two famous studies that involved the mistreatment of subjects. Not surprisingly, the victims of some of the most abusive research practices were members of disadvantaged groups.

The three social psychological studies that generated the most discussion about subjects' rights are Milgram's obedience experiments (Box 2.2), Zimbardo's Stanford

---

Box 2.2   Two Experiments That Raised Questions About the Ethical Treatment of Research Subjects

Two studies played a significant role in generating discussion about the ethical treatment of human subjects within social psychology and in other fields. Both studies were experiments, one biomedical in nature, and the other social psychological. Neither study is considered acceptable by today's standards.

The Tuskegee Syphilis Study (1932–1972): In this medical experiment, researchers funded by the U.S. Public Health Services followed 399 low-income African American men with syphilis and collected data to study the natural course of the illness. Many of the participants were not informed that they had syphilis and were denied treatment for the disease and any related medical problems. The study continued until 1972, even though penicillin became the standard treatment for syphilis in the 1940s. The study ended when a public health official went to the press (Brandt 2000).

The individuals who unknowingly took part in the Tuskegee Syphilis Study and their families have received some monetary compensation from the U.S. government. Moreover, in 1997, 25 years after the study was initiated, President Bill Clinton apologized to the study's victims. If you're interested, go to the following web address to view the transcript of President Clinton's apology: http://clinton4.nara.gov/New/Remarks/Fri/19970516-898.html.

Milgram's Obedience Studies (1960s): In a series of laboratory experiments, psychological social psychologist Stanley Milgram told subjects they were participating in a study on learning. Subjects were told that they would be teaching another subject to remember word pairs by administering increasing levels of electric shocks when they incorrectly matched a word to its pair. The switches used to deliver the shocks were labeled with information about the number of volts being administered (ranging from 15 to 450), and above the levers for the strongest shocks there were phrases such as "Extreme-Intensity Shock," Danger—Severe Shock," and "XXX." The subjects (the "teachers") were instructed to give progressively stronger shocks to another subject (really a confederate of the experimenter) in an adjoining room, even when this individual would scream, kick the wall, and beg for the experiment to stop. Whenever the subject wanted to stop, the experimenter would urge the teacher to continue administering the shocks. The (dependent) variable of interest was how far the teachers went on the shock generator. Many were willing to give someone shocks of 450 volts. In reality, no shocks were given, but the subjects did not know this until they were debriefed at the end of the experiment (Milgram 1963). Many of the participants experienced high levels of stress during these experiments and left the lab knowing they had the capacity to harm someone just because a person with authority told them to do so.

The subjects in Milgram's experiment did not express any regrets about their participation in the study when they were later surveyed (Milgram 1974). Nonetheless, Milgram was accused of violating his subjects' rights, and the legitimacy of his research on ethical grounds is still being debated within social psychology and related fields of study.

PHOTO 2.3

U.S. health care worker getting blood samples from men for use in the Tuskegee syphilis study.

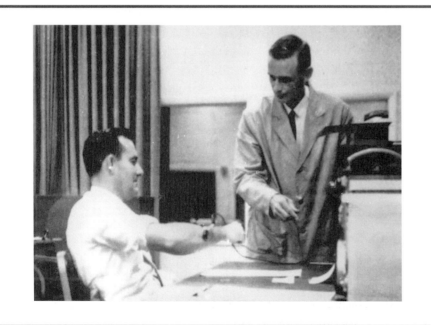

PHOTO 2.4

Professor Stanley Milgram (on right) prepares subject for participation in an experiment on obedience.

Prison Experiment (pages 38–39), and Laud Humphreys' Tearoom Trade (page 51). After these studies were published, there was much debate about their legitimacy and about whether the researchers had gone too far. This debate ultimately led to a greater awareness of the ethical issues associated with conducting research with human subjects.

Institutional Review Boards and Codes of Ethics

To reduce the likelihood that subjects' rights will be violated, researchers using humans as subjects must have their prospective studies reviewed and approved by outside boards. Prior to collecting their data, social psychologists typically have their studies evaluated by their college or university's human subjects committee, often referred to as the **institutional review board (IRB)**. To further ensure the ethical treatment of subjects, most professions that involve research have developed a code of ethics that all members are expected to adhere to. The American Sociological Association, the national association for professional sociologists (there is a division of this organization specifically for social psychologists), has posted their Code of Ethics on their website (http://www.asanet.org/images/asa/docs/pdf/CodeofEthics.pdf). Sections 11, 12, and 13 pertain specifically to the research process.

The general rule regarding the use of human subjects is that the expected benefits of the study to particular groups or the larger society must outweigh any potential harm to the subjects. In social psychological research (vs., e.g., medical studies), this means that the risks to subjects must be minimal. Even so, potential participants must be told of these risks, participation must be voluntary, and the researcher must obtain participants' consent before beginning the study.

Experiments, Surveys, and Observational Research

The key ethical issue in experimental research pertains to the use of deception. Subjects are never told the true purpose of the experiment beforehand because knowing what the study is about is likely to affect their behavior. How, then, can they really consent to participate?

The key ethical issue associated with survey research is confidentiality. The researcher must protect the confidentiality of participants' responses. Because survey results are usually presented at the aggregate level, identification of individuals based on published results is unlikely.

The primary ethical issue associated with overt participant observation also has to do with confidentiality. Sometimes it is difficult to protect subjects' identities, given the detailed nature of these analyses. Researchers always use fictitious names for participants, the groups to which they belong, and the communities they live in. Still, given the level of detail that characterizes these studies, participants who read the research report are likely to recognize themselves and others.

It would be difficult these days for a covert study like Humphreys's (1970) Tearoom Trade to gain IRB approval, given the potential risk to the subjects. (If the wrong person got hold of the data, it could have devastating consequences for the participants.) Thus, covert nonparticipant observation (like the study of customers of adult bookstores) has become more popular despite the fact that the information gathered is more limited.

You may be required to conduct a research project as part of your social psychology course or for a senior seminar or capstone course for your major in sociology or some other program. If you are collecting your own data, you might be required to obtain approval from your school's human subjects committee or IRB. You may not need IRB approval if the study you are planning to conduct is nonthreatening and the results will only be used within the context of your class. (This means your findings will never be published or presented outside of the classroom.)

If you engage in secondary data analysis, depending upon the policy at your school, you may not need to obtain IRB approval because you will not actually collect the data. If you do need IRB approval, this application should be relatively easy to complete because the data are already available. One of the benefits of secondary data analysis is that the researcher avoids the potential ethical issues associated with the data collection phase of the research process.

What Do You Think?

You're on the college's committee to decide whether these proposed research studies are ethical and should be approved. Tell what your decision is, and why.

- Willa has proposed a study of college students' political views. In particular, she wants to determine whether students have the same party affiliation and views about public policies, such as welfare and health care reform, as their parents. She plans to administer an anonymous survey in sociology classes to approximately 300 students. She will use the data she gathers for a paper, which she will present at an on-campus research conference. The results she presents in her paper and at the conference will be in aggregate form so that no particular individual's responses can be identified.
- Sam wants to conduct a study on illegal drug use at his college for his senior project. He knows some people who use drugs and plans to attend some of their parties, where he will conduct 10 in-depth interviews. The interviews will focus on when and why participants began using drugs.

CHAPTER SUMMARY

The key determining factor in the selection of a methodology is the research question under investigation. Thus, there is a relationship between the face of social psychology within which a researcher is working and the method of data collection used. Large-scale surveys are the best way to measure the outcomes (patterns of perception and behavior) studied by researchers working within the social structure and personality (SSP) tradition. Because social psychologists aligned with the group processes and structures (GPS) face of social psychology can control the composition of the groups they study, they are able to collect their data using laboratory experiments. GPS studies differ from the experiments conducted by psychologists, which examine variables specific to the immediate social encounter. In contrast, GPS studies focus on the effects of inequality at the societal level on group behavior. The social processes of interest to symbolic interactionists (SI) are most accessible through the use of qualitative methods—participant observation and in-depth interviews. The methods of data collection discussed in this chapter, the face of social psychology within which they are used, and their strengths and weaknesses are summarized in Table 2.2.

Key Points to Know

- **There are two general research orientations within social psychology: qualitative and quantitative.** These types of research serve very different purposes.

- **Quantitative research focuses on outcomes, rather than processes, and is used to determine whether independent and dependent variables are causally related.** These deductive studies, involving surveys or experiments, are designed to *test* theories.

- **Qualitative research is descriptive and focuses on social processes.** These studies, based on either participant observation or in-depth interviews as a stand-alone method, involve inductive logic. After researchers collect their data, they develop theories to explain their observations.

- **It is important for the researcher to have a representative sample if generalizability to a larger population is a goal of the study. Sampling is an especially important issue in survey research.** Representative samples are drawn in some random fashion so that they include individuals with characteristics similar to the characteristics of the people in the population the researcher wants to know about.

- **Empirical studies are evaluated based on three criteria: validity, generalizability, and reliability.** Validity refers to the accuracy of a study's findings. Generalizability is a sampling issue and requires that the individuals who participate in the study adequately represent the population of interest. Reliability is reflected in a consistency in results across analyses and is a product of consistent measures, interpretations, and samples.

- **It is conventional to evaluate the results of social psychological studies based on surveys or experiments in terms of their internal**

TABLE 2.2

Methods of Data Collection Used by Social Psychologists

FACE OF SOCIAL PSYCHOLOGY	RESEARCH ORIENTATION	METHOD	PURPOSE	STRENGTHS	WEAKNESSES
	Quantitative			Reliability and generalizability	Validity
Social structure and personality		Survey	Causal, testing theories	External validity/ generalizability	Internal validity
Psychological/group processes and structures		Experiment	Causal, testing theories	Internal validity	External validity/ generalizability
	Qualitative			Validity	Reliability and generalizability
Symbolic interactionism		Participant observation	Description, developing theories	Validity	Reliability and generalizability
		In-depth interviews	Description, developing theories	Validity	Reliability and generalizability

and external validity. Internal validity reflects the degree to which researchers can conclude that independent and dependent variables are causally related, based upon their study findings. External validity pertains to the generalizability of a study's results.

- **Provided the sample is representative of the target population, survey research is high in external validity. Survey research tends to be lower in internal validity, given the potential for spurious relationships.**

- **Experiments tend to be high in internal validity but may lack external validity.**

- **Validity is the main strength of qualitative methods, including participant observation and in-depth interviewing, whereas reliability and generalizability are their limitations.** Symbolic interactionists, the social psychologists who most frequently use qualitative methods, argue that human social behavior is complex and requires detailed analysis in natural settings. Therefore, they feel that it is unreasonable to expect social psychological studies to meet evaluative criteria designed for the natural sciences.

- **Due to their more narrow focus, quantitative studies are lower than qualitative analyses in overall validity but higher in reliability and generalizability.**

- **In conducting research with human subjects, there are ethical issues that must be addressed before beginning a social psychological study.** Social psychologists must have the approval of their school's institutional review board (IRB) before collecting their data.

Terms and Concepts for Review

Causal relationship	Operationalization
Convenience sample	Operational definition
Correlation	Overt participant observation
Convert nonparticipant observation	Participant observation
Covert participant observation	Population
Cross-sectional data	Positive relationship
Debriefing	Qualitative research
Deductive reasoning	Quantitative research
Dependent variable	Random assignment
Ethnographic research	Random sampling

Terms and Concepts for Review (*Continued*)

Experiment	Range
External validity	Reliability
Generalizability	Representative sample
Grounded theory	Response rate
Hypothesis	Sample
Independent variable	Secondary data
In-depth interview	analysis
Index	Snowball sample
Inductive reasoning	Spurious relationship
Institutional review board (IRB)	Standard deviation
Internal validity	Subculture
Longitudinal data	Survey
Mean	Theory
Methodological empathy	Triangulation
n	Validity
Negative relationship	Variable

Questions for Review and Reflection

1. Suppose that you want to know how much time students at your school spend studying during a typical week. Your friend suggests that you hand out questionnaires at his upcoming party because many students are likely to attend. Is this a good idea? Explain why or why not.

2. What is a snowball sample? When do researchers use this sampling strategy? Imagine that you are planning to study the gamer identity. What would be the best way to get a snowball sample of students attending your school who regularly play online video games?

3. Describe the relationship between face of social psychology, research question, and methodology. How would a symbolic interactionist and a social psychologist working within SSP differ in their approach to the study of Greek life on your campus? Focusing on the relative strengths and weaknesses of qualitative and quantitative research, discuss the potentially complimentary nature of their studies.

4. Which method of data collection discussed in this chapter presents the greatest risk to study participants? Discuss the ethical issues associated with the use of the method. Which of the methods discussed in the chapter, excluding secondary data analysis, is the least likely to result in negative outcomes for the subjects? Is there any situation in which the use of this method might be ethically questionable?

CHAPTER 3

Symbolic Interactionism and Related Perspectives

PHOTO 3.1

How people perceive the effects of marijuana is rooted in social interaction and feedback from others.

In his classic study of marijuana users, Becker (1963) argues that the experience of being high is socially constructed. The following exchange between Becker and one of his study participants illustrates the role of others in shaping users' perceptions. The participant is a jazz musician recounting his early experiences with marijuana.

RESEARCHER: Did you get high the first time you turned on?

PARTICIPANT: Yeah, sure. Although, come to think of it, I guess I really didn't. I mean, like the first time it was more or less of a mild drunk. I was happy, I guess, you know what I mean. But I didn't really know I was high, you know what I mean. It was only after the second time I got high that I realized I was high the first time. Then I knew something different was happening.

RESEARCHER: How did you know that?

PARTICIPANT: How did I know? If what happened to me that night would of happened to you, you would've known, believe me. We played the first tune for almost two hours—one tune! Imagine, man! We got on the stand and played this one tune, we started at nine o'clock. When we got finished, I looked at my watch, it's a quarter to eleven. Almost two hours on one tune. And it didn't seem like anything.

I mean, you know, it does that to you. It's like you have much more time or something. Anyway, when I saw that, man, it was too much. I knew I must really be high or something if anything like that could happen. See, and then they explained to me that that's what it did to you, you had a different sense of time and everything. So I realized that that's what it was. I knew then. Like the first time, I probably felt that way, you know, but I didn't know what was happening (Becker, 1963:51).[1]

According to Becker (1963), people learn how to define the physiological effects of marijuana as pleasurable through face-to-face interaction with more experienced users. Seasoned users teach novices how to moderate their intake of the substance to avoid extreme, and thus potentially uncomfortable, symptoms. Experienced users also reinforce the view that the effects of the drug are enjoyable.

Becker's work emphasizes the role of the social context and others' reactions in providing the framework within which physiological cues are evaluated. His work is an excellent example of a symbolic interactionist study. Like some of the symbolic interactionists whose research we discussed in previous chapters, Becker used in-depth interviews to collect his data. His snowball sample consisted of 50 individuals. Some participants were musicians, whereas others held more conventional blue-collar (manual labor) or professional jobs. Becker's theory about the social nature of marijuana's effects was based on the results of a systematic analysis of his subjects' experiences.

In Chapter 10, we will discuss the symbolic interactionist literature on drug use and other forms of deviance (violations of social norms), as well as recent changes in the legal status of marijuana and the population's views on this issue. The purpose of this chapter is to familiarize you with symbolic interactionism and the various strains of thought within or related to this theoretical tradition. Symbolic interactionist analyses discussed in earlier chapters include Besen's (2006) study of teens working at coffee shops, Kurien's (2005) article on identity construction among Indian American college students, and Hurst's (2007) analysis of class identity among college undergraduates from working-class backgrounds.

THEORETICAL FRAMEWORKS

Symbolic interactionism is a theoretical framework that emphasizes symbolic communication and the social construction of meanings through face-to-face interaction. **Theoretical frameworks** (also called theoretical perspectives) within sociology, and within sociological social psychology more specifically, provide researchers with sets of concepts and specify how these concepts are related. It is within theoretical frameworks that more specific social psychological theories explaining social phenomena are developed. For example, working within the symbolic interactionist framework, Becker (1963) developed his theory about how people learn to experience marijuana intoxication as pleasurable.

In Chapters 1 and 2, we introduced the concept of face, or type, of social psychology. A theoretical framework is a bit more specific than a face, which is a research tradition or orientation. In fact, within a given face of social psychology, such as the symbolic interactionist tradition, there are usually coexisting theoretical frameworks. These theoretical frameworks are related in that they share common assumptions and methodologies.

Symbolic interactionism, which itself contains two schools of thought is the most prominent theoretical framework within the symbolic interactionist face of

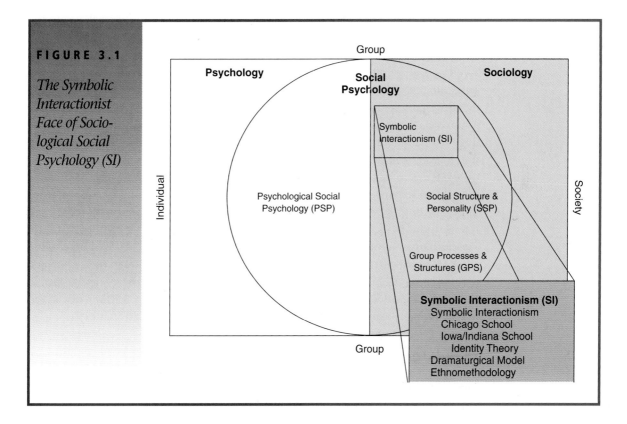

FIGURE 3.1

The Symbolic Interactionist Face of Sociological Social Psychology (SI)

social psychology. In addition, there are two other related theoretical frameworks within this face of sociological social psychology: (1) the dramaturgical approach and (2) ethnomethodology (Petras and Meltzer 1973). Figure 3.1 shows the different theoretical frameworks within the symbolic interactionist face of sociological social psychology. We discuss each of the theoretical frameworks in detail in subsequent sections of the chapter.

SYMBOLIC INTERACTIONISM (SI)

George Herbert Mead, a philosopher at the University of Chicago during the early part of the twentieth century, is regarded as the most significant contributor to the symbolic interactionist tradition. *Mind, Self, and Society* (1934) is the primary treatise on symbolic interactionism based on Mead's social philosophy. This book was compiled from lecture notes from Mead's social psychology course, which were put into book form by his students following his death in 1931 (Ritzer and Goodman 2004).

Communication as an Exchange of Significant Symbols

In *Mind, Self, and Society,* Mead argues that people communicate through the exchange of significant symbols. A symbol is something that represents something else. A **significant symbol** is a gesture that brings out the same meaning in oneself as it does in another. Thus, a significant symbol has the same meaning to the person initiating it as it does to the individual toward whom it is directed. Within this culture, for example, a raised hand in class usually means that a student has a question. In most classroom contexts, the raised hand becomes a significant symbol because there is a shared understanding that the initiator of the gesture is requesting permission to ask a question or make a comment. Because humans communicate through the exchange of significant symbols, including language, most of our interactions have an underlying symbolic component.

According to Mead (1934), symbolic communication occurs both *within* and *between* individuals. People converse with themselves in the form of complex thought. The capacity to have a conversation with oneself (mind) emerges as children develop what Mead called the "self." We will discuss the processes through which the self develops in detail in Chapter 6. Here we focus on the nature of the self and its implications for our understanding of human social behavior. See Box 3.1 for a discussion of how humans compare to other animals in communication and cognition.

Mead's Self

Using terminology introduced by the Harvard psychologist William James (1890), Mead (1934) describes the **self** as the process of interaction between two phases: the "I" and the "me."[2] According to Mead, the "**I**" is the subject phase of the self, our spontaneous reactions to people, situations, and events. The "I" remains largely unconditioned, or untrained, and is never fully within our control. It is, however, frequently constrained or redirected by the "me." The "**me**" is the object phase of the self, which allows for self-reflection and evaluation through the process of role taking.

Taking the role of another, called **role taking** or **perspective taking**, involves viewing oneself as an object from the perspective of another individual, a

Box 3.1   Animal Communication and Cognition

The degree to which animals communicate and have higher-level cognitive abilities has been debated extensively. According to Mead (1934), it is our ability to communicate using language that underlies our ability to think and sets us apart from other animal species.

Some contemporary symbolic interactionists have challenged this assumption. Drawing on the results of research conducted with animals over the last 30 years, they argue that communication can occur without spoken language and that animals, and animals and humans, routinely communicate with one another. Furthermore, they argue that animals have subjective experiences (i.e., they are mentally aware of what they are doing or feeling) and the capacity for thought (Alger and Alger 2003; Irvine 2004; Sanders and Arluke 1993).

In her biography of the chimpanzee Nim Chimpsky, journalist Elizabeth Hess (2008) chronicles the life of one of the most controversial research subjects in the history of primatology. Nim was a central character in the debate about the differences between humans and animals. Raised from infancy in a human family, Nim was taught American Sign Language (ASL) in an attempt to show that the ability to learn language is not unique to humans. Naming the chimp Nim Chimpsky was a poke at the famous American linguist Noam Chomsky and his notion that humans are the only species genetically programmed for language acquisition.

After years of data collection, the researcher in charge of the project (primatologist Herbert Terrace) concluded that he and his team had not succeeded in teaching Nim how to communicate using language (Terrace 1980). Many of Nim's handlers, interviewed by Hess, tell a different story. They are adamant that Nim could talk and think. After misbehaving, Nim would often sign, "Sorry." Having picked up some of the habits of his caretakers, he was known to ask for a cigarette or some marijuana (Hess 2008).

Although he could use signs to make requests, Nim never learned the rules of language (grammar) or how to combine words into meaningful phrases. Consistent with Chomsky's assertion, the ability to communicate using spoken language appears to be specific to humans (Rivas 2005).

This does not, however, mean that animals cannot communicate with one another or with humans or that they have no mental life (Savage-Rumbaugh, Shanker, and Taylor 1998). Although humans and animals have different abilities (or different degrees of ability) when it comes to communication and cognition, many sociological social psychologists feel that Mead's view of the experiences of animals was too rigid.

PHOTO 3.2

Woman using signs to communicate ith Nim Chimpsky

group, or society at large (the generalized other). It is through role taking that people are able to gain a sense of others' expectations and coordinate their behaviors. Thus, it is our capacity for role taking that makes social interaction possible and allows for the creation and maintenance of society. If people couldn't view themselves through the eyes of others, they would not be able to construct shared meanings or to align their conduct with that of other individuals. Behavior would be haphazard, and people would have little regard for the consequences of their actions (Schwalbe 1991a, 1991b).

Within a given social context, social behavior is the product of an interaction between the "I" and the "me." We react with the "I" and immediately gauge the appropriateness of our response by viewing ourselves through the eyes of others (the process of role taking). Insofar as the spontaneous "I" fails to conform to prevailing normative expectations, the "me" redirects or reshapes the "I," bringing it into line with these broader social standards.

Although we may seek to channel our "I" responses in particular ways in many situations, it is important to keep in mind that the "I" is what allows for creativity and spontaneity in human behavior. It is what prevents us from acting like overly programmed robots. Our capacity to respond in unique and unfettered ways in any social setting is, for Mead, an important part of the human experience. Due to the "I," behavior is never predetermined.

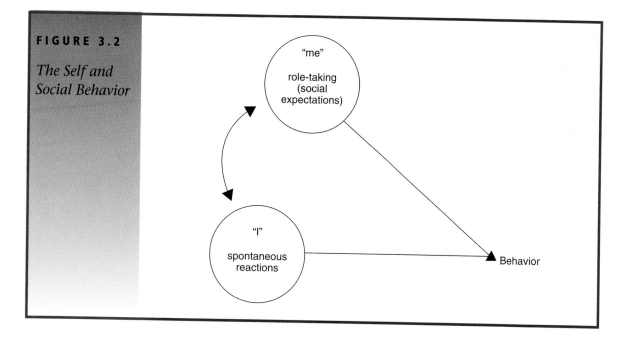

FIGURE 3.2

The Self and Social Behavior

We do, however, regulate our behavior much of the time. The extent to which the "me" constrains, or modifies, the "I" depends upon the social context within which behavior occurs. Mead (1934) used the creation of art as an example of a situation where the "me" steps back and the "I" is given greater latitude. Can you think of any other settings where the "I" is likely to exert a strong influence on your behavior? Any social context that is low in normative regulation is conducive to this type of response. When a setting is low in normative regulation, the rules governing behavior are loose, and you can relax and act without much reflection about how your behaviors will be perceived by others.

In structured situations with high levels of normative regulation (e.g., a job interview, a court appearance, and a college classroom), the "me" plays a larger role in shaping an individual's behaviors. Still, there is always a spontaneous component to our action (the "I") that we cannot fully control, even when we would like to do so. We can modify our immediate reactions so that they are socially appropriate, but there is often that split second when the "I" seeps through.

Think about the popular television programs involving competitions, shows like *American Idol, Project Runway,* and *Top Chef.* Viewers are ultimately presented with two final contestants, but they do not yet know who has won. The announcer then gives the name of the runner-up, the person in second place. Watch that individual's face the next time you catch a scene like this. For just a moment, you can see the disappointment (the autonomic, uncontrollable "I" response). Then, within a split second, the "me" kicks in, and the runner-up smiles broadly and excitedly congratulates the winner—the "appropriate" behavior.

PHOTO 3.3

The runner-up in this competition is not demonstrating good sportsmanship. Acting gracious when you have lost a competition is a learned behavior.

What Do You Think?

- When was the last time you saw someone's "I" slip through (in a face-to-face encounter) for that split second before the person was able to consciously regulate his or her facial expressions, gestures, and other behavior? Where did this occur?
- When and where was the last time this happened to you? How did it make you feel?

Key Premises of Symbolic Interactionism

It was Herbert Blumer, a student of Mead's, who named Mead's perspective "symbolic interactionism" (Blumer 1969). Blumer was also instrumental in codifying the central tenets of this theoretical framework. According to Blumer (1969), the three premises of the symbolic interactionist perspective are as follows:

1. People act toward objects, events, and others based on their meanings.

2. Meanings emerge through the course of social interaction. Meanings are created as actors respond to things (objects, events, and other actors and their behaviors) in their environment. Thus, meanings are rooted in behavior.

3. Meanings are subject to modification through self-communication (mind) as individuals interpret and respond to the things they encounter. Within a given social context, meanings change as people's behavior changes.

Henslin (2007) makes explicit the way these premises apply to real-world interactions in his analysis of the experiences of the survivors of a plane crash in the Andes Mountains. The plane, carrying members of a rugby team from Uruguay and some of their family members and friends, crashed en route to Santiago, Chile, in October of 1972. This story may sound familiar. The events that occurred following the crash were portrayed in *Alive* (1993), a popular film starring Ethan Hawke and Vincent Spano.

After more than two months in a desolate area with subzero temperatures, the sixteen remaining crash survivors were in a dire situation, with little hope of being rescued. They were starving. They needed nourishment or they would die. Without adequate supplies, their only option was the flesh of the individuals who had perished in the crash.

Premise 1: Meanings shape behavior.
At first, the idea of eating human flesh was repugnant to the survivors, as it probably seems to you, and they were unwilling to engage in this behavior. The human body was regarded as sacred, a view consistent with values acquired in childhood. Given the meaning accorded to the human body, crash survivors were unable to bring themselves to eat the flesh of dead companions and crew members.

Premise 2: Meanings emerge through social interaction and are rooted in behavior.
As time passed, the survivors came to realize that they had no choice but to consume the bodies of individuals who perished in the crash or they too would die. As a group, they decided they had to start eating the corpses. Within this context, the crash survivors negotiated a new normative order, one that would enable them to eat human bodies while still maintaining positive self-views. Through face-to-face interaction, they developed a set of rules about who could eat what, when they could eat, and how much they could eat. First, they would eat those individuals they did not know personally (members of the flight crew) before any family members or friends. There were certain body parts that were off limits (e.g., genitals and heads). Fat could be consumed at any time, whereas muscle tissue was rationed. Individuals who would be venturing out to seek help were allowed to eat the largest portions of the protein-rich muscle meat.

Premise 3: Meanings change as behaviors change.
Clearly, the meaning of the dead bodies had changed. They were no longer something sacred, to be revered and treated in the conventional manner (i.e., buried). They were food, and this new meaning was reflected in the

group members' subsequent behaviors. The crash survivors became accustomed to the new system, so much so that individuals even brought "snacks" (e.g., a human hand) with them to bed in the evening (Henslin 2007).

How could this happen, you might ask? How could a group of people so radically change their perceptions of what is morally right and wrong? And how could they change their definition of the human body from something sacred to something edible? The answer is that the transition was gradual, and the new norms emerged over a number of days as the group responded to their dire situation. When they were finally rescued, the survivors (all Roman Catholics) were given absolution by the Church. Church officials deemed their behavior appropriate because they had a moral obligation to survive (Henslin 2007).

It is often relatively easy to identity social patterns and processes in situations that require substantial adjustment on the part of the individuals present, as in the 1972 Andes flight disaster. As noted by Henslin (2007), studying social interaction in such an extreme condition makes clear the processes of negotiation that occur in everyday social life but go largely unnoticed because of their more subtle and routine nature.

What Do You Think?

- How would you have acted if you were one of the survivors of the plane crash just described? Would you have eaten human flesh in order to survive?
- Think of a situation in which your behavior, or the behavior of someone you know, surprised you because it was out of the ordinary. What happened?

The Social Construction of Reality in Everyday Situations

From a symbolic interactionist perspective, our interactions with others involve the continual construction and negotiation of reality—how we interpret situations and how we view ourselves and others. We participate in these processes every day, although we rarely think about them or record them. Think about your current classes, for example. It is likely that each one has a slightly different tone, which reflects both prior and current interactions between the students and the professor. In some classes, students speak more freely and less formally than in others. Within some general parameters, the structure of a given college class is negotiated by the individuals present in the encounter, and it changes with alterations in their behaviors. Imagine, for instance, that a professor makes a joke, so everyone feels more at ease and student participation increases, which in turn leads the professor to respond to students in a less formal manner. This example illustrates the extent to which we are active participants in creating our everyday realities. It is this participation in the constructing of reality that is the focal point of symbolic interactionism.

For the symbolic interactionist, the meaning of an action (e.g., a raised hand in class) is defined not by the act itself or solely within the individual, but through the behaviors (responses) of others. As such, meanings are malleable and vary over time and across social settings. Although they serve as guides for behavior, meanings are never set or predetermined. Meanings continuously change as social interactions unfold and participants interpret and respond to the reactions of others.

Given its emphasis on face-to-face interaction and the social construction of meaning, symbolic interactionism is more inherently social in its focus than other micro-level perspectives, in particular psychological social psychology (House 1977). Symbolic interactionism is distinct from regular sociology and the more macro orientations within sociological social psychology (SSP and GPS) because it views human beings as relatively free from social constraints.

We say relatively free because Mead's conceptualization of the self allows for the regulation of behavior through the socially based "me." Nonetheless, from the SI perspective, people are viewed as creators of society. That is, the SI orientation emphasizes the importance of face-to-face interactions in the creation and maintenance of meanings and (more generally) society. Symbolic interactionism emphasizes agency—individuals' capacity to act in a self-directed manner. In choosing certain behaviors over others, people have the potential to produce, reproduce, or alter social structures through their interactions with others.

It is important to recognize that symbolic interactionism does not deny the existence of social phenomena that exist above and beyond any one individual or interactive setting. In fact, contemporary symbolic interactionists emphasize the fact that people's social encounters occur within the context of a larger society. In their view, social structure (statuses, roles, and macro-level societal patterns) shapes people's social experiences by making it more or less likely that certain individuals will be present in particular settings at particular points in time (Stryker and Vryan 2006). Social structure also constrains people's actions. Prevailing societal patterns make it more or less likely that people will act in various ways, but these patterns do not determine individuals' actions (Snow 2001).

For example, as a college student you are likely to attend class, study, and socialize with other students because that's what students are supposed to do. However, how and when you engage in these activities is not set in stone. In fact, you have a lot of latitude in terms of how you play the role of student. You make choices: you select your friends, develop your own study habits, and decide how to allocate your time. When you make choices, you are exhibiting agency.

THE TWO SCHOOLS OF SYMBOLIC INTERACTIONISM

As noted at the beginning of the chapter, there are two types of symbolic interactionism. They are distinguished by the degree to which they embrace the concept of agency. That is, they differ in the extent to which they emphasize the spontaneous, creative elements of human social behavior versus social constraint resulting from social structure. The two schools of symbolic interactionism are named after the institutions where they developed: (1) the University of Chicago and (2) the University of Iowa and Indiana University (Meltzer and Petras 1970; Weigert and Gecas 2003). We review these perspectives in the following sections.

Chicago School Symbolic Interactionism

Chicago school symbolic interactionism is the variant of symbolic interactionism that is the least structural in focus. This orientation is associated with the work of a number of individuals from the University of Chicago, including Mead and Blumer, whose contributions we described in the preceding section.

Situational Definitions

W. I. Thomas, a contemporary of Mead's, is also associated with Chicago school SI. In particular, Thomas emphasized the importance of people's definitions of the situation in shaping their responses to the broader social environment. **Situational definitions** are perceptions. Thomas argued that situational definitions, which may or may not coincide with objective facts (what actually occurs in any given interaction), must be taken into consideration when studying human social behavior (Thomas and Thomas 1928).

THE COLLEGE CLASSROOM

Situational definitions often vary across individuals. In a well-known study, introduced in Chapter 2, two renowned symbolic interactionists, David Karp and William Yoels (1976), applied the concept of situational definition to the college classroom. They were interested in the social construction of meanings within this context. As noted in Chapter 2, they opted to use nonparticipant observation and a survey to collect their data because participant observation (the method of choice for most symbolic interactionists) would have been disruptive to the classroom setting.

Karp and Yoels (1976) argued that professors view the classroom as an arena for the discussion of ideas. Thus, professors define the situation as one where high levels of engagement are appropriate. Students, on the other hand, define the college classroom as a setting in which information is to be *given* to them rather than *created* by them. They regard themselves as idea seekers rather than active participants in the creation of knowledge. From their perspective, participation is not central to the learning process, and talking too much is a violation of classroom norms (Karp and Yoels 1976).

Professors and students also had different views about the reason for students' lack of participation in classroom discussions. The professors in Karp and Yoels's study assumed that students were hesitant to speak up in class because they did not want to look dumb in front of their peers. This was not something that students reported feeling concerned about. Instead, on the end-of-term survey they listed lack of preparation (i.e., they hadn't done the reading) as the main reason they did not participate in class.

In each of the ten classes Karp and Yoels observed, there were a few students (less than 10% of the class) who participated, typically by answering questions posed by the professor, whereas the majority of the class was silent. The nontalkers knew that they could count on the few talkers to carry the discussion, which made it unlikely that the professor would call on them. Karp and Yoels call this the **consolidation of responsibility** because it is similar to the diffusion of responsibility that takes place in emergency situations (see Chapter 1, p. 10). This consolidation of responsibility (the fact that nontalkers can count on a few of their fellow students to participate enough so that no one gets called on), combined with students' view of the teacher as the provider of knowledge, made lively discussions within the classroom unlikely.

Creating a classroom atmosphere conducive to the exchange of ideas can be difficult, especially in large classes. Although much has changed in the thirty-plus years since Karp and Yoels conducted their study, more current research (Howard 2002) suggests that the consolidation of responsibility has persisted.

What Do You Think?

- What about your courses? How many students participate, and who are they? Do students respond to the comments of other students, or are their comments mainly in response to questions from the professor?
- If there's variation across classes, list the characteristics that seem to make a difference. What is it (the professor, the subject matter, the structure of the room, etc.) that increases student participation? How much of an issue is student preparation?
- Compare your responses with one or two of your classmates. As a group, come up with three strategies that professors might use to encourage student participation in their classes. How are students likely to respond to these changes?

FAN-CELEBRITY ENCOUNTERS

Although faculty and students may have different expectations when it comes to student participation, their competing definitions of the classroom rarely result in direct confrontations. Ferris's (2001) analysis of fan-celebrity encounters, based on data gathered using participant observation, provides an example of a social context within which discrepant situational definitions can result in explicit conflict and, in extreme cases, legal action.

Fans desire interaction with the celebrities they admire. Generally, celebrities, like everyone else, demand that their privacy be respected. When overzealous fans

PHOTO 3.4

Fans seeking contact with Eric Bana, who plays the villain Nero in the film *Star Trek*.

seek celebrities out in restaurants, malls, the beach, and other public settings, celebrities often get angry. In some instances, they experience fear.

Some of the fans with whom Ferris (2001) completed in-depth interviews indicated that they went to great lengths to make contact with celebrities. They followed celebrities from prestaged events, such as conventions and other planned public appearances, to restaurants or airports. One woman even went so far as to deceive the mother of one of her favorite soap opera stars at a golf tournament. The fan posed as a friend of the actor in order to get his mother's home address. Presumably, she planned to stake out the mother's house. Maybe the actor visits his mother regularly. If he does, the woman might get to see him in his real life.

From the perspective of the fan, this type of behavior is not problematic, and the celebrity whom she was seeking to contact had nothing to worry about. From the perspective of the celebrity, this kind of aggressive pursuit may be viewed as a threat to the celebrity's security. There have been instances where celebrities have been killed by fans (e.g., John Lennon's murder outside his New York City apartment in 1980), which certainly reinforce these concerns. Behaviors like those of the woman described in the preceding paragraph are not likely to be viewed by celebrities as harmless and fun. Instead, they are defined as stalking (Ferris, 2001), a crime for which a perpetrator can be sent to jail.

What's Distinctive About Chicago School SI

Chicago school symbolic interactionism is known for its emphasis on the importance of gaining access to the subjective realities (the situational definitions) of the individuals studied (e.g., college students and their professors or fans seeking contact with the stars they admire), the social construction of meaning, the use of qualitative methods (in particular, participant observation and in-depth interviews) to accomplish this task, and the development of theories rooted in data.

THE CONSTRUCTION OF MEANING IN GROUP ENCOUNTERS

Focusing on social interactions in everyday settings, Chicago school symbolic interactionists often study how people negotiate power and status within the context of their face-to-face interactions. For example, Schippers (2008) studied low-income African American girls in middle school and their White middle-class mentors (female college students). Schippers found that they constructed a status hierarchy though their face-to-face interactions that differed from that within the larger society. Although middle-class Whites are of higher status than low-income African Americans within society in general, the power dynamic that emerged over the course of the girls' interactions with their mentors favored the girls. The girls made clear their preference for African American over White mentors, and they routinely challenged their (White) mentors' authority. Obviously, the girls' dominant status in interactions with their mentors did not alter macro-level patterns of racial inequality. However, the girls and their mentors did create new meanings for race through their social interactions. These meanings challenged, rather than reproduced, macro-level social inequalities (Schippers 2008). Like most SI analyses within the Chicago school, Schippers's (2008) study was qualitative in orientation and used data from in-depth interviews with the mentors, as well as the mentors' field notes.

Becker's (qualitative) research on marijuana users, described at the beginning of this chapter, also illustrates the application of Chicago school symbolic interactionism. (See Box 3.2 for Becker's view on Chicago school SI and methodology.) In addition, the SI studies discussed in Chapters 1 and 2 (qualitative analyses of teens working in coffee shops and of conceptions of social class among college undergraduates with working-class roots) are within the Chicago school tradition.

When people mention symbolic interactionism, unless otherwise specified, it is safe to assume that they are referring to the Chicago school variety. Chicago school SI is considered the dominant theoretical perspective within the realm of **microsociology** (sociological analyses within a micro-level unit of analysis, typically the individual) and is thus the framework after which the first face of sociological social psychology is named.

Iowa and Indiana School of Symbolic Interactionism

The second strain of symbolic interactionism is associated with the work of the sociologist Manford Kuhn, a member of the University of Iowa's sociology department from the mid-1940s through the early 1960s (Melzer and Petras 1970). Since the late 1960s, the work of Sheldon Stryker and other social psychologists affiliated with the sociology department at Indiana University has been

Box 3.2   A Note on Chicago School Symbolic Interactionism and Methodology

- How does social class affect Greek life on your campus?
- How does social class influence students' social relationships in the high school you attended?
- In what ways does social class shape students' experiences and the meanings they construct in these social contexts?

According to Becker and Geer (1957), two Chicago school symbolic interactionists, these kinds of questions are difficult for people to answer during an interview for three reasons:

1. People are often unaware of the everyday patterns that are of interest to sociological social psychologists, or the patterns may be such a routine part of their existence that people do not believe they are worth mentioning.
2. Participants, who are not themselves sociologists, rarely have insight into why they do what they do. Many of our behaviors are habitual and do not generate much reflection.
3. There is often a discrepancy between situational definitions and objective reality. People are biased in their perceptions, and the information they provide to interviewers may not reflect the interactions that actually happened. This is not because they are lying but because situational definitions are skewed by many factors (e.g., prior experiences, desires, and group allegiances or affiliations).

What would you tell a researcher about social class and students' experiences in your high school or college? How might the three issues discussed above affect your responses?

Participant observation gives researchers access to most, if not all, aspects of subjects' daily lives. Thus, it often yields more valid information than in-depth interviews.

Sometimes participant observation is not an option because of the topic under investigation (e.g., how social class influences Greek life on a college campus, or how it shapes students' social relationships more generally). In such cases, Becker and Geer (1957) argue that researchers must be cautious when interpreting their findings. They must recognize that there is likely to be information that is missing or misreported. (This would be an even greater problem on a survey, given its more narrow focus.) Heeding this warning, Becker (1963) notes the care he took in analyzing his interview data from marijuana users when formulating his theory about the subjective nature of drug-induced experiences.

part of this second strain of symbolic interactionism (Weigert and Gecas 2003). **Iowa/Indiana school SI** places a greater emphasis on social structure than the Chicago school does. This distinction is illustrated in Figure 3.3.

What's Distinctive About Iowa/Indiana School SI

Whereas Chicago school symbolic interactionists focus on the path from selves (individuals) to society, Iowa/Indiana school symbolic interactionists are concerned primarily with the effects of society on the self. Thus, Iowa/Indiana school SI is often referred to as **structural symbolic interactionism** (Meltzer and Petras 1970; Stryker 1980). Although this orientation is similar to social structure and

FIGURE 3.3

The Self-Society Relationship

Chicago School SI

Self ——————————————→ Society

"I" ←——→ "me"

Iowa/Indiana School SI

Society ——————————————→ Self
"me"

Note: Stryker (1980)

personality, discussed in the next chapter, Iowa/Indiana school symbolic interactionists are a distinct group in that they are highly concerned (more so than SSP researchers) with Mead's concept of self. However, instead of focusing on the meanings that emerge within a given social context as the result of the interplay between the "I" and the "me" (the focus of Chicago school symbolic interactionists), they study the content of people's self-concepts, a part of the socially derived "me" (self as object).

The **self-concept** refers to the characteristics, thoughts, and feelings that people attribute to themselves (Kinch 1967, Rosenberg 1979). In particular, Iowa/Indiana school symbolic interactionism is noted for its emphasis on the link between the roles people play and the content of their self-concepts. Insofar as society is relatively stable (the statuses people occupy persist over time), the content of people's self-concepts should be relatively stable and thus measurable (Stryker 1980).

MEASURING THE SELF-CONCEPT

Given their emphasis on stability in the content of the self-concept, symbolic interactionists working within the tradition of the Iowa/Indiana school tend to be quantitative in orientation and use surveys to collect their data. Kuhn and McPartland's (1954) Twenty Statements Test (TST) is an example of a measure of the self-concept that can be included on a written questionnaire.

Students commonly respond to the TST by listing the statuses they occupy (e.g., student, sister, athlete, Catholic, friend). According to Kuhn and McPartland (1954), the TST results validate the assumption that statuses and their associated roles (the behaviors that people who occupy a particular status engage in) serve as sources of social identity.

How many statuses did you list in response to the TST? Did you list any statuses associated with the group affiliations you identified in Chapter 1 (page 21)?

Not surprisingly, Kuhn and McPartland found that college students who belonged to unconventional religious groups were more likely than students who participated in mainstream religions to list a religious denomination as one of their first responses to the TST. Religious self-identification (viewing oneself in terms of one's religious affiliation) is probably less pronounced for members of common,

What Do You Think?

How do you see yourself? Take out a sheet of paper and write down your answers to the Twenty Statements Test. Here are the test instructions (taken verbatim from Kuhn and McPartland 1954: 69). Kuhn and McPartland usually gave students 12 minutes to complete the test.

> *There are twenty numbered blanks on the page below. Please write twenty answers to the simple question "Who am I?" in the blanks. Just give twenty different answers to this question. Answer as if you were giving the answers to yourself, not to somebody else. Write the answers in the order that they occur to you. Don't worry about logic or "importance." Go along fairly fast, for time is limited.*

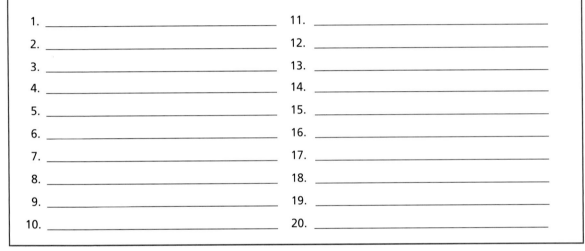

1. _____
2. _____
3. _____
4. _____
5. _____
6. _____
7. _____
8. _____
9. _____
10. _____

11. _____
12. _____
13. _____
14. _____
15. _____
16. _____
17. _____
18. _____
19. _____
20. _____

widely accepted religious denominations because this status is not regarded as a distinctive social characteristic.

We have seen similar results to the TST among our students in regard to gender and race/ethnicity. Women and students of color are more likely than men and Whites to list their gender or race as self-defining.

Family Roles and College Students' Self-Concepts

Couch's (1962) classic study on the relationship between family role specialization and the content of college students' self-concepts provides an excellent illustration of SI research within the Iowa/Indiana school. Survey data were gathered from college students taking an introductory sociology course. The questionnaire included measures of the degree to which household tasks were divided based upon gender (i.e., the degree of role specialization) in each student's family of origin. Students also completed the TST. As is common, females were more likely than males to list gender-based statuses (woman or daughter) in response to the TST.

Role specialization (the independent variable) was positively associated with self-identification as a man or a son among male participants, but it was negatively related to self-identification as a woman or daughter among females (the dependent variable). In families where task assignment (e.g., buying groceries, cooking meals, earning money for the family) is based on gender, the relative status of men and women is likely to be striking. Given their high status, it is not surprising that men from these kinds of families were inclined to think of themselves in terms of their gender, whereas the women (the subordinate group) defined themselves in terms of other statuses. Both the men and women in the study sample responded in ways that reflected their group's position within society's stratification system.

Family role specialization is still common. In fact, the experiences of contemporary college students are not that different from those of their parents when it comes to who did most of the housework in their family when they were growing up (typically their mothers) (Goldberg et al. 2012). Thus, Couch's (1962) findings probably apply to current students. Among college students today, males are more likely than their female counterparts to support a traditional division of household labor. This suggests that gender ideologies (beliefs about the appropriate roles for men and women) are shaped by the position of one's group (male vs. female) within society's stratification hierarchy (Goldberg et al. 2012).

SOCIETY, THE SELF-CONCEPT, AND BEHAVIOR

In addition to examining the link between social structure and the content of people's self-concepts, Iowa/Indiana school symbolic interactionists have focused on how the self-concept shapes behavior. In particular, Stryker's (1980) **identity theory** emphasizes the relationship between the statuses people occupy, the content of their self-concepts, and how they choose to act in various social situations. In Stryker's view, how we see ourselves shapes the kinds of social encounters we seek out. Therefore, responses to survey questions that measure the content of the self-concept can be used to predict patterns of behavior (Stryker 1980). For example, research suggests that high school students who view themselves as individuals who do science, math, and engineering (SME) are more likely than their peers to engage in subsequent activities that have a SME component. Because adolescents' SME identities are rooted in social relationships, increasing high school students' involvement in SME-based activities with peers should have long-term effects (e.g., the selection of a college major in one or more of these fields and entrance into a SME career).

Interestingly, the self-concepts of females appear to change more readily than those of males as the result of new relationships. This is probably because girls are taught to value social connection more than boys are. Therefore, school programs that provide opportunities for the cultivation of meaningful relationships centered on SME activities may have more of an impact on females' future careers than on males' future careers. This finding is notable given the small number of women currently working in SME fields (Lee 2002).

Working within the Iowa/Indiana school of SI, identity theorists have also specified the ways that emotions help people to maintain consistency between their self-concepts and their behaviors (Burke and Stets 2009). We discuss research guided by identity theory in greater detail in the chapters on self and identity and on emotions.

Comparing Iowa/Indiana School to Chicago School SI

The main purpose of Iowa/Indiana SI research is specifying the link between the structure of society and the content of people's self-concepts. Most studies within this tradition, including Couch's (1962) analysis and the research by Lee (2002) just described, are quantitative in orientation. Chicago school SI studies, like Becker's research on the social construction of marijuana intoxication and the analyses of competing situational definitions, are qualitative in orientation.

Q: Given what you know about different units of analysis (micro versus macro), from Chapter 1, how else might one distinguish between the Iowa/Indiana and Chicago schools of symbolic interactionism?

A: In Chicago school SI research, the unit of analysis is the individual. In contrast, most studies within Iowa/Indiana school SI, including Couch's (1962) and Lee's (2002) research, focus on the group. The Iowa/Indiana unit of analysis might be, for example, women versus men or racial/ethnic minorities versus Whites. Thus, we can say that Iowa/Indiana school SI is more macro in focus than Chicago school SI.

RELATED THEORETICAL FRAMEWORKS

In addition to symbolic interactionism (both the Chicago and Iowa/Indiana school variants), the symbolic interactionist face of social psychology includes the **dramaturgical perspective** and **ethnomethodology**. Along with Chicago school SI, these theoretical frameworks are referred to as microsociology.

The Dramaturgical Perspective

The sociologist Erving Goffman, who earned his doctoral degree at the University of Chicago in the early 1950s (around the same time as Howard Becker), was instrumental in the development of the dramaturgical model. Like Mead, Goffman focused on the concept of self. However, Goffman was specifically interested in the strategies people use to convey to others that they really are who they claim to be (i.e., that the self they are presenting is authentic) (Reynolds 1993). We treat the dramaturgical model as a distinct theoretical framework because this perspective provides a unique set of concepts, which Goffman and others working within this tradition have used to direct their analyses.

As suggested by the term "dramaturgical," Goffman focused on the theatrical aspects of social life. From this perspective, people are viewed as actors who stage performances that enable them to convey desired self-images to others. Goffman argued that the social context within which an interaction occurs shapes the extent to which people strategically manipulate their behaviors to create a particular impression.

For example, in one of his well-known books, *The Presentation of Self in Everyday Life* (1959), Goffman makes a distinction between two spheres of activity: the "back region" and the "front region." The **back region** refers to situations that are low in normative regulation. These are settings where we feel free to let the "I" govern more of our actions, to use Mead's terminology. In the **front region**, where most of our social interactions take place, behavior requires more calculation and conscious monitoring. Thus, the "me" phase of the self exerts more of an influence within the front region.

Goffman illustrates the difference between the back and front regions (also called the back stage and the front stage) with his description of a hotel restaurant. The kitchen is the back region, where workers let their guard down and behave in ways that might be regarded as shocking to diners (e.g., drying socks on the stove and cleaning fish with spit). If you have ever worked in a restaurant, you know about some of the things that go on behind the kitchen door. Workers tend to be protective of this space, in recognition of its contrast to the more public, front arena. The front region is the dining room, where wait staff work to make a positive impression on customers (Goffman 1959). When customers are difficult, they must keep smiling and do their best to please them ("The customer is always right.").

Think about your behaviors. The back region represents settings where you need not worry about the self you convey to others. When you are angry or frustrated, you are free to express yourself, as you might do in your home, at your friend's apartment, or in any situation in which you are among people you do not feel the need to impress. The front region, on the other hand, encompasses all of your public encounters (e.g., at work, school, parties, or the mall) where your guard is up and you restrain yourself from engaging in behaviors that would not be viewed positively. Like wait staff on the dining room floor, people adopt self-presentational strategies designed to convey favorable self-images within the front region. They do so by monitoring their behavior and by strategically revealing or concealing information about themselves to the other individuals present.

People also use what Goffman (1959) called props to aid in their front region performances. **Props** include objects associated with the impression one is trying to make. Some examples of props would be the diplomas on a therapist's office wall, the stethoscope around a doctor's neck, a particular style of dress, or even some trendy glasses worn under the assumption that they make one look smart or fashionable. Again, the goal from the dramaturgical perspective is to convey a positive image to others. This central feature of social life is referred to as impression management. **Impression management** involves self-presentations that are designed to gain the support or approval of others. We all engage in impression management.

When individuals fail in a public (front region) performance and are unsuccessful in conveying the desired impression to others, they experience embarrassment. People typically go to great lengths to avoid this emotion, but we have all experienced situations when we unintentionally do something unflattering. For example,

PHOTO 3.5

When people choose eyeglass frames they often seek feedback from others. In addition to correcting one's vision, the "right" glasses can help people convey a desired self-image.

a student slips and falls going up steps on the way to class, a professor's fly is down during a lecture, or someone makes an obvious mistake during a presentation at work.

As Goffman points out, these kinds of social blunders create discomfort among the audience, as well as in the person who has failed to convey a positive impression. In this sense, embarrassment is contagious and can spread to everyone who is present in an interactive encounter. When this happens, all witnesses have a stake in alleviating the tension and will do what they can to help the person who has failed in his or her performance save face. **Saving face** means recovering from, or avoiding, public disgrace. Strategies for accomplishing this vary with the social context in which the transgression has occurred. When they can get away with it (when the deception is not too obvious), people often choose to simply ignore a faux pas. They pretend they did not see the fall, the open zipper, or notice the error. This enables the person who slipped up to save face and facilitates the recovery of the situation's normative structure (Goffman 1956).

What Do You Think?

■ Form a group with three or four of your classmates. Have each group member describe the two most embarrassing things that ever happened to him or her. Have one of your group members record the following information:

1. The nature of each embarrassing incident (its cause and what made it so embarrassing).
2. How the witnesses of each of the embarrassing events reacted. Were they also uncomfortable?
3. Whether the witnesses of the embarrassing event actively helped the person who failed to convey a positive impression save face.
4. Whether the individual who fell short in his or her self-presentation was appreciative of their efforts, if they did so. (We usually are appreciative, provided no one draws further attention to our faux pas.)

■ How similar are your group members' stories? Describe any noticeable themes concerning the nature of, or people's reactions to, embarrassing encounters.

Grades and Impression Management Among College Students

Albas and Albas's (1988) study of college students' impression management strategies following the return of graded examinations provides a good illustration of the use of face-saving techniques and other dramaturgical processes. Students who get an A on an exam usually want others in the class to be aware of their success. However, as you know, there is an unwritten code of classroom conduct concerning such matters. Is it acceptable to announce to the class that you got a 99% on a test? How would other students react? How would they view someone who engaged in this kind of behavior?

Using data from classroom observations, in-depth interviews, and student journals, Albas and Albas found that A students (Aces) were much more strategic in revealing their grades. They did not simply blurt out their scores, as that would have been seen as highly inappropriate and they would have been viewed as braggarts. Still, they wanted others in the class to know they did well. Many Aces resolved this tension by revealing their grades in more subtle ways. For example, one student reported leaving an exam face up on the desk where it could readily be seen by others. Another individual nonchalantly yawned and stretched, holding a test up in the air so that others could see it. Albas and Albas refer to these behaviors as "accidental" revelation.

Like the Aces, students who scored poorly on exams (Bombers) were strategic in how they handled themselves in this front region performance. Although their goal was concealment rather than revelation, they wanted their actions to seem spontaneous and unpracticed. They would, for example, pretend to lose the exam in a stack of papers. Using less subtle strategies, some Bombers folded the test so that the grade was not visible or placed the test in their binder. These and other patterns described in Albas and Albas's study are summarized in Table 3.1.

Not surprisingly, students' impression management strategies varied in accordance with the nature of the interactive context. Aces acted differently with other Aces than they did with Bombers. They were much more up front about their grades with other Aces. In interactions with Bombers, Aces were modest, often saying that

Aces' strategies for revealing good grades *Repressed bubbling:* Let a bit of the "I" (jubilation over grade) slip out, but control reaction *"Accidental" revelation:* Subtly make exam visible to others (e.g., stretch with paper in hand) *Passive persuasion:* Give positive sign (e.g., smile) so someone asks about grade *Active persuasion:* Engage others in conversation about exam so someone asks about grade *Question-answer chain:* Ask others how they scored so that they will inquire about grade *Foot-in-door:* Ask peer about specific question and follow reply with inquiry about grade *Selective revelation:* Brag to someone other than students in class (e.g., family members) **Bombers' strategies for concealing poor grades** *Absenteeism:* Skip class when exam is returned if poor grade is anticipated *Lying about grade:* Blatant deception; indicate that grade is higher than that earned *Emphatic concealment:* Signs to ward off grade inquiries (e.g., no eye contact); hide test paper *Subtle concealment:* "Accidentally" conceal exam (e.g., lose exam in stack of papers) *Air of nonchalance:* Act as though grade is unimportant (e.g., never look at score)	**TABLE 3.1** *Students' Impression Management Strategies After the Return of Graded Exams (Albas and Albas 1988)*

TYPE OF ENCOUNTER

Ace-Ace	bragging acceptable, critical review of exam questions, sharing of study strategies
Bomber-Bomber	secretive, "pity parties," excuses for poor performance, scapegoat by blaming the professor ("hate-the-professor-fest")
Ace-Bomber	concealment, apologetic revelation of grade, face-saving behaviors focusing on difficulty or unfairness of exam, displays of sympathy
Bomber-Ace	encounters largely avoided; when forced, "gracious and congratulatory"; use of disclaimers to save face (e.g., "I didn't study.")

the exam was unfair or exceptionally difficult in order to help the Bombers save face. Within this context, they revealed their score apologetically and, if a Bomber appeared especially upset, they concealed their grade. These behaviors were designed to minimize embarrassment on the part of the Bombers (and among the Aces themselves, who were at risk for experiencing the embarrassment associated with others' failures).

In interaction with Aces, Bombers often commented that they did not study or that they had put forth little effort on the exam (face-saving techniques). Among themselves, Bombers had "pity parties," made excuses for their performance, and blamed the professor for their poor grades (referred to as a "hate-the-professor-fest").

Other Research on Self-Presentational Strategies and Impression Management

Other studies within the dramaturgical tradition have focused on self-presentational strategies in a variety of settings, including singles bars (Snow, Robinson and McCall 1991), public restrooms (Cahill et al. 1985), and high-end hotels (Dillard et al. 2000). These types of analyses are qualitative in orientation and typically involve participant observation, nonparticipant observation, or in-depth interviewing.

An alternative, quantitative approach to the study of impression management focuses on individuals' awareness of the extent to which they are likely to be evaluated by others. This survey-based literature bridges the disciplines of sociology and psychology. Many of these studies, typically conducted by psychological social psychologists, use the **public self-consciousness** scale (presented in Box 3.3) to measure how much individuals focus on the self-evaluative nature of their public performances. The psychological trait measured by the public self-consciousness scale is a concern with impression management. This chronic concern has been associated with (1) a fear of negative evaluation (Martin and Leary 2001), (2) a susceptibility to embarrassment (Edelmann 1985), and (3) a tendency to withdraw from embarrassing social encounters (Froming, Corley, and Rinker 1990).

Box 3.3   The Public Self-Consciousness Scale

Please answer each of the following questions, using the following scale, where 0 = "extremely uncharacteristic of me" and 4 = "extremely characteristic of me."

0————————1————————2————————3————————4

extremely uncharacteristic of me   *extremely characteristic of me*

_____ 1. I'm concerned about what other people think of me.
_____ 2. I usually worry about making a good impression.
_____ 3. I'm concerned about the way I present myself.
_____ 4. I'm self-conscious about the way I look.
_____ 5. I'm usually aware of my appearance.
_____ 6. One of the last things I do before leaving my house is look in the mirror.
_____ 7. I'm concerned about my style of doing things.

_____ Total

Scores Among a Sample of College Students

Males (n = 179):   Mean = 18.9   SD = 4.0
Females (n = 253):   Mean = 19.3   SD = 4.0

Note: Fenigstein et al. (1975).

Average public self-consciousness scores for a college sample are presented by gender as a benchmark with which you can compare your score. Note that there is not an appreciable gender difference in levels of public self-consciousness among college students. Other studies have yielded similar results.

Ethnomethodology

Ethnomethodology is a theoretical framework related to symbolic interactionism that emphasizes the ways that people create meaning in their day-to-day lives. The name, coined by its founder, Harold Garfinkel, joins two common terms: *ethno* (cultural group) and *methodology* (a set of rules or procedures used in the process of inquiry). Ethnomethodology focuses on how members of a society make sense of the situations they encounter (Heritage 1984). Like Chicago school SI, ethnomethodology directs researchers' attention to face-to-face interactions in natural settings. Thus, despite some fundamental differences between the two perspectives (noted next), ethnomethodology can be considered a part of the symbolic interactionist face of social psychology.

Nonetheless, ethnomethodologists do envision a somewhat different role for the social psychologist than that defined by symbolic interactionists. As discussed in the preceding section, symbolic interactionism emphasizes the social construction of meanings that vary across groups and social settings. From this standpoint, the SI researcher's job is to enter into the minds of the individuals under study and document their unique perspectives, as well as the motivations behind their behaviors. Rather than focusing on the nature of the meanings people produce through their interactions with others, ethnomethodologists are concerned with *how* people impose order on their social encounters so that they are meaningful.[3]

Ethnomethodologists argue that people share a common set of rules, which they use to make sense of the world around them (see Box 3.4). **Accounts** are the explanations people generate to give meaning to their experiences in specific situations. From the perspective of an enthnomethologist, accounts themselves are the events that should be studied (Garfinkel 1967).

The accounting procedures people use to create meaning are taken for granted and rarely the subject of reflection. Therefore, the accounts may be difficult for the social psychologist to access through the observation of everyday social interaction. However, when the taken-for-granted rules that govern behavior are violated, the means through which reality is constructed become explicit. (Note the similarity of this argument to Henslin's point about extreme situations and studying the social construction of meaning on pages 73–74) Garfinkel illustrated this by having his students break the rules in a series of breaching experiments.

Breaching experiments involve the intentional violation of social norms in order to create situations in which people must struggle to maintain their sense of reality. Breaching experiments make evident the fragile nature of realities and how readily they are disrupted when people fail to apply the basic rules of social

Box 3.4   Making Sense of Everyday Situations

Well-known ethnomethodologist Aaron Cicourel (1973) identifies six procedures used in the interpretation of situations and the creation of meaning. According to Cicourel, these interpretive procedures enable people to recognize the relevance of social norms and to translate them into behaviors that serve to maintain a coherent sense of reality. Note the central role of language and communication in this process.

1. *The reciprocity of perspectives.*[1] Actors assume that their immediate experiences are the same as others present within the encounter, that they are receiving the same type of information with the same meanings, and that their verbal accounts of the situation will be understood.
2. *Normal forms.* People assume that their partners in interaction will share their view of what is normal within their culture.
3. *The et cetera assumption.*[2] Drawing on a common stock of shared knowledge, people can be expected to fill in the blank when information is left out of verbal accounts.
4. *Retrospective-prospective sense of occurrence.* People can expect that ambiguous statements will subsequently be clarified. Thus, in conversation, they continuously reinterpret previous statements within the context of later utterances.
5. *Talk as reflexive.* Verbal accounts simultaneously create and reflect reality. Talk is part of the accounting process and is relied on to communicate recognizable aspects of the situation. Thus, talk (as distinct from the content of speech) is regarded as a central feature of social interaction and people expect that its presence will give a sense of normalcy to the encounter.
6. *Descriptive vocabularies as indexical expressions.*[3] The descriptive vocabularies used in any given situation reflect both prior and current experiences and thus require a sense of context to capture their full meaning. Descriptive vocabularies are significant in that they provide people (including social psychologists conducting research) with clues as to how to fill in what has been left unsaid. People tend to take this for granted.

To what degree do you employ these interpretive procedures throughout the course of your interactions with others? These assumptions about the nature of the social order are so commonplace that we are largely unaware of the extent to which they impact our behavior and make society as we know it possible.

1.   Schutz (1953, 1955).
2.   Garfinkel (1964).
3.   Garfinkel (1967).

interaction (Mehan and Wood 1975). They also show how people go about reconstructing a coherent sense of reality by accounting for, and thereby imposing order on, situations disrupted by the unexpected and bizarre behaviors of others.

In one breaching experiment, Garfinkel's students acted as though they were boarders in their own homes. They spoke to their relatives in a formal manner and asked permission before doing things that do not require permission within the context of everyday interactions among individuals in close relationships (e.g., taking a snack from the refrigerator). Family members often responded with hostility when the social order was challenged in this fashion, and their explanations of the students' behaviors are telling. They believed the student was either not feeling well, working too hard in school, tired from working at a job that required late hours, or upset due to a fight with a fiancé (Garfinkel 1967: 48). As evidenced in these accounts, parents and other family members went to great lengths to impose order on the situation by drawing on past experiences and knowledge of the students' current lives (Garfinkel 1967).

According to Garfinkel (1967), lay people and professional sociologists use similar methods for making sense of the social world. Like professional sociologists analyzing unfamiliar social groups, people search for meaningful patterns through the interpretation and reinterpretation of the behaviors of self and others. Borrowing from Mannheim (1952), Garfinkel calls this procedure the documentary method. When employed by the social psychologist, the **documentary method** involves the analysis of interactions in natural settings using qualitative methods. Thus, despite their somewhat different foci, ethnomethodologists and Chicago School symbolic interactionists share a common methodological approach.

Using the documentary method, including participant observation, in-depth interviews, and the textual analysis of recorded conversations, ethnomethodologists have analyzed a variety of real-world situations in which the nature of reality is debatable. They have studied everyday reasoning and reality construction in a halfway house (Wieder 1974), in courtrooms (Pollner 1987), and in the presentation and definition of gender (Currah and Moore 2009; Garfinkel 1967). Ethnomethodologists have also focused on how commonsense understandings of society (taken-for-granted understandings about how society operates) are reproduced through social interaction. This provides insight into how inequalities based on class, gender, and race within society are perpetuated over time (e.g., Cicourel and Kitsuse 1963; Pascale 2008; Stokoe 2006).

Take a Break

- Go to YouTube and view at least three breaching experiments. Most of these video segments have been posted by students taking a sociology course and are accessible when you search for "breaching experiment" or "norm violation."
- Note how startled people are when the norm violations occur. How do they make sense of what's going on?
- Consider doing a breaching experiment with some of your classmates. If you plan to do this, make sure to have your norm violation approved by your professor before you carry out the exercise. If you plan to videotape the breaching experiment (this is not necessary), keep in mind that there are ethical issues surrounding videotaping people without their permission. You will need to check with your professor, and possibly with your university's IRB, to find out if, and how, this can be managed.

Talk About Race and the Reproduction of Social Inequality

A recent analysis by Whitehead (2009) on how people talk about race exemplifies research in ethnomethodology. This study was based on the analysis of recorded conversations from a daylong employment race training workshop attended by 15 White and minority participants. As noted by the author, the workshop was an ideal setting for studying conversations about race. People are likely to be especially conscious of what they say about race during a race training workshop.

According to Whitehead (2009), when people mention others' race, it makes their own race stand out and introduces race as a potential explanation for their behavior. Thus, they run the risk of being perceived as endorsing commonsense knowledge about race (i.e., common understandings of race) within society. Whites fear that this will make them appear racist, and racial/ethnic minorities fear that they will be perceived as overly sensitive to the potential for racial bias. On the other hand, not mentioning race may also be problematic because others are inclined to interpret an actor's behaviors as being racially oriented, regardless of his or her intentions. As a result, people must consciously manage how they talk about race.

The workshop participants did this by (1) talking about race only in general terms, thereby discounting its use in explaining the experiences of any specific group (e.g., African Americans, Latinos, or Asians); (2) offering racial accounts as relevant, but limited, to specific situations; and (3) alluding to, but not explicitly stating, the relevance of race to particular events. Whitehead sees these patterns as significant in that they reveal the conversational strategies (what people say about race and how they say it) through which commonsense knowledge about race is reproduced. This, in turn, provides insight into how racial inequality at the (macro) societal level is perpetuated through individuals' (micro-level) encounters. Thus, like the other studies discussed in this chapter, Whitehead emphasizes people's active roles in the construction and reproduction of the social order.

AGENCY VERSUS STRUCTURE WITHIN THE SI FACE OF SOCIAL PSYCHOLOGY

All sociological social psychologists acknowledge the effects of societal norms and stratification on people's social experiences. However, the extent to which they emphasize the power of these social forces (social facts), versus the role of individuals in the construction of their realities (agency), depends upon the face of sociological social psychology they are working in.

As illustrated in Whitehead's study of conversations about race and throughout this chapter, sociologists working within the SI orientation emphasize agency over structure. They view individuals as active in the creation of society. (An exception is Iowa/Indiana school of symbolic interactionism, which focuses more on the effects of society on individuals.) SI researchers argue that we cannot understand the nature of society without understanding the interactional processes upon which it is based.

EVALUATING SI RESEARCH

The studies discussed in this chapter reflect this theme. They focus on individuals' interactions with others and on their subjective realities. Thus, they are qualitative in orientation.

Strengths of SI Research

It is by studying behavior in micro-level social encounters that SI researchers have provided insight into how macro-level societal patterns are reproduced, or challenged, by people's everyday behaviors. Research in the SI face of sociological social psychology also gives us information about the unique experiences of particular groups within society. The qualitative studies common within the SI orientation provide a level of detail not found in most quantitative analyses. With their focus on face-to-face interactions in real-world settings, they provide insight into facets of people's everyday lives that cannot be accessed in any other way.

Limitations of SI Research

Qualitative research within the SI orientation is sometimes criticized for lacking rigor, given its subjectivity and limited generalizability. Moreover, researchers working within the SI face of sociological social psychology (excluding those associated within the Iowa/Indiana school tradition) have been criticized for emphasizing the individual over social structure. Some general (macro) sociologists and sociological social psychologists working within the GPS or the SSP orientation feel that SI researchers don't pay enough attention to the impact of broader social forces on people's experiences.

SI researchers have countered that more macro perspectives, which focus on patterns of perception and behavior at the aggregate level, overlook the nuances of social life. In their view, social psychologists must study people's micro-level interactions and their subjective interpretations in order to capture the essence of human social behavior.

CHAPTER SUMMARY

The symbolic interactionist face of social psychology includes Chicago and Iowa/ Indiana school symbolic interactionism, the dramaturgical perspective, and

TABLE 3.2

Symbolic Interactionism and Related Perspectives

PERSPECTIVE	UNIT OF ANALYSIS	PRIMARY FOCUS	METHODOLOGY	STUDIES
Chicago school symbolic interactionism	Individual/interaction	Social construction of meaning, situational definitions	Participant observation (with in-depth interviews)	Teens working in coffee shops (Besen, Ch. 1) Indian American students' identity construction (Kurien, Ch. 1)
			In-depth interviews	Fan-celebrity encounters (Ferris) working-class students' identities (Hurst, Ch. 2) Social basis of marijuana's effects (Becker)
		Situational definitions	Observation, survey	Reasons for nonparticipation in college classes (Karp and Yoels)
Iowa school symbolic interactionism	Group	Link social structure, self and interaction	Survey	Measuring the content of students' self-concepts (Kuhn and McPartland) Family role-specialization and self-identification based on gender (Couch)

TABLE 3.2
(Continued)

PERSPECTIVE	UNIT OF ANALYSIS	PRIMARY FOCUS	METHODOLOGY	STUDIES
Dramaturgical model	Individual/interaction	Self-presentational strategies	Participant observation, observation, in-depth interviews	Students' postexam impression management strategies (Albas and Albas)
Ethnomethodology	Individual/interaction	Methods through which reality is constructed	Breaching experiments, documentary method (participant observation, textual analysis of conversations)	Reproduction of commonsense understandings of race through conversation (Whitehead)

ethnomethodology. With the exception of Iowa/Indiana school SI, which is more structural in orientation, these theoretical frameworks focus on individuals and face-to-face interaction in natural settings. They do, however, address different aspects of everyday life. These distinctions are highlighted in Table 3.2, which includes a summary of each theoretical framework discussed in this chapter, as well as the studies we have used to illustrate each type of social psychological research. Given their subject matter, with the exception of analyses within the Iowa/Indiana school tradition, these studies are qualitative in orientation.

Key Points to Know

- **Chicago school symbolic interactionism is the dominant theoretical framework within the symbolic interactionist face of sociological social psychology.** Research within this tradition and within the two related theoretical frameworks (the dramaturgical perspective and ethnomethodology) is referred to as microsociology. → micro-level

- **The concept of the self, as a process of interaction between the "I" and the "me," is central to the symbolic interactionist perspective.** The extent that social expectations, brought into awareness through the process of role taking (the "me") versus impulses (the "I"), govern social action depends upon the social context in which the behavior occurs. The higher the level of normative regulation within a given social setting, the more likely the "me" is to reshape our "I" responses, making them consistent with social expectations.

- **Because they regard the "I" as giving social action a spontaneous component, Chicago school symbolic interactionists view human social behavior as unpredictable and unique to the social context within which it emerges.** They focus on the social construction of meanings, which are fluid and have a subjective component.

- **Chicago school SI emphasizes the construction of meanings through social interaction and the importance of people's subjective experience. Chicago school SI research is qualitative in orientation and studies behavior in natural settings.** Its goal is to access the unique perspectives (situational definitions) of the individuals under study and to analyze their actions within this context.

- **Iowa/Indiana school SI emphasizes the relationship between the statuses people occupy and the content of their self-concepts (the "me" phase of the self).** Assuming stability in self-concepts rooted in the structure of society, researchers working in the Iowa/Indiana school tradition use surveys to study people's reflective self-perceptions and to look for patterns at the group level. Iowa/Indiana school studies are similar to social structure and personality research but are considered symbolic interactionist because of their focus on the self.

- **The dramaturgical model is a variant of symbolic interactionism. The dramaturgical model views social life as consisting of staged performances designed to convey positive impressions to others.** Like Chicago school SI, the dramaturgical model focuses on face-to-face interaction and acknowledges the effects of social context (back vs. front region) on behavior.

- **Social psychologists working within the dramaturgical framework study the process of impression management and the strategies people use to avoid embarrassment in public settings.** These qualitative analyses often involve in-depth interviews or participant observation.

- **Ethnomethodology is a perspective related to symbolic interactionism that focuses on how people make sense of everyday situations.** Ethnomethdologists are similar to symbolic interactionists in their interest in the social construction of meaning and their use of qualitative methods to study social behavior in natural settings. However, rather than studying the meanings that emerge through social interaction, ethnomethodologists focus on the accounts people generate to make the situations they encounter meaningful.

- **Both symbolic interactionists and ethnomethodologists regard language and communication as central features of social life.** For the symbolic interactionists, language is the basis of mind and allows for the construction of meaning. According to ethnomethodologists, people create and maintain a sense of reality through the (verbal) accounting process.

- **The symbolic interactionist face of social psychology (with the exception of the Iowa/Indiana school) emphasizes agency over structure.** Whereas sociologists who are more macro in orientation regard this as problematic, sociological social psychologists working within this tradition argue that micro-level interactions bear direct study because they are the basis of society.

Terms and Concepts for Review

Accounts	Iowa/Indiana school of SI
Back region	"me"
Breaching experiments	Microsociology
Chicago school SI	Props
Consolidation of responsibility	Public self-consciousness

Terms and Concepts for Review (*Continued*)

Documentary method	Role taking (perspective taking)
Dramaturgical perspective	Saving face
Ethnomethodology	Self
Front region	Self-concept
"I"	Significant symbol
Identity theory	Situational definition
Impression management	Structural symbolic interactionism
Iowa/Indiana school SI	Theoretical framework

Questions for Review and Reflection

1. The notion that situational definitions shape behavior is central to the symbolic interactionist perspective. Give an example, from your own experience or from a public (media) account, of an instance where two or more people arrived at different definitions of the same incident or interaction. What impact did these varying situational definitions have on people's behavior?
2. Decide whether the following research questions would be of greater interest to a Chicago school symbolic interactionist or to an Iowa/Indiana school symbolic interactionist. Explain the basis for each of your decisions.
   a. How do status differences emerge among middle school children? What does it mean for someone to be of high social status, or popular, within this social setting?
   b. To what extent do college students' self-concepts reflect the various statuses they occupy and the roles they play (e.g., member of a school athletic team, resident assistant, tutor, or friend)?
   c. When and how do college students form study groups? What kinds of social interactions occur during study group sessions?
3. List three social situations where impression management is a key concern. List three social settings where people tend to be unconcerned about the images they convey to others. Which list was easier to come up with? Discuss the implications of this.
4. How do Chicago school SI and ethnomethodology differ in focus? From the perspective of an ethnomethodologist, why are breaching experiments a useful method for the study of everyday life?

ENDNOTES

1. The statements presented here were taken verbatim from the cited monograph, but the format of the text was modified by adding the labels "Researcher" and "Participant."
2. Like James, Mead is associated with the school of philosophical thought called pragmatism. John Dewey, Mead's friend and colleague at the University of Chicago (Jahoda 2007), was another pragmatic philosopher whose work had a substantial impact on Mead's thinking. In general, pragmatists define meaning and truth in terms of everyday

activities. From this perspective, an idea is true insofar as it is effective when put into practice (Honderich 2005).

3. Whereas symbolic interactionism has its roots in pragmatism, ethnomethodology is associated with a school of thought in philosophy called phenomenology and, in particular, with the work of Alfred Schutz. Phenomenology locates meaning in subjective experience rather than in social processes (Gallant and Kleinman 1983).

CHAPTER 4

Social Structure and Personality

Social norms within college classrooms influence the likelihood that students will offer comments and ask questions. As you know from the previous chapter, symbolic interactionists have studied the interactional processes through which these norms are created and maintained and the degree to which they reflect competing situational definitions between students and professors.

PHOTO 4.1

Status characteristics, including gender, race/ethnicity, and age, influence people's social interactions in college classrooms and other social settings.

SSP ANALYSES OF THE COLLEGE CLASSROOM

In contrast, researchers working within the social structure and personality (SSP) tradition have focused on the effect of social stratification on people's thoughts and behaviors within college classrooms. For example, they have looked at how faculty race and gender influence students' perceptions of their professors and how their perceptions affect classroom dynamics. Recall that race and gender are status characteristics associated with inequality at the macro level.

Research suggests that African American professors are less likely than White faculty to be viewed by students as credible sources of information (Harlow 2003; Hendrix 1997). This may lead to less positive teaching evaluations.

You may be familiar with RateMyProfessors.com, a website where college students from across the country evaluate their professors. In a recent study, Reid (2010) analyzed student ratings of faculty posted on RateMyProfessors.com by professor race and gender. Professor race/ethnicity and gender were determined using photos posted on department webpages or on other public websites. All of the online ratings for professors from the top 25 liberal arts college in the United States whose race/ethnicity and gender could be determined were included in the study.

White professors (n = 3,079) received, on average, more positive evaluations of their courses than professors who were Asian (n = 238), Latino (n = 130), or Black (n = 142). On average, Black professors received the lowest student ratings. Black males (n = 81) were especially likely to be given negative reviews (Reid 2010).

It is safe to assume that these differences in professor ratings are due to status beliefs associated with race/ethnicity (societal beliefs about the relative abilities of racial/ethnic minorities and Whites) and not differences in the preparation or abilities of minority and White professors. Due to prevailing status beliefs, managing interactions with students and gaining their respect often requires extra work on the part of minority faculty, which takes time and can be emotionally draining (Harlow 2003).

Harlow (2003) discusses how professor race intersects with gender in its effects on faculty-student interaction. She interviewed 58 professors (29 African Americans and 29 Whites) at a large state university with a predominantly White student population. Among the study participants, Black male professors were the most likely to report that students challenged their intellectual authority, whereas Black female professors were more likely than faculty in other race-gender categories to report that their students perceived them as mean and intimidating.

Despite these differences, many of the African American faculty interviewed by Harlow (2003) did not believe that race significantly influenced their interactions with students. Presumably this was because acknowledging the extent to which race affected their experiences in the classroom would have been disempowering. How African Americans are perceived and treated within this society is not within the control of these professors (Harlow 2003).

Students' status characteristics (including gender, race/ethnicity, and socioeconomic background) also influence classroom dynamics from elementary school through college (Ansalone 2001; Buchmann, DiPrete, and McDaniel 2008; Downey and Pribesh 2004; Sadker, Sadker, and Zittleman 2009; Trujillo 1986). Status characteristics have important consequences for students' self-concepts and aspirations and play a role in the reproduction of existing patterns of inequality. We discuss studies on stratification within schools (in the section titled "Tracking") later in this chapter.

For SSP researchers, bias in the classroom reflects the relative power of individuals who occupy various positions within society (e.g., racial/ethnic minorities vs. Whites, females vs. males), irrespective of the unique characteristics of the particular students or teachers in any given interactive encounter. It is not that social psychologists working within this framework do not believe that people vary in their perceptions and actions in random ways (i.e., in ways that do not reflect their positions within the structure of the larger society). They simply view these micro-level characteristics as less relevant to the study of social behavior. Sociological social psychologists working within the SSP tradition focus on causal agents that transcend the immediate settings within which social interaction occurs. To these researchers, the idiosyncratic qualities of the individuals present in any given social encounter are of little interest.

SSP researchers view individuals' perceptions and behaviors as products of macro-level social forces rather than micro-level personal characteristics. Thus, acknowledging the existence of race, gender, and class bias within schools or in any other social context need not be equated with the notion that members of dominant groups (Whites, men, and the socioeconomically advantaged) are bad or malicious people. It is the current organization of society (inequality at the macro level), rather than ill will on the part of any particular individual, that is seen as the root of these patterns.

SSP AS A FACE OF SOCIOLOGICAL SOCIAL PSYCHOLOGY

The social structure and personality face of social psychology is closest to general (macro) sociology in that the main unit of analysis is macro (large-scale social processes or groups, typically defined by social class, race/ethnicity, and gender). Within this context, the term **personality** is defined as relatively stable psychological attributes, which include attitudes, values, beliefs, motives, perceptions, and feelings (House 1981).

Given its focus on perception and behaviors at the group level, much of the research on social structure and personality is survey based. In fact, to a large degree, the growth of social structure and personality as a distinct face of sociological social psychology was tied to the development of survey methods (House 1977). With the use of representative samples, survey procedures enable researchers to study patterns of perception and behavior among large numbers of individuals and yield results that are generalizable to the larger society.

Early Research

Among the first researchers to work within SSP, Stouffer and associates (1949) used what were then newly developed survey methods to study the perceptions and attitudes of military personnel during World War II. One of their most interesting results, published in their classic book *The American Soldier,* pertains to the mismatch between soldiers' actual (objective) opportunities for advancement and their subjective assessments of their likelihood of being promoted. Paradoxically, soldiers in the Military Police, a branch of the Army with a relatively low rate of promotion, were more optimistic about their chances for upward occupational mobility than individuals in the Air Corps, a division with a relatively high promotion rate.

The mismatch occurred because the Military Police were using other individuals in their division as their point of reference when assessing their own careers and their likelihood of advancement. **Reference groups** serve as standards for comparison when people evaluate their personal characteristics and experiences. These groups are typically selected on the basis of contextual factors (e.g., geographical proximity) and social relationships. Thus, reference groups are often groups to which one belongs, but they need not be.

Given the low promotion rate in their division, most of the members of the Military Police studied by Stouffer and his colleagues had coworkers who had yet to advance in rank. As a result, they believed that they were faring at least as well as their peers and were optimistic about their own chances for advancement. Soldiers in the Air Corps, on the other hand, thought they were lagging behind others because many of the individuals in their division had already been promoted. Thus, despite their greater objective opportunities for advancement than members of the Military Police, members of the Air Corps experienced what Stouffer and associates (1949) termed relative deprivation. **Relative deprivation** results from the perception that one is less well-off than members of his or her reference group (Merton 1968; Merton and Rossi 1968).

Social Stratification and Its Consequences

In the 1950s and 1960s, sociological social psychologists became increasingly interested in aspects of social structure related to systems of stratification and their effects on aspirations, self-evaluations, and attitudes (Spenner 1988). Following in this tradition, most contemporary studies within SSP take stratification as their starting point (McLeod and Lively 2006). The main emphasis of these studies is on relationships between groups with differential access to societal resources and on the influence of a group's position within the stratification hierarchy on its members' social experiences. This emphasis is reflected in the literature on racial and gender bias in the classroom, which we described at the beginning of this chapter.

SSP and Theory

The social structure and personality face of social psychology is defined largely by its research foci and not by a particular theoretical framework. This, in addition to its macro focus, makes it very different from symbolic interactionism, discussed in Chapter 3.

Given the absence of an overriding theoretical framework, sociologists working within SSP utilize a variety of social psychological theories to explain social behavior. Some of these theories are from within sociology and some are from within psychology. In this chapter and in the topical chapters in the second part of the book, you will see that SSP researchers at times employ theories that are specific to a particular area of study. Because these analyses sometimes include concepts from role theory (a theoretical framework within general sociology), we begin by providing a brief overview of this perspective.

Role Theory

Role theory, sometimes called **structural role theory**, has its roots in cultural anthropology and the structural functionalist tradition within general (macro) sociology. Role theory provides researchers with a set of concepts that draw their attention to the social expectations associated with various structural positions and to patterns of behavior at the macro level. In particular, role theorists focus on statuses and roles (Stryker and Statham 1985).

STATUSES AND ROLES

Statuses are the recognized social positions within a society. Thus, when sociological social psychologists use the term "status," they are not necessarily referring to one's economic or social standing. Within sociological social psychology, statuses include positions, such as student, worker, athlete, and friend. Statuses also include dimensions of stratification, such as social class, gender, and race/ethnicity.

Every status comes with a **role**, which is a set of norms (i.e., rules) about how one should behave, think, and feel (Heiss 1981). Whereas you occupy a status, you play a role. For example, when you occupy the student status, there are certain expectations about how you should act. Some of these expectations are that you sit facing the instructor in class, take notes, convey to the instructor that you are paying attention and interested in the course material (even if you aren't), and raise your hand when you have a question. These expectations attached to the status of student are shared among members of our society and thus place constraints on our behaviors. Whereas students who follow the rules tend to receive positive feedback from their teachers and peers, those who violate the role expectations attached to their student status often receive negative sanctions from others.

Can you imagine what would happen if you blatantly texted your friends, surfed the web, or posted pictures on Facebook during a lecture? Even more extreme, what if you answered your cell phone and spoke loudly in the middle of one of your classes, and then moved your desk out of its row so that you sat apart from all of the other students in the class (assuming that you are in a classroom with movable seats) so that you could speak more privately? How would the professor respond to you? How would your fellow students respond?

Conformity to the expectations of a particular role is encouraged through the application of sanctions, and over time, role expectations are internalized. That is, we often come to see the required behaviors of a status as not just something we have to do but as something we *should* do. It just makes sense to us that students should pay attention in class, or at least appear as though they are doing so, and that they should sit and face the front of the room without changing the location of their desks. Most students don't even think to act in an alternative manner. Would it even have crossed your mind before now to talk on the phone in class or to move your desk to a more favorable location within the room?

As you might have guessed, roles are social facts. They exist above and beyond any one of us. Do your specific behaviors as a student (e.g., how you act in class, how much time you spend studying, how frequently you miss class, whether and when you do your assigned reading) in any way affect what people within society at large expect of students? No individual is powerful enough to change society's role expectations, even if that person has lots of money and is highly regarded. Nonetheless, role expectations influence our individual behaviors. If you fail to conform to the student role, there are usually consequences, in terms of grades and even continued enrollment at your school.

In addition to providing guidelines for our behavior, roles tell us what actions we can anticipate or expect from others within society. Thus, roles define many of our daily activities and interactions by telling us who should do what, and when and where they should do it (Biddle 1979).

What Do You Think?

- Have you or someone you know ever violated the role expectations attached to the student status? How chronic and serious was this violation? What happened as a result of this behavior?
- What can students who have violated the role expectations associated with being a student do in order to redeem themselves (i.e., in order to once again be regarded as a legitimate occupant of the student status or to regain that status)? Whom do they have to convince?

SOCIAL INSTITUTIONS

Social institutions provide the contexts in which many of our status-role relationships occur. **Social institutions** are clusters of patterned status-role relationships

PHOTO 4.2

The student role set includes academic, social, and organizational roles.

that have developed over time to meet one or more societal needs. For example, status-role relationships among students, professors, school administrators, clerical staff, coaches, and others at the macro level, and the relatively stable and predictable patterns of behavior they generate, make up the institution of education. (You probably mentioned people in these positions when you answered the second question in the What Do You Think? exercise you just completed.)

The institution of education serves an important societal function. It teaches individuals the knowledge and skills they need to function within society and, in particular, within the workplace.

Social psychological research within SSP also suggests that education plays a role in reproducing the class structure within society even though we aren't always aware of this. Would you believe that education helps to keep the children of poor people poor and the children of rich people rich? We talk about this later in this chapter.

Other social institutions include religion, politics, the economy, and the family. The statuses we occupy in relation to the family, education, and other social institutions often involve multiple roles. The term **role set** is used to refer to the various roles attached to a particular status (Merton 1957). There are, for instance, multiple roles associated with being a student: academic (attending classes and studying), social (hanging out with friends), and organizational (involvement in campus and community organizations). Each of these roles entail interaction with individuals in related statuses (e.g., professors, other students, and university staff and administrators).

ROLE STRAIN

Role strain occurs when individuals have difficulty meeting their role obligations (Goode 1960). **Intrarole conflict**, a type of role strain, results in situations where the roles associated with a particular status are in opposition. For example, as a student you need to study for an exam, but your friends want you to go out with them instead. When the role expectations associated with more than one status conflict, people experience a type of role strain referred to as **interrole conflict** (Sarbin and Allen 1968). Interrole conflict occurs when, for example, you have to work at your off-campus job, but you also need to study for an upcoming exam.

Other interrole conflicts emerge when the nature of a role, such as worker or parent, is incongruent with an individual's status characteristics or his or her self-concept (Stryker and Statham 1985). For instance, men who work in jobs that are occupied mainly by women (e.g., men who are flight attendants, kindergarten teachers, librarians, or nurses) report that people routinely question their career choice and their masculinity. As a result, they often start questioning their own masculinity and whether they are in the right job (Simpson 2005).

A third type of role strain, **role overload**, arises when people do not have enough time or emotional resources to fulfill the role expectations associated with one or more of their statuses (Goode 1960; Coverman 1989). This kind of situation might sound familiar. You've experienced role overload if you've ever found it difficult, if not impossible, to read for your classes, study for exams, write papers, work, spend time with your friends, spend time with your family, and finish tasks you've taken on as a member of one or more groups or organizations. People experiencing role overload just can't do everything they are supposed to do within the allotted time frame.

We all have a stake in the role performances of others if social interaction is to maintain its stable and predictable character. Thus, when individuals fail to fulfill the role obligations associated with one or more of the statuses they occupy, people typically react with surprise and anger. As a result, most of us fulfill the role expectations placed upon us most of the time. In fact, as we noted earlier, most role performances are so routine that we rarely question their legitimacy. These behaviors seem automatic (Stryker and Statham, 1985).

In general, structural role theory emphasizes the stability and predictability of people's role performances and downplays individuals' capacities for creativity and innovation. Researchers working within this tradition examine which statuses, as a part of the social structure, influence our responses to situations. Thus, structural role theory has enhanced our understanding of the nature of the link between macro-level structural factors and patterns of individual perception and behavior. As we explore some of the SSP research, you will see the ways in which concepts central to role theory, including role conflict and role overload, have been used to explain the patterns of individual attitudes, feelings, and behaviors produced by social structure.

THE THREE PRINCIPLES THAT GUIDE RESEARCH IN SSP

There are three general principles, identified by House (1981), that define the focus of research within SSP. (See Figure 4.1 for an overview of this face of sociological social psychology.) They are (1) the components principle, (2) the proximity principle, and (3) the psychology principle.

The Components Principle

The **components principle** involves the identification of the specific components of the larger social system that are the most relevant for understanding the aspect of personality or behavior under investigation (House 1981). There are many different components, or parts, of society that can be explored as possible explanations for variations in individual-level psychological processes and actions. SSP researchers, also called structural social psychologists, have focused on all of the following:

- organizational characteristics of societies or communities (e.g., type of economic system)

- large-scale processes within society (e.g., urbanization, industrialization)

- individuals' positions within the social structure (e.g., social class, race/ethnicity, and gender)

- specific dimensions of a status such as social class (e.g., education or occupation)

What makes these SSP studies similar is that the causes of individuals' attitudes, feelings, and behaviors are located within the structure of society (House 1977; McLeod and Lively 2006).

By applying the components principle, researchers can document existing societal patterns and identify which aspects of social structure are important for understanding different individual-level outcomes. The examples of research in social structure and personality discussed in previous chapters illustrate the application of this principle. In Chapter 1 we showed that White teenagers are more likely to work for pay than their African American counterparts, and that immigrant youths are less likely than their American-born counterparts to engage in delinquent behavior. In our discussion of teacher-student relations at the beginning of this chapter, we also illustrated some of the ways race and gender shape the experiences of college students and faculty.

Although the application of the components principle helps us uncover the relationships between social structure and individuals' attitudes and behaviors, it does not help us understand how social positions mold or shape us to produce these patterns. What are the processes by which a person's race, gender, and social class influence his or her perceptions and actions? Numerous studies show, for instance, that the status of immigrant (immigrant vs. nonimmigrant) affects youths' likelihood of being delinquent, but without further investigation we do not know why this is the case. What is there about being an immigrant that leads to lower rates of delinquency?

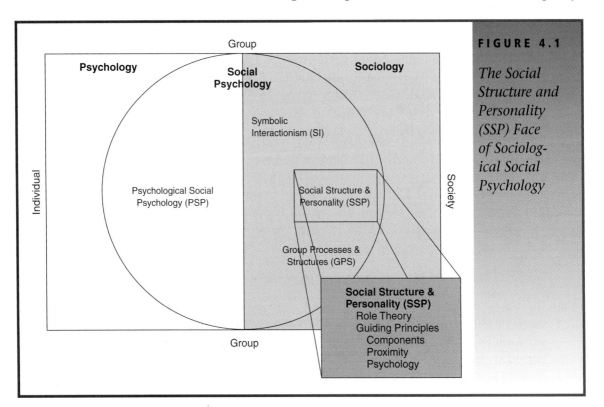

FIGURE 4.1

The Social Structure and Personality (SSP) Face of Sociological Social Psychology

The Proximity Principle

In order to understand the preceding question, researchers must apply what House (1981) defines as the proximity principle. The **proximity principle** addresses the ways the broader social structures affect us through more proximate (immediate) life conditions. Going back to our previous example, research suggests that immigrant youths are less likely to engage in delinquent behaviors than their American-born counterparts in part because they have more positive relationships with family members and are more closely monitored by their parents (Bui 2009).

As illustrated in this example, the proximity principle directs our attention to **meso-level** phenomena (McLeod and Lively 2006). "Meso" means "in between"; in this case, the conditions and experiences in between social structure and the individual. Typically, meso level refers to people's social networks, which include their family members and friends.

The term **Social network** is used to refer to the people with whom we interact on a regular basis, often within the context of particular institutions, such as the family. The term "social network" also refers to the links or connections that exist between the members of these groups (Felmlee 2006). Social networks serve as one intervening (proximal) link between the most macro structures within society and the individual. For example, stratification (a macro-level phenomenon) affects our immediate social environments, including—but not limited to—where we live, where we go to school, and the types of jobs we are likely to have. As a result, we experience the effects of stratification through our daily interactions with others in these areas of our lives.

Thus, proximate conditions are mediating variables. A **mediating variable** explains why a particular independent variable (cause) affects a particular dependent variable (outcome). In the research on immigrants and delinquency we just discussed, family relationships (a mediating variable) help to explain why immigrant status (the independent variable) reduces delinquency (the dependent variable).

What do You Think?

- Why do college undergraduates who are affiliated with the Greek system drink more than other students? Describe at least three proximal conditions that could serve as links between Greek participation and student drinking.
- Social class is positively related to health. That is, socioeconomically advantaged individuals have better health than individuals at the bottom of the stratification hierarchy. Identify three proximal conditions that are likely to mediate the class-health relationship.
- Compare your responses to these questions with one or two of your classmates.

The Psychology Principle

The third guiding proposition for research on social structure and personality, the **psychology principle** (House 1981), directs social psychologists' attention toward the ways people process and incorporate macro-level structures (components principle) into their personal experiences. To this end, social structure and personality researchers seek to determine how individuals' proximal social environments enter into their minds and affect their behaviors (McLeod and Lively 2006). The psychology principle, along with the components and proximity principles, summarized in Figure 4.1, are presented as more detailed prescriptions for the SSP researcher in Box 4.1.

Structure Versus Agency Within SSP

Researchers in SSP study people's interactions with others within various institutional contexts, such as the family (the proximity principle), and their thoughts and feelings (the psychology principle). When they do so, they assume that the patterns they observe result largely from people's positions within the structure of society and the roles that they play (the components principle). They also assume that these patterns of behavior are not caused by idiosyncratic preferences or reactions to individuals and social settings, which vary among members of particular groups (e.g., men and women, Whites and racial and ethnic minorities, or individuals who belong to a particular social class). This means that SSP researchers focus on structure over agency.

Box 4.1 Conducting Research in SSP

1. **Components principle**: First, the researcher should select the most relevant components of social structure, given his or her topic of interest, for investigation. Relevant components often include one or more of the statuses that serve as a dimension of stratification within our society (i.e., gender, class, or race/ethnicity).

2. **Proximity principle**: The researcher must then determine which proximate environments (e.g., the family, school) and relationships (e.g., with a spouse, children, or friends) affected by the components under investigation shape personality and behavior. The researcher should treat proximate conditions as mediating variables in the causal chain and assess the degree to which these variables explain the relationship between the components of social structure under investigation and the psychological and behavioral outcomes of interest.

3. **The psychology principle**: It is also part of the researcher's task to specify how the components of social structure under investigation, and the proximate environments and relationships they influence, become incorporated into people's perceptions, feelings, and behaviors.

Note: House (1981).

It is important to note that researchers in SSP acknowledge that the relation-ships they observe will apply to most members of a target group, but not to every-one. For example, although immigrant status affects the likelihood that individuals will engage in delinquency, it does not *determine* that outcome. That is, not all non-immigrant (i.e., American-born) youths engage in delinquency, and most do not. Even those with similar proximal environments may act differently. This means that the effects of social structure on perception and behavior of interest to structural social psychologists are **probabilistic**. Effects are probabilistic when they are likely but not guaranteed. Social psychologists can determine which status characteristics (e.g., immigrant status) are likely to lead to a given outcome (e.g., delinquency) through their association with a given set of proximal variables (e.g., relationships with parents), but due to the complexity of social life, there will always be variations from the overall pattern.

The General SSP Model

Figure 4.2 illustrates the general SSP model linking societal characteristics to pat-terns of thought, feeling, and behavior at the individual level via proximate envi-ronments and social relationships. Note the multiple levels of analysis (macro, or structural; meso, or proximal; and micro, or individual) involved in conceptualizing these relationships. SSP researchers assume that personality characteristics and the patterned behaviors they generate serve to reproduce (or, insofar as they change, will alter) social structure. (The mechanisms through which this occurs are not always directly addressed, a point we discuss in the following section.) Thus, we include dual causal arrows on the left-hand side of Figure 4.2. We made the arrow from individuals' psychological states to society (the dashed line) less pronounced than the solid arrow from society to individuals' perceptions, feelings, and behaviors to show that SSP research emphasizes the effects of macro-level societal characteristics on individuals.

As you have probably already noticed, social structure and personality is a research orientation that can be used to help us understand a variety of individual-level psychological processes and behaviors. Sociologists working within this tradition have examined the relationship between a wide array of macro-level structures (e.g., social institutions, stratification) and individual-level outcomes, including happiness, delinquency, social mobility, self-esteem, depression, discrim-ination, and collective action.

The application to a particular topic of all three of the principles specified by House (1981)—the components principle, the proximity principle, and the psy-chology principle—gives us the fullest understanding of how social structures affect individuals. But in reality it is somewhat rare for any specific study to apply all three principles. In most SSP studies, one or two of the principles guides the research. That is, they focus on part, rather than all, of the SSP model depicted in Figure 4.2.

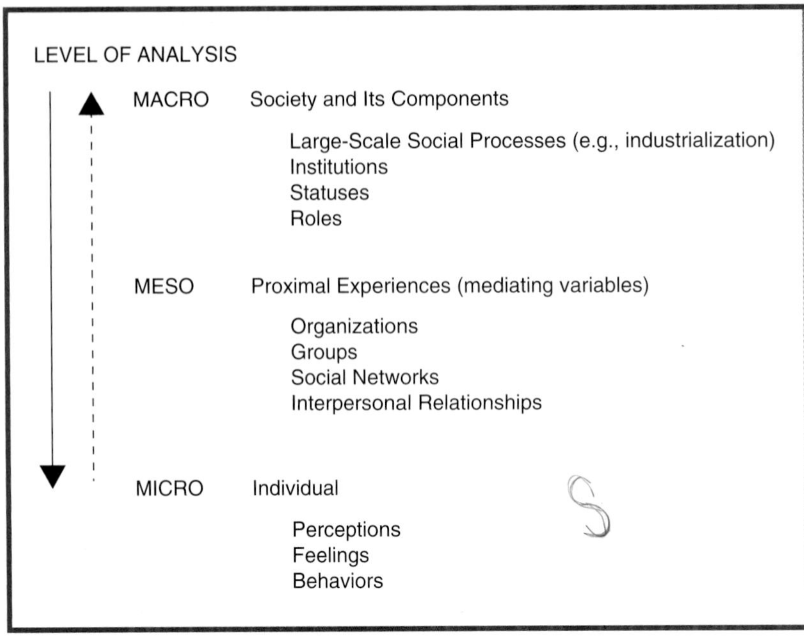

LEVEL OF ANALYSIS

MACRO   Society and Its Components

Large-Scale Social Processes (e.g., industrialization)
Institutions
Statuses
Roles

MESO   Proximal Experiences (mediating variables)

Organizations
Groups
Social Networks
Interpersonal Relationships

MICRO   Individual

Perceptions
Feelings
Behaviors

FIGURE 4.2

The General Social Structure and Personality Model

Given this, the most complete understanding of the effect of social structures on individuals often develops over time and can be found in reading the collective body of research on a given subject (vs. a single study). Throughout the topical chapters in the second part of this text, we review relevant research from within the social structure and personality tradition, as well as studies from within the other faces of sociological social psychology. In the following section, we summarize some of the most prominent research literatures within SSP.

PROMINENT RESEARCH IN SSP

Studies in SSP are often categorized by the context, or setting, they focus on. The focus of most contemporary work in SSP is the effects of stratification on psychology and behavior. The social contexts (proximate environments) that have received the most attention by SSP researchers are the workplace, schools, and the family. This is not surprising, given their importance to social life (McLeod and Lively 2006). Because it is not possible to review all of the literature pertaining to each of these contexts, we focus on those studies that are the most well-known and best illustrate the three guiding principles of the SSP face of social psychology. In the absence of any overriding theoretical framework, it is these principles, or research guidelines (see Box 4.1), that define social structure and personality as a distinct subfield.

Many analyses within the SSP literature examine multiple social institutions, often highlighting their interrelationship (e.g., work and family, family and education). This is the case in much of the research described in the following sections. For ease of presentation, we categorize these studies in terms of the proximate environment that serves as their focal point.

Work

Research on the relationship between social class, work experiences, and personality by Melvin Kohn and Carmi Schooler is one of the most influential bodies of literature within the social structure and personality framework (Mortimer and Lorence 1995; Spenner 1988). Kohn and Schooler demonstrated that work conditions—in particular, variations in job complexity, supervision, and control over the work process—explain class differences in personality. White-collar professional jobs, an indicator of middle-class standing, involve high levels of **occupational self-direction** in that they are complex, involve little supervision, and give individuals substantial latitude in terms of how and when the work is done. On the other hand, manual labor and other working-class jobs are characterized by low occupational self-direction because the work is routine, closely monitored, and individuals have few opportunities for independent decision making.

Occupational self-direction leads to a **self-directed orientation** (i.e., a sense of personal responsibility, trustfulness, and an openness to change), as well as to self-confidence and psychological well-being. It also leads to the ability to view issues from multiple perspectives, a personality characteristic called "ideational (or intellectual) flexibility." Given the work experiences of middle-class workers, these psychological attributes are more common among the middle class than among the working class (Kohn and Schooler 1969; Miller et al. 1979).

Class differences in work experiences also explain class differences in parenting styles. That is, the personality characteristics cultivated by the work environment affect how parents raise their children. Whereas working-class parents tend to value in their children characteristics associated with success in blue-collar jobs (e.g., obedience and conformity), middle-class parents tend to value attributes associated with success in white-collar professional occupations (e.g., curiosity and self-control) (Kohn 1969).

Data from the 2010 General Social Survey showing a link between occupational status and the characteristics people value in children are presented in Table 4.1. It is important to note that social psychologists do not make moral judgments about the patterns they observe. Thus, they do not regard one set of values as better than another. Rather, they view variations across groups as predictable reactions to very different sets of social experiences.

Although Kohn and Schooler initially focused on the United States, the patterns they observed generalize to other societies, including Poland and Japan,

MOST IMPORTANT FOR CHILDREN TO:	OBEY (%)	THINK FOR SELF (%)	N	TABLE 4.1
Education				*Characteristics*
< High school	31.4	23.7	207	*Valued in*
High school	14.9	39.0	664	*Children by*
Junior college	13.3	52.2	90	*Indicators of*
College	4.4	57.0	388	*Social Class,*
Occupation				*U.S. Adults in*
Nonprofessional/technical	17.1	37.7	799	*2010*
Technical/technical support	15.1	43.4	53	
Managerial/professional	6.3	56.5	382	

Note: Smith, Tom W., Peter V. Marsden, and Michael Hout. 2011. General Social Surveys, 1972–2010 [machine-readable data file] / Sponsored by National Science Foundation.—NORC ed.—Chicago, IL: National Opinion Research Center [producer]; Storrs, CT: The Roper Center for Public Opinion Research, University of Connecticut [distributor].

despite some notable differences in values across cultural contexts. For instance, Japanese culture is much more group oriented and places less of a value on individual achievement than U.S. culture (Schooler 1996). The consistency in the study results across societies provides additional support for the notion that work conditions are proximate experiences that link social class (a component of social structure) to personality characteristics. Experiences at work spill over into other spheres of social life (the psychology principle) and affect cognitive functioning, as well as people's orientations toward themselves, their children, and the larger society.

In turn, the psychological outcomes associated with self-direction on the job increase individuals' likelihood of moving up in the occupational hierarchy, thus providing insight into the mechanisms through which systems of stratification are reproduced. Education is also viewed as an important part of this process because it facilitates the development of the kinds of intellectual skills required for success in middle-class, professional occupations (Kohn and Schooler 1969, 1982; Schooler 1996; Schooler, Mulatu and Oates 2004).

Gender, Race, and Occupational Mobility

In her award-winning book *Men and Women of the Corporation*, Kanter (1977) draws attention to how gender, another status characteristic, affects both personality and social mobility in work settings. In her comprehensive study, Kanter used data gathered in detailed interviews to provide an in-depth analysis of the experiences of individuals working in a large, hierarchical organization.

The majority of the clerical workers in the company Kanter studied were women, and they exhibited traits commonly associated with femininity within this society. In particular, they wanted constant praise from their (male) bosses, and they regularly engaged in workplace gossip.

Kanter (1977) argues that these characteristics result from the occupation of a low-status job, a proximate condition associated with gender, rather than any innate or inborn tendencies in women. People of low status tend to be insecure and require continual reassurance. Similarly, when workers lack authority and resources within the formal organizational structure, they seek informal avenues for securing power. Through gossip, people receive information they may not otherwise have access to, and that information provides them with a sense of greater control over their lives (Burt 2005; Foster 2004). Kanter purports that men are as likely as women to exhibit "praise addiction" and engage in gossip when they experience low status and disempowering work conditions.

See Box 4.2 for a news article that makes a similar argument about power and infidelity. Note that women with power are as likely to cheat on their spouses as their male counterparts.

Focusing on issues pertaining to occupational mobility, Kanter (1977) also offers a structural analysis of the psychological motivations behind patterns of discrimination within the organization she studied. Very few women and racial and ethnic minorities made it to the upper rungs of management within this company. Surprisingly, given this pattern, the White male managers (who decided which employees did, and did not, get promoted) did not exhibit negative attitudes toward women or minorities. What, then, was motivating their behavior?

Kanter argues that organizational uncertainty was at the root of their actions. Upper-level managers' day-to-day work experiences were rife with uncertainty. This was due to their lack of control over broader market forces; the substantial time lag between managerial decisions and their outcome; and the hierarchical structure of the organization itself, where multiple tiers of actors were required to put any managerial decision into effect. Because there were so many aspects of their jobs they couldn't control, managers felt that it was important to surround themselves with people they could trust, people who would think and act like them. Inevitably this meant they promoted other White males from advantaged socioeconomic backgrounds. By doing so, managers could at least have some degree of control over their work outcomes. It was not that the managers were conspiring against women and minorities. They were simply less accustomed to working with members of these groups and felt unsure of how women and racial/ethnic minorities would handle everyday situations and potential crises. To ensure their success in an unstable work environment, the managers opted to bring others just like themselves into their inner circle. Thus, women and minorities were locked out of the upper rungs of management irrespective of their personal attributes.

Kanter calls this process the **homosocial-homosexual reproduction of the managerial ranks** and emphasizes its structural roots. She notes that the managers making decisions about whom to promote were not necessarily

Box 4.2   Power Players

Does being a politician make you more likely to be unfaithful?

By J. Bryan Lowder
Slate Magazine
Posted Wednesday, June 15, 2011, at 1:30 PM ET

Anthony Weiner's extramarital sexting, Arnold Schwarzenegger's love child, and the Dominique Strauss-Kahn scandal has led to a lot of handwringing about the prevalence of philandering among politicians and to speculation about why politicians risk their families and their careers to cheat. Is it possible that politicians are more prone to infidelity than the rest of us?

Yes, actually. According to a forthcoming psychological study, politicians, executives, industrialists, generals—basically anyone with power—are indeed more likely to cheat than their underlings. The psychologists, led by Joris Lammers of Tilburg University, surveyed 1561 readers of a weekly magazine for professionals. Respondents were asked to rate their level of professional power and then to answer questions regarding their sexual history. According to the researchers' findings, a higher level of self-perceived power correlates strongly with increased incidence of infidelity and with the belief that one could get away with cheating if one wanted to.

But it's not necessarily the case that power, in itself, is what leads to cheating. Lammers' work suggests that confidence in one's ability to attract a partner—a trait often *exhibited* by the powerful—is the strongest corollary to infidelity. Lammers' research also seems to demonstrate that female power-brokers are no less likely to fool around than their male counterparts, casting doubt on the idea that men are naturally more inclined to extramarital escapades.

In the population at large, infidelity has remained steady for the past two decades, with surveys finding that about 20% to 25% of respondents have cheated at one time or another. (Subjects define infidelity in different ways: For some, sexual intercourse is the standard, while for others, mere emotional involvement constitutes betrayal.) Among men and women over 60, however, infidelity is up: from 5% in 1991 to 15% in 2006 for women and from 20% to 28% for men over the same time period. For comparison, 15% of women and 20% of men under 35 report having cheated.

conscious of their motivation or of its outcomes. Nonetheless, the consequences for the women and minorities denied opportunities for occupational mobility were as negative as they would have been had the discrimination been conscious and intentional.

Table 4.2 shows the gender and race distributions of managerial workers in 2010 and in 1980, around the time of Kanter's study. Although the percentage of women and people of color in upper management increased during these 30 years, these positions are still dominated by males and by Whites. Given this, it is safe to assume that Kanter's findings are relevant to the contemporary workplace.

PHOTO 4.3

Former Represen-
tative Anthony
Weiner (D-NY)

Alienation

Alienation is another work-related outcome that has garnered the attention of SSP researchers. **Alienation** refers to the separation of self and experience. It is a concept developed by the social historian Karl Marx (1818–1883), who is still a highly influential figure within the discipline of sociology. Alienation occurs when people lack control over their work and thus become estranged from the work process and from their basic human nature (Hodson 2007). Alienation has been measured using survey questions that focus on the degree to which work is perceived as dull, unrewarding, and of little intrinsic value (indicators of self-estrangement). Surveys also measure the degree to which individuals feel as though they lack control over their lives (Mottaz 1981; Seeman and Anderson 1983).

	FEMALE (%)	RACIAL/ETHNIC MINORITY (%)	
Managers, 1981[1]	27.5	5.8	**TABLE 4.2**
Managers, 2010[2]	38.2	18.4	*Gender*
Chief executives, 2010	25.5	10.8	*and Racial*
General/operations managers, 2010	29.9	15.0	*Composition* *of Managerial*
Administrative services managers, 2010	34.4	18.5	*Positions,* *United States,* *1981 and 2010*

[1]Data are from the 1982 U.S. Census Bureau, Statistical Abstract of the United States. The category "manager" includes managers and administrators, excluding farm.

[2]Data for 2010 are from the 2012 U.S. Census Bureau, Statistical Abstract of the United States. Current census occupational codes differ from those used in 1982. Occupations most compatible with the earlier definitions of manager and administrator are presented in the table.

Factors that predict alienation include a sense that one's work is meaningless and that one has little or no autonomy. **Autonomy** refers to the level of control employees have over how and when they complete their jobs and is thus related to the concept of self-direction discussed earlier. Because individuals toward the bottom of the class hierarchy tend to have little autonomy at work, they are the groups most likely to experience alienation (Mottaz 1981). Hence, social class is a key structural component that affects alienation (a psychological state) through its effects on people's work conditions (proximate experiences).

Workers who experience alienation are at risk for heavy drinking (Greenberg and Grunberg 1995; Parker and Brody 1982; Seeman and Anderson 1983; Seeman, Seeman, and Budros 1988). Erickson (1986) suggests that this is another spillover effect from work to other social spheres, and that substance abuse may be one way to blunt the psychological consequences of a disempowering work environment.

Job Satisfaction

Other SSP researchers interested in job characteristics and their consequences have focused on more positive outcomes, most notably job satisfaction. A comprehensive study of full-time workers eight years post-high school (Nguyen, Taylor, and Bradley 2002) suggests the following patterns:

• That autonomy, or freedom at work, is the strongest determinant of job satisfaction.

- That race, but not gender, affects job satisfaction. In particular, Black employees are less satisfied with their jobs than their White counterparts. This is not surprising because African Americans are less likely to benefit from the worker role than Whites (Jackson 1997).

- That income is positively associated with job satisfaction. This effect is stronger among males than among females (Nguyen et al. 2002), a finding consistent with prevailing societal expectations concerning work and gender.

- That work hours are not associated with job satisfaction.

- That people are the most satisfied in professional jobs. This association persists when levels of autonomy are held constant (Nguyen et al. 2002), indicating that professional jobs have pleasing attributes in addition to autonomy.

Table 4.3 lists the 10 most satisfying jobs. Not surprisingly, these professional positions all provide their occupants with a substantial degree of freedom and control over their work.

PHOTO 4.4

Work on an assembly line can be alienating because workers often have little control over what they do and how they do it. Expanding workers' responsibilities, job rotation, and involving workers in company decision making may be ways to reduce worker alienation (Blauner 1964, Blumberg 1968)

THE 10 MOST SATISFYING JOBS	THE 10 LEAST SATISFYING JOBS	
1. Clergy	1. Roofers	**TABLE 4.3**
2. Physical therapist	2. Waiters/servers	*Occupations*
3. Firefighters	3. Laborers (except construction)	*with the*
4. Education administrators (e.g., deans, principals, and superintendents)	4. Bartenders	*Highest and Lowest*
5. Painter, Sculptors and Illustrators	5. Hand packers and packagers	*Levels of Job*
6. Teachers	6. Freight, stock, and material handlers	*Satisfaction*
7. Authors	7. Apparel clothing salespersons	
8. Psychologists	8. Cashiers	
9. Special education teachers	9. Food preparers	
10. Operating engineers	10. Expediters (e.g., customer service clerks, complaint desk)	

*Job satisfaction was measured by asking the questions "On the whole, how satisfied are you with the work you do? Would you say you are very satisfied, moderately satisfied, a little dissatisfied, or very dissatisfied?" Rankings are based on the mean score for a particular occupation, with numbers being assigned to each category (i.e., 1 = very dissatisfied, 2 = a little dissatisfied, 3 = moderately satisfied, and 4 = very satisfied); n = 27,587.

Note: General Social Survey, 1988–2007. Adapted from Smith (2007).

What Do You Think?

- Form a group with three or four of your classmates. Choose three of the most satisfying jobs listed in Table 4.3 and identify their similarities and differences. In addition to autonomy and control over the work process, what do you think makes these jobs appealing?
- Have someone in your group record the job each group member hopes to get after completing his or her education. As a group, discuss and evaluate the characteristics of the occupations you have listed. Talk about how the occupations might relate to outcomes such as alienation and job satisfaction.

School

The studies reviewed in the previous section show that experiences at work are one set of proximate conditions that link social class to personality and subsequent occupational mobility. The role of schools in the social mobility process is also of substantial interest to SSP researchers.

The Wisconsin Model of Status Attainment

Education has long been recognized as the gateway to social mobility, but not everyone has access to this resource. Early research on social mobility in the United States showed a strong effect of father's social class on men's levels of educational attainment (Blau and Duncan 1967). The **Wisconsin model of status attainment**, named for the institution where it was developed (the University of Wisconsin–Madison), extended this literature by identifying some of the social psychological processes through which social class influences educational and occupational achievement.

Kohn and Schooler's research (page 116) focuses on *intragenerational* mobility and links self-direction at work to a self-directed orientation and subsequent occupational advancement. In contrast, research on status attainment seeks to explain patterns of intergenerational mobility. **Intragenerational mobility** is social mobility that occurs over the course of an individual's lifetime, whereas **intergenerational mobility** refers to an individual's location in the class structure relative to that of his (most studies of intergenerational mobility have focused on males) parents. Note that Kohn and Schooler's research also addresses processes of relevance to intergenerational mobility, or the lack thereof, by focusing on social class and the socialization of children.

The Wisconsin model of status attainment (Otto and Haller 1979; Sewell and Hauser 1980) is summarized in Figure 4.2. This figure is a path model. **Path models** show the direct and indirect effects of an independent variable, like social class, on a particular outcome, in this case educational attainment. A direct effect is evident when an independent variable influences a dependent variable directly, rather than through some other third variable. For example, the effect of gender on height illustrates a direct effect because generally men are taller than women. Indirect effects are mediating effects, discussed earlier in the chapter with regard to the proximity principle.

Social psychologists working within the social structure and personality face of social psychology often use path models to represent complex causal relationships between different sets of variables. As shown in Figure 4.3, class background (components principle) influences adolescent males' levels of education (measured up to 15 years after their high school graduation). The influence of class is felt both directly and indirectly, through its effects on academic achievement; parental expectations, peers' educational plans, and discussions with teachers (proximity principle); and college aspirations. Social influences (relationships with parents, peers, and teachers) also affect educational attainment both directly and indirectly, through their effects on students' educational aspirations.

The social-psychological processes in the middle of Figure 4.3 (intervening, or mediating, variables in the causal chain) explain much of the impact of class

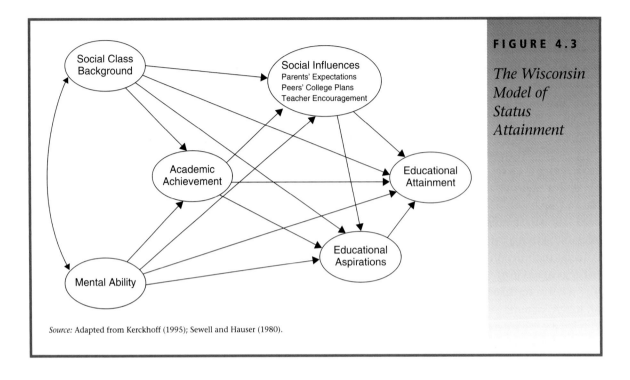

FIGURE 4.3

The Wisconsin Model of Status Attainment

Source: Adapted from Kerckhoff (1995); Sewell and Hauser (1980).

background (the independent variable) on educational attainment (the dependent variable). These relationships are an important part of the social mobility process because education affects the kinds of jobs people get and how much they are paid (Jencks, Crouse, and Mueser 1983; Otto and Haller 1979; Sewell and Hauser 1980). (Note: In Figure 4.3, the double arrow between social class and mental ability, measured using standardized tests, means that these two variables are correlated. We address this relationship later in the section on tracking).

Socialization within the family and at school is believed to be the key mechanism through which class affects aspirations and subsequent educational and occupational outcomes (psychology principle). Presumably, students internalize messages they receive about the viability of college from parents, teachers, and peers (Otto and Haller 1979).

Although initial research on status attainment focused on males, most of the processes represented in Figure 4.2 also apply to females (Looker and Pineo 1983; McClendon 1976). However, due to patterns of race-based discrimination within schools and in society at large, the status attainment model better fits the experiences of White than minority students (Portes and Wilson 1976).

Take a Break

Watch an interview with activist and award-winning author Jonathan Kozol about his 2005 book *The Shame of the Nation*. The interview, focusing on racial inequalities in our school system, aired on the 2005–2006 season of the PBS program *This Is America*. The interview is in three parts, which may be accessed sequentially from the following three web addresses, respectively:

http://www.youtube.com/watch?v=UR6yFsGMrqc (Part 1, 9:59 minutes)

http://www.youtube.com/watch?feature=endscreen&v=XxjmehzWR-9w&NR=1 (Part 2, 9:02 minutes)

http://www.youtube.com/watch?v=6dQe983ypvk&NR=1&feature=end-screen (Part 3, 7:45 minutes)

Q: If you were interviewing Jonathan Kozol about his research and his experiences as an activist, what would you ask him?

Tracking

Public schools are funded with local tax dollars. Thus, there is substantial stratification among schools, and less-advantaged students (including racial and ethnic minorities) from low-income areas tend to attend those institutions with the fewest economic resources and the lowest college placement rates. Studies of stratification *within* schools also indicate that tracking reflects students' positions within the broader society's structure and affects their aspirations. **Tracking** is the placement of students into different classes or courses of study based on perceived ability. It usually involves ability grouping within an elementary school setting and the sorting of students into different curricula (e.g., vocational vs. college preparatory) in middle and high school (Oakes 2005).

Tracking is believed to facilitate learning and is viewed as a way to increase students' options in terms of course content. It is also assumed that early placement decisions are made based on valid assessments of academic aptitude. (Note that these placement decisions exert a strong influence on later placements and on curriculum "selection" in high school; we use quotation marks to indicate that this "selection" is rarely an unconstrained choice.) However, class background is a primary determinant of track placement. Race/ethnicity also influences the type of coursework to which students are exposed, although much of this difference is due to the relationship between class and race (with minorities disproportionately represented at the bottom of the stratification hierarchy within the larger society) (Brewer, Rees, and Argys 1995; Lucas 1999). Given the effects of class and race/ethnicity on track placement, assuming this process is legitimate (i.e., that it reflects group differences in academic ability) implies that lower-class youths and racial and ethnic minorities are less intelligent than their upper-class and White counterparts.

Structural social psychologists (and most other individuals aware of the association between class, race, and track placement) reject this notion and question the validity of the measures of academic aptitude or IQ upon which placement decisions are based. SSP researchers point to differences in vocabulary and intellectual flexibility, rather than innate intelligence, as the primary sources of variations in test scores across social classes (as reflected in the correlation between class and mental ability in the Wisconsin model of status attainment, in Figure 4.2). Recall that intellectual flexibility is an acquired (i.e., learned) cognitive ability that enables individuals to view a problem or social issue from multiple perspectives (Kohn and Schooler 1982).

Children's college expectations are shaped within the family and coincide with their parents' educational and work experiences, as well as with the expectations of their peers and teachers (Figure 4.2). Given the association between socioeconomic background and track placement, tracking exacerbates class differences in educational attainment. Students are well aware of their placement within the tracking system, and those individuals at the bottom of the hierarchy often participate in peer cultures that devalue education as a way to compensate for their low status (MacLeod 1995; Morris 2005; Willis 1977). Students' peer cultures, combined with the limited investment in students within the non-college preparatory tracks by teachers and school administrators, drastically reduces lower-class students' likelihood of making the transition to college (Oakes 2005; Lucas 1999). Nevertheless, the practice of tracking persists and is especially prominent in schools that are heterogeneous in terms of the class composition of the student body (Lucas and Berends 2002).

What Do You Think?

Describe the tracking system in your high school. Was the student body at your school diverse in terms of social class and race/ethnicity? Focusing on the overall patterns, who was in the upper-track classes and who was in the lower-track (non-college preparatory) courses? You might ask one or two of your friends the same questions. How do your experiences compare?

Family

As indicated in the preceding sections, much of the SSP literature on work and schools has examined the effects of social class on psychological orientation and mobility processes. The family is the proximal context through which another status characteristic, gender, has been shown to exert a strong influence on both personality and behavior.

Gender and the Division of Household Labor

Remember the letter to Annie's Mailbox at the beginning of Chapter 1? "On Strike" felt that the women in her family were overburdened because the men did little work around the house, and as a result, she was angry. At the end of this section, we discuss this case and its structural context from a social psychological perspective.

Numerous SSP studies have focused on gender and the division of household labor, invoking concepts from role theory. In her highly influential book *The Second Shift*, sociologist Arlie Hochschild (1989) studied 50 working women with young children and their spouses in depth, some for up to a period of eight years. She found that in most families, women bore the burden of the household tasks. As a result, these women were highly stressed. Stress often translates into **psychological distress**, which reflects feelings of depression, anxiety, or anger. These kinds of feelings may be bothersome, but they are not necessarily severe enough to result in a clinical diagnosis. Unlike mental disorders (you either have one or you don't), psychological distress is typically measured on a continuum ranging from low to high (Ross and Mirowsky 2006).

Structural social psychologists (e.g., Lennon 1998) have suggested that role overload, a type of role strain that we discussed earlier in the chapter, is the primary source of the psychological distress associated with the second shift. However, the relevance of the second shift to contemporary family life has recently been called into question because men and women work the same amount (about 65 hours per week for married fathers and married mothers) when both paid and unpaid (domestic) labor are taken into consideration. Data also suggest that husbands are doing more around the house now than ever before (Bianchi, Robinson, and Milkie 2006).

Despite the fact that husbands are helping more, women still do most of the housework and child care—about twice as much as men (Bianchi et al. 2006; Press and Townsley 1998). Meeting these obligations often requires multitasking (i.e., combining domestic tasks with work and other activities) (Offer and Schneider 2011). Table 4.4 shows the results of a 2007 Gallup poll, based on a nationally representative sample of married couples, focusing on the division of household tasks. Note the discrepancy in perceptions by gender. For instance, 21% of the husbands said that they were the one most likely to wash the dishes, whereas only 10% of the wives indicated that this was the case. In general, these results are consistent with the contention that men tend to overestimate their housework contributions (Press and Townsley 1998).

There are, however, sizable discrepancies in husbands' and wives' estimates of their participation in male-dominated tasks, including maintaining the car and yard work. That aside, men are clearly more likely to do what are regarded as male

Gallup's Social Series Lifestyle Poll (December 2007) examined gender differences in the performance of household tasks. One of the questions on the survey asked the 594 married couples, "Who is the most likely to do each of the following in your household?"

As indicated in the following table, the report of who does what in the household varies by the gender of the respondent.*

TABLE 4.4

Who Does the Housework?

	HUSBANDS (%)		WIVES (%)		ALL RESPONDENTS (%)	
	SELF	SPOUSE	SELF	SPOUSE	HUSBAND	WIFE
Keep the car in good condition	79	6	20	58	69	13
Do yard work	63	8	17	51	57	12
Wash dishes	21	38	60	10	16	48
Do grocery shopping	20	44	63	12	16	53
Prepare meals	18	49	67	10	14	58
Care for children on daily basis**	12	45	64	5	10	68
Clean the house	8	56	60	3	6	61

*Reported responses exclude "neither" or no answer.

**This question was given only to couples with children under the age of 18.

Note: Adapted from Newport (2008).

activities, like fixing the car and taking care of the lawn, tasks without concrete deadlines. Women, on the other hand, appear to be largely responsible for caring for children and running the household (e.g., shopping and preparing meals), jobs that cannot be put off from one day to the next. These results are consistent with Hochschild's (1989) groundbreaking work and with a number of other studies within SSP (Bianchi et al. 2006; Legerski and Cornwall 2010; Press and Townsley 1998).

Research also suggests that levels of economic contribution from paid work may influence the gender balance of household tasks. Recent data indicate that mothers, who typically do more of the domestic labor, do work significantly fewer hours outside of the home than fathers (Bianchi et al. 2006; OECD 2012). However, that is not the only reason why they do more housework. **Gender roles** (the expected behaviors of males and females within a given society) also affect the income-housework relationship.

As children, people usually develop gender ideologies (beliefs about what it means to be male or female) that coincide with prevailing gender roles. Moreover, they adopt gender strategies, which are plans of action for dealing with problems or conflicts within their households and elsewhere. These gender strategies reflect their gender ideologies, as well as their immediate circumstances, such as their work situations and how much money they earn (Hochschild 1989).

Hochschild's (1989) research on the second shift revealed that husbands who earned substantially higher incomes than their wives did very little around the house. Husbands who earned close to the same as their wives did somewhat more domestic labor. However, husbands who were unemployed did very little and, in most instances, none of the housework. Thus, the ratio of husband's to wife's income did not predict men's participation in housework activities in a linear fashion. (A linear relationship is evident when one variable consistently increases, or decreases, with increases in another variable.)

Hochschild asked about this in her qualitative interviews with the married couples. The women whose husbands were unemployed acknowledged that their partners were not fulfilling traditional gender role expectations because they were not the family's breadwinner. Unemployment comes with a substantial cost to male self-esteem and identity. As a result, these women indicated that they were willing to take on extra housework in order to make their husbands feel like kings within the home. This is called balancing. Women took on more housework in order to allow their unemployed husbands to feel positive about their status in at least one sphere of life. Their husbands were not successful in the realm of work, but this was offset by their superior standing within the context of their family (Hochschild 1989).

If these women were willing to work harder to compensate for their unemployed husbands' failure to meet societal expectations concerning the masculine gender role, it is likely that prevailing gender-role expectations explain other women's willingness to do housework. Gender roles are relevant to women's lives even when they think they are unfair, want their husband to do more around the home, and are angry about his lack of participation (like "On Strike," who wrote the letter to Annie's Mailbox about the men in her family). Often men can't understand why women do such a good job cleaning the house and then feel put out for doing so. Sociological social psychologists can help people put their interpersonal conflicts into a broader structural context in order to gain insight into the motivations behind their behaviors.

As role theorists have noted, people fulfill the role expectations attached to the statuses they occupy in order to avoid negative feedback from others. Women recognize that, given prevailing gender role expectations, they will be the ones to suffer the consequences if the house goes untended. Even if they themselves do not believe that women should be doing the housework, they know that many people do subscribe to this view. Thus, women know that having a messy house is likely to result in negative evaluations from others, a consequence that most of us would rather avoid.

Think about how you might view a female, versus a male, who has an exceptionally messy dorm room or apartment. When it comes to housework, men have much more latitude than their female counterparts. If a married couple has a dinner party and the guests arrive to find a dirty house, who is going to be held accountable? It is likely

COMIC 4.1

that the wife is the one who will be regarded as negligent in fulfilling her role obligations. For this reason, women may find it difficult to leave housework unattended.

Furthermore, if a woman does opt to stop doing housework, her husband might get fed up and decide to leave the marriage. Given the usual gender differences in earnings, this could have negative financial, as well as interpersonal, consequences. Hence, women are not exactly in the best position to bargain about housework. Because women as a group lack power relative to men, they have more to lose when they are faced with gender-based interpersonal conflicts (Coontz 1997).

As members of the dominant group, men may not always recognize the negative economic and personal consequences that a woman who refuses to do housework might face. This lack of awareness is not because they are men per se, but because of their advantaged status. Again, structural social psychologists believe that it is position, rather than gender itself, that shapes people's perceptions or behaviors. The implication of this is that women would be behaving like men, and men like women, with regard to housework if their relative statuses were reversed. Structural social psychologists do not view idiosyncratic personality characteristics, which vary within gender (i.e., among men or among women), as an important part of this process.

So what does all of this mean for "On Strike," who wrote the Annie's Mailbox letter? According to Cootnz (1997), placing problems concerning the division of household labor within the context of the broader social forces out of which they arise may help to diffuse this kind of situation. Although it may not change the men's behavior, seeing the division of the tasks during family get-togethers for what it is (a reflection of gender inequality at the macro level) may alleviate some of "On Strike's" anger toward the men and make the men in her family more open to her perspective. From this standpoint, Annie's reply is misguided because it takes the letter writer's problem out of its social context and denies its relationship to the asymmetrical power relations that exist between women and men at the societal level. Annie's advice does nothing more than facilitate the reproduction of this system of inequality.

As women gain equality with men in the labor force, change in societal expectations concerning the distribution of domestic work are likely to follow. But this type of change tends to be gradual. As shown in Figure 4.4, Americans have become increasingly less traditional in their gender-role attitudes over the years (a trend that

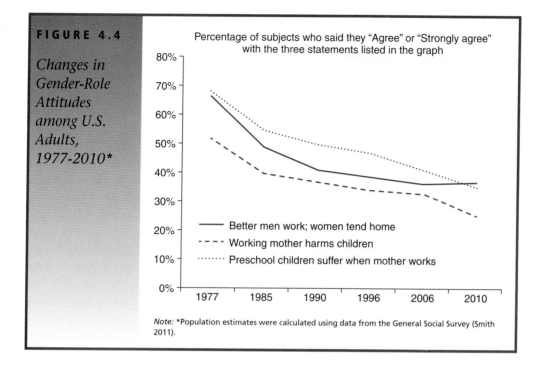

FIGURE 4.4

Changes in Gender-Role Attitudes among U.S. Adults, 1977-2010*

Percentage of subjects who said they "Agree" or "Strongly agree" with the three statements listed in the graph

—— Better men work; women tend home
- - - Working mother harms children
······ Preschool children suffer when mother works

Note: *Population estimates were calculated using data from the General Social Survey (Smith 2011).

coincides with the increase in men's participation in household tasks and activities, documented by Bianchi et al. 2006).

This kind of attitudinal change typically occurs on a cohort basis. A **cohort**, or age cohort, is a group of individuals born at a particular time who thus share a common set of experiences. To say that change in attitudes about the family and gender roles occurs on a cohort basis implies that they are associated with age and change at the group level. Shifts in attitudes over time take place as one age cohort dies out and is replaced by a new generation of individuals socialized in a different structural context (Alwin and McCammon 2004). Not surprisingly, Baby Busters (individuals born from 1965 to 1981) are more likely to believe that parents should share child care responsibilities equally than Baby Boomers (born from 1946 to 1964), who are more likely to subscribe to this view than individuals born before 1946 (Bianchi et al. 2006).

If you were born after 1981 (some researchers say after 1980), you are part of the Millennial Generation. Although Millennials view the family as important, they tend to reject traditional gender roles (Winograd and Hais 2011).

What Do You Think?

Reconsider the situation of "On Strike." How do your current thoughts about her dilemma compare to your initial reactions, when you read her letter to Annie's Mailbox in Chapter 1? How would a structural social psychologist respond to her letter?

LIFE COURSE RESEARCH

SSP researchers working in a subfield called "life course" study the social experiences and attitudes of particular age cohorts, such as the Baby Boomers or the Millennial Generation. Other structural social psychologists focus on intragenerational changes in role expectations and their psychological consequences from a **life course perspective**. These researchers are especially interested in role transitions and variations in social relationships across the age spectrum.

Given its centrality to social life, life course research often focuses on the family as a proximate environment linking age-related life experiences to psychological outcomes. For example, Mirowsky and Ross (2010) show that middle-aged individuals (individuals age 35–55) have the lowest levels of depression. They attribute this to marriage (the young and the old are the least likely to be married), as well as to the stable work lives and economic well-being characteristic of individuals within this age range.

Not surprisingly, economic cycles affect people's levels of psychological well-being. Individuals in late-middle or old age may be the most resilient to downturns in the economy. This is because their incomes are more likely to have already reached their peak; they have, on average, more wealth; and they are less likely to have children at home than younger people (Mirowsky and Ross 2010). However, it is interesting to note that female Baby Boomers had substantially higher levels of depression at midlife than women from previous generations, due largely to macro-level economic changes that made it difficult to balance work and family roles (Putney and Bengtson 2005).

We discuss the life course perspective and various studies within this tradition in greater detail in the chapter on socialization and in the chapter on mental health.

EVALUATING SSP RESEARCH

The studies reviewed in the previous sections illustrate some of the key issues of interest to researchers working within the SSP face of social psychology. Unlike sociologists who work within the symbolic interactionist face of social psychology, SSP researchers focus on causal factors that exist above and beyond individuals and their interactive settings.

Strengths of SSP Research

The strength of SSP research is its emphasis on the social processes that link macro-level social structures such as status characteristics and social roles to micro-level perceptions, feelings, and behaviors. The nature of the link between macro- and micro-level phenomena is an issue of interest to many sociologists, even if they themselves do not study these kinds of social processes. Because they tend to be survey based, studies within SSP often yield findings that are generalizable to the larger population.

The breadth of research generated within the social structure and personality face of social psychology, as illustrated in the research reviewed in this chapter, is another major strength of this orientation. However, because sociological social psychologists who work within SSP do not have an overriding theoretical framework to guide their research, it is sometimes difficult to see the commonalities between the various bodies of literature this research tradition has generated (e.g., studies on social class, work conditions, and personality; and research on gender, housework, and psychological distress). Making these links clear is one of the focal points of this chapter.

A third strength of the social structure and personality orientation is that the research it generates, like work within general (macro) sociology, often has policy implications. For example, Kanter's analysis of work within a large hierarchical corporation supports affirmative action and other social policies that counter pressures toward similarity and subsequent discrimination based on gender and race. Kanter's work shows that it is the structure of the corporation itself, not individual-level characteristics (prejudice), that results in the homosocial-homosexual production of the managerial ranks. Consequently, individual-level interventions (e.g., diversity training workshops designed to change mangers' attitudes about women and minorities) are not likely to be effective.

Similarly, simply telling disadvantaged youths that school is important is likely to have little effect on their academic performance. Tracking based on class and race/ethnicity within, as well as inequality between, schools lowers students' aspirations and creates patterns of resistance that run counter to the educational process. Given this, many individuals have called for a radical shift in the way in which schools in this country are organized. It is structural social psychologists' emphasis on societal patterns—and their documentation of the link between class, race/ethnicity, and track placement and its consequences—that has led to this recommendation.

Limitations of SSP Research

Although identifying the structural causes of perception and behavior may be seen as a strength of SSP, structural social psychologist have been criticized, particularly by symbolic interactionists, for overemphasizing general patterns and overlooking many of the nuances of social life. The survey analyses common within SSP focus on differences between groups within society but not on differences in the experiences of individuals within these social categories. Despite some notable commonalities associated with social class, race/ethnicity, gender, and age, people within these social categories can have very different social experiences. Moreover, social interactions continually produce meanings that may not generalize across individuals or social settings, and these emergent meanings shape people's perceptions and their subsequent behaviors. Because research on social structure and personality fails to take this into account, many symbolic interactionists view SSP analyses as too deterministic to be of much value.

A related limitation of SSP research, also noted frequently by social psychologists who work within the more micro-level SI tradition, is the tendency for structural social psychologists to overlook the reciprocal nature of the relationship between individuals and society. Whereas society shapes our perceptions and behaviors, the broader social forces that constrain us are themselves a product of our face-to-face interactions as they occur at the collective level. That is, we produce—and reproduce—society through our relationships with others.

Although structural social psychologists acknowledge this, they have tended to direct their attention more toward the effects of society on the individual than to the effects of individuals on society (Rosenberg and Turner 2004). There are some exceptions, including research on status attainment, which focuses specifically on the reproduction of the class structure. Kohn and Schooler, and researchers studying the consequences of tracking, have also identified some of the mechanisms through which social class is reproduced within and across generations (work conditions and experiences within the family and in school). However, other prominent bodies of literature within SSP (e.g., studies on gender and housework) have been less concerned with how the patterns identified influence broader social structures.

A final criticism of SSP literature comes from individuals who work within this face of sociological social psychology (e.g., McLeod and Lively 2006; Thoits 1995). They argue that researchers who study social structure and personality do not always make clear how social structure affects personality (the psychology principle). Structural social psychologists have been relatively thorough in their identification of the components of society that shape people's everyday experiences (status characteristics such as class, race/ethnicity, gender, and age), as well as the proximate environments through which they operate (e.g., work, the family, and schools). However, the mechanisms through which individuals' experiences become integrated into their psyches are not always explicated.

INTEGRATING PERSPECTIVES: RESEARCH ON SOCIAL COGNITION

Psychological theories have provided researchers with some of the concepts needed to develop more complete models of the link between social structure and psychological states (Thoits 1995). For example, there is a growing literature on **social cognition** that emphasizes the relationship between current social arrangements, particularly racial inequality, and the cognitive structures (schemas) that enable people to process the information they encounter.

Cognitive schemas are mental representations containing information about objects, people, and events. They are generalizations based on the sum total of an individual's past experiences, and they have organizational structures that affect how information is processed and stored (Fiske and Taylor 2008). Studies on the effects of cognitive schemas on perception and memory as they relate to issues of interest to sociological social psychologists are discussed in the chapters on self and identity and on prejudice and discrimination. These analyses are also of relevance to social psychologists trained in psychology because they provide a means for linking internal psychological processes to aspects of the broader social environment (Thoits 1995). Again, it is through combining perspectives that social psychologists develop the most complete and accurate depiction of social life.

CHAPTER SUMMARY

Research on social structure and personality emphasizes the relationship between societal patterns, in particular stratification, and individual's perceptions, attitudes, and behaviors. Given this, most of the research within this face of sociological psychology is survey based. Because studies on SSP have been governed by a set of general principles, rather than by distinct and coherent theoretical frameworks, research within this tradition is more eclectic than that within the other faces of sociological social psychology (including the symbolic interactionist tradition). The bodies of literature reviewed in this chapter, and the manner in which they reflect the key principles of the SSP face of social psychology, are summarized in Table 4.5.

Key Points to Know

- **Social structure and personality is the most macro face of socio-logical social psychology.** Thus, it is closer to general (macro) sociology than the more micro-level symbolic interactionist framework.

- **In most SSP analyses, the unit of analysis is the group, typically defined based on social class, race/ethnicity, or gender.** Some SSP researchers, especially those working within the life course tradition, have also focused on age.

- **The development of social structure and personality as a distinct face of sociological social psychology coincided with the develop-ment of survey methods.** Surveys allow researchers to assess patterns of perception and behavior among large groups of individuals and yield results that are generalizable to the larger population.

- **Some studies within the realm of social structure and personality are guided by concepts specified by role theory. More generally, SSP research reflects the components principle, the proximity principle, and the psychology principle.**

- **Research within the social structure and personality face of social psychology analyzes social phenomena at multiple levels.** Studies within this tradition seek to identify how macro structures (the components

RESEARCHER(S)	COMPONENT	PROXIMATE ENVIRONMENT/ EXPERIENCES	CAUSAL MECHANISM(S) (PSYCHOLOGY PRINCIPLE)	OUTCOMES
Kohn and Schooler	Social class	Work conditions (self-direction)	Socialization, spillover from work to other spheres of social life	Self-directed orientation, psychological well-being, intellectual flexibility, parental values
Kanter	Gender, Race/ Ethnicity	Work conditions (power, control)	Reactions to low-status position, pressures toward similarity	Praise addiction, gossip, discrimination
Varied	Social class	Work conditions (autonomy)	Spillover from work to other spheres	Alienation, substance use, job satisfaction
Sewell and Hauser, and others	Social class, race/ ethnicity	Family; school relations with parents, peers, and teachers	Socialization, reflected appraisals affect educational aspirations	Status attainment (education, occupation)
Varied	Social class, race/ ethnicity	School (tracking), peer relations	Academic preparation, socialization, aspirations	Transition to college
Hochschild and others	Gender	Family, division of household labor (second shift), role overload	Stress	Psychological distress

TABLE 4.5

Summary of Prominent Research Literatures/ Studies in SSP

principle) translate into thoughts, feelings, and behaviors at the micro level (the psychology principle). Thus, these analyses also focus on the meso level—namely, the proximate conditions and relationships through which components of social structure affect individuals (the proximity principle).

- **Work, schools, and the family are the proximate environments most frequently studied by SSP researchers.** Most of these analyses focus on the effects of stratification (based upon class, race/ethnicity, and gender) on people's social experiences.

- **Research on social structure and personality has a number of notable strengths. They stem from its emphasis on societal**

characteristics that exist above and beyond any one individual, group, or interactive context. The strengths of SSP include the explication of the macro-micro link and breadth of coverage. Structural social psychologists provide insight into how social inequality at the macro level affects people's day-to-day lives across a range of social settings. By locating the root causes of individuals' perceptions and behaviors within the structure of society, they also draw our attention to avenues for intervention that have the potential to change existing societal patterns. Thus, their analyses often have important policy implications.

- **Although the emphasis on social structure as a fundamental cause of personality and behavior is often regarded as the strength of this perspective, it can also be viewed as its primary weakness.** Symbolic interactionists, in particular, have argued that research on social structure and personality overlooks the creative and spontaneous ways in which people construct society.

- **Research on social structure and personality has also been criticized for failing to fully realize the psychology principle.** Many of the analyses within the social structure and personality orientation fail to specify the mechanisms through which aspects of social structure become incorporated into psychological processes. Some recent developments in the area called social cognition address this issue.

Terms and Concepts for Review

Alienation
Autonomy
Cognitive schema
Cohort
Components principle
Gender roles
Homosocial-homosexual reproduction
   of the managerial ranks
Intergenerational mobility
Interrole conflict
Intragenerational mobility
Intrarole conflict
Life course perspective
Mediating variable
Meso level
Occupational self-direction
Path model
personality

Probabilistic
Proximity principle
Psychological distress
Psychology principle
Reference group
Relative deprivation
Role
Role overload
Role set
Role strain
Self-directed orientation
Social cognition
Social institution
Social network
Status
Structural role theory
Tracking
Wisconsin model of status attainment

Questions for Review and Reflection

1. Why do SSP researchers tend to use surveys as a method of data collection? Why isn't a qualitative method, such as participant observation, appropriate within this context?

2. Suppose you were advising someone on how to conduct a research project within SSP. The topic of interest is the use of illegal drugs. What instructions would you give this individual?

3. What do the studies discussed in this chapter on work, schools, and family have in common? Which of these bodies of literature did you find the most interesting or insightful? What makes this research stand out to you in this way?

4. How have your views and behaviors been shaped by broader social forces? What are the main advantages of considering how your experiences reflect the structure of society? Discuss the main strengths and limitations of the social structure and personality face of social psychology. How have researchers working within SSP addressed the issue of agency?

CHAPTER 5

Group Processes and Structures

Your group memberships encompass a wide range of relationships, involve varying levels of commitment, and serve a number of functions. When asked to categorize common group affiliations, a sample of college undergraduates (n = 40) placed 40 groups with a diverse array of properties into four distinct categories, presented in Table 5.1 (Lickel et al. 2000).

Intimacy groups (most notably the family) are primary groups. **Primary groups** serve important socialization and support functions. Emotional ties are strong among the members of primary groups, and these affiliations are stable over time because people value the relationships upon which they are based. Primary groups are in contrast to task, or secondary, groups. People interact with individuals in **secondary**

groups because the groups serve specific purposes (e.g., completion of an assigned task) rather than for the sake of the relationships themselves (Cooley 1909).

As you know from Chapter 4, social categories such as gender and race/ethnicity exert strong influences on people's social experiences, regardless of whether they are aware of these effects. Is it surprising that the social categories female, Black, and Jew (but not male, White, and Protestant) were included in the groups listed in Table 5.1? As we noted in Chapter 4, people frequently define themselves in terms of status characteristics that distinguish them from dominant groups because these characteristics are salient and readily recognized as determinants of their social experiences.

Finally, people routinely have superficial, fleeting encounters in public or semi-public spaces with individuals who are in a specific location for similar reasons. (These are the loose affiliations listed in Table 5.1.) Although such encounters may be viewed as being of little importance, students recognize these situations as indicative of a particular type of group experience (Lickel et al. 2000).

What Do You Think?

- Go back and look at your list of group affiliations (from the exercise on page 21). Which groups are the most important to you? Why?
- How similar are your group affiliations to those listed in Table 5.1? Where in Table 5.1 (into which category or categories) would you put your most important group affiliations?

TABLE 5.1 *Categories of Groups*	INTIMACY GROUPS	TASK GROUPS	SOCIAL CATEGORIES	LOOSE ASSOCIATIONS
	Members of a family	Airline flight crew	Citizens of America	People at a bus stop
	Romantic relationship	Company committee	Citizens of Poland	People in line at a bank
	Friends	Coworkers assigned a project	Women	Audience at a movie
	Local street gang	Members of a jury	Blacks	People in same neighborhood
	People having dinner together	Cast of a play	Jews	Students at a university
	Roommates	Student campus committee		Students in a class
	Students studying together	Local environmental organization		Residents in retirement home
		Support group		People at a classical concert
		Employees of local restaurant		People at an athletic contest
		People working in same factory		
		Rock band		
		Orchestra		
		Labor union		
		Members of a political party		
		Sports team		
		Plumbers		
		Teachers		
		Doctors		
		University social club		

Note: Adapted from Lickel et al. (2000).

Kimberly Ann [handwritten note]

GROUPS IN EVERYDAY LIFE

Given the centrality of groups to social life, social psychologists have a long history of studying their structures and functions (Jahoda 2007). Sociological social psychologists who work within the group processes and structures (GPS) face of social psychology are interested in the link between individuals and the larger society, as well as the consequences of social inequality. GPS researchers have examined how members of groups develop expectations for others' behaviors, acquire and use power, maintain intimate relationships, and respond to people who have characteristics that differ from their own. These analyses have focused primarily on small groups, often in controlled laboratory settings.

Groups Versus Social Networks

Small groups are characterized by three characteristics: (1) propinquity (i.e., physical proximity), (2) perceived similarity, and (3) common outcomes (a shared fate) among their members. They include **dyads** (two-person groups) and **triads** (three-person groups), as well as more complex structures that meet the three criteria just listed. Small groups are more than the sum of the characteristics or attributes of their members. They are entities that exist above and beyond individuals, and they have the power to shape individuals' perceptions and behaviors (Campbell 1958).

Much of GPS research on small groups focuses on task-oriented (secondary) groups. Other GPS studies focus on a related construct: the social network. Whereas the behaviors of group members are interdependent and governed by shared normative expectations, **social networks** are comprised of autonomous actors who occupy positions within a larger structure. Their positions within a network may be different, and they may play different roles. Thus, network members do not necessarily share a common fate or goal (Emerson 1981). For example, a work network might be composed of managers, technology personnel, and clerical staff. These individuals have different ranks within the corporate structure and different kinds of skills. Given their different roles and resources, these individuals do not necessarily have the same interests or degree of control over the behavior of others.

Note that the term "social network" is used somewhat differently within the context of the group processes and structures face of social psychology than it is within the social structure and personality framework (discussed in the previous chapter). In SSP, the concept of social network refers generally to those group members with whom individuals regularly interact in proximate environments (e.g., work, school, and the family). In GPS, social networks are typically an independent variable rather than an intervening (proximal) variable. For example, GPS researchers have developed precise measures of social network structure and assessed its effects on the use of power. We discuss research on social networks later in the chapter (in the section titled "Social Exchange Theory").

RESEARCH IN GROUP PROCESSES AND STRUCTURES (GPS)

There are three distinct theoretical frameworks that have guided research within the group processes and structures (GPS) tradition. In this chapter, we will focus on these theoretical perspectives and the research they have generated. As in previous chapters, we use specific empirical studies (in this case, mostly laboratory experiments) to illustrate the ways the three theoretical frameworks within GPS have directed researchers' attention to particular aspects of group life.

Experimental Sociology

As you know from previous chapters, symbolic interactionists typically use qualitative methods, and SSP research tends to be survey based. In contrast, research within the group processes and structures tradition tends to be experimental. Each of the three theoretical traditions within this face of social psychology makes predictions about the effects of independent variables that are subject to the researcher's control. Thus, they can be manipulated by the researcher so that their effects on group members' perceptions and behaviors can be assessed. For example, researchers can manipulate the relative status of an interaction partner and measure its effect.

Categorizing these types of studies as part of a distinct face or orientation within sociological social psychology is a relatively recent development. In fact, research on group processes and structures (Berger 1992) was not fully recognized as a unique literature until the early 1990s. This designation was largely a response to the growth in experimental studies on small-group dynamics and their relationship to social structure published in sociology journals in late 1980s and early 1990s, a trend that has persisted over the years (Harrod, Welch, and Kushkowski 2009).

THREE THEORETICAL FRAMEWORKS WITHIN GPS

The three theoretical frameworks within the group processes and structures face of sociological social psychology, shown in Figure 5.1, are (1) expectations states theory (which includes status characteristics theory), (2) social exchange theory, and (3) social identity theory.[1] Although they have somewhat differ foci, these theoretical frameworks reflect a set of themes common to the face of sociological social psychology in which they are located. These themes include

- an emphasis on how small-group dynamics reflect broader societal patterns (e.g., social inequality based on gender, class, or race/ethnicity);

- how social inequality at the macro level is reproduced in small-group encounters; and

- the use of controlled laboratory experiments by researchers addressing these issues.

Note that social identity theory is different from identity theory. Identity theory is a structural symbolic interactionist model within the SI, rather than the GPS, face of sociological social psychology.

In Chapters 1 and 2, we gave some examples of research in GPS (studies on the effects of gender and education on susceptibility to social influence). These studies are within the expectations states tradition.

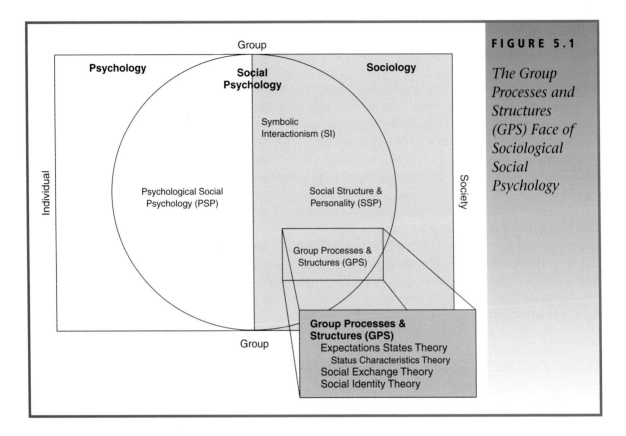

FIGURE 5.1

The Group Processes and Structures (GPS) Face of Sociological Social Psychology

Expectation States Theory

Expectation states theory (Berger, Conner, and Fisek 1974) focuses on the development and maintenance of inequality within small task-oriented groups. The key assumption underlying expectations states theory (EST) is that, within small task-oriented groups, status structures emerge in accordance with the anticipated contributions of individual group members (Meeker 1981).

Status structures are subjective rankings of group members based on their perceived likelihood of moving the group toward the successful completion of its goals (Ridgeway and Walker 1995). In any small task-oriented group, a status structure develops as a function of group members' performance expectations for themselves and for others.

Performance expectations are assessments of one's own and other individuals' likely contributions to the completion of the group's assigned tasks (Berger, Wagner, and Zelditch 1985). For example, you might expect that your study partner will be able to help you more than you will be able to help him or her prepare for an upcoming exam. This assessment may or may not be accurate. Performance expectations are perceptions that may or may not correspond to individuals' actual abilities (objective reality). Thus, they are similar to the SI concept of situational definition (Wagner, 2007).

Expectation states theory is based on the assumption that the status structures that develop within small task-oriented groups are consensual in that members share and subscribe to the emergent normative order (Ridgeway 1984). Research suggests that status structures in groups composed of relative equals emerge quickly, often by the end of the standard one-hour laboratory session. Some individuals talk more than others, are given more opportunities to provide input, are evaluated more positively following their contributions, and are less subject to influence by other group members when disagreements arise (Correll and Ridgeway 2006).

Once developed, status structures within small groups tend to reproduce themselves. That is, they result in what social psychologists call a self-fulfilling prophecy. A **self-fulfilling prophecy** exists when an initial assessment, regardless of whether it is true, generates subsequent perceptions and actions that result in its confirmation (Merton 1968). The self-fulfilling prophecy is a powerful process that operates across a variety of social contexts. Status begets status through the increased opportunities for action and positive evaluations accorded to high-status group members, which reaffirm their position within the group. When initial performance expectations are low, individuals are given fewer opportunities to contribute to the group and receive less positive evaluations for their input, irrespective of its content or merit. This, in turn, reinforces their low status, which results in fewer action opportunities, and so forth.

Given the self-fulfilling nature of group dynamics, understanding *how* an individual initially becomes the beneficiary of positive performance expectations is important. Consider groups composed of individuals who enter into the interaction as status equals. Characteristics such as presentational style, eye contact, and position (e.g., sitting at the head of the table) result in initial patterns of status differentiation, which are then reproduced through subsequent interactions (Meeker 1981). Personal characteristics associated with social dominance in group encounters are listed in Box 5.1.

Once status structures are established, they readily become legitimated. That is, their underlying behavioral patterns (with more frequent and more positively evaluated actions by high-status members) become normalized and are viewed as the way the group should function. After this occurs, any violation of the existing status structure is likely to be regarded as inappropriate, and those who engage in this type of deviant behavior will be sanctioned (Ridgeway and Walker 1995).

Status Characteristics Theory

Outside of a laboratory setting, it is unlikely that all of the individuals present within a group encounter will be of equal status. Berger and associates developed **status characteristics theory (SCT)**, a subtheory within the expectation states tradition. SCT theory explains how status characteristics influence the creation and

Box 5.1   Personal Characteristics Associated With Dominance in Group Encounters

Appearance (e.g., style of dress, hair style)

Assertive speech (e.g., use of commands vs. requests)

Maintenance of eye contact

Glaring

Strutting

Erect posture

Advancing toward (vs. retreating from) others

Leaning forward when speaking

Use of sweeping hand and arm gestures to emphasizes speaking points

Absence of nervous gestures (e.g., touching face or hair, fidgeting)

Vertical head movements (i.e., nodding)

Stern facial expression

Note: Ketrow (1999), Mazur (1985), and Pavitt (1999).

PHOTO 5.3

What visual cues are preset to help you determine who is dominant and who issubservient in the pictured interaction?

maintenance of status structures in small task-oriented groups. The experiment on gender and susceptibility to influence that was used to illustrate GPS research in Chapter 1 is within the SCT tradition. We reviewed a second SCT study, on education and social influence, in the section on experimental sociology in Chapter 2.

Recall that status characteristics are varying attributes that are tied to societal beliefs about competence and worthiness. Think about the last time you participated in a group project. Who were the other group members? What characteristics did they share, and in what notable ways did they differ from one another? Were you aware of these differences at the time, and did they shape group members' expectations of one another? Sociological social psychologists who work within GPS, and within the expectations states tradition more specifically, argue that we are often unaware that people's status characteristic affects our assessments of their abilities. Nonetheless, they almost always do. Status characteristics theory explains why and how this happens.

Specific status characteristics refer to attributes or abilities that are only relevant in certain situations (e.g., math skills or artistic talent). Studies suggest that favorable information about a group member's task-relevant specific status characteristics results in positive performance expectations. Such expectations, in turn, result in more opportunities to contribute to the group task, more positive performance evaluations, and greater social influence (Berger et al. 1977).

As you know from earlier chapters, people's locations within the structure of society (in particular their gender, race/ethnicity, and socioeconomic standing as indicated by their education or occupation) also influence performance expectations in task groups and the subsequent group dynamics. These attributes (gender, race/ethnicity, and social class) are referred to as **diffuse status characteristics** because they shape others' expectations across social contexts. Diffuse status characteristics have powerful effects on patterns of interaction within group settings because they are tied to broad cultural notions about individuals' levels of competence. These cultural notions are called status beliefs.

Recall from our discussion of SCT in Chapter 1 that **status beliefs** refer to sets of assumptions about a particular group within society relative to another (e.g., men vs. women). They are the hierarchical components of cultural stereotypes. **Stereotypes** consist of (unfounded) beliefs about members of a particular group that make them distinct from others in people's minds. As such, they typically have a nonhierarchical component (e.g., girls like pink). Stereotypes also contain status beliefs such that, regardless of their other content, one group is regarded as better, smarter, and more sophisticated than another. For example, boys are better than girls at math (Correll and Ridgeway 2006).

Status beliefs tend to associate the dominant group with active, goal-directed behaviors, whereas members of the subordinate group are regarded as more communal or socially oriented in nature. This distinction is especially strong with regard to gender because traditional gender roles reflect this type of differentiation (men are viewed as breadwinners and women as caregivers) and because men and women interact in cooperative settings, such as the family, more regularly than with members of different racial/ethnic groups or different social classes (Ridgeway 2001).

SCT researchers are especially interested in the effects of diffuse status characteristics like gender, race/ethnicity, and indicators of social class (education and occupation). This is because they influence group interaction even when they are not relevant to the task at hand. **Status generalization** is the process through which diffuse status characteristics are associated with task-relevant abilities and thus influence performance expectations and subsequent behaviors within group settings (Berger et al. 1977).

By manipulating the relative status of members of task-oriented groups, researchers have studied the status generalization process in controlled laboratory settings. You have already read about examples of such research in the studies on education and social influence by Moore (1968) and on gender and social influence by Pugh and Wahrman (1983). The literature on status characteristics and group behavior has grown substantially since the 1980s. Overall, the greatest attention in SCT literature has been given to gender, followed by race/ethnicity and social class. Numerous studies suggest that these three diffuse status characteristics significantly affect group members' performance expectations, evaluations, and task-related behaviors (Driskell and Mullen 2006).

However, diffuse status characteristics influence performance expectations and subsequent behavior among group members only when they are salient. For example, gender translates into more action opportunities and positive evaluations for males than females only in mixed-sex groups. In single-sex groups, gender is not a source of differentiation and is thus of little consequence. These results suggest that there is no status characteristic that affects perception and behavior in every social context. Group composition matters.

The nature of the group task may also make a difference (Meeker 1981). For example, Dovidio and associates (1988) found that gender differences in verbalizations (speech initiations and frequency of speech) varied with the group's purpose. The same was true for gender differences in nonverbal behaviors associated with power, such as maintaining eye contact while speaking, avoiding eye contact while listening, and gesturing.

The subjects in this laboratory experiment (n = 48) were randomly assigned to mixed-sex dyads, and each group was asked to describe how to perform one of three tasks: changing oil in an automobile (stereotypically male), sewing (stereotypically female), or vegetable gardening (gender neutral). In the oil-changing group, males initiated more speech and talked significantly more often than females. Males also displayed more of the nonverbal behaviors associated with dominance. These patterns were reversed in the sewing condition. Females initiated more speech, talked more frequently, maintained more eye contact while speaking and less while listening, and gestured more frequently than their male partners.

Interestingly, in the gender-neutral gardening condition, men displayed significantly more of both the verbal and nonverbal behaviors indicative of power within an interactive context than women did. These differences were, however, less pronounced than those observed among the subjects describing how to change oil (the task associated with masculinity). Thus, this study suggests that males are likely to have the status advantage unless the group's task is perceived as explicitly feminine.

In many of the activities associated with work (and with school), males and members of other dominant groups (i.e., Whites and the socioeconomically advantaged) are assumed to be the most adept. SCT researchers argue that these diffuse status characteristics will exert an influence on perception and behavior in most group settings unless something happens to suggest that they are not related to people's task-related abilities. Thus, the burden of proof is on actors to show that a particular status characteristic is irrelevant to the group's assigned task. Otherwise, the status characteristic will influence perceptions and behavior in a manner consistent with prevailing patterns of inequality within the larger society (Correll and Ridgeway 2006).

What Do You Think?

- Write down five things that you think most men are good at. Then write down five things that you believe most women do well. Have one or two of your friends do the same. How consistent are the characteristics you and your friends listed?
- Compare the attributes of men and of women from your lists. Which set of traits is more likely to result in success within a school or work environment?

MULTIPLE STATUS CHARACTERISTICS

In everyday life, it is uncommon for people to find themselves in group settings where only a single status characteristic is salient. Therefore, it is important to understand how people combine information about various statuses when making assessments about group members' likely contributions.

Berger and associates (1977) argue that people form performance expectations based on multiple status characteristics by combining information about an individual's diffuse and specific status characteristics. First, information about positive status characteristics and information about negative status characteristics are combined into two distinct subsets. Then, the two subsets are averaged to yield an overall performance expectation. As this occurs, information about each of the individual's status characteristics is weighed in accordance to its perceived task relevance, and those attributes believed to be the most relevant to the situation at hand exert the strongest influence on the emergent perception.

The context in which information about a status characteristic is introduced is also important. Information that is consistent with other information people have about a given individual's status characteristics will be given less weight than information that runs counter to what they already know about that person's statuses (Berger et al. 1977). Thus, when a group task requires difficult calculations, learning that Mara, an African American woman, is an accomplished mathematician will have a greater effect on performance expectations than learning the same thing about Joseph, a White male. This is because in Mara's case the positive specific status characteristic math ability is in the opposite direction of two negative diffuse status characteristics (female, minority), whereas in Joseph's case the positive specific status characteristic math ability is in the same direction as two positive diffuse status characteristics (male, White).

The effects of various combinations of diffuse and specific status characteristics on performance expectations are computed using complex mathematical equations. Although people may not consciously execute the process these equations represent, they act as though they do (Correll and Ridgeway 2006). Research on task groups within which multiple status characteristics are made salient strongly supports the existence of these patterns (Berger et al. 1992). Thus, SCT provides insight into how macro structures (namely, systems of stratification based on gender, race/ethnicity, and social class) combine to affect individuals' face-to-face interactions. Because status structures reflect the structure of the broader society, and are reproduced within the context of small groups in predictable ways, SCT also explicates the nature of the effects of individuals on society. This reciprocal process is depicted in Figure 5.2.

As shown in Figure 5.2, macro-level status beliefs shape group members' perceptions and behaviors in micro-level social encounters. These interactions, in turn, reinforce the status beliefs and the initial performance expectations that created them in a self-fulfilling prophecy.

INTERVENTION

SCT offers some relatively concrete strategies for intervention. Specific status characteristics (e.g., information about an ability known to be related to the group's task) can be introduced into social situations to counter the effects on group dynamics of diffuse status characteristics such as gender, race/ethnicity, and class (Berger and Webster 2006). It is also possible, although more difficult, to eliminate the influence of diffuse status characteristics on group members' perceptions and behaviors. We discussed one technique that had this effect in Chapter 1.

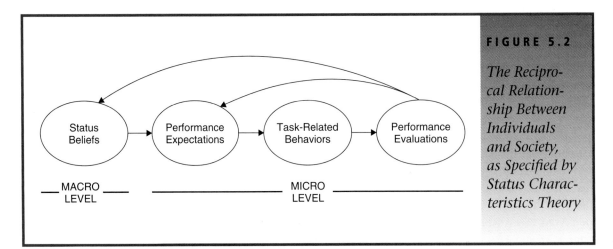

FIGURE 5.2

The Reciprocal Relationship Between Individuals and Society, as Specified by Status Characteristics Theory

Q: Do you remember the study by Pugh and Wahrman (1983) on gender and social influence? (See pages 15–17.) What was their main finding? How did they eliminate the effects of gender on susceptibility to social influence?

A: They showed their subjects that women outperform men on a related task prior to beginning the experimental trial. Doing so reduced the effect of gender on performance expectations (usually lower for women) and thus on difference in susceptibility to social influence (usually higher among females). Among the subjects who received that intervention, females were no more likely than their male counterparts to change their response when they were told that their partner gave a different answer (Pugh and Wahrman 1983).

Telling individuals that no one is likely to excel on a given task has also been used to counteract the status generalization process and subsequent patterns of bias that emerge in small-group encounters. This is referred to as the incompatible complexity manipulation.

Tasks that are complex and require a variety of different abilities exhibit a characteristic called **incompatible complexity**. Insofar as a task is complex and requires distinct abilities that do not overlap, it is unlikely that any single person will have all of the skills necessary to complete the task successfully. This inhibits the perception that some people will be good and others bad at generating the desired task outcomes. Informing subjects in mixed-race groups that they will be completing a task of this nature prior to the onset of the group interaction eliminated race differences in both verbal and nonverbal task-related behaviors in one SCT experiment (Goar and Sell 2005).

Social Exchange Theory

The second theoretical framework within GPS, **social exchange theory** (Blau 1964; Homans 1961), directs researchers' attention to patterns of interaction within both primary (intimacy) and secondary (task) groups. In this sense, it is broader in its applications that expectations states theory.

Research on social exchange processes focuses on power. Sociologists define **power** as the degree to which a person is able to impose his or her will on another (Weber 1968). Drawing on **behaviorist psychology**, which focuses on the effects of rewards and punishments on behavior, social exchange theorists argue that power is exercised through the administration of reinforcement (rewards) and punishment. **Rewards** are positive consequences (e.g., social acceptance, money, or a promotion at work), which may vary in value depending upon the social context in which behavior occurs. **Punishments**, on the other hand, are negative outcomes (poor evaluations from others, fines, or being fired). Punishments have perceived costs, which people seek to avoid, that may change across individuals and social settings. **Noncoercive (reward) power** is exercised when an actor produces change in another's behavior through the control of rewards. **Coercive power** involves the use of punishments to produce change in another person's behavior (Homans 1974).

Power-Dependence Relations

For social exchange theorists, power is a property of the social relation (the unit of analysis) rather than of an individual or a group. In what social exchange theorists refer to as a **power-dependence relation**, actors' abilities to secure desired rewards from other sources serve as the structural basis for power. From this perspective, structurally based power reflects two factors: (1) what an actor has to offer in terms of resources (i.e., rewards) and (2) the number of potential exchange partners who can provide the resources the actor is seeking. The resources might be money, knowledge, experience, respect, love, or whatever is desired within the context of a given encounter (Emerson 1962).

To illustrate this model, consider your job prospects following your graduation from college. When you are offered a job, you will want to negotiate a good salary. This is usually the most important resource an employer has to offer. Your skill set is what you have to offer in return. If there are other people the employer can hire with similar work-related skills to your own, you will have less power in the negotiation and will probably end up with a lower starting salary. The employer is dependent on you only insofar as she is unable to hire someone else with your skill set. She has exerted power if you take the job at the salary she offered, even though it is less than what you asked for.

Having work-related skills that are superior to other job candidates gives you more structurally based power. This is because it leaves the employer with few exchange alternatives. You should be able to use this power to negotiate a higher salary than the one initially offered.

Note that the power exerted in a power-dependence relation need not equal the actual (structurally based) power that one actor has over another (Emerson 1962). For example, a supervisor has power over his subordinates within a work context, but supervisors vary in the degree to which they manage (or, from the perspective of their subordinates, micromanage) their employees' behaviors. That is, they vary in their use of power. When power embedded in a social structure is used in a manner that is deemed appropriate, it is legitimized. Asking a subordinate to modify work-related behaviors that are deemed unprofessional is typically considered a legitimate use of power. These days, however, in most work settings it is not legitimate for a boss to ask a subordinate to engage in non-work-related tasks, such as picking up dry cleaning.

TYPES OF POWER-DEPENDENCE RELATIONS

There are two types of power-dependence relations: balanced and unbalanced. In a **balanced relation**, the parties in the exchange have equal power. In an **unbalanced relation**, one actor has more power than the other due to the possession of valued rewards and other exchange options.

In general, the actor with the power disadvantage in an unbalanced relation is more likely to initiate exchange. When an unbalanced relation persists over time, exchange outcomes (i.e., the rewards received) tend to increasingly favor the less dependent party. The rewards the less dependent actor in the exchange (i.e. the actor with power) receives will increase until they reach the level at which the disadvantaged actor could obtain the same rewards from an alternative exchange partner.

It is important to remember that in this model power and its use are determined not by the individual characteristics or motivations of specific actors but by the structure of the relations themselves (Molm and Cook 1995). Social exchange theorists focus on the effects of the structural context in which the exchange of resources occurs. It is their emphasis on structure, versus people's personal characteristics, that makes the social exchange framework inherently sociological.

POWER IN EXCHANGE NETWORKS

Exchange relations often occur within the context of (power) exchange networks. An **exchange network** consists of two or more interconnected exchange relations. Exchange relations (each involving a power-dependence relation between two actors) are connected when the nature of the exchange in one relation affects the nature of exchange in the other (Emerson 1962).

Much of the social exchange literature has focused on negatively connected exchange networks. In a **negatively connected exchange network**, exchange in one relation reduces exchange in another. For example, when students are required to work in pairs on a class project, once a given individual chooses her partner, she is no longer available to others in the class as a potential work partner. Thus, her likelihood of engaging in an exchange relation with her other classmates decreases, and the potential rewards associated with these other (alternative) alliances diminish. **Opportunity costs** reflect the potential rewards that are lost when an actor chooses one exchange partner over others (Emerson 1981).

Figure 5.3 shows two negatively connected network structures used in research on the effects of structural position (i.e., position within an exchange network) on the use of power. These representations illustrate how structural context affects power (Cook and Emerson 1978).

As shown in Figure 5.3, Actor A in the unbalanced network has a distinct power advantage over individuals in other positions. This is because B-A exchanges are worth 24 points, whereas B-B exchanges are only worth 8 points. As a result, the actor in position A within the network has more desirable exchange alternatives than actors in position B. Although the value of the resources to be exchanged between the occupant of position A and the three occupants of network position B is consistently high (24 points), the alternatives to an exchange with the actor in position A available to actors in position B are less rewarding (only 8 points).

In contrast, each relation in the balanced network in Figure 5.3 is of equal value, and all four actors have the same exchange alternatives. Thus, power is equally distributed in the balanced negative network.

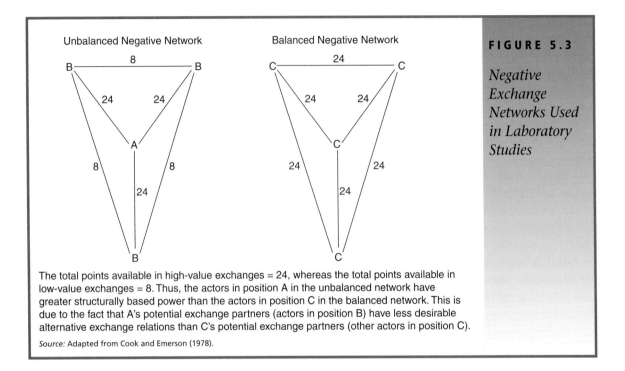

FIGURE 5.3

Negative Exchange Networks Used in Laboratory Studies

The total points available in high-value exchanges = 24, whereas the total points available in low-value exchanges = 8. Thus, the actors in position A in the unbalanced network have greater structurally based power than the actors in position C in the balanced network. This is due to the fact that A's potential exchange partners (actors in position B) have less desirable alternative exchange relations than C's potential exchange partners (other actors in position C).

Source: Adapted from Cook and Emerson (1978).

STUDYING NEGOTIATED EXCHANGE IN THE LAB

A **negotiated exchange** is one in which actors bargain over resources. In Cook and Emerson's (1978) classic study of the use of power in negotiated exchanges, 112 subjects (56 males and 56 females) were randomly assigned to a particular network position (the independent variable). The two experimental groups, which differed only in terms of their network position (their level of structurally based power), consisted of actors in position A in the unbalanced network and actors in position C in the balanced network in Figure 5.3. These network positions (A, unbalanced; or C, balanced) served as levels of the independent variable. Because the balanced network was composed of four actors, each occupying position C, one individual's exchange outcomes were selected at random for analysis from each network.

The exchanges of interest were between actors in network positions A and B in the unbalanced network and between actors in position C (i.e., C-C exchanges) in the balanced network (Figure 5.3). B-B exchanges among participants in the unbalanced network were not examined in this study.

The use of power was the outcome (dependent variable) of interest. The use of power was reflected in the exchange behaviors of individuals in either position A or position C in one of the two four-person networks depicted in Figure 5.3. The dependent variable was measured as the number of reward points subjects earned across trials. Subjects were given 3 cents for each point at the end of the experiment.

The exchange networks studied were either all male or all female. Study participants were placed in separate rooms and interacted with other network members over the computer. Each subject was given a sheet listing potential trade agreements, which included the amount of resources he or she must offer for a given number of reward points. Subjects were also told the rate of pay per point received (3 cents).

Exchanges were negotiated among study participants through a series of three steps: (1) network members sent exploratory preliminary offers; (2) members paired off and negotiated formal offers; (3) once accepted, formal offers were recorded and the experiment progressed to the next trial. Each negotiation was structured so that one partner's gain was another's loss. The maximum profit was either 8 or 24 points. For example, if one partner received 15 points in a particular exchange, his or her partner received 9 points for a total of 24 points.

During the first 20 of the 40 trials, subjects were aware only of the reward points they had been given but not of the points received by the other three individuals in their exchange network. At the end of trial 20, the researchers revealed other network members' reward points to all subjects so that they could compare the other subjects' points to their own.

Remember, exchange theorists make a distinction between power (defined in terms of resources and alternatives) and its use. As expected, the use of power was substantially greater among the occupants of position A in the unbalanced network than position C in the balanced network. This was due to the structure of the networks in which these actors were operating. Again, Actor A in the unbalanced network had more power than Actor C in the balanced network because Actor C's potential exchange partners had better alternatives than Actor A's potential exchange partners (see Figure 5.3). Still, the use of power (measured as the number of reward points acquired) among individuals in position A in the unbalanced network did not reach equilibrium. That is, the use of power never reached the point at which the power-disadvantaged partner (occupants of position B) could obtain equal rewards from an alternative partner (other occupants of position B). Thus, individuals in position A in the unbalanced network did not use their power to secure rewards as much as they could have.

Interestingly, women were as likely as men to use power when its consequences (their gains relative to others) were not evident (exchanges 1–20). When it was made clear that the exchange outcomes (reward points) were unequally distributed, thereby invoking norms concerning equity, women in a position of power (position A) were less likely to use their advantage to secure additional points than their male counterparts (Cook and Emerson 1978). This probably reflects prevailing societal norms pertaining to gender: men should be competitive, whereas women should be caring.

There was also some evidence that women were more likely to form commitments. **Commitment** in an exchange relation is evidenced when an actor engages in long-term exchanges with a partner even when doing so is not advantageous (i.e., there are better exchange options). In Cook and Emerson's (1978) study, this meant that females were more likely than males to skip phase 1 of the negotiation process outlined above and immediately begin an exchange with their partner from a previous exchange.

Although this experiment does not supply us with information as to why this was the case, gender differences in commitment within this context may reflect prior patterns of gender role socialization and women's greater aversion to risk relative to their male counterparts (Cook and Emerson 1978). Actors often form commitments when engaging in negotiated exchanges characterized by uncertainty (Lawler and Yoon 1996).

HOW TO INCREASE POWER IN A NEGOTIATED EXCHANGE

By manipulating structural power within the laboratory, researchers have gained a sense of when, and to what extent, people are likely to reward their partners in interaction. They have also identified ways that the balance of power within a negotiated exchange relation might be altered.

To illustrate, consider an individual (Nora) who has a small business that involves selling jewelry produced and sold at small, individually owned craft stores to large retail chains. She has a contract with Mr. Gutierrez, a local business owner, and much of her revenue comes from her commission on the sale of his goods.

Nora would like to negotiate a better contract with Mr. Gutierrez, for whom she sells a large number of goods. She is by far the best salesperson in the region; no one can match the amount of merchandise she moves. Therefore, she feels that she deserves a higher commission.

Although the value of what Nora has to offer is high (her proven sales ability), Mr. Gutierrez is her primary client. Without this contract, her business would not make it. Unfortunately, he is aware of Nora's lack of alternative exchange partners (other businesses) and has been able to use it to his advantage. He has rejected Nora's demand for a raise. In this case, the local business owner has been able to use his structurally based power to ensure the maintenance of a work contract in his favor.

This does not sit well with Nora, who starts considering her options. Ultimately, she realizes that she needs to expand her client base (i.e., her exchange network) so that she has more exchange alternatives and is thus less dependent upon Mr. Gutierrez. A larger exchange network would place her in a much better position should she try to negotiate a new contract sometime in the future. **Network expansion** is a way to increase one's structurally based power at work or in other settings (Emerson 1962). To give another example, you are likely to get a better deal when you buy a car if four (instead of just one or two) local dealers have the model you are interested in buying.

STUDYING RECIPROCAL EXCHANGE IN THE LAB

Many of your exchange relations occur over time, and the rewards you hope to receive are not guaranteed as they are in a negotiated exchange. Relations between family members, romantic partners, and friends are rooted in these kinds of reciprocal transactions, called **reciprocal exchanges**. The reciprocal transactions upon which these relationships are based involve paired but separate contributions. The transaction is initiated by a reward, which may or may not be reciprocated at some point in the future (Emerson 1981).

Think about the last time you attended a party. Who invited you? The individual who told you about the party probably expects that you will do something nice for him or her sometime. It may not be tomorrow or later this week, but at some point it is likely that you will do so. You might help him or her study for an exam, take him or her to lunch, or invite him or her to your next party.

Research on reciprocal exchange in the laboratory has focused on the use of both rewards and punishments. As was the case in Cook and Emerson's (1978) study of negotiated exchange processes described in the preceding section, the subjects in experiments involving reciprocal exchanges used reward power less frequently than they could have. This is probably because the use of reward power in a reciprocal exchange requires individuals to forgo short-term rewards for more long-term benefits. Individuals who are not experienced with these types of reinforcement contingencies may not be able to use their structural advantage effectively in order to maximize the rewards received within the context of their exchange relations (Molm 1987). Abilities related to information processing, behavioral monitoring, and risk taking may be required for the effective use of reward power within this context (Molm 1990).

Subjects participating in computer-mediated reciprocal exchanges are even less willing to use coercive power (punishment), despite the fact that it is an effective tactic for increasing the value of the rewards received (Molm 1994). Individuals appear to avoid the use of punishment (e.g., subtracting points from an exchange partner during an experimental trial) primarily because they fear retaliation in future interactions. Interestingly, actors in an exchange relation are hesitant to use coercive power because they fear the loss of future rewards, not punishment. Thus, coercive power tends to be used only when the potential for rewards in an exchange is so low that it is of little consequence.

These experimental findings clearly have relevance outside of the laboratory. They suggest that the use of coercive tactics is most likely among individuals who have nothing left to lose when it comes to relationship benefits. This condition applies to employees about to be laid off; political factions not taken seriously by mainstream political parties; married individuals whose spouses no longer care about them (Molm 1997); and college students who receive few rewards from coworkers, friends, or romantic partners.

Trust

As a rule, people use power less in reciprocal than in negotiated exchange relations. As you might expect, given their more long-term nature, reciprocal exchanges also yield higher levels of commitment, positive affect, and trust than negotiated exchanges (Molm 2003; Molm, Schaefer, and Collet 2007). **Trust** exists when an actor believes that another person or group will act in his or her interest, because they have incentive to do so or because they care about the actor's well-being (Cook, Hardin, and Levi 2007).

Social exchange theorists are especially interested in the role of trust in contemporary society. The conventional wisdom is that that we need to increase trust within the context of businesses and other organizations, as well as within society's institutions. In their book *Cooperation Without Trust?* Cook, Hardin, and Levi (2007) reject this notion. They argue that trust in relationships often perpetuates racism and hinders productive economic exchanges. (Kanter's study, described in Chapter 4, is a good illustration of how trust in relationships can lead to gender and racial discrimination in a work setting.) Although trust enhances interpersonal relationships, it is often detrimental in broader social and economic contexts. Organizations and institutions, including the government, can be considered substitutes for trust relations insofar as they protect individuals from unethical and unfair treatment by others through rules and regulations (Cook et al. 2007).

Research on Social Exchange in Intimate Relationships

Focusing on social exchange outside of the laboratory, GPS researchers have studied the balance of power in romantic relationships and its consequences. These studies focus on dyads and are more micro in orientation than the research on social exchange processes described in the preceding sections.

In a dyad, **equity** reflects the balance of rewards between relationship partners. In an equitable relationship, each partner gives rewards proportional to those received. In an inequitable relationship, one partner contributes more and receives less, or contributes less and receives more, than the other (Walster, Walster, and Berscheid 1978).

Most of the literature on equity in intimate relationships (a type of reciprocal exchange) is survey based. This is because the focus of this research is on the balance of rewards over time, which would be difficult to study in the laboratory. Sprecher's (1986) study of equity and emotion in college students' dating relationships provides a good example of this type of analysis. The students in her sample (n = 402) were given a questionnaire designed to measure the degree of equity in their romantic relationships. (Students who were not currently involved with a romantic partner were excluded from the study.) They were also asked to report the frequency with which they experienced various negative and positive emotions.

Students were placed into three relationship categories, based on the degree of equity they perceived in their interactions with their romantic partners: (1) overbenefiting inequity (their perceived rewards were greater than their perceived contributions), (2) equity (their perceived contributions matched their perceived outcomes), and (3) underbenefiting inequity (their perceived relationship inputs were greater than their perceived rewards). See Box 5.2 for the measure of equity used in this study and a summary of students' answers. If you're in a relationship, see where you fall on this 1–7 scale. Do you perceive your relationship to be equitable?

As expected, students in equitable relationships experienced more satisfaction, joy, and contentment than those who reported experiencing either under- or

---

Box 5.2   Measuring Equity in College Students' Dating Relationships

Sometimes things get out of balance in a relationship and one partner contributes more to the relationship than the other. Consider all the times when the exchange in your relationship has become unbalanced and one partner contributed more than the other for a time. When your relationship becomes unbalanced, which of you is more likely to be the one who contributes more?

1. My partner is much more likely to be the one to contribute more.
2. My partner is somewhat more likely to be the one to contribute more.
3. My partner is slightly more likely to be the one to contribute more.
4. We are equally likely to be the one to contribute more.
5. I am slightly more likely to be the one to contribute more.
6. I am somewhat more likely to be the one to contribute more.
7. I am much more likely to be the one to contribute more.

Responses of college students involved in a romantic relationship (n = 402)

28% = Overbenefiting from relationship (response options 1, 2, or 3)

29% = Equitable relationship (response option 4)

43% = Underbenefiting from relationship (response option 5, 6, or 7)

Note: Sprecher (1986).

---

overbenefiting inequity. Overall, underbenefiting inequity was more strongly associated with emotion than overbenefiting inequity. In particular, individuals who perceived themselves as contributing more than they were getting out of the relationship (underbenefiting inequity) experienced high levels of anger. Men in this type of relationship also experienced hate and resentment, whereas underbenefiting women experienced sadness and depression. As noted by Sprecher (1986), these latter differences are consistent with research suggesting that, due to lifelong patterns of socialization, women are more likely than men to internalize perceived failures, putting women at risk for depression, whereas men are more likely to direct their emotions toward others.

Interestingly, students who were overbenefiting also experienced anger. This suggests that people respond to inequity with negative emotions, regardless of the direction of the imbalance.

Males, but not females, who perceived themselves as overbenefiting in their current romantic relationship also felt guilty. Perhaps this reflects gender differences in the resources individuals bring to their romantic relationships. Overbenefiting females may have received an abundance of tangible resources (material goods), whereas overbenefiting males received more intangible resources (e.g., love). Intangible rewards, when in excess, may have a greater potential to make people feel guilty (Sprecher 1986).

In a subsequent study, Sprecher, Schmeeckle, and Felmlee (2006) found that men and women in relationships that were balanced in terms of emotional involvement were more satisfied with their relationships and experienced more positive and fewer negative emotions. Their relationships also tended to be more stable over time than relationships characterized by unequal emotional investments across partners. A number of other studies (e.g., Hatfield et al. 1982; Pillemer, Hatfield, and Sprecher 2008) have yielded similar results, suggesting that equity is an important determinant of relationship quality.

In addition, Sprecher and associates (2006) found that individuals who indicated that they were less emotionally involved in their romantic relationship than their partner (overbenefiting inequity) perceived greater control over whether the relationship continued. This is consistent with Waller's (1938) principle of least interest (Sprecher et al. 2006). The **principle of least interest** states that the person with the greater ability to reward (or punish) another has the least to lose should the relationship end. This gives this individual greater power than his or her relationship partner (Thibaut and Kelley 1959; Waller and Hill 1951; as cited in Homans, 1974).

What Do You Think?

- Have you ever felt disempowered in a personal relationship (either a romantic relationship or a friendship)? Why did you feel this way?
- Consider your disempowered relationship (or the disempowered relationship of someone you know) from the perspective of social exchange theory. How might resources (rewards) have affected your power within the relationship? What about exchange alternatives? How might people's exchange alternatives affect their intimate relationships? (Note: We discuss these issues in more detail in Chapter 11, on personal relationships.)

Social Identity Theory

The literature reviewed in the previous sections focuses on relations within groups (or intragroup relations). The third theoretical framework within the GPS face of social psychology is social identity theory (Tajfel 1978). It has a somewhat different focus: relations between groups (or intergroup relations).

Although social identity theory (SID) is not a part of the GPS tradition as originally identified by Berger (1992), there has been a tremendous growth in the number of studies on social identity theory published in academic journals in sociological social psychology in recent years (Harrod et al. 2009). This increase, as well as some core similarities between social identity theory and the theoretical frameworks discussed earlier in the chapter (namely, a focus on the link between micro and macro processes and an experimental orientation), merits the inclusion of social identity theory in this chapter.

Social identity theory (Tajfel 1978) views groups as cognitive constructs (i.e., they exist within people's minds) and has its roots in the work of social psychologists trained in psychology. From this perspective, a group exists when three or more individuals define themselves in terms of shared characteristics that make them distinct from other people (Hogg 2006a).

The main premise of social identity theory is that people psychologically identify with groups, and that this affects the way they view themselves and others. **Social identities**, as cognitive constructs, are constructed through a process of self-categorization (us vs. them) and reflect people's *perceived* group memberships. Using terminology introduced by sociologist Graham Sumner (1906), social identity theorists call the groups you identify with **in-groups** and the groups you don't belong to **out-groups**. Stop a minute and think about your in-groups. How many can you list?

The process of self-categorization results in negative stereotypes, negative attitudes (prejudice), and discriminatory behaviors directed toward out-group members. This happens across social contexts, as in-group/out-group distinctions form based upon any salient distinguishing attribute (Tajfel 1982).

Why People Form Social Identities and Devalue Out-Groups

According to **self-categorization theory** (Turner 1985), the cognitive dimension of social identity theory that focuses on the construction of group-based social identities (Hogg 2006a), self-categorization occurs for two main reasons: (1) it enables people to focus on those aspects of the social environment that are meaningful in a particular interactive context and (2) it serves a self-enhancement function. A key assumption underlying the social identity framework is that people have a need to see themselves in a favorable manner in relation to others. It is because of this that they tend to make self-flattering comparisons between the groups to which they belong and relevant out-groups (Hogg, Terry, and White 1995).

Do you remember what it was like being in elementary school? Within this setting, children often identify with others assigned to the same class ("I'm in room 212"or "My teacher is Ms. Kruse."), the in-group. Peers in the same grade who are in other classes are the out-group. Fellow students in the out-group aren't as smart, or they aren't as good at sports, or they aren't as funny as members of the in-group. We do the same thing in college. Students attending our school are smarter, better athletes, and more likely to get good jobs than individuals at other institutions.

Contextual factors, including structural conditions (social stratification), often support the view that one group is superior to another, as in the case of Whites versus racial/ethnic minorities. (Again, we want to stress that social psychologists don't believe this is true, but they recognize the existence of these beliefs within society at large.) Members of subordinate groups may use varied strategies to enhance their status in the face of negative societal beliefs about their group's attributes. For example, the may compare themselves to groups lower in the stratification hierarchy. Or they may focus only on positive dimensions of their group or actively seek social change (Hornsey 2008). Nonetheless, patterns of prejudice and discrimination at the macro level make in-group favoritism among members of dominant groups (e.g., Whites) in everyday social encounters especially likely to have negative consequences.

Application: A Class Divided

In 1968, shortly after the assassination of Dr. Martin Luther King, Jr., Jane Elliott, a third-grade teacher in Riceville, Iowa, executed a classroom exercise geared toward teaching the children in her all-White class a lesson about discrimination. She divided the class by eye color (blue vs. brown) and told the children that blue-eyed people were smart, clean, and responsible, whereas brown-eyed people were dumb, dirty, rude, and untrustworthy. Within this context, eye color became a salient dividing characteristic, and the blue-eyed children were nasty toward their brown-eyed counterparts, to whom they felt superior. In response, the brown-eyed children showed signs of demoralization and, in some cases, aggression.

Later that day, Ms. Elliott reversed the roles (brown-eyed children were better than their blue-eyed counterparts). A similar pattern emerged with the group on top (those with brown eyes) discriminating against their blue-eyed peers. Interestingly, scores on academic tasks completed that day varied in accordance with students' positions in the hierarchy. That is, the children's ability to successfully complete classroom exercises reflected their relative status at the time each task was completed, providing concrete evidence in support of the self-fulfilling prophecy (see page 145).

Although Jane Elliot's eye-color exercise was not designed as a test of social identity theory, the exercise is consistent with the theory's key premises. Social identity theory emphasizes the fact that a characteristic such as eye color, something of little consequence within most interactive contexts, once salient, can serve as the basis for self-categorization, stereotypes, and subsequent patterns of prejudice and discrimination.

Self-categorization often occurs based upon race/ethnicity because of its visibility and salience due to broader structural inequalities. However, Jane Elliott's eye-color exercise shows how social environments might be changed to facilitate the recategorization of in-groups versus out-groups and the effects of this kind of manipulation on perception and behavior.

Take a Break

In 1985, PBS *Frontline* aired the follow-up to a film produced in 1970 about the impact of Jane Elliott's eye-color exercise on her third-grade class. The episode, called "A Class Divided," shows footage from the 1970 film, as well as interviews with the individuals students in Ms. Elliott's class, now adults, as they attended a school reunion.

You may view "A Class Divided" at the following web link: http://www.pbs.org/wgbh/pages/frontline/shows/divided/. This is a powerful film that provides a good illustration of the self-categorization process and the social construction of in-groups and out-groups.

Minimal Groups

Social identity theorists have used the minimal groups procedure to study the self-categorization process in more controlled settings. **Minimal groups** are created in the laboratory by giving experimental subjects feedback on a task that results in self-categorization based upon a trivial characteristic, without any face-to-face contact (Hogg 2006b). Here the term "minimal" refers to researchers' creation of social conditions that meet the minimum requirement for social identification and intergroup discrimination (Tajfel 1982).

In his classic minimal groups experiment, Tajfel (1970) had subjects estimate the number of dots in a series of images. Putting subjects into groups based on whether they had consistently underestimated or overestimated the number of dots presented on a screen was enough to result in favoritism toward the in-group (either dot under- or overestimators) on a subsequent task. (The group assignment was random and had nothing to do with their actual task performance.) The subsequent task involved allocating money to other study participants. When making the monetary allotments, subjects knew only which group the other study participants were in. They knew nothing about their other characteristics, such as their gender or race/ethnicity.

Within this context, subjects gave more money to in-group than to out-group members (Tajfel 1970). Thus, information about an inane perceptual difference (dot under- or overestimation) was enough to cause in-group/out-group distinctions and discrimination. Many experiments, using a variety of trivial tasks, have yielded similar results (Diehl 1990).

Contemporary Research on Social Identities

Like Tajfel's original (1970) study, much of the current research on the formation of social identities focuses on experimentally induced minimal groups. The purpose of these studies is to assess the mechanisms underlying the effects of the self-categorization process and the construction of social identities on intergroup relations.

Other studies within the social identity framework focus on racial/ethnic prejudice and discrimination. Most of these analyses are experimental. We discuss a number of these studies in Chapter 12, which focuses on prejudice and discrimination. Here we illustrate the kind of research social identity theorists do by describing studies on two other topics: national identity and the relationship between political identity and behavior.

THE CONSTRUCTION OF NATIONAL IDENTITIES

In their innovative field experiment, Hopkins and Moore (2001) examined the construction of national identities and how they affect individuals' perceptions of people from another country. Recall that a field experiment is like a laboratory experiment in that the researchers randomly assign their subjects to different levels of an independent variable. The only notable difference between field and laboratory experiments is that field experiments occur in a real-world setting.

In Hopkins and Moore's (2001) study, 60 Scottish participants living in the town of Dumfries, Scotland, completed a questionnaire that focused on their perceptions of members of their community and of residents of Carlisle, a nearby town just across the border, in England. Despite the fact that Scotland and England have been united as a single country since the beginning of the 18th century, as the study authors point out, the Scottish have a strong sense of national identity. As a result, they perceive themselves as distinct from the English, even though both Scottish and English individuals are considered British.

The purpose of Hopkins and Moore's study was to determine whether the content of subjects' stereotypes of residents of the nearby English community, Carlisle, would be affected by making salient their identity as Scots versus their identity as British citizens. Either the Scottish or British identity was made salient (the manipulation of the independent variable) by having subjects complete a preliminary task that primed the target identity. **Priming** occurs when people are exposed to something that makes certain information more readily accessible in memory (Fiske and Taylor 2008). In this case, a particular identity (Scottish or British) was primed by asking subjects to describe the Scots and the English (condition 1, designed to make the Scottish identity salient) or the Germans and the British (condition 2, designed to make the more global British identity salient). From a list of adjectives, the subjects in condition 1 were asked to select the five adjectives that best described the Scottish and the five adjective that best described the British. In condition 2, subjects were asked to choose the five adjective that best described Germans and five adjectives that best described the British.

Following the completion of this task, all subjects were asked to select the five adjectives that best described the residents of their town, Dumfries, and the five adjectives that best described the residents of Carlisle, the nearby English community. The dependent variables were the degree of perceived similarity between the in-group (Dumfries) and the out-group (Carlisle) and the content of subjects' stereotypes (descriptions) of Carlisle residents.

As is typically the case, in-groups were rated much more favorably than out-groups across both conditions. Whereas the Scottish perceived themselves as warm, tradition-loving, and passionate, they regarded the English as arrogant, boastful, and conceited (condition 1). Similarly, whereas the British were said to be warm, courteous, and honest, the Germans were perceived as arrogant, loud, and rude (condition 2). Judgments of Dumfries (the in-group) and Carlisle (the out-group) showed a similar pattern.

However, as predicted, perceived in-group/out-group similarity (measured as the degree of overlap in the adjectives listed to describe residents of Dumfries and residents of Carlisle) was affected by the identity prime (Scottish or British). Perceived similarity was greater in condition 2, in which the shared British (vs. German) identity was made salient, than in condition 1, in which the Scottish (vs. the English) identity was made salient. Similarly, the content of the Carlisle stereotype was less negative among the subjects in condition 2 than among subjects in condition 1.

As noted by the study authors, the results of this experiment suggest that nations are defined subjectively (i.e., they are social constructions and not objectively defined entities) and that national identities are malleable. Like group-based social identities, national identities shift in relation to social cues.

POLITICAL IDENTITIES AND BEHAVIOR

Although they are somewhat less common than experiments, some studies within the social identity framework are based on the analysis of survey data. The advantage of these kinds of analyses is that they directly reflect people's perceptions and behaviors as they occur outside of the laboratory, in everyday social encounters.

For example, Greene (2004) used data from a questionnaire administered to a regional sample (n = 302) to assess the relationship between party identification and political attitudes. He found that self-categorization as a Democrat or Republican increased individuals' positive feelings about the party with which they identified. It isn't surprising that people have positive attitudes toward their political party. However, it is interesting to note that the effect of party identification on party attitudes is independent of (and thus not due to) the effects of strength of party affiliation or political ideology (liberal to conservative). We know this because when conducting his statistical analyses, Greene (2004) held strength of party affiliation and political ideology constant in the manner described in Chapter 2.

Having a partisan political identity (Democrat or Republican) was also associated with partisan political behaviors (e.g., wearing candidate buttons, actively campaigning on behalf of one's party, donating campaign funds, and voting in the primary). Again, this is to be expected. However, it is important to recognize that the effect on behavior of having a partisan political identity was evident when levels of party affiliation and political ideology were held constant. That is, social

COMIC 5.1

identification as Democrat or Republican affected respondents' political activities independent of the effect of the strength of their political affiliation or their political ideology.

Social identities have been shown to emerge in response to minimal social cues (like feedback about one's perceptions of clusters of dots). As a result, Greene (2004) suggests that any actions politicians can take to increase social identification with their party are likely to result in a more active, more partisan group of supporters. This could, in turn, impact the outcome of an election, especially in the case of a close race.

What Do You Think?

■ What's the difference between (political) party identity and political ideology (liberal to conservative)? What can politicians do to increase the extent to which people identify with their political party (remember, this is an us vs. them mentality)? Form a group with two or three of your classmates and make a list of strategies.

■ Also consider how television advertisements are used before an election to facilitate people's identification with a particular political party. Give one or two examples of political ads you've seen that seem to serve this function. If it's difficult to remember specific political advertisements, or if you want some additional examples, consider checking some political websites. Look at websites for political action committees, like American Crossroads (conservative) or America's Families First Action Fund (liberal), which fund political ads. How does the information presented on these websites, including the format and the language, facilitate the process of party identification?

EVALUATION OF GPS RESEARCH

As evidenced by the studies described in the preceding sections, research within the group processes and structures tradition is quite different from the kinds of analyses conducted within the other two faces (SI and SSP) of sociological social psychology. In particular, many GPS studies use standard experimental protocols. Such studies include research on susceptibility to social influence, the use of power within social exchange networks, and identify formation in studies of minimal groups.

Strengths of GPS Research

The consistency in the measurement of key variables and in the procedures used in each set of analyses (e.g., in SCT studies on social influence), along with their experimental nature, has made it possible for GPS researchers to reach some definitive conclusions about the nature of group dynamics. Experimental studies are high in internal validity. Thus, experimental sociologists (and social identity theorists, who tend to be psychologists) working within the GPS face of social psychology have been able to pinpoint with a high degree of certainty the causes of inequality in group encounters.

Identifying the causes of patterns of perception and behavior in group settings has enabled GPS researchers to develop interventions for reducing inequality. They can reduce inequality both within groups (e.g., by manipulating task instructions in small groups or through network expansion) and between groups (e.g., by making a particular characteristic more or less salient through the manipulation of social cues). This ability to develop interventions for reducing inequality is another major strength of research within the group processes and structures tradition.

Limitations of GPS Research

Given the macro orientation of GPS research, its limitations are similar to those of studies within social structure and personality. The same concerns about agency and micro-level variations in perception and behavior, discussed with regard to research in SSP, apply to GPS research. Given its focus on broad societal patterns, research in GPS tends to overlook the individual and the ways that people respond to their environments in active and creative ways.

Other limitations of GPS research are largely methodological. Although experimental sociology has its benefits, it also has some drawbacks. In particular, conducting group research within the laboratory may undermine the external validity or generalizability of the studies' results. There are two reasons for this, which we discussed in Chapter 2. First, an artificial laboratory setting may result in patterns of group behavior that differ from those that occur in everyday life. Second, most laboratory experiments, including those conducted within the GPS tradition, have used college undergraduates as subjects. College students have characteristics that set them apart from the population at large. They tend to be from relatively affluent families, and in many schools they are predominantly White.

How serious are these issues? That is, does the artificial laboratory setting and the reliance on college samples seriously undermine the external validity of GPS laboratory experiments? Social psychologists who work within this framework would say, "Probably not." As indicated earlier in the chapter, the processes they have studied (e.g., status generalization, the use of power within exchange relations, and self-categorization) have been shown to exist outside of the lab. They might also add that the benefits of their experimental approach, as outlined previously, outweigh the associated costs.

Once again, when evaluating a methodology's strengths and weaknesses, one must consider the purpose of the research. Whereas laboratory experiments may not be an appropriate method for SI or SSP researchers, they are well suited to the research questions generated within the GPS tradition.

CHAPTER SUMMARY

Research within the group processes and structures face of sociological social psychology has been guided by three theoretical frameworks: expectations states theory, social exchange theory, and social identity theory. These perspectives have directed researchers' attention to patterns of bias in task-oriented groups, to the effects of structural position on the use of power in exchange networks, to equity in intimate relationships, and to intergroup relations. Because most of these processes are amenable to study in a controlled setting, much of GPS literature is experimental. The studies used to illustrate each of the three theoretical frameworks within the GPS tradition are summarized in Table 5.2. Although research in GPS is eclectic, it reflects some common themes, including an emphasis on identifying the manner in which social inequality at the macro level affects perception and behavior.

TABLE 5.2

Summary of Studies Illustrating the Group Processes and Structures Face of Social Psychology

RESEARCHERS	FRAMEWORK	FOCUS	METHOD	RESULTS
Dovidio and associates	Expectation states/status characteristics	Effect of gender on interaction in small task-oriented groups	Experiment	Nature of task (stereotypically male, female, or neutral) affected relationship between gender and group interactions
Goar and Sell	Expectation states/status characteristics	Effect of race on interaction in small task-oriented groups	Experiment	Manipulating task instructions (incompatible complexity) reduced the negative effects of race status on perception and behavior
Cook and Emerson	Social exchange	Effect of network structure on exchange behavior	Experiment	Use of power in negotiated exchanges was affected by network position (i.e., the value of alternative exchange relations)

TABLE 5.2

(Continued)

RESEARCHERS	FRAMEWORK	FOCUS	METHOD	RESULTS
Sprecher	Social exchange	Inequity and emotion in students dating relationships	Survey	Both under-benefiting and overbenefiting inequity resulted in negative emotions (in particular, anger)
Hopkins and Moore	Social identity/ self-categorization	Effect of priming on self-categorization and national identity	Experiment	Scottish participants perceived English neighbors as more similar to themselves when the British identity was made salient; British versus Scottish identity also reduced negative stereotypes
Greene	Social identity/ Self-categorization	Self-categorization and political identity	Survey	Having a partisan political identity influenced feelings and partisan behavior independent of effect of political ideology or strength of affiliation

Key Points to Know

- **Social psychologists working within the group processes and structures tradition often study small groups.** Small groups are characterized by propinquity (or physical proximity), similarity, and a shared fate among their members.

- **There are three theoretical frameworks within the GPS face of sociological social psychology: (1) expectations states theory, which includes status characteristics theory; (2) social exchange theory; and (3) social identity theory.** Whereas expectations states theory and social exchange theory focus on *intragroup* relations, social identity theory focuses on *intergroup* relations.

- **According to status characteristics theory, men, whites, and the socioeconomically advantaged are given more action opportunities and evaluated more favorably in task groups than women, racial and ethnic minorities, and people with few socioeconomic resources**. Since individuals who contribute more to the group tend to be given more action opportunities and receive more positive evaluations, initial patterns of bias in task groups tend to result in a self-fulfilling prophecy. Status characteristics theorists have developed strategies for disrupting the process that initiates this cycle which results in more egalitarian patterns of group interaction.

- **Working within the social exchange tradition, researchers have studied how power affects exchange behavior within the context of exchange networks. From this perspective, power is structurally determined and reflects an actor's exchange alternatives (i.e., number of potential exchange partners), as well as his or her degree of control over valued resources.** Studies suggest that reward power is rarely used to its full capacity due in part to norms pertaining to the importance of equity. Coercive (punishment) power also tends to be underutilized, but this is primarily because people fear a loss of future rewards. People can increase their structurally based power through network expansion.

- **At the micro level, research on exchange in romantic relationships suggests that a balance (equity) between reward inputs and outputs increases both positive emotions and relationship stability.**

- **The third GPS framework, social identity theory, focuses on social cognition and the psychological processes underlying in-group favoritism.** Research suggests that social identities, and their consequences, can be altered by making particular social characteristics salient.

- **The emphasis on intervention and its potential for social change is a main strength of research in the group processes and structures face of social psychology.** The experimental basis of much of the GPS literature has made it possible for researchers to identify precisely how macro-level social inequalities influence people's social behaviors. Experiments also allow researchers to test the effectiveness of various strategies for altering common patterns of group interaction.

- **Research within the group processes and structures tradition has been criticized for its emphasis on social interactions in artificial**

(laboratory) environments. Nonetheless, many of the interactional processes GPS researchers have observed within the lab reflect broader societal patterns that transcend any particular group encounter and address issues of substantial relevance to everyday life.

Terms and Concepts for Review

Balanced relation	Priming
Behaviorist psychology	Principle of least interest
Coercive power	Punishment
Commitment	Reciprocal exchange
Diffuse status characteristics	Reward
Dyads	Secondary group
Equity	Self-categorization theory
Exchange network	Self-fulfilling prophecy
Expectation states theory	Small groups
Incompatible complexity	Social exchange theory
In-group	Social identity
Minimal groups	Social identity theory
Negatively connected exchange network	Social networks
Negotiated exchange	Specific status characteristic
Network expansion	Status beliefs
Noncoercive (reward) power	Status characteristics theory (SCT)
Opportunity costs	Status generalization
Out-group	Status structures
Performance expectations	Stereotype
Power	Triads
Power-dependence relation	Trust
Primary group	Unbalanced relation

Questions for Review and Reflection

1. Status characteristics theorists assume that all statuses that serve as dimensions of stratification within this society will affect small-group interactions in a similar manner. Thus, from this perspective, it doesn't matter whether you study gender, race/ethnicity, or social class; the results should be similar. Why is this? Moreover, why do status characteristics theorists expect the results of their laboratory experiments to generalize to real-world social encounters?
2. Make a distinction between power and its use. Give an example of a time when you had structurally based power over someone but didn't use it. What kind of social exchange was this (negotiated or reciprocal)? What influenced your behavior in this encounter?

3. What are the main premises of social identity theory? Apply social identity theory to the relationship among fraternities or sororities on a college campus. What predictions would social identity theory make about the attitudes and behaviors of Greek participants toward in-group members and members of out-groups (other fraternities or sororities)?

4. Briefly summarize the results of one research study from within each of the three theoretical frameworks within GPS. What do these studies have in common, and how do they reflect the main themes of the GPS face of sociological social psychology?

ENDNOTE

1. Expectation states theory not only provides researchers with a set of concepts that direct their attention to particular aspects of social life (the role of a theoretical framework within social psychology) but also specifies a set of propositions that can be converted into hypotheses and directly tested (like the income-happiness example in Chapter 1). Given this, expectation states theory is a theory rather than a theoretical framework (Meeker 1981). This distinction (between theoretical framework and theory) is not important given the purpose of this chapter. Thus, for ease of presentation, we will refer to expectations states theory as a theoretical framework, like the other perspectives within GPS (social exchange theory and social identity theory).

PART II

Topics Studied by Sociological Social Psychologists

CHAPTER 6

Socialization Throughout the Life Course

PHOTO 6.1

This toddler, shown with an iPad, was born into a high-tech world. Thus, her experiences are likely to be quite different from those of individuals in previous generations. Children today are much more technologically advanced than prior age cohorts, with their cell phones, voicemail, MP3 players, cable and satellite television, movies on demand, and laptop computers. Most children (84%) have Internet access at home and spend an average of one to two hours per day on the computer. About a fourth of this time is spent visiting social network sites, such as Facebook.

Other common computer-mediated activities include playing interactive games, watching videos on YouTube, surfing the web, and sending and receiving instant messages and emails (Rideout, Foehr, and Roberts 2010).

There have been some concerns about the impact of this heavy use of computer-mediated technology on cognition and behavior. Contemporary youths multitask much more frequently than children in previous generations. This may have negative consequences for how effectively they process information or complete tasks (Ophir, Nass, and Wagner 2009).

The significance of the widespread use of technology within this society has yet to be determined. Discussions about its effects, do, however, highlight the role of the culture into which children are born in shaping their abilities and behaviors.

KEY CONCEPTS

Culture refers to everything within society that is learned and thus passed on from one generation to the next. **Material culture** refers to tangible objects created by humans (e.g., a house, a desk, a cell phone, or a computer), whereas **nonmaterial culture** consists of things we cannot see or touch, including values, norms, beliefs, and knowledge. Language is also an important part of nonmaterial culture.

Socialization is the process through which people develop the ability to communicate using language, an understanding of societal norms and values, and the knowledge and skills required for participation in society. It is the process through which they acquire their society's culture. Socialization is an important topic of study within sociological social psychology because it explains how society comes to exert such a strong effect on the perceptions and behaviors of individuals.

Primary socialization refers to the acquisition of language and of core cultural norms and values that occurs during childhood. **Secondary socialization** occurs in adulthood and often builds upon what people have learned as children. Social psychologists refer to the individuals, groups, organizations, and social institutions that shape people's perceptions and behaviors throughout the life course as **agents of socialization**. Box 6.1 lists the various agents of socialization of interest to sociological social psychologists.

Box 6.1 Agents of Socialization Commonly Studied by Sociological Social Psychologists

Family	Religion
Schools	Sports
Peers	Preschool/day care centers
Media	Clubs/social groups

PRIMARY SOCIALIZATION

Theories and research on primary socialization address what is commonly referred to as the **nature-nurture question**: are people, their attitudes, preferences, and behaviors products of genetic or biological factors (nature) or the social environments they experience (nurture)? That is, to what degree are our perceptions and actions the result of socialization versus innate biological and genetic factors?

Socialization begins at birth. Thus, there is widespread agreement that family members—in particular, parents—are especially important in the lives of young children. Beyond that, different perspectives on primary socialization vary in the degree to which they emphasize the importance of nurture versus nature in the developmental process.

Psychological Approaches to Child Development

Psychological approaches to the study of child development emphasize biological factors, as well as the role of parent-child relationships, in the emergence of various characteristics and skills. We focus here on Freud's psychoanalytic model and Piaget's cognitive developmental approach. These perspectives differ from the sociological approaches discussed throughout the chapter in that they place a greater emphasis on biological determinants of perception and behavior. However, it is important to have some familiarity with them. Freud's model was popular at the time when Mead was writing and is often used as a point of reference in discussions of Mead's more socially based symbolic interactionism. Moreover, a prominent model of the socialization process within sociological social psychology called the interpretive approach, discussed later in the chapter, expands on Piaget's model of cognitive development.

Personality

The Austrian biologist and clinical psychologist Sigmund Freud developed the first and most influential model of the nature and formation of personality. Here, **personality** refers to ways of perceiving and responding to the world that are stable across social settings. Note the difference between how personality is defined within this context and the broader manner in which this term is used within the social structure and personality orientation, discussed in Chapter 4.

Freud (1923) argued that personality has three components: the id, the ego, and the superego. The **id** refers to innate, irrational, and unconscious drives that affect people's behaviors. The **ego**, in contrast, represents rational thought processes. The ego is given energy by the id insofar as it can meet the id's demands for gratification. The third component of the personality structure, the **superego**, emerges out of the ego when children internalize parental norms and values. It represents our conscience. Because the id (biological nature) is in direct opposition to the superego (social values and norms), the ego (rational thought processes) must serve as a mediator, meeting the id's demands in a manner that is consistent with broader societal standards.

According to Freud (1949) personality develops in a series of psychosexual stages, each of which involves a key set of interactions between children and their parents. The order of Freud's stages, and their physical manifestations (e.g., in the oral stage, infants seek stimulation to the mouth), are biologically based. Because the developmental process is biologically driven, it is presumed to continue even in the face of less-than-optimal social relations. However, in Freud's view, problematic parent-child interactions during childhood have long-term negative consequences, and personality disorders or problems experienced in adulthood are traceable to early parent-child conflicts. From this perspective, changing personality after it is formed is difficult and requires years of intensive therapy, called psychoanalysis.

Although Freud acknowledged the importance of the environment (nurture) in this developmental process, he focused on a relatively narrow range of interactions between children and their parents. Thus, his psychoanalytic theory of personality is more within the nature camp than the nurture camp.

Cognitive Development

Focusing on the development of mental abilities, Swiss psychologist Jean Piaget offered another famous stage theory of child development. Piaget's (1926) theory of cognitive development emphasizes the physiological underpinnings of the intellectual skills that emerge as children mature. However, it is through interaction with the broader social environment that children encounter the stimuli necessary for these abilities to be realized. Piaget felt that children have an innate tendency to react to environmental challenges in ways that reflect their level of cognitive development, as well as their broader social milieu. Thus, they are active participants in the primary socialization process (Corsaro 1997).

Piaget proposed a series of developmental stages through which knowledge is constructed. These stages, summarized in Box 6.2, reflect an increasing capacity for generalization and abstract thought on the part of the child.

Social Learning Theory

Social learning theory, associated with the work of Albert Bandura, is another theoretical framework within psychology that focuses on primary socialization. Drawing on the behaviorist tradition in psychology, social learning theorists emphasize the effects of the environment—patterns of reinforcement (reward) and punishment—on people's acquisition of behaviors, beliefs, and attitudes. Because social learning theory specifies some of the mechanisms through which socialization occurs (reinforcement and punishment), this perspective has some appeal to sociological social psychologists, despite its micro-level focus.

Box 6.2   Piaget's Stages of Cognitive Development

Sensorimotor stage (birth to 2 years old): Children experience the world through their senses (touching, tasting, smelling, looking, and listening). It is during this stage that they discover the *rule of object permanence*—an understanding that objects exist even when you can no longer see them.

Preoperational stage (2 to 7 years old): Children begin to learn how to use symbols and language and how to communicate with others. However, they have not yet developed the capacity for perspective taking or complex thought.

Concrete operational stage (7 to 11 years old): During this stage, children begin to develop logic and reasoning skills through the classification, ranking, and separation of objects. They are able to make causal connections.

Formal operational stage (11 years and up): During this stage, adolescents develop abstract reasoning and critical thinking skills. They learn how to think hypothetically or theoretically. Progression into, and within, this developmental stage is facilitated by education and autonomous work environments.

Bandura (1977) argued that people learn from both indirect, or vicarious, and direct forms of reinforcement or punishment. **Vicarious, or indirect, reinforcement or punishment** occurs when someone observes another individual being rewarded or punished for engaging in a particular behavior and this experience affects his or her likelihood of enacting that behavior. Vicarious reinforcement is the process that underlies role modeling, another key concept associated with the social learning framework.

Role modeling occurs when people acquire behaviors by observing others. In Bandura's original social learning experiment (Bandura, Ross, and Ross 1961), children observed adult models beating a Bobo doll, an inflatable toy designed to serve as a punching bag with a mallet (For video footage of Bandura's classic Bobo doll experiment search Youtube using the terms Bobo doll and Bandura). When given the opportunity to do so, the children who had seen the adult model rewarded for beating the Bobo doll imitated their behavior. Children were most likely to copy the actions of same-sex adult models, suggesting that perceived similarly increases the frequency with which observational leaning takes place.

Symbolic Interactionist Approaches

Because socialization is an ongoing process rooted in children's interactions with others, much of the sociological social psychological literature on this topic is symbolic interactionist in orientation. Symbolic interactionist models of primary socialization focus on the concept of self rather than personality. The **self** refers to the process of interaction between the "I" (biologically based impulses) and the "me" (social expectations) described in Chapter 3. Unlike personality, which is often assumed to have a biological basis, the self is predominantly social in origin. Thus, the symbolic interactionist approach to primary socialization emphasizes nurture over nature.

The Development of the Self

Like his predecessors, George Herbert Mead (1863–1931), considered the founder of symbolic interactionism, postulated a stage theory of primary socialization. For Mead (1934, 1964), primary socialization is the process through which the "me" phase of the self develops. The "me" is the phase of the self that underlies human's capacity for role taking. As discussed in Chapter 3, **role taking** (or perspective taking) is the ability to view oneself from the perspective of others and to plan patterns of action that meet the expectations of others and broader societal standards.

In an initial **preparatory stage**, children exhibit recognition that there are roles in society other than their own by imitating significant others (a term coined by Sullivan, 1940, that is often applied to Mead's work). Although people currently use the term **significant other** to designate a romantic partner, within symbolic interactionism it means anyone important to a child, including parents, siblings, and peers.

In the **play stage**, children learn how to take the role of another individual behaviorally by participating in role-play activities with peers. Common role-play activities within this category include "house" or "school." Mead argued that these activities are important in the development of the "me" phase of the self. It is by taking on the role of someone else behaviorally (e.g., by playing the role of teacher when playing "school" with friends) that children learn how to take the role of another individual at the cognitive level.

In the **game stage**, children interact in larger groups and play games, like baseball, which have multiple, interrelated positions and complex rules. Mead posited that children refine their role-taking abilities in this stage of development. During the game stage, children learn to negotiate tiers of social expectations (individual level and societal level). Playing baseball requires each team member to imagine what others expect of him or her as the occupant of a particular position (e.g., catcher or pitcher). At the same time, each team member must also have an understanding of the larger group, or team, goal (to win the game). Mead argued that, in games, children learn how to organize individual expectations in a group expectation and develop a sense of the generalized other. The **generalized other** is an understanding of broader societal values and norms, as well as the recognition that one is an individual member of a larger group (Corsaro 1985).

To effectively participate in society, people must have an understanding of the expectations placed upon them as individuals, given their various roles, and as members of the society. For example, you are expected to behave in particular ways as a daughter or son, as a student, as an athlete, as a participant in one or more campus organizations, or as an employee. At the same time, there are obligations placed on you as a member of this society (e.g., you should never hurt someone else in order to get your way). You are also expected to adhere to these broader societal norms when you interact with others.

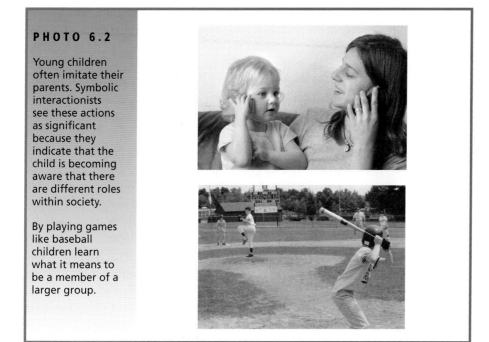

PHOTO 6.2

Young children often imitate their parents. Symbolic interactionists see these actions as significant because they indicate that the child is becoming aware that there are different roles within society.

By playing games like baseball children learn what it means to be a member of a larger group.

We gain a sense of social expectations through taking the role of one or more specific others. This makes it clear to us what we should be doing as a student, brother, friend, or employee. In order to gain an understanding of broader societal expectations (social norms), we must view ourselves from the perspective of society at large (the generalized other). It is through the kinds of relationships that characterize the game stage that children acquire this capacity.

Although Mead felt that individuals develop the ability to take the role of another and an understanding of broader social obligations by early adolescence, from this perspective, socialization is a lifelong process. This is because our understandings of ourselves and others have the potential to change every time we interact with others.

What Do You Think?

Are you the same person that you were in high school? Do you see the world in the same way? What relationships or activities were instrumental in creating any changes in the way in which you view yourself and others?

Language and Primary Socialization

Drawing on Mead (1934), symbolic interactionists regard the acquisition of language as central to the primary socialization process. Language mediates the development of the capacity for role taking and thus underlies our ability to synthesize individual and broader societal expectations in the manner outlined in the previous section.

As noted in Chapter 3, language, as a system of significant symbols, is a powerful tool, one that enables us to conceptualize events that go beyond our immediate experience. Language allows for complex thought (mind) and the self-regulation of behavior in that it underlies our ability to imagine others' responses to potential actions and to reflect back on past occurrences and reactions.

People's first memory is often of something that happened when they were about three to four years old (Bruce, Dolan, and Phillips-Grant 2000; Usher and Neisser 1993). This is the point in time at which most children become proficient in spoken language. However, children in this age range are not able to explain events they experienced during the preverbal period using their newly acquired language skills. This suggests that language forms the basis for autobiographical memories (Simcock and Hayne 2002).

There is also some evidence that available linguistic categories (words in a language) shape people's perceptions of their environments. This argument, associated with the work of the anthropologist Edward Sapir and his associate, Benjamin Whorf, is called the **Sapir-Whorf hypothesis** (Hoijer 1954). It is also referred to as the linguistic relativity hypothesis.

Most languages have words that are difficult to translate into another language. Thus, whenever you go from one language to another, some of the original writer's intended meaning may be lost. For example, in Italian the word *magari* is frequently used in conversation. It expresses or conveys feeling and may change with the context within which it is used (e.g., as an adverb it may mean "yes," whereas as an exclamation it may mean "No!"). There is no equivalent term in English. Thus, it is difficult for someone who speaks Italian to explain what this word means in English.

There may also be variations in the language commonly used across groups within a given society. To illustrate this, and its consequences, we often ask the students in our social psychology classes if they are familiar with cattle. We live in the Midwest, so we usually have at least one or two students in class who grew up on a farm and know about the various types of cows common in the region. When these individuals are driving and see a cow along the side of the road they don't just see a cow, they see a Holstein (this is a black and white dairy cow), a Jersey (a brown dairy cow), an Angus (a black cow raised for its beef), and so forth. Those of us without these labels at our disposal are much more general in our perceptions: we see a cow.

The notion that language affects perception is the primary rationale for what some people call "politically correct" speech. Presumably, replacing words with negative connotations with neutral or positive terms (called euphemisms) will change the way the population perceives a certain event or group of individuals. See Box 6.3 for a list of commonly used terms and their predecessors. As they

Box 6.3   Common Euphemisms and the Terms They Replaced

Word	Replacement (Euphemism)
Died	Passed away; in a better place; departed
Blind	Visually impaired
Deaf	Hearing impaired
Short	Vertically challenged
Old person	Senior citizen; elderly
Mortician	Funeral director
Janitor	Custodian; custodial engineer
Garbage man	Sanitation worker
Garbage dump	Landfill
Poor	Underprivileged; low income
Fired	Laid off; let go
Unemployed	Between jobs
Pornography	Adult entertainment
Crazy	Mentally ill
Drunk	Under the influence; intoxicated
Dormitory	Residence hall
Nursing home	Retirement home; assisted living facility
Illegal immigrant	Undocumented worker

acquire these and other words, children are learning to perceive the world in particular ways.

The Effects of Social Isolation

Historical accounts of children denied human contact are further testaments to the relationship between language and thought. Since the mid-eighteen hundreds, there have been a number of documented cases of **feral children**—children raised in the wild who are completely unsocialized. There have also been cases of children who have suffered severe abuse at the hands of their caretakers (Davis 1940, 1947). One such individual, given the pseudonym Genie (because, like a Genie, she emerged from seclusion into the world), was found in a town close to Los Angeles, California, in 1970. Genie had been locked in a closet since infancy. When she was discovered at the age of 13, Genie was nonverbal, salivated heavily, spat regularly, and appeared to have no awareness of temperature (hot or cold) (Rymer 1993).

Like Genie, most children isolated from birth never develop the mental abilities characteristic of adults with more normative social histories. Often, it is difficult to determine whether a particular child's cognitive deficits are physiological or social in origin. This was the case with Genie, as it was unclear whether she was mentally retarded at birth. However, the pattern observed among children denied human contact has been consistent. Individuals who haven't developed a language before reaching puberty, the critical period for language acquisition (Lenneberg 1967), have not been able to do so. As a result, they have permanent cognitive impairments. Symbolic interactionists emphasize the importance of social contact in the development of the self and the capacity for higher-level thought. It is through interaction with others, including parents, siblings, and, later, with peers, that children learn language and develop cognitive skills.

Take a Break

View a 2007 an episode of the National Geographic program *Is It Real?* on feral children. The program is available in segments on YouTube (search "feral children and National Geographic"). It is also available via Netflix.

A short (10 minute) segment of the video can be viewed at the following web address: http://watchdocumentary.org/watch/feral-children-video_789e80944.html.

If you're interested, you can watch the PBS *Nova* documentary *Secret of the Wild Child* (1994), the story of Genie, at the following web address: http://www.youtube.com/watch?v=hmdycJQi4QA.

Through the application of Mead's model, one can pinpoint the nature of the deficits observed in Genie and other children denied social contact. Children isolated from birth have no means of communicating with others, and thus they are unable to communicate with themselves within their minds. Without language, they have no capacity for role taking, or self-reflection, and they have no ability to evaluate the likely consequences of various courses of action. Thus, their behaviors are products of the "I," with which we are born, rather than the socially derived "me."

Studies of Children's Social Worlds

Symbolic interactionists have been studying the social worlds of children as they relate to primary socialization processes since the late 1960s. These analyses are based on naturalistic observation of children's everyday social experiences. As such, they focus on the intersection between constraint (societal values and norms as reflected in the actions of parents, teachers, and other adults) and agency (the face-to-face interactions through which meanings are created and reproduced). Although children's social encounters are regarded as products of broader social forces, children are viewed as active participants in the socialization process (Cahill 2003). Key symbolic interactionist studies of children's socialization experiences at home, in schools, and in other social environments are summarized in Table 6.1. Like most symbolic interactionist research, these (ethnographic) studies are qualitative in orientation.

TABLE 6.1	PUBLICATION TITLE	SAMPLE	RESEARCHER/DATE
Classic Symbolic Interactionist Studies of Children's Social Worlds	**PRESCHOOL/ELEMENTARY SCHOOL AGE**		
	Peer Power: Preadolescent Culture and Identity	Elementary-school children	Adler and Adler (1998)
	Language Practices and Self-Definition: The Case of Gender Identity Acquisition	Preschool-aged children	Cahill (1986)
	Play, Games and Interaction: The Contexts of Childhood Socialization	Children aged 3–8	Denzin (1975)
	Sex Differences in the Games Children Play	Children aged 10–12	Lever (1976)
	Peer Interaction in Day Care Settings: Implications for Social Cognition	Children in day care	Mandell (1986)
	Gender Play: Boys and Girls in School	Elementary-aged children	Thorne (1993)
	PREADOLESCENT/ADOLESCENT		
	The Cycle of Popularity: Interpersonal Relations Among Female Adolescents	Middle school girls	Eder (1985)
	With the Boys: Little League Baseball and Preadolescent Culture	Boys participating in Little League baseball	Fine (1987)
	From Nerds to Normals: The Recovery of Identity Among Adolescents From Middle School to High School	High school males and females	Kinney (1993)
	The Meaning of Meanness: Popularity, Competition, and Conflict Among Junior High School Girls	Junior high school girls	Merten (1997)

The Interpretive Approach

The **interpretive approach** to the study of primary socialization, developed by sociologist William Corsaro, synthesizes elements of symbolic interactionism and Piaget's cognitive developmental model. Interpretive sociologists view primary socialization as a continuous creation and reorganization of knowledge. This process is shaped by children's developing cognitive skills and by the expansion of their interactive encounters to contexts beyond that of the family. From this perspective, socialization occurs as individuals participate in a series of peer cultures, in school and other social contexts, throughout childhood and adolescence (Corsaro and Eder 1990).

Children's Peer Cultures

As illustrated in Table 6.1, symbolic interactionists have a history of studying children's peer groups and how meanings are constructed within this context. Interpretive analyses build upon this tradition by emphasizing the creative and spontaneous aspects of children's peer relationships (Musolf 1996).

Peer cultures are subcultures characterized by shared activities, values and concerns that emerge in children's face-to-face interactions with other youths. They arise in social interaction and reflect, but rarely mimic, adult culture. They are creative productions that reshape information from the larger (adult) society to fit the concerns of the peer group, a process called **interpretive reproduction** (Corsaro and Eder 1990). The term "interpretive" is used to convey the spontaneous and innovative aspects of children's peer cultures, whereas the term "reproduction" acknowledges children's active role in both the creation and modification of culture (Corsaro and Fingerson 2006).

Milkie's (1994) analysis of the role of the media in the production of gender among middle school students is a good example of a study within the interpretive tradition. Although we discuss gender socialization in detail in the next section, we present this example here because it provides a clear illustration of the concept of interpretive reproduction. The sixth through eighth graders from which participant observational data were gathered took information from the larger culture, including movies popular at the time, and integrated it into their group activities in unique and creative ways.

The following excerpt from Milkie (1994: 374), reproduced verbatim, illustrates this process. As is standard, the names given to the various participants, all boys (as is often the case, the interactions of the children studied tended to be gender segregated), in the interaction are fictitious. The film being discussed is *The Quest for Fire*, a popular movie from the early 1980s set in the prehistoric era. The designation // is used to indicate that someone has taken over and completed a phrase started by another participant in the dialogue. Information about the nonverbal gestures and laughter that took place during the exchange is included in double parentheses.

MATT: How b'out—what about when that lady, she's holdin' on to her arm, she's layin' there goin' ((holds up arm and makes a silly face)) "Uunh, unh, unh."
PAUL: An there's blood drippin' out of her arm an the next thing you see is that dude //
GREGG: Chewin' // on her arm.
PAUL: chewin' on her arm. That'd be funny if she's hop down ((in female voice)) "Oh, I need to do my nails." ((mimes using a nail file)) ((Everyone laughs.))

As the author notes, there is no scene in *The Quest for Fire* during which a woman (or cavewoman, given the setting of the film) files her nails. Thus, the boys' interpretations of the film were unique and involved both the exaggeration and embellishment of its content in a manner consistent with prevailing gender stereotypes. Although their conversation reflects prevailing societal beliefs about gender, it is not solely a product of these social facts. Rather, through their interaction with peers, the boys in the study actively created meanings that reflected spontaneous elements of the interactive encounter, and the unique inputs of particular group members, as well as broader societal patterns (Milkie 1994). It is through these kinds of interactions with friends that children creatively respond to, and in some cases reproduce, macro-level phenomena (Corsaro and Eder 1990), such as cultural stereotypes pertaining to gender.

Structural Approaches

Unlike the symbolic interactionist and interpretive models just described, research on socialization within the social structure and personality face of sociological social psychology emphasizes the transmission of knowledge, beliefs, and skills from society to the child. (Note: Given the focus of the group processes and structures orientation, there are few studies on socialization within this face of sociological social psychology.) In particular, SSP researchers study the effects of social class on the socialization process. As you already know from Chapter 4, social class influences the characteristics parents value in their children and children's experiences at school.

Patterns of communication within the family have also been related to social class, and these differences explain, in part, the association between socioeconomic background and educational track. Children from middle-class families are likely to be more familiar with the type of speech used to elaborate upon and analyze complex ideas or events because their parents talk this way. They do so because they are required to use this style of speech in their white-collar, professional jobs. This kind of language is rarely required in blue-collar, manual labor positions.

Middle-class children's familiarity with elaborated speech places them at an advantage relative to their working-class peers when it comes to educational testing, as this style of speech matches the kind of language used in these assessments (Bernstein 1972). Again, it is not innate intellectual ability that distinguishes between children from different class backgrounds. Rather, it is their social experiences and, in this case, familiarity with the kind of speech used by teachers, school administrators, and other professionals that differentiates between children from working- and middle-class families. Nonetheless, this difference has educational consequences (unfairly so, from a sociological standpoint) and is one reason why working-class children tend to be placed in their schools' low-tier academic or vocational tracks.

More contemporary research points to other class differences in children's socialization experiences. In particular, middle-class parents use their economic resources to actively facilitate their children's social and cognitive development. They enroll them in structured activities (e.g., sports and music lessons) and teach them how to be assertive in interactions with individuals in positions of authority, such as doctors and teachers. Power differences between adults and children are minimized in middle-class families, and children's activities often supersede other family pursuits. For these reasons, middle-class children have a sense of entitlement uncommon among working-class youths (Lareau 2002).

In working-class families, children are treated as subordinates by their parents, a pattern consistent with the hierarchical nature of the parents' work experiences (Bernstein 1972; Laureau 2002). Working-class youths also spend more time than middle-class children interacting with members of their extended family. In addition, given their social experiences, working-class parents frequently teach their children to avoid people with authority. Thus, children from working-class backgrounds often lack the negotiating skills of their middle-class counterparts. This puts them at a disadvantage when dealing with administrators and other professionals and exacerbates class-based inequalities in how people are treated in various institutional settings.

Although race/ethnicity itself has minimal effects on the processes of socialization in families just described (Lareau 2002), racial and ethnic minorities are disproportionately represented at the bottom of the class structure. Thus, race/ethnicity affects these aspects of the primary socialization process indirectly via social class.

Poverty

Regardless of their racial/ethnic background, children who live in poverty face a host of environmental and interpersonal factors that impede their development. Poor children are more likely than their more advantaged counterparts to live in high-crime neighborhoods; to attend poor quality schools; and to experience stressors associated with disease, disability, and substance use (Aber et al. 1997; Brooks-Gunn and Duncan 1997; Moore et al. 2009).

The constant strain associated with having too little money to make ends meet also takes its toll on parent-child relationships (Kaiser and Delaney 1996; McLoyd and Wilson 1991) and increases the likelihood of parental divorce. In fact, according to the U.S. Census Bureau, poverty has been a major contributor to rising divorce rates in this country (Hernandez, 1993).

Parental Divorce

Almost half of all marriages end in divorce (Schoen and Canudas-Romo 2006) and over 20% of children currently live in single-parent families (U.S. Census Bureau 2012). Much of the negative impact of parental divorce on children's development results from the decline in the standard of living experienced by mothers and their children as the result of this change in family structure (McLanahan and Percheski 2008).

Other (nonsocioeconomic) effects of parental divorce on primary socialization are less clear cut (Putney and Bengston 2002). It is, for example, true that adolescents whose parents have divorced are at risk for the use of alcohol and other drugs. However, it is important to note that it is not the change in family structure itself that causes an increase in these behaviors. Rather, it is changes in the kinds of interactions children have with their parents and peers, which coincide with changes in family structure, that have the greatest effect on patterns of adolescent substance use.

Adolescents from single-parent families are less closely monitored by their parents than adolescents in two-parent homes, especially when the custodial parent is the father. As a result, they are more likely than children from two-parent families to spend time with friends in unsupervised settings, which is associated with alcohol and marijuana use. Adolescents living in stepfamilies, on the other hand, frequently report conflict with their parents. Poor quality parent-child relationships are, in turn, related to a risk for substance use. The implication of this is that parents, whatever the structure of their household (two biological or adoptive parents, single parent, or stepfamily), can shape their children's behavior by altering the nature and quality of their relationships with them (Crawford and Novak 2008).

ISSUES OF INTEREST PERTAINING TO PRIMARY SOCIALIZATION

Topics pertaining to primary socialization of particular interest to sociological social psychologists include how children learn about gender, how they develop the capacity for moral reasoning, and the role of the media as an agent of socialization. We discuss these issues in the following section.

Gender Socialization

Within the family, and later in other social contexts, children learn what it means to be male or female within a given society. Thus, gender socialization is an integral part of the primary socialization process.

We talked earlier about the role of nature (biology) versus nurture (environment) in child development. The nature-nurture debate is especially salient when it comes to gender and the origin of differences in perceptions, preferences, and behavior between men and women.

What Do You Think?

Read the news article in Box 6.4. Note that it was really the child's sex that was a secret. Because the child's sex was not revealed, people don't know to what gender category that child belongs. Do you think it was difficult for the parents to keep their child's sex a secret? How did their choice to withhold their child's sex affect the way that people perceived and treated this infant?

Box 6.4   Canadian Couple Won't Reveal Child's Gender

Ever since the 1970s when Marlo Thomas and Friends introduced the idea of raising gender-neutral kids in the *Free to Be . . . You and Me* record, parents have encouraged their boys to play with dolls and their girls to build with blocks.

A Toronto couple is taking this concept to a more controversial extreme by keeping the gender of their 4-month-old baby a secret. They have no plans to reveal whether their child named Storm is a boy or a girl. They say it will be up to Storm to deliver the news when he (or she) is old enough and ready.

The parents, Kathy Witterick, 38, and David Stocker, 39, hope to raise their child in a world that's "unconstrained by social norms about males and females," according to the *Toronto Star*. They want their child to freely grow into his (or her) own person and to find his (or her) true self unhindered by gender stereotypes.

Only a handful of people know whether baby Storm is a boy or a girl: the parents, of course; Storm's brothers, Jazz, 5, and Kio, 2; a close family friend; and the two midwives who delivered Storm at home in a birthing tub.

You might assume Storm's appearance would give the gender away, but photographs posted on the *Toronto Star* depict a blonde-haired baby that looks no more like a boy than like a girl—there's really no way of telling. The parents mix up the pronouns they use when referring to their child. They dress Storm in pink one day and blue the next, and often the baby is wearing gender-neutral colors like red. What's more, Storm's longhaired brothers are often wearing more girlish colors and they're mistaken for females.

The parents alerted friends and family of their idea to keep Storm's gender under wraps in an email: "We've decided not to share Storm's sex for now—a tribute to freedom and choice in place of limitation, a stand up to what the world could become in Storm's lifetime (a more progressive place? . . .)."

Their announcement was met with mixed reactions. The grandparents were slow to warm up to the idea. Many friends were supportive but a few were confused, even angered. Some feared that Storm would grow into a child who's bullied by peers.

Reactions in the Internet world have been equally conflicted. Some criticize the parents for treating their child like a lab rat and others applaud their efforts to fight against societal pressures. Many point out studies indicating that male and girl behaviors are influenced by prenatal development, not only by societal pressures. They say boys will go after toys that are stereotypically male even if you push dolls on them.

Over at BabyCenter, one reader chimes in: "I see this backfiring in the future when the kid is confused as hell going through puberty and the social outcast throughout their life. You can have a girl and let her play with doll and truck and roll in the mud and not pressure her to 'act' like a girl. And little boys can enjoy playing dress up and playing with dolls too. We are given our gender for a reason and if we were meant to be neutral we'd all be hermaphrodites."

At Babble, one reader writes in: "I think there are great points to what this family is doing, I wouldn't be able to keep my baby's gender a secret, but it's not for me to judge this families choice to raise their children in what seems like a loving, healthy way."

Is it possible to raise a gender neutral child? Do you think the parents are helping Storm or just messing the child up by keeping his (or her) gender a secret?

Note: Graff (2012).

http://blog.sfgate.com/sfmoms/2011/05/24/canadian-couple-wont-reveal-childs-gender/

Gender Differences in Abilities and Behavior

There is greater variation within each sex than between sexes in most characteristics (Costa, Terracciano, and McCrae 2001). This means that gender differences in anything are rarely as large as people presume them to be. Most gender differences reported within the academic literature are small and vary in magnitude with the setting in which the research was conducted (Hyde 1990; Maccoby and Jacklin 1974).

Bearing this in mind, here are a few of the observed gender differences reported in the research literature. This research was conducted mainly by psychologists, who are more likely than sociologists to study cognitive abilities:

- Men do better than women on tests of math and science ability. Men also tend to have better spatial abilities than women and thus perform better on mental rotation tasks (Halpern 2004) like the one shown in Figure 6.1.

- Women outperform their male counterparts on tests of verbal ability (Halpern 2004).

FIGURE 6.1

Examples of pairs of figures presented to subjects in a mental rotation experiment (Shepard and Metzler 1971). The two figures in panel A are the same, as are the two figures in panel B. They are simply presented from different vantage points and can be rotated so that they look exactly the same. The two figures in panel C are different. Even with rotation, these two figures will never match.

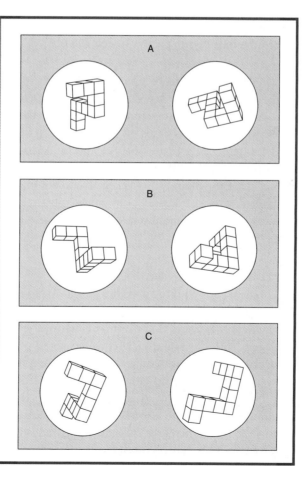

- Men are more aggressive than women (Bettencourt and Miller 1996). However, contrary to conventional wisdom, there is no experimental evidence that women are kinder or more cooperative than men (Balliet et al. 2011).

Many psychologists posit that gender differences in abilities and behaviors are due to a combination of biological and social influences. Although sociological social psychologists do not deny the existence of biologically based differences between the sexes, they believe that the social environment (nurture) has a much more significant impact on perception, ability, and behavior than biology (nature). This is, in fact, a central tenet of the discipline of sociology. The following bodies of literature support this position.

Evidence That Gender Socialization Begins at Birth

Because socialization begins at birth, it is impossible to disentangle the effects of nature from those of nurture on people's thoughts and actions. However, the literature on gender socialization suggests that boys and girls are raised very differently and that this has important consequences for their development, which lends support to the nurture perspective (Block 1983).

Q: You might have heard that the brains of men and women look different when they are viewed using scanning devices. Does that mean that gender differences in cognitive abilities are biologically based?

A: Recent studies based on magnetic resonance imaging (MRI) do show some gender differences in brain structure and function, which may underlie gender differences in spatial skills and mathematical ability. It is, however, important to remember that the brain is highly reactive to environmental stimuli. Although there is a tendency to regard gender difference in brain structure and operation as innate or hardwired, they could just as easily be due to gender differences in social experiences (Hyde 2007).

TWO CLASSIC STUDIES

Two of the most well-known studies pertaining to early socialization focused on the impact of infants' genders on the ways adults perceived them. Rubin, Provenzano, and Luria (1974) found that parents evaluated their newborn children in a manner consistent with prevailing societal beliefs about gender. Male infants were rated as more alert, stronger, and more coordinated than female infants, who tended to be viewed as softer, finer, and littler, especially by fathers. This was despite the fact that hospital records indicated no gender differences in infants' size or birth weight.

In a related experiment focusing on the impact of gender labels, Condry and Condry (1976) had college students evaluate a nine-month old infant's reactions to various stimuli. Half of the subjects, determined at random, were led to believe that the infant was male. The other subjects were led to believe that the infant was female. All subjects were then shown a videotape in which the infant encountered four stimuli: a teddy bear, a buzzer, a doll, and a jack-in-the-box.

Whether subjects thought the infant was male or female did not influence their ratings of the child's reactions to either the teddy bear or the buzzer. It was fairly clear that the infant showed a positive response to the teddy bear (smiling and laugher) and a negative (fear) response to the buzzer. The infant's reaction to the jack-in-the-box was the most ambiguous, and it was interpreted within the context of the gender label.

The child in the film reacted to the jack-in-the box with increased agitation and, finally, by crying. Whereas subjects who believed the infant was female tended to interpret this response as fear, the students who believed the infant was male thought this reaction was indicative of anger. As noted by the study authors, this shows that simply knowing the gender of a child can influence how his or her behavior is perceived.

CONTEMPORARY PATTERNS

Contemporary analyses suggest that things have changed some since the 1970s. For example, in their study of expectant parents, Plant and associates (2000) found that only men who embraced gender stereotypes concerning the experience and expression of emotion were more likely to interpret a male, versus a female, infant's ambiguous expressions as anger. However, Plant and associates (2000) also found that college students interpreted adults' displays of emotion in gender-stereotyped ways. Slides of the same ambiguous poses mixing anger and sadness tended to be interpreted as anger when the target was male and as sadness when the target was female. Moreover, female (but not male) targets expressing anger were often viewed as sad.

A second sample of college students showed support for cultural stereotypes concerning gender differences in the frequency with which people experience various emotions. With the exception of anger and pride, these individuals believed that women experience and express emotions more frequently than men. The emotions considered more common among women included awe, disgust, fear, sadness, happiness, love, surprise, shyness, sympathy, and guilt (Plant et al. 2000).

The belief that there are gender differences in emotive experiences is likely to shape the ways parents interact with their infants. Parents may expect young girls to be more socially connected. Mutual gazing (looking directly at someone) is one sign of social engagement. Gender differences in this behavior emerge at between 13 and 18 weeks of age. These differences are not evident at the time of birth, suggesting that mutual gazing is learned as children interact with parents and other individuals, and not innate (Leeb and Rejskind 2004).

Language, acquired largely through social interaction within the family, is also an important component of early gender role socialization, as it plays a significant role in the formation of gender identity. The use of the labels "boy" and "girl" facilitate the child's emerging awareness of gender categories and are associated with participation in "gender-appropriate" behaviors (Cahill 1983, 1986), including gender-typed play.

Prior to the point at which children become aware of gender categories (before the age of 17 months), the selection of activities and toys is notably less gendered than it is after gender self-labeling occurs (Zosuls et al. 2009). For example, both boys and girls prefer dolls to toy cars at one year of age. By 18 months, the time frame during which children become aware of gender categories and their associated expectations, boys show a clear preference for cars over dolls. This pattern is consistent with a nurture (versus nature) explanation (Jadva, Hines, and Golombok 2010).

Social psychologists have also pointed to the role of toys in the socialization of gender roles (e.g., Pomerleau et al. 1990). In general, "boys" toys promote active exploration and innovation, whereas "girls" toys promote a concern with appearance and caring behaviors (Blakemore, Owen, and Centers 2005).

What Do You Think?

List three to five popular toys designed for boys and three to five popular toys designed for girls.

- What types of attitudes and behaviors do these toys reinforce?
- Get together with two or three of your classmates to see how much your lists overlap. Note how many of you played with these, or other, gender-typed toys.

Buying toys for children is a taken-for-granted activity that rarely involves reflection on its potential consequences. Thus, parents and other individuals who purchase toys for children may not consider whether they reflect their values and beliefs about gender (Nelson 2005). In describing contemporary culture, Fine (2010) argues that we live in a "half-changed world," in which parents have "half-changed minds" when it comes to gender. Empirical studies confirm this kind of ambiguity among 21st-century parents and make a distinction between perception and practice.

Although many parents regard gendered toys as inappropriate, they are more likely to select gender-stereotyped than gender-neutral toys when they play with children, especially boys (Wood, Desmarais, and Gugula 2002). Similarly, many contemporary parents embrace non-gender-stereotyped characteristics in their children, but they temper this with concerns about gender-inappropriate behavior, especially when it comes to their sons. The messages boys receive concerning the appropriateness of their behaviors often include explicit rejections of "icons of femininity" such as stereotypically female toys and clothing. Moreover, whereas girls are encouraged to participate in a wide range of activities traditionally considered to be masculine, boys are encouraged to engage in stereotypically feminine activities in only three areas: empathy; nurturing; and domestic tasks, in particular cooking (Kane 2006).

It is also clear that parents still have different sets of expectations for their sons and daughters when it comes to the distribution of household tasks. On average, girls spend about 30% more time than boys on household chores (eight vs. five hours per week), and they are less likely than boys to be paid for cleaning and cooking (University of Michigan Institute for Social Research 2007). These differences reflect the gendered division of domestic labor among adults and persist despite the fact that gender-role attitudes have become substantially more egalitarian in recent years (Brooks and Bolzendahl 2004).

Gender Differences in Children's Peer Relationships

As children mature, they develop relationships with individuals outside of the family and peers, in particular, become increasingly influential in the socialization process. Schools, preschools, and daycare centers facilitate the creation and maintenance of peer cultures by providing opportunities for children to interact regularly and to build friendships. They also serve as agents of gender socialization when they provide activities that reinforce gendered attitudes and behaviors. For example, sports such as football place a high value on toughness and physical aggression, characteristics of the traditional male role. On the other hand, female-dominated activities like cheerleading place a high value on attributes associated with traditional conceptions of femininity, including physical attractiveness, and emphasize sexuality, as well as athletic prowess.

Sports, cheerleading, and other extracurricular activities often form the basis for peer group membership. When they do so, they tend to facilitate patterns of social interaction that both mirror and produce macro-level social inequalities based on gender, as well social class and race (Adams and Bettis 2003; Eder and Parker 1987). However, structured extracurricular activities, and the values and behaviors they cultivate, are not usually prominent features of students' lives until the middle or high school years.

Perhaps the most distinct feature of young children's peer groups is that they tend to be gender segregated (Thorne 1993). This reflects children's early recognition of gender as an important organizing category (Corsaro and Fingerson 2006). Beginning in elementary school, girls tend to progress through a series of best friends, emotionally intimate relationships centered on self-disclosure and empathy. Boys, on the other hand, interact in larger groups. Within this context, peer relationships center on physical activities, in particular sports.

Gender differences in the kinds of interactions children have with their peers may give rise to different cognitive styles. There is some evidence that girls are more adept at taking the role of a specific other, an ability that emerges in the play stage, whereas boys are more proficient in the application of general rules and principles (the generalized other), an ability that emerges through participation in complex games (Lever 1976). (Note: We discuss children's friendships and the interactional processes through which individuals develop expectations for their romantic relationships in detail in Chapter 11.)

PHOTO 6.3

In middle and high school structured extra-curricular activities often reflect prevailing gender roles. Adolescents who participate in these activities are learning how to present themselves as males or females. They are learning how to "do gender."

PHOTO 6.4

Young children's peer interactions are often gender segregated. Through interaction with same-sex peers, boys and girls acquire different sets of expectations and skills.

CONSEQUENCES

A related literature suggests that there is a notable gender difference in perspective taking among adults. Perspective taking is often measured using items from Davis's (1980, 1983) Interpersonal Reactivity Index (IRI). The IRI measures the frequency with which individuals' take the perspective, or role, of another individual, a capacity that emerges in the play stage of development.

The IRI is presented in Box 6.5. Go ahead and compute your score. The higher your score, the more likely you are to engage in perspective taking. Benchmarks for a college sample are provided by gender for comparison.

Note that a related measure, the public self-consciousness scale, was presented in Chapter 3. Both public self-consciousness and perspective taking are traits presumed to transcend any particular interactive encounter and were, not surprisingly, developed by psychologists. Because most symbolic interactionists are qualitative in orientation and focus on socialization processes (e.g., how gender roles are acquired) over socialization outcomes (e.g., gender differences in perception or behavior), they are less concerned with these kinds of stable dispositional characteristics. Nonetheless, these attributes have applicability to the primary socialization process, as outlined by Mead and other symbolic interactionists.

The public self-consciousness scale measures reflexive role taking—the degree to which people recognize that they will be evaluated by others in the social encounters. As you may recall, there are no gender differences in public self-consciousness. However, the perspective taking items in Box 6.5 yield higher scores among women

Box 6.5   Measuring Perspective Taking

For each item below, please indicate how well it describes you by choosing the appropriate number on the following scale.

```
      0———————————1———————————2———————————3———————————4
Does not describe me well                              Describes me very well
```

Item	Response
1. I sometimes find it difficult to see things from the "other guy's" point of view.*	_____
2. I try to look at everybody's side of a disagreement before I make a decision.	_____
3. I sometimes try to understand my friends better by imagining how things look from their perspective.	_____
4. If I'm sure I'm right about something, I don't waste much time listening to other people's arguments.*	_____
5. I believe that there are two sides to every question, and I try to look at them both.	_____
6. When I'm upset with someone, I usually try to "put myself in his shoes" for a while.	_____
7. Before criticizing somebody, I try to imagine how I would feel if I were in their place.	_____
*Total Score	_____

*Items number 1 and 4 should be reverse coded before you compute your score on the perspective-taking index. This is necessary because someone who says these statements describe them well (e.g., they respond with a 4 to each question) is not someone who readily takes the perspective of other people. This is the opposite of what a high score means for each of the other five statements. Reverse coding these items means changing the scores in the following manner: 1 = 4, 2 = 3, 3 = 2, 4 = 1. For example, if you answered question 4 with a 4, give yourself a score of 1 in the space provided. If you responded with a 3, give yourself a 2, and so forth. Questions in an index are often worded like this in order to minimize the bias that occurs when someone answers all of the questions in the same way without really reading them.

Scores among a College Sample

Males (n = 579):   Mean = 16.8   SD = 4.7
Females (n = 582):   Mean = 18.0   SD = 4.9

Source: Davis (1980)

than among men (Davis 1980; O'Brien et al. 2013). This suggests that women engage in role taking more frequently than their male counterparts. From a symbolic interactionist perspective, women demonstrate what is called a propensity for role taking. **Role-taking propensity** refers to the readiness with which people use their role-taking skills. Interestingly, given women's greater propensity for role taking, men and women are equally adept role takers. That is, they are equally effective role takers when they choose to put this skill to use (Schwalbe 1991a).

Gender differences in peer interaction, and the types of activities the characterize children's peer cultures, are the likely root of the observed difference in role-taking propensity. Symbolic interactionists do not deny that human social behavior has a biological component (Mead's "I"). However, they do feel that it is people's social experiences, and not biological factors, that shape the self, perception, and behavior.

Cross-Cultural Research

Cross-cultural studies offer additional evidence that gender differences in perception and behavior are learned rather than innate. In her classic study of gender in New Guinea, the anthropologist Margaret Mead found notable differences in the characteristics of men and women across tribes (Mead 1935). Other, more recent analyses also show substantial variation in what are regarded as gendered personality characteristics (e.g., assertiveness among men and warmth among women) and cognitive skills (e.g., spatial and mathematical abilities), as well as in gender roles, across societies (Costa, Terracciano, and McCrae 2001; Else-Quest, Hyde, and Linn 2010; Hoffman, Gneezy, and List 2011; Nanda 1999).

Moral Reasoning

Through social interaction, within the family and later in school and with peers, children also acquire a sense of a morality. **Morality** is a conceptualization of what is good or right and bad or wrong. **Moral reasoning** is the ability to determine right from wrong and to evaluate actions and their likely consequences. Because this cognitive skill underlies the self-regulation of behavior, the development of the capacity for moral reasoning is regarded as one of the most important outcomes of the primary socialization process.

According to Kohlberg (1969, 1976), children develop the capacity for moral reasoning in a series of hierarchical stages. These stages, which build upon Piaget's model of cognitive development described earlier, occur at three more general levels of reasoning: preconventional, conventional, and postconventional.

Children at the preconventional level make moral decisions based on the desire to avoid punishment from someone in a position of authority. At the second, conventional level, moral reasoning is based on meeting the expectations of others and the social consequences of action. Finally, postconventional morality, the most sophisticated level of moral reasoning, emphasizes the recognition of individual rights and conformity to shared standards and duties.

The following examples illustrate these distinctions:

- **Preconventional morality**: Don't commit murder because you could be sent to prison if you kill someone.

- **Conventional morality**: Murder is wrong because it violates the expectations of others and will have negative consequences for the family members and friends of the victim.

- **Postconventional morality**: Murder is wrong because taking a human life is a harmful act that violates internalized societal standards.

Kohlberg argued that females presented with hypothetical moral dilemmas tend to reason at the conventional level, whereas males tend to respond to these dilemmas by employing postconventional logic. Thus, from this perspective, men have a more highly developed sense of morality than their female counterparts.

In her classic book *In a Different Voice,* the psychologist Carol Gilligan (1982) challenges Kohlberg's notion that men have superior moral reasoning abilities than women. She argues that men and women tend to approach moral dilemmas differently, but one way is not superior to another. Women, she argues, tend to apply the morality of caring. The **morality of caring** emphasizes the social consequences of action (conventional moral reasoning) and requires the ability to take the role of a specific other. It requires viewing a moral dilemma within context and considering factors relevant to that specific situation. Alternatively, men favor the application of the morality of justice. The **morality of justice** involves the application of general rules and standards (postconventional moral reasoning), without regard for specific situational factors. It requires an assessment of the situation from the perspective of the generalized other.

The origin or these differences, according to Gilligan (1982), is early socialization and differential participation in play activities versus games. This argument is a direct application of Mead's symbolic interactionism. Girls, who spend more time than boys honing their ability to take the role of a specific other in the play stage, more readily apply this skill when facing moral quandaries. In contrast, boys, who spend more time in the game stage, hone their ability to take the role of the generalized other and regularly exercise this skill through the application of general societal rules when faced with moral dilemmas.

Gilligan's claims are contentious. Some studies offer support for this distinction, whereas others fail to find any notable gender differences in moral reasoning. A systematic analysis of studies on moral reasoning suggests that there is an association between gender and the manner in which people approach moral dilemmas. Gender explains about 16% of the variation in research participants' application of the morality of caring, and about 17% of the variability in their use of the morality of justice, across studies (Jaffee and Hyde 2000). The rest (over 80%) of the variation in the use of the two styles of moral reasoning across research subjects is related to factors other than gender. These factors include the nature of the moral dilemma (presented to subjects vs. self-generated) and the social context within which the moral problem was rooted (e.g., a work vs. a family setting) (Clopton and Sorell 1993).

In everyday life, moral reasoning involves balancing competing impulses to act in different ways in particular social contexts. That is, it involves an interaction between the "I" (impulse) and the "me" (social expectations, brought into awareness through the process of role taking). In most situations, people take multiple roles and choose actions that are aligned with these competing perspectives. This means that they must simultaneously employ both the morality of caring and justice. It also suggests that moral reasoning has a behavioral, as well as a cognitive, component (Schwalbe 1991b).

Have you ever done something when you were with your friends that you felt was wrong? Most of us have at one time or another. When adolescents act in a manner that is acceptable to other group members, even if their behavior is in opposition to their personal standards or broader societal norms, we say they are subject to peer pressure. Often this type of behavior is rationalized by focusing on one's loyalty to his or her friendship group, which provides guidelines for behavior (norms) that supersede those acquired within the family or in other institutional contexts (Sykes and Matza 1957). This shift in allegiance, from, for example, family to friends, occurs over time as group members construct meanings through their face-to-face interactions. Symbolic interactionists study the processes through which adolescents, and members of other social categories, acquire moral codes that are distinct from those of the larger society. We discuss some of these studies in Chapter 9.

Focusing on patterns of behavior at the macro level, SSP researchers have pointed to the link between societal characteristics and morality. In capitalist societies, for example, the emphasis placed on maximizing profits may inhibit moral action among individuals seeking to increase their economic gains (Schwalbe 1988). The structure of the organization within which people work may also hinder, or promote, morally responsible behavior, independent of the characteristics of individual actors (Chambliss 1996; Vandenburgh 1999).

Children and the Media

Children in the United States watch a lot of television—on average, about 15 hours per week (University of Michigan Institute for Social Research 2007). Whether viewing violence on television puts children at risk for aggressive behavior is a question of interest to social psychologists. Because they focus on role modeling, studies that address this issue can be considered to be within the social learning tradition, described earlier in the chapter.

There is some evidence that exposure to violent video clips desensitizes subjects by making them less emotionally reactive to this type of behavior (e.g., Krahe et al. 2011). However, these studies pertain only to reactions within the laboratory. Surveys focusing on people's actual viewing behavior suggest that media exposure has little effect on aggression. Without added information about individuals' reactions to the material encountered, the amount of time spent watching violent television

PHOTO 6.5

Children spend a lot of their time watching television and often incorporate what they see into their play activities with peers.

programs has a negligible effect on aggressive behavior among either males or females (Paik and Comstock 1994; Wood, Wong, and Chachere 1991).

There is, however, some evidence that viewing violent television in childhood increases adults' risk for aggression under certain conditions. Children who (1) identify with same-sex television characters who engage in violence and (2) perceive the television violence as realistic may be at risk for aggressive behavior later in life. In one high-profile study, the researchers collected data on how many hours children ages 6-9 spent watching television, how much they acted like aggressive adult characters they had seen on television programs (character identification), and how real they thought the violence they saw on television was (perceived realism). Viewing time, character identification, and perceived realism explained about 10% of the variation in the study participants' levels of aggression fifteen years later, when they were in their early twenties (Huesmann et al. 2003). This means that 90% of the variation in aggression among the study participants when they were in their early twenties was due to factors unrelated to their exposure to television violence during childhood.

A series of related studies show that time spent playing violent video games explains close to 4% of the variation in aggressive behavior (Anderson et al. 2010). This suggests that 96% of the variation in aggressive behavior across individuals is due to characteristics and experiences other than exposure to violent video games.

Note that this (4%) is quite a bit less than the effect of gender on moral reasoning (about 17%), discussed earlier in the chapter. To give you another benchmark, alcohol use explains about 50% of the variation in aggression among 16-year-olds (Huang et al. 2001). As illustrated by this comparison, the quantitative literature on media exposure and violence provides little evidence that this is a pressing social problem.

However, symbolic interactionist and interpretive approaches to the study of the role of the media in the primary socialization process suggest that these kinds of analyses may be too narrow in focus to capture the various ways the media might influence young children and adolescents. From this perspective, peer cultures provide the link between the content of television and films and children's perceptions and behaviors, which may not include explicit acts of violence. Through interactions with peers, children routinely transform information from the media, which may include violent imagery, to fit their ongoing concerns. Children may not imitate the violence they see on television or in films. However, given its pervasiveness, this imagery is likely to become a part of their peer culture in one way or another.

SECONDARY SOCIALIZATION

Not all socialization occurs in childhood. Symbolic interactionist analyses of secondary (i.e., adult) socialization processes have focused mainly on professional educational or work contexts. Professional socialization reflects pressures to conform rooted in institutional norms and participants' desires for social prestige. It is within this context that superiors (supervisors or teachers) reshape individuals by reinforcing particular sets of values and norms (Mortimer and Simmons 1978).

Some of this process occurs informally. In most organizations, there is a lot for any new employee to learn that is not in the company handbook. This information is acquired only through interaction with others, including peers.

Have you ever had a job where there were sets of informal rules that governed workers' behaviors? In companies without a formal dress code, for example, it is likely that there are norms concerning dress that must be learned through interaction with and observation of others. There may also be norms governing the exchange of gifts on holidays and birthdays. These are not written anywhere, and this may be something that no one thinks to tell the newbie. It is only by spending time there and talking informally with others that new hires learn what is acceptable behavior among individuals in their unit or division.

Similarly, in graduate school, a lot of learning takes place outside of the classroom. For example, as a graduate student in sociology, you learn what it means to be a teacher and a researcher. You learn how to interact with undergraduates by serving as a teaching assistant and how to prepare for and act at professional conferences. This is something that is missing from online master's or PhD programs, where interaction between students and between students and faculty is of a more limited nature.

Life Course Research

Studies on secondary socialization within the life course tradition focus on people's experiences as they age. These analyses focus on role transitions (e.g., marriage, parenthood, and retirement); on the unique experiences of particular generations; and on developmental stages and the attitudes, values, and behaviors that accompany them.

Role Transitions

Role transitions occur when people either exit a role they have occupied for some time (e.g., retirement) or enter into a new role (e.g., becoming a college student, getting married, or having a child). Entering a new role often involves a process of **anticipatory socialization**, during which people start thinking and acting like someone who occupies the role they are planning to transition into. For example, expectant parents who start reading parenting books and buying infant clothing and toys are undergoing an anticipatory socialization process.

Parenthood is an important role transition. Although becoming a parent is often a positive experience, it can have negative connotations when it is unplanned or it occurs before other role transitions, such as entrance into the workforce or marriage (Jackson 2004).

Similarly, retirement is often perceived as stressful when it is sudden and occurs without adequate preparation. Even when retirement is planned, it can lead to declines in psychological well-being if people have poor health or financial concerns. This means the retirement years are often more difficult for individuals who are poor and for racial/ethnicity minorities. Minority status is associated with financial hardship across the life course (Flippen and Tienda 2000; Hogan and Perrucci 1998). Having too few economic resources is a major contributor to both psychological distress and physical health problems (Kahn and Fazio 2005; Travis and Velasco 1994; Williams et al. 1997). Thus, racial and ethnic minorities may find the postretirement years more difficult than Whites.

In general, the ease with which individuals adapt to role transitions, including the movement into parenthood or retirement, is influenced by the following five factors:

1. The rewards offered by the new and old roles;

2. The clarity of the norms associated with the new role;

3. The visibility of new roles to others within society;

4. The extent to which transitions are supported by broader social institutions (e.g., the family, education, and the economy);

5. The compatibility between old and new roles (Mortimer and Simmons 1978).

You might consider some of the role transitions you have experienced. Most notable, perhaps, is the movement from high school student to college student. Those of you who took college courses while you were in high school, or worked on developing new study strategies likely to enhance your college performance, were engaging in behaviors designed to ease your transition into the college student role as part of an anticipatory socialization process.

"College student" is a fairly visible role within families and society at large, and it offers many social and economic rewards. Moreover, transitioning into the role of college student is couched within relationships between high schools and colleges and universities (e.g., high school guidance counselors provide students with information about colleges and college admissions counselors often recruit at area highs schools). The transition from high school student to college student has also been routinized. There are standard application deadlines and testing requirements; students make campus visits and, once they have committed to a particular school, attend orientation sessions; and so forth. Finally, there is at least some consistency in the behaviors expected of high school and college students (e.g., attending class, studying, taking exams, and socializing with fellow students). All of these factors make the transition from high school to college seem relatively natural. The transition from high school to work is likely to seem much more drastic.

What Do You Think?

Form a group with two or three of your classmates. Discuss the following questions.

- Do students share a common set of expectations about what they should, and should not, be doing? Is there agreement on this issue within your group?
- Do professors share college students' understanding of the student role? What about parents? What do professors and parents expect from college students? Give some examples.

What can you conclude based on your group members' responses? Is the college student role clearly defined? How might this affect the ease with which people make the transition from high school to college student?

Cohort Effects

SSP researchers who study the life course also consider how both the contexts and meanings of socialization vary across age cohorts. Family roles have changed tremendously over the past 50 years, with substantial increases in women's labor force participation, dual career families, and single-parent and blended families (Luftey and Mortimer 2006). These differences explain some of the differences in attitudes, values, and behaviors across generations. In particular, individuals in the Millennial Generation (born 1981–2000) are less likely to value having a successful marriage, place a higher value on being a good parent, and are more optimistic about the state of the nation than previous generations (Taylor and Keeter 2009).

Sociological social psychologists working within the life course tradition are interested in the experiences of young adults in relation to their broader sociohistorical context. In the 1950s and 1960s, the average age of marriage was 23 for men and 20 for women. Today, men, on average, marry at the age of 29 and women at 27 (U.S. Census Bureau 2011). Furthermore, college enrollments have more than quadrupled in the last 60 years (Jamieson, Curry, and Martinez 1999). Currently, over 50% of individuals between the ages of 18 and 21 are college undergraduates (U.S. Bureau of the Census 2010). These demographic shifts have had a substantial impact on the identities and behaviors of contemporary youths (Johnson, Crosnoe, and Elder 2011).

EMERGING ADULTHOOD: A NEW DEVELOPMENTAL STAGE

By the 1970s, it was widely acknowledged that adolescence was expanding (Furstenberg 2008). It was within this context that a new developmental stage, called emerging adulthood (Arnett 2000), came into being. **Emerging adulthood** spans from the end of high school into the midtwenties. In emerging adulthood, individuals straddle adolescence and mature adulthood. A reflection of demographic changes such as those described in the preceding paragraph in the United States and other Western societies, emerging adulthood is characterized by identity exploration; instability; financial dependence; low social control; and a propensity for risk behaviors, including substance abuse (Arnett 2000, 2005; Arnett and Taber 1994).

The use of alcohol and other drugs may serve ritual functions within this context (Hawdon 2005; Wolburg 2001). In less developed societies, the transition from adolescence to adulthood is marked by formalized rites of passage (Van Gennep 1960). Rites of passage involve three stages through which individuals become segregated from and then reintegrated into the larger social system. It is during the second phase of the rite of passage, the liminal stage, during which individuals are separated from and perceived as distinct from the broader society, that societal norms lose much of their regulatory power (Van Gennep 1960; Turner 1969).

College students clearly occupy a **liminal status**. A liminal status is an interstructural position because it is "betwixt and between" two statuses that occur in a developmental sequence (e.g., adolescence and adulthood) (Turner 1969). As emerging adults, college students have more freedom than adolescents, but they have yet to enter into mature adult roles. Thus, they experience a temporary suspension of the rules of conduct that apply to other members of society. This lack of constraint, as well as the communal living arrangements typical of traditional college students, has created a social environment conducive to high rates of binge drinking (Butler 1993; Crawford and Novak 2006).

Binge drinking is defined as four or more drinks in one sitting for females and five or more drinks in a sitting for males (Wechsler and Toben 2001). Despite its negative long-term effects on people's brains (Hermens et al. 2013), binge drinking is common at this nation's colleges and universities. It is estimated that 45% of college under-graduates engage in this practice (Hingson et al. 2009). As a response to high levels of binge drinking and the rise in related accidents and alcohol-related deaths on college campuses, school administrations have implemented various programs designed to reduce the prevalence of this behavior, with some success (Saltz 2004/2005).

Although it is not commonly recognized as a remedy for the high levels of alcohol abuse on college campuses, there is some evidence that service requirements reduce student drinking (Weitzman and Chen 2005; Weitzman and Kawachi 2000). Presumably these types of commitments counter the lack of social constraint asso-ciated with liminality by facilitating students' integration into more mature adult society (Crawford and Novak 2006). Many students reduce their levels of alcohol consumption after they graduate from college and transition into adult roles, such as work, marriage, and parenthood (Bachman et al. 1997; Christie-Mizell and Peralta 2009; Miller-Tutzauer, Leonard, and Windle 1991). Similarly, college undergraduates who report that they are ready for adult role obligations exhibit lower levels of alco-hol use and heavy drinking than their peers (Blinn-Pike et al. 2008; Willoughby and Dworkin 2009). Future research is needed to assess the nature of the anticipatory socialization process through which students prepare for adult roles and its implica-tions for college drinking.

What Do You Think?

Why do college students drink? Think about the people you know at your school. Is drinking less common among those individuals with additional role responsibilities associated with internships, full-time jobs, leadership roles in campus organizations, or family responsibilities (e.g., taking care of chil-dren)? If you use alcohol, would you drink less if you had more structured role responsibilities?

CHAPTER SUMMARY

Socialization is an important topic within sociological social psychology because, from this perspective, virtually everything we know is learned. Symbolic interaction-ists are especially interested in the process of primary socialization, through which the self and mind develop. The research literature on socialization addresses this and other issues. This literature is broad in scope and expands disciplines (sociology, psychology, and anthropology), as well as faces of sociological social psychology (symbolic interactionism and SSP). These studies have demonstrated the importance of the environment (nurture) in shaping perceptions and behaviors across the life course. It is through interaction with others that children acquire the knowledge and skills required for participation in society. Proximate social contexts (e.g., work or school), as well as the larger society, within which interaction occurs are also important in shaping adults' perceptions and behaviors.

Key Points to Know

- **Socialization is the process through which individuals acquire the knowledge and skills necessary for participation in society.** The literature on primary (childhood) socialization includes theories of child development focusing on personality, cognitive development, and the emergence of the self.

- **For symbolic interactionists, the development of the "me" phase of the self is the most significant aspect of the primary socialization process.** The "me" phase of the self, rooted in the ability to communicate using a language, develops as children progress through a series of stages. Role taking begins with imitation in the preparatory stage. Then, through interaction with peers, children learn how to take the role of a specific other during the play stage. In the subsequent game stage, they learn how to view themselves as objects from the perspective of society at large (the generalized other). The capacity for role taking allows for the self-regulation of behavior and thus makes society as we know it possible.

- **The interpretive approach to socialization emphasizes children's creative responses to inputs from the broader society.** Within the context of their peer cultures, children and adolescents may reproduce, modify, or challenge prevailing cultural beliefs, values, and norms.

- **Structural approaches to socialization focus on the link between parents' economic resources and children's experiences in the home and in schools.** Studies within this tradition have examined the relationship between parents' work experiences and how they interact with their children, as well as the link between children's socialization experiences and track placement. SSP researchers have also focused on the impact of parental divorce and poverty on children's opportunities, aspirations, and behaviors.

- **The nature-nurture question, central to the literature on primary socialization, is especially relevant to the subject of gender.** Some psychologists emphasize the role of nature (biology) in determining gender differences in perception and behavior. In contrast, symbolic interactionists, proponents of the interpretive approach, and SSP researchers emphasize the role of social factors, including relationships with parents and peers, in shaping these outcomes.

- **The research literature on gender socialization provides strong support for the nurture position.** Evidence that socialization begins at birth, as well as the results of studies on gender and peer relationships, support this perspective. Cross-cultural variation in gender roles is also consistent with the notion that gender differences in perception and behavior are socially based.

- **Given its impact on the self-regulation of behavior, moral development is a topic of substantial interest to social psychologists.** There are some gender differences in the manner in which people respond to hypothetical moral dilemmas. Women tend to focus more on the social consequences of action (the morality of caring) than men, who are more likely than women to consider broader societal standards (the morality of justice) when faced with moral questions. However, in most situations, both orientations come into play as people anticipate the reactions of specific others and society in general (the generalized other) before choosing a course of action.

- **Although social psychologists believe that the media is an important agent of socialization, there is little evidence of a direct link between media exposure and violence.** The impact of the media on children is more subtle and presumably operates through its effects on their peer cultures.

- **Secondary (or adult) socialization builds on the knowledge, beliefs, values, and norms acquired during primary socialization processes.** Research on secondary socialization has focused largely on adults' experiences in school, at work, and within the family.

- **Within the life course tradition, SSP researchers have focused on role transitions, the experiences of particular age cohorts or generations, and developmental stages such as emerging adulthood.** As emerging adults, contemporary college students occupy a transitional status. Thus, they experience less normative regulation than other individuals and are relatively free to engage in risk behaviors such as binge drinking. Service requirements may reduce binge drinking on college campuses by integrating students into more mature adult society.

Terms and Concepts for Review

Agents of socialization	Peer culture
Anticipatory socialization	Personality
Conventional morality	Play stage
Ego	Postconventional morality
Emerging adulthood	Preparatory stage
Feral children	Primary socialization
Game stage	Preconventional morality

Terms and Concepts for Review (*Continued*)

Generalized other	Role modeling
Id	Role taking
Interpretive approach	Role-taking propensity
Interpretive reproduction	Role transition
Liminal status	Sapir-Whorf hypothesis
Material culture	Secondary socialization
Morality	Self
Morality of caring	Significant other
Morality of justice	Socialization
Moral reasoning	Social learning theory
Nature-nurture question	Superego
Nonmaterial culture	Vicarious, or indirect, reinforcement and punishment

Questions for Review and Reflection

1. Individuals with antisocial personality disorder (called sociopaths) appear to have little regard for other people. They commit murder, or engage in other violent acts, without seeming to understand how their behaviors affect others, or that they are in violation of societal norms. Discuss the potential social roots of these deficits with reference to the development of the "me" phase of the self.

2. What is the nature-nurture question and how does it relate to gender? Have you noticed any gender differences in the mind-sets or behaviors of the students at your school? If so, consider their origin. How would a sociological social psychologist explain these patterns?

3. What is secondary socialization? Where does secondary socialization usually occur? Drawing on your personal experiences, describe a setting where the individuals present experienced a notable shift in attitudes, values, or behaviors. How and why did these changes occur?

4. What were your parents doing when they were your age? What were they like? If you don't know from prior conversations, ask them. Compare their biographies to yours. Discuss the manner in which your experiences reflect recent demographic shifts and contemporary beliefs about the transition to adulthood.

CHAPTER 7

Self and Identity

These paintings were done by individuals with schizophrenia, a psychiatric disorder characterized by incoherent and irrational thoughts and behaviors. Individuals who suffer from schizophrenia often depict their disease as fragmenting or distorting their sense of themselves and reality (Wadeson and Carpenter 1976). Their perception, affect, and behavior lack stability and consistency. This is in contrast to nondisordered individuals, for whom the self organizes both thought and action into coherent and meaningful patterns.

SELF, SELF-CONCEPT, AND IDENTITY

As noted in earlier chapters, the self is a process of interaction between biology (the "I") and social expectations brought into awareness through role taking (the "me").

The self-concept is socially based and is the object of our self-reflections (the "me"). **Identity**, a related construct, serves as the basis upon which individuals categorize and present themselves. Identities are socially based and are part of the self-concept (Owens 2006).

Sociological social psychologists are interested in the content of people's self-concepts, including their identities, and how they shape their perceptions, emotions, and behaviors. From this perspective, the self-concept gives the stability and predictability to people's behaviors that serve as the basis for society.

We focus on the self, the self-concept, and identity in this chapter and illustrate why these topics are so important to social psychologists seeking to understand people's social experiences. The research we discuss in doing so is notably interdisciplinary. Unlike some of the topics covered in this book, the nature of the self and its consequences for everyday life are of interest to social psychologists trained in psychology, as well as in sociology. This is because the self is so fundamental to social life.

SELF-PERCEPTION AND AFFECT

A significant portion of the literature on the nature and function of the self focuses on people's self-concepts, how we come to view ourselves in particular ways, and the affective consequences of this social process.

The Looking-Glass Self

Charles Horton Cooley, an early contributor to the symbolic interactionist perspective, was one of the first social psychologists to discuss the link between social relationships and the content of the self-concept. According to Cooley (1902), other people serve as mirrors (called looking glasses at the time at which he was writing) in that they reflect images back to us. These images are called **reflected appraisals**.

For Cooley (1902), the **looking-glass self** is rooted in the following three processes:

1. We imagine how we appear to another individual.

2. We imagine how that person judges us.

3. We react to this perceived judgment with emotions such as pride or mortification.

Thus, from this perspective, our understanding of ourselves, who we are, our sense of our competencies and weaknesses, and our self-evaluations are shaped solely by the feedback we receive from others.

As you might imagine, not all reflected appraisals are given equal weight in defining the content of people's self-concepts. In general, reflected appraisals from individuals who are regarded as important, and whose opinions are valued, will be the most influential.

Imagine that you are getting ready to apply to graduate school or for your ideal job and the person who sits next to you in your senior seminar, whom you barely know, assures you that, because you're so smart, you're going to get in (graduate school) or get it (the job). This might make you feel good, but it's not likely to have as large of an effect on your evaluation of yourself as a similar statement made by your favorite professor.

Time is also of essence in the operation of the looking-glass self. Our self-concepts rarely change overnight, but they shift in content as we receive messages from others about who we are, how we are, and what we are, or are not, capable of achieving. Feedback that is pervasive and consistent will ultimately affect how one sees oneself.

What Do You Think?

How has your self-concept been influenced by the feedback you received from others? List the individuals whose assessments of you, either explicit or more subtle and never openly stated, have played a significant role in shaping your view of yourself.

When asked who has influenced how they see themselves, most people will list parents, teachers or coaches, and long-term friends as a key source of information about what they are like. This is because much of the content of our self-concepts is formed in childhood as a product of our early socialization experiences.

Self-Esteem

Expanding upon Cooley's earlier work, social psychologists use the term **self-esteem** to refer to an individual's overall, or global, self-evaluation. Self-esteem is typically measured on surveys using the Rosenberg Self-Esteem Scale (Rosenberg 1965). These items are presented in Box 7.1.

Sources of Self-Esteem

Self-esteem has three main sources: reflected appraisals, social comparisons, and self-perceptions. As suggested by Cooley, the messages about ourselves that we receive from others (reflected appraisals) are a primary source of an individual's sense of self-worth. We also compare ourselves to others (reference groups) and evaluate our characteristics and achievements within this context. Finally, we observe and

Box 7.1   The Rosenberg Self-Esteem Scale

Indicate the extent to which you agree or disagree with each statement using the following response options.

1 = Strongly agree
2 = Agree
3 = Disagree
4 = Strongly disagree

Item	Response
I feel that I am a person of worth, at least on an equal plan with others.	_____
I feel that I have a number of good qualities.	_____
All in all, I am inclined to feel that I am a failure.*	_____
I am able to do things as well as most other people.	_____
I feel I do not have much to be proud of.*	_____
I take a positive attitude toward myself.	_____
On the whole, I am satisfied with myself.	_____
I wish I could have more respect for myself.*	_____
I certainly feel useless at times.*	_____
At times I think I am no good at all.*	_____
Total score	_____

*Score needs to be reverse coded (4 = 1; 3 = 2; 2 = 3; 1 = 4) before total score is computed because high scores on these items in their original format mean low self-esteem.

Note: Adapted from Rosenberg (1965).

College student samples*

Mean = approximately 32
Range: 10–40

*Data are from multiple samples of college undergraduates (Gentile, Twenge, and Campbell 2010).

evaluate our own role performances. The outcomes of these kinds of self-assessments (self-perceptions) contribute to self-esteem primarily when they emerge in relation to situations over which people perceive at least some degree of control (Rosenberg and Pearlin 1978).

Structural Influences

In general, the effects of status characteristics on individuals' self-evaluations are smaller than what one might expect. Among adults, social class has a moderate (positive) effect on self-esteem, presumably because people feel personally responsible for their economic position (McMullin and Cairney 2004; Rosenberg and Pearlin 1978).

Insofar as they are even aware of class divisions, young children are less likely than adults to feel responsible for their economic status. Thus, self-esteem and class are unrelated among this age group (Rosenberg and Pearlin 1978).

Class and self-esteem are positively related among adolescents. However, self-esteem is more strongly associated with personal accomplishments (e.g., grades and a number of friends) than with parents' financial and employment status among individuals in this age range (Wiltfang and Scarbecz 1990). Similarly, characteristics like emotional stability and conscientiousness have a greater effect than income on self-esteem among young adults (Erol and Orth 2011).

Although gender differences in self-esteem are minimal among adults (Kling et al. 1999; Galambos, Barker, and Krahn 2006), adolescent males often exhibit higher self-esteem than adolescent females. This is the case across race/ethnicity, with one exception. Among African Americans, researchers have not observed a gender gap in self-esteem during adolescence (Bachman et al. 2011).

Social psychologists have speculated as to why this is the case. One common explanation focuses on body image. Concerns about body image increase with puberty (O'Dea and Abraham 1999). However, among adolescents, body image is inversely related to self-esteem mainly among White girls (Vogt Yuan 2010). Presumably this reflects cultural differences in appearance norms and definitions of attractiveness. Black girls, in particular, may be more likely than their White counterparts to receive positive messages about their bodies from family members and people in their local communities. These positive messages may make them less vulnerable to criticisms from others and media imagery (Franko and Roehrig 2011).

During adolescence, African Americans have the highest self-esteem, followed by Whites and Hispanics (Bachman et al. 2011). However, by the age of 30, Hispanics as well as African Americans have higher self-esteem than Whites (Erol and Orth 2011). Although these patterns refute the notion that the advantages associated with dominant group membership necessarily result in positive self-images, (if this were the case, Whites would have higher self-esteem than racial/ethnic minorities), racial/ethnic differences in self-esteem are relatively small. Moreover, the relationship between race/ethnicity and self-esteem is influenced by other status characteristics (e.g., class, age, and gender) (Bachman et al. 2011; Erol and Orth 2011; Gray-Little and Hafdahl 2000).

Interestingly, the belief that one will be evaluated based upon one's status characteristics, including race and gender, may have a bigger impact on self-esteem than the positions themselves. Adults who perceive that they are judged based upon their status characteristics have lower self-esteem than individuals who believe that they are evaluated based upon their personal attributes in various social settings. Evidently, being viewed as a member of a social category, rather than as an individual, erodes people's sense of distinctiveness, which has negative implications for how they feel about themselves (Jaret, Reitzes, and Shapkina 2005).

Self as a Cognitive Structure

Other approaches to the study of the content of people's self-concepts are more psychological in orientation. Before we say any more, read the following passage (verbatim from Smith and Swinney 1992:315–316). We'll explain its significance to our discussion of the self-concept before the end of this section.

The process is as easy as it is enjoyable.
This process can take anywhere from about 1 hour to all day.
The length of time depends on the elaborateness of the final product.
Only one substance is necessary for this process.
However, the substance must be quite abundant and of suitable consistency.
The substance is best used when it is fresh, as its lifespan can vary.
The lifespan varies depending on where the substance is located.
If one waits too long before using it, the substance may disappear.
This process is such that almost anyone can do it.
The easiest method is to compress the substance into a denser mass than it held it
    its original state.
This process gives a previously amorphous substance some structure.
Other substances can be introduced near the end of the process to add to the
    complexity of the final product.
These substances are not necessary.
However, many people find that they add to the desired effect.
At the end of the process, the substance is usually in a pleasing form.

Close your eyes and think about what you did last weekend for one minute. Now, without looking back at the previous paragraph, jot down everything you remember about the passage you just read on a separate sheet of paper. Were you able to remember what you read? Did it make sense?

What if you were told beforehand that the title for the passage was "Building a Snowman"? Reread the passage with that title in mind. Does it make sense now? Is it easier to remember its contents?

The time it takes to read the passage is notably less when individuals are initially given the title beforehand. They read it faster than individuals not provided with this information, and they have better recall of its different components. This is because the title activates a cognitive schema that pertains to the activity in question (snowman building) and information is encoded into and stored within that cognitive structure (Alba and Hasher 1983).

Interestingly, when people reflect back upon information that has been processed schematically, they often remember things that were not really there (Alba and Hasher 1983; Bransford and Johnson 1972; Smith and Swinney 1992). Thus, students who initially read the passage about building a snowman with the title given beforehand may remember aspects of this ritual that were not actually in the text they read (e.g., "You make eyes using coal."). This is how schemas work once they are activated.

After people integrate new information into that already stored within the relevant schema, they lose track of what was just encountered and what they already knew.

Whenever new information is received, processing it requires attention, description, and integration into our existing knowledge structures. This sequential process necessarily involves the activation of cognitive schemas, like the schema for building a snowman from our previous example. Your schema for building a snowman is likely to be activated whenever you encounter information that you recognize as relevant to this activity, and this schema will affect how this information is processed.

People have **self-schemata**, composed of information stored in memory about their personal attributes, which facilitate the processing of information of relevance to the self. Much of the research on the self and schematic processing has been conducted by social psychologists trained as psychologists because it focuses on factors within the individual (attention and information processing).

How Self-Schemata Function

The content of self-schemata is built up over time as people categorize and evaluate their social behaviors. An important part of the self-concept, self-schemas may pertain to specific situations or events (e.g., attending class or a rock concert) or traits (e.g., intelligence or shyness). As such, self-schemata contain images, as well as verbal descriptions.

Once people have developed a self-schema in a particular domain they make quick and certain judgments about themselves in that area; have a good memory for information pertaining to that area; resist self-relevant information that is in opposition to the content of that schema; and evaluate new information in terms of its relevance to that schema. Thus, information that does not fit well within the realm of our existing self-schemata is often disregarded. It is not processed, categorized, or stored in long-term memory (Markus 1980). The implication of this is that people's views of themselves tend to be reinforced even in the face of contradictory information or feedback.

Research suggests that some people have self-schemata that are chronically accessible. They are high in a form of self-awareness called private self-consciousness (Fenigstein et al. 1975).

The survey questions used to measure **private self-consciousness** (or private self-awareness) are presented in Box 7.2. Individuals who score high in this measure tend to be highly aware of their internal states, including their thoughts and their emotions. Thus, they regularly scrutinize themselves, their feelings, and their motivations. Complete the Private Self-Consciousness Scale and see how you compare to other college students.

Private self-consciousness is associated with public self-consciousness (or public self-awareness), discussed in Chapters 3 and 6, but only minimally. Although there are no gender differences in public self-consciousness among adults, women score higher on private self-consciousness than men. This suggests that woman are more likely than men to reflect upon their internal states (Fenigstein et al. 1975).

Box 7.2   Private Self-Consciousness Scale

For each of the following items, please indicate how well it describes you by choosing the appropriate number on the following scale.

0————————1————————2————————3————————4

Extremely uncharacteristic of me   *Extremely characteristic of me*

Item   **Response**

1. I'm always trying to figure myself out.   _____
2. I reflect about myself a lot.   _____
3. I'm often the subject of my own fantasies.   _____
4. I never scrutinize myself.*   _____
5. I'm generally attentive to my inner feelings.   _____
6. I'm constantly examining my motives.   _____
7. I sometimes have the feeling that I'm off somewhere watching myself.   _____
8. I'm alert to changes in my mood.   _____
9. I'm aware of the way my mind works when I work through a problem.   _____
10. Generally, I'm not very aware of myself.*   _____

                                                                              Total score   _____

*Items 4 and 10 should be reverse coded (0 = 4, 1 = 3, 2 = 2, 3 = 1, 4 = 0) before computing your total score, as high scores on these items indicate low levels of private self-consciousness.

Note: Fenigstein, Scheier, and Buss (1975).

_____

Scores among a college sample (Fenigstein et al. 1975)

Males (n = 179):   Mean = 25.9   SD = 5.0
Females (n = 253):   Mean = 26.6   SD = 5.1

As noted in Chapter 4, there has been an increase in the attention given to schemas and social perception by sociological social psychologists working within the social structure and personality tradition. We discuss some of these studies in greater detail toward the end of the book in the chapter on prejudice and discrimination.

The literature on self-schemata is also of interest because it enhances our understanding of some common psychological disorders, in particular depression. People suffering from depression may be more sensitive than other individuals to negative evaluations from others (Pietromonaco and Markus 1985). The sensitivity to negative interpersonal feedback observed among depressed individuals is distinct from private self-consciousness, which results in a sensitivity to all (both positive and negative) self-relevant feedback. Some social psychologists have suggested that their sensitivity to negative evaluations makes depressed people more realistic in

PHOTO 7.2

Individuals suffering from depression may exhibit cognitive biases that lead them to perceive feedback from others more negatively than non-depressed people.

their assessments of self-relevant feedback than other individuals. That is, they have suggested that in order to maintain their positive self-concepts, nondepressed people tend to unconsciously overlook any negative feedback they get from others. Depressed people may be less likely to do this.

This model, called the depressive realism hypothesis, has received inconsistent support (Dobson and Franche 1989). However, depressed people do appear to be more accurate than nondepressed individuals in predicting negative events (Shrauger, Mariano, and Walter 1998). This is presumably because they process self-relevant information with a negative bias (Beyer 2002). Given their negative self-schemata, depressed people process negative information faster (Moretti et al. 1996) and remember it better than nondepressed individuals (Watkins et al. 1996). These cognitive tendencies may undermine the effectiveness of some therapies.

THE SELF-CONCEPT AND BEHAVIOR

Although conceptualizing the self-concept as cognitive schemata provides a useful framework for studying the effects of self-knowledge on perception, this literature tells us little about why we act in particular ways. We discuss the link between self and behavior in the following section.

Self-Esteem and Behavior

We discussed self-esteem, how it is measured, and how it varies across groups in an earlier section of the chapter. Here we focus on self-esteem as an independent variable.

The consequences of self-esteem have been widely studied. Across analyses, self-esteem has been associated with a number of positive outcomes, including both life satisfaction (Diener and Diener 1995) and happiness (Furnham and Cheng 2000).

Self-esteem may also have long-term consequences for individuals' physical, psychological, and economic development. Adolescents with lower self-esteem become less-well-adjusted adults than their high-self-esteem peers and are at risk for later obesity, cardiorespiratory problems, depression, anxiety, criminal behavior, low educational attainment, and unemployment (Trzesniewski et al. 2006). More-over, although differences in self-esteem do not explain race differences in wealth (e.g., White > Black and Hispanic), within each racial group adolescents with high self-esteem are more likely than adolescents with negative self-concepts to be finan-cially successful during middle age (Mossakowski 2012).

The effects of self-esteem on perception and behavior are especially notable when they are viewed in the aggregate. The impact of self-esteem on any one indica-tor (from depression to financial success) may be small to moderate. However, when taken together, the large number of outcomes linked to self-esteem means that how people feel about themselves is likely to affect their lives in significant ways (Swann, Chang-Schneider, and McClarty 2007).

The Dramaturgical Model and Impression Management

A desire for self-esteem may also motivate people to present themselves to others in favorable ways. Recall our discussion of Goffman's dramaturgical model from Chapter 3. Goffman (1959) argued that people engage in behaviors that are likely to receive positive feedback from others. Thus, they manage the impressions they convey to others through a strategic presentation of self.

Note, however, that in Goffman's view impression management is not necessar-ily deceptive, or even conscious. Think about your self-presentation in the last class you attended. Most likely, within this interactive encounter you were managing the image you conveyed to others so that you could effectively claim the identity of stu-dent, which is what you believe yourself to be. This means you were controlling the information you presented and directing the attention of your fellow students and your professor to this aspect of yourself. Presumably, you were also monitoring your behavior so as to avoid acting in ways that would result in embarrassment.

Were you conscious of how you were presenting yourself to the others in the classroom? Often social behavior is so routine or habitual that we aren't even aware that we're engaging in impression management. In other instances, impression management is a conscious activity motivated by a desire for self-enhancement. When this is the case, people's self-presentational strategies sometimes involve deception.

Deceit is evidenced when individuals intentionally mislead others through their use of language. As a broader and more frequently used form of communication,

feigning involves nonverbal strategies (e.g., dress, posture, and demeanor) that increase the likelihood that one will be perceived in the desired manner. Although equally as deceptive and strategic as deceit, feigning is less explicit and thus more difficult for others to openly question or reject (Goffman 1959).

Psychological and Situational Factors Related to Impression Management

Some people may be more prone to impression management than others. As indicated in Chapter 3, people high in public self-consciousness are especially concerned about how others view them. This is because this form of self-awareness makes them more attentive to self-evaluative feedback than other individuals (Buss 1980). As a result of this perceptual tendency, individuals high in public self-consciousness are more likely than other people to engage in impression management across social settings (Buss and Briggs 1984).

Settings that make people aware, or conscious, of others evaluations' also facilitate impression management. These environments include job interviews; public presentations (e.g., lectures and speeches); and formal events, such as weddings, religious services, and graduations (Buss and Briggs 1984).

In general, the drive for self-enhancement appears to be strongest in short-term encounters and may play less of a role in shaping behavior in more long-term, stable relationships (e.g., friendships or marriage) (Burke and Harrod 2005). Thus, people are the most likely to adopt a strategic presentation of self when they are around strangers or individuals they do not know well (Buss and Briggs 1984).

What if you are in a situation with strangers or people you know only superficially that makes it difficult to covey a positive impression? What strategies might you use to present a favorable self in an unfavorable setting?

Cahill and associates (1985) address this issue in their qualitative analysis of interaction rituals in public bathrooms. Bathrooms are back regions, where we engage in behavior (defecation) viewed as dirty and profane. However, public restrooms create a "ritually delicate" situation because, outside of the stall, we are on display to the bathroom's other occupants.

Everyone knows why they, and others, are there, and people convey respect for others in public bathrooms by minimizing contact. Individuals who are strangers acknowledge the presence of another by establishing brief eye contact and then looking away. This ritual validates each individual present in the setting (ignoring someone would be a slight) while making it clear that there will not be further attention or scrutiny. People who know one another will typically converse, but they keep it brief. Men, in particular, may engage in "urinal talk" with people who are familiar, but this conversation almost always occurs without eye contact. Toilet stalls typically prohibit conversation.

The stalls in public restrooms enable us to escape direct observation, and the privacy they offer is regarded as inviolate. This is illustrated when someone accidently opens the door to an occupied stall, at which time they almost always apologize profusely.

Because bathroom stalls give us privacy, it is odor that makes us most vulnerable to self-disenhancement in public restrooms. Smells readily permeate beyond the stall into the public area. When this happens, others help the offending party save face by pretending they don't smell anything. When the other occupants are strangers, the individual responsible for the foul odor will typically exit the restroom quickly without making eye contact (Cahill et al. 1985). Nonetheless, he or she may still experience some degree of embarrassment.

Structural Symbolic Interactionist Approaches

Other models linking the self to behavior are within the Iowa/Indiana school of symbolic interactionism. Given their emphasis on social structure (statuses and roles), this research is similar to research in the social structure and personality face of sociological social psychology.

Identities and Behavior

As you may recall from Chapter 3, identity theory (Stryker 1980) focuses on the effects of the content of people's self-concepts on their behaviors. From this perspective, identities are internalized statuses. Because of how they are formed, these kinds of identities are sometimes referred to as **socially based identities**.

According to identity theory, identities are rank ordered within the self-concept in a salience hierarchy. **Identity salience** refers to the readiness with which people enact the roles associated with a particular status (Burke and Stets 2009). Identity salience is different from related concepts, such as importance, in that it does not imply that people are conscious of their identities or their behavioral implications (Stryker and Serpe 1994).

Identity salience is a function of the number of relationships individuals have with other people based on a particular identity, called **commitment**. Once an identity becomes salient, people will choose to engage in role behaviors associated with that identity whenever they have the opportunity to do so. Thus, current social relationships with individuals based on an identity (commitment) cause identity salience, which in turn causes the individual to engage in identity-relevant behavior in future social encounters (Styker 1980).

These relationships are depicted in Figure 7.1. As shown in the figure, it is the content of the self-concept (identities) that links society (statuses and role relationships) to relatively stable and predictable role-related behaviors. The desire for support for, or verification of, our salient identities is presumed to be the motivating force underlying this process (Stryker 1980).

Identity verification (the path from identity salience to identity-relevant behavior in Figure 7.1) occurs when there is a match between situational meanings and

FIGURE 7.1

Identity Theory

Commitment ――――――→ Identity Salience ――――――→ Behavior

Note: Stryker (1980)

the meanings that define a particular identity, called an **identity standard** (Burke 2006). Thus, identities and behaviors are linked through shared meanings. For example, if someone defines femininity in terms of tenderness (the identity standard), and defines oneself as feminine, then that individual must act in ways that are likely to be viewed by self and others as tender (vs. rough or harsh) (Burke and Reitzes 1981). Similarly, if being a student means studying hard, then an individual who defines himself or herself as a student must regularly engage in this behavior in order for this identity to receive verification.

Note the level of specificity of this model. Identity theory is a theory proper in that it specifies testable relationships between key variables. These variables—commitment, identity salience, and behavior—can readily be measured on a survey. For example, college students are often asked to respond to questions about their current social relationships (commitment) and behaviors. Identity salience is measured using an abbreviated version of the Who Am I Test, described in Chapter 3, involving 5 rather than 20 responses (Stryker 1980).

Take a look at your answers to the Twenty Statements Test, presented in Chapter 3 on page 82. Most people list statuses in response to this question. How many of your first five responses to the TST were statuses? Most significant for identity theorists is the status you listed first. This is your most salient identity. Don't worry if you didn't list any statuses in response to the Who Am I Test. Although identity theorists are only interested in the statuses people list on the TST, other sociological social psychologists take into consideration all of an individual's answers to this question. We discuss their work, and the significance of responses to the TST other than statuses, later in the chapter.

For many college students, student is the most salient identity. This is because so many of their interactions with others are based on their occupation of this status. If student is your most salient identity, identity theory predicts that you will enact behaviors consistent with the student role whenever you are able to do so. This is because the feedback you get from others when you engage in these behaviors is needed for confirmation (verification) of this identity.

This model depicted in Figure 7.1 pertains to any salient identity, not just student. You may have listed athlete or friend or president of your sorority or fraternity as an initial response to the TST.

At the aggregative level, individuals' desires for self-verification ultimately reproduce existing structural arrangements. That is, people seeking to reinforce their self-concepts by engaging in role-related behaviors reinforce the social structures within which the positions they occupy are located. Although identity theorists embrace this assumption, the focus of the model is on the link between self and behavior at the micro level. Numerous studies based on the analysis of survey data support this theory (Burke and Stets 2009).

The Role-Person Merger

Reversing the order of the processes depicted in Figure 7.1, it may be possible to predict the content of people's self-concepts by observing their behaviors. Sometimes people synthesize self and role, giving rise to the role-person merger.

The **role-person merger** occurs when an identity is so entrenched within an individual's self-concept that he or she engages in behaviors related to it even when it is not appropriate to so do. That is, the individual seeks verification for this identity even when it means engaging in behaviors that are incongruent with prevailing situational norms (Turner 1978). When this happens, it is safe to assume that the identity in question is highly salient.

Examples of the role-person merger include the following:

- The student who studies for an exam during a religious service.

- The professor who grades papers at a rock concert.

- The father who puts his arm in front of a friend sitting in the passenger seat of his car when he is driving and comes to a stop sign (as he would do with his child).

- The comedian who converses with family members by telling a series of jokes.

- The older sister who bosses her college roommates around as though they were younger siblings.

What Do You Think?

Form a group with two or three of your classmates. Come up with three cases of the role-person merger that differ from the examples just given, as witnessed by one or more of your group members. Record the following information:

■ The identity in question, given the inappropriate behaviors observed. List also the observed identity-relevant behaviors in opposition to prevailing situational norms.

■ How others present in the interactive encounter reacted to this individual's situationally inappropriate behavior.

   Did your group have difficulty coming up with examples of the role-person merger? What does this tell you about the relationship between the content of people's self-concepts and their behaviors?

Although anyone can experience the role-person merger, it is most likely to occur under the following conditions:

- When other people consistently identify an individual with a particular role.

- When the role in question is relevant to a wide range of situations.

- When the role is evaluated positively

- When the role is frequently played in public settings

- When entrance into the role was difficult and required a high degree of sacrifice (in terms of time, money and relationships) or training

- When an individual is effective in playing the role.

Role strain (when the demands associated with a role are difficult to fulfill or stressful for other reasons) may also increase the likelihood that someone will come to identify with and enact behaviors associated with a particular identity (Turner 1978). Imagine a writer who is having difficulty getting started on her next book and is experiencing substantial distress as a result. Despite the fact that she is not actually writing, she thinks and talks about her inability to do so constantly, which may in turn increase her level of psychological discomfort.

The Verification of Self-Conceptions

Like their socially based identities, there is also ample evidence from within psychological social psychology that people seek confirmation for their beliefs about themselves (called self-conceptions), even when they are negative (e.g., Swann et al. 1992; Swann, Wenzlaff, and Tafarodi 1992). One especially telling study focused on college students' self-views and the potential stability of their relationships with their roommates.

Do you remember your first day of college? Were you matched with a roommate, someone whom you had never met before? Many students have this experience when they move into the dorm at the beginning of their freshman year.

Sometimes individuals maintain long-term friendships with their freshman roommate, whereas others move on quickly and find other living arrangements. When is this most likely to happen? That is, when do students want to continue living with their current roommate and when do they desire an end to this relationship? This was the question investigated by Swann and Pelham (2002).

In this study, over 100 pairs of freshmen roommates close to completing their first semester in college were each asked to rate themselves and their roommate on five characteristics (intelligence, attractiveness, sociability, artistic ability, and athletic ability). They were also asked to indicate whether they wanted to continue living with their current roommate. The purpose of the study was to predict which students wanted to stay with their current roommate by looking at (1) whether their

PHOTO 7.3

The beginning of the school year marks a significant shift in behaviors and relationships for many college students. "Move in day" may be especially notable for incoming freshmen, who are often leaving home for the first time.

roommates' evaluations of them were positive and (2) the degree of overlap between how they viewed themselves and how their roommate saw them in relation to the five domains under investigation (intelligence, attractiveness, etc.).

Think about the two motivations underlying the self-concept—behavior relationship, discussed earlier in the chapter.

1. The desire for **self-enhancement**, a motivation underlying the process of impression management, which is the focus of Goffman's dramaturgical model.

2. The desire for **self-verification**, the underlying motivation for engaging in identity-relevant behaviors, according to identity theory.

How might these motives relate to college freshmen's roommate preferences?

Q: What about the college freshmen who had positive views of themselves across the five areas examined? When would they be most likely to want to continue living with their current roommate?

A: In this instance, a desire for self-enhancement or for self-verification should yield the same results. Freshmen with positive self-views should want to continue to live with roommates who also think well of them. The maintenance of this relationship would both enhance and verify their self-images. Swann and Pelham (2002) found that this was the case: individuals with positive self-conceptions wanted to stay with roommates who confirmed their positive self-views.

Q: What about the college freshmen with negative self-views? When would they be most likely to want to maintain their current living arrangement?

A: It is in this instance that a desire for self-verification should yield a different pattern of results than a desire for self-enhancement. If these students were motivated by a desire for self-enhancement, then they should have wanted to maintain relationships with roommates who saw them positively. On the other hand, if they were motivated by a desire for self-verification, freshmen with negative self-conceptions should have wanted to continue living with roommates who viewed them negatively. Thus, it is the freshmen with negative self-conceptions that are of particular interest in this study.

Among this group, Swann and Pelham (2002) found that the desire for self-verification superseded any potential desires for self-enhancement (impression management). Students with negative self-conceptions had a greater interest in continuing to live with roommates who thought negatively of them. If they had a roommate who saw them in a positive light, they were less likely to want to maintain that relationship.

You might be asking why this would be the case. Why would someone prefer to be around an individual who views him or her negatively rather than positively?

Research suggests that people seek verification for their self-concepts, regardless of their content, in relationships that persist over time because this enhances their sense of control; provides reassurance that they do, in fact, know themselves; and makes interaction flow more smoothly (Swann, Stein-Seroussi, and Giesler 1992). The preference for self-verification, even in the face of a negative self-concept, may explain the link between low self-esteem and the variety of negative outcomes, discussed earlier in the chapter. It also provides an explanation for the self-fulfilling prophecy.

The Self-Fulfilling Prophecy

As noted in Chapter 5, the self-fulfilling prophecy occurs when an initial assessment that is false results in a shift in self-expectations and behavior that ultimately lead to its confirmation. Rosenthal and Jacobson (1968) call this the **Pygmalion effect**, named for the mythological Greek sculptor Pygmalion who made his statue of a woman real by wishing it so.

In their classic study on the power of expectations in shaping future outcomes, Rosenthal and Jacobson (1966) showed that elementary school children selected at random and identified as high ability outperformed their peers on an IQ test at the end of the school year simply because of their positive label. The high-ability students (20% of the students in the school where the study was conducted) were not really any smarter than the other children. However, they were alleged to have scored high on an IQ test given at the beginning of the term. Their teachers were told that they scored high on the test, supposedly a measure of the potential for rapid intellectual growth, and that they were likely to exhibit exceptionally large academic gains over the course of the year. As a result, their teachers expected them to be the best students in the class and treated them accordingly. These students internalized the messages they received from their teachers (reflected appraisals) and rose to the challenge. Thus, labeling student in this fashion induced a self-fulfilling prophecy.

Much of the literature on the self-fulfilling prophecy comes from studies conducted in schools. These analyses suggest that low teacher expectations may have especially negative consequences for students from lower class backgrounds and racial minorities (Jussim and Harber 2005).

Parents' expectations of their children may also impact their subsequent behaviors in a self-fulfilling manner. Middle school students whose mothers thought they would drink when they were teenagers were more likely than their peers to think that they would become teenage drinkers. As a result, they were more likely than other students to use alcohol when they were in high school (Madon et al. 2008). Similarly, students drank more when they were in high school when their mother and father overestimated their risk for future alcohol use when they were in the seventh grade (Madon et al. 2004).

Mothers' beliefs about their children's academic performance when the children are in middle school, measured as estimated grades, affects student's educational aspirations and their likelihoods of going to college in a similar manner. Interestingly, this effect occurs independent of that of students' actual grades, suggesting that children internalize their mothers' assessments and confirm them, even if they are untrue. Even when mothers' estimates of their middle schoolers' grades were not accurate, they affected the students' future academic performances (Scherr et al. 2011).

What Do You Think?

- Have you or someone you know experienced the self-fulfilling prophecy firsthand? Who was the source of the expectations that influenced your self-concept and behavior, or the self-concept and behavior of someone you know?
- The research literature on the self-fulfilling prophecy has focused mainly on the expectations of teachers and parents. What other individuals are likely to influence the self-concepts and behaviors of adolescents and young adults?

GPS RESEARCH ON INTERGROUP RELATIONS AND SOCIAL IDENTITIES

Within the group processes and structures tradition, social identity theorists focus on how the groups to which people belong shape their self-definitions. As you may recall from Chapter 5, social identity theory focuses on the self-categorization process, people's perceptions of in-group versus out-group members, and the link between social identity (in-group identification) and behavior. Thus, this body of literature is distinct from the studies reviewed in the previous section. Whereas we use the term "identity" (or socially based identity) to refer to internalized statuses that are reinforced as individuals enact relevant social roles, we use the term "social identity" to designate a self-categorization based upon an individual's membership in a particular group.

According to social identity theory, people seek to enhance their self-esteem through identification with an in-group that is perceived as having positive qualities (e.g., a winning team or, more broadly, a dominant racial/ethnic group) (Owens 2006). Thus, individuals with negative self-concepts may be especially motivated to evaluate members of out-groups negatively (Long and Spears 1997).

Identity Threat

Desires for self-enhancement may also influence individuals' reactions to **identity threat**. Threats to social identities occur when people receive negative information about in-group members or anticipate structural changes that make their group's status precarious. Members of dominant groups tend to respond with increases in out-group derogation and offers of assistance that cultivate dependence rather than autonomy among out-group members when their social identities are threatened (Branscombe and Wann 1994; Nadler, Harpaz-Gorodeisky, and Ben-David 2009).

In situations providing opportunities for cross-group evaluation, threats to social identities among members of dominant groups may result in compensatory actions. For example, in one study, White teachers who received feedback suggesting that they did not hold egalitarian attitudes pertaining to race gave significantly more favorable ratings to essays ostensibly written by Black, but not White, students. This pattern was not observed among White teachers whose egalitarian self-images were not challenged (Harber, Stafford, and Kennedy 2010). For many Whites, being non-racist is a core element of their self-image. When this identity is threatened, they seek to reestablish it by showing a positive bias toward members of the out-group (racial/ethnic minorities).

Threats to White individuals' views of themselves as nonracist may also affect their selection of reference groups. In a recent experiment, White college undergraduates completed a test designed to threaten their view of themselves as nonprejudiced (the experimental condition) or a personality inventory (the control condition). Following this manipulation, subjects were asked to select a set of documentaries for viewing. Each documentary was described as either featuring highly prejudiced or egalitarian (nonprejudiced) subjects. Students whose egalitarian identities were just threatened were more likely than individuals in the control group to choose videos focusing on people who were prejudiced, thereby enabling them to validate the threatened identity. Viewing films focusing on highly prejudiced subjects would make them appear more egalitarian in comparison (O'Brien et al. 2010).

Among members of low status groups, reactions to identity threat (e.g., receiving negative information about one's racial/ethnic group) include psychological disengagement from the group or adoption of the belief that in-group members vary substantially in their characteristics and behaviors. Psychological disengagement is evidenced by ambivalent attitudes toward in-group members and is most likely to occur among individuals whose initial in-group identification is weak. Having a weak in-group identification means that membership in the group is not viewed as important. Embracing the belief that in-group members differ from one another is a more common response to identity threat than psychological disengagement among individuals whose identification with the in-group (measured in terms of the importance of group membership) is initially strong (Pagliaro et al. 2012).

Outside of the laboratory, in schools, identity threat among members of non-dominant groups has been measured in terms of students' experiences of race-based discrimination. In the absence of perceived discrimination, simultaneously maintaining a strong national and minority identity (i.e., being attached to both the larger society and the minority community) is associated with positive academic outcomes. However, among students who frequently experience unfair or hostile treatment due to their minority status, maintaining these dual identities may have negative consequences. These individuals tend to be less successful academically than minority students who self-identify solely as a racial/ethnic minority. Thus, in order to equalize students' educational opportunities, it is important for majority groups to accept and support the social identities of racial and ethnic minorities (Baysu, Phalet, and Brown 2011).

IDENTITY CONSTRUCTION AND MAINTENANCE

The construction of social identities based on in-group/out-group distinctions is the main focus of social identity theory. We discussed this theoretical framework in detail in Chapter 5 on research on group processes and structures. Thus, we focus here on research on the construction and maintenance of identities as they are defined by sociological social psychologists working within the symbolic interactionist face of social psychology.

Symbolic Interactionist Approaches

From a symbolic interactionist perspective (the Chicago school variety), identity construction is an ongoing, flexible process that varies across groups and individuals. As noted in previous chapters, most symbolic interactionist studies focus on self and identity (e.g., Kurien's study of Indian American college students and Hurst's analysis of working-class college students).

The symbolic interactionist literature on identity construction also encompasses studies of the content of the self-concepts of individuals following role transitions. The role transitions of interest to symbolic interactionists include going to college, marriage, parenthood, divorce, and retirement. Response to life changes such as those that accompany chronic disease, disability, or a terminal illness have also been studied by researchers working within the SI face of sociological social psychology. Analyses of role transitions and responses to life changes within SI are typically qualitative in orientation and focus on the social processes through which selves are created, modified, and maintained through face-to-face interaction. These analyses also focus on the meanings of events and social relationships to the study participants.

Structural symbolic interactionist approaches to the study of self and behavior within the Iowa/Indiana school of SI—namely, identity theory—focus on the maintenance of identities over time and across interactive settings. They are usually survey based. The difference between Iowa/Indiana and more traditional (Chicago school) symbolic interactionist studies of identity and behavior can readily be seen in the research literature on the transition to college.

Application: Studying the Transition to College

As noted earlier, role transitions, such as beginning college, provide an arena in which identity construction is likely to occur. A study by Karp and associates (1998) within the Chicago School of SI highlights some of the expectations and concerns of high school students getting ready to go away to school.

The individuals they interviewed (n = 21) recognized the college years as a time when people experience significant identity changes and find out who they really are, apart from the constraints imposed by their current social roles and relationships. Many of the soon-to-be college freshmen were pleased to note that going away to school would enable them to drop one or more undesirable identities. Because they would be removed from the people (e.g., family members and childhood friends) who provided the basis for their maintenance, these individuals expected to have a greater degree of control over how others viewed them than they did in high school.

Although they looked forward to exploring new relationships and creating new identities in college, the participants in Karp and associate's study expressed concerns about their ability to do so effectively. Thus, this transitional period between high school and college was characterized by anxiety and fear, as well as excitement.

Interestingly, all of the participants in this study indicated that they sought to limit the uncertainty associated with going away to school by selecting a college where someone like them would easily fit in and feel comfortable. They did this by visiting various campuses and observing the students (the way they dressed and carried themselves) and by evaluating the overall friendliness of the environment. Doing so gave them a greater sense of control over the direction their lives were taking and helped ease some of their anxieties about moving into the college student role (Karp et al. 1998).

What Do You Think?

- How did you feel when you started college? How does your experience compare to those of the students interviewed by Karp and associates?
- Most of the high school students interviewed by Karp and associates were from affluent families. How might the experiences of individuals from lower- or working-class backgrounds moving from high school to college differ from those of described in the preceding section?
- How did your class background influence the way in which you experienced the transition to college?

Although students often develop new identities during the college years (Jones 2009), quantitative studies of high school and college students' identities, conducted by structural symbolic interactionists, suggest that there is at least some degree of stability in their self-concepts during this time frame. These quantitative analyses, designed as tests of identity theory, focus on patterns of behaviors among larger samples. Overall, they suggest that students seek out activities and relationships that verify precollege athletic and recreational, extracurricular, and social identities (Serpe and Stryker 1987). Common college student identities (e.g., academic, extracurricular, athletic and recreational, social, and dating) also show a fair degree of stability over the course of the first semester of the freshmen year (Serpe 1987). Thus, college students' experiences can best be characterized as consisting of both identity construction and continuity.

IDENTITY CHANGE

According to identity theory, people will enact the roles associated with their salient identities whenever they have the opportunity to do so. Although college students may have ample opportunities to select activities and develop relationships that allow for at least some reinforcement of their precollege selves, there are other changes that make this more difficult. What happens when individuals are unable to verify their identities through their interactions with others? That is, what happens when there is a mismatch between situational meanings and an identity standard (the meanings that define a particular identity)?

This is likely to occur in the aftermath of a life event (e.g., a fire in the home, the acquisition of a substantial sum of money, or the loss of a friendship) or a role transition that requires a new set of responsibilities, such as becoming a parent. Research suggests that, in these situations, individuals modify their identity standard so that it matches their new behavioral patterns.

Similarly, individuals with incompatible identities that cannot simultaneously be verified because they have conflicting meanings (e.g., a nontraditional gender identity and a traditional spousal identity) will also experience identity change. Which of the two identities undergoes the most revision in response to this discrepancy will depend upon the number of interactions with others the individual has based on each identity (i.e., commitment) and thus their relative salience.

Irrespective of their direction, these types of changes occur gradually and may thus go unnoticed (Burke 2006). This is in contrast to the construction of new identities, which, as noted in the previous section, tends to involve more drastic and conscious changes in the content of people's self-concepts.

THE REAL SELF

As indicated in the preceding sections on the self-concept, cognition, and behavior, most social psychologists embrace the notion that the self is multidimensional rather than a unitary entity. Thus the self-concept is composed of self-schemas, identities, or social identities, which serve as frameworks for the processing of social information and direct our behaviors.

In his classic article on self and culture, structural symbolic interactionist Ralph Turner (1976), the author of the article on the role-person merger, described earlier, argues that we perceive ourselves as having a real, or core self, that represents our true nature. For some of us, what we recognize as our "**real self**" is located in social institutions and the roles we play (e.g., son or daughter, student, athlete, and friend). That is, the real self is found in the socially based identities within our self-concept (the "me" phase of the self). For others, the real self is located in impulsive, spontaneous, uncontrolled reactions to situations, people, and events (Mead's "I").

The locus of the real self (what it is anchored in) has implications for how we evaluate our experiences (Turner 1976). For example, imagine that you are in a monogamous relationship and encounter someone other than your partner and find that you are attracted to this individual. How would you respond to this situation?

According to Turner (1976), it depends upon whether you locate your real self in institutions or impulse. Individuals who define the real self in terms of institutionalized roles ("institutionals") would probably regard this experience as anomalous and accord it little meaning because it is counter to their role as a partner in a committed relationship. Individuals who define their real selves in terms of impulse ("impulsives") are likely to view this situation differently. They may embrace this type of spontaneous emotion and regard it as highly telling or significant. Perhaps this is a potential soul mate.

Evidence of a Cultural Shift

Historically, the number of available social roles was limited and most role behaviors occurred within the family. These roles defined almost all of people's social interactions. Thus, individuals readily identified with these sets of social expectations and saw them as indicative of who they really were (i.e., they located the real self in institutions).

In contemporary society, people play multiple roles, rooted in a variety of social institutions, with permeable boundaries and questionable outcomes. Given this, Turner (1976) argues that we have experienced a cultural shift in locus of self, such that an increasing percentage of the population anchors their real, or true, selves in spontaneous emotions and other impulsive experiences rather than in social institutions.

Researchers measure **locus of self** with the Twenty Statements Test. Whereas identity theorists look at the number and order of statuses listed in response to the TST, sociological social psychologists interested in assessing the nature of students' real selves have used the following four-category scheme to code students' responses to the Who Am I question.

1. **Category A**: Physical characteristics

2. **Category B**: Social roles attached to the statuses one occupies (e.g., identities such as student)

3. **Category C**: Descriptions of personal characteristics or preferences

4. **Category D**: Responses not inherently linked to institutional structures (e.g., "I am a spot in the universe.") (McPartland 1965)

In general, category A and D responses are rare and are almost never an individual's modal (most common) response type. Most students' answers to the TST fall into category B or C.

Code your responses to the TST on page 82. Do you have more responses in category B (social roles and identities) or in category C (idiosyncratic traits, preferences, and other non-institutionally based characteristics)?

Whereas people who anchor their real self in institutions should respond to the Twenty Statements Test by listing a majority of category B responses, individuals who exhibit an impulse orientation should list more category C responses as self-defining (Turner 1976; Hartley 1968 cited in Zurcher 1977). Therefore, if you have more C than B responses, you are an impulsive. If you have more category B than C responses, you are an institutional. Does that classification fit with your view of yourself and the way in which you evaluate your experiences? (If you're not sure, review the distinction between the two self-loci in the previous section.)

You might be wondering how you compare to other students. In the 1950s, over half of a college sample listed primarily social roles (in category B) in response to the TST (Hartley 1968 cited in Zurcher 1977). By the late 1960s, the percentage of institutionals was lower, as more students provided adjectives and preferences (category C responses) than social roles as self-descriptions (Zurcher 1972, 1977), consistent with Turner's (1976) contentions. More recent studies (Babbitt and Burbach 1990; Grace and Cramer 2002; Roscoe and Peterson 1983; Snow and Phillips 1982) have yielded similar results, suggesting that this trend was not merely a reflection of the individually oriented culture of the 1960s and 1970s. In Grace and Cramer's (2002) analysis, the majority of the students surveyed (over 90%) listed a majority of category C responses (reflective descriptions or preferences) when asked to define themselves using twenty statements.

Whether contemporary students define their real selves in terms of institutional roles or unique personal characteristics is open to question. In a 2011 study (Crawford and Novak 2011) only 60% of an undergraduate sample listed more category C than B responses to the TST. Although this suggests the possibility of a shift in self-locus, back toward the institutional (vs. impulse) orientation observed prior to the 1960s, more research is needed to determine whether this is a prevailing societal pattern.

Take a Break

In a visually oriented version of the Who Am I Test, individuals are asked to take pictures that describe themselves and how they see themselves. Here are the instructions students are typically given (taken verbatim from Ziller 1990:34).

We want you to describe to yourself how you see yourself. To do this we would like you to take (or have someone else take) 12 photographs that tell who you are. These photographs can be of anything just as long as they tell something about who you are. You should not be interested in your skill as a photographer. Keep in mind that the photographs should describe who you are as you see yourself. When you finish you will have a book about yourself that is made up of 12 photos.

Complete this exercise using the camera on your cellular phone or a digital camera. If possible, make print copies of your photographs. What patterns emerged in your set of photos? How do they compare to your written responses the Twenty Statements Test? What do they imply about who you are? Consider comparing your pictures with those of some of your classmates.

SSP RESEARCH ON GENERATIONAL CHANGES IN THE SELF-CONCEPTS OF YOUTHS

In recent years, a number of studies on changes in the self-concepts of youths have been published. These analyses include measures of some of the concepts we have discussed in this and in previous chapters, in particular self-esteem and perspective taking. Despite the fact that some of their authors are psychological social psychologists, the issue these studies address place them within the social structure and personality face of sociological social psychology.

Studies using the Rosenberg (1965) scale (see Box 7.1) suggest that self-esteem has increased substantially among middle school students, and slightly among high school and college students, over the past 25 years (Gentile, Twenge, and Campbell 2010). Conversely, there is some indication that perspective taking (measured in college student samples using the Davis items presented in Box 6.4) decreased slightly during this time frame (Konrath, O'Brien, and Hsing 2011).

Current research reports on changes in the self-concept across age cohorts also focus on narcissism. In fact, this particular dimension of the self has received a lot of media attention following the publication of the book by psychologist Jean Twenge entitled *Generation Me* in 2006. This popular book is based on the results of studies measuring narcissism among college samples using the Narcissistic Personality Inventory or NPI (Raskin and Terry 1988). This index is designed to assess levels of narcissism in nonclinical populations (narcissistic personality disorder is a clinical disorder included in the *Diagnostic and Statistical Manual* of the American Psychiatric Association). The NPI consists of multiple survey questions focusing on the extent to which individuals feel superior to others, exhibit vanity and exhibitionism, have a sense of entitlement and authority, and are self-sufficient and exploitive of others (see Box 7.3 for an Internet link to an online version of the NPI).

Twenge's (2006) key argument in *Generation Me* is that today's young adults (the Millennial Generation) tend to be highly narcissistic. In a related set of academic articles (Twenge et al. 2008; Twenge and Foster 2010), Twenge and her colleagues assessed changes in scores on the NPI among college samples between the years 1980–2009. Based on the results of their analyses, they conclude that narcissism is at an all-time high and that this reflects a notable cultural shift in personality.

Are young adults really more narcissistic now than ever before? Perhaps, but there has been a fair amount of debate concerning the validity of Twenge's conclusions. In particular, it is important to note that *Generation Me,* and Twenge's scholarly articles on the increase in narcissism in this country (Twenge et al. 2008; 2010),

---

Box 7.3   Online Version of the Narcissistic Personality Inventory

If you're interested, go to the following *USA Today* website to view an online version of the Narcissistic Personality Inventory: http://usatoday30.usatoday.com/news/health/2009–03–16-pinsky-quiz_N.htm.

This version of the NPI has been given to celebrities, who tend to have high scores. This is the subject of a popular book, coauthored by psychologist Drew Pinsky (a.k.a. Dr. Drew), titled the *Mirror Effect*. The book is also discussed on the *USA Today* website.

are based on samples of college students. Thus, they are not representative of all young adults living in the United States. This is critical to the evaluation of her findings. There is a substantial correlation between parents' economic resources, as well as race/ethnicity, and college attendance. Given this, it is not appropriate to make generalizations about all of the Millennial Generation (or any cohort) based on data collected from only those individuals who are enrolled in college, predominantly Whites and those from middle- and upper-class backgrounds.

As a side note, the same argument applies to the literature on the real self, discussed in the preceding section, which is also based on nonrepresentative college student samples. Interestingly, this criticism has never visibly emerged in relation to this literature, presumably because these analyses were read by fewer people and are less inherently controversial than the narcissism studies. It is one thing to say that the way in which people define their real selves has changed and quite another to state that the current generation is characterized by a pathological personality trait (truth of the claim aside, it is clearly a more touchy subject).

What Do You Think?

How do you feel about this issue?

- If you're a member of the Millennial Generation, do you think your generation is more narcissistic than previous generations? If you're not a Millennial, how do you think current adolescents and young adults differ from the youth of your generation?
- Do you think that social class makes a difference in the attitudes and behaviors of current adolescents and young adults?

The Narcissistic Personality Inventory, used in almost all of the research on this topic, includes questions that also assess leadership, social effectiveness, and self-confidence. Thus, it has been suggested that much of the increase in "narcissism" among college students over the past 25 years is due to changing gender roles, which have led to increases in self-confidence and self-sufficiency among college women (Trzesniewski and Donnellan 2009). Consistent with this interpretation, Twenge and associates (2008, 2010) found that increases in narcissism were greater among women than among men during the time frame under investigation.

Trzesniewski and Donnellan's (2009) used data from the Monitoring the Future Survey, collected from nationally representative samples of U.S. high school students since 1976, in order to assess changes in the characteristics of individuals from different generations. The primary change in attitudes between the mid-1970s and 2006 is that members of the Millennial Generation have higher educational expectations and are more skeptical about the notion that hard work will result in a good job than individuals in previous generations. There have not, however, been any notable changes in the personality characteristics such as self-esteem or individualism among U.S. high school students during this 30-year time frame. Thus, Trzesniewski and Donnellan (2009) conclude that recent generations, including the Millennials, are more similar to than they are different from prior age cohorts.

SELF AND IDENTITY IN THE POSTMODERN ERA

Envisioning much more widespread and substantial changes than those discussed in the previous sections, postmodern theorists posit that society has undergone a radical transformation in recent years. This, they argue, has had a profound impact on identity and the self-concept more generally. (An increase in narcissism, albeit limited in scope, would be consistent with the kind of changes associated with postmodernity.)

Postmodern is the label applied to late-stage capitalist societies, in which people are presumed to have qualitatively different experiences than those of individuals who lived in the previous (modern) era. Whereas modern societies are characterized by relatively stable and meaningful relationships and shared beliefs, the postmodern world is characterized by a sense of rapid transformation fueled by the growth in information technologies, widespread consumption, the commodification of images and culture (people profit from selling images, values,

---

Box 7.4 Postmodern Versus Modern Values

MODERN VALUES	POSTMODERN VALUES
Acceptance of new ideas	Absence of truth
Faith in science	Quality of life
Concern with social affairs	Romantic life
Awareness of local and international events	Tolerance of diversity
Individualism	Free expression
Secularism	Expression and display of uniqueness

Note: Inglehart and Welzel (2005), Lash (1990), and Cheung and Leung (2002).

and lifestyles rather than tangible physical objects), and the decline of modern values (Sandstrom and Fine 2003). See Box 7.4 for a list of postmodern, versus modern, values.

The postmodern world is fragmented and shallow. In a postmodern society, everything is fluid and social relationships are fleeting. Thus, from this perspective, there is no single theoretical framework that can be used to explain people's experiences because everyone's subjective reality is different (Ritzer 1996), a notion that is not inconsistent with the position of (Chicago school) symbolic interactionists (Weigert and Gecas 2005).

Through the use of new technologies (e.g., cell phones, video conferencing, email, social networking sites like Facebook, and the Internet), people's social contacts have expanded, but they are more transient and superficial in their nature. As a result, some social psychologists have argued that the self has no stable locus or anchorage and has become so overextended that it no longer serves as a source of consistent or coherent meaning (Gergen 1991).

Other social theorists have suggested that it is primarily through narratives, made public in personal journals and autobiographies or constructed semipublically in self-help and support groups, that a coherent self is maintained within the context of postmodernity (or, as some theorists have argued, late modernity) (Giddens 1991; Holstein and Gubrium 2000). Within this context, identities are constructed through consumption. However, because these identities are idiosyncratic, strategically cultivated, and lack depth, they may readily be dropped or modified when doing so serves the needs or desires of the individual (Lash 1990).

Have widespread social changes, including recent technological advancements, radically altered people's social relationships and experiences? Many people do communicate with others through email and other computer-mediated devices. But this does not necessarily reduce the time they spend interacting with others in face-to-face encounters (Boase et al. 2006). Moreover, survey data collected over the past 50 years suggests that the quality of individuals' social relationships has changed very little since the 1970s. People still have close and stable relationships with others (Fischer 2011).

Although the world has certainly changed, the degree to which movement into the postmodern era has altered the basis of people's core relationships, the construction of meaning, and thus the structure and function of the self has been the topic of much debate (Sandstrom and Fine 2003). Many social psychologists do not acknowledge the postmodern point of view (e.g., Owens 2006), whereas other explicitly reject the postmodernist approach to the study of the self and social life (e.g., Maines 1996; Smith 1994). Consistent with the latter position, the literature discussed in this chapter suggests that the self still reflects and shapes our social interactions in ways that are relatively stable, predictable, and perceived as meaningful.

CHAPTER SUMMARY

The self-concept reflects our prior social relations and shapes both our perceptions and behaviors. As illustrated throughout this chapter, how and why this occurs has been the focal point of many social psychological analyses. Because the origin, nature, and function of the self has been studied by social psychologists trained in psychology, as well as sociology, this literature is eclectic and covers topics ranging from how people process and recall self-referent information to the effects of social structure (statuses and roles) on individuals' behaviors. Although the content of people's self-concepts may have changed some in recent years, the self still serves as an important organizer of human thought and action.

Key Points to Know

- **The content of people's self-concept is rooted in reflected appraisals.** We respond to this self-referent feedback with negative or positive affect.

- **Self-esteem refers to an individual's global self-evaluation.** It is based on reflected appraisals, social comparisons, and self-perceptions. Studies suggest that self-esteem has long-term effects on physical health, mental health, criminal behavior, and wealth.

- **Psychological social psychologists have studied the effects of self-schemata on information processing and memory.** People attend to and remember self-referent information that is consistent with the content of their self-schemata. Thus, self-schemata can be resilient to change.

- **The self-concept is linked to behavior through two basic processes: self-enhancement, which often underlies the process of impression management, and self-verification.** Self-enhancement motives may be especially strong when the people interact with strangers or individuals they know only superficially. In more long-term relationships, behavior tends to be motivated more by a desire for self-verification.

- **Within the structural symbolic interactionist framework, identity theory specifies the link between social structure (the statuses people occupy), the content of self-concepts (a salience hierarchy of identities), and behavior.** An identity becomes salient when commitment is high. Once an identity becomes salient, people will seek to verify that identity through the enactment of identity-relevant behaviors whenever they have the opportunity to do so.

- **The literature on social identities within the group processes and structures face of social psychology focuses on the construction of identities within the context of intergroup relations.** When these identities are threatened, members of dominant groups enhance their self-concepts by devaluing out-group members and engaging in compensatory behaviors. Members of nondominant groups respond to identity threat by psychologically distancing themselves from the group or by emphasizing within-group variability.

- **Most socially based identities (i.e., those of interest to identity theorists) are relatively stable. However, people often construct new identities when their social environments change.** Studies of the transition to college suggest that students engage in both identity construction and maintenance at this juncture.

- **There have been some changes in self locus and in the content of people's self-concepts in recent years.** More college students locate their real self in spontaneous emotions and reactions today than in the 1950s. Although contemporary college students use their role-taking skills somewhat less readily than they did in previous generations, reported generational increases in narcissism may be a methodological artifact.

- **Postmodern theorists argue that the nature of the self and its role in social life have been radically altered by widespread social change.** These claims are contentious and have been rejected by many social psychologists.

Terms and Concepts for Review

Commitment	Pygmalion effect
Deceit	Real self
Feigning	Reflected appraisals
Identity	Role-person merger
Identity salience	Self-enhancement
Identity standard	Self-esteem
Identity threat	Self-presentation
Locus of self	Self-schemata
Looking-glass self	Self-verification
Postmodern	Socially based identity
Private self-consciousness	

Questions for Review and Reflection

1. Why is self and identity such an important topic of study for social psychologists? Distinguish between these terms and, in about 8 to 10 sentences, summarize the research discussed in this chapter. What study or studies did you find the most interesting? Why does this research stand out to you in this manner?

2. Discuss the difference between the two motivations underlying the self-behavior relationship: self-enhancement and self-verification. Give an example of a time when your behavior was governed by a desire for self-enhancement. Describe a time when your main goal was to receive confirmation from others for the way that you see yourself.

3. Compare Chicago school and more structural Iowa/Indiana school symbolic interactionist approaches to the study of role transitions. How have these models been used to explain students' experiences during the transition to college? How does your experience making the transition from high school to college compare to the results of the studies on this topic discussed in the chapter?

4. How has the content of people's self-concepts changed in recent years? Is the self still a useful construct? Support your argument with reference to at least two of the studies discussed in this chapter.

CHAPTER 8

Emotions and Social Life

PHOTO 8.1

The impact of the widespread use of the social networking site Facebook on people's emotional well-being has been the subject of a number of recent studies. According to sociological social psychologists Hui-Tzu Grace Chou and Nicholas Edge (2012), the more time people spend on Facebook, the less happy they are and the more likely they are to believe that life is unfair.

Q: What underlies the link between Facebook, happiness, and perceptions of fairness?

A: Chou and Edge (2012) say social comparison processes. People compare themselves to this online reference group, who tend to restrict their postings to positive information about themselves and their families. These social comparisons, in turn, lead to negative self-evaluations, which may result in emotions such as sadness and perceptions of injustice.

Social psychologists argue that these and other emotions are an integral part of our social experience. Without emotion, society as we know it would not be possible.

We address this issue in this chapter as we discuss the relationships between cognition, culture, emotion, and behavior. As in the previous chapter, we focus on research by social psychologists trained as sociologists. However, where relevant, we also discuss some classic studies on emotion conducted by psychologists. It is through the integration of research from across the different faces of sociological social psychology, and from within psychology, that we gain the fullest understanding of the nature and functions of emotion in social life. We begin by defining some key terms used within the social psychological literature on emotions.

IMPORTANT TERMS

Social psychologists use the term **affect** to refer to positive and negative evaluative states (e.g., like or dislike). **Emotions** are more complex than affective states and are inherently social. They have physiological, cognitive, cultural, and behavioral components (Thoits 1989), which we identify and discuss later in the chapter.

A related concept, sentiment, highlights the social nature of people's emotive experiences (Stets 2003). **Sentiments** are socially constructed patterns of sensations, cultural meanings, and expressive gestures that pertain to a social object, most often another individual. They include love, loyalty, friendship, patriotism, grief, sorrow, and nostalgia (Gordon 1981).

"Feeling" and "mood" are two other terms used in discussions of emotion. The term **feeling** refers to an individual's subjective experience of an emotion. A **mood**, on the other hand, is a chronic affective state that is typically less intense than an emotion. Because they are less directly tied to particular events or situations, moods are of less interest to sociological social psychologists than emotions (Thoits 1989).

CATEGORIES OF EMOTION

There are two general categories of emotion: primary emotions and secondary emotions.

Primary Emotions

Primary emotions are emotions that occur in all humans. These emotions are presumed to be physiologically distinct and rooted in the evolution of the species. They are unsocialized and do not involve higher-level cognitive processes. Thus, they are evident even in infancy, and they occur cross-culturally (Kemper 1987).

They include fear, anger, happiness, sadness, and probably surprise and disgust (Turner and Stets 2005).

The **James-Lange theory of emotion** (James 1884; Lange 1885) links different kinds of physiological arousal to distinct emotions, such as fear. For example, if it's late at night and you encounter someone you don't know in your residence, you will experience physiological changes such as increased heart rate and trembling, which you will recognize as fear. From this perspective, every emotion is tied to a unique type of physiological arousal.

Zajonc's (1989) more recent arguments in support of a vascular theory of emotion are based on a similar notion. According to this view, changes in facial expressions lead to changes in blood flow, which result in temperature changes in the brain. These changes, in turn, give rise to the experience of particular emotive states.

In a well-known experiment designed as a test of this theory (Strack, Martin, and Stepper 1988), college students rated cartoons while holding a pen either with their lips or with their teeth (see Figure 8.1). Whereas the teeth condition resulted in a smile, the lips condition inhibited this facial expression. The cover story was that the researchers were assessing people's ability to complete tasks with body parts not typically used for this purpose, as might be required in the case of a physical disability. Thus, subjects did not associate the pen exercise with a particular facial expression, which meant that individuals in the "teeth" condition were not aware that they were smiling.

As the researchers expected, students in the pen-in-teeth condition reported that they were more amused by the cartoons than the individuals in the pen-in-lips condition. Have you ever heard the phrase "Just smile and you'll feel better." This suggests that this platitude may actually be true. Facial movements associated with smiling lead to physiological changes in the brain, due to vascular changes that reduce brain temperature, which give rise to positive affect (Zajonc, Murphy, and Inglehart 1989).

Conversely, the absence of facial feedback associated with emotions, due to neurological disease or, as is now relatively common, the use of Botox (Botulinum toxin), may inhibit emotions. Botox is injected into the facial muscles to reduce, or prevent, facial wrinkles. It is commonly used among actresses who are concerned

FIGURE 8.1

This figure shows the technique used in Strack et al.'s (1988) study to induce positive affect.

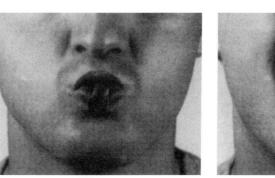
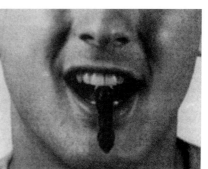

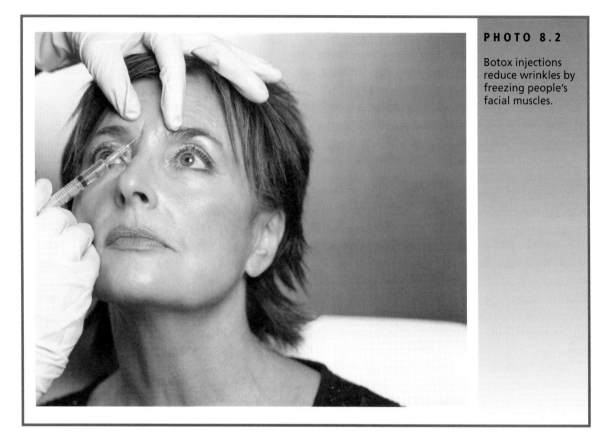

PHOTO 8.2

Botox injections reduce wrinkles by freezing people's facial muscles.

about aging out of the industry (as you probably know, it is often difficult for older actresses to get desirable roles). Botox reduces wrinkles by freezing the individual's facial muscles in the areas in which the shots are given (usually around the eyes, on the forehead, or in the nasolabial folds around the mouth).

Interestingly, subjects using Botox reacted with less emotion to a series of video clips than individuals in the (no Botox) control group in a recent experiment. This finding supports the notion that facial movements may create, or strengthen, particular feelings (Davis et al. 2010).

Note the studies reviewed in this section, laboratory experiments, were conducted by psychological social psychologists. Although these findings are of limited interest to sociological social psychologists, who focus on the social origin of emotions, it is important to recognize that physiological changes may themselves affect our emotive experiences.

Secondary Emotions

Given their inherently social basis, sociological social psychologists (and some psychologists) focus on secondary emotions. Unlike primary emotions, **secondary emotions** are socially constructed. Thus, they are acquired through socialization, as people learn to pair physiological arousal that emerges in particular situations with culturally defined labels (Thoits 1989).

There are many secondary emotions, including sentiments such as pride, shame, guilt, and resentment (Kemper 1987; Thoits 1989). Secondary emotions are uniquely human because they emerge only when a bodily sensation is given a cognitive label. The cognitive labels that give meaning to our affective experiences are based on the immediate situation within which behavior occurs, as well as on broader cultural factors.

Labeling Based on Situational Cues

Schachter and Singer's (1962) famous study of the social determinants of the emotions anger and euphoria illustrates the importance of situational cues in shaping people's emotive experiences. The subjects in this study were told that they would be given a vitamin injection as part of a study on the effects of vitamins on vision (the cover story). In reality, they were given either an injection of adrenaline or a placebo (saline). Adrenaline increases arousal and results in an elevated heart rate, sweating, and tremor. (Note that given Given the physiological effects of adrenalin, Schachter and Singer's experiment would not pass an institutional review board today. The risk to subjects would be considered too great).

Some of the subjects in the adrenaline condition in Schachter and Singer's (1962) experiment were told that they could expect increases in physiological arousal as the result of the shot. Others were not given this information.

After the injections were given, subjects were placed in a room with a confederate of the experimenter. In the anger condition, subjects were asked to complete a written questionnaire including items that most people would perceive as rude. For example, they were asked to report how many family members they had who "do not bathe or wash regularly," with response options that excluded "none." The confederate of the experimenter acted as though he was annoyed with the questions and verbalized his ostensible displeasure with the questionnaire's content.

In the euphoria condition, subjects were placed in a room in a state of disarray. It contained paper, folders, and some hula hoops. The confederate of the experimenter began flying paper airplanes. Then he engaged in a game of basketball, during which he tossed balls of paper into the wastebasket. Finally, he grabbed a hula hoop and twirled it on his arm, saying "Hey, look, this is great."

The purpose of this manipulation (anger vs. euphoria) was to provide the subjects injected with adrenaline with a cognitive label for their physiological arousal. Schachter and Singer (1962) hypothesized that those individuals who were given adrenaline and were unaware of the side effects of the shot would mislabel their physiological arousal as either anger or euphoria, in accordance with the social setting in which they were placed and the confederate's behavior.

This is exactly what they found. An assessment of subjects' self-reported emotional states at the end of the experiment, as well as the observation of their behavior when they were in the room with the confederate, revealed the expected pattern of results. Subjects in the anger condition injected with adrenaline and not informed about the effects of the shot appeared angry, whereas subjects who received the adrenaline without a warning about the side effects reported and acted as though they were euphoric. These individuals were aroused, and not knowing that this was caused by the shot they received, they labeled the arousal as an emotion (either anger or euphoria) based on available situational cues.

Subjects in the placebo condition, and those individuals given adrenaline and informed of the shot's physiological consequences, had quite different experiences than the latter subjects. The placebo subjects did not experience the physiological arousal that gives rise to emotions. Thus, those in the "anger" group did not appear to be as angry as the subjects placed in that setting who were given the injection of adrenaline and not informed of its effects. Nor did the placebo subjects in the "euphoria" condition seem to experience this emotion the way that adrenaline-uninformed subjects did. Although the subjects in the adrenaline-informed group were aroused due to the shot, they correctly attributed their elevated heart rate, sweating, and tremor to the "vitamin" injection. Thus, they had no reason to define their physiological arousal as an emotion.

This study provided the basis of Schachter and Singer's (1962) **two factor theory of emotion**. The two-factor theory states that emotions have two components: physiological arousal and a cognitive label. People become aroused and they label that arousal as an emotion based upon what is going on around them.

Based on their findings, Schachter and Singer (1962) argue that all emotions are rooted in the same physiological reactions. People experience them as specific, or distinct, emotions only insofar as they label this arousal differently in different social contexts. From this perspective, when you're arguing with someone, you label the arousal you experience as anger. If it's dark out, you're alone, and you hear footsteps behind you, you label the same physiological arousal as fear. However, when you experience this kind of central nervous system activation after acing an exam, you define it as joy.

What Do You Think?

Think about the last time you experienced anger, fear, or joy. Evaluate your experience in relation to Schachter and Singer's two-factor theory of emotion. Do your experiences seem consistent with their argument?

Some later studies did not replicate Schachter and Singer's (1962) findings, fueling criticism that their argument may be overstated. Other studies have, however, yielded results consistent with their two-factor theory.

Experiments designed to test the effects of cognitive labeling on emotive experience would be expected to yield inconsistent results insofar as environmental manipulations themselves induce emotions. In particular, subjects may become aroused *due to* an environmental manipulation, like the anger or euphoria conditions in Schachter and Singer's study, and label that experience as a particular emotion. Thus, inconsistencies within the research literature do not necessarily negate the two-factor theory of emotion (Thoits 1989).

With this in mind, Thoits (1989) offers a more flexible account of emotive experience that distinguishes between primary and secondary emotions. Primary emotions may coincide directly with specific, and unique, forms of central nervous system activation. On the other hand, secondary emotions probably have a similar physiological basis and emerge through a cognitive labeling process. Most contemporary social psychologists agree with this assessment.

Cultural Factors

Most sociological social psychologists accept the validity of Schachter and Singer's (1962) two-factor theory of emotion. However, they see the two factors, physiological arousal and labeling based on situation cues, as only a part of the equation. There are also broader social forces, existing above and beyond any given person or interactive setting, that shape people's emotive experiences.

Every culture has a vocabulary pertaining to emotive experience. As noted earlier, language plays a role in shaping people's perceptions (remember the Sapir-Whorf hypothesis and the cow example from the chapter on socialization). Thus, the labels available for different emotions within a particular culture, and beliefs about their origin and interrelationship, influence people's experiences and the degree of distinction they make between different types of feeling (Gordon 1981; Wierzbicka 1999). See Box 8.1 for a list of emotions unique to particular cultures.

Box 8.1   Emotions From Around the Globe

Label/phrase	Language	What it means
Uttori	Japanese	Enraptured by the loveliness of something
Ai bu shi shou	Chinese	So delighted with something that one can't keep one's hands off it
Sekaseka	Bemba (Congo and Zambia)	To laugh without reason
Bas-bhualadh	Scottish Gaelic	Clapping one's hands from joy or grief
Bel hevi	Tok Pisin (Papau New Guinea)	The heavy sinking feeling that accompanies extreme sadness (literally, belly heavy)
Termangu-mangu	Indonesian	Sad and not sure what to do
Hiraeth	Welsh	Feeling of sadness between homesickness and nostalgia
Saudade	Portuguese	The longing for things that might have been

Note: de Boinod (2005).

Across social settings, **emotion norms** also shape the way we experience and express emotion. **Display rules** tell us how we should express our emotions, and failing to adhere to these norms will typically generate negative reactions (Hochschild 1979, 1983). For example, students who cheer loudly or cry when they receive their exam grade in class are violating a display rule and are likely to receive negative feedback from their peers (some of the "Aces" and "Bombers," described in Chapter 3, attested to this fact). Other violations of display rules likely to get a reaction include laughing at a funeral; laughing or crying during a formal presentation (e.g., a speech) or performance (e.g., a band concert); laughing when people tell you about something negative that happened to them; hitting someone who has made you angry while working on a group project; laughing or snickering when being admonished by a teacher; or crying on a daily basis, which may be defined as reflective of an illness (depression).

The inappropriate expression of emotion—that is, the expression of emotion in a manner that is not consistent with prevailing emotion norms—is considered to be one of the overt indicators of mental illness (American Psychiatric Association 2013). Young children are also chronic violators of display rules, as they have not yet learned these norms or acquired the role-taking skills necessary to gauge others' responses to their behavior. Because they are observable, violations of display rules are often obvious.

Feeling rules are social norms that tell us how we should and shouldn't feel in particular situations. Violations of feeling rules tend to be more private affairs than the violation of display rules. People can readily hide the fact that they are violating a feeling rule by acting appropriately and by keeping how they are feeling to themselves (Hochschild 1979, 1983).

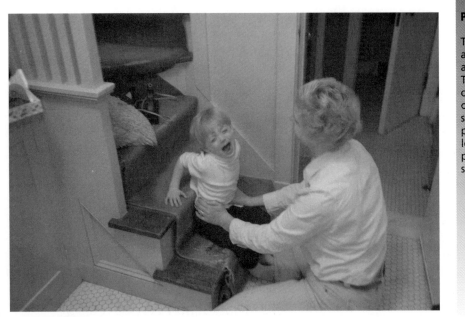

PHOTO 8.3

Temper tantrums are common among children. The ability to control, or channel one's emotions in socially appropriate ways, is learned during primary socialization.

The following scenarios illustrate the violation of feeling rules: an individual's father dies and she doesn't feel sad; someone feels sad for weeks after the death of a celebrity he did not know personally (most people would think this is excessive); or a student experiences rage (vs. anger or sadness) after failing an exam. In these situations, people are likely to perceive their feelings (or the lack thereof) as inappropriate and may attempt to change them so that they are consistent with social norms.

What Do You Think?

- Think of a time when you violated a display rule. What did you do, and what were the consequences of your violation of this emotion norm? Describe any changes in your behavior that occurred in response to the reactions of others to your nonnormative behavior.
- Can you think of a time when you violated a feeling rule? If so, what feeling rule did you violate? What, if anything, did you do to change your feelings so that they were more consistent with societal expectations?

Emotion Management

In most social contexts, people express emotions in a manner viewed as appropriate by others. **Emotion management**, also called emotion work, is the process through which we strive to control our feelings so that they meet the expectations of others present in the social encounter and broader societal standards (Hochschild 1979, 1983).

We asked you to describe some situations in which you may have managed your emotions so that your behavior and feelings were consistent with prevailing emotion norms. That was probably relatively easy to do. Most of us have reigned in, or sought to modify, our emotions at one time or another.

The strategies that people use to manage their emotions fall into two general categories, identified by Hochschild (1979, 1983): surface acting and deep acting. **Surface acting** involves displaying emotions in a manner appropriate to the social setting. This is a part of the process of impression management (Rafaeli and Sutton 1989) and often requires hiding one's true feelings or pretending to have a particular feeling (e.g., playing off the disappointment one feels after receiving a failing score on an exam by acting as though getting such a low score is funny). Thus, surface acting involves some deception and is likely to be perceived by the actor as inauthentic.

Deep acting, on the other hand, involves conscious attempts at changing the way one feels so that it is consistent with one's behaviors and prevailing feeling rules (Hochschild 1983). This might mean convincing yourself that you really don't care about a poor exam score; trying not to feel too sad when someone you barely know dies, even if you admire that person (you're allowed some grief, but not as much as would be acceptable with the loss of someone you were more intimately involved with); and trying to believe that you're happy with your life, or your current (romantic) relationship, even if this isn't the case.

Much of the literature on emotion management has focused on the workplace. Workers are often required to manage their emotions on the job. Individuals in service industries (e.g., flight attendants, wait staff, customer service representatives, and salespeople), in particular, are expected to be happy and friendly. Because it is important to appear authentic (fake smiles are not good for public relations), they are expected to manage their feelings, as well as their behaviors. Thus, within a capitalist economy, emotions have become a commodity. People aren't just selling their labor; they're selling their feelings. Emotion management at or in relation to work is called **emotional labor** (Hochschild 1983).

Table 8.1 lists occupations in the United States that require among the highest levels of emotional labor. Emotional labor was measured by assessing the degree to which jobs required caring for others, interacting with customers, being present in situations involving conflict, dealing with people who are angry or unpleasant,

JOB	FEMALE (%)
Lawyers	33
Correctional institution officers	23
Registered nurses	93
Bill and account collectors	70
Sheriffs, bailiffs, and other law enforcement officers	18
Dispatchers	51
Social workers	70
Public transportation attendants	78
Therapists	73
Receptionists	97
Sales counter clerks	64
Managers, marketing, advertising, and public relations	37
Sales workers, mechanical equipment	9
Sales workers, apparel	80
Waiters and waitresses	77
Public relations specialists	63
Administrators, education and related fields	60
Sales workers, electronics	26
Teachers, special education	82
Counselors, educational and vocational	69

TABLE 8.1

Twenty Jobs That Require High Levels of Emotion Management

Note: Adapted from Bhave and Glomb (2009).

working with the public, and communicating with individuals outside of the organization (Bhave and Glomb 2009).

As shown in Table 8.1, some of the occupations requiring a lot of emotional labor are dominated by men (e.g., correctional officers), whereas others are predominantly female (e.g., registered nurses). However, the degree to which the occupants of a job must demonstrate concern about the emotions of others tends to vary with the position's gender composition. For example, prison guards have power over inmates and are not required to assess and respond to the prisoners' emotional needs. This is not the case for nurses, who are expected to care about their patients' feelings.

Other occupants of female-dominated jobs, like receptionists, must regularly defer to others. Given their subordinate status within the larger society, the women in these jobs are likely to find it especially difficult to deflect the negative emotions of the customers with whom they have contact (Hochschild 1983).

Hochschild (1983) has expressed concern about the consequences of the commodification of emotion for the individual. In particular, people who engage in emotional labor may become estranged from their feelings. They may no longer view their emotive experiences as meaningful and indicative of who they are or what they really feel. Thus, they may no longer perceive their emotions as part of a core or authentic self (Hochschild 1983).

The notion that people potentially define their core, or real, selves in terms of their emotions probably sounds familiar. It is consistent with Turner's (1976) argument that many individuals locate their real selves in their impulsive experiences.

Expanding upon Turner's thesis, Gordon (1989) suggests that how people define their emotions is shaped by the anchorage of the real self. Individuals who define themselves in terms of impulse may experience emotions as more intense and short-term than people who locate their real selves in institutions.

Whereas emotion work is likely to involve controlling or redirecting emotions in a socially prescribed manner among individuals who are institutionally oriented, impulsives may resist this. Individuals who locate their real self in impulsive experiences typically seek to reduce their inhibitions and release their emotions. Thus, they may find it especially difficult to work in settings where their emotions are regulated by company policies (Gordon 1989).

Interestingly, it is surface, rather than deep, acting that appears to have the most negative psychological consequences, including perceived estrangement from one's feelings, as well as emotional exhaustion or burnout (Wharton 2009). There is some evidence that deep acting, that is emotion work that generates feelings consonant with those expected of one in a particular job, may enhance the extent that individuals value being a member of the organization they work for and their levels of job satisfaction (Agrawal and Sadhana 2010; Godwyn 2006).

In retail settings, where emotional labor is at its peak, deep acting is most likely to have positive consequences when the job involves long-term customer relationships and workers have autonomy and can control the kinds of relationships they construct within this context (Godwyn 2006).

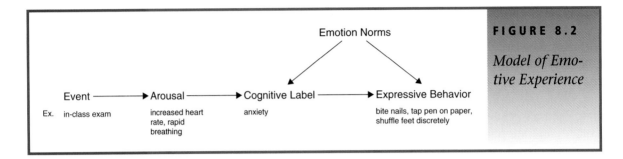

FIGURE 8.2

Model of Emotive Experience

What Do You Think?

Form a group with two or three of your classmates. Compile a list of the various jobs you have held (part time or full time, including current jobs).

- What kind of emotional labor do these jobs require?
- Which of these jobs requires the most emotional labor? Why?
- How difficult are these emotional requirements for the jobs' occupants? Group members with experience in these jobs should lead this part of the discussion. If a job was (or is) clearly temporary, consider how that might have affected (might affect) its occupants' reactions.

Group members should also consider the jobs they plan to obtain after they graduate. Evaluate the extent to which these jobs require emotional labor and how this influences their perceived desirability.

Model of Emotive Experience

Figure 8.2 depicts the components of people's emotive experiences, discussed in the preceding section: precipitating situations or events, physiological arousal, the cognitive label that identifies this experience a particular emotion, and expressive gestures. Prevailing cultural norms, and the characteristics of the setting in which interaction occurs, shape how we label, as well as express, our emotions (Thoits 1989).

EMOTION AS SOCIAL CONTROL FROM A SYMBOLIC INTERACTIONIST PERSPECTIVE

Although culture shapes individuals' emotive experiences, emotions emerge within the context of people's face-to-face interactions and play a significant role in the self-regulation of behavior at the micro level. Much of the literature on emotion as social control comes from within the symbolic interactionist face of sociological social psychology. It includes analyses of emotions produced by the process of role taking and their consequences, a key concern of traditional (Chicago school) symbolic interactionists, as well as research within the dramaturgical tradition on emotions and self-presentation.

Reflexive Role Taking and the Self-Regulation of Behavior

Reflexive role taking (viewing oneself as an object through the eyes of others) results in a variety of emotions, including pride. As noted in our discussion of the looking-glass self in Chapter 7, people experience pride when they believe that they have received positive evaluations from others.

Because it is rooted in the evaluations of others, pride promotes normative conduct. However, there are three other emotions associated with the process of reflexive role taking—embarrassment, shame, and guilt—that play an even greater role in regulating people's behaviors. People behave in an appropriate manner most of the time in order to avoid experiencing these emotions. Thus, they provide the basis for the relatively stable patterns of behavior that characterize society (Shott 1979).

Embarrassment and Shame

As noted in earlier chapters, **embarrassment** is the physiological arousal that arises when social norms, including display rules, are violated in public encounters. We feel embarrassed when we take the role of others, evaluate the quality of our self-presentation through their eyes, and recognize that we have failed to convey a positive impression.

Shame, on the other hand, occurs when someone realizes that an individual, a group to which they belong, or society at large (the generalized other) views them as deficient in some way. When the person someone is does not match the person he or she would like to be, that individual will experience the sense of inadequacy that characterizes shame.

The perceived self-deficiencies that give rise to shame may be based, in part, on failed public performances. Thus, people who experience shame are also likely to feel embarrassed. However, because embarrassment is situation specific, individuals frequently feel embarrassed without experiencing shame (Shott 1979).

College students are often the focus of studies on the nature and function of embarrassment and shame, and they indicate that these emotions have notably different origins. They associate embarrassment with relatively trivial and surprising incidents (e.g., falling on the stairs on the way to class), whereas they attribute shame to the revelation of personal flaws (e.g., that one is dishonest or unintelligent). College students also report that shame is more intense and longer in duration than embarrassment (Miller and Tangney 1994).

Despite its transient nature, embarrassment is an unavoidable aspect of social life. Everyone, even those most competent of social actors, experiences embarrassment at one time or another (Goffman 1959).

As you know, people will go to great lengths to avoid embarrassment in public settings. This includes behaving in a manner consistent with social norms and helping others save face by pretending that one has not noticed their transgressions. The avoidance of the negative self-assessment that underlies shame, on the other hand, may involve the regulation of both private and public behaviors (Shott 1979).

BEHAVIORAL INDICATORS OF EMBARRASSMENT AND SHAME

People often blush when they are embarrassed. Moreover, they frequently engage in what sociologist Thomas Scheff (1990) calls **hiding behaviors**. They stammer, repeat words, pause frequently and for longer than is typical, and speak softly. They also avoid eye contact with others and cover their face with their hands. It is as though they are trying to avoid scrutiny of themselves and their perceived failures by distancing themselves from the encounter (Scheff 1990).

Scheff and a colleague (Suzanne Retzinger) observed these indicators of embarrassment, along with expressions of surprise, in their analysis of "moment of truth" revelations in episodes of the television show *Candid Camera* (Scheff 1985, 1990). This television program ran for many years. Unwitting participants were filmed in unusual situations, which they did not realize were staged. The purpose of the show was to watch their reactions to the situation itself and to the disclosure that it wasn't real.

Variants of this program have aired on television in recent years and currently include *Scare Tactics* (originally hosted by Shannen Doherty, followed by Stephen Baldwin and, most recently, Tracy Morgan) and *Punk'd*, with Ashton Kutcher. If you have seen any of these shows, you know that they are fairly effective in their mission of embarrassing their victim.

Shame, versus embarrassment, is frequently displayed by individuals who have been caught engaging in a behavior regarded by others as abhorrent (e.g., molesting a child), which has resulted in potentially irreparable damage to the way in which others view them. Like embarrassment, shame may result in hiding behaviors, especially when individuals are asked to discuss their deficiencies publically. These types of responses (e.g., covering one's face, avoiding eye contact, and speaking softly) are sometimes evidenced in television interviews during which the perpetrator admits his or her transgressions and asks for forgiveness or acceptance.

Because shame is so damaging to a person's self-concept, when feasible (e.g., when the individual hasn't been caught on tape), it often results in the denial of any wrongdoing. Or people experiencing shame will emphasize the reasons for which they are not responsible for their actions. This rarely happens when individuals experience the related emotion, guilt. This is because guilt is not directly tied to our sense of self the way that shame is (Tangney and Dearing 2002).

Guilt

Whereas shame involves a perceived self-deficiency, guilt arises in response to a specific behavior (Tangney and Dearing 2002). The desire to avoid the experience of guilt is the main reason why people behave in a responsible and moral fashion. Note that the desire to avoid shame may also lead to moral conduct, but shame is not directly tied to the morality of an individual's actions the way that guilt is. For example, someone might experience shame after flunking out of school or getting fired from a job for poor performance, but the behaviors leading to these outcomes are not regarded as immoral.

Guilt emerges when individuals take the role of the generalized other (society at large), evaluate their behaviors within the context of societal norms, and recognize that they have acted immorally. Guilt is an especially powerful regulator of behavior because it is not necessarily linked to the appraisals of specific others. No one else need know that one has violated a norm (or law) for that person to experience guilt following the transgression. In this sense, guilt is a more private emotion than embarrassment or shame (Shott 1979).

Parents often recognize the power of guilt in shaping their children's behaviors. Once children internalize the household rules, parents no longer need to monitor them constantly. Children police themselves, as any transgression will result in the unpleasant feeling we label guilt.

The capacity for guilt emerges with the synthesis of the generalized other in early adolescence, during the game stage. However, studies of children's reactions to various social situations suggest that they begin developing the ability to experience guilt as a distinct emotion by the age of about 4 or 5 (Mascolo and Fisher 1995).

Embarrassability and Other Dispositional Differences

Although everyone experiences embarrassment, shame, or guilt at some point in their life, some people have a dispositional sensitivity to these emotions. A susceptibility to embarrassment is called **embarrassability**. People high in embarrassability are more prone to embarrassment across social encounters than is typical (Modigliani 1968). As a result, they are more likely than other people to avoid potentially embarrassing situations and to become flustered when embarrassing transgressions occur (Miller 2009).

Embarrassability can be measured using a standard set of survey questions. These items are presented in Box 8.2. This embarrassability index (Modigliani 1966) captures the contagious aspect of embarrassment, described by Goffman (1959), as a number of the questions assess individuals' reactions to the embarrassing behaviors of others.

How does your score compare with those of other college students (compare your score to the mean score for your gender)? Note that women usually score higher

Box 8.2 Measuring Embarrassability

Please indicate how you would personally feel in each situation using a 9-point scale ranging from 0 = "not the least embarrassing" to 9 = "extremely embarrassing."

0——1——2——3——4——5——6——7——8——9

Not at all embarrassing   extremely embarrassing

Item	Response
1. You slip and fall on a patch of ice in a public place, dropping a package of groceries.	_____
2. You are a dinner guest, and the guest seated next to you spills his plate in his lap while trying to cut some meat.	_____
3. A group of friends are singing "Happy Birthday" to you.	_____
4. You discover you are the only person at a social occasion without formal dress.	_____
5. You are watching an amateur show and one of the performers who is trying to do a comedy act is unable to make people laugh.	_____
6. You are calling someone you have just met for the first time in order to arrange a date.	_____
7. You are muttering aloud to yourself in an apparently empty room when you discover someone else is there.	_____
8. You walk into a bathroom at someone else's house and discover that it is occupied by a member of the opposite sex.	_____
9. You are in the audience watching a play when it suddenly becomes clear that one of the actors has forgotten his or her lines, causing the play to come to a standstill.	_____
10. You are being lavishly complimented on your pleasant personality by your partner on your first date.	_____
11. You notice that your professor has forgotten to zip his fly.	_____
12. You enter an apparently empty room, turn on the light, and surprise a couple making out.	_____
13. You are talking to a stranger who stutters badly due to a speech impediment.	_____
14. Your mother or father has come to visit you and was accompanying you to college.	_____
15. You are a dinner guest and cannot eat the main course because you are allergic to it.	_____
16. You are alone in the elevator with your professor who has just given you a bad grade.	_____
17. You walk into a room full of people you do not know and are introduced to the whole group.	_____
18. You trip and fall while entering a bus full of people.	_____
19. You are opening some presents while the people who have given them to you are watching.	_____
20. You ask someone on crutches if they have had a skiing accident and they tell you they were crippled by polio as a child.	_____
21. You have forgotten an appointment with your professor, and remember it as you meet him or her in the entrance the next day.	_____

22. You are talking in a small group that includes a blind person, when someone next to that person unthinkingly makes a remark about everyone being as blind as a bat. _____

Total score   _____

Note: Modigliani (1966), as modified by Edelmann (1987) with minor changes.

College males (n = 97)   College females (n = 110)
Mean = 89.4   Mean = 100.5
SD = 25.1   SD = 25.6

than men on this measure. Presumably, this reflects women's high propensity for role taking relative to men (see Box 6.5) or gender differences in other characteristics acquired during the primary socialization process.

People also vary in their susceptibility to shame and to guilt. In general, individuals prone to shame are at risk for low self-esteem, depression, and anxiety. A dispositional susceptibility to guilt, on the other hand, has largely positive consequences, in particular social connectedness and the enactment of behaviors defined by most people as moral. Dispositional susceptibilities to shame and guilt are usually learned in childhood and may reflect parents' childrearing practices (Tangney, Youman, and Stuewig 2009).

Empathic Role Taking and Sympathy

Sympathy is another role-taking emotion that serves a self-regulatory function. It involves empathy, taking the perspective of another person, and sharing in his or her feelings. As such, sympathy strengthens the bond between individuals and gives rise to prosocial behavior (Clark 1987; Shott 1979).

Rules for Giving and Receiving Sympathy

The process of sympathizing is highly regulated in this culture, as it is governed by a clearly defined set of emotion norms. People are not only expected to feel sorry for someone who has had something bad happen (a feeling rule), they are expected to actively express sympathy for others (a display rule). Typically, this means listening to someone talk about their illness, divorce, breakup, crisis, accident, mistake, or loss; making it clear through one's demeanor that the person's problem is being taken seriously; and providing emotional and more tangible types of support, such as offering someone a ride when his or her car is broken, as needed. Failure to engage in these displays of sympathy is not likely to be well received and will result in negative reactions from others (Clark 1987).

PHOTO 8.4

People in the U.S. often express sympathy by giving flowers to a person who has suffered an illness, trauma, or loss.

There are also norms governing sympathy claims (requests for sympathy). Clark (1987) offers the following guidelines for managing sympathy requests.

1. Don't pretend you need sympathy when this isn't the case. That is, don't make up or exaggerate claims in order to manipulate others into giving you sympathy. If you do this, when you really need sympathy, people won't believe that your claim is legitimate.

2. Don't ask for too much sympathy. You shouldn't ask for sympathy too frequently or for too long period of time. This requires too much effort on the part of the sympathizers.

3. Claim sympathy when it is appropriate to do so. People are likely to distance themselves from someone who never needs their support.

4. Reciprocate. Individuals who fail to give sympathy are likely to get little in return.

Clark (1987) calls the sympathy individuals are due from others their sympathy margin. A **sympathy margin** is like an account that accrues credits and debits as a function of the merit of one's claims to sympathy in the eyes of others and the extent to which they have abided by sympathy rules in the past. Thus, the rules of sympathy etiquette may affect the balance of power in people's relationships (those to whom a sympathy debt is owed experience an increase in power). They may also be used to enhance one's prestige through public displays (Clark 1987). Thus, there is a notable strategic, as well as cultural, aspect to the process of sympathizing (Turner and Stets 2005).

What Do You Think?

Can you think of an example where someone (you, an individual you know personally, or a media figure) made a public display of sympathy? What was the primary motivation for doing so? Was this display of sympathy effective in achieving this end? Why was or wasn't it effective?

Identities and Emotion

The relationship between socially based identities, emotion, and behavior is another topic of interest to social psychologists working within the symbolic interactionist face of social psychology.

Identity Control Theory

Identity control theory (ICT) (Burke 1991) is an extension of Stryker's (1980) identity theory that emphasizes the role of emotion in the self-verification process. In general, self-verification is associated with positive emotions (e.g., self-esteem). On the other hand, failure to receive confirmation for a salient identity results in negative emotions (e.g., distress and anxiety), even when the feedback received from others is positive (Burke and Stets 2009).

According to ICT, the identity process is a cybernetic feedback loop in which ongoing situational meanings associated with salient identities usually match individuals' identity standards (the meanings individuals attach to their identities) (Turner and Stets 2005). A **cybernetic model** is like a thermostat, where outputs are used as benchmarks for the control of inputs. In the case of a heating system, for example, the output is the temperature of the air. When the temperature drops to a certain point, the heater turns on and runs until the temperature reaches the desired level, at which point the system turns off.

In the **identity control system**, feelings are the outputs that indicate whether the system needs realignment. Positive feelings are associated with the verification of salient identities and signify that the system is functioning smoothly. In contrast, negative feelings arise in response to unverified identities and signal that the system is in need of adjustment.

Typically, the negative emotion generated by disruptions to the identity control system is strongest when the source of the discrepant (non-self-verifying) feedback is from significant others, such as family members, friends, and others with whom the individual has a close relationship. Non-self-verifying feedback from significant others is likely to prompt notable changes in behavior (strategic attempts to receive self-verifying feedback for the identity in question) or perception (changes in one's identity standard) (Burke and Stets 2009). From this perspective, it is emotional reactions to discrepancies between situational meanings associated with a given identity and an individual's identity standard that underlie the relationship between self-concept and behavior.

Affect Control Theory

Affect control theory (ACT) (Heise 1977) is another prominent cybernetic model of the identity-behavior relationship within the symbolic interactionist tradition. Like ICT, ACT is based on the assumption that emotions signal the manner in which an individual is experiencing a situation (Robinson, Smith-Lovin, and Wisecup 2006). However, ACT is broader in scope than ICT in that it focuses on culturally shared views (vs. self-views) about what a given identity means (Turner and Stets 2005).

Affect control theorists argue that people frame events by generating cognitive labels, mediated by language. These cognitive labels, in turn, give rise to situational definitions that result in affective meanings (Robinson and Smith-Lovin 2006).

ACT focuses on two categories of affective meaning: fundamental sentiments and transient impressions. **Fundamental sentiments** are affective meanings about identities and behavior that are shared by societal members and thus transcend any given situation. **Transient impressions**, on the other hand, are the affective meanings tied to particular events or situations (Turner and Stet 2005).

Both fundamental sentiments and transient impressions reflect the three universal dimensions of affect identified by Osgood and associates (1957, 1975), termed evaluation (good, nice vs. bad, awful), potency (powerful, big vs. weak, little) and activity (fast, noisy, young vs. slow, quiet, old). Scores on each dimension range from −4.23 to 4.23, where 0 indicates neutral meaning (Heise 1999).

There are evaluation, potency, and activity (EPA) profiles available for numerous identities, behaviors, personal characteristics, and social settings. The identity of a social worker, for instance, has the following EPA profile: moderately good (evaluation score = 1.77), slightly powerful (potency score = .96), and slightly active (activity score = .39). ACT predicts that an individual with this identity will enact behaviors (e.g., help, aid, and trust) with similar EPA scores and thus similar meanings (DeCoster 2002). Other identities, their EPA profiles, and consonant behaviors are shown in Box 8.3.

The key premise of ACT, called the **control principle**, is that people strive to keep transient impressions in line with fundamental sentiments. When discrepancies between transient impressions and fundamental sentiments, called **deflections**, occur, people will engage in behaviors that repair the situation so that the transient impression matches the fundamental sentiment. For example, given common cultural meanings, an employee correcting a boss generates a deflection, which

Box 8.3 EPA Profiles for Identities and Behaviors With Similar Meanings

E = Evaluation
P = Power
A = Activity

IDENTITY	E	P	A	BEHAVIOR	E	P	A
Surgeon	3.02	2.82	.99	Heal	2.94	2.76	1.18
Great grandmother	2.05	.70	−1.11	Snuggle	2.52	1.24	−1.48
Honeymooner	2.26	1.09	1.84	Cheer	2.56	1.72	2.35
Toddler	1.44	−1.39	1.33	Escape	1.37	.63	1.35
Boss	.48	2.16	.94	Discipline	.66	1.76	.83
Subordinate	−.44	−1.61	−.41	Beg	−1.64	−1.76	−.34
Librarian	1.07	−.70	−1.79	Whisper to	.85	.19	1.30
Bully	−2.61	1.17	1.38	Assault	−2.52	1.10	1.50
Brat	−2.42	−.93	1.60	Scream at	−1.79	.45	2.03
Wife abuser	−3.69	−2.15	.39	Rape	−3.10	−.59	1.07

Note: Adapted from Nelson (2007).

can be repaired if the employee engages in a behavior that indicates admiration for the boss or the boss instructs or counsels the employee. These actions would confirm our fundamental sentiments about bosses, employees, and correcting (Robinson et al. 2006).

We also expect the identities and behaviors in Box 8.3 to go together because they share common meanings (based on their evaluation, power, and activity ratings). Note the most positive identity in Box 8.3, associated with the most positive behavior, is "surgeon" and "heal," respectively. A surgeon (3.02, 2.82, .99) assaulting someone (−2.52, 1.10, 1.50) would generate a large deflection. Similarly, the identity "great grandmother" is evaluated positively, despite a moderate power and low activity rating, and is expected to coincide with a positive, moderate power and low activity behavior (snuggle). A great grandmother (2.05, .70, −1.11) who screams at someone (−1.79, .45, 2.03) will generate a deflection because this identity and behavior do not have similar meanings.

According to the **reconstruction principle**, people redefine situations by altering the characteristics of the people present in the encounter whenever deflections are too large for repair. There is, for instance, no behavior that can repair the deflection created by a mother who abandons her child, an action highly inconsistent with the fundamental sentiment attached to the identity of "mother." Thus, people will redefine this actor by assigning her an alternative identity (e.g., bully) (Robinson and Smith-Lovin 2006).

Could the deflection associated with a surgeon who assaults or with the grand-mother who screams at someone be repaired? The grandmother might repair the discrepancy between her identity and behavior by acting in a loving manner. It would, however, be more difficult to repair the deflection created by the surgeon who assaulted someone because the discrepancy between identity and behavior is notably larger. Thus, he or she may also be redefined as a bully, the identity with the EPA profile similar to the behavior in question, assault.

Deflections also arise when feedback disconfirms an individual's own identities. In general, situations in which transient impressions are more negative than the fundamental sentiments associated with an identity result in negative emotions. Deflections in which transient impressions are more positive than identity-relevant fundamental sentiments, on the other hand, result in positive emotions. Interestingly, this does not inhibit the tendency toward self-verification among people with negative self-images, discussed earlier. Research suggests that people will seek out interactions with others that verify their negative self-concepts even when doing so means forgoing interpersonal feedback that would create deflections that would make them feel better (Robinson and Smith-Lovin 1992).

Tests of ACT often use mathematical equations developed to predict behaviors that produce transient impressions that match fundamental sentiments in specific situations or to predict actors' responses to deflections (Robinson and Smith-Lovin 2006). Researchers use a computer program called INTERACT (Heise and Lewis 1988) to complete the required calculations. If you want more information about this program and ACT, check out the ACT website: http://www.indiana.edu/~socpsy/ACT/index.htm.

Studies comparing participants' responses to events with the results of INTERACT simulations support the tenets of ACT. These analyses have enabled social psychologists to more clearly define what it means to be a normal social actor and to understand the motivations behind people's social behaviors (Robinson and Smith-Lovin 2006).

Take a Break

If you haven't already seen it, watch the film *Equilibrium,* starring Christian Bale and Emily Watson. It's available through most major distributors (e.g., Netflix, Hulu, Blockbuster). It is an action film (a warning for those who don't favor this genre), but it makes an interesting statement about emotions and humanity.

EMOTION AS A PRODUCT OF GROUP PROCESSES AND STRUCTURES

Social psychologists working within the group processes and structures face of social psychology focus on social exchange and emotions and on the role of emotions in the reproduction of status differences in task groups.

Social Exchange and Emotion

People experience global emotions as the result of the exchange process, which they attribute to objects, including themselves, others, or social units (Lawler 2001). These emotions are important outcomes of the exchange of resources, as individuals are motivated to maximize positive, and minimize negative, feelings across social encounters (Homans 1961). Given this motivation, negative emotions as the result of the social exchange process are likely to result in the termination of an exchange relationship, especially when there are other alternatives (potential exchange partners).

Recall that negotiated exchanges involve explicit agreements as to the terms of the trade and include transactions like buying a computer from a friend or paying someone for tutoring. If someone feels the exchange is successful, they will feel proud. Shame, on the other hand, results from the belief that one should have negotiated a better result (Lawler 2001).

Have you ever felt good, or bad, about yourself following a negotiated exchange? Buying a car is one transaction that often results in feelings of self-deficiency. People believe that they should have gotten a better deal (they're afraid that they have been ripped off) and may think that they appeared unsophisticated or stupid, which results in shame. It is the shame associated with being taken advantage of financially that often makes the victims of fraud (e.g., mail and phone scams) hesitant to take legal action.

Unlike negotiated exchanges, reciprocal exchanges include serial transactions that occur over time, in which subsequent rewards are expected but not guaranteed. Sympathizing, discussed in the previous section, is a form of reciprocal exchange in which sympathizers expect a return at a later date, when something bad happens giving them a legitimate sympathy claim.

In reciprocal exchanges, shared situational definitions result in emotional responses among both the giver (pride) and the receiver (gratitude) (Lawler 2001). Moreover, reciprocal exchanges generate high levels of trust and feelings of liking for one's exchange partner (Molm, Takahashi, and Peterson 2000).

In general, people experience more emotions directed toward other actors in reciprocal than in negotiated exchanges because the longer time lag between exchanges makes it easier to view actors' contributions as separate events. Although the emotions that result from negotiated exchanges are relatively strong, they are more readily directed toward the group (the exchange relation) than toward individual actors (Lawler 2001).

Distributive Justice and Equity

Distributive justice, defined as perceived fairness (Homans 1961), also affects the emotions people experience as the result of the exchange of resources. Research suggests that equity leads to positive emotions (e.g., gratefulness) in negotiated exchanges (i.e., when people bargain over something), whereas inequity has negative emotional consequences. The negative emotions associated with inequity in negotiated exchanges include distress and resentfulness among individuals who are under-benefitting (contributions greater than rewards), and guilt among those who are overbenefitting (rewards greater than contributions), from the exchange (Hegtvedt 1990). These findings are largely consistent with the results of research on college students' dating relationships (Sprecher 1986), a form of reciprocal exchange.

Interestingly, the perception that the distribution of rewards in an exchange relationship is fair, even when it's not from an objective standpoint, reduces the distress associated with overbenefitting inequity. Because individuals experiencing overbenefitting inequity often regard their situation as fair, they are not substantially more distressed than individuals in equitable relationships (Hegtvedt 1990).

Status and Emotion in Task-Oriented Groups

Whereas exchange theorists point to the degree of equality in a relationship (equity) as a source of emotion, status characteristics theorists emphasize the role of emotion in the maintenance of social inequality. Think about the last time you worked with others on an assignment. Who contributed the most to the completion of the group's task and who was regarded the most positively? Status characteristics theory suggests that this will be the same person. Were these patterns evident at the beginning of the encounter? They probably were because status begets status in group interactions.

Socioemotive Behaviors and the Reproduction of Status Structures

The manner in which people express their emotions in task-oriented groups helps explain why this occurs. Within group settings, positive **socioemotive behaviors** include agreeing with someone, acting friendly or dramatizing (e.g., telling a joke), whereas negative socioemotive behaviors include disagreeing with someone, acting unfriendly, or exhibiting tension. In general, interactions within task-oriented groups are characterized by more positive than negative socioemotive behaviors, which helps to perpetuate their existing status structures.

The status hierarchy within task groups limits the expression of negative socio-emotive behaviors in three ways. First, the task-related suggestions and behaviors of high-status group members are usually evaluated favorably and result in few challenges. Second, on those occasions when high-status individuals are questioned, they punish lower-status challengers with negative socioemotive behaviors, which serve as a source of social control and reduce the likelihood of future disagreements. Finally, given their disadvantaged position, low-status group members are more likely than high-status members to attribute negative responses from other group members to themselves. As a result, they experience depression rather than anger in the face of challenges from others, which inhibits their expression of negative socioemotive behaviors.

Because negative socioemotive behaviors occur so infrequently, status struggles are kept at a minimum within most task groups. Thus, solidarity is maintained and their status structures are reproduced (Ridgeway and Johnson 1990).

The patterns of emotive expression through which a group's status structure is maintained are difficult to disrupt because they tend to reproduce themselves. High-status individuals are rarely challenged and are able to readily overcome negative socio-eomotive responses from others, which reinforces their dominant status. Although this makes life difficult for members of disadvantaged groups (e.g., women and minorities), there are ways in which emotions can be managed to combat this negative cycle.

Using Emotion to Combat the Self-Fulfilling Nature of Group Interactions

The results of a series of laboratory experiments (Lovaglia and Houser 1996) suggest that people experiencing positive emotions are readily influenced by others, whereas negative emotions make them resistant to others' contributions. Negative emotions have an especially strong (negative) effect on susceptibility to influence among high-status group members. Thus, individuals with low status given macro-level patterns, including women and racial/ethnic minorities, may increase their influence by eliciting positive emotional reactions among those above them in the status hierarchy. They may be especially well positioned to do this when they themselves are experiencing negative emotions. This is because low-status individuals are less likely to underestimate their own abilities relative to others when they are feeling bad than when they are feeling good (Lovaglia and Houser 1996).

Drawing on these results, Lovaglia and Houser (1996) offer the following tips for members of disadvantaged groups seeking to influence their supervisors as they compete for promotions and raises at work.

1. Don't alter, or suppress, your negative emotions. It is okay to feel frustrated and angry about your subordinate position because this will make you less likely to overestimate the abilities of your peers.

2. Behave appropriately. That is, mask your negative emotions and act in a manner consistent with prevailing display rules so that you are not evaluated negatively.

3. Engage in behaviors that induce positive emotions in your supervisor or in other individuals with power in the organization. This will make them easier to influence. You can do this by participating in activities that show that you are interested in the success of your group, division, or team (Lovaglia and Houser 1996).

These tips may also be useful in other social contexts that are hierarchical in nature or have hierarchical aspects (e.g., student-professor relations in educational settings). Although research on emotion and behavior within the group processes

PHOTO 8.5

Status characteristics such as gender influence the status hierarchies that emerge in task groups. Because people in task groups tend to agree more than disagree and to act in a friendly manner, a group's initial status structure is usually reproduced.

and structures tradition is often conducted in the laboratory, it provides information that readily applies to the workplace and other social settings.

EMOTION WITHIN THE SOCIAL STRUCTURE AND PERSONALITY TRADITION

Structural social psychologists have studied the distribution of psychological distress, as well as positive emotions such as happiness and life satisfaction, within society in accordance with the statuses that people occupy (namely, gender, class, race/ethnicity, and age). This is, in fact, one of the most prominent literatures within the social structure and personality face of social psychology. We discuss this research in the chapter on mental health and thus do not focus on these analyses here.

Outside of the mental health literature, structural theories of emotion fall into two categories, those that focus on interaction rituals and those that emphasize power and status (Turner and Stets 2006). We illustrate these approaches to the study of emotion in the following sections.

Interaction Rituals

Interaction ritual theories focus on the positive and negative energy that emerges in interaction (Turner and Stets 2006). For example, Collins (1981, 1990), the most well-known theorist working in this area, argues that group interactions involving a shared focus of attention and a common mood (e.g., anger, friendliness, enthusiasm, etc.) generate a kind of emotional contagion. People get caught up in others' emotions as the encounter establishes a rhythmic aspect. Individuals at a funeral, for instance, become sadder as its rhythms develop. On the other hand, people become increasingly more sociable as a party unfolds (Collins 1990).

What Do You Think?

Describe a situation in which the emotions of group members were in sync and became more intense as the event progressed. How did this escalation in emotional tone influence your behavior?

When positive or negative energy emerges and intensifies in group encounters, it generates positive self-feelings and solidarity among group members. This happens even when the emotional tone of the group is negative (e.g., sadness), as in the case of a successful funeral. Collins refers to the positive feelings and group solidarity that emerge in group interactions as **emotional energy**.

Within this framework, situations in which individuals lacking in power must take orders from others are low in emotional energy. In these contexts, individuals typically feel drained and alienated from the group. In contrast, group encounters high in emotional energy include religious services, weddings, military ceremonies, initiations, and graduations, as well as funerals and parties.

When emotional energy is high, aspects of an interaction ritual that served as its focal point (e.g., particular objects or ideas) become symbols. Represented cognitively, as such, they have the power to invoke feelings of group membership even when people are alone. It is in this manner society gets into the mind of the individual.

Symbols also influence people's behaviors. Individuals are expected to show respect for the group and its symbols, and the feelings of solidarity they generate, by participating in subsequent interaction rituals through which the group and its symbols are venerated (Collins 1990). At the aggregate level, these interaction rituals give rise to macro phenomena, including social institutions and the patterned behaviors that characterize social structure more generally (Collins 1981).

Collins' ritual interaction model is summarized in Figure 8.3. From this perspective, it is the maximization of emotional energy that serves as the motivating force behind human social behavior (Summers-Effler 2006).

FIGURE 8.3

Collins's Model of Ritual Interaction

rhythmic synchronization

Ritual Interaction ⟶ Emotional Energy ⟶ Symbols

Group encounters with shared focus
awareness of shared focus
common mood

group solidarity
positive sense of self

invoke feelings of group membership

Note: Collins (1980).

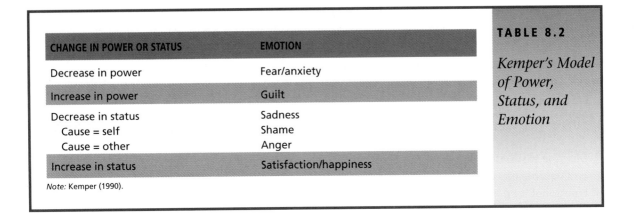

CHANGE IN POWER OR STATUS	EMOTION
Decrease in power	Fear/anxiety
Increase in power	Guilt
Decrease in status	Sadness
Cause = self	Shame
Cause = other	Anger
Increase in status	Satisfaction/happiness

TABLE 8.2

Kemper's Model of Power, Status, and Emotion

Note: Kemper (1990).

Power, Status, and Emotion

Other theories within the social structure and personality face of social psychology emphasize the effects of power (authority) and status (prestige or honor) on people's emotive experiences (Turner and Stets 2006). The most well-known example of this approach is Kemper's (1978) **power and status theory of emotions**.

From this perspective, gains in power increase positive emotions (security), declines in power result in negative emotions (fear and anxiety), and the abuse of power gives rise to guilt. Similarly, whereas increases in status result in satisfaction or happiness, the loss of status has negative emotional consequences. The negative emotions associated with a loss in status include shame, when individuals feel responsible for the loss; anger, when one attributes loss of status to someone else; and sadness (Kemper 1978, 1990). Kemper's model of power, status, and emotion is summarized in Table 8.2.

Responses to 9/11

Kemper (2002) uses changes in power and status associated with the terrorist attacks on September 11, 2001, to predict people's emotional responses to these events. The likely emotional reactions of various groups to 9/11 are summarized in Table 8.3.

As shown in Table 8.3, New Yorkers and Americans in general are expected to have experienced anger in response to 9/11 because the terrorist attacks (action by another) resulted in a decline in the dominant standing of the United States globally. This loss of status should also have resulted in sadness. In fact, all but two of the groups listed in Table 8.3 (radical Islamists and the individuals defined by the United States as terrorists, which includes members of Al-Qaeda) should have felt sadness due to declines in status.

Similarly, all of the groups except radical Islamists and terrorists should have experienced fear resulting from a decrease in power.

TABLE 8.3	GROUP	ANGER	SADNESS	FEAR	HAPPINESS	SHAME	GUILT
Predicted Reactions to Terrorist Attacks on September 11, 2001	New Yorkers/most Americans	X	X	X			
	Airport security agents		X	X		X	X
	Pacifists		X	X			
	Radical Islamists				X		
	Moderate Islamists		X	X		X	
	U.S. allies		X	X			
	Terrorists				X		
	U.S. Muslims		X	X		X	

Note: Reprinted with minor modifications from Kemper (2002).

- Americans would have feared another terrorist attack.

- U.S. allies would have feared an attack in retaliation for their support of the United States.

- Airport security agents would have been afraid they would be fired.

- Pacifists would have been afraid that the U.S. military would harm civilians.

- Moderate Islamists would have feared that U.S. retaliation would extend to them.

- Similarly, U.S. Muslims would have feared that they would be held responsible for the behaviors of the attackers.

Terrorists and radical Islamists, who realized increases in status due to the attacks on 9/11, should have felt happiness rather than fear. In contrast, moderate Islamists and U.S. Muslims would be expected to have experienced shame (the emotion that results from a loss in status for which an individual feels responsible) because the terrorists stated that they were acting in the name of Islam.

Airport security agents may also have experienced shame, insofar as they felt responsible for letting the terrorists through their various checkpoints. Moreover, if airport security agents believed that they used their power inappropriately by failing to prevent the attacks, they would have felt guilty (Kemper 2002).

Interestingly, an analysis of texts sent from over 85,000 pagers (a precursor to cell phones) in the United States on September 11, 2001, shows that many Americans initially responded to the events that unfolded with sadness, fear, and anger. However, as the day progressed, anger became the dominant emotion expressed in the texts (Back, Kufner, and Egloff 2010), suggesting that the locus of the status loss associated with the terrorist attacks (the actions of others) was especially salient.

CHAPTER SUMMARY

Many of the emotions we experience are rooted in our capacity for role taking and are shaped by broader cultural forces. As such, they allow for the self-regulation of behavior, signal the presence of unexpected or inconsistent social information, facilitate the maintenance of social relationships, and both reflect and perpetuate the distribution of power within the larger society. Although the various literatures discussed in this chapter vary in their focus, they share a common theme: emotions are central to the operation of society. They give meaning, predictability, and continuity to our experiences. Without emotion, society as we know it would cease to exist.

Key Points to Know

- **There are two general categories of emotion: primary emotions and secondary emotions.** Primary emotions are similar across cultures and may involve distinct kinds of physiological arousal. Secondary emotions, which include sentiments, are socially constructed and are thus of greater interest to sociological social psychologists.

- **Secondary emotions have multiple components, including a triggering event or situation, physiological arousal, a cognitive label, and expressive behaviors.** The cultural context in which interaction occurs shapes the manner in which secondary emotions are experienced. People frequently manage their emotions so that they are consistent with prevailing emotion norms.

- **Display rules tell us how emotions should be expressed, whereas feeling rules tell us how we should feel in particular situations.** Surface acting occurs when people change their behaviors but not their feelings. Deep acting requires the management of feelings. Studies of emotion management in the workplace suggest that surface acting may have the most negative consequences for the individual, including a sense of estrangement from one's emotions.

- **Symbolic interactionists emphasize the self-regulatory function of role taking emotions such as embarrassment, shame, and guilt.** The public failures that result in embarrassment, and the self-deficiencies that underlie shame, are tied to the reactions of others. Guilt, which arises when a person's behavior fails to meet broader societal standards, is an especially powerful regulator of behavior because it manifests even when no one other than the perpetrator knows about a transgression.

- **Like embarrassment (and, to some degree, shame), sympathy has dramaturgical element.** There are rules that govern how sympathy should be expressed and when an individual may legitimately claim sympathy from others. People strategically present themselves in ways that maximize the sympathy they are entitled to receive.

- **Structural symbolic interactionists view emotions as signals of discrepancies between identities and the feedback received from others (identity control theory) or between identities, emotions, events, and behavior (affect control theory).** People respond to this information by adjusting either their behaviors or their perceptions of self and others.

- **Research within the group processes and structures tradition focuses on the emotions that result from the exchange of resources.** People experience more emotions directed toward other individuals, including trust and liking, in reciprocal than in negotiated exchanges. In both negotiated and reciprocal exchanges, individuals underbenefitting from an exchange relationship are likely to experience anger or resentment. In contrast, overbenefitting inequity leads to feelings of guilt. Overbenefitting inequity may not cause high levels of distress because individuals who are overrewarded tend to perceive their situation as fair.

- **Studies of task-oriented groups have linked socioemotive behaviors to group solidarity and the maintenance of their status structures.** Members of nondominant groups may combat the self-fulfilling nature of this process through the strategic manipulation of their emotions and the emotions of those above them in the status hierarchy.

- **Theories of emotion within the social structure and personality face of social psychology focus on ritual interactions and on power and status.** Collins's ritual interaction model explains how transient emotions occurring in group contexts result in more enduring emotions, symbols, and group solidarity. Kemper's power and status theory of emotion draws our attention to the structural origin of particular emotions and makes predictions about individuals' emotional reactions to situations and events (e.g., 9/11).

Terms and Concepts for Review

Affect	Hiding behavior
Affect control theory (ACT)	Identity control system
Control principle	Identity control theory (ICT)
Cybernetic model	Interaction ritual theories
Deep acting	James-Lange theory of emotion
Deflection	Mood

Terms and Concepts for Review (*Continued*)

Display rules	Power and status theory of emotion
Distributive justice	Primary emotion
Embarrassability	Secondary emotion
Embarrassment	Reconstruction principle
Emotion	Sentiments
Emotional energy	Shame
Emotional labor	Socioemotive behavior
Emotion management	Surface acting
Emotion norms	Sympathy
Feeling	Sympathy margin
Feeling rules	Transient impressions
Fundamental sentiments	Two-factor theory of emotion
Guilt	

Questions for Review and Reflection

1. Describe the last time you experienced each of the following emotions: embarrassment, shame, and guilt. What situations gave rise to these emotions and how did they affect your subsequent behaviors? Why do symbolic interactionists regard these three role-taking emotions as central to social relationships and the functioning of society?

2. Describe an inequitable work relationship or friendship. If possible, draw on your personal experience. If you can't come up with a good personal example, use the experiences of someone you know or have heard about from others or via some form of media to illustrate the ways in which inequity can manifest in this context. How did the participants in this relationship feel, and how did their feelings affect their behaviors? To what degree were their experiences consistent with the predictions of social exchange theory?

3. Suppose that a student violates one of the rules of his or her fraternity or sorority and the president of the organization decides to expel this individual from the group. When, according to Kemper's power and status theory of emotion, would the fraternity or sorority president feel guilty for taking this course of action? Why, from this perspective, might the student who was expelled feel sadness and shame after receiving this punishment?

4. Which of the approaches to the study of emotions described in this chapter provides the greatest insight into the nature and functions of emotions? Why do you believe this to be the case? What do the various approaches to the study of emotions discussed in this chapter have in common?

CHAPTER 9

Deviance and Social Control

How would you describe the person sitting on a towel, in her swimsuit, reading in a computer lab where classes are regularly held? How would you view this college student if you encountered her in the same position outside, as in the photo on the right? This is the same person, dressed the same way, engaging in the same behavior. Yet, how we evaluate this individual depends on the social setting she is in. Outside, this student appears normal. In the computer lab, the student in the picture is likely to be regarded by others as deviant (i.e., outside of the norm) because she is wearing inappropriate classroom attire and acting in a way that is unusual in this setting.

WHAT IS DEVIANCE?

Deviance refers to behaviors that violate social norms and result in negative sanctions or reactions from others. Deviance can range from relatively trivial (e.g., sitting backward in your desk during class) to serious (e.g., murder) behaviors. In addition, although we most often focus on negative or bad behaviors, behavior that is defined as positive or good by society may be considered deviant by others if it is outside the range of societal expectations. For example, although cleanliness is considered to be a good thing, someone who is excessively clean (e.g., someone who takes multiple showers a day or cleans his or her house constantly) is likely to be seen as strange, different, or deviant by others.

Do you know anyone who is eccentric? People often use this term to describe individuals who violate social conventions, called folkways. **Folkways** govern the way in which we keep our houses, what and when to eat, how we dress, and how we spend our leisure time, among other things. **Mores**, on the other hand, pertain to more serious issues. For instance, they prohibit murder or the enactment of behaviors that harm other people in other ways.

Laws, a third type of social norm, are formally codified and enforced by the state through the institution of criminal justice (the criminal justice system). Laws often, but do not always, correspond to societal mores. For example, laws against murder coincide with most people's moral code, whereas laws against speeding on the highway and on other public roads are not perceived as moral imperatives.

Deviance includes all norm violations, including transgressions that violate both informal norms (those that taken for granted but rarely put in writing; e.g., wearing appropriate clothing to class) and formal norms (those that are written down; e.g., organizational rules or policies and laws). **Crime** is a subcategory or type of deviance that occurs when someone breaks the law.

The term "deviance" also applies to people's personal characteristics. Individuals with particular attributes (e.g., people who are overweight, mentally ill, addicted to substances, or much taller or shorter than average) are often regarded by others as abnormal (Kaplan 2006). Table 9.1 includes a list of deviant behaviors, crimes, and deviant attributes that have been recently studied by sociological social psychologists. You can see here that deviance as a subfield of study is quite broad in its focus.

Historically, sociologists have referred to research on deviance as the study of "nuts and sluts" (Gibbs 1981). This (tongue-in-cheek) label reflects the breadth of work in this subfield (behaviors that are unconventional, as well as those that are illegal) and the fact that it was, and is still to some extent, a bit controversial. The study of deviance delves into behaviors that some people might prefer not to know about, and it reminds us that pressing life questions (what is good or moral behavior and what behaviors are wrong or bad) rarely have definitive answers that apply to all individuals in all social settings. Regarding this latter point, the literature on deviance serves as a reminder that conceptions of good and bad, right and wrong, and normative/ and deviant are subjective.

Deviance as a Social Construction

You can't have good, desirable behavior without its bad, undesirable counterpart. Thus, although moral boundaries (what's good vs. bad) change, there will always

TABLE 9.1		
Some Topics of Recent Articles on Deviance by Sociological Social Psychologists	Body-building subculture	Dirt eating
	Snitches	Corporate crime in the pharmaceutical industry
	Prisoner's wives	Commercial burglary
	Heroin abusers	Suicide among dentists
	Child molesters	Ex-psychiatric inpatients
	Mental illness	Bug chasers (men who try to get infect with HIV)
	Homosexuality	Incest
	Physical disabilities	Involuntary psychiatric hospitalization
	Marijuana use	Belief in UFOs
	Employee theft	Sexual asphyxia
	Strippers	Johns (men who go to prostitutes)
	Cybersex	Gambling
	Dogfighting	Academic cheating
	Middle-class coke dealers	Female patrons of male strip clubs
	Sexual harassment	Wives of alcoholics
	Poaching	Serial murders
	Police who snitch	Morticians and funeral directors
	Fraternity gang rape	Satanic cults
	Homelessness	Self-injurers
	Shoplifters	Medicare and Medicaid fraud

be behavior regarded as deviant in every society. Drawing attention to deviant behavior helps make clear to people within a society what constitutes moral conduct. Moreover, identifying and responding to deviance promotes social unity among individuals whose behaviors are normative and lawful (Durkheim 1895).

Whether a behavior is considered deviant is a function of social factors. People define a particular behavior as bad, wrong, or immoral when it violates societal expectations for appropriate behavior within a given social context. Because there is variation in norms from culture to culture, across groups within a society, and within the same culture over time, we need to know the context in which a behavior occurred before we know if it will be seen by others as normal or deviant. Because norms also vary across situations and across statuses, the immediate social context in which behavior occurs and the characteristics of the actor will also determine whether an act is considered deviant or not.

The following examples illustrate the manner in which definitions of deviance vary: cross-culturally, across groups (or subcultures) within a given society, over time, across situations, and across statuses:

- Cultural variation: Wearing your shoes inside your house in the United States is common and is typically not considered deviant. However, entering someone's home without first removing your shoes in Japan violates prevailing social norms and would be viewed as offensive.

- Subcultural or group variation: In some peer groups, drinking heavily and its consequences (e.g., disclosing more information in conversation than is typical among nonintoxicated individuals) are valued, viewed as fun or funny, and expected of group members. In other peer groups, drinking to excess and the lack of self-regulation associated with alcohol intoxication are regarded as highly deviant and to be avoided.

- Changes over time: Having tattoos was once considered highly deviant. However, today it is fairly common to see individuals with multiple tattoos (DeMello 1995). Although views on this behavior have changed, tattoos are still seen as less deviant within certain subcultures (e.g., heavy metal musicians and their fans) and among particular social categories (e.g., adolescents and young adults). There are also norms concerning the number of tattoos people should have and how visible they should be, which affect whether this form of body modification is defined as deviant (Adams 2009). The following photos illustrate some of these rules. What about the first photo, the one of the man with tattoos on his upper body and neck? Is this person deviant?

- Situational variation: It's normative to wear a swimsuit when you're sitting around a pool with friends or sunbathing outside your house. On the other hand, this attire is so inappropriate to the college classroom that it is likely to generate stares, comments, and snickers from those who are present. In fact, if someone wore a swimsuit to class, like the individual in the picture at the beginning of the chapter, it would probably be quite disruptive to the lecture or activities the professor had planned. If class were in session, the professor would probably ask the student dressed in swimwear to leave the room.

- Variations across statuses: In this society, it is common for women to carry personal belongings in a purse. What if a male carried a purse? How would you evaluate this person and his behavior? In this culture, this individual would most likely be seen as deviant. He has clearly violated the expectations of what it means to be a male in this society.

Because deviance depends upon the cultural and situational context in which it occurs, and the social characteristics of the actor, no behavior is in and of itself

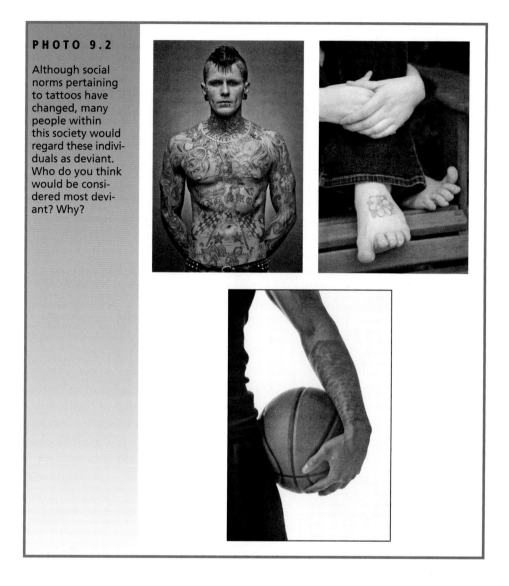

PHOTO 9.2

Although social norms pertaining to tattoos have changed, many people within this society would regard these individuals as deviant. Who do you think would be considered most deviant? Why?

deviant. An act is deviant only when people define it as such. It is for this reason that social psychologist regard deviance as a social construct.

Q: What about murder? Isn't killing someone inherently bad or deviant?

A: Killing someone is not always defined as murder. We need information about the context within which the killing occurred to know if it was murder and therefore deviant. Was it a soldier who killed someone during wartime? Did someone kill another person in self-defense? Did the state carry out the death penalty to punish someone for a crime he or she committed? Did a corporation sell unsafe products resulting in the death of individuals? Did an individual intentionally shoot someone in order to take his or her possessions? Whether a particular act of killing is considered murder within this society varies across the social contexts just described (e.g., carrying out the death penalty vs. shooting someone during a robbery) and is therefore a social construction.

WHY STUDY DEVIANCE?

Because definitions of deviance are relative, they are often arbitrary. As a result, access to important societal resources—power, money, and prestige—influences who makes the rules and to whom they apply. This makes deviance a topic of substantial interest to sociological social psychologists, who study how macro-level societal patterns, including inequality between groups, shape people's perceptions and behaviors. Because psychologists are less likely to address this issue, almost all of the social psychological research on deviance has been conducted by sociological social psychologists.

Types of Deviance

There are two general categories of deviance of interest to sociological social psychologists: unmotivated and motivated. **Unmotivated deviance** occurs when people recognize that an individual is failing to meet others' expectations because they are unable to do so. Unmotivated deviance usually arises as a result of physiological factors (e.g., a physical deformity that makes someone look different, a cognitive disability that makes it impossible for an individual to understand social norms, or an illness that makes it difficult for someone to fulfill their role obligations), unresolvable role conflicts, or a lack of resources. **Motivated deviance**, on the other hand, refers to situations in which (a) an individual can, but chooses not to, behave in accordance with prevailing group norms or (b) an individual belongs to a group with norms that others within society consider to be deviant. Social psychologists who study deviant behavior focus primarily on motivated deviance (Kaplan 2006).

MECHANISMS OF SOCIAL CONTROL

There are three mechanisms of social control that encourage conformity and thus reduce motivated deviance among members of society. They are commonly referred to as formal control, informal (or interpersonal) control, and internal (or self) control.

When someone breaks the law, he or she has committed a crime and may be sanctioned by the state for this violation. In the case of crimes, the state has the authority to punish individuals and typically does so through the use of fines, community service, or incarceration. This is a type of **formal control**. Formal control refers to sanctions imposed by authorized individuals to encourage conformity. Another example of formal control is the use of suspensions by a university to encourage students to follow the university's rules for conduct, which are usually spelled out in the university's student handbook (or some comparable document).

A second type of social control, **informal control**, operates through interpersonal feedback and is rooted in our capacity for embarrassment. We discussed how embarrassment facilitates the self-regulation of public behavior in the previous chapter. We behave in an appropriate (normative) manner when we are around others in order to avoid experiencing embarrassment, the emotion that emerges when an individual fails in a public performance.

Whereas informal control requires the presence of others, a third type of social control, internal control, is not directly tied to others' reactions. **Internal control** operates through guilt. People experience guilt when they engage in behavior perceived as immoral, even if no one else is aware that they have violated a societal rule (a norm or the law).

In many instances, all three mechanisms of social control (formal, informal, and internal) are in place at the same time and, as a result, the likelihood of rule violation is very low. For example, not only is murder against the law (formal control), most people believe that others would reject them if they were a murderer (informal control), and the vast majority of Americans view murder as immoral and wrong (internal control). As a result, formal, informal, and internal control mechanisms are present in most situations, resulting in relatively low rates of murder relative to other rule violations.

Q: What if some of the elements of social control are missing? Which of the three mechanisms of social control is the most effective in regulating behavior by itself, and which form of social control is the least effective in doing so?

A: In general, internal control is the most effective regulator of behavior because it involves feelings of guilt. Because guilt is not tied to the reactions of others, an individual can't escape it by simply hiding his or her behaviors. Shame may also serve as a mechanism of internal control, but only when it isn't tied to the responses of specific others (this would make it a type of informal control).

Formal control, on the other hand, is the least effective form of social control because it applies only to those situations in which we think our behaviors are, or will be, visible to agents of social control. Agents of formal social control represent social institutions and include police officers, school administrators, teachers, bosses, religious leaders, and mental health and health officials.

Informal control is somewhere in between internal and formal control when it comes to regulating behavior. The presence of almost anyone is enough for interpersonal concerns to shape our behaviors. However, informal control doesn't occur when we are alone.

What Do You Think?

How might the three types of social control (formal, informal, and internal) influence college students' likelihoods of cheating on exams and papers?

- Get together with two or three of your classmates and come up with at least four reasons why students don't cheat. Have someone in the group write them down.
- Next, determine which form of social control underlies each of the reasons for not cheating. There is likely to be some variability (e.g., some reasons for not cheating reflect formal control mechanisms, others reflect informal control, and so forth).
- When are students most likely to cheat on tests and exams? Explain.

SOCIETAL PATTERNS

Although most people conform to societal norms in most settings, this is not always the case. Research on deviance and crime suggests the following patterns.

Deviance Among Youths

Much of the literature on deviance (vs. crime) has focused on youths. These survey-based analyses often use measures of delinquency similar to the one you completed in Chapter 2 (Box 2.1). The following patterns have been documented among adolescents.

- Social class effects on delinquency vary with the type of offense under investigation. Research suggests that class background is positively related to theft. Theft is the most common among adolescents from affluent families. In contrast, social class is negatively related to violence. Violence is most common among adolescents from poor families.

- Race is not independently related to general delinquency when parents' socioeconomic status is taken into consideration, with one exception. Black females have higher rates of violence than their White counterparts.

- Males are more likely to engage in deviant behaviors than females (Triplett and Jarjoura 1997).

Deviance Among Adults

Most studies of deviance among adults have focused on crime, the violation of norms that have been formally codified into law. Presumably, this is due to two factors: the availability of data (government data on crime are readily accessible to social psychologists and other social scientists) and concerns about the well-being of the population (crime often has more negative consequences than other deviant behaviors).

In opposition to prevailing cultural stereotypes, social class is not associated with overall crime rates. There is, however, a relationship between social class and the type of crime committed. In general, the lower class are more involved in what are considered traditional street crimes, while the upper class are more likely to commit offenses such as embezzlement or fraud (Rosoff, Pontell, and Tillman 2004; Tittle, Villemez, and Smith 1978).

As is the case in analyses of race and juvenile delinquency, there are few race differences in crime among adults who are in the same social class. This suggests that the higher rates of crime observed among racial and ethnic minorities (in particular, Hispanics and Blacks) in comparison to Whites are due to economic factors (Haynie, Weiss, and Piquero 2008; Kaufman 2005).

There are, on the other hand, notable gender differences in criminal behavior. Crime rates are higher among males than among females, especially for violent offenses. However, the gender gap in some crimes (robbery, burglary, and motor vehicle theft) has been steadily decreasing since the 1960s (O'Brien 1999). This is presumably due to women's increased financial independence and changing gender roles, which accord women more latitude today than in the past. As gender equality has increased within this society, women's and men's attitudes and behaviors have become more similar.

RESEARCH ON THE CAUSES OF DEVIANCE WITHIN SOCIAL STRUCTURE AND PERSONALITY

Approaches to the study of deviance within social structure and personality locate the causes of deviant behavior and crime in the organization of society rather than within individuals. Thus, they focus on identifying the social conditions that produce high rates of deviance and help us to understand some of the patterns described in the previous section. This literature is well developed and encompasses a number of theories that specify the conditions under which people are likely to become deviant with a high degree of precision. Their unifying theme is an emphasis on the intervening interpersonal and psychological mechanisms that link social structure to deviant behavior.

Structural Strain Theory

Strain theories focus on the psychological states that result from structural conditions. The most well-known **strain theory** was developed by Robert K.

Merton (1938, 1968). The crux of this theory is that anomie causes deviance and crime.

Anomie is a term familiar to most sociologists. According to Durkheim (1897), anomie occurs when societal norms lose their regulatory power and don't exert a strong enough influence on people's aspirations and behaviors. People experiencing anomie often aren't sure how they should act. Thus, anomie causes frustration and is associated with an increase in suicide, a type of deviant behavior. Durkheim (1897) argued that rapid social change is one cause of anomie.

Merton, like Durkheim, attributed deviance to anomie. However, Merton (1938) argued that the conditions that produce anomie are built into the structure of American society. He focused on the gap between what people are socialized to aspire to and what they might realistically achieve given prevailing patterns of social inequality (Merton 1938).

Within this culture, people are socialized to desire many goals. However, Merton (1938) argued that financial or material success is emphasized as being of the utmost importance. Americans are encouraged to strive for economic success, and most individuals in this society have internalized this message: they want to be rich.

Society also defines the appropriate or legitimate means for becoming rich, which include education, hard work, and landing a good job. Conformity, or abiding by the norms of society, means that an individual is seeking material success through these avenues.

Although Merton felt that all societal members desire economic success, he recognized that not all members of society have access to the legitimate means for achieving it. This creates strain, which may lead individuals to turn to alternative (nonlegitimate) means for making money. From this perspective, nonlegitimate means for making money include crimes like dealing drugs or robbery.

Merton (1938) argued that strain is more common among the lower class because this is the group with limited access to the legitimate means to achieve success. Because they lack access to the legitimate means to success, individuals toward the bottom of the stratification hierarchy should be more likely than their more socioeconomically advantaged counterparts to engage in monetary-based crimes. Strain (the gap between aspirations and opportunities) is hypothesized to be the intervening variable in this causal chain. Being lower class increases strain, which in turn puts one at risk for participation in criminal activities.

The relationships between class, strain, and crime are depicted in Figure 9.1. Survey analyses using measures consonant with Merton's conceptualization of

Social Class ⟶ Strain ⟶ Deviance

FIGURE 9.1

Structural Strain Theory

strain (e.g., Farnworth and Leiber 1989; Vowell and May 2007) have yielded results that are largely consistent with his theory.

What Do You Think?

- Why are you in college? Do you know anyone with similar goals to your own who was not able to continue their education for financial or other reasons? How have they responded to this situation? Does Merton's strain theory provide an explanation for their reactions?
- Consider the policy implications of Merton's model. If crime is caused by structural strain, what might be done to reduce this type of behavior?

Social Comparison Processes and Relative Deprivation

Although Merton's theory was developed to explain financially motivated crimes among the lower classes, it may also apply to more affluent individuals. As you know, research in social structure and personality has shown that reference groups shape both our aspirations and our self-evaluations. When people fall short of the financial benchmark set by their selection of a reference group, they experience relative deprivation.

Insofar as these individuals feel that they cannot enhance their economic standing through legitimate means, they may be at risk for deviant behavior.

Box 9.1   The U.S. Housing Crisis

The U.S. housing crisis arose due to subprime lending. High interest loans, sold by banks to private-sector bondholders, were given to home buyers who were unable to qualify for traditional home mortgages because they had low incomes or poor credit. Brokering these mortgages was highly profitable for the banking industry.

The primary targets of this predatory lending were low-income racial/ethnic minorities and recent immigrants. These individuals were knowingly being issued loans that they couldn't afford, given their financial standing.

Although it may have become normative within banking, this is considered, by most people, to be a highly deviant business practice. Other deviant behaviors geared toward increasing profit within the industry included the manipulation of property appraisals by subprime lenders to justify higher loan amounts (stated property values were often well outside of normative parameters) and the intentional misrepresentation of loan applicants' incomes and employment histories by mortgage brokers (U.S. Department of Housing and Urban Development 2010).

The high default rate on subprime mortgages drove the then-high price of housing down (i.e., the housing bubble burst) and ultimately resulted in huge losses for the banks and bondholders. As a result, banks are giving less money in loans and credit, and their lenders are worried about their creditworthiness, which has had a negative impact in the United States and on the global economy.

Thus, aspects of Merton's theory, in particular the concept of anomie, can be used to explain financially motivated crimes committed by individuals who most of us would consider to be fairly well off. These individuals include company CEOs and chief financial officers or, as in the case of the recent housing crisis, home mortgage brokers. If they are making less than members of their reference groups (e.g., friends, top company officials, or others working in the industry), these latter individuals may engage in criminal behaviors, or behaviors that violate the spirit of the law that others within society are likely to view as deviant, in order to increase their earnings. See Box 9.1 for a discussion of some of the deviant business practices of home mortgage lenders before the housing bubble burst in 2007, resulting in a downturn in the economy in the United States and globally.

General Strain Theory

Focusing on nonfinancial, as well as economically motivated, forms of deviance, Agnew (1992; 2000) extended Merton's concept of strain to include a wider range of precipitating social conditions. According to his **general strain theory**, strain results from the failure to achieve economic or noneconomic goals, racial discrimination, the removal of positive stimuli (e.g., the death of a parent, the termination of a romantic relationship), or the introduction of negative stimuli into someone's life (e.g., being bullied at school, having arguments with parents). The presence of strain from these sources increases individuals' levels of stress, especially when the events causing strain occur around the same time. Stress, in turn, results in negative emotions including frustration, unhappiness, and anger, which translate into various forms of deviant behavior.

General strain theory has been subject to many empirical tests. These (survey-based) analyses suggest that general strain explains participation in a wide range of deviant and criminal activities, including the violation of military rules (Bucher 2011), corporate crime (Passas 1990), alcohol and drug use (Agnew and White 1992), bullying (Patchin and Hinduja 2011), and gambling (Eitle and Taylor 2011).

Social Control Theory

Whereas strain theories emphasize the structural roots of deviant behavior, control theories locate the cause of deviance within the individual. Hirschi's (1969) social control theory is most well-known theory within this tradition. Because it focuses on the individual, at the micro level, Hirschi's control theory is not itself a structural model. However, it has been used by sociological social psychologists working in the social structure and personality orientation to address structural issues. We review Hirschi's theory here and then discuss its more macro-level extensions by social structure and personality (SSP) researchers.

Main Premises

Social control theory (Hirschi 1969) was developed to explain juvenile delinquency. It is based on the assumption that all individuals have the potential to become deviant. From this perspective, we are all motivated to break the rules because it often offers a quick and easy way to get what we want or need.

Given this general tendency to deviate from social norms, **social control theory** focuses on explaining why individuals conform, rather than why they deviate. Note that the strain theories discussed in the previous section focus on why people deviant from societal norms. Social control theorists argue that it is the social bond that individuals have to conventional (mainstream) society that constrains (controls) them and encourages conforming behavior. Therefore, individuals who are weakly bonded to society are more likely to violate the law than those with strong bonds (Hirschi 1969).

Bonds to Society

According to Hirschi (1969), there are four dimensions of the social bond: attachment, commitment, involvement, and belief. **Attachment** refers to adolescents' emotional ties to important people in their lives, including parents, peers, and school personnel. Individuals who are attached to other people care about what they think and are sensitive to their feelings and expectations. They don't want to jeopardize their relationships with these individuals or risk hurting or disappointing them, which keeps them from breaking the rules. Thus, attachment operates through informal control.

The second dimension of social bonding, called **commitment**, refers to the investments that individuals have made in conventional activities and goals such as education. Participation in conventional educational activities and endeavors gives adolescents a stake in following the rules. If they get caught breaking the rules, they have a lot to lose. A high school student who has received a scholarship to an Ivy League school, for instance, could lose this opportunity for a prestigious, tuition-free education if she gets arrested dealing drugs. Thus, this individual is less likely to engage in this behavior than someone without such a potentially bright future.

The third element of the social bond, **involvement**, refers to the time and energy spent participating in conventional activities, such as sports, school clubs, studying, and youth groups. The more time adolescents spend in these conventional activities, the less time they have available for participation in deviant activities.

Finally, the dimension of social bonding, called **belief**, relates to the degree that individuals accept and believe in societal values and rules, including the law. Thus, it reflects an individual's propensity for internal or self-control. An individual who does not see the rules or laws as fair or worthy of obeying will be more likely to violate them across social settings.

The main proposition of social control theory is straightforward: the stronger adolescents' levels of attachment, commitment, involvement, and belief, the lower their likelihoods of engaging in delinquent behavior. Socialization and participation in societal institutions are presumed to be important in the formation of strong bonds to society. However, Hirschi's theory does not directly address why the bonds of some individuals are stronger than others or whether social bonds vary with individuals' positions within the structure of the larger society.

Macro Extensions

As noted earlier, some researchers have expanded Hirschi's (1969) control theory in an attempt to address issues of interest to social psychologists working within the social structure and personality face of social psychology. For example, the study by Bui (2009), reviewed in Chapter 1, linked parental attachment (low child-mother conflict), one dimension of social bonding, to low levels of delinquency among immigrant youths.

Other analyses linking bonds to society to social structure have focused mainly on gender. This literature indicates that males do **not** have higher levels of deviance than females because they have weaker bonds to conventional society (Jensen and Eve 1976; White and LaGrange 1987). However, weak social bonds have been associated with participation in delinquency among both males and females in a number of studies (e.g., Chapple, McQuillan, and Berdahl 2005; Sampson and Laub 1993).

RESEARCH ON HOW DEVIANCE IS LEARNED

Although the theories described in the previous section have provided some insight into why people become deviant (limited economic opportunities and other strains or weak bonds to society), in order to truly understand when and why people deviate from social norms, we need to know something about the processes through which deviant behaviors are acquired. As you might expect, sociological social psychologists take the stance that people learn deviant behavior the same way that they learn to behave in a normative manner: through their socialization experiences.

Many deviant behaviors are learned during childhood or adolescence, whereas others are acquired later in life, typically at work or in other organizational settings. In either case, the initiation of deviant behavior almost always occurs in groups or as the result of an individual's group affiliations (Kaplan 2006).

The Symbolic Interactionist Model Revisited

We discussed Becker's (1963) study of the experiences of marijuana users at the beginning of Chapter 3, on symbolic interactionism. Becker (1963) argues that these individuals had to learn how to interpret and respond to the physiological effects of this drug. Getting high was not an inherently pleasant experience. Rather, the participants in Becker's study learned from more seasoned users to interpret their physiological sensations in a positive manner as they became socialized into a sub-culture of jazz musicians in which marijuana use was common.

Among the larger society at the time in which Becker was writing, most people regarded marijuana use as highly deviant. Thus, Becker refers to his participants as "Outsiders." Symbolic interactionists emphasize the relative nature of deviance, and the qualitative literature on this topic, including Becker's (1963) analysis, provides illus-trations of how individuals learn what others within society define as deviant behavior.

Q: Is marijuana use still considered deviant in this society? Do you think its legalization for medical use in a number of states has affected people's views on this issue?

A: An analysis of data from the General Social Survey suggests that it may have. In 1975, it was estimated that only 22% of the U.S. adult population sup-ported the legalization of marijuana. This percentage increased slightly each year throughout the 1970s, then dipped in the 1980s and 1990s (with a low of 17% in 1990). Since 1993, support for the legalization of marijuana has steadily risen, with larger increases following the legalization of marijuana for medical use by five states (California, Alaska, Oregon, Washington, and Maine in 1996–1999). By 2000, it was estimated that 34% of the population believed that marijuana should be legal. In 2010 (15 states and the District of Columbia allowed for the use of medicinal marijuana by the year's end), it was estimated that 48% of the U.S. adult population supported the legalization of this substance. As this figure indicates, there is currently a lack of consensus in this society as to whether marijuana use is a deviant behavior (assuming that support for the legalization of marijuana coin-cides with the perception that its use is not problematic or abnormal, which seems likely).

In the 2012 election, marijuana use was legalized for recreational use in two states—Colorado and Washington. It is too soon to tell what effect this might have on the population's attitudes, but social scientists will be able to monitor this using the biannual data from the General Social Survey.

Take a Break

For additional insight into on how views of marijuana use have changed in the United States, check out the film *Reefer Madness* (1936), available for stream-ing online at http://archive.org/details/reefer_madness1938.

This cult classic was a serious attempt to reduce drug use when it was pro-duced. The film's message was "Don't smoke marijuana because it will make you crazy." Regardless of their views on the legalization of marijuana for medic-inal or other purposes, most contemporary viewers find this movie entertaining.

Differential Association Theory

Differential association theory is a well-known theory of delinquency that is generally consistent with the premises of symbolic interactionism. Developed in the 1930s by Edwin Sutherland (1939), it is similar to the symbolic interactionist approach, illustrated in Becker's (1963) study of marijuana users, in that it emphasizes the importance of socialization and the social processes through which deviance is learned.

Despite this, the research Sutherland's theory has generated is largely quantitative in orientation. Many of these studies measure specific perceptions and behaviors, as well as the nature of individuals' (usually adolescents') group affiliations, called differential associations. Differential associations are measured using survey questions, which usually focus on how frequently adolescents' friends engage in delinquent behavior.

Main Premises

Sutherland (1939) argued that individuals learn to be deviant through their associations with others. Within these contexts, people are socialized to perceive the world and act in certain ways. Whereas some individuals acquire beliefs and norms that differ from those of the broader society, others learn to conform to conventional societal definitions and rules. Thus, according to this theory, anyone can become a deviant or a criminal. It is the social environment, and not innate characteristics or predispositions within individuals, that result in deviant actions. People who grow up in high-crime neighborhoods and are regularly exposed to criminal activities, for example, learn to define these behaviors as normative and are taught the tools of the trade (e.g., how to deal or buy drugs) as part of the socialization process.

Given its applicability to virtually any social setting, differential association theory is able to explain a wide range of deviant behaviors, including both the crimes of the rich and of the poor. Sutherland himself used his theory to explain why some individuals engage in **white-collar crime**, defined as crimes committed by people of relatively high status in the course of their occupation (Sutherland 1940), or become professional thieves (Sutherland 1937).

Although people can learn from a wide range of associations within primary groups, Sutherland emphasized the importance of the family and peers as agents of socialization. Consistent with this tenet, research suggests that association with deviant peers is one of the strongest correlates of delinquency (Warr 2002).

Differential association theory predicts that it is the association with delinquent peers that leads to an individual to engage in delinquent behavior. However, it is possible that the relationship occurs the other way around. That is, there could be some other factor that causes an individual engage in delinquent behavior, and then once a person becomes delinquent, they begin to associate with others who participate in similar (delinquent) activities.

To address this issue of reverse causality, recent studies have examined the direction of the relationship between peer relations and delinquency using longitudinal data. Most analyses show that the causal arrow goes both ways, from peers to delinquency (as predicted by Sutherland) and from delinquency to interaction with deviant peers (Thornberry et al. 1994). This reciprocal relationship is depicted in Figure 9.2. The double plus sign on the arrow from peers to delinquency represents the results of an analysis of a large nationally representative dataset. The study results suggest that the effect of associations with delinquent peers on delinquency is notably larger than the effect of delinquency on adolescents' peer relationships (Matsueda and Anderson 1998).

Differential Reinforcement Theory

Ronald Akers's (Akers 1998; Burgess and Akers 1966) **differential reinforcement theory** extends Sutherland's theory of differential association by specifying the mechanisms through which deviance is learned. Drawing on social learning theory (page 178), Akers argues that deviance is often acquired through imitation (role modeling) and reinforcement. Acts that are reinforced through reward or the avoidance of discomfort are likely to be repeated, whereas acts that result in punishments are likely to be avoided. Thus, individuals are most likely to engage in criminal behavior when differential associations result in definitions favorable to violating the law and this misconduct is reinforced by others with whom they have close relationships (Burgess and Akers 1966).

Application: Social Learning and Stalking

Stalking is a relatively recent construction, as antistalking laws were not enacted until the 1990s. They were, in part, a response to some high-profile cases of celebrity stalking, in particular the death of Rebecca Schaeffer in 1989, star of the then-popular sitcom *My Sister Sam*. We discussed the issue of celebrity stalking in Chapter 3, where we focused on competing situational definitions between fans pursuing contact with their favorite stars and the celebrities who were often frightened by behaviors they viewed as stalking.

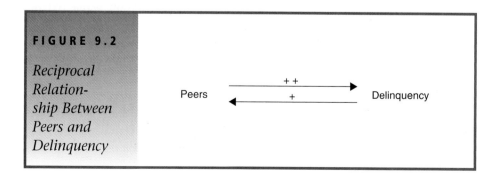

FIGURE 9.2

Reciprocal Relation-ship Between Peers and Delinquency

Peers   + +   Delinquency
          +

According to the U.S. Department of Justice (2009), stalking includes unwanted phone calls, letters, or email; unwanted gifts; following and spying; or spreading rumors via the Internet or other means. Based upon these criteria, it is estimated that over 3.5 million people are victims of stalking in the United States (about 14 out of every 1,000 individuals 18 or older). Most of these cases go unreported. Not surprisingly, given prevailing gender roles and patterns of socialization, the majority of stalking victims are female, whereas the majority of stalkers are male. Most victims of stalking, irrespective of their gender, know the offender (U.S. Department of Justice 2009).

In their analysis of survey data from a large sample of college students (n = 15,000), Fox, Nobles, and Akers (2011) evaluated the explanatory power of four constructs central to differential reinforcement theory (the independent variables in their study) with regard to the issue of stalking:

1. Beliefs about stalking (positive definitions of stalking)

2. Whether individuals had friends who engaged in, or were the victims of, stalking (differential associations)

3. Whether stalking is worth the risk, given its relative costs and benefits (costs versus rewards)

4. How friends would react if the respondent were to stalk someone or be stalked by someone (reinforcement)

Whether respondents engaged in stalking behavior or were themselves a victim of stalking were the two outcomes under investigation (the dependent variables).

Definitions of stalking and the measure of differential associations (having friends who engaged in stalking) predicted whether or not respondents had ever stalked someone, confirming the authors' hypothesis that stalking is learned behavior. Similarly, positive definitions of stalking and differential associations with victims of stalking were significantly associated with being a stalking victim, suggesting that responses to stalking may also be learned.

Interestingly, the belief that one would receive positive feedback from friends if one was stalked (peer reinforcement) also increased respondents' likelihoods of being the victim of a stalker. Thus, changing positive perceptions about stalking among victims' friends, as well as among the victims of stalking themselves (along with the implementation of strategies that facilitate their empowerment, such as those used in cases of intimate partner violence), may be a way to reduce the prevalence of this behavior.

The positive definitions of stalking observed among the perpetrators of this behavior, a key correlate of this form of deviance among the study respondents, might also be altered through cognitive or behavioral interventions (Fox et al. 2011). However, because stalking is a gendered phenomenon that reflects prevailing patterns of inequality and beliefs about the legitimacy of patriarchy (Kamir 2001), without widespread change in the balance of power between men and women at the macro level, it is likely to remain a pervasive social problem.

OVERVIEW AND EVALUATION OF STRUCTURAL AND LEARNING THEORIES

In general, a review of the empirical literature suggests that concepts that distinguish differential reinforcement theory from differential association theory (i.e., imitation and reinforcement) predict levels of deviance reasonably well. However, differential associations (in particular, having friends who engage in deviant behavior) are more strongly related to the commission of crimes and other acts of deviance, including stalking, across studies (Fox et al. 2011; Pratt et al. 2010).

In addition, research indicates that relationships with deviant peers, and susceptibility to their influence, is highest among adolescents with weak social bonds (e.g., low levels of attachment to their parents), which is what actually increases their risk for deviance. Social bonds themselves have few effects on delinquency independent of their relationship to individuals' peer relations. Thus, socialization processes are necessary to explain the link between bonds to conventional society and deviant behavior (Erickson, Crosnoe, and Dornbusch 2000; Matsueda and Heimer 1987). This has led some sociological social psychologists to conclude that differential association theory is superior to social control theory when it comes to explaining crime and deviance (Matsueda and Heimer 1987).

Differential association is also a better predictor of deviant behavior than the strain theories reviewed toward the beginning of the chapter. Still, these structural models do explain some of the variation in individuals' participation in deviant activities (Neff and Waite 2007; Vowell and Chen 2004).

The strength of structural perspectives, in general, is that they direct our attention to the root of the situational definitions that give rise to behaviors deemed as problematic (e.g., stalking). It is through the application of multiple theoretical perspectives, and levels of analysis, that sociological social psychologists gain the most complete understanding of the factors that give rise to various social behaviors, including deviance.

THE CONSEQUENCES OF BEING CONSIDERED DEVIANT

The previous sections focused on identifying the factors that put individuals at risk for deviance and the processes through which behaviors deemed nonnormative by conventional society are acquired. Sociological social psychologists are also interested in what happens to people who are regarded by others as deviant.

The Symbolic Interactionist Approach

Labeling theory, the dominant symbolic interactionist approach to the study of deviance (and arguably the dominant perspective on deviance within sociological social psychology), addresses this issue. Unlike research on the legal process or the functioning of the criminal justice system, labeling theorists focus on the social and psychological consequences of labeling at the micro level.

Given its symbolic interactionist roots, labeling theory (also called societal reaction theory) is firmly entrenched in Cooley's looking-glass self and the notion that people's self-concepts are shaped by how they are perceived and treated by others. Labeling theory arose largely out of the work of Becker (1963), discussed earlier in this chapter, as well as that of Lemert (1972), Kituse (1962), and Scheff (1966). The following section includes a synthesis of the concepts and ideas introduced by these individuals.

Main Premises of Labeling Theory

Labeling theorists point out that everyone engages in deviant behavior. We all violate social norms at one time or another throughout the course of our lives.

What Do You Think?

Refer back to your score on the delinquency measure presented in Chapter 2 (Box 2.1). Although this is a relatively limited measure of individuals' engagement in deviant behavior, you can still get a feel for just how common rule violations are. Did you score above a zero? If you did, do you consider yourself to be a deviant? Do others see you as a deviant? Why or why not? Would you expect your score to be higher if the measure had included other types of deviant acts? The fact that the average score on this measure and others like it is greater than zero (the mean for this index was 4.31) supports labeling theorists' assumption that we all violate social norms at one time or another.

Primary deviance is behavior in violation of social norms that is not defined by others within society as deviant. Whereas we all engage in deviant behavior (acts of primary deviance), only some of us are singled out and labeled as deviant by agents of social control (e.g., police officers, school administrators, or teachers). Sometimes these individuals don't notice a norm violation, or if they do notice it, they don't label the individual as deviant. They may excuse the norm violation or downplay its significance (e.g., he was having a bad day, it was unintentional, she's under a lot of pressure, it's just what kids do). Thus, most of us suffer no significant consequences a result of our participation in deviant activities. We are basically regarded as a good person by others. We may make mistakes from time to time, but they are seen as transitory behaviors and not indicative of who we are.

This is not the case for the individual who is labeled as deviant. In this situation, behavior is seen as reflective of the individual. Others come to view the person as a deviant and see their behaviors and actions through the lens of this label. They are quick to notice behaviors that are consistent with the label that has been applied and see any rule violation as an indication that the label is correct.

They are also likely to engage in **retrospective labeling**. Retrospective labeling occurs when people reflect back on the past behaviors of the individual in question and interpret them in a manner that fits the new (deviant) label. For example, someone is labeled an "alcoholic." Once this label is applied, her friends start talking about this party and that party during which her behavior was totally out of control, due to her drinking problem. Insofar as no one thought twice about her drinking prior to the application of the label "alcoholic," retrospective labeling has occurred.

Being defined as deviant can have a profound effect on the self-concept of the individual who has been so labeled. Others begin to treat him differently than in the past, in a way that is consistent with the new label. They may not trust him or find him credible. If something goes wrong, they may readily place the blame on him. As a result of this kind of treatment, people who have been labeled as deviant are likely to starting seeing themselves as a deviant.

This is facilitated by their isolation from nondeviant individuals. In extreme cases, people labeled as deviant are put in prisons or mental hospitals. In less extreme situations, they are simply avoided by people not identified as deviant because the latter individuals do not want to be associated with someone viewed in this negative fashion (i.e., they seek to avoid guilt by association).

Once isolation from normal, nondeviant society occurs, the only people a person labeled as deviant has left to interact with are those individuals who have been similarly labeled. Within this context, interaction between deviants, whose only shared characteristic may be their deviance, often results in the formation of what labeling theorists call a **deviant subculture**. Once a deviant subculture is formed based on group members' common deviance, its norms tend to facilitate their participation in subsequent acts of deviance. Within the group, these behaviors are considered normative.

Secondary deviance is deviant behavior that occurs after a person has been labeled. Whereas the cause of primary deviance is varied, the cause of secondary deviance is the labeling process itself. This is highly consistent with the Thomas theorem, a key premise of symbolic interactionism: when situations (or people) are defined in a particular way, regardless of the accuracy of this assessment, they become this. Although it is the label itself that produces the secondary deviance, these new behaviors are used to justify the initial labeling. Thus, labeling someone as deviant frequently gives rise to a self-fulfilling prophecy.

Due, in part, to its controversial message—namely, that labeling someone is bad because it causes more deviance—labeling theory has had its critics over the years. However, many studies support it central propositions (Grattet 2011; Link and Cullen 1990).

To summarize, a person is singled out and labeled as deviant. As a consequence of the fact that he has been labeled in this manner, this individual begins to see himself as deviant and interacts primarily with other people who have been similarly labeled. This in turn results in the person committing further acts of deviance, which are taken as an indication that the initial label was accurate. This process is depicted in Figure 9.3.

You might be wondering why this happens. We can find our answer in the literature on the self-concept. People have a need for self-verification. Thus, they seek confirmation for the way that they see themselves, even when their identities or self-conceptions are negative. What makes this process especially problematic when it comes to deviance and labeling is that who gets labeled as deviant reflects broader patterns of inequality within society and is thus subject to substantial bias.

Status and Labeling

One of the authors once asked some of her students to rate various behaviors in terms of their degree of deviance. Overall, these individuals reported that murder, robbery, and rape are highly deviant acts, whereas speeding on the highway and taking two newspapers from a machine for the price of one are normative. (The students themselves generated the list of potentially deviant behaviors. Perhaps someone had recently engaged in paper stealing, which made it salient at the time at which the excercise was completed.) Interestingly, whereas behaviors such as murder, robbery, and rape were consensually defined as deviant (i.e., there was agreement across students that these are deviant actions), some behaviors were defined as deviant by some students but not by others. These low-consensus behaviors included drinking alcohol, having multiple sex partners, and engaging in homosexual sex.

Surveys of the population's attitudes toward various issues reveal a similar pattern. Table 9.2 includes data pertaining to two sexual behaviors, homosexuality and premarital sex, from the 2010 General Social Survey. Remember, GSS data are based on a representative samples, so these figures are generalizable to the adult population in the United States.

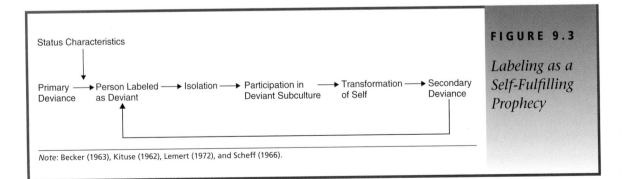

FIGURE 9.3

Labeling as a Self-Fulfilling Prophecy

Note: Becker (1963), Kituse (1962), Lemert (1972), and Scheff (1966).

As shown in Table 9.2, there is substantial variation in how people view these behaviors. Not everyone agrees that these acts are deviant (or normative). For homosexual sex, for example, the split is about 50/50. Approximately half of the sample (53%) indicated that homosexuality is wrong, whereas the rest of the survey participants (47%) reported that this behavior is acceptable.

Not surprisingly, the extent to which people perceive homosexual and premarital sex as deviant varies by status characteristics such as education, race, gender and age, and by religious participation. Note the large differences in views about homosexuality by education and by religious participation, and the large effect of religious participation on beliefs about premarital sex.

Despite the fact that definitions of deviance vary across individuals and groups within society, it is those individuals at the top of the stratification hierarchy who

TABLE 9.2

Perceptions of Homosexuality and Premarital Sex Among U.S. Adults, 2010

	HOMOSEXUALITY WRONG	PREMARITAL SEX WRONG
Total sample	53%	31%
n	3068	3231
Education		
Less than college	60%	34%
College graduate	36%	23%
Race		
Minority	64%	38%
White	50%	29%
Gender		
Male	56%	25%
Female	51%	36%
Age		
40 and under	43%	24%
Over 40	59%	34%
Attend: religious services		
Less than once a month	37%	14%
Once a month or more	70%	50%

Note: Smith, Tom W., Peter V. Marsden, and Michael Hout. 2011. General Social Surveys, 1972–2010 [machine-readable data file] / Sponsored by National Science Foundation.—NORC ed.—Chicago, IL: National Opinion Research Center [producer]; Storrs, CT: The Roper Center for Public Opinion Research, University of Connecticut [distributor].

have the greatest ability to impose their definitions of deviance on others, and those individuals who lack socioeconomic resources who are the least able to resist these labels. Given this, labeling serves to control the behaviors of those at the bottom of the class structure. Low-status members of society often run the risk of being formally labeled, and experiencing the consequences of this process, if they don't conform to middle- and upper-class norms (Adler and Adler 2011).

What Do You Think?

People are also labeled as deviant when their behaviors do not conform to the expectations for someone of their gender or age. Discuss this with one or two of your classmates.

- Come up with at least three behaviors that are considered deviant for males but not females and at least three behaviors that are considered deviant for females but not for males.
- Give an example of two or three behaviors likely to be regarded as deviant because they are age inappropriate.

Even among people who commit the same transgressions, lower-class individuals are more likely than upper-class individuals, and racial and ethnic minorities are more likely than Whites, to be defined as deviant (Chambliss 1973; Link and Cullen 1990; Tapia 2011). Although the behaviors that result in a deviant label may vary across social contexts and with the whims of the labeler, labeling theorists emphasize the fact that it is people with certain social characteristics (in general, the socially disadvantaged) who are most likely to be labeled as deviant.

This is a serious issue, given the effects of labeling on individuals' self-concepts and subsequent behaviors. Although the negative spiral depicted in Figure 9.3 can be disrupted, it is not always easy to do so. Often there must be some major change in a labelee's social environment for that individual to break out of this cycle.

High school students making the transition to college are often happy they are going away to school because they recognize that it will give them a clean slate (Karp et al. 1998). Research on the consequence of labeling (Chambliss 1973) suggests that this kind of change in environment can be of great benefit to individuals who have been labeled as deviant. This is because it increases their likelihoods of receiving interpersonal feedback that confirms nondeviant identities.

Deviant Selves

A deviant label, whatever its source, is often a stigmatizing one. A **stigma** is a trait or characteristic that causes one to lose prestige and social status in the eyes of others.

Thus, it results in an individual's identity being discredited or spoiled (Goffman 1963). In order to avoid this, some individuals actively resist the labeling process. Resistance is most likely to occur when the individual labeled as deviant has power that is equal to or greater in magnitude to that of the labelers or is able to maintain relationships with others based on prior nondeviant identities.

MANAGING STIGMA FROM A DRAMATURGICAL PERSPECTIVE

Goffman (1963) discusses a number of strategies that are used to minimize the effects of having a stigmatized identity. They all involve mechanisms for controlling the information that is given to others in order to reduce the likelihood that labeling will occur or its negative impact.

Some individuals opt to conceal their deviance in order to avoid potential negative consequences associated with labeling. **Passing** involves deliberating concealing the stigmatized characteristic and acting as someone who does not possess a stigmatizing characteristic. This technique is often employed by individuals who have a stigmatized attribute that they can readily hide. Historically, the term "passing" has been used to describe the behaviors of light-skinned African Americans who posed as Whites in order to avoid being the victims of racism. In a similar manner, an alcoholic may choose not to reveal his addiction to others due to the negative attitudes about substance abusers within this culture.

A second technique, **covering**, refers to self-presentational strategies that minimize or keep the stigmatized characteristic from being the focal point of interactions, even though others are aware of its existence. For example, a sick person who takes multiple medications hides them before anyone comes over so that others are not reminded that he has a particular illness. If you're interested, go to the following web address for a summary of a book in which the author reflects upon, among other things, his attempts to cover his homosexuality: http://www.nytimes.com/2006/01/22/books/review/22altho.html.

If an individual is not able to conceal or cover her stigma, or if attempts at doing so fail, she may openly disclose her deviant identity to others with the hope that they will accept her anyway. **Disclosure** might also be undertaken to alleviate the burden of living with a secret, with a goal toward casting the stigmatized identity in a positive light, or for preventative reasons. People may respond more favorably to a revelation about a person's stigmatized identity when that information comes directly from that individual, instead of from someone else in the form of gossip.

Through the use of a related technique, **deviance disavowal**, individuals openly acknowledge their stigma and try to present themselves in a positive light (Goffman 1963). The stigma associated with certain characteristics or behaviors is sometimes managed this way within a group context or through some type of collective effort (Adler and Adler 2011; Herman 1995). There are many voluntary associations for individuals with stigmatized identities, including the National Stuttering Project, Overeaters Anonymous, and Gamblers Anonymous. These groups are often organized to provide support for members, to give information and advice, and to create opportunities for people to meet others who face similar issues.

Other associations (e.g., the Gay Liberation Front, COYOTE, AIDS Coalition to Unleash Power) are formed for the purpose of political activism, as well as support, with a stated goal of changing people's views of the behavior in question. These groups usually focus on stigmatized identities that are either involuntary (e.g., physical or mental disabilities) or arise as the result of behaviors that, although regarded by some as deviant, are not illegal (Adler and Adler 2011).

DEGRADATION CEREMONIES AND THE USE OF ACCOUNTS

When a member of society breaks the law and the violation is consensually regarded as serious (e.g., they commit murder, molest a child, or steal large sums of money), his or her actions often result in public shaming. If society were to allow this behavior to go unchecked, it would call into question our understanding of the world—who we are and what we believe in. Through denunciation rituals, people are able to express their collective moral outrage at the perpetrator's behavior and validate their understandings of what is good and bad by ostracizing this individual from the group or society (Garfinkel 1956).

Degradation ceremonies are rituals designed to transform the identity of an individual and to expel them from membership in the group. Through a standard set of rituals, the identity of the individual is transformed into something as dishonorable, disreputable, and deviant. The denouncer often suggests that the individual's old identities are accidental and that it is the new one that is real. "What he is now is what, 'after all,' he was all along" (Garfinkel 1956:422).

Garfinkel (1956) discusses the conditions required for a successful degradation ceremony. For a degradation ceremony to be effective, people denouncing a perpetrator must complete the following steps.

1. They must make their claims public so that there is widespread recognition that the perpetrator is not as he or she appears but is rather different or out of the ordinary.

2. They must get others to see the perpetrator and behavior as one and the same and thus reflective of a particular type rather than as unique individual who engaged in a particular behavior.

3. They must show this type to be devalued by contrasting it with its opposite, which is good and desirable.

4. They must speak not as private individuals but as public figures who represent the community and their shared values.

5. They must show that they have a right to speak for the group.

6. They must create distance by distinguishing themselves and others who are law-abiding as good and thus as different from the perpetrator, who is bad or immoral.

7. Finally, they must ensure that the denounced person is ritually separated from a place within the legitimate social order. The perpetrator must be made an outsider (Garkfinkel 1956).

The criminal justice system itself (investigation, prosecution, and conviction of offenders) has elements of a degradation ceremony because it has the power to transform an individual's identity from a law-abiding member of the community to a convicted felon (Benson 1985; Einstadter and Henry 2006). The "perp walk" is part of this process.

Degradation ceremonies also include the public outcry and denunciation that occur when a politician falls from grace because of a scandal or when an individual has been accused of a serious crime. Some recent examples of individuals subject to highly public degradation ceremonies include Mark Sanford, the former governor of South Carolina, a vocal advocate of "family values," who had an extramarital affair; Martha Stewart, known for her home-oriented crafts and products, for insider trading; and ex-Penn State football coach Jerry Sandusky, for child molestation.

PHOTO 9.3

The "perp walk" is often part of a public degradation ritual.

What Do You Think?

Can you think of any other highly visual outrage ceremonies recently represented on television, in newspapers, or on the Internet? If so, to what extent were the steps identified by Garfinkel evident in the condemners' verbal statements and behaviors? How did you feel when you were exposed to this information? Did you feel anger or outrage at the perpetrator's behavior? How did you feel about the perpetrator?

The kind of public labeling associated with a degradation ceremony makes it difficult for its target to maintain a positive sense of self or convey to others that he or she is more than a criminal. However, criminals and others who have been publicly labeled as deviant can minimize the effects of a degradation ceremony if they can undermine one or more of its required elements (Garfinkel 1956). For example, the continual and visible support of family members and friends may reduce the impact of a degradation ceremony on how a perpetrator is viewed by showing that he or she has identities other than that of "criminal."

In addition, individuals convicted of crimes may account for their actions in an attempt to thwart their transformation from law-abiding citizen to criminal (Benson 1985). In this context, **accounts** are excuses or justifications for behavior that are designed to relieve individuals of responsibility for their actions (Scott and Lyman 1968). In the case of criminals, accounts are often used to deny that there was criminal intent, which demonstrates to others that they are not really deviant. Alternatively, a criminal may suggest that his crime represents only one behavior and is not indicative of who he is as a person, thereby negating the claims of the denouncers (Benson 1985).

TECHNIQUES OF NEUTRALIZATION

Accounts may also be used to reduce the guilt and shame associated with the violation of society's rules. According to Sykes and Matza (1957), most people who engage in deviant behavior have internalized the general norms of society and believe in the moral validity of the law. Thus, they often develop rationalizations (accounts) about why it was okay to break the rules or violate the law in a particular situation. This neutralizes the negative affect associated with their deviant actions.

Techniques of neutralization, as identified by Sykes and Matza (1957), commonly take one or more of the following five forms:

1. **Denial of responsibility**: The individual denies any responsibility for the behavior or its consequences by arguing that it was not his or her fault (e.g., due to peer pressure), that it was unintentional (e.g., an accident), or that it was beyond his or her control (e.g., due to biological drives or bad parenting). As illustrated in the previous section, this technique of neutralization is commonly used by criminals trying to counteract a degradation ritual.

2. **Denial of injury**: The perpetrator argues that no one was hurt by his or her behavior. They may use particular language to cultivate this meaning. For example, instead of stealing a car, it was just "borrowed." Or, in the case of white-collar crime, no individual was harmed when the perpetrator embezzled money from her company.

3. **Denial of victim**: The violator transforms the victim into the one who is responsible for what happened to them (e.g., they got what they deserve) or into the wrongdoer (they shouldn't have been out so late). Alternatively, the perpetrator may claim that there was no victim. In the case of employee theft, for instance, one might claim that the corporation is hardly affected by such a small loss.

4. **Condemnation of condemners**: The perpetrator shifts the focus away from his or her own acts to the motives and behaviors of the one who disapproves of the rule violation (e.g., teachers, the police, or his or her parents). They might argue that that person is a hypocrite, corrupt, or unfair (Sykes and Matza 1957). Police are out to get gang members, or federal regulators targeting particular industries are making crimes out of standard business practices in order to enhance their own careers. The argument about career enhancement is often made in regard to prosecutors when individuals convicted of white-collar crimes talk about their trials (Benson 1985).

5. **Appeal to higher loyalties**: The deviant individual sacrifices the demands or rules of the larger society for those of smaller groups to which he belongs. A gang member or a rogue police officer might justify behavior that is harmful to others by emphasizing how it benefits his friends or work colleagues. Similarly, someone might rationalize breaking the law by stealing food if the food is for her family (Sykes and Matza 1957).

Each of these techniques of neutralization serves to redefine the situation so that the behavior in question is viewed as acceptable. Thus, techniques of neutralization enable individuals to engage in deviant acts without serious damage to their self-image or feelings of guilt or shame. They can maintain a positive self-concept despite their participation in activities that others' within society view negatively. See Box 9.2 for an application of techniques of neutralization to student cheating.

Deviation From Norms Within Groups

Up to this point, we have said little about the manner in which deviance is studied within the group processes and structure face of social psychology. Given its focus, social psychologists aligned with this orientation have not studied deviance with the same degree of depth as those working within the other two faces of sociological social psychology (social structures and personality and symbolic interactionism). They have, however, discussed the extent to which some of the processes discussed

Box 9.2   College Student Cheating

Cheating in college is a pervasive problem among American college students. It's estimated that over two-thirds of college students cheat on tests, homework, and assignments (Klein et al. 2007; Whitley 1998). Students who have participated in research on this topic have given the following accounts for their behaviors, suggesting that they regularly use the techniques of neutralization specified by Sykes and Matza (1957). By reducing the shame and guilt associated with cheating, these kinds of accounts may be used to neutralize the effects of some of the informal and internal controls you identified in the exercise earlier in the chapter.

Denial of responsibility

"Here at . . . you must cheat to stay alive. There's so much work and the quality of materials from which to learn, books, professors, is so bad there is no other choice." (McCabe 1992)

"Everyone has test files in Fraternities, etc. If you don't, you're at a great disadvantage." (McCabe 1992)

"I couldn't do the work myself." (McCabe 1992)

"I was taking the test and someone in another part of the room was telling someone else an answer. I heard it and just couldn't not write it down." (Labeff et al. 1990)

Denial of injury

"These grades aren't worth much therefore my copying doesn't mean very much. I am ashamed, but I'd probably do it the same way again." (McCabe 1992)

"If I extend the time on a take home it is because I feel everyone does and the teacher kind of expects it. No one gets hurt." (McCabe 1992)

Condemnation of condemners

"The TAs who graded essays were unduly harsh." (McCabe 1992)

"It is known by students that certain professors are more lenient to certain types, e.g., blonds or hockey players." (McCabe 1992)

"Major exams are very important to your grade and it seems that the majority of instructors make up the exams to try and trick you instead of testing your knowledge." (LaBeff et al. 1990)

Appeal to higher loyalties

"I only cheated because my friend had been sick and she needed help . . . it (cheating) wouldn't have happened any other time." (Labeff et al. 1990)

"I personally have never cheated. I've had friends who asked for help so I let them see my test. Maybe some would consider that to be cheating." (Labeff et al. 1990)

Is cheating OK? Professors, school administrators, and many students think it's not. It gives an unfair advantage to individuals who break the rules and is likely to reinforce the notion that unethical behaviors are okay for instrumental purposes. What might college and university professors and administrators do to minimize student cheating?

earlier in the chapter apply to interaction in small groups organized for the purpose of accomplishing some goal.

Status Violation Theory

In particular, **status violation theory** (Wagner 1988), an expansion of status characteristics theory, focuses on how members of task-oriented groups respond to behaviors deemed inappropriate given an actor's status characteristics (e.g., gender, race/ethnicity, or level of task-related expertise). Insofar as group members consistently behave in a nonnormative manner (e.g., a low-status member challenges high-status group members on multiple occasions), status violation theory predicts that they will be accorded a new status, that of "deviant." In combination with their other status characteristics, this deviant status is expected to influence other group members' expectations, and evaluations, of the actor. Because the status of deviant is regarded as negative, this process should inhibit the extent to which individuals defined in this manner are given opportunities to contribute to the groups' outcomes and lead to more negative evaluations of their task performance.

Most people are aware of the potential for labeling within task groups, which increases their likelihood of behaving appropriately. Thus, within the context of small group encounters, the labeling process may serve a social control function similar to that observed in other social settings (Wagner 1988). Albeit largely untested, the results of a recent experiment (Youngreen and Moore 2008) offer some support for status violation theory.

The effects of deviant identities that are not themselves constructed during the group interaction (e.g., deviant identities that individuals bring with them to the group encounter, such as "criminal" or "drug addict") on task-group behavior have not been systematically examined by sociological social psychologists working within the group processes and structures tradition. However, it is likely that they would function much like other diffuse status characteristics, including gender and race/ethnicity.

Other Perspectives

Like social psychologists who have studied deviance as a status characteristic, whose work we described in the previous section, social identity theorists have focused on how deviance emerges within groups and on how other group members treat deviants. In general, these studies suggest that group members who engage in nonnormative behaviors are marginalized, unless their deviance makes others look upon the group more favorably (Hogg and Reid 2006).

Within the social exchange framework, it is assumed that behaving in a deviant manner with regard to the process of exchange itself (e.g., withholding rewards from an exchange partner in a manner perceived as inappropriate) will reduce the rewards received in future exchanges with a given actor. Failing to meet others' expectations may also reduce an individual's desirability as an exchange partner, especially in the case of reciprocal exchange relations, such as marriage or friendship. Given their desire to maximize rewards, and minimize losses, it is assumed that people will behave in accordance with prevailing group norms insofar as it is in their interest to do so.

CHAPTER SUMMARY

Sociological social psychologists have sought to identify the structural conditions that give rise to deviance, how deviant behaviors are learned, and the social experiences of individuals considered deviant. The theories governing their analyses, and the faces of sociological social psychology they represent, are summarized in Table 9.3. As illustrated throughout the chapter, these theories direct our attention to prevailing societal patterns and to the micro-level interactions they generate. Because deviance is socially constructed and reflects macro-level inequalities between social groups, understanding the causes and consequences of this type of behavior provides us with important information about how society operates.

Key Points to Know

- **Deviance is socially constructed, which means that no behavior is in and of itself deviant.** Behaviors are defined as deviant only in relation to prevailing social norms. Whether an act is considered deviant also depends upon the situation within which it occurs and the status characteristics of the actor.

- **Deviance is a topic of interest to sociological social psychologists, not only because it is a regular occurrence, but also because it reflects the concerns of their home discipline—the manner in which inequality at the macro level influences individuals' everyday social experiences.** The study of deviance is still somewhat controversial, albeit less so than in the past, because it directs our attention to behaviors that make some people uncomfortable.

- **Patterns of deviance at the societal level vary by gender, class, and race. Most racial/ethnic differences in crime among adults, and delinquency among youths, are due to socioeconomic factors. Thus, they are really class differences.**

- **Structural theories emphasize the relationship between social class and crime.** Research on the causes of deviance suggest that people engage in financially motivated crimes when they are socialized to aspire to culturally defined goals but are denied the legitimate means for obtaining these ends. Other kinds of strain (e.g., discrimination or

	THEORY	FACE OF SOCIAL PSYCHOLOGY	PRIMARY RESEARCH QUESTION	EMPIRICAL SUPPORT
TABLE 9.3 *Theories of Deviance Summary*	Structural strain (Merton)	Social structure and personality	What causes economically motivated crimes?	Moderate
	General strain (Agnew)	Social structure and personality	What causes crime and other forms of deviance?	Strong
	Social control (Hirschi)	Social structure and personality (extensions of theory)	Why aren't more people deviant more of the time?	Moderate
	Symbolic interactionist (e.g., Becker)	Symbolic interactionist	How is deviance learned?	Strong
	Differential association (Sutherland)	Symbolic interactionist	How is deviance learned?	Strong
	Differential reinforcement (Akers)	Psychological (social learning)/symbolic interactionist	How is deviance learned through patterns of reinforcement and punishment?	Moderate
	Labeling (many theorists)	Symbolic structures	What happens to people labeled as deviant?	Strong
	Status violation (Wagner)	Group processes and structures	What happens to people labeled as deviant in task groups?	Some

the loss of something or someone who is valued) also result in deviant behavior.

- **Social control theory attributes delinquency to weak social bonds.** Extensions of this theory within the social structure and personality face of social psychology have investigated the link between social structure and social bonding. A number of these studies have focused on gender. Social bonds do not explain males' higher levels of delinquency than their female counterparts.

- **At the micro level, symbolic interactionists focus on the social processes through which deviance is learned. Two theories of deviance (differential association theory and differential reinforcement theory) share a similar concern, although the research they have generated is largely quantitative in orientation.** Research showing a strong effect of adolescents' peer affiliations on their levels of delinquency supports the main premises of these theories.

- **Labeling theory is the dominant symbolic interactionist approach to the study of deviance. Rather than focusing on the causes of deviance, labeling theorists direct their attention to the effects of status characteristics, in particular social class and race/ethnicity, on who gets labeled and on the consequences of the labeling process.** Being labeled as deviant has negative effects on individuals' self-concepts and subsequent behaviors, and the self-fulfilling prophecy it generates may be difficult to disrupt without some major change in the target's social environment.

- **Degradation ceremonies involve the public shaming of criminals who have engaged in behaviors consensually regarded as immoral.** These rituals provide a forum for law-abiding individuals to collectively express their outrage and serve to remind us of what is means to be good and moral.

- **Individuals use a variety of strategies to manage deviant selves.** They may minimize the stigma associated with a deviant identity by hiding or selectively revealing information about their identity or by affiliating with others with similar characteristics for social or political reasons. People may also neutralize their deviant behaviors through the use of accounts, which enable them to deny responsibility for their actions, deny that their actions are harmful to others, or view their behaviors as appropriate given their group loyalties or the actions of others.

- **Status violation theory suggests that individuals who violate task-group norms will be accorded the status of "deviant," which is likely to generate negative performance expectations and evaluations.** Although there is some empirical support for this perspective, there is little research on how deviant identities developed prior to joining the group influence members' perceptions and behaviors. Given its focus, there are fewer systematic analyses of deviance within the group processes and structure tradition than there are within the other two faces of sociological social psychology.

Terms and Concepts for Review

Accounts	Formal control
Anomie	General strain theory
Appeal to higher loyalties	Informal control
Attachment	Internal control
Belief	Involvement
Commitment	Labeling theory
Condemnation of condemners	Laws
Covering	Mores
Crime	Motivated deviance
Degradation ceremony	Passing
Denial of injury	Primary deviance
Denial of responsibility	Retrospective labeling
Denial of victim	Secondary deviance
Deviance	Social control theory
Deviance disavowal	Status violation theory
Deviant subculture	Stigma
Differential association theory	Strain theory
Differential reinforcement theory	Techniques of neutralization
Disclosure	Unmotivated deviance
Folkways	White-collar crime

Questions for Review and Reflection

1. What do sociological social psychologists mean when they say that deviance is socially constructed? What factors influence whether an act, or an individual, is defined as deviant?

2. Apply at least three of the theories of deviance discussed in this chapter to the topic of college student drinking. Which theory offers the best explanation of this behavior? Discuss the utility of combining perspectives.

3. Consider a high school student who regularly skips class to hang out with friends in the local park. What factors are likely to influence whether this student is labeled as deviant by teachers and school administrators? What is likely to happen to this individual if labeling occurs?

4. Reality shows are quite popular these days. Some of these programs focus on revealing or analyzing some form of deviance (e.g., shows such as *My Strange Addiction, Intervention,* and *Obese and Expecting*), whereas others provide an inside look into an atypical family's day-to-day life (e.g., *Little People, Big World; 25 Kids and Counting;* and *Sister Wives*). Why are these television programs so popular? Please make reference to the literature on deviant selves when responding to this question. (If you aren't familiar with any of the programs listed, look a few of them up online. You'll get the gist of their focus.)

CHAPTER 10

Mental Health and Illness

Stress is something we hear a lot about these days. Stress is the body's reaction to threatening situations and events. Thus, it is a biological state (Wheaton 1999).

Although social psychologists rarely measure stress itself, as a state of physiological arousal, they frequently measure the psychological and emotional consequences of stress on survey questionnaires. To what extent do you exhibit common signs of stress? Use these response options to answer the following questions.

0 = never
1 = almost never
2 = sometimes
3 = fairly often
4 = very often

_____ 1. In the last month, how often have you been upset because of something that happened unexpectedly?

_____ 2. In the last month, how often have you felt that you were unable to control the important things in your life?

_____ 3. In the last month, how often have you felt nervous and "stressed"?

_____ 4. In the last month, how often have you found that you could not cope with all the things that you had to do?

_____ 5. In the last month, how often have you been able to control irritations in your life?

_____ 6. In the last month, how often have you felt that you were on top of things?

_____ 7. In the last month, how often have you been angered because of things that happened that were outside of your control?

_____ 8. In the last month, how often have you found yourself thinking about things that you have to accomplish?

_____ 9. In the last month, how often have you been able to control the way you spend your time?

_____ 10. In the last month, how often have you felt difficulties were piling up so high that you could not overcome them?

_____ Subtotal 1 (total score for questions 1–10)

Use these response options to answer the next set of questions.

4 = never
3 = almost never
2 = sometimes
1 = fairly often
0 = very often

_____ 11. In the last month, how often have you dealt successfully with irritating life hassles?

_____ 12. In the last month, how often have you felt that you were effectively coping with important changes that were occurring in your life?

_____ 13. In the last month, how often have you felt confident about your ability to handle your personal problems?

_____ 14. In the last month, how often have you felt that things were going your way?

_____ Subtotal 2 (total score for questions 11–14)

_____ TOTAL INDEX SCORE (Subtotal 1 + Subtotal 2)

The Perceived Stress Scale (PSS) (Cohen, Kamarck, and Mermelstein 1983), which you just completed, is a measure of perceived stress-related outcomes that is often administered to college students. High scores mean high levels of perceived stress. What was your score? The average score on the PSS for college students, a benchmark with which you can compare your score, is between 23 and 24 points (the standard deviation is about 7 points) (Cohen et al. 1983). Scores on this measure do not notably vary by gender or year in school (Cohen et al. 1983; Pettit and DeBarr 2011).

Note that the PSS is not used for clinical purposes, so a high score on this index doesn't mean you have a psychiatric disorder or that your perceptions are in any way pathological. It simply means that you have recently exhibited a lot of the perceptions and feelings associated with a high level of stress.

WHAT CAUSES STRESS?

Write down five things that cause stress. If you have ready access to a computer or cell phone from which you can access the Internet, you might also consider running a quick search for "causes of stress." What comes up? We found websites (a lot of them) focusing on the following issues.

- Problems pertaining to work

- Problems within the family (conflict between spouses or between parents and children)

- Poor health

- Having a relative or close friend who is ill or has died

- Financial troubles

This isn't too far off, according to sociological social psychologists. These are all stressors that have been associated with psychological well-being within the research literature on the social psychology of mental health.

Stressors are external conditions that cause stress. Whereas stress occurs inside the individual, stressors (e.g., getting divorced or losing a job) are located within an individual's social environment. Sociological social psychologists who study stress have focused on the relationship between stressors and **psychological distress** (the psychological manifestation of stress).

Sociological Versus Psychological Approaches to the Study of Stress

In news articles and online discussions or blogs, people often overlook how stress is distributed within society. Not everyone experiences high levels of stress, despite the fact that most of us would probably say that we're really stressed if we were asked about stress in our lives.

Research has shown that some people's life experiences consistently result in more stress, and thus psychological distress, than others (Wheaton 1999). In general, members of disadvantage groups face economic and social conditions that make them more prone to psychological distress than other individuals.

The ways that social inequality at the macro level affects people's social experiences, and thus their risk for stress and its negative effects, is the focus of much of the social psychological research on mental health conducted by sociologists. Psychologists also study stress and its consequences, but they typically take a much more micro-level approach to this topic. They study stress at the individual level and are much less likely to take into consideration how a group's location within the stratification hierarchy shapes its members' day-to-day experiences, thereby increasing or decreasing their likelihoods of experiencing psychological distress. As you may have guessed, it is studies by social psychologists working within the social structure and personality face of social psychology that dominate the research literature on stress within sociological social psychology. Iowa/Indiana school symbolic interactionists have a similar orientation to SSP researchers and have also contributed to the stress literature.

Chicago school symbolic interactionists study mental health but, given the focus of this face of sociological social psychology, they do not typically analyze the ways that stress is distributed across groups within society. Rather, much of their work is on the experiences and identities of individuals who are mentally ill. Many of these studies are within the labeling tradition. We discuss (Chicago school) symbolic interactionist perspectives on mental health later in the chapter. Given the focus of the group processes and structures face of social psychology, there are few studies on mental health and illness in this research tradition.

MODELING THE STRESS PROCESS

SSP researchers who study when and why people experience stress focus on the relationships between three main constructs: stressors, resources, and distress.

Distress Versus Disorder

Psychological distress serves as the dependent variable in most studies on the stress process, and measures of psychological distress are continuous rather than discrete in nature. Thus, low scores on a distress index indicate psychological well-being (mental health), whereas high scores reflect the kind of unpleasant psychological states presumed to manifest when individuals experience high levels of stress.

The Perceived Stress Scale, discussed in the previous section, is really a measure of perceived psychological distress because it includes items measuring how frequently people feel angry, nervous, and generally stressed, as well as other outcomes presumed to result from the exposure to stressors. Box 10.1 contains questions commonly used to measure how frequently individuals experience symptoms associated with psychological distress on general population surveys, based on large nationally or regionally representative samples of U.S. adults. These items are from a measure called the Brief Symptom Inventory (or BSI).

The BSI (Derogatis 1975, 1993) includes 53 questions designed to assess individuals' levels of depression, anxiety, hostility, somatization (physical symptoms with a psychological cause), and some other dimensions of psychological distress. Although the BSI is not used to determine whether someone has a psychiatric disorder, it measures psychological symptoms presumed to be of clinical relevance (Derogatis 1975). Thus, it is different than the Perceived Stress Scale, described earlier,

---

Box 10.1 The Brief Symptom Inventory

During the past 7 days, how much were you distressed by _____?
Response options range from 1 = "not at all" to 4 = "extremely."

SAMPLE QUESTION	SUBCALE
Feeling hopeless about the future	Depression, 6 questions
Feeling so restless you couldn't sit still	Anxiety, 6 questions
Having urges to break or smash things	Hostility, 5 questions
Pains in the heart or chest	Somatization, 7 questions
Having to check and double check what you do	Obsession-compulsion, 6 questions
Feeling others are to blame for most of your troubles	Paranoid ideation, 5 questions
Never feeling close to another person	Psychoticism, 5 questions
Feeling afraid to travel on buses, subways, or trains	Phobic anxiety, 5 questions
Feeling that you are watched or talked about by others	Interpersonal sensitivity, 4 questions
Feelings of guilt	Other symptoms, 4 questions

Note: Derogatis (1975).

---

which has no clinical basis and emphasizes individuals' appraisals of their current situation (Cohen et al. 1983).

Actually, the PSS is a better measure for college students than the BSI. College students score higher than other groups on the BSI (Cochran and Hale 1985), potentially because of the nature of the college student role itself. College students are often living away from their family for the first time, and they typically balance multiple roles, many of which may be new to them. The BSI has been found to be a less accurate measure of distress among college students than it is among more mature adults (Hayes 1997). Thus, it is more appropriate for use on general population surveys than on questionnaires administered to college student samples.

Stressors

Stressors come in many different forms and vary in terms of whether they are discrete (one-time occurrences) or continuous in duration (relatively long term). The types of stressors most frequently studied include major traumas, negative life events, and chronic strains.

Major traumas are events that are perceived as extremely disturbing. Although they may have long-term consequences for their victims, major traumas are often discrete events. Examples of discrete major traumas are being raped or witnessing a murder. Childhood sexual abuse that occurs over a period of years is an example of a major trauma that is chronic, rather than discrete, in nature.

Life events are discrete events that require adjustment on the part of the individual. Life events can be positive (e.g., getting married, moving to a new city, or starting college), as well as negative (e.g., the death of a loved one, getting fired, or getting divorced) (Wheaton 1999). Research suggests that positive life events have minimal effects on psychological well-being (Sarason, Johnson, and Segal 1978). Thus, most contemporary stress researchers focus on negative life events, which have been shown to have negative psychological effects.

Chronic strains include ongoing problems, like conflict at work or with one's spouse, as well as role strains (e.g., having to do too many things at once on a day-to-day basis) (McDonough and Walters 2001; Turner, Wheaton, and Lloyd 1995). These kinds of stressors are distinct in that they occur over an extended period of time. Whereas getting divorced is a negative life event, having marital problems is a chronic strain. Not having enough money to meet one's needs is another common chronic strain. Because they continue over time, chronic strains may deplete an individual's ability to effectively manage them. People often get burned out when they face stressful circumstances that are long term in their duration. Thus, chronic strains often have more detrimental psychological effects than negative life events (Wheaton 1999).

Temporal Order

Stressors can also be classified with regard to their temporal order. **Primary stressors** include major traumas, negative life events, and strains that give rise to other (secondary) stressors. **Secondary stressors** are caused by primary stressors and may help to explain why some primary stressors have such strong effects on psychological well-being. **Stress proliferation** occurs when something bad happens (a primary stressor) and this leads to one or more other (secondary) stressors. When this occurs, an individual's level of psychological distress is likely to be quite high (Pearlin 1999).

For example, major traumas experienced during childhood are primary stressors that have substantial effects on adults' levels of distress. This is largely because they put them at risk for a host of secondary stressors, including negative life events (e.g., divorce) and chronic strains (unemployment, relationship difficulties) throughout the course of their lives.

What Do You Think?

How might divorce, a negative life event, result in other (secondary) stressors? What other life events, or chronic strains, are likely to give rise to secondary stressors?

Coping Resources

SSP researchers emphasize the fact that stressors do not always cause psychological distress. This is because some people have social and psychological resources that enable them to cope with the stressors that befall them. **Coping resources** include social support and aspects of people's self-concepts, in particular self-esteem and mastery.

Social Support

Social support is an important coping resource, one that is rooted in people's ties to others. More specifically, social support is information received from others that leads individuals to believe that they are "cared for and loved," "esteemed and valued," and a member of "a network of communication and mutual obligation" (Cobb 1976:300).

Social support can be measured on a survey using a single indicator or a series of items. Sometimes survey respondents are simply asked to report whether they have someone they can talk to about their problems. Box 10.2 includes items from a more detailed measure of social support used within the stress literature.

In the absence of any major stressors, the amount of social support an individual receives has a minimal impact on psychological well-being. However, when people are exposed to one or more significant stressors, social support has a substantial effect on their emotional states. When bad things happen, individuals with low levels of social support are at a much higher risk for psychological distress than people with high levels of social support. This is called a **buffering effect**. Social support buffers (or minimizes) the effects of stressors on distress (Cobb 1976; Turner 1981). As a result, social support is an important coping resource. We all experience stressors at one time or another, at which point social support becomes important to our emotional well-being. Study after study has shown that individuals who are socially isolated are at a substantial risk for negative psychological outcomes (Turner 1999).

Self-Esteem and Mastery

Self-esteem and mastery also reduce the negative effects of stressors. As described in Chapter 7, self-esteem reflects one's overall, or global, self-evaluation. **Mastery** refers to the degree to which people believe that they have control over the forces that shape their lives. As such, it is the opposite of fatalism (Pearlin and Schooler 1978) and is similar to the concept of perceived control (Ross and Mirowsky 2006). Although mastery and self-esteem are correlated (Pearlin et al. 1981), they are distinct constructs. This means that someone with high self-esteem is also likely to be high in mastery, and someone low in self-esteem is likely to be low in mastery. However, this isn't always the case. There are some people who have positive self-concepts

Box 10.2   Measuring Social Support

The following items are from the friends subscale of a social support index used within the research literature (Turner and Turner 2005). Similar questions about spouses, other family members, and coworkers are also given to survey respondents, and all of the items are added up into a composite social support score.

Response options

1 = Not at all like my experience
2 = Much like my experience
3 = Somewhat like my experience
4 = Very much like my experience

Item	Response
1. I feel very close to my friends.	_____
2. I have friends who would always take the time to talk over my problems, should I want to.	_____
3. My friends often let me know that they think I'm a worthwhile person.	_____
4. When I am with my friends, I feel completely able to relax and be myself.	_____
5. No matter what happens, I know that my friends will always be there for me, should I need them.	_____
6. I know that my friends have confidence in me.	_____
7. I feel that my friends really care about me.	_____
8. I often feel really appreciated by my friends.	_____

How would you answer these questions? Do you perceive your friends as supportive? Studies suggest that it is perceived, not the actual amount, of social support people receive that affects their psychological well-being (Wethington and Kessler 1986).

who don't feel like they can control their environment, and there are some people with negative self-concepts who believe that they have control over their lives.

Whereas coping resources such as self-esteem and mastery reflect how people view themselves, **coping strategies** refer to the things people do to minimize the negative effects of stressors. Effective coping strategies (1) alter or eliminate the problematic situation, (2) change the way in which a problematic situation is perceived in order to reduce its threat, or (3) enable individuals to manage their emotional reactions to problematic situations.

Interestingly, psychological coping resources (self-esteem and mastery) are more important than coping strategies (what people actually do to manage negative events and situations) when it comes to reducing the distress associated with work-related stressors. When dealing with marital conflict, on the other hand,

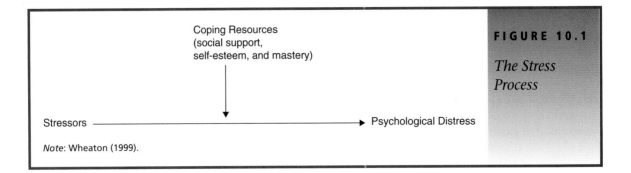

Coping Resources
(social support,
self-esteem, and mastery)

FIGURE 10.1

The Stress Process

Stressors ──────────────────────────────────────▶ Psychological Distress

Note: Wheaton (1999).

coping strategies are more important than coping resources for battling distress (Pearlin and Schooler 1978).

Most SSP researchers who study the stress process, depicted in Figure 10.1, focus on the general population. They typically assume that distress is a type of mental illness (Aneshensel and Phelan 1999), which may or may not result in clinical disorder. The presence of a psychiatric disorder, such as clinical depression, is an all-or-none proposition. Either a person is disordered or they are not. Whether or not people have a diagnosable psychiatric disorder is rarely the focus of research on the stress process (Ross and Mirowsky 2006).

SSP researchers focus on psychological distress rather than clinical disorders because continuous distress measures provide more valid representations of people's emotive states. Measures of psychiatric disorder are more narrow in focus (disorder present or disorder absent) than distress indices, and they fail to capture the kind of information necessary to effectively compare the experiences of various groups within society (Mirowsky and Ross 1989).

SOCIAL STRUCTURE AND PSYCHOLOGICAL DISTRESS

As noted earlier, individuals toward the bottom of the stratification hierarchy (lower-class individuals, racial/ethnic minorities, and women) have higher levels of psychological distress than their more advantaged counterparts (middle- and upper-class individuals, Whites, and men) (Pearlin 1989; Turner and Lloyd 1999). Being single, versus married, also reduces psychological well-being (Turner and Marino 1994).

What Do You Think?

Why might the major dimensions of stratification within this society (class, race/ethnicity, and gender) and marital status influence individuals' likelihoods of becoming distressed?

Two models have been proposed as explanations for the high levels of psychological distress observed among disadvantaged groups and the unmarried. They are referred to within the literature as the "differential exposure" and the "differential vulnerability" (or "differential access to resources") models (Aneshensel 2009).

The Differential Exposure Model

SSP researchers have suggested that group differences in levels of psychological distress are due to variations in the number of stressors individuals are exposed to. Thus, according to the **differential exposure model**, stressors mediate (explain) the effects of statuses such as class, race/ethnicity, and gender on psychological distress. Members of disadvantaged groups have high levels of distress *because* they experience more stressors than other individuals (see Figure 10.2). The differential exposure model is not typically used to explain unmarried individuals' high levels of distress.

The Differential Vulnerability Model

The second explanation for observed differences in levels of psychological distress between groups emphasizes group differences in coping resources, including self-esteem, mastery, and social support. From this perspective, members of disadvantaged groups are at risk for psychological distress because they have lower levels of these resources than their more advantaged counterparts. As a result, they are less able than members of advantaged groups to cope with negative life events, chronic strains, and other stressors. This approach is called the **differential vulnerability model** because it is differences in coping resources, not different levels of exposure to stressors, that is presumed to result in high levels of psychological distress among disadvantaged groups (see Figure 10.3).

The link between age, perceived control, and mental health is readily explained by the differential vulnerability model. Psychological resources, in particular mastery, reach their peak during middle age, which is why psychological well-being is highest among individuals in this age range.

Social psychologists argue that disadvantaged groups have fewer coping resources than advantaged groups because of their prior experiences. In particular,

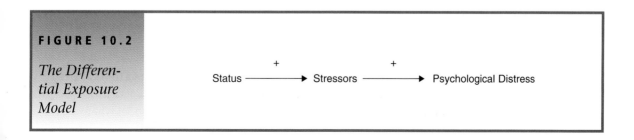

FIGURE 10.2

The Differential Exposure Model

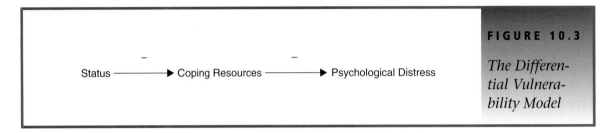

FIGURE 10.3

The Differential Vulnerability Model

having a low level of mastery or sense of control over one's environment is often a realistic assessment among individuals who lack money and power (Ross and Mirwosky 2006). Research also suggests that, over time, chronic financial strains wear away at the self-concept, diminishing both self-esteem and mastery (Pearlin et al. 1981), as well as social support (Aneshensel 2009). There is a limit to how much support family members and friends are willing, or able, to provide. The differential vulnerability model has been used to explain differences in levels of distress across marital status, as well as across class, race/ethnicity, and gender.

Explaining Status Effects on Mental Health

Survey research based on data from large, representative samples of U.S. adults offers some support for both the differential exposure and differential vulnerability models. These analyses have led SSP researchers to reach the following conclusions about individuals' status characteristics and psychological distress:

- The effect of social class on psychological distress is due largely to stressor exposure, which is higher among the lower classes (Turner and Avison 2003; Turner and Lloyd 1999), and to the lack of perceived control (low mastery) characteristic of individuals who lack economic resources (Turner and Lloyd 1999). Thus, both the differential exposure and differential vulnerability models explain class differences in mental health.

- Much of the effect of race/ethnicity on psychological distress is due to the fact that racial and ethnic minorities experience more stressors than Whites (Turner and Avison 2003). Thus, the differential exposure model explains much of the effect of race on mental health. The differential vulnerability model is less relevant within this context.

- Women's high levels of psychological distress are, in part, due to their low levels of mastery relative to men (Kessler and Essex 1982; Turner and Lloyd 1999). Gender differences in distress are not, however, due to gender differences in stressors exposure (McDonough and Walters 2001; Turner and Avison 2003). Thus, the differential vulnerability explanation has received more support than the differential exposure model when it comes to gender.

- The exception to the latter pattern is married parents. Among married parents, women are more distressed than men due to a greater occurrence of role strain, resulting from difficulties in balancing work and family roles (Simon 1992).

- Social support explains much the effect of marital status on distress. On average, married people are better off psychologically than their unmarried counterparts because being married is associated with high levels of social support (Turner 1999). This finding is consistent with the differential vulnerability model.

Socially Based Identities, Self-Complexity, and Psychological Distress

Working within the Iowa/Indiana school of symbolic interactionism, identity theorists have focused on the psychological effects of people's role involvements. In general, the accumulation of socially based identities increases psychological well-being (Thoits 1983). However, having multiple identities based on roles with requirements that must be fulfilled (e.g., worker, spouse, and parent) may have negative psychological consequences insofar as it leads to role strain. People with multiple identities sometimes experience role overload (a type of role strain) because they simply have too much to do. Nonetheless, the social benefits derived from identities with required and time-sensitive duties seem to counteract any distress associated with role overload. Moreover, having multiple identities based on roles that are voluntary, with responsibilities that can readily be dropped or put off (e.g., friend, neighbor, athlete, or group member), reduces distress by increasing both self-esteem and mastery (Thoits 2003).

Having multiple role-based identities may also be beneficial if it reduces an individual's degree of investment in any one set of identity-relevant activities or relationships. People with multiple identities should be less affected by negative feedback in any given identity domain than individuals with few identities (Thoits 1983).

If, for example, "student" is someone's only identity and she fails an exam, the consequence of this for how she sees and feels about herself is likely to be large. If, on the other hand, someone has multiple identities in addition to student (e.g., volunteer, worker, and spouse), that same negative event (failing an exam) is not likely to have as much of an effect on her emotions. Thus, having multiple identities should buffer the impact of identity-relevant stressors on psychological distress.

Consistent with this proposition, Linville (1987) found that college students with multiple domains of self were less likely to react to stressors with depression, insofar as their domains of self were independent. **Domains of self** are cognitive schemata that reflect the different ways that people view themselves. They include identities (e.g., student, son or daughter, athlete) and distinct sets of relationships or behaviors that may be associated with more than one identity (e.g., social, school-related, friendly, or loyal).

Domains of self are independent when the social interactions and relationships they are rooted in don't overlap. Overlap occurs when the social interactions someone has pertaining to different domains of self are in the same setting or involve the same people.

Linville calls the number of domains of self people have and the degree to which they overlap **self-complexity**. An individual with a complex self-structure has multiple domains of self that are independent of one another. Because failures in one domain of self are unlikely to spill over into other self-domains, self-complexity is like not having all of your eggs in one basket (Linville 1985). As such, self-complexity may serve as an important coping resource, reducing individuals' psychological vulnerability to stressors.

Having low self-complexity may make people prone to psychological distress in response to negative events (Linville 1985, 1987). To illustrate, consider John, who has low self-complexity because he has only four overlapping domains of self—husband, father, caring person, and responsible. The roles of husband and father occur in the same context (family) and both involve what John is likely to perceive as caring and responsible behaviors. This means that a failed role performance related to any of John's four domains of self is likely to reverberate throughout his self-concept. An event or interaction suggesting that he is not responsible, for instance, will make John question his ability to perform the roles of father and spouse. Thus, an indication that he is not responsible may also lead John to wonder if he is really caring (a good father and spouse would be). This situation is likely to result in high levels of psychological distress.

What Do You Think?

How complex is your self-concept? Have you had something negative happen in one domain of self that spilled over into others? If so, how did this make you feel?

Status Effects

General population surveys don't include measures of self-complexity. This construct would be difficult to measure within the context of a standard interview. However, surveys often include measures of the roles people play. Results based on data from one community sample suggest that having multiple roles is beneficial for both women and men (Sachs-Ericsson and Ciarlo 2000).

On the other hand, having multiple roles does not appear to be as beneficial for racial/ethnic minorities as it is for Whites. In particular, racial and ethnic minorities do not experience the reductions in distress associated with the accumulation of roles among Whites. Presumably this is because patterns of racial prejudice and discrimination at the macro level limit the social rewards associated with various roles (e.g., worker, group member) for members of nondominant racial/ethnic groups. Limited role-related benefits may explain, in part, racial and ethnic minorities' high levels of distress in comparison to their White counterparts (Jackson 1997).

STUDYING PSYCHIATRIC DISORDER

Psychiatric disorder is defined in the ***Diagnostic and Statistical Manual*** of the American Psychiatric Association **(DSM)** as a disturbance in thought, emotion, or behavior that results from pathology within the individual and causes distress or disability (American Psychiatric Association 2013). The terms "psychiatric disorder" and "psychological disorder" are used interchangeably within the stress literature and are distinct from psychological distress (a continuous variable). However, distress may ultimately lead to psychological disorder when stressor exposure exceeds an individual's coping resources (Wheaton 1999). Stressor exposure often exceeds coping capacity among individuals who experience combat during a war.

Application: Explaining Racial/Ethnic Differences in PTSD Among War Veterans

There are substantial race differences in the prevalence of chronic combat-related posttraumatic stress disorder (PTSD) among war veterans (Roberts et al. 2011). SSP researchers have sought to determine why this is the case by applying the concepts and models described earlier in the chapter.

For example, Dohrenwend and associates (2008) use the differential exposure and vulnerability models, described earlier in the chapter, to explain racial/ethnic differences in PTSD among Vietnam veterans. The data used in Dohrenwend and associates' study are from the National Vietnam Veterans Adjustment Survey or NVVAS (n = 260). The current DSM criteria for PTSD include exposure to a traumatic event or series of events; intrusive symptoms (e.g., memories or flashbacks) associated with the event(s); the avoidance of reminders of the event(s); changes in thoughts, emotions, and arousal due to the event(s); and impairment in social or occupational functioning that persist for at least a period of one month (APA 2013).

The rates of current PTSD for Vietnam veterans, from Dohrenwend and associates' (2008) study, are presented in Table 10.1. As shown in Table 10.1, race/ethnicity is clearly related to PTSD years after individuals' military service ended. Note that the incidence of combat-induced PTSD (cases occurring during or immediately following military service) did not vary by race/ethnicity (data not shown).

PHOTO 10.1

Exposure to combat during a war is a major trauma. It is estimated that from one third to one half of the individuals who experience combat suffer from post-traumatic stress (APA 2013).

Across racial/ethnic groups, there was a strong association between exposure to war zone stressors and risk for long-term or chronic PTSD. Moreover, differential exposure to stressors across racial/ethnic groups explained some of the racial/ethnic differences in PTSD shown in Table 10.1. The NVVAS data revealed that Blacks experienced more severe stressors during the war than their White counterparts. This differential exposure to stressors explained most of Blacks' higher rate of PTSD than Whites. Hispanic veterans' stressor exposure during the war was somewhat higher than that of the White veterans, but this did not explain the greater risk for chronic PTSD among Hispanics than among Whites.

	BLACK	HISPANIC	WHITE
Has current PTSD	33.0%	32.9%	18.7%
n	70	84	94

Note: Dohrenwend et al. (2008).

TABLE 10.1

PTSD by Race/Ethnicity Among Vietnam War Veterans

Risk factors for PTSD include low educational attainment (less than high school) and being young (under the age of 19) at the onset of one's military service. Hispanic veterans had the least formal schooling and were, on average, younger than Blacks and Whites when they went to Vietnam. Low levels of education and being young at the time of their service increased Hispanics' vulnerability to chronic PTSD (Dohrenwend et al. 2008).

Thus, both the differential exposure model and the differential vulnerability model provide insight into racial/ethnic differences in rates of chronic PTSD among Vietnam War veterans. If you're interested, go to the following website to read more about Dohrenwend and associates' (2008) study of PTSD among Vietnam War veterans in a CBS news article: http://www.cbsnews.com/2100–500368_162–1908799.html.

Q: Why would race/ethnicity affect rates of current PTSD but not the incidence of PTSD among Vietnam vets, and are Dohrenwend and associates' (2008) results likely to generalize to veterans of other wars (e.g., the Gulf War, the Iraq War, the war in Afghanistan)?

A: The incidence (i.e., onset) of PTSD is not associated with individuals' degree of exposure to war-zone stressors (Dohrenwend et al. 2008). Thus, the onset of PTSD may be more strongly related than chronic PTSD is to personal characteristics that do not vary systematically by race/ethnicity.

Data from Gulf War veterans suggest that racial and ethnic minorities may still be at greater risk for the development of long-term PTSD symptoms than their White counterparts (Fulco, Liverman, and Sox 2000). Along with stressor exposure and prewar demographics, including education, limited access to treatment may be a factor that increases the risk for chronic PTSD across cohorts of war veterans (Seng, Kohn-Wood, and Odera 2005).

Adversity Throughout the Life Course

Working within the life course tradition, SSP researchers have sought to determine how status characteristics such as race/ethnicity and class influence mental illness trajectories. Many of these analyses have focused on the effects of stressor exposure, beginning with early traumas. Major traumas experienced during childhood and early adulthood, including active military combat, reduce the accumulation of the social and psychological resources necessary for individuals to effectively cope with subsequent stressors. Thus, major traumas put people at risk for additional stressors (stress proliferation) and mental illness. The poor and racial/ethnic minorities are among the individuals most likely to experience early traumas and thus the escalating vulnerability to stressors and distress across the life course that major traumas trigger (George 1999). Because poor mental health inhibits people's ability to function effectively, early adversity plays a role in the reproduction of the stratification hierarchy within society (Thoits 2010).

SSP Research on Mental Health and Public Policy

Modifying the social conditions that give rise to the plethora of stressors experienced by the economically and socially disadvantaged might be the starting point of programs designed to improve mental health (Turner 2003). In particular, government policies should target children whose exposure to poverty and other stressors puts them at risk for poor mental health throughout the life course (Thoits 2010).

Programs that increase social support often improve the mental health of individuals with psychological difficulties and are thus central to most clinical interventions. However, programs that target social support will not alleviate the status gap in mental health that persists at the macro level (Aneshensel 2009). As a result, structural social psychologists emphasize prevention over treatment.

THE SOCIAL CONSTRUCTION OF PSYCHIATRIC DISORDER

Other sociological social psychologists focus on how mental illness is diagnosed and treated within this society. Many people assume that the DSM categories used to diagnose psychiatric disorders are objective indicators of who is and is not mentally ill. Sociological social psychologists who study the nature of psychiatric disorder reject this notion. These latter individuals, who typically align with the symbolic interactionist tradition, focus on labeling processes and on the subjective nature of societal definitions of mental illness.

The DSM and the Dominance of the Medical Model

The DSM, often referred to as the Bible of psychiatric diagnosis, is used widely in the diagnosis of psychiatric disorders, including PTSD, discussed in the previous section. Although the DSM does not focus on specifying the causes of various disorders, inclusion in the DSM is often taken to mean that a particular set of symptoms represents a disease with a biological basis. If a condition is not in the DSM, then it's not considered a legitimate disorder. If a condition is included the manual, then the assumption is that people who meet the diagnostic criteria presented have an illness.

Sociologists who study psychiatric disorders have expressed concern about how psychiatric disorders are diagnosed and about the dominance of the medical model within this society. The **medical model of mental illness** is based on the assumption that mental disorders are biologically based diseases. Sociological social psychologists don't deny that some psychiatric disorders may have a biological component. However, they remind us that, like everything else, psychiatric disorders are cultural products, specific to a particular society at a particular point in time. Of particular interest are the social processes through which sets of symptoms become defined as a psychiatric disorder. Defining mental illness is subjective (there are no objective standards for determining what is or is not a mental illness) and can be highly contentious.

For example, homosexuality was listed as a psychiatric disorder until it was removed from DSM II in 1973. In response to the more permissive cultural climate of the 1970s, as well as persistent challenges by activists calling for homosexuality to be recognized as a normal behavioral variant, homosexuality was replaced by sexual orientation disturbance in the 1973 edition of the DSM. This conciliatory gesture was not satisfactory from the perspective of gay rights activists. In response to social pressures, in DSM III (1980), sexual orientation disturbance was replaced by ego-dystonic homosexuality (Kirk and Kutchins 1992; Spitzer 1981). Ego-dystonic homosexuality was a diagnosis given to homosexuals who were disturbed by their sexual orientation. By the publication of DSM III–R (1987), homosexuality had been dropped as a diagnostic category.

DSM diagnostic categories are often modified as cultural definitions of what constitutes deviance change. Thus, psychiatric disorders are socially constructed. What's included in the DSM is determined by the interests of clinicians; researchers; pharmaceutical companies, which often have ties to the individuals on the panel that determines what goes into the manual (Cosgrove et al. 2006); and the groups affected by the inclusion of particular diagnostic categories. Thus, the negotiations through which decisions about the content of the DSM are made are highly contentious. While the American Psychiatric Association purports that DSM diagnostic categories are based on the results of empirical research (Regier et al. 2011), the political and economic interests of different groups play a major role in shaping the content of the manual.

Medicalization and Its Consequences

Since its original publication in 1952, many disorders have been added to the DSM. The increase in the number of psychiatric disorders reflects the cultural trend referred to as "medicalization."

Medicalization is the process through which a behavior or set of behaviors or perceptions is defined as a disease. Because medical interventions are used to treat most diseases, drug treatment is usually the prescribed course of action once medicalization has occurred (Olafsdottir 2011). Conditions that have been medicalized and are now considered as diseases include attention-deficit/hyperactivity disorder (ADHD) (Timimi and Leo 2009); social anxiety disorder (Cottle 1999); and premenstrual dysphoric disorder (PMDD), a severe form of premenstrual syndrome (PMS) (Figert 2010).

ADHD is, in effect, the medicalization of childhood (Timimi 2004; Timimi and Leo 2009), as young children, especially those who begin school earlier than average, tend

PHOTO 10.2

In school children are expected to follow the rules and behave in a respectful manner.

to be restless and highly active (Elder 2010). Similarly, social anxiety disorder is what was once the normal variant in perception and behavior called shyness (Cottle 1999).

Scientists often advocate for the medicalization of a condition because once it is considered a legitimate disease they are better able to secure large research grants in order to study it (Figert 2010). Drug companies also have a financial stake in the process of medicalization, as their medical interventions are lucrative (e.g., the drug Paxil for the treatment of social anxiety disorder) (Cottle 1999). Eli Lilly, the company that makes Prozac, repackaged that drug in a pink capsule as Sarafem, a treatment for PMDD, right before their patent for Prozac ran out. Presumably, this was because their Prozac revenues were likely to drop once the drug could be produced in generic form (Daw 2002).

In contrast to scientists and drug companies, those individuals who will be considered disordered as the result of the medicalization of a set of symptoms or behaviors often resist this process. In the case of PMDD, feminist groups have argued that this disorder undermines the credibility of women by making it seem like they are all prone to monthly bouts of irrationality and rage (Figert 2010).

With the publication of DSM V in 2013, PMDD became an official psychiatric disorder, included in the section of the manual on depression. PMDD was in an appendix in the previous (1994) edition of the DSM, as a condition that required further study.

Social (pragmatic) communication disorder (SCD) and hoarding disorder are two of the psychiatric disorders in DSM V that were not in the earlier version of the manual. SCD is the new label for individuals who can't effectively communicate with other people for social purposes. Hoarding disorder, previously defined as a symptom of obsessive compulsive disorder, is now a separate disease, presumed to have a distinct physiological cause. In addition, Internet gaming disorder is described in DSM V and listed as a condition to be investigated for potential inclusion as an official disorder in the next version of the manual. How the existence of these new diseases will affect individuals in or outside of a clinical setting is open to question.

Although the sociologists who study medicalization and its consequences may not self-identify as social psychologists, their research addresses issues of interest to sociological social psychologists—how prevailing societal norms, values, and beliefs shape individuals' social experiences. Their arguments are also highly consistent with labeling theory, the main symbolic interactionist approach to the study of mental illness. The cultural dominance of the medical model serves as the backdrop for some of labeling theorists' key points about the diagnosis and treatment of psychiatric disorders.

The Labeling Theory of Mental Illness

Social psychologists who study mental illness from a labeling perspective (many, but not all, of them are symbolic interactionists) emphasize the fact that mental illness is a class, or type, of deviance. As noted in Chapter 8, what we define in this culture as mental illness often involves the violation of emotion norms. People violate display rules by expressing, or failing to express, emotions in an appropriate manner (Pugliesi 1987). Or their emotions in a particular situation don't match what they think they should feel (Thoits 1985).

Other norm violations associated with mental illness include hearing voices (auditory hallucinations), talking to oneself in public, and believing that one is being persecuted by someone or something when this isn't the case (paranoid delusions). These latter symptoms are associated with schizophrenia, a serious mental disorder that characterizes much of the population in in-patient treatment facilities. **Schizophrenia** is a type of psychosis, meaning that the individual experiencing these symptoms has had a break with reality. Recall the distorted pictures drawn by individuals with schizophrenia, presented at the beginning of Chapter 7.

Unlike most forms of deviance, the symptoms of schizophrenia, or behaviors we take as indicative of other mental illnesses, cannot be readily classified using our standard vocabulary for norm violations. Although they are viewed as problematic, they are not crimes, perversions, incidences of drunkenness, or cases of poor manners (Scheff 1963). Thus, they fall into the category of behavior that Scheff refers to as residual deviance.

Residual deviance is a catchall category for leftovers—those behaviors that violate social norms for which we have no specific label. According to Scheff (1963, 1966), residual deviance is fairly common and has multiple sources, ranging from the bio-logical (an imbalance in neurotransmitters in the brain) to the social (exposure to stressors). Usually residual deviance goes unnoticed or ignored by others and is thus transitory. That is, these behaviors typically remain acts of primary deviance because they are never defined, or labeled, by others as significant. However, if acts of resid-ual deviance are formally labeled, an individual experiences the process of self and behavioral change outlined in the previous chapter in the section on labeling the-ory. People who are labeled as mentally ill are isolated from others, the deviant label is internalized, and the frequency with which they engage in deviant behavior (secondary deviance) increases. Thus, for Scheff, it is labeling itself that results in the stable patterns of nonnormative behavior that we define as mental illness.

Societal Functions of the Concept of Mental Illness

In his critique of modern psychiatry, Thomas Szasz (1970) argues that labeling some-one as mentally ill serves two basic functions. First, it provides a global explanation for behaviors that are regarded as abhorrent and otherwise unexplainable (e.g., why a mother drowned her children or why someone killed multiple people and con-sumed their flesh). This provides a sense of order to the rest of society—individuals who would never behave in this kind of deviant fashion (Szasz 1970). Even if attrib-uting someone's behavior to a mental illness alleviates some of the perpetrator's responsibility for his or her crime, the process through which this abdication occurs in enmeshed in a public degradation ritual. This degradation ritual, which usually includes a trial and television interviews about the case with mental health profes-sionals, reminds the rest of us that this behavior is unacceptable.

Whether a crime is attributed to a mental disorder can be a contentious process, as legal and lay definitions of mental illness often differ. A person must not under-stand that his or her behavior violates the law for them to be considered legally insane. Of course, some people not deemed insane by the courts are likely to be viewed as mentally ill by your average person. The heinous nature of their behavior is enough to convince most of us that they must have been mentally ill. Surely, no sane person would commit such an action. It is in this sense that the concept of mental illness makes comprehensible the incomprehensible.

What Do You Think?

Can you think of an example of a news story that illustrates the use of mental illness as an explanation for behavior that is otherwise incomprehensible? If not, do a quick search of the Internet. Try the search terms "face eating" and "crime" to read about a recent case that will probably make you ask, "Why would some-one do this?" The answer, "Because he is mentally ill" is consistent with Szasz's argument about the explanatory function of the concept of mental illness.

The second function of the concept of mental illness and the labeling process, according to Szasz (1970), is that it gives medical doctors (psychiatrists) and the state (institutional psychiatry) the power to control the behaviors of individuals whose actions do not meet the standards of the dominant culture. Historically, it was lower-class individuals, racial/ethnic minorities, and women who were often placed in mental institutions against their will by family members or the state. If someone is deemed mentally ill, the state has the right to incarcerate them indefinitely for the protection of themselves and others within society.

Two Important Studies

We discussed research in support of labeling theory in the previous chapter. Thus, we focus here on the two studies that drew people's attention to issues pertaining to the labeling of mental illness: Goffman's (1961) analysis of life in the mental hospital and Rosenhan's (1973) "On being sane in insane places."

THE MENTAL INSTITUTION FROM A DRAMATURGICAL PERSPECTIVE

Sociologist Erving Goffman, founder of the dramaturgical perspective, went undercover, posing as a staff member in a psychiatric hospital, in order to study everyday

PHOTO 10.3

State mental institutions, at one time called insane asylums, are usually set apart from the rest of society. Many state-run mental institutions have closed since the 1950s, due to concerns about the care provided to mental patients in institutional settings and a lack of funding. (Ohio, 1946)

life in this context. His purpose was to experience firsthand what life was like in this type of total institution.

Total institutions are agents of resocialization that are designed to alter people's behaviors through a process of retraining or reprogramming. Psychiatric hospitals and prisons are good examples of total institutions. **Resocialization** is the process through which people are reprogrammed with new values and norms following what others perceive as one or more serious transgressions. To this end, total institutions are physically separated from the rest of society. This physical segregation removes patients (or inmates, in the case of a prison) from individuals with whom they have preexisting relationships. Total institutions are also all encompassing in that their staff controls every aspect of the lives of the individuals who reside within them, including their style of dress, when they get up and go to bed, when and what they eat, and what they do with their time (Goffman 1961).

Goffman talks about the moral implications of this kind of existence, emphasizing how people's views of the world and of themselves are fundamentally altered. Although people may have unique experiences, there are commonalities across individuals as they move through the series of phases that make up the career of the mental patient. The phases mental patients go through include their admission to the hospital, their time as psychiatric inpatient, and their exit from the facility. Viewing these transitions as a career is useful because it draws our attention to sets of social conditions, and reactions, which unfold over time and transcend any one individual (Goffman 1961).

According to Goffman, who is and is not admitted to the mental institution typically reflects contingencies such as their geographic proximity to the facility and status characteristics such as class, race/ethnicity, and gender. Remember, from a labeling perspective, who is and is not labeled as deviant is largely a function of factors other than the nature of their behavior.

The primary process of interest, from a dramaturgical perspective, is the **mortification of self** that to occurs among psychiatric inpatients. Everything within the mental hospital, from its location to the standard attire and routines conferred upon patients, is designed to eradicate (or kill) the selves they came in with. This is the first phase of the resocialization (relearning) process, called **desocialization**, through which the slate is cleared. The self of the inmate is worn away because any kind of unique self-presentation, which requires props (e.g., a particular style of dress) and certain freedoms, is prohibited within the total institution.

Goffman argued that mental institutions do a pretty good job of desocializing patients. Once desocialization is complete, the reprogramming, or resocialiation, is supposed to occur. This is where mental institutions and other total institutions, like prisons, juvenile detention facilities, or in-patient alcohol and drug rehabilitation programs, fall short. There is rarely the implementation of a coherent strategy for rebuilding new, nondeviant selves. Thus, people begin viewing themselves as nothing more than mental patients, delinquents, or substance abusers, which results in subsequent acts of secondary deviance. This process continues even after they are released from the hospital, which may ultimately result in their reinstitutionalization.

ON BEING SANE IN INSANE PLACES

Rosenhan, a psychologist, reached a set of conclusions similar to Goffman based on the results of his famous study "On being sane in insane places." Focusing on the diagnosis of mental illness, Rosenhan (1973) argues that determining who is and is not mentally ill is not easy. Unlike diagnosing a physical illness, like cancer, there are no diagnostic tests that indicate insanity. Thus, even mental health professionals may have difficulty distinguishing the insane from the sane.

In order to evaluate this proposition, Rosenhan had eight pseudopatients (himself and seven other individuals) feign symptoms of mental illness in order to gain admission into various psychiatric hospitals. They pretended they were hearing voices, a symptom of schizophrenia, which was enough to get all of them admitted.

Once in the hospital, they were instructed to act normal. They were also asked to take notes on their experiences, as any participant observer would do. Initially, they hid their note-taking activity, afraid that it would blow their cover. However, they soon realized that, as a mental patient (most were given the label "schizophrenic"), it didn't matter. It was just another symptom of their disorder. When pseudopatients were observed taking notes by doctors or other hospital staff, this behavior was simply taken as evidence of their paranoia.

What the pseudopatients quickly came to realize was that once you're in a mental institution, there is nothing that you can do to prove your sanity. Once the label of mental patient (or, more specifically, schizophrenic) is applied, everything you do is interpreted within the context of that label.

As a result, it wasn't so easy for Rosenhan's pseudopatients to get out of the hospital since their release required the determination of sanity by hospital staff. One person was in a facility for 52 days. Moreover, all but one of the pseudopatients was released with the label "schizophrenic in remission," rendering all of their subsequent behaviors equally suspect.

Thus, as suggested by Scheff (1963) and Szasz (1970), the label "schizophrenic" (or mentally ill, more generally) may be much like the label of "witch." Like witchcraft, the concept of mental illness is subjective and can be applied to any action. Furthermore, once the label of "witch" is applied, there is little someone can do to prove he or she is not this category of person. Historically, witches were innocent of the charge only if they drowned after being thrown into the water, which of course made their guilt or innocence a moot point.

Like Goffman, Rosenhan talks about the powerlessness of the patient within the context of the mental hospital. Individuals in this role are treated more like an object than a person, a process that Rosenhan calls **depersonalization**. Those with the most power, the psychiatrists, were the individuals who spent the least amount of time interacting with patients, given the patients' undesirable and stigmatized status (Rosenhan 1973).

When considering the context of Rosenhan's study, it is important to note that he is a psychologist by training. Psychologists have a PhD in clinical or counseling psychology and often provide therapy to individuals who are mentally ill. Although psychiatrists may do the same, they are medical doctors. Thus, in institutional settings, it is usually the psychiatrists who call the shots. As a rule, medical doctors have more power than other health professionals within this society. As medical doctors, psychiatrists also have the ability to prescribe medication, whereas psychologists do not. Rosenhan's study was largely perceived as a critique of psychiatry, from the perspective of a psychologist, who also happens to be a labeling theorist.

Because Rosenhan's study was published in the prestigious journal *Science,* it was read by individuals both within and outside of the mental health field. On one hand, his study was applauded as an important wake-up call because it brought the subjective nature of psychiatric diagnosis and its negative consequences to the public's attention. On the other hand, those who questioned Rosenhan's conclusions expressed concern that his study would make people who were ill afraid to seek treatment. Rosenhan's study, and the labeling model more generally, have also been criticized on methodological grounds (Gove and Fain 1973; Millon 1975).

Take a Break

Watch the film *Girl, Interrupted*. This movie is based on the book with the same title, an account of the author's, Susanna Kaysen's, experiences as a mental patient during the 1960s. The film is a good adaptation of Kaysen's book, and it serves as an excellent illustration of central tenets of the labeling theory of mental illness, including Goffman's and Rosenhan's arguments. If you've seen this movie before, consider watching it again with these propositions in mind.

One Flew Over the Cuckoo's Nest, based on the book by Ken Kesey, provides another good illustration of the labeling process and its consequences. This award-winning movie came out in 1975 and was quite influential. In fact, it is often cited as one of a number of precursors to the widespread deinstitutionalization of mental patients in this society, discussed in the following section. It gave people insight into the deplorable state of inpatient psychiatric care and how involuntary institutionalization, and various treatments (e.g., electroconvulsive therapy), were used to control deviant behavior, under the guise of medical care. If you haven't seen this movie, we highly recommend that you watch it.

Evaluating the Qualitative Literature on the Experiences of Mental Patients

Both Goffman (1961) and Rosenhan (1973) used participant observation to gather their data. Critiques of labeling theory as it pertains to the issue of mental illness have argued that analyses on life in the mental hospital by Goffman and by Rosenhan are subjective and lack validity. They have also pointed to the many survey-based studies showing that patients in mental hospitals have largely positive attitudes toward their treatment and its outcomes (Millon 1975; Weinstein 1979).

Proponents of the labeling perspective have responded to these charges by noting that participant observation allows researchers to study social processes and to access detailed information about mental patients' lives not available to researchers using other methodologies (i.e., experiments and surveys). As a result, they note, qualitative studies of the inpatient experience address a different issue than quantitative (survey) research on patients' attitudes. Whereas qualitative research uncovers the nature of social processes, surveys document the outcomes of a process, including attitudes. People may have positive attitudes toward a psychiatric hospital, and the care they received there, even when their experiences in the institution were quite negative (Essex et al. 1980).

Think about initiation rituals for membership in certain groups (e.g., fraternities and sororities). These rituals are often unpleasant and require recruits, or pledges, to engage in behaviors that non-group members consider excessively harsh.

People are more likely to value their membership in a group when they have to work hard to get in. If they don't feel positively about the group, their attitude and their behavior (participation in rigorous preinitiation rituals) will be inconsistent. This inconsistency is likely to result in a negative mental tension (Aronson and Mills 1959) called **cognitive dissonance** (Festinger 1957). The desire to avoid, or reduce, cognitive dissonance explains why people feel so good about a group that has put them through so much. Holding a positive attitude toward the group is consonant with the rigorous hazing ritual one just completed (Aronson and Mills 1959).

The fact that mental patients given surveys about their stay in the hospital were most likely to report that their experiences were positive when their commitment was voluntary (Weinstein 1979) supports this argument. If one checks oneself into a mental hospital, a negative experience is likely to generate cognitive dissonance. This tension can be alleviated by adopting a more positive attitude about one's stay in the hospital.

Contemporary Patterns

There has been a large-scale movement toward the **deinstitutionalization** of mental patients in this country. In 1955 there were over 500,000 individuals residing in state mental hospitals. By the mid-1990s, the number of psychiatric inpatients had decreased to about 100,000 (Dowdall 1999).

The reasons for this trend, which began in the 1950s, include the increasing use of psychotropic drugs, which reduce many of the symptoms of schizophrenia and other severe disorders, and concerns about the quality of care patients received in mental institutions (Scheid and Brown 2010). There was also a financial incentive to limit the number of individuals with mental illness in state-funded institutions. Inpatient care is expensive. Thus, it is cheaper to treat people in the community (Scull 2011).

Today, people who are seriously ill and can't pay for private care receive services through community mental health centers. During crisis periods, people with mental illness might receive inpatient care, but their stays are usually brief, on average less than two weeks (Center for Disease Control 2009).

Because inpatient care, especially on a long-term basis, is much less common today than it was during the 1960s and 1970s, some of the original arguments of labeling theorists may be less applicable than in the past. As a result of deinstitutionalization, class and race/ethnicity have much less of an impact on the amount of time patients spend in psychiatric hospitals today than in the 1950s and 1960s (Pavalko, Harding, and Pescosolido 2007). Nonetheless, people receiving inpatient psychiatric care are likely to experience depersonalization and stigma, and institutionalization may be used for social control purposes.

In a study by Rosenbaum and Prinsky (1991) a researcher posing as a concerned parent contacted 12 psychiatric hospitals. This individual gave the following story to the person on the phone.

> My son John has me worried. He's fifteen and in the last year or so he's started listening to heavy metal music and I'm concerned. I've been reading in the paper about kids listening to that music and how influential it is. He wears his hair very strange—it's spiked and lined with unnatural colors. He doesn't wear the cloths my wife buys him. Instead he wears ragged jeans, T-shirts with skulls and stuff on them and a leather jacket and often black wristbands with studs on them. He really looks like a bum. His room is a mess and the walls are covered with these awful looking posters. I'm sure he's not taking drugs and drinking because his school work is fine and he's there every day. He doesn't seem depressed and he's not violent or suicidal like all the reports say he should be. When I ask him about his appearance and choice

PHOTO 10.4

Adolescents who participate in the heavy metal subculture may be considered by those outside the subculture to be dangerous to themselves and others.

of music, he just says, 'everyone at school dresses that way and listens to the same music.' But, when he brings his friends over, it's like having a bunch of weirdos in the house. They just sit in his room listening to that music and I've heard some of the songs—they really are about suicide, the devil and all that. I'm really worried about him. I think he needs help to get is head on straight and get away from his friends.

(Rosenbaum and Prinsky 1991:532–533)

The researcher intentionally omitted any mention of 5t any symptoms of mental illness or the presence of substance use, violence, or suicidal tendencies. Nonetheless, representatives at 10 out of the 12 hospitals contacted (83%) recommended that the son, John, be admitted for evaluation. Albeit based on a small, nonrepresentative sample of hospitals, these findings are notable. The study authors argue that they support the notion that people in this society tend to view youth subcultures involving popular music as dangerous and that labeling, and institutionalization, is used to control deviant behavior among adolescents, a group that lacks power.

Rosenbaum and Prinsky's (1991) results are also consistent with the charge that psychiatric hospitals admit patients for financial reasons. Vandenburgh (1999) provides numerous examples of aggressive marketing practices used within the largely unregulated, for-profit psychiatric industry in Texas during the 1980s and 1990s. Psychiatric hospitals would, for example, send representatives to local high schools to screen students for mental illness. Then, without disclosing their tie to the facility, they would recommend large numbers of students for inpatient evaluation. Parents who were concerned about their children's safety were easily persuaded to admit them for inpatient care when they were told, often without just cause, that their child was a danger to him or herself. These youths would remain in the hospital until their parents' insurance ran out, at which point they were deemed cured.

The subjective nature of psychiatric diagnosis, and thus of distinguishing the mentally ill from the sane, makes psychiatric care an arena open to abuse. Rosenbaum and Prinsky (1991) report that the private (for-profit) hospitals contacted in their study were more likely than the state facilities to recommend inpatient care for John. All of the six private facilities recommended hospitalization, suggesting that economic incentives on the part of the institutions in question might have affected the evaluations given.

The treatment of adolescents in hospital settings with no clinical justification for doing so increased nationwide during the 1980s and 1990s (Weller et al. 1995). Although their average length of stay has decreased due to insurance restrictions associated with managed care, the frequency with which adolescents are treated for mental health problems in inpatient settings has continued to increase (NIMH 2011). Labeling theory can help us to understand some of these individuals' experiences.

Labeling theory also remains relevant to our understanding of the experiences of individuals who have been labeled as mentally ill and treated outside of an institutional context. "Mental patient," or "mentally ill," is still a stigmatized identity that can have a significant impact on people's lives outside of, as well as within, the hospital. Link and associates' (1989) modified labeling theory addresses this latter issue.

The Modified Labeling Theory

The crux of the **modified labeling theory** is that individuals with mental illness, like everyone else, recognize that being mentally ill is stigmatized within this society. Thus, when people are diagnosed with a mental illness they realize that negative cultural beliefs about mental illness apply to them. At this point, individuals who have been formally labeled may employ the strategies for managing a stigmatized identity discussed in the previous chapter. They may also withdraw from social encounters out of the fear that they will be perceived or treated negatively. These reactions to stigma shape people's subsequent social experiences and have negative effects on their self-concepts and social relationships. Thus, although treatment for mental illness is often effective, the stigma associated with the label of mental patient is likely to counteract its benefits (Link and Phelan 1999).

In support of the modified labeling theory, research suggests that formal labeling has negative effects on people's social networks. The more individuals expect their diagnosis to result in devaluation and discrimination, and the more they use withdrawal as a self-presentational strategy, the more limited their social networks become. This shift is important because social networks serve as the basis of an important coping resource, social support. Thus, being formally diagnosed with a mental illness may increase individuals' vulnerability to future psychopathology (Link et al. 1989).

Regarding this, it is important to recognize that the modified labeling theory is in no way blaming mentally ill individuals for the negative consequences associated with labeling. Anyone labeled as mentally ill within this society is likely to be subject to this process because mental illness is stigmatized in this culture (Link and Phelan 1999).

Much of the contemporary social psychological literature on mental illness and labeling focuses on the issue of stigma and its effects on the day-to-day experiences of people who are mentally ill. The results of surveys of individuals with psychiatric disorders (Wright, Gronfein, and Owens 2000) and of attitudes toward mental illness among the general population (Pescosolido et al. 2007, 2010) support the central tenets of the modified labeling approach.

What Do You Think?

How do adolescents view mental illness? What does having a psychiatric diagnosis (e.g., ADHD) mean to adolescents? How would this label affect an adolescent's relationships with his or her peers?

- What theoretical framework would lead a sociological social psychologist to ask these kinds of questions?
- Propose a study that addresses these issues. Indicate which method of data collection you would use and why you would select this methodology over others. Who would be in your sample? Consider completing this part of the exercise with one of your classmates.

Identity and Illness Careers Among Individuals With Depression

Qualitative research also suggests that the subjective nature of psychiatric disorder and the stigma it carries can have a profound effect on the identities of individuals with mental illness. In his influential book *Speaking of Sadness,* symbolic interactionist David Karp (1996) focuses on the illness careers of 50 individuals suffering from depression as they sought to cope with their condition.

Depression is characterized by persistent feelings of sadness or hopelessness, feelings of worthlessness, impaired cognition, and thoughts of death (APA 2013). Depression is relatively common, as it is estimated that almost one fifth of the population (17%) will suffer from these symptoms at some point throughout their lives (Kessler 2010). However, as noted by Karp, depression is highly ambiguous as a medical condition because there is no biomedical test or indicator that one fits into this category, as there is with many physical diseases (e.g., cancer or AIDS). Given its subjective nature, many people experience uncertainty when they receive a diagnosis of depression (Karp 1996).

Karp's (1996) in-depth interviews revealed remarkable similarities in the experiences of depressed individuals. His study participants' narratives indicated that they progressed through a series of stages, each of which was characterized by a turning point for their identity. The stages were derived by Karp from the interview data using a grounded theory approach. As Karp notes, the similarity in nature and ordering of the trajectory he observed across participants, and its implications for the manner in which they viewed themselves, makes the concept of career an especially apt metaphor within this context.

Karp's research suggests that the career of a depressed person has the following four sequential phases:

1. **An initial period of inchoate feelings.** At this time, individuals have not yet labeled their experience as depression, and they tend to attribute their pain to their current situation, typically their family relationships. The underlying assumption is that once their situation changes they will feel better.

2. **The realization that something really is wrong.** At this juncture, individuals experience a change in perception and begin to locate their problem within themselves, instead of in their social circumstances. However, the label of "depression" is not typically applied until the following (crisis) stage.

3. **Crisis.** There is usually a concrete event or series of events that precedes the transition into the third phase in the illness career of individuals with depression (e.g., going away to college, the escalation of problems at work). This is the time when people receive a diagnosis and begin therapy or are admitted to a psychiatric facility. At this point in their careers, many of the respondents in Karp's study reported that they engaged

in a form of retrospective self-labeling. Through the lens of their new diagnosis of depression, they reinterpreted their life histories, focusing on prior instances in which their perceptions and behaviors reflected their illness.

However, getting a diagnosis can be a double-edged sword. On one hand, having a label for one's condition provides an explanation for behaviors and feelings that were difficult to comprehend before the diagnosis. On the other hand, individuals understand that a diagnosis of depression carries with it a certain stigma. It is because of the stigma associated within mental illness that many of Karp's participants indicated that they were selective in their revelation of their condition to new friends, coworkers, and acquaintances, so as not to be judged negatively or devalued.

4. **Acceptance of the illness identity.** The final stage in the careers of individuals with clinical depression manifests as they seek to understand the cause of their illness and assess their prospects for the future. Whether Karp's participants felt they had moved beyond their depression, or recognized it as a more long-term feature of their lives, depended on how old they were they first experienced symptoms and the chronicity of their disease. In particular, individuals who experienced the initial symptoms of depression during childhood tended to view their illness as permanent as they created interpretive frameworks for their lives.

As in the crisis stage, people in the acceptance stage frequently grapple with whether, or when, to go public with their diagnosis as they construct a strategy for moving forward (Karp 1996). Interestingly, the narratives of depressed individuals are very similar to those of homosexuals, supporting the notion that there are general processes through which people resist, cope, and adapt to stigma. As with homosexuality, "coming out" of the depression closet may be a lifelong process, as individuals continually experience new situations and relationships in which they may be judged negatively once their illness identity is revealed (Ridge and Ziebland 2012).

Taken together, the studies reviewed in this section illustrate the extent to which common beliefs about mental illness within this society shape individuals' micro-level experiences. From a practical standpoint, they show that societal beliefs are a key point of intervention and that changing these perceptions would improve the lives of individuals with mental illness. This may, however, be difficult to accomplish because people tend to process information in a manner that confirms the beliefs they hold about the mentally ill and other groups within society (Corrigan and Penn 1999). We discuss various approaches for changing cultural stereotypes in greater detail in Chapter 12, on prejudice and discrimination.

STRUCTURAL PERSPECTIVES ON TREATMENT

How mental illness is treated is a focal point of research within the labeling tradition, discussed in the previous section. Taking a different approach, social structure and personality researchers have studied the role of social networks in the initiation of, and in people's responses to, psychiatric treatment, most of which occurs on an out-patient basis.

The **network episode model** or NEM (Pescosolido and Boyer 1999) is the most comprehensive model addressing the issue of treatment within this research tradition. From this perspective, the characteristics of people's relationships with others and beliefs about the effectiveness of mental health care shape their treatment trajectories.

The NEM provides an explanatory framework for some of the group differences in treatment utilization documented within the research literature. For example, women are more likely to use mental health services than men. SSP researchers applying the NEM have linked this difference to the fact that females have larger and more care-oriented social networks than their male counterparts (Pescosolido and Boyer 1999).

Other analyses within social structure and personality have focused on responses to mental illness within the family. These studies suggest that caring for someone who is mentally ill tends to increase people's levels of psychological distress (Lefley 2010), especially when the ill individual is relatively young, unemployed, and low in social functioning (Harvey et al. 2001).

There is some evidence to suggest that race/ethnicity affects the extent to which individuals experience the care of a family member with mental illness as burdensome. Among individuals with similar class backgrounds, Black caregivers are less likely than their White or Latino counterparts to evaluate their situation negatively. Surprisingly, mediating variables like the quality of social support received, religious involvement, and beliefs about mental illness do not explain the relationship between race/ethnicity and attitudes toward caring for mentally ill family members (Stueve, Vine, and Struening 1997).

Presumably, race differences in responses to a family member's mental illness reflect the less individualistic, more group-oriented values and norms, characteristic of African American's kinship networks, versus those of Whites. Given the positive effects of family integration on patients' prognoses, a pattern that exists cross-culturally (see Box 10.3), relationships within the family may have a more positive impact on the experiences of individuals with mental illness than the reliance on mental health professionals (Horwitz and Reinhard 1995).

SSP researchers are starting to explore racial/ethnic differences in caregiving in greater detail. Their emphasis is on macro-structural and cultural, as well as micro-level relational, factors. This approach to the study of caregiving is distinct from that found in more individually oriented fields such as nursing and social work. Given their focus on the interplay between Individual and Society, SSP researchers are well

Box 10.3   Individuals With Severe Mental Illness Fair Better in Developing Societies Than in Technologically Advanced Societies

Although reports within the research literature indicate that the prevalence of schizophrenia is consistent across societies (between 2 to 4 cases per 1,000 population), there are substantial cultural differences in the prognosis for individuals experiencing these symptoms. In opposition to conventional wisdom, researchers have found that individuals suffering from schizophrenia in developing countries (e.g., Nigeria and India) fair better than individuals in technologically advanced societies such as the United States, the United Kingdom, and Denmark (Lefley 2010). This is due to differences in how individuals with mental illness are treated within these societies.

In North America and in Europe, there are treatment bureaucracies that facilitate formal labeling and geographic segregation between the mentally ill and the healthy. Individuals with schizophrenia live in inpatient facilities or in parts of the community where there is low-income and subsidized housing. This facilitates a labeling process from which individuals may find it difficult to recover, even if their symptoms subside. Even without treatment, the symptoms of schizophrenia often come and go.

In less technologically advanced non-Western societies, individuals with psychotic symptoms often remain within the family. This makes it easier for them to transition back into their regular roles should their symptoms remit. Moreover, when mental illness is attributed to forces outside of the individual, like possession by a spirit, ill people are not themselves viewed as flawed. Thus, once their symptoms subside, these individuals are seen as the same selves they were before the possession. There is also minimal stigma because the deviant behaviors are believed to have been the result of forces outside of the afflicted person's control (Waxler 1979). Although we tend to think our way of responding to mental illness is superior to that of developing societies, the available data do not support this assumption.

positioned to provide new insights into group differences in responses to mental illness within the family context and their consequences in this and other societies (Avison and Comeau 2013).

CHAPTER SUMMARY

Given prevailing cultural beliefs, and the dominance of the medical model, many people view mental health and illness as biological constructs and believe that being diagnosed as mentally ill has positive consequences insofar as an individual is receiving treatment. As illustrated throughout this chapter, social psychological approaches to the study of mental illness from within sociology challenge these views by showing how psychological distress and disorder are distributed in a nonrandom fashion throughout society and reflect patterns of inequality at the macro level. By emphasizing the structural causes of psychological well-being, they point toward interventions (e.g., public policies designed to reduce heavy exposure to childhood traumas common among individuals born into families at the bottom the stratification hierarchy) that go beyond individual psychotherapy. In terms of treatment, labeling theorists remind us of the history of, and potential for, the abuse of power when it comes to inpatient psychiatric care. Moreover, they illustrate the importance of broader societal beliefs in shaping people's responses when they, or others, experience symptoms of mental illness and receive a formal diagnosis, irrespective of whether they are treated within or outside of a hospital setting.

Key Points to Know

- **Most of the research on mental health and illness within sociological social psychological lies within the social structure and personality or within the symbolic interactionist face of social psychology.** Given the focus of the group processes and structures orientation, there are few studies on this topic within this tradition.

- **Structural social psychologists point to the fact that members of disadvantaged groups (lower class individuals, racial/ethnic minorities, and women), as well as the unmarried, tend to have high levels of psychological distress (e.g., symptoms of depression).** They have attempted to explain these differences by focusing on stressor exposure and vulnerability due to a lack of coping resources.

- **The distribution of stressors and coping resources by class, race/ethnicity, gender, and marital status explains much of the gap in distress levels between groups.** Stressor exposure accounts for most of the relationship between social class, and race, on levels of psychological distress. Lower-class individuals also tend to have poor mental health because their social experiences result in low levels of perceived control or mastery, which makes them more vulnerable to the effects of stressors. Coping resource, in particular mastery, explain in part why women are more distressed than men. Individuals who are unmarried are more distressed than their married counterparts due to lower levels of social support.

- **High self-complexity is beneficial for mental health, as is holding multiple identities.** However, Whites benefit more than racial and ethnic minorities from the occupation of multiple roles.

- **Many sociologists, including labeling theorists, question the legitimacy of the construct of mental illness.** Rather than viewing psychiatric disorders as (biological) diseases, they argue that they are forms of deviance labeled as "illnesses" so that individuals' behaviors can more readily be controlled. Two classic studies within the labeling tradition, by Goffman and by Rosenhan, support for this position.

- **Although the deinstitutionalization of mental patients has rendered some of labeling theorists' original arguments less relevant today than in the past, this model still provides a useful**

framework for understanding the experiences of individuals diagnosed with a mentally illness. People still receive inpatient care, during which they are likely experience depersonalization and the mortification of self; institutionalization is still used to control behaviors that are deviant but not necessarily indicative of an illness, especially among adolescents; and stigma is still very much a problem both within and outside of the institution.

- **Contemporary research within the modified labeling tradition emphasizes the issue of stigma. From this perspective, regardless of whether they are treated within or outside of the mental hospital, mental patients realize that their condition is stigmatized, which influences the ways in which they interact with others.** Numerous studies show that societal attitudes toward mental illness are highly negative and that this affects the day-to-day lives of individual who are mentally ill.

- **Symbolic interactionist research on the construction of identities among people diagnosed with depression suggests that individuals' illness careers involve a series of stages through which they come to terms with their diagnosis.** Because dealing with stigma is a part of this process, this literature is consistent with the central tenets of the modified labeling theory.

- **Caring for a family member with mental illness can be distress producing.** In general, African Americans are less likely than Whites to perceive caring for a mentally ill relative as burdensome. This may have positive implications for the mentally ill relatives' prognoses.

Terms and Concepts for Review

Buffering effect	Medical model of mental illness
Chronic strains	Modified labeling theory
Cognitive dissonance	Mortification of self
Coping resources	Network-episode model (NEM)
Coping strategies	Primary stressor
Deinstitutionalization	Psychological distress
Depersonalization	Residual deviance
Desocialization	Resocialization
Diagnostic and Statistical Manual (DSM)	Schizophrenia
Differential exposure model	Secondary stressors
Differential vulnerability model	Self-complexity
Domains of self	Social support

Terms and Concepts for Review (*Continued*)

Life events	Stress
Major traumas	Stress proliferation
Mastery	Stressors
Medicalization	Total institution

Questions for Review and Reflection

1. Freshmen just beginning college sometimes exhibit high levels of psychological distress. Use the differential exposure and differential vulnerability models to explain why this might be the case.
2. In what way does the nonrandom distribution of psychological distress within society contribute to the reproduction of the class structure and what might be done to intervene in this negative cycle?
3. How would a sociological social psychologist respond to the following statement? *Diagnosing and treating mental illness is just like diagnosing and treating physical ailments like cancer.*
4. How, according to the modified labeling theory, does the stigma associated with mental illness in this society affect mental patients' social interactions? Suppose that you were diagnosed with depression. Would you conceal this identity from others? When would you be most likely to do so, and why might you want to hide your illness in these situations?

CHAPTER 11

Personal Relationships

*I didn't know if there ever was a choice, really. I was already in too deep.
Now that I knew—if I knew—I could do nothing about my frightening
secret. Because when I thought of him, of his voice, his hypnotic eyes, the
magnetic force of his personality, I wanted nothing more than to be with
him right now.*

—Bella Swan

This quotation, from the first book in the *Twilight Saga* (Meyers 2005: 139), provides an excellent illustration of the strong and sometimes overpowering feeling we refer to as romantic or passionate love. As popular myth would have it, we often fall in love with someone who is less than appropriate as a relationship partner, based on his or her status characteristics or social background. In this case, Bella, a human teenager, has fallen in love with Edward, a vampire—not a good match in their social world. This provides much of the storyline for this book, as well as the three subsequent novels about their relationship.

The *Twilight* books, and the films based on them, are popular among adolescents and young adults. Given prevailing cultural beliefs about love and intimate relationships, we enjoy reading and watching television programs and movies about love in this society, even though they are rarely realistic (Galician 2004). We discuss romantic love, and its origins, as well as other dimensions of personal relationships, in this chapter.

KEY CONCEPTS

Personal relationships are defined by the interdependence that exists between interaction partners. In a **personal relationship**, one actor's behavior is shaped by the actions of the other. Moreover, in a personal relationship, people interact with one another as unique individuals rather than as occupants of particular statuses (Blumstein and Kollock 1988). Personal relationships include friendships, as well as romantic partnerships. We use the term **romantic relationship** to refer to dating relationships and marriage, as distinct from friendships.

Personal relationships, romantic or not, are intimate relationships. **Intimacy** refers to feelings of closeness that emerge with the disclosure of information that is highly personal. **Physical intimacy** involves touching and sexual activity, as in the case of romantic relationships, especially marriage (Berscheid and Reis 1998).

When most people think of marriage, or marriage-like romantic relationships, they also think about love. What, exactly, is love, and what does it mean to be in love?

SOCIAL PSYCHOLOGICAL RESEARCH ON LOVE

Love is complex, and it comes in different forms. Psychologists who study love have focused on identifying and measuring different types of love. One of the most well-known classification schemes (Berscheid and Walster 1978; Hatfield and Walster 1978) distinguishes between companionate and passionate love. **Companionate love** is manifest in the affection we feel for the individuals with whom we share our lives. It involves feelings of closeness, emotional intimacy, comfort, and friendship. **Passionate love**, on the other hand, is reflected in an intense longing for another person. It is the experience that people associate with falling in love. Passionate love brings about fulfillment and ecstasy when it is reciprocated and anxiety and despair when it is not (Hatfield 1988).

Hatfield and Sprecher's (1986) Passionate Love Scale (PLS) is the most widely used measure of this construct (Graham 2011). The PLS is composed of 30 survey questions that assess the cognitive, emotional, and behavioral components of this experience. Most measures of romantic love within the social psychological literature are similar in orientation to the PLS (Hatfield, Bensman, and Rapson 2012).

Box 11.1   Questions From the Passionate Love Scale (PLS)

Respondents completing the PLS are instructed to fill in the blanks with the person they love passionately (if they are in love), the last person they loved passionately (if they are not currently in love), or the person they came closest to caring about in that way (if they have never been in love).

Response options range from:

1————2————3————4————5————6————7————8————9————10

Not at all true   Definitely true

	MEAN SCORE FOR COLLEGE SAMPLE*	
	MEN	WOMEN
I sense my body responding when _____ touches me.	7.88 (1.37)	7.45 (1.61)
Sometimes I feel I can't control my thoughts: they are obsessively on _____.	6.12 (2.19)	5.83 (2.52)
I would feel despair if _____ left me.	7.18 (2.10)	7.53 (2.15)
For me, _____ is the perfect romantic partner.	6.24 (2.34)	6.40 (2.23)
I possess a powerful attraction for _____.	7.08 (1.89)	6.87 (1.69)
I feel happy when I'm doing something to make _____ happy.	8.29 (1.13)	8.33 (1.04)

*Standard deviations are in parentheses.

Note: Hatfield and Sprecher (1986).

Given this overlap, we use the terms "passionate love" and "romantic love" interchangeably throughout the chapter.

Box 11.1 includes the subset of items from the PLS, along with average scores for a college sample. Note that there are no gender differences in responses to these questions or in overall scores on this measure (Hatfield and Sprecher 1986).

Passionate Love as the Misattribution of Arousal

As indicated by the items in Box 11.1, passionate, or romantic, love involves feelings of intense arousal. Social psychologists (Bersheid and Walster 1974; Walster 1971) have argued that people sometimes infer that they are experiencing passion for someone when, in reality, they are aroused for some other reason. From this perspective, passionate love involves both arousal and a cognitive label, as suggested by the Schachter and Singer's (1962) two-factor theory of emotion. People experience increased heart rate and other signs of sympathetic activation due to environmental stimuli, which they misattribute to another person (Berscheid and Walster 1974; Walster 1971). This process is especially relevant at a relationship's onset and may explain what we call "love at first sight."

In one famous experiment (Dutton and Aron 1974), male subjects encountered a female confederate of the experimenter on either a platform bridge that was low to the ground or on a high bridge that extended across a river gorge (the bridge type was the independent variable). The extension bridge was high enough, and flimsy enough, to increase physiological arousal (manifest as increased heart rate, sweating, and tremor) in the experimental subjects. The dependent variable was whether subjects would seek further contact with a female confederate of the experimenter who interviewed them on the bridge (either platform or extension).

Interestingly, male subjects interviewed on the extension bridge (the high arousal condition) were more likely than male subjects interviewed on the platform bridge (the low arousal condition) to try to contact the female interviewer when provided with the opportunity to do so at the end of the experiment. Presumably, this was because subjects interviewed on the suspension bridge misattributed the physiological arousal they experienced on the bridge to the presence of the female interviewer and assumed that they were attracted to her. Other studies show a similar pattern and suggest that people readily associate physiological arousal from a variety of sources to the individuals in their presence (Cantor, Zillman, and Bryant 1975; White, Fishbein, and Rutstein 1981).

Alcohol may contribute to interpersonal attraction in this manner. People feel pleasant due to the physiological effects of alcohol intoxication. They then misattribute this feeling to the person they are interacting with at that moment and label the arousal as physical attraction.

Note, however, that physiological arousal is misattributed only to those individuals who exhibit characteristics perceived as appropriate for a romantic or sexual partner. The (heterosexual) male subjects in Dutton and Aron's (1974) study, for example, did not infer that they were attracted to the person conducting interviews on the suspension bridge when that individual was male. Only a female interviewer elicited this perception. Thus, societal beliefs concerning the type of person one should find physically attractive provide boundary parameters for the misattribution of arousal and the experience of romantic passion.

What Do You Think?

Think about the last time you felt attracted to someone you just met. What was going on around you? What might you have been responding to other than your partner in interaction?

Love Styles

The experience we define as passionate, or romantic, love is reflected in two of six love styles originally described by Lee (1973). **Love styles** are psychological orientations, or approaches to love, composed of complexes of attitudes and beliefs about love, which lead to particular types of romantic behavior. The six love styles are **eros**, characterized by strong physical attraction and the intense emotion we associate with passionate or romantic love; **mania**, the obsessive component of passionate love that vacillates between pain and ecstasy; **storage**, a companionate or "*best friends*" approach to love; **pragma**, manifest as a "shopping around" approach to love conducive to activities such as online dating; **agape**, evidenced in sacrifice and putting the needs of one's partner above one's own; and **ludus**, reflected in manipulation, dishonesty, a lack of intimacy, and a large number of sexual partners (Hendrick and Hendrick 2006).

These different approaches to love have been measured using a series of survey items. Complete the questions in Box 11.2 to determine your dominant love style.

Box 11.2   Determining Your Dominant Love Style

Complete the Love Attitudes Scale (Short Form) (Hendrick, Hendrick, and Dicke 1998). The subscale with the highest total score indicates your dominant love style.

Instructions

Some of the items refer to a specific love relationship, whereas others refer to general attitudes and beliefs about love. Whenever possible, answer the questions with your current partner in mind. If you are not currently dating anyone, answer the questions with your most recent partner in mind. If you have never been in love, answer in terms of what you think your responses would most likely be (verbatim from Hendrick and Hendrick 1986:394).

Response options

1 = strongly disagree, 2 = moderately disagree, 3 = neutral, 4 = moderately agree, 5 = strongly agree

Eros (named for the Greek god of love)

_____ My partner and I have the right physical chemistry between us.
_____ I feel that my partner and I were meant for each other.
_____ My partner fits my ideal standards of physical beauty/handsomeness.
_____ Total score

Mania (erratic, obsessive)

_____ When my partner doesn't pay attention to me, I feel sick all over.
_____ I cannot relax if I suspect that my partner is with someone else.
_____ If my partner ignores me for a while, I sometimes do stupid things to try to get his/her attention.
_____ Total score

Storage (emergence over time)

_____ Our love is the best kind because it grew out of a long friendship.
_____ Our friendship merged gradually into love over time.
_____ Our love relationship is the most satisfying because it developed from a good friendship.
_____ Total score

Pragma (pragmatic)

_____ A main consideration in choosing my partner was how he or she would reflect on my family.
_____ An important factor in choosing my partner was whether he or she would be a good parent.
_____ One consideration in choosing my partner was how he or she would reflect on my career.
_____ Total score

Agape (spiritual, selfless love)

_____ I would rather suffer myself than let my partner suffer.
_____ I cannot be happy unless I place my partner's happiness before my own.
_____ I am usually willing to sacrifice my own wishes to let my partner achieve his or hers.
_____ Total score

Ludus (latin for "sport" or "game")

_____ I believe that what my partner doesn't know about me won't hurt him or her.
_____ I have sometimes had to keep my partner from finding out about other lovers.
_____ My partner would get upset if he or she knew of some of the things I've done with other people.
_____ Total score

What is your dominant love style? Historically, college males have been more likely than college females to exhibit the ludus, eros, and agape orientations toward love. College women have exhibited more pragmatic, storgic, and manic love attitudes than men.

These patterns are consistent with traditional gender roles. Breadwinners can afford to focus on passion (eros) and to have multiple partners (ludus). More practical, safer approaches to love (storage and pragma) are a better bet if you are, or will be, financially dependent upon a romantic partner. Mania is rooted in insecurity, also making it potentially more common among those groups low in power (women), as reflected in their financial dependency. On the flipside, agape may be higher in men insofar as they believe that it is their duty to financially support their partner (Hendrick et al. 1984; Hendrick, Hendrick, and Dicke 1998). As women gain equality with men in the workplace, these gender differences in love styles are likely to diminish.

The love style you favor may affect how you experience the process of falling in love. Whereas a person who favors either eros or mania is likely to be hit hard by this experience, someone who favors pragma will perceive falling in love as much less intense. An individual for whom ludus is the dominant love style may never fall in love (Hendrick and Hendrick 2006), and an individual high in agape may be prone to relationships in which they play a caretaking role. Research suggests that the passion associated with falling in love is most likely to last when it exhibits the characteristics of eros (intense emotion) but not mania (obsession) (Acevedo and Aron 2009).

Relationships are also more stable, and partners more satisfied, when understandings of love are shared. Every individual has a story about what love is, which influences his or her approach to love (love style) and shapes his or her relationship outcomes. These love stories reflect people's personal experiences, as well as broader social forces (Sternberg 1996).

Macro-Level Structural and Cultural Influences on Definitions of Love

As you know, social psychologists working within the social structure and personality face of sociological social psychology are especially concerned with the effects of society on the individual. Thus, they have focused on the ways people's conceptions of love are shaped by societal characteristics. They view this as critical to understanding how people within this culture experience love in intimate relationships (Felmlee and Sprecher 2006).

From a historical standpoint, the emphasis on romantic love as the basis for marriage is a relatively new phenomenon. Romantic love did not emerge in Western cultures until the 19th century. Prior to this, people married for more practical reasons, such as security or to maintain an alliance between families, as is often the case in contemporary non-Western cultures (Coontz 2005).

Although the concept of romantic love has a long history among the European nobility, it changed radically with the onset of European capitalism. At this juncture, popular novels played a central role in the creation and perpetuation of the link between romantic love and marriage among the new middle class. These novels (e.g., Jane Austen's *Pride and Prejudice,* published in 1813) reflect the individualist ethos of English capitalism. Love is portrayed as a test of an individual's virtue, as couples must struggle to overcome adversity in order to be together. These stories typically end with a marriage where there is both autonomy and self-discovery. The characters meet, fall in love (usually at first sight), and live happily ever after once they overcome the obstacles in their path (Swidler 2001).

The economic changes that provided the new middle class with enough leisure time to read romantic novels also created a dichotomy between emotion and self-development within people's households. This dichotomy had a profound effect on beliefs about love and its relation to gender. Before capitalism, and the movement of economic production from within the family to outside of the household, both men and women were responsible for caring for and about family members. By the late 1800s, the family and economic production had become separate spheres of activity, and gender roles were polarized. Economic production and the acquisition of material resources were the responsibility of men, whereas love and attachment within the family were considered to be the domain of women. Within this context, cultural images perpetuated conceptions of love as tender, expressive, and weak. Love was the essence of femininity. Masculinity, on the other hand, was associated with self-development through separation, independence, and power.

However, this pattern was not self-sustaining. Wives had fewer children and started working, which made them less willing to play a subordinate role within the family, and the expansion of leisure time left husbands with more time at home. As a result, Americans moved toward a more androgynous form of love. By the 1970s, the cultural blueprint for love emphasized autonomy and self-fulfillment for husbands and wives, open communication, and more flexible roles than those adhered to in prior generations (Cancian 1987). The separation of sexuality from reproduction has also helped to create a context where love is less tied to traditional gender roles and thus more egalitarian than in the past (Giddens 1992).

Although people still subscribe to the romantic love ideal, the basis of passionate or romantic conceptions of love, in-depth interviews with married couples suggest that many individuals reject this as mythological "movie" love in favor of "real" love. Unlike romantic love, which is sudden, intense, and never-ending, real love grows slowly over time, is rooted in compatibility, and does not necessarily last forever.

Nonetheless, even those individuals who consciously reject the idea of romantic love in favor of a more realistic, practical model sometimes vacillate between the two views. That is, they recognize the fictional aspects of romantic love, yet they can't help but feel the pull, or influence, of this way of conceptualizing love. This is because the mythical romantic view of love is grounded in the institution of marriage, which still serves as the dominant model for love relationships in this culture.

Marriage itself has the characteristics of passionate love. It's all or nothing (you either are or aren't married); you may be married to only one person; and, even in the face of a high divorce rate, marriages are meant to be forever ("Til death do us part"). Thus, the institution of marriage perpetuates the romantic love myth, even among individuals whose experiences have led them to reject its validity. How people think about their romantic relationships, and what they expect from their partners, reflect this orientation (Swidler 2001).

Symbolic Interactionist Perspectives on Love

Focusing on people's face-to-face interactions, symbolic interactionists have studied the social processes through which people acquire beliefs about love and expectations for their marital and marriage-like relationships. Much of the symbolic interactionist literature on socialization focuses on peer relationships in childhood. Children's peer interactions tend to be gender-segregated at this stage of development, and it is within this context that they develop particular abilities and orientations (e.g., the capacity for empathy and an understanding of societal values and norms). From a symbolic interactionist perspective, peer cultures mediate the effect of societal beliefs and norms on individuals' everyday social experiences.

In their analysis of children's peer interactions, Thorne and Luria (1986) emphasize the role of peer culture in shaping individuals' understandings of love and romance. Based on observational data collected on elementary school playgrounds, Thorne and Luria documented the gendered nature of children's emerging conceptualizations of romantic relationships. As in other studies (Lever 1978; Maccoby and Jacklin 1974; Zarbatany, McDougall, and Hymel 2000), the girls Thorne and Luria (1986) observed spent a lot of time talking about love and romance and who liked whom within dyads. These dyads were often composed of best friends. Research on children's friendships networks suggests that girls' relationships with their best friends are often more exclusive than those of boys. That is, boys are more likely to share their best friend with someone else. Boys who have a best friend are also more likely than girls to respond to a friendship offer from a peer.

It is common for a third person to initiate a friendship with someone who has a best friend, or for someone who has a best friend to initiate a friendship with someone else. Boys who are best friends tend to respond to a newcomer by expanding their friendship network. In contrast, when a third individual becomes part of a friendship network, girls are more likely than boys to transition back to the best friend dyad over time. This means that one of the three friends is likely to be dropped from the network (Eder and Hallinan 1978). Among girls, best friendships are transitory and often end when a new person comes into the picture and pairs up with one of the original partners. Being best friends is a temporary arrangement that ends, sometimes abruptly, and then begins again with someone else.

By having a series of best friends, girls become adept at cultivating and terminating intense, emotionally intimate relationships. They also learn to associate intimacy with self-disclosure and emotional support. Being "best friends" is considered special, and girls who are best friends are expected to share secrets and display empathy (understanding) and sympathy (shared feeling). Girls' best friendships center on emotional intimacy. This emphasis on communication and emotional intimacy shapes girls' expectations for their future romantic relationships.

Whereas young girls are entering and exiting a series of emotionally close "best friend" relationships, young boys are participating in shared activities with many friends. Boys are more likely than girls to interact in large groups. Within this context, core activities with friends involve communal rule breaking, resulting in an emotionally charged atmosphere, characterized by shared physiological arousal. It is often within these settings that young boys are first exposed to pornographic magazines and learn about what is considered sexually arousing. These encounters provide the scripts for boys' later romantic relationships. These scripts emphasize physiological arousal and sexuality, rather than verbal intimacy and emotion—the dominant themes for girls (Thorne and Luria 1986).

Among adults, men are more likely than women to connect love with sex and shared activities, and women are more likely than men to express affection through communication. In particular, among individuals who report high levels of love for their spouse, wives are more likely than husbands to compliment and to accommodate their partners by refraining from critical comments and potentially aggravating behaviors and by listening to them when they talk (Schoenfeld, Bredow, and Huston 2012). These results are compatible with the literature on gender and love styles, described earlier. Economic inequality between women and men at the macro level, in conjunction with expectations cultivated and reproduced within early peer cultures, results in gender differences in definitions of, and expressions of, love.

Men and women also differ in their attitudes toward sex. Women are less likely than men to believe premarital sex is acceptable, presumably for the same reason that they are less likely than men to exhibit the ludus love style. On the other hand, men are less tolerant than women of homosexuality. Table 11.1, based on data from the 2010 General Social Survey, shows heterosexual respondents' answers to a question about the acceptability of homosexuality. As shown here, heterosexual males have substantially more negative attitudes toward homosexual relationships than do heterosexual females.

Thorne and Luria (1986) make an interesting point about gender, early peer group interactions, and the norm of compulsory heterosexuality. It is within the context of boys' group interactions, characterized by high levels of arousal, that touching becomes minimal and what Thorne and Luria call "fag" talk emerges. **"Fag" talk** refers to the use of terms like "fag" and "homo" by young children who may not know what these words mean, other than the fact that they are derogatory, as verbal taunts. Often "fag" talk is directed toward marginalized individuals, such as boys who lack athletic skills or don't fit in socially for other reasons. With some greater awareness of the meanings of the terms they're using, adolescents often engage in "fag" talk on school busses (deLara 2008) and in other social contexts where peer interaction routinely occurs (Pascoe 2007).

TABLE 11.1		MEN	WOMEN
Attitudes Toward Homosexuality Among Heterosexual Men and Women, 2010	Sexual relations between two adults of the same sex:		
	Wrong	52.3%	43.5%
	Sometimes wrong	9.8%	6.1%
	Not wrong at all	37.8%	50.4%
	n	407	423

Note: Smith, Tom W., Peter V. Marsden, and Michael Hout. 2011. General Social Surveys, 1972–2010 [machine-readable data file] / Sponsored by National Science Foundation.—NORC ed.—Chicago, IL: National Opinion Research Center [producer]; Storrs, CT: The Roper Center for Public Opinion Research, University of Connecticut [distributor].

"Fag" talk is common among boys but not girls. Thorne and Luria (1986) speculate that the context of children's peer interactions play a role in establishing this difference. In the physically charged climate associated with boys' communal rule breaking, "fag" talk may serve as a source of social control, minimizing the emergence of same-sex sexual encounters, which might otherwise occur given the sexually charged atmosphere. Girls, who are more likely to interact in dyads, without this group arousal, are in a context less conducive to sexual relationships. This may be why "fag" talk is rarely observed among females in this age range and why physical contact between girls is not prohibited by peer norms the way that it is among young boys (Thorne and Luria 1986). These differences may serve as the underpinnings for gender differences in heterosexual adults' attitudes toward homosexuality.

SEX ON COLLEGE CAMPUSES: THE HOOKUP CULTURE

Much of the current literature on heterosexual sexual relationships focuses on the attitudes and behaviors of the Millennial Generation. Like previous age cohorts, today's young adults expect that they will get married and have children. They regard marriage as important, and they believe that love and fidelity are critical to a successful relationship (Scott et al. 2009). However, there is consensus within the research literature that dating among young adults is different than it used to be, especially on college campuses. In particular, the pattern referred to as "hooking up" has received a lot of attention in recent years.

Hooking up is a common college practice that involves casual sex (Glenn and Marquardt 2001). As such, it is broadly defined. As it is used by college students and other young adults, hooking up does not have a precise definition and may be used to refer to kissing, sexual intercourse, or something in between (Bogle 2008; Regnerus and Uecker 2011).

Hooking up is rooted in the changing societal norms pertaining to gender and sexuality that began in the 1960s, and it has altered the ways young adults approach dating. Members of the Millennial Generation aren't any more likely to have sex than Baby Boomers were when they were coming of age in the 1960s and 1970s. However, Millennials are more likely to have casual sex than previous generations (Armstrong, Hamilton, and England 2010).

The **hookup culture** is the term used to refer to the social settings and groups where prevailing norms support casual sex. The hookup culture is not specific to college campuses. Nonetheless, colleges and universities provide a social climate that facilitates hookups. In the college environment, students are likely to encounter individuals from similar backgrounds, who may even know their friends. Thus, people who don't know one another feel less like strangers on college campuses than they do in other settings. The belief that the college years are the time for letting loose and partying also fosters an atmosphere conducive to hookups (Bogle 2008).

As a side note, the kind of relationship referred to as "friends with benefits" does not fall into the hookup category. **Friends with benefits** is the label used to refer to a sexual relationship between friends that is not romantic in nature. Friends-with-benefits relationships tend to be more stable than hookups, which are "one night stands" (Hughes, Morrison, and Asada 2005). There has been little research on friends-with-benefits relationships.

In contrast, there are a number of studies on hooking up. Many of these analyses focus on college undergraduates. This research suggests that hooking up may be somewhat less common among college students than recent articles expressing concern about this behavior in newspapers and magazines would lead us to believe. One national survey of college undergraduates does suggest that most students (70%) participate in the hookup culture. However, the seniors who completed the latter survey reported an average of three or fewer hookups during their college years, suggesting that this behavior is not a routine occurrence (as cited in Armstrong et al. 2010).

Who Hooks Up?

There are no gender differences in the frequency with which college students hook up, but there are other group differences in this behavior. In general, racial and ethnic minorities, students from lower- and working-class backgrounds, and gays and lesbians are less likely to participate in the hookup culture than Whites, students from affluent families, and heterosexuals (Bogle 2008; Owen et al. 2010).

Religiosity (how religious someone is) also reduces the likelihood that young adults hook up for sex outside of a committed relationship (Burdette et al. 2009; Penhollow, Young, and Bailey 2007). Religious youth appear to be similar to previous generations in terms of their sexual behaviors, often engaging in premarital sex, but doing so within the context of a committed relationship (Uecker 2008). Nonetheless, the nature of sexual relationships has changed for some segments of this society.

What Do You Think?

How common is hooking up at your school? Is this behavior normative among your friendship group? Do you have friends with different views on this issue than your own? If so, consider the ways that these individuals differ from you in terms of their social characteristics and experiences.

What the changes in dating associated with the hookup culture mean for the current cohort of young adults and subsequent generations remains to be seen. Social psychologists tend to be cautious when assessing the consequences of changing sexual and relationship norms. In fact, in their recent article based on the analysis of the results of 94 studies on heterosexual dating published within the past 35 years, Eaton and Rose (2011) conclude that the gender dynamic associated with dating has changed little within this society. Men have more power than women within the hookup culture, due largely to the **sexual double standard** (the cultural belief that it's okay for men but not women to have multiple sex partners).

However, things are certainly no worse than in prior generations, before hooking up became common. Men have always been in the dominant position, and women in the subordinate position, in intimate relationships.

Eaton and Rose (2011) attribute longstanding gender inequality in sexual and romantic relationships to the persistence of gender inequality in business and politics at the macro level. They cite friendships, given their egalitarian nature, as models for dating and marital relationships. As women gain equality with men at the societal level, romantic relationships may move in this direction.

FRIENDSHIP

Friendships are nonkin, nonromantic personal relationships (Blumstein and Kollock 1988) that are voluntary and relatively flexible in their trajectory. In contrast to other relationships, such as business partnerships or marriage, people readily end or modify friendships without any formal notification or change in a publically recognized status. Nonetheless, there are shared "cultural images" or "codes of conduct" for friends that exist at the macro level, which shape individuals perceptions and behaviors. Although there is substantial variability in the content of people's friendships, most people adhere to the normative standards of their society (Suttles 1970).

Children acquire an understanding of friendship, and what it entails, primarily through their interactions with peers. As noted earlier, many of children's peer interactions are gender segregated (Lever 1978; Maccoby and Jacklin 1974; Thorne and Luria 1986; Zarbatany, McDougall, and Hymel 2000). However, as they progress into adolescence, cross-gender interactions, and friendships, become more common (Crosnoe 2000). Interestingly, participation in opposite-gender friendships is associated with more intimate same-gender friendships, measured in terms of perceived self-disclosure, caring, and help and guidance, for boys but not girls. Thus boys, as well as girls, appear to develop the capacity for empathy and other skills required for emotional intimacy through friendships with females (Zarbatany et al. 2000).

Research suggests that both boys and girls focus on shared activities when describing their friendships with boys, and that girls place a greater emphasis on verbal intimacy in their friendships with other girls than they do in their friendships with boys (McDougall and Hymel 2007). These patterns persist into adulthood (Aukett, Ritchie, and Mill 1988; Caldwell and Peplau 1982).

What Do You Think?

List three things that you expect from your female friends. List three things you expect from your male friends. Do you have the same expectations of your same- and opposite-gender friendships? Compare notes with one or two of your classmates.

TABLE 11.2		SAME-SEX FRIEND (N = 139)	OPPOSITE-SEX FRIEND (N = 142)
Characteristics College Students Value in Their Friends*	Warmth and kindness	6.85 (1.91)	7.58 (1.18)
	Expressiveness and openness	6.70 (1.95)	7.11 (1.58)
	Sense of humor	7.04 (1.62)	7.06 (1.58)
	Physical attractiveness	3.27 (2.11)	4.32 (2.14)
	Intelligence	5.78 (1.84)	6.48 (1.61)
	Social status	4.06 (2.24)	4.34 (2.18)

*The values presented are mean scores. Standard deviations are in parentheses.
Each item was scored from 1 = "not at all important" to 8 = "extremely important."
Note: Adapted from Sprecher and Regan (2002).

Characteristics College Students Value in Their Friends

The literature on adults' friendships focuses more on the characteristics people desire in their friends than on the interactions through which these expectations are constructed and reproduced. Some of the characteristics college students value in their friends are listed in Table 11.2 (the higher the mean score, the more important the characteristic). These data are from the results of a study by Sprecher and Regan (2002).

As shown in Table 11.2, warmth and kindness, expressiveness and openness, and a good sense of humor are regarded as more important in friendships than attractiveness, intelligence, and social status. However, college students do value attractiveness and intelligence in their friends, especially when they are of the opposite gender (the between-groups difference, same vs. opposite sex, for status was not strong enough to indicate a real effect). This is not surprising because opposite-sex friendships often develop into something more romantic (Sprecher and Regan 2002). How do the characteristics listed in Table 11.2 compare to your lists?

THE TRAJECTORY OF PERSONAL RELATIONSHIPS

In addition to studying the nature of people's friendships, and their romantic relationships, social psychologists have examined how personal relationships develop and progress. There is a consensus within this literature that personal relationships have a trajectory that is consistent across individuals. Thus, various models of the development and maintenance of personal relationships have been proposed (Levinger 1974; Thibaut and Kelley 1959). Although different models emphasize somewhat different factors, there is agreement that personal relationships involve the following phases: **initiation**, an initial ("getting to know you") stage; a period of **negotiation** and establishment of behavioral patterns; followed by a period of **maintenance** and, in some cases, **dissolution** (Backman 1981). Social psychologists have studied people's experiences at each of these stages.

Initiation: Person Perception and Attraction

People make rapid judgments about other individuals, often in less than 10 seconds. These assessments change little with increased contact (Ambady and Rosenthal 1993). Thus, it is important to understand the basis of people's initial evaluations of others.

The way people present themselves, regardless of who they really are, influences how they are viewed by others. Thus, people go to great lengths to convey positive impressions across social settings. We discussed the process of impression management in detail in an earlier chapter. Thus, we focus here on other, less strategic, factors that affect person perception.

Research suggests that common perceptual biases influence people's initial impressions and facilitate, or inhibit, attraction. Because (internal) perceptual processes are, in general, of greater interest to psychologists than to sociologists, most studies on person perception and attraction have been conducted by psychological social psychologists. These analyses provide important information about the attraction process and why some people are regarded more favorably than others in social encounters with strangers. Because these studies focus on aspects of the social setting that researchers can easily manipulate, they tend to be experimental.

Application: How to Make Common Perceptual Biases Work in Your Favor

Here's what we know from this literature. Because the desire to make a favorable impression is close to universal (Goffman 1959), we present this information as a set of tips for enhancing attractiveness (something that is, potentially, in all of our interest).

1. *Make yourself consistently visible.* The more you are seen by people, the more likely they are to find you appealing. This is because repeated exposure itself increases liking. This is called the **mere exposure effect** (Zajonc 1968).

   The mere exposure effect may be due to the ease with which familiar information is processed (Reber, Schwarz, and Winkielman 2004) or with covert (undetectable) muscle movements mirroring those enacted in prior encounters in which a person was present. These muscle movements may result in physiological changes that translate into positive feelings (Moreland and Topolinski 2010), much like the changes in blood flow associated with smiling that make people feel happier.

2. *Put yourself in a situation that requires behaviors likely to be viewed positively.* People typically attribute others' behaviors to personal characteristics, even when their actions are the product of situational factors, such as the enactment of a particular social role. This is why people often assume that celebrities have the traits of the characters they play on television or in film. For example, one soap star who played a particularly evil character once reported that a fellow customer in a grocery store purposely stamped on her foot as retribution for her character's bad behavior. In the same vein, playing a role with negative connotations will make you less attractive, whereas more desirable behaviors, even if they are required as part of your job or some other role, will make you more appealing to others.

Our tendency to misattribute situation-specific behaviors by others to personal characteristics is called the **fundamental attribution error** (Ross 1977). The fundamental attribution error may be due, in part, to the salience of the individual in people's perceptual field. Whereas the people we're observing grab our attention, situational constraints like cultural norms and role expectations are themselves invisible. Perhaps this is why people are more likely to attribute their behavior to internal versus situational causes when they view videotapes of their actions (as in Storms 1973). However, the fundamental attribution error is more common in the United States than in other cultures, which suggests that this perceptual bias also reflects the individualistic orientation that characterizes this society (Miller 1984; Morris and Peng 1994). The perception that the will of the individual is more important than structural factors in shaping behavior is more prevalent in the United States than it is in other counties (Gilens 1996; Lepianka, Gelissen, and van Oorschot 2010).

3. *Gravitate toward situations that induce positive affect.* As discussed earlier in relation to passionate love, people sometimes misperceive the source of their feelings, attributing physiological arousal to another person, rather than to its environmental source. The tendency to misattribute arousal generated by a situation to an individual means that you are more likely to be attractive to others in a social context that generates positive feelings (e.g., a party) than in a setting that does not elicit emotion or has negative connotations (Griffitt 1970).

4. *Emphasize the ways that you're similar to those around you, but don't reveal too much information about yourself.* You've probably heard the statement, birds of a feather flock together or, alternatively, that opposites attract. So which is it? Do people prefer individuals who are like or unlike themselves in terms of their appearance, attitudes, and behavior?

Research suggests that people tend to like individuals with similar attitudes (Neimeyer and Mitchell 1988), personality traits, and status characteristics (e.g., gender and race) to themselves (Tenney, Turkheimer, and Oltmanns 2009). Even similarity in more trivial characteristics can increase attraction. For example, in class, college students tend to sit next to other individuals who resemble themselves in terms of hair length, hair color, and whether or not they wear glasses, as well as race and gender (Mackinnon, Jordan, and Wilson 2011). We may not be conscious of it, but these kinds of physical attributes affect our behaviors.

According to the **matching hypothesis** (Walster et al. 1966), people are more likely to consider someone as a potential mate if they are similar to themselves in physical attractiveness, intelligence, and other desirable characteristics. This increases the likelihood that the relationship will be equitable in terms of what are perceived as important resources. The results of studies focusing on college students (Berscheid et al. 1971) and non-college adults (Folkes 1982; Murstein 1972) conducted in the 1970s and 1980s, when matching was a popular topic, are largely consistent with this proposition. More recent research using data from an online dating service also support the matching hypothesis (Taylor et al. 2011). Overall, the research literature provides little support for the notion that opposites attract (Berscheid and Reis 1998).

However, ambiguity may facilitate liking. The more people know about an acquaintance, the less likely they are to like them. This is because knowledge increases perceptions of dissimilarity. The more you find out about someone, the more you are likely to realize that he or she isn't really that much like you after all. Hence, in initial encounters, before an association has progressed to a relationship, keeping self-disclosure to a minimum may increase the extent to which one is perceived as attractive by a potential partner (Norton, Frost, and Ariely 2007).

5. *Never underestimate the power of physical attractiveness.* Studies consistently show that people like others whom they perceive to be physically attractive (Byrne, London, and Reeves 1968; McKelvie and Matthews 1976), even if they recognize that they're out of their league when it comes to dating (Taylor et al. 2011). Furthermore, being regarded as physically attractive often leads to other positive assessments. Once we have a positive view of people, or attribute a positive trait to them, we tend to assume they have other valued characteristics. This is called the **halo effect** (Thorndike 1920). The halo effect explains why being perceived as physically attractive has so many benefits. People assume that attractive people are more intelligent, more successful, and more competent than their less comely peers (Dion, Berscheid, and Walster 1972; Landy and Sigall 1974). Well aware of the significance of the halo effect, defense attorneys routinely require that their

PHOTO 11.2

Beauty is in the eye of the beholder: in a society envisioned by *Twilight Zone* creator and writer, Rod Sterling, looking piggish is the norm.

clients look their best when they appear in court. Research has consistently shown that attractive defendants receive lighter sentences (Sporer and Goodman-Delahunty 2009).

However, it is important to recognize that what is and is not defined as attractive may vary across groups within a society and is culturally determined. The picture, "Beauty Is in the Eye of the Beholder," is a clip from a famous episode of the television program *The Twilight Zone* (Eye of the Beholder, 1960). In this episode, what people would consider an attractive woman is deemed ugly within a society in which the norm is to look piggish. The photo is of a doctor (smoking a cigarette, a common behavior in 1960) and a nurse in the hospital where the woman has had surgery to make her look the way she should—like everyone else. The point of the story: nothing is inherently beautiful or ugly. We define things as such only in relation to prevailing societal beliefs and norms.

Propinquity

Propinquity, or physical proximity, is an important precursor to the initiation of most relationships because it increases the likelihood that social interaction will occur between two individuals. As a reflection of broader societal patterns, propinquity is shaped by factors such as social class, race/ethnicity, gender, and age. Our social worlds, including the neighborhoods where we live and the schools we attend, are segregated based on these status characteristics.

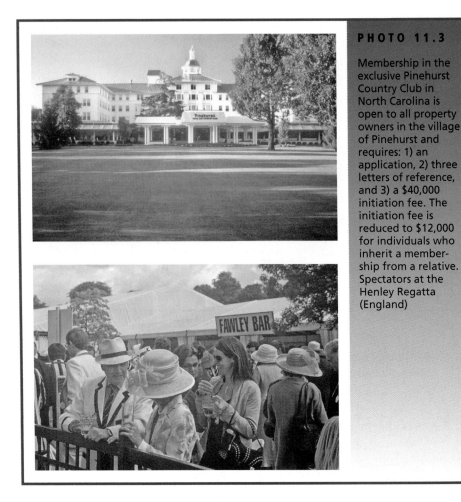

PHOTO 11.3

Membership in the exclusive Pinehurst Country Club in North Carolina is open to all property owners in the village of Pinehurst and requires: 1) an application, 2) three letters of reference, and 3) a $40,000 initiation fee. The initiation fee is reduced to $12,000 for individuals who inherit a member- ship from a relative. Spectators at the Henley Regatta (England)

When we think of segregation, we often think of people at the bottom of the stratification hierarchy as separate from others. However, segregation occurs at every level of the class spectrum.

In the *Bohemian Grove and Other Retreats: A Study in Ruling Class Cohesiveness*, sociologist William Domhoff describes the social settings in which the superrich hobnob. The Bohemian Grove is an exclusive campground belonging to San Francisco's all-male Bohemian Club, originally populated by artists and musicians and, more recently, elite businessmen. Although Domhoff's book was initially published in 1974, his arguments are as relevant today as they were then. With whom does one interact with at the Bohemian Grove and in similar settings, like prestigious country clubs? With other individuals who are among the wealthiest members of society. Regardless of where they are in the class structure, people have the most regular contact with individuals from similar backgrounds.

As a result, people's social networks exhibit what social psychologists call **homophily**. This means that they are composed of individuals who are alike in their demographic and social characteristics. People's social networks are the most homogenous (i.e., they exhibit the most homophily) when it comes to race/ethnicity, followed by age, religion, education, and occupation (McPherson, Smith-Lovin, and Cook 2001).

Environmental factors also determine whom we connect with. Research suggests that people are more popular when their office, house, apartment, or dorm room is located in a high traffic area, or they use a common walkway or elevator, so that they come into regular contact with others. This makes the costs of physical engagement minimal (Backman 1981).

How the environment is structured has a large effect on the initiation of friendships. In a study of recruits in a state police academy, for example, Segal (1974) found that student surname was a better predictor of who became friends than characteristics such as religion, marital status, age, ethnicity, level of education, or organizational memberships. This was because trainees were seated alphabetically in their classes.

Think of how the structure of the physical environment affected your transition to college. Where you live is likely to have had a tremendous impact on the friendships you developed. Who have you become friends with on campus? College

PHOTO 11.4

College students often develop friendships with other students who live in their dorm. Some of these friendships last throughout the life course.

students often become friends with their roommates or with other individuals who live in their residence hall (Griffin and Sparks 1990; Menne and Sinnett 1971).

College is also the setting where many people first encounter their romantic partner. Current estimates indicate that about 10% of couples meet in college.

However, physical proximity is less critical to the development of romantic relationships these days than in the past. Today, about one in five romantic relationships begins online. Thus, the Internet is replacing other social contexts, including school and work, as a primary venue in which couples meet. Individuals with more limited dating markets, including gays, lesbians, and middle-aged heterosexuals, are the most likely to meet their romantic partner online (Rosenfeld and Thomas 2012).

We discuss the effects of recent technological developments on personal relationships in greater detail toward the end of the chapter. Although the Internet and other computer-mediated technologies have altered the way we interact with others and expanded our pool of potential mates and friends, physical proximity continues to play a significant role in the development of personal relationships. Most people still meet relationship partners in face-to-face encounters (Sprecher 2009).

Cultural and Group Norms

While the opportunities for interaction accorded by physical proximity are an important precursor to relationship development, cultural norms also increase, or decrease, people's likelihood of forming personal relationships. For example, people typically marry someone of their same class background, race/ethnicity, and religion, who is similar in age and of the opposite gender (Jepsen and Jepsen 2002; Lehmiller and Agnew 2011; Rosenfeld 2008). We may not always recognize the extent that this is the case, but the choice of a spouse or any romantic partner is highly constrained by what people within a given society have been socialized to view as acceptable. There are many potential relationship partners (really, anyone is a potential partner) who are simply off our radar given their demographic or social characteristics.

Family members also exert a fair degree of control over the choices we make when it comes to the selection of a romantic partner, or friends, even though they play less of a role as the instigators of these relationships than they did in prior generations (Rosenfeld and Thomas 2012). Even after they leave home, parental attitudes shape children's behavior through financial and other less tangible means (e.g., shame and guilt). Would it be okay, from the perspective of your parents, or other family members, for you to marry, date, or even befriend someone who has been convicted of a serious crime?

Friends, teammates, and coworkers may also react negatively if someone becomes involved in a personal relationship, romantic or otherwise, with someone they view as unacceptable because of their characteristics. This type of interpersonal (informal) control can be quite effective in regulating people's behaviors.

What Do You Think?

Can you think of a time when you or someone you know dated, or befriended, someone who wasn't considered acceptable by family members or friends. On what basis did they reject this individual as an appropriate choice for a relationship? What happened as the result of their reaction? Did the relationship end?

The structural and perceptual factors that shape our relationship decisions are summarized in Figure 11.1. Social structure creates opportunities for interaction, and cultural and group norms make particular individuals viable candidates for personal relationships. Among these potential partners, mere exposure, perceptual biases leading people to misattribute positive characteristics and feelings to a certain individuals, and perceived similarity in characteristics and potential contributions to the relationship all increase liking. This, in turn, increases the probability that an association will progress to a personal relationship.

The Initial Stage of a Relationship

Once initiated, relationships grow as their partners become increasingly interdependent and establish routine patterns of interaction. During the initial stage of a relationship, self-presentational concerns remain heightened. In those instances when a first impression is positive enough to result in subsequent interaction, self-disclosure becomes the focal point of people's impression management strategies.

Studies of the initial stage in an emerging relationship suggest that people adhere to a norm of reciprocity, disclosing information of a nature comparable to

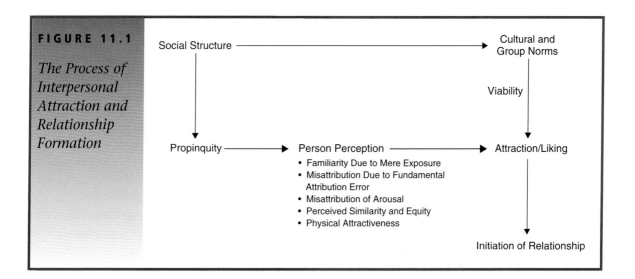

FIGURE 11.1

The Process of Interpersonal Attraction and Relationship Formation

that disclosed by their partner. As a relationship progresses, each individual's revelations become increasingly more intimate. This, in turn, facilitates the disclosure of more intimate details of one's thoughts and experiences. Thus, self-disclosure is both the source and consequence of intimacy in a developing relationship. It is through the process of escalating revelation that intimacy grows and people transition from independent actors to an interdependent unit (Backman 1981).

Q: Have you ever had someone tell you too much? Most of us have. Hence the term "too much information" (TMI), with which you are probably familiar. But how much self-disclosure is too much?

A: It depends upon the context of the relationship and how far it has progressed. For example, people may hold back more in friendships with work colleagues, keeping the relationship less intimate, than they might in other social contexts. Also, as noted earlier in the chapter, disclosing too much when you first meet someone is not a good strategy because it counters the positive effect of perceived similarity. However, once a relationship has been established, self-disclosure is associated with a number of positive outcomes in dating relationships, including confidence in one's partner and relationship satisfaction (Sprecher and Hendrick 2004).

In friendships, self-disclosure is also important because it is perceived to be the foremost indicator of intimacy. Still, even in a close friendship, people may be viewed as revealing too much when the content of their disclosures make their partner uncomfortable. Revelations about one's sexual activities to someone who believes such information is best kept to oneself would fall into this category (Monsour 1992).

Role Negotiation

As a relationship progresses, partners begin negotiating their respective roles within the partnership. Much of what we know about role negotiation and the establishment of norms within relationships comes from structural symbolic interactionists, who emphasize the interplay between social constraint and agency and the role of the self in shaping patterns of behavior. From this perspective, altercasting is central to the process of role negotiation (Backman 1981). **Altercasting** occurs when someone projects an identity consistent with his or her own goals onto another individual (Weinstein and Deutschberger 1963).

The extent that a projected identity matches an individual's self-concept affects the success of this process. Whereas people readily accept an identity that is consistent with the way they view themselves, they tend to resist identities that contradict their core self-conceptions (Blumstein 1975). Should the relationship continue, this resistance is likely to result in a battle over competing situational definitions concerning the nature of the relationship and the responsibilities of each partner. Who wins will be determined by the partners' relative power.

There are four main sources of power in intimate relationships. Two are structural, in that they reflect patterns of inequality at the macro level, and two are relational, because they emerge within the context of the relationship itself. The two **structural bases of power** are gender and socioeconomic resources (education, occupational standing, and personal earnings). The two **relational bases of power** are relative love or liking (who likes or loves their partner more) and an individual's opportunities for other equally or more beneficial relationships relative to those of his or her partner (Cast 2003; Thibaut and Kelley 1959). Recall the principle of least interest (Waller 1938). Power lies in the hands of the partner who has the least to lose should the relationship end. The two relational sources of power reflect this basic premise.

Although gender serves as a basis of power in many heterosexual relationships, giving men greater control than women over the negotiation of roles within this context, this effect appears to operate through socioeconomic resources. In one study of newly married couples (Cast 2003), men were no more likely than women to impose identities on their spouse when the partners had similar levels of education and equally prestigious occupations. However, gender is likely to affect the balance of power within an intimate relationship among partners with equal socioeconomic resources who hold traditional gender role attitudes (Cast 2003). Because people's self-conceptions and identities are rooted in the responses of others, partners' self-concepts are likely to change in a manner consistent with the negotiated role structure of the relationship, whatever its nature (Burke and Cast 1997).

The relationships between structural and relational power, altercasting, roles, self, and behavior are presented in Figure 11.2. Although these processes have been studied primarily within the context of marriage, they are relevant to other kinds of relationships, including friendships. Within a friendship, relational characteristics (relative liking and relationship alternatives) may be more important determinants of power than structural attributes (education or gender). Similarly, relational bases of power may be more important than structural bases of power in shaping the outcomes of college students' dating relationships (Grauerholz 1987).

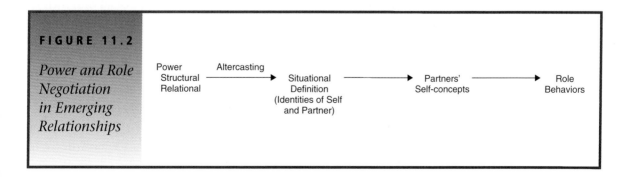

FIGURE 11.2

Power and Role Negotiation in Emerging Relationships

Power
Structural ——— Altercasting ———> Situational ———> Partners' ———> Role
Relational   Definition   Self-concepts   Behaviors
                                    (Identities of Self
                                    and Partner)

Relationship Maintenance

One defining characteristic of personal relationships is that they persist over time. Most studies of the maintenance of personal relationships have focused on romantic partnerships. As these relationships grow and develop, individuals typically experience increasing levels of relationship commitment (Michaels, Acock, and Edwards 1986).

Recall that social exchange theorists define commitment as repeated exchanges with the same partner, even in the face of more rewarding exchange alternatives (Cook and Emerson 1978). In a romantic relationship, commitment is considered to be high when an individual intends to stay in the relationship (Crawford et al. 2003; Sprecher 1988).

See Box 11.3 for a measure of commitment commonly used within the research literature on romantic relationships, along with benchmarks for comparison. If you're in a relationship, compute your commitment score and compare it to the mean for the relevant subgroup (dating, exclusively dating, living together, etc.). If you're not currently dating someone, think about someone you know who is in a romantic relationship and respond to these questions as you think he or she would answer them. Alternatively, you might ask this person to complete the measure. Note that, on average, commitment increases as people progress from casual dating to engagement and marriage.

Working within the social exchange tradition, social psychologists have identified a number of factors that increase commitment in college students' dating relationships. They include the following.

> ***Love for one's partner:*** Feelings of love for one's partner increase commitment (Crawford et al. 2003).
>
> ***Sex:*** Sexual involvement increases relationship commitment among dating couples (Simpson 1987).
>
> ***Relationship alternatives:*** Both the perception that one's partner could readily be replaced, as well as the attractiveness of potential alternative partners, decrease individuals' levels of commitment to their relationship (Crawford et al.2003; Floyd and Wasner 1994; Sprecher 2001).
>
> ***Relationship satisfaction:*** In general, people who are satisfied with their relationship report high levels of relationship commitment (Michaels, Acock, and Edwards 1986; Sprecher 2001).

In earlier discussions of social exchange theory, we focused on the concept of equity (when the benefits and costs of a relationship are equal). Equity may increase relationship stability by increasing commitment, although these variables have not been consistently related across studies (Floyd and Wasner 1994; Lujansky and Mikula 1983; Sprecher 2001).

Box 11.3   Measuring Relationship Commitment

Answer each of the following four questions using the response options provided and then add these scores to get your total commitment score.

QUESTION	SCORE
1. How committed are you to your partner? Response options: 1 = "extremely uncommitted" to 9 = "extremely committed"	_____
2. How often have you seriously considered ending your relationship with your partner? Response options: 1 = "several times" to 9 = "never"	_____
3. How likely is it that you will try to end the relationship with your partner during the next year? Response options: 1 = "extremely likely" to 9 = "extremely unlikely"	_____
4. How likely is it that you will try to end the relationship with your partner during the next 5 years? Response options: 1 = "extremely likely" to 9 = "extremely unlikely"	_____
Your total commitment score	_____

Subgroup Norms (College Undergraduates and Graduate Students)

	OCCASIONAL/REGULAR DATING	EXCLUSIVE DATING	LIVING TOGETHER (NOT ENGAGED)	ENGAGED	MARRIED
Mean	5.3	7.3	7.3	8.0	8.1
n	26	181	69	41	73

Note: Sprecher (1988).

Relationship Dissolution

The fourth, and final, stage of personal relationships involves their dissolution. Because friendships are more flexible than other relationships and often end gradually (Suttles 1970), most of the literature on the termination of relationships has focused on romantic partners.

When and why do romantic relationships end? Social psychologists have identified a number of the factors that lead to the termination of both dating and marital relationships.

Factors Associated with Premarital Breakups

Research suggests that, among dating couples, breakups are caused by the following four interpersonal factors.

1. *Time.* The less time partners in a relationship spend together, the more likely they are to break up.

2. *Alternatives.* People are more likely to end a dating relationship when they think they have better options (Felmlee, Sprecher, and Bassin 1990).

3. *Sexual behavior and attitudes.* Couples that are not sexually active are more likely to break up than sexually active couples. Couples who are sexually active are especially likely to stay together when the partners are not oriented toward casual sex (Simpson 1987).

4. *Social support.* Dating couples are less likely to stay together when they don't receive support for the relationship from family members and friends, illustrating the power of group norms in shaping people's relationship choices.

Research also suggests that, interracial relationships are less likely to persist than relationships where partners are of the same race, even among couples with similar levels of support for the relationship from family members and friends (Felmlee et al. 1990). This illustrates the extent that broader societal, as well as group norms, can affect the stability of individuals' intimate relationships. Patterns of prejudice and discrimination, and the resultant stigma conferred upon interracial couples, may increase their levels of stress and thus increase their chances of breaking up.

The Consequences of Breaking Up

Breakups themselves can be stressful. Sprecher and associates (1998) conducted a survey of approximately 300 young adults who had experienced the dissolution of a nonmarital romantic relationship within the past year. Among these individuals, the following characteristics were associated with psychological distress due to the breakup (listed in order of their importance).

- The conditions surrounding the breakup, in particular the nonmutuality of alternatives. **Nonmutual alternatives** is a state prior to the dissolution of a relationship where one's partner becomes interested in someone else when one has no similar (competing) interest in an alternative partner.

- Having been committed to and satisfied with the relationship prior to the breakup.

- Being the one who initiated the relationship to begin with.

- Having a partner initiate the breakup.

Gender was also associated with high levels of psychological distress (female higher than male), but only in the weeks immediately following the breakup. Thus, gender had less of an impact than the relationship characteristics just listed (non-mutual alternative, commitment, etc.) on young adults' reactions to the dissolution of a romantic relationship (Sprecher et al. 1998).

Divorce

Ending a marriage is different from ending a dating relationship. The investment in a marriage is usually higher than in a nonmarital relationship. Married couples are also more likely than nonmarried partners to have children, which may make separating more difficult.

STRUCTURAL DETERMINANTS OF DIVORCE

Like interracial dating relationships, interracial marriages are less stable than endogamous marriages. **Endogamous marriages** are marriages between people of the same group, in this case, the same race/ethnicity. On average, interracial marriages are 21% more likely to end than endogamous marriages. Couples where the husband is Black and the wife is White are especially likely to experience difficulties due to prevailing patterns of prejudice and discrimination. Thus, their risk for divorce exceeds that of all other groups (Zhang and Van Hook 2009).

Race is also an important predictor of divorce among the general population. Among same-race couples, Asian Americans have the lowest divorce rate and African Americans, the highest, notably higher than that reported among Whites. Hispanics have a divorce rate only slightly higher than that of Whites.

Education, an important socioeconomic resource, reduces the risk for divorce across racial/ethnic groups (Gibbs and Payne 2011), except among Black males. Although neither household income nor the income of husbands relative to that of their wives is associated with divorce among African Americans (Orbuch et al. 2002), Black men who have divorced often cite financial strains as the main reason for the dissolution of their marriage (Lawson and Thompson 1999).

SOCIAL EXCHANGE PROCESSES AND DIVORCE

Other factors associated with divorce emerge through interactions between spouses and increase the perceived costs, versus benefits, of remaining in the relationship (Levinger 1982). The most common reason for divorce is poor relationship quality (Amato and Hohmann-Marriott 2007). Declines in marital quality may result from incompatibility due to partners' differential development (i.e., growing apart) (Amato and Previti 2003) or interactional patterns characterized by hostility, anger, stubbornness, inconsideration, defiance, or rejection (Matthews, Wickrama, and Conger 1996).

Other commonly cited reasons for divorce include infidelity and drug or alcohol use, actions likely to reduce perceived relationship benefits. Unlike dating couples, very few married couples cite better alternatives as a reason for breaking up (Previti and Amato 2003).

Finally, attitudes toward marriage affect people's likelihoods of getting divorced. Individuals with prodivorce attitudes are more likely to divorce than individuals who view marriage as a permanent arrangement. This is because prodivorce attitudes lead to low levels of marital investment. When investment in a marriage is low, the quality of the relationship tends to decrease. Low relationship quality, in turn, increases the risk for divorce (Amato and Rogers 1999).

The series of survey questions used to measure prodivorce attitudes are presented in Box 11.4. Calculate your score on this measure. How do you compare to the sample of married adults (data from college students are not readily available)? Save your score. We'll talk more about this in a later section of the chapter.

THE CONSEQUENCES OF DIVORCE

Ending a marriage often has negative psychological consequences. For some individuals, these effects dissipate rather quickly. For others, they persist and may cause more long-term problems. In general, adults tend to recover from divorce faster when they are educated, they are employed, and they receive social support from a new relationship partner (Amato 2000).

What about children? Do they suffer from parental divorce? Most people would probably say that they do. The extent to which parental divorce has negative consequences for children has been debated within the research literature. Some high-profile studies suggest that the children of divorce are psychologically and socially impaired throughout life, whereas others indicate that parental divorce has no lasting effects. The truth is somewhere in the middle (Amato 2003).

Adults from intact families are better off psychologically and socially than individuals whose parents divorced when they were children. Adults who grew up with both biological or adoptive parents have lower levels of distress, higher life satisfaction, better family relationships, and more friendships and community involvements than adults who experienced parental divorce during childhood. However, these effects are relatively small (Amato and Booth 1991). Overall, it is estimated that no more than 10% of adults who experienced parental divorce as a child suffer serious reductions in well-being during adulthood as a consequence (Amato 2003). Research also suggests that divorces that are amicable and do not reduce the quality of children's relationships with their parents do not have any more negative long-term consequences than living with parents whose marriage is unhappy (Amato and Booth 1991).

Box 11.4   Measure Your Attitudes Toward Divorce

Use the response options given to answer each of the following questions and then total your score for each subscale.

<u>Subscale 1</u>
Response options: 1 = "strongly agree," 2 = "agree," 3 = "disagree," 4 = "strongly disagree"

_____ 1. Couples are able to get divorced too easily today.
_____ 2. If one spouse becomes physically or mentally disabled, the other person should stay in the marriage regardless of his or her happiness.
_____ 3. Marriage is for life, even if the couple is unhappy.
_____ 4. In marriages where parents fight a lot, children are better off if their parents divorce or separate.
_____ Total subscale 1

<u>Subscale 2</u>
Response options: 1 = "strongly disagree," 2 = "disagree," 3 = "agree," 4 = "strongly agree"

_____ 5. It is OK for people to get married, thinking if it doesn't work out, they can always get a divorce.
_____ 6. The personal happiness of an individual is more important than putting up with a bad marriage.
_____ Total subscale 2

Add your scores for the subscale 1 and subscale 2 to get your total score.

_____ Total score (subscale 1 + subscale 2)

Mean = 13.92   Standard deviation = 2.29

n = 1,032 married respondents

Note: Amato and Rogers (1999).

Thus, adults from intact and nonintact families may differ most when it comes to their own risk for divorce. It has been well documented that having parents who divorced increases people's chance of getting divorced themselves (Wolfinger 2003). Research suggests that it is attitudes toward divorce and not socialization (the acquisition of poor relationship skills) that underlies this effect. The transmission of divorce across generations is strongest when the parents got along well prior to the breakup of their marriage. Moreover, witnessing frequent disagreements and arguments between parents does not itself put individuals at risk for divorce. People from families characterized by marital discord whose parents stayed together are not any more likely to get divorced than individuals whose parents rarely fought. This latter finding suggests that the transmission of divorce from one generation to the next occurs because having parents who divorced reduces the degree to which people view marriage as a lifelong commitment (Amato and DeBoer 2001).

What Do You Think?

How did you score on the measure of prodivorce attitudes presented in Box 11.4? Were you substantially more, or less, prodivorce than the average (benchmark) score? Are your parents still married? What other factors might have shaped your attitudes about marriage and divorce?

CONTEMPORARY TRENDS

In the following section, we discuss recent trends in relationships resulting from changing attitudes and behaviors at the macro level, as well as the advent of new technologies. These patterns, and their impact on personal relationships, are of particular interest to sociological social psychologists working within the social structure and personality tradition, given their focus on the link between macro-level societal characteristics and people's social experiences.

Same-Sex Couples

Same-sex marriage has become increasingly more acceptable in the United States. Some states allow for civil unions, which give gay and lesbian partners similar rights to married couples. Same-sex marriage has been legalized in a number of other states. According to a recent Gallup poll, 50% of the population now supports the legalization of same-sex marriages (vs. 40% in 2009) (Newport 2012).

The number of same-sex couples living in the United States has increased drastically in recent years. In 2006 there were five times as many same-sex households as there were in 1990, a growth rate over 20 times that of the overall population (Gates 2007). Currently, there are almost one million same-sex couples living in this country, about 0.8% of all households (O'Connell and Feliz 2011).

Over the course of the past 20 years, increasing attention has been given to gay and lesbian families within the research literature. In general, studies suggest that there are more similarities than differences between heterosexual and same-sex couples (Van Eeden-Moorefield et al. 2011). Although gay and lesbian couples experience less conflict within their relationships than heterosexual couples, this difference is minimal. Furthermore, same-sex and heterosexual couples do not differ in relationship satisfaction, frequency of sex, partner evaluations, or in the characteristics associated with relationship quality and stability (Kurdek 2006). Thus, there appear to be basic social processes that apply to all dyadic relationships, regardless of the partners' sexual orientation (Kurdek 2006, 2008).

Nonetheless, the stigma associated with homosexuality may serve as a source of ongoing stress for gay and lesbian couples and put these relationships at risk. Gay and lesbian partners get less social support for their relationship from family members than their heterosexual counterparts, which may increase their chances of breaking up (Kurdek 2004). This is an issue in need of further research. To date, there is little information available about the dissolution of gay and lesbian relationships (Van Eeden-Moorefield et al. 2011).

Cohabitation Among Heterosexual Couples

Cohabitation among heterosexual couples is another relationship trend that bears mention. Cohabitation has grown steadily in popularity since the 1970s and has been a normative family form since the 1990s (Kennedy and Bumpass 2008). Today, approximately 60% of young adults cohabitate with an opposite-sex partner before marrying (Payne 2011).

Research suggests that cohabitation increases the risk for divorce, but only when the couple lives together before becoming engaged. This is called the **cohabitation effect**. SSP researchers have explained the cohabitation effect by focusing on group differences in relationship commitment. Cohabitation implies less of a commitment than marriage or engagement. Yet it is often difficult to end a relationship when you're living with someone, even if your commitment to the relationship is low. Thus, it is normative for cohabitating couples to marry (Payne 2011), so much so that social psychologists have suggested that cohabitation be considered a part of the marriage process (Manning and Cohen 2012).

Given the social pressures pushing them toward marriage, cohabitating couples who would split if they weren't living together often stay together and eventually marry. Once they get married, these latter individuals are at risk for divorce because their relationships are characterized, on average, by lower commitment than other couples who marry. When cohabitation occurs after an engagement, it is not associated with a risk for divorce because couples who get engaged before living together tend to be highly committed to their relationship (presumably, that's why they get engaged). Note, then, that cohabitation itself doesn't cause divorce. Rather, it is low relationship commitment, which occurs most frequently among couples who live together before becoming engaged, that increases the risk for divorce.

Due to their high levels of commitment going into marriage, couples who cohabitate only after an engagement are no more likely to divorce than couples who do not live together before getting married (Stanley et al. 2010). Given this pattern, and the fact that cohabitation has not replaced the institution of marriage, as many people feared it would when it started becoming popular, it is fair to say that cohabitation has not radically altered the course of people's romantic relationships.

The Internet and Personal Relationships

The growth in the use of the Internet is another trend of interest to social psychologists who study personal relationships. Over the course of the past 20 years, the Internet has become a central feature of most people's lives. It has drastically increased people's access to information, but has it radically altered the nature of their personal relationships?

As the Internet was gaining in popularity in the 1990s, social scientists expressed concerns that heavy use would decrease people's participation in face-to-face encounters, leaving them with minimal social support and low psychological well-being (e.g., Kraut et al. 1998). This has not come to pass. According to a large-scale national study of Internet use and its consequences by the Pew Research

PHOTO 11.5

Although social networking has grown in popularity among adults, e-mail, web searches, and getting news are the most common online activities (Purcell 2011).

Center, Internet use has positive rather than negative social consequences, primarily because of its effects on people's social networks (Boase et al. 2006).

Some sociological social psychologists study the composition of people's social networks and the nature of the relationships between network members (Felmlee 2006). These researchers distinguish between two kinds of network connections: core ties and significant ties. **Core ties** are the individuals that people have close relationships with. Core ties include family members, a romantic partner, close friends, or anyone else you have an intimate relationship with. People's relationships with their significant ties are less intimate. **Significant ties** are individuals that people aren't especially close to, but they are more than just acquaintances (Boase et al. 2006). Significant ties might include members of a group that you belong to (e.g., a political organization or a school club) whom you know fairly well but would not consider good friends.

What Do You Think?

Think about your social network. Jot down the names, or initials, of your core ties and, in a second column, the names or initials of your significant ties. How many core ties do you have? How many significant ties do you have?

On average, Americans have 23 core ties and 27 significant ties. Whereas females have more core ties than males, males have more significant network ties than females do. Although race/ethnicity is not associated with the size of people's social networks, education does affect network composition. College graduates tend to have more network ties than individuals with lower levels of educational attainment.

Interestingly, Internet users have larger social networks than nonusers—an average of 37 versus 30 individuals, respectively. This is because Internet users have more significant (but not core) ties than people who don't go online.

People who use the Internet report that doing so has helped them make major decisions, pertaining to their career, their health, their finances, or other issues. People use the Internet to access information of relevance to their lives and to seek support from members of their social networks via email. However, there is no evidence that the use of email reduces non-computer-mediated social contacts. To the contrary, the use of email is associated with more, rather than fewer, interactions with network members in person and over the phone (Boase et al. 2006).

Psychological Well-Being and Social Development

Adolescents spend more time on the Internet than any other group. Thus, a number of studies on Internet use have focused on individuals in this age range. The results of these analyses are fairly clear-cut. The Internet has positive effects on social integration and well-being when it is used to connect with friends. However, the Internet may have negative effects when it is used for solitary purposes, such as surfing the web, or to communicate with strangers in, for instance, public chat rooms (Valkenburg and Peter 2009). Safety is a concern in these online environments. Adolescents often post personally identifying information online, making it easy for potential predators to locate them (Williams and Merten 2008).

Despite potential safety issues, Internet encounters in public or semipublic forums may facilitate adolescents' social development. Adolescents frequently experiment with new identities over the Internet. Through anonymous online communications, they have the opportunity to engage in a kind of role-play that is not possible in face-to-face encounters. By pretending to be someone they're not online, adolescents get a sense of what it is like to be in different position and to have characteristics that differ from their own attributes (Valkenburg, Shouten, and Peter 2005). These kinds of social interactions, albeit more sophisticated in terms of their content, are comparable to the face-to-face role-play activities of children that serve an important socialization function.

Social media sites also provide forums where adolescents negotiate identities through interactions with friends. Although parents and other adults are sometimes shocked by the content of adolescents' online postings, which often include comments about the use of alcohol and other drugs or sexual references, they are not atypical for this age group. Adolescents' face-to-face conversations with peers are likely to be similar in content to their Internet communications. Thus, from a developmental perspective, the main function of social media is its provision of an additional venue for peer interaction (Williams and Merten 2008).

The results of a study of Dutch adolescents suggest that the use of social media is associated with positive outcomes, including enhanced self-esteem and life satisfaction (Valkenburg, Peter and Shouten 2006). Similar effects have been observed among college students in the United States (Ellison, Steinfield, and Lampe 2007). Presumably, this is because the use of social media increases social integration. Consistent with this interpretation, Kim and Lee (2011) found a positive association between number of Facebook friends and happiness among a college student sample. Having a lot of friends on Facebook may increase happiness by making people feel validated (Kim and Lee 2011).

Friendship

Think about what it means to "friend" someone on Facebook. Does this suggest any kind of deep or committed relationship? For most people, it does not. Thus, friendship within this context implies a fair degree of superficiality.

Although Facebook and other social media may have trivialized the concept of friendship, they have not radically altered it. Research suggests that how people define their friendships, and the content of their interactions, is similar in online and face-to-face encounters. Moreover, communicating with people online, versus in person, appears to facilitate self-disclosure, which serves as the basis for intimate relationships (Amichai-Hamburger, Kingsbury, and Schneider 2012).

WHO BENEFITS THE MOST FROM INTERNET USE?

Research suggests that males in early to middle adolescence benefit most from online interaction with peers. Boys in this age range often avoid self-disclosure in face-to-face interactions, due to prevailing patterns of gender socialization and beliefs about masculinity. Given their low level of self-disclosure in face-to-face encounters, communicating over the Internet increases the frequency of self-disclosure more among adolescent males than it does among other groups.

Individuals who are socially adept also reap more benefits from online communications than other people. Research suggests that the Internet is used more for social purposes by socially competent than by shy or socially anxious adolescents (Valkenburg and Peter 2009).

Although college students with low self-esteem perceive the Internet as a more appealing forum for self-disclosure than face-to-face encounters, their Facebook postings often generate negative feedback (Forest and Wood 2012). Thus, individuals who are not successful in their self-presentations in face-to-face settings may also be unsuccessful in their online communications.

Romantic Relationships

As noted in the section on relationship initiation, meeting a romantic partner on the Internet has become relatively common. With two exceptions, the factors leading to an initial attraction between partners, described earlier in the chapter, are less relevant to relationships that begin online than they are to those that begin face to face. The two exceptions are physical attractiveness and similarity.

Physical attractiveness is an important determinant of relationship opportunities in online dating (Taylor et al. 2011). The more appealing an individual's posted photo, the more responses he or she is likely to receive.

Perceived similarity may also affect individuals' assessments of potential mates on Internet dating sites (Hitsch, Hortacsu, and Ariely 2010). In fact, some online dating services (e.g., eHarmony) emphasize the importance of similarity in the formation of lasting relationships and the effectiveness of their matching process for bringing compatible people together (Sprecher 2009).

The extent to which committed relationships result from the use of online dating services is open to question. Although eHarmony claims it is responsible for 2% of all U.S. marriages, this statistic has not been verified by social scientists. If you're interested, go to the following website for a *Wall Street Journal* article critiquing company-generated statistics on the success of their online dating services: http://online.wsj.com/article/SB124879877347487253.html.

The other significant difference between online and traditional dating pertains to the preliminary stage of a relationship. Computer-mediated communication may have a number of advantages early on in a relationship. They include the following:

1. *More control over one's self-presentations.* People have time to think about what they want to say when communicating over the Internet versus in person.

2. *More balanced communication.* Individuals who are shy may easily be dominated in a face-to-face conversation. However, on the Internet they can write long, detailed messages without being interrupted.

3. *More flexibility in timing.* The asynchronous nature of online communication enables people to respond when it is most convenient to do so.

These factors make it relatively easy for people to get to know one another. However, once individuals who initiated contact online meet in person and begin dating, the relationship is likely to unfold in the typical manner. After a relationship has developed, people who met online engage in the same kinds of activities as individuals who met in face-to-face encounters (Sprecher 2009).

Couples who had their first contact online are as satisfied with their relationships as people who met through family members, friends, in a bar, at work, or at college. Only two kinds of couples have higher levels of relationship satisfaction than individuals who met online—those who met in primary or secondary school and those who met in church (Rosenfeld and Thomas 2012). (Note that couples who met in school or in church are likely to be similar in terms of their social backgrounds and beliefs.) Couples who met online are no more likely to break up than couples who initially met in person (Rosenfeld and Thomas 2012).

Take a Break

For a fun movie about online dating, check out *Must Love Dogs,* staring Diane Lane and John Cusack. This 2005 film is available at most video stores and via the online distributors Netflix and Hulu.

INTERNET INFIDELITY AND ITS CONSEQUENCES

What about the Internet and infidelity? The Internet makes it relatively easy to meet new people, or to reconnect with old friends and romantic partners. Thus, the Internet, and social networking sites in particular, may increase individuals' likelihoods of having affairs.

Reliable statistics on the prevalence of infidelity within marriage and other committed relationships due to Internet relationships are hard to come by (Hertlein and Piercy 2006). Despite this, the conventional wisdom is that Internet affairs have become a serious social problem. It has also been suggested that infidelity associated with the pervasiveness of the Internet has increased the divorce rate.

Available data suggests that this is not the case. The increase in rates of infidelity in recent years is more pronounced among women, presumably due to their gains in the workplace. An Internet effect would be expected to increase infidelity across gender. Furthermore, there is no evidence that Internet access is associated with divorce (Kendall 2011). Given this, claims about the Internet, infidelity, and the dissolution of relationships are probably overstated.

Mobile Phones and Personal Relationships

Cellular phones are another relatively new means of communication with the potential to affect individuals' relationships. Although research on this topic is limited, a recent study of college students (Hall and Baym 2011) suggests that regular mobile phone use between friends, including both calling and texting, increases relationship satisfaction by increasing their dependence upon one another. However, at the same time, frequent cell phone contact creates feelings of overdependence, which reduces relationship satisfaction.

As a result of this tension, college students often have mixed feelings about friendships involving constant maintenance through phone calls and text messages. These relationships enhance their levels of social integration, but they are also perceived as constraining (Hall and Baym 2011). As stated succinctly by a participant in a (qualitative) study on college students' feelings about the pervasiveness of mobile phone use:

> [Y]eah, it's a pain in the butt. Because before (you had the cell phone) you could have excuses to get away from people. You could say, "Oh, I wasn't home" or whatever. And now, they know that you're ignoring them because you have that voice-mail. And if they get forwarded straight to voice-mail, they know that you are denying their call and they're not happy. There is no way you can get away from it (cell phone) and just have quiet time. (Aoki and Downs 2002:355).

Teenagers have similar complaints. Although they recognize the social benefits of cell phone use, many teens report that they get irritated when they get a text message when they're busy (Lenhart et al. 2010). Adolescents expect rapid responses to texts or missed calls to their friends. Individuals who don't hear from their friends right away often feel slighted.

The continuous connection to others offered by technologically mediated communication may undermine adolescents' ability to develop a sense of independence and autonomy. Before deciding how they think or feel about something, teenagers request input from their friends. The friends, with cell phones at their sides, offer almost immediate feedback. Thus, among contemporary youths, there is little self-refection on situations or emotions that occurs in private (Turkle 2011).

Additional research is needed to determine how cell phones have shaped teens' social relationships. The social impact of Twitter, another form of electronic communication popular among adolescents and young adults, is also in need of more systematic investigation. Despite its asymmetrical nature (communication is not reciprocal), research suggests that Twitter may promote social integration and provide participants with a sense of community (Gruzd, Wellman, and Takhteyev 2011).

CHAPTER SUMMARY

The literature on personal relationships is diverse and encompasses contributions from each of three faces of sociological social psychology. Symbolic interactionist analyses have pointed to the social origin of people's relationship expectations and how power affects the negotiation of roles within an emerging relationship. Within the group processes and structures tradition, social exchange theorists have identified factors associated with relationship commitment. Focusing on changing norms concerning college students' dating, the increasing acceptability of same-sex marriage and cohabitation, and the advent of computer-mediated technologies, social psychologists working within the social structure and personality face of social psychology have illustrated the ways that broader social forces shape the content of people's relationships. Together with psychological research on the nature of love and attraction, these analyses provide a comprehensive body of knowledge about a central feature of social life—our ties to others. Although things have changed in recent years, especially with the advent of computer-mediated forms of communication, research suggests that the content and trajectory of personal relationships have not been radically altered.

Key Points to Know

- **Personal relationships (including romantic partnerships and friendships) involve interdependency between participants and the acknowledgement of people's unique characteristics.** Partners in an interpersonal relationship treat one another as individuals and not solely as occupants of statuses.

- **There are six different types, or styles, of love (eros, mania, storage, pragma, ludus, and agape). Passionate or romantic love, which is likely to be the most intense among individuals high in eros or mania, has physiological, as well as cultural, components.** Due to their similar characteristics, the institution of marriage helps to perpetuate the romantic love myth within this culture. Both marriage and romantic love are all-or-none propositions and are expected to last forever.

- **Symbolic interactionists have linked children's interactions with peers to adults' expectations for romantic relationships.** In romantic relationships, females focus more on emotional intimacy and verbal self-disclosure than their male counterparts, who emphasize sex and shared activities.

- **Dating norms have changed on college campuses, and sex outside of a committed relationship is more common now than in the past.** Despite this, young adults' heterosexual sexual and dating relationships may not be substantially different from those of the previous generation.

- **Social exchange theorists have shown that college students value warmth and kindness, expressiveness and openness, and a good sense of humor in both their same- and opposite-sex friends.** Physical attractiveness and intelligence are also viewed as important characteristics in friends of the opposite sex.

- **Personal relationships have a trajectory that is consistent across individuals and includes the following stages: initiation; an initial stage where people get to know one another; role negotiation; maintenance; and, in some cases, dissolution.** First impressions are important in that they tend to be fairly stable. Thus, the factors associated with people's initial assessments of others have received a lot of attention within the social psychological literature.

- **Common perceptual biases, processes of primary interest to psychological social psychologists, affect whom people find attractive. Propinquity also plays an important role in the initiation of personal relationships and cultural and group norms determine who is, and is not, a viable relationship partner.** Family members and friends serve as agents of informal control when it comes to our relationships. Selecting a romantic partner, or even a friend, who others we care about disapprove of is likely to make us feel guilty or shameful.

- **People embarking upon a relationship get to know one another through a process of mutual self-disclosure.** Disclosing too much, or disclosures regarded as inappropriate based upon their content, may have negative consequences.

- **Power affects the negotiation of roles within an emerging relationship.** The two structural sources of power in marital relationships are gender and socioeconomic resources. Relational sources of power include who likes or loves the other more and who has more alternative partners.

- **Much of the literature on relationship maintenance comes from within the social exchange tradition. Studies suggest that commitment is highest in romantic relationships when people love their partner, have few alternative partners, and they are satisfied with the relationship.**

- **Factors associated with divorce include race (Black higher than White, Hispanic higher than Asian), having a low level of education, and partner behaviors that reduce relationship benefits.** The attractiveness of alternative partners is less predictive of divorce than it is of the breakup of committed nonmarital relationships. The main consequence of divorce for children is that it increases their own risk for divorce by reducing the likelihood that they view marriage as a lifelong commitment.

- **Research suggests that same-sex couples are similar to their heterosexual counterparts when it comes to the content of their relationships, that cohabitation among heterosexual couples has not replaced marriage, and that the Internet has more positive than negative social consequences.**

Terms and Concepts for Review

Agape	Ludus
Altercasting	Maintenance stage
Cohabitation effect	Mania
Companionate love	Matching hypothesis
Core ties	Mere exposure effect
Dissolution stage	Negotiation stage
Endogamous marriage	Nonmutual alternatives
Eros	Passionate love
"Fag" talk	Personal relationships
Friendships	Physical intimacy
Friends with benefits	Pragma
Fundamental attribution error	Propinquity
Halo effect	Relational basis of power
Homophily	Romantic relationships
Hooking up	Sexual double standard
Hookup culture	Significant ties
Initiation stage	Storage
Intimacy	Structural basis of power
Love styles	

Questions for Review and Reflection

1. Compare research on the expectations people have for their friends and romantic partners conducted by symbolic interactionists with studies on this topic conducted by social exchange theorists. Discuss the ways these approaches to the study of personal relationships differ in their focus and the potentially complimentary nature of the research findings across the two traditions.

2. Think about your current romantic partner or, if you're single, your best friend. How did you initially meet? Discuss the extent that propinquity, norms, and perceptual tendencies increased the likelihood that the two of you would establish a personal relationship.

3. Describe the relationship between power and the negotiation of roles in a relationship. How have increases in educational attainment and labor-force participation among women and changes in gender roles in the past 50 years influenced the balance of power in heterosexual romantic relationships?

4. What are your personal experiences with the Internet? Do you think it has impacted your life in a positive way? Compare your assessment with the research literature on the social and psychological consequences of Internet use.

CHAPTER 12

Prejudice and Discrimination

PHOTO 12.1

Oblio and his dog Arrow (*The Point*, 1971)

The animated film *The Point* (1971) is a fable about a round-headed child, Oblio, who stands out because everyone else has a cone-shaped head. In order to fit in, he wears a pointed hat. However, because Oblio is different, he is ultimately banished from his village. Upon his return, he grows a point, but everyone else loses theirs and becomes rounded. The point of the story (this kind of play in words is a central part of the film's narration) is that societies change, what is perceived as good or bad is subjectively rather than objectively determined, and that individuals shouldn't be devalued or discriminated against based upon how they look or because they are different from others.

Given its positive message, presented in a way that children can easily under-stand, *The Point* was often used in elementary schools in the 1970s to introduce the topic of diversity. Although the animation may be regarded as rudimentary given current standards, it has a catchy soundtrack by Harry Nilsson (a famous singer-songwriter from that era), who also wrote the story. Dustin Hoffman was the film's original narrator. (Note that the version of the film currently being sold is narrated by former Beatle Ringo Starr.)

In the post-civil rights era, diversity and acceptance have become a part of public discourse within this culture. Although these are laudable goals, social psy-chologists argue that we still have a way to go. Talking about prejudice and dis-crimination, without widespread structural change, is not likely to significantly alter the nature of intergroup relations within this society and the existence of social inequality.

How much of a problem are prejudice and discrimination within the United States, and how can prejudice and discrimination within this society be reduced? We address these issues in this chapter, drawing on research from within each of the three faces of sociological social psychology and, where relevant, studies conducted by social psychologists trained in psychology.

Much of the social psychological research on prejudice and discrimination focuses on race/ethnicity. These are the studies we emphasize in this chapter (recall that a number of studies pertaining to gender discrimination were covered in earlier chapters). Racial/ethnic prejudice and discrimination are important topics for socio-logical social psychologists because, like gender, race/ethnicity is a major dimension of stratification within this society.

IMPORTANT CONCEPTS

You are already familiar with some of the terms social psychologists use when study-ing prejudice and discrimination based on race/ethnicity, such as race (a group regarded as distinct due to characteristics that are *perceived* to be genetic in origin) and ethnicity (a group *perceived* as distinct due to cultural factors). A related con-cept, **minority**, is a status conferred based on a group's socioeconomic standing, not numbers. Minority groups lack access to important societal resources and are, as a result, toward the bottom of society's stratification hierarchy. Thus, women are considered a minority group. African Americans, Native Americans, and Latinos are some of the racial and ethnic minority groups that have been studied by sociological social psychologists.

The ethnic category Latino includes individuals of Latin American descent, including Mexicans, Puerto Ricans, Cubans, and individuals from other Spanish-speaking cultures. (The term "Latino," "Latina" for women, and "Hispanic" are often used interchangeably.) Latinos and other racial/ethnic minority groups are viewed as different from the dominant group (non-Hispanic Whites) and are often the targets of negative attitudes and poor treatment.

There are some other groups defined as racial/ethnic minorities because they are subject to similar patterns, even though they are not, on average, socioeconomically disadvantaged. These groups include Asian Americans, as a general category, because some Asian Americans (e.g., Pacific Islanders) have few socioeconomic resources, and Jews.

The virtues of the dominant group often become the vices of minority groups whose relative economic standing is perceived as threatening to members of the dominant group. **Moral alchemy** is the perceptual process through which the same behavior is seen as positive when it is exhibited by members of one group and negative when it's exhibited by members of another group, typically one that is the target of prejudice and discrimination within the broader society. For example, members of the dominant group (White Christians) are viewed as hardworking, driven, and thrifty, whereas Jews who engage in the same behaviors are perceived as competitive, ruthless, and stingy (Merton 1948). These unfounded overgeneralizations are examples of cultural stereotypes.

We defined stereotypes in Chapter 4 as cognitive structures (schemas) composed of beliefs about members of particular groups and their attributes, which affect the way people process information and what they remember. Racial/ethnic stereotypes affect how members of certain groups are perceived and influence people's affective reactions to the individuals they encounter.

Status beliefs pertaining to race/ethnicity are the hierarchical component of racial/ethnic stereotypes because they are rank ordered from low (or bad) to high (or good). Status beliefs associate negative attributes (e.g., low ability and laziness) with racial/ethnic minorities and positive attributes (e.g., high ability and industriousness) with Whites. As noted in earlier chapters, sociological social psychologists do not believe that these assessments are true. They simply recognize their existence as societal patterns (Berger, Rosenholtz, and Zelditch 1980).

There are other aspects of racial/ethnic stereotypes that are not hierarchical. For example, a preference for certain foods is often associated with membership in a particular racial/ethnic group. However, racial/ethnic stereotypes are largely hierarchical in nature in that one group is viewed as inferior, the other as superior. Thus, they coincide with and are presumed to serve as the basis for prejudice (Bodenhausen and Richeson 2010).

Most of us have an understanding of racial/ethnic prejudice as it occurs at the individual level. It's a term we often encounter in everyday conversation or read or hear about in the news. At the micro level, prejudice is a feeling about individuals who belong to a group (often a racial/ethnic group) other than one's own. People make judgments about out-group members without knowing anything about them personally. Thus, prejudice is an attitude based on an overgeneralization, as it applies to all members of a target group without regard for individual variation within that group (Fiske 1998). This is the definition of prejudice typically used within the psychological literature.

Sociological social psychologists define prejudice in more macro terms. Symbolic interactionist Herbert Blumer (1958) emphasizes the importance of perceived advantage in the creation and perpetuation of racial/ethnic prejudice. From this perspective, **prejudice** is a collective sentiment that emerges from the relationship between groups within society, and the shared perception of superiority among members of the dominant group that transcends the feelings of any one individual. Although there is often substantial variability in what dominant group members believe and feel about members of a subordinate group, they share a sense of the position of this group relative to their own. Racial/ethnic prejudice is this shared feeling of superiority among members of the dominant racial/ethnic group (i.e., Whites) within society.

This is the definition of prejudice that we use throughout the chapter. When talking about racial/ethnic prejudice at the micro level, we use the term "negative racial attitudes," or we say prejudice at the individual level. Individuals with **negative racial attitudes** are demonstrating individual-level (or micro-level) prejudice.

Like racial prejudice, self-esteem reflects macro-level, as well as micro-level, processes. As discussed in the section on social identity theory in Chapter 5, social identity theorists argue that people form social identities (us vs. them) in part so that they can feel good about themselves. Consistent with Blumer's (1958) perspective on prejudice, social identity theorists argue that it is the shared desire for self-enhancement (the desire to increase self-esteem) on the part of members of the dominant group (Whites) that underlies the maintenance of racial prejudice within society (Bobo 1999).

Institutional Discrimination and Racism

Whereas prejudice is a feeling that exists within individuals, discrimination is a behavior. Racial/ethnic **discrimination** occurs when someone is treated in a particular way because of his or her race/ethnicity. Discrimination is often a micro-level phenomenon (i.e., it's an action committed by one individual toward another). However, discrimination also occurs at the societal level. Often discrimination results from the way social institutions (e.g., the education system, the criminal justice system, and the political system) operate. This kind of discrimination, which occurs at the societal level, usually on a large scale, is called **institutional discrimination**.

The Anti-Drug Abuse Act of 1986, which required harsher minimal mandatory sentences for the possession of crack cocaine than for cocaine in its powder form, is an example of institutional discrimination. The sentencing disparity under this law was 100 to 1. This means that to get the same minimal sentence as someone arrested for possessing 1 gram of crack cocaine, a person would have to have 100 grams of powder cocaine when they were arrested. Among cocaine users, African Americans are more likely to use crack, whereas Whites favor powder. This is largely due to economic resources: powder cocaine is more expensive than crack. Thus, among individuals arrested for possessing the same amount of cocaine, Blacks were more likely to be sent to prison and were given longer sentences than their White counterparts.

The gap in the minimum mandatory sentence for crack versus powder cocaine was reduced to a ratio of 18 to 1 by the Fair Sentencing Act of 2010. However, the law still results in harsher penalties for African Americans than Whites who engage in the same behavior, an outcome one Massachusetts judge called "both unjust and racist" (Liptak 2011:A12).

Racism is commonly defined as the belief that racial/ethnic minority groups are inferior to Whites. However, sociological social psychologists argue that racism is not just inside people's heads. It is embedded within the structure of society. From this standpoint, racism refers to negative racial attitudes and discriminatory behaviors that are consistent with broader institutional patterns. Thus, members of racial/ethnic minority groups can have negative attitudes toward, or discriminate against, Whites, but this is not indicative of racism. This is because prejudice or discrimination on the part of racial/ethnic minorities is not consistent with, and thus does not help reproduce, society's power structure. (Similarly, gender-based discrimination against men is not sexism because it goes against broader institutional patterns and does not reinforce existing social inequalities.)

This definition of racism focuses on the consequences of behavior and not the behavior itself, outside of its social context. Thus, it acknowledges an important fact: the same action does not always have the same outcome. Having to pay a $5,000 fine will be of much less consequence to a millionaire than to someone with no savings who lives paycheck to paycheck.

To illustrate this proposition as it pertains to race/ethnicity, we focus on relations between African Americans and Whites. Discrimination against African Americans by Whites is more damaging than discrimination perpetrated by African Americans against Whites. This is due to patterns of inequality at the macro level. Whites have more money and power than African Americans, which means that their discriminatory behaviors will have more negative outcomes. For example, discriminatory hiring practices that are unfavorable to African Americans on the part of White managers are more damaging in their consequences than discriminatory hiring practices unfavorable to Whites on the part of African American managers. This is because most managers are White (82% as of 2010) and because African Americans, but not Whites, are likely to be discriminated against in other social contexts. This makes their exclusion from any given job more costly.

Acknowledging this distinction, sociological social psychologists define **racism** as prejudice and discrimination, at both the individual and institutional level, directed toward members of racial and ethnic minority groups. Cultural stereotypes about the characteristics of racial and ethnic minorities (but not Whites, due to their advantaged position in the stratification hierarchy) are also considered racist.

What Do You Think?

Is it considered acceptable for an African American comedian to make jokes that portray Whites in a negative way? What if a White comedian told jokes that were derogatory toward African Americans? Why are these situations different?

STATUS BELIEFS AND BEHAVIOR

In order to understand the effects of race/ethnicity on people's perception and behavior, it is important to understand the nature of the broader societal context within which they occur. Much of the research literature on status characteristics theory within the group processes and structures tradition focuses on how societal beliefs about gender translate into patterns of bias, through negative performance expectations and evaluations, in small groups encounters.

Status beliefs pertaining to race/ethnicity have similar effects on perception and behavior in group settings. Due to status generalization processes (people in groups assume that Whites will be better than members of racial/ethnic minority groups at the task at hand), Whites are given more opportunities to contribute to the group task and their input is viewed more favorably than that of racial/ethnic minorities. This serves to reproduce racial/ethnic inequalities because people evaluated favorably are given more opportunities to participate, and so forth. At the macro level, these inequalities reproduce the status beliefs that create them (Goar and Sell 2005; Webster and Driskell 1978).

Status beliefs may also affect the self-concepts, and the behaviors, of the individuals they denigrate. In their classic study on the effects of stereotypes on test performance among college undergraduates, Steele and Aronson (1995) found that Black students scored lower than White students on a version of the Graduate Record Exam (GRE), a test required for admission into most doctoral programs. However, this occurred only when the study subjects were told prior to taking the test that it measured intellectual ability. When Black and White students in a second experimental condition were given instructions indicating that the test was a problem-solving task unrelated to intellectual ability, there were no race differences in students' test scores.

It is status beliefs concerning the academic abilities of Blacks versus Whites, the hierarchical component of cultural stereotypes pertaining to race/ethnicity, which underlie this effect, called stereotype threat. **Stereotype threat** refers to recognition on the part of individuals that anything they do has the potential to confirm a negative stereotype about their group. This induces anxiety, which undermines their performance, resulting in a self-fulfilling prophecy.

Stereotype threat is a process that can affect anyone, insofar as they are in a setting (e.g., school or work) where negative stereotypes about a group to which they belong are salient. However, African Americans and Latinos are especially vulnerable to this process given the nature of prevailing cultural stereotypes that rank them lower on intelligence than other groups. Using data from a nationally representative sample of college freshman (n = approximately 4,000), Massey and Fischer (2005) found that stereotype threat significantly reduced grades among African Americans and Latinos relative to Whites and Asians. Stereotype threat was measured as the degree to which students believed in cultural stereotypes about their racial/ethnic group and felt that others shared this view.

ATTITUDES AND BEHAVIOR

In addition to studying the stereotype-behavior relationship, social psychologists have examined the link between negative racial attitudes (prejudice) and discrimination. There have been many studies that have focused on this topic over the years. Overall, they suggest that the relationship between prejudice and discrimination at the individual level is weaker than one might think. On average, negative racial attitudes explain only about 13% of the variation in discriminatory behavior (Schutz and Six 1996).

This isn't surprising when one considers the social psychological literature on the attitude-behavior relationship more generally. Research dating back to the 1930s (LaPiere 1934) consistently shows that attitudes don't predict how people act (Ajzen and Fishbein 2005).

The Effect of Social Norms

Most of our behaviors are shaped by normative constraints, regardless of how we feel (LaPiere 1934). Because overt discrimination is considered inappropriate in most social contexts, many Whites avoid engaging in this type of behavior when it is clear to others and to themselves that this is what they are doing.

Whites are especially likely to discriminate against African Americans when social norms defining appropriate behavior are unclear. For example, Whites are less likely to help an African American than a White individual in need of assistance before, but not after, a request for help is made. An explicit request for help makes it clear that helping is an appropriate response. Failing to do so would be in violation of a norm.

Whites also tend to discriminate against African Americans when they can justify their discriminatory behavior by focusing on non-race-related factors. For example, White subjects in groups who witness an emergency are less likely to offer assistance when the victim is Black than when the victim is White because they can justify nonintervention by assuming that others will help (i.e., diffusion of responsibility serves as a rationalization for not helping a Black person). Rates of helping do not vary by the race of the victim when White subjects are the sole witness of the emergency (as cited in Gaertner and Dovidio 1986).

Pressures Toward Similarity

Pressures toward similarity also influence the behaviors of individuals in positions of power, especially when the outcomes of their decisions are uncertain. Remember Kanter's (1977) analysis of race- and gender-based discrimination in a large, hierarchical company? We discussed this study in detail in the section on work in Chapter 4. Within the company Kanter studied, almost all of the top-level managers were White males. Although these White men did not harbor explicitly prejudiced attitudes toward racial and ethnic minorities or women, when deciding whom to promote, they consistently chose other White males. They did so because they felt comfortable with these individuals. The managers felt they could trust other White males to interpret and respond to situations the way that they would. As a consequence, even in the absence of explicit prejudice, racial/ethnic minorities and women were locked out of the upper rungs of management. This is a further testament to the fact that individuals need not have overtly negative racial attitudes in order to engage in discriminatory behavior.

Evidence That Behaviors Predict Attitudes

There is also ample evidence that individuals' behaviors, whatever their source, shape their attitudes, and not the reverse. According to **self-perception theory** (Bem 1967, 1972), our behaviors provide us with information about our internal states, including our feelings. The central tenet of self-perception theory is that people observe their own behaviors, much like they observe the behaviors of others, and assume that they hold attitudes that are consistent with their actions. Behavior shapes attitudes mainly in situations where people can't find an external cause for their behavior and are not aware of any strong preferences. When this is the case, they make an **internal attribution** and locate the cause of their behavior within themselves (Bem 1967).

Self-perception theory was developed within psychological social psychology as an alternative to the theory of cognitive dissonance. Recall that cognitive dissonance is the negative tension that arises when people behave in a way that is inconsistent with their attitudes. The theory of cognitive dissonance states that people alleviate this tension by changing their attitudes so that they match their behaviors (Festinger 1957).

Numerous studies (mostly laboratory experiments) designed to induce a particular type of behavior show that individuals form attitudes that are consistent with their actions (Cooper 2007). For example, in a series of experiments focusing on racial attitudes (Leippe and Eisenstadt 1994), White college students assigned at random to write an essay in favor of giving a higher percentage of scholarship money to Blacks at their school, and thus a lower percentage of scholarship money to White students, had more positive feelings about African Americans after completing the essay than other study subjects.

Whether cognitive dissonance or self-perception theory better explains the effect of behavior on attitudes has been heavily debated. Self-perception theory may be a better explanation for the effect of behavior on attitudes when people do not have strong feelings about the issue at hand to begin with, or their behavior is only marginally inconsistent with their initial feelings. Cognitive dissonance, on the other hand, may better explain the effect of behavior on attitudes when people do have strong preferences that run counter to their actions (Fazio, Zanna, and Cooper 1977). In either case, there is agreement that behaviors often precede attitudes. This has implications that we discuss in the section on intervention at the end of this chapter.

THE CURRENT RACIAL CLIMATE

The following quotations are from a qualitative study of the work experiences of African American pilots. Three of the men interviewed for the study made the following statements about encounters they had on or related to their job. The text is verbatim from the authors' transcribed interviews and is presented, as such, in their article, with the interviewer's questions in brackets:

> I was like, "Well did you think this was going to be a problem having two black students?" And he was like, "Well honestly, yeah. I did. Nobody told me you guys were black, I saw you guys come out the elevator, I was like, Aw shit. Black guys." So we're just kind of looking at him like, "For real?" "It's crazy because I thought you guys wouldn't know anything, and that I was going to have to lower the bar to get you through! I didn't know black people could learn."
>
> —Young African-American male, discussing a recent encounter with an instructor

> Yes. I had a passenger leave the plane. [Why?] She didn't want to be flown by a black person. Out of Waco. [How do you know that?] Cause she said it.
>
> —First Officer, talking about a recent airplane passenger

> I do have to suppress my emotions at work. You can't be seen as having angry black man syndrome! [Which is what?] Every time your emotions are being worked up— some [white] people take greater offense. . . . If they've never been ordered or told to do something by a woman or a person of color, it becomes a problem.
>
> —Pilot, Captain, discussing his relationships at work over past ten years and his attempts to manage his emotions

You might be wondering what year this study was conducted. These data were collected in 2010–2011! The citation for the article is Evans and Feagin (2012).

Despite the fact that most Whites today would deny that they have negative attitudes toward racial/ethnic minorities, or that people's race affects how they treat them, racial/ethnic minorities report incidents of discrimination across social settings (Deitch et al. 2003; Gallup 2001; Langer and Craighill 2009). Moreover, controlled experiments show that an individual's race or ethnicity routinely affects the decisions of people in positions of power in schools (Elhoweris et al. 2005), medical evaluations (Schulman et al. 2009), and job interviews.

Race/Ethnic Discrimination in Hiring Decisions

In two recent field experiments (Pager and Western 2012) conducted in Milwaukee, Wisconsin, and in New York City, researchers measured discrimination based on race in the hiring process. The eight testers in Milwaukee were Black and White males, age 21 to 24, who were similar in height, weight, physical attractiveness, verbal skills, and self-presentational styles. They were also given equivalent educational backgrounds, employment histories, and local residences. The same was true for the ten testers in New York City, who were either Black, Latino, or White. Altogether, the testers in the two studies visited close to 700 employers (350 in Milwaukee and 340 in New York) while ostensibly applying for entry-level jobs listed in city newspapers.

The independent variable in both studies was the race of the job applicant, and the dependent variable was whether the applicant was called for a second interview or given the job. To control for the number of applications placed, the dependent variable was measured as the percentage of callbacks received out of the total number of employers visited by individuals within each racial category.

The results were consistent across the two experiments and showed substantial discrimination, especially toward African Americans. In Milwaukee, 34% of the White applicants, versus 14% of the equally qualified Black applicants, received callbacks from potential employers. White applicants also received more callbacks than equally qualified Latino applicants in the New York study, although the lowest percentage of callbacks was among Blacks (14%, vs. 25% for Latinos and 31% for Whites).

Interestingly, follow-up surveys completed by the testers indicated the Black and Latino job applicants were unaware of any negative perceptions on the part of potential employers. This suggests that the employers were hiding their biases and refutes the notion that racial/ethnic minorities are likely to interpret ambiguous responses from others as indicative of discrimination.

The notion that minorities overreport incidents of discrimination is often used to challenge the validity of the results of self-report data on discrimination from surveys (as noted earlier, these studies indicate that racial/ethnic minorities experience discrimination in many settings). The results of the two field experiments on racial/ethnic discrimination in the hiring process suggest that the survey results are accurate and that overreporting of discrimination is not an issue (Pager and Western 2012).

What Do You Think?

- How might you conduct an experiment to test racial discrimination?
  1. What setting would you focus on? Choose a context that is different from those discussed in the previous section.
  2. How would you measure your independent and dependent variables?
  3. What results would you expect?
  4. What is the main strength of this kind of study? What are its limitations?
- Consider completing this exercise with one or two of your classmates.

Proportional Representation as an Indicator of Discrimination

Discrimination experiments are useful because they provide concrete evidence of bias in specific settings. However, as you may have discovered in the exercise you just completed, it isn't always easy, or even possible, to assess the presence of discrimination using an experiment. Only a relatively narrow range of behaviors and encounters can be studied in this manner. Given this, researchers often use **proportional representation** to assess racial fairness at the organizational, regional, or national level.

A group is proportionally represented in a particular domain (e.g., a school or an occupation) when the percentage of people from a particular racial/ethnic group in that context matches the percentage of people from that group who live in the United States. Groups from which there are proportionally fewer people in the target domain than in the population as a whole are underrepresented, whereas groups that exceed their percentage in the population are overrepresented.

African Americans are overrepresented in prisons, given their frequency of drug use. In 2005, only 12% of illegal drug users were African American, but 34% of the individuals arrested for drug offenses, and 45% of the individuals in state prisons for drug offenses, were Black (Mauer 2009). These statistics reveal a significant bias in the criminal justice system, due in part to the 1986 federal minimal sentencing law.

African Americans are also overrepresented in police traffic stops due to the process referred to as racial profiling. **Racial profiling** is a police practice in which individuals are targeted (e.g., stopped or searched following a traffic stop) because of their race or ethnicity (Warren and Farrell 2009). The term also applies to the screening of individuals in airports, where people whose appearance or surnames are perceived to be like those of Arabs or Muslims are treated as potential terrorists (Bonikowski 2005).

Most research studies of racial profiling have focused on traffic stops and searches. These analyses show that racial profiling exists, and that Black males are the most common targets of this practice (Brunson and Miller 2006; Warren et al. 2006; Weitzer and Tuch 2004).

TABLE 12.1 *Educational Attainment by Race/Ethnicity, United States 2010*	RACE/ETHNICITY	WHITE	BLACK	HISPANIC	ASIAN OR PACIFIC ISLANDER*
	College degree or more	30.3%	19.8%	13.9%	52.4%

*Pacific islanders are individuals of Micronesian, Melanesian, and Polynesian heritage, including Native Hawaiians, Samoans, and Guamanians.

Note: U.S. Census Bureau, Statistical Abstract of the United States (2012; table 221, p. 151).

In 2010, Arizona passed a law requiring police officers to assess the immigration status of anyone encountered in a routine stop (traffic and otherwise) who is suspected of being an illegal immigrant. This law is highly contentious. Those who oppose the recent Supreme Court ruling (it upheld the law in June 2012) have argued that the Arizona law is a violation of people's civil rights and that it facilitates racial profiling.

If society were egalitarian, there would be no racial profiling or other racial/ethnic biases in the criminal justice system. Racial/ethnic minorities would also be proportionally represented in colleges and universities and among the highest status occupations. As shown in Table 12.1, people of color are underrepresented in higher education. The same is true in high-status occupations (Table 4.2, p. 120).

Race/ethnicity also determines where people live. Neighborhood segregation is often socioeconomic in origin because social class and race/ethnicity are highly correlated, and where people live is determined, in part, by their economic resources. However, even among the middle class, there is substantial residential segregation among Blacks and Whites in metropolitan areas across the country. This is because middle-class Blacks are proportionately underrepresented in middle-class neighborhoods, due largely to housing discrimination (Adelman 2004).

Despite ample evidence that discrimination is common at the individual and at the institutional level, most Whites fail to recognize how prevailing societal patterns limit the opportunities of racial and ethnic minorities. Contemporary attitudes toward racial and ethnic minorities, and the beliefs upon which they are based, tend to reflect unconscious biases and emphasize individual over societal causes of racial/ethnic inequality.

Cognitive Biases and Contemporary Racial Attitudes

Psychological social psychologists often study cognitive processes. Within this research literature, a number of studies indicate that people process information pertaining to race/ethnicity in a biased manner. For example, researchers have shown that people associate central aspects of the American identity with Whiteness (Devos and Benaji 2005). They call this the **American = White bias**.

Much of the American = White effect occurs at the subconscious level and can be measured using implicit associations. **Implicit associations** are characteristics people associate with members of particular groups, even though they are unaware that they are doing so. For instance, people more readily associate American symbols (like the flag, a dollar bill, and Mount Rushmore) with Whites than with Blacks or Asians. Psychological social psychologists have documented this bias by measuring the amount of time it takes and the accuracy with which experimental subjects are able to classify sets of stimuli presented to them on a computer screen (Devos and Benaji 2005).

Implicit and Explicit Attitudes

Even individuals who don't think they are prejudiced tend to harbor these unconscious biases. Moreover, without being aware of it, people in this society prefer Whites to members of other racial/ethnic groups, even when levels of familiarity are held constant to rule out the mere exposure effect described in the previous chapter (Dasgupta et al. 2000).

Although this bias is stronger among Whites than among racial/ethnic minorities, even the latter individuals tend to show a preference for Whites (Livingston 2002). This is a reflection of dominant cultural beliefs and patterns of socialization. Almost everyone within this society, regardless of his or her race/ethnicity, absorbs the prevailing cultural belief that Whites are the superior group. (We discuss some of the ways in which many minority parents combat this bias during our discussion of the primary socialization process later in this chapter.)

The results of a large-scale nationally representative study of racial attitudes in the United States by the Associated Press (n = 1,071) illustrate the pervasiveness of this pattern. Participants, selected at random, were initially contacted by phone or by mail and were given the survey online. Individuals who did not have a computer were provided with a laptop and an Internet connection at no cost to them (GfK Group 2012).

The online survey included a segment in which participants rated neutral images as either less pleasant or more pleasant. The images were rated after faces of people of different races briefly appeared on the computer screen. Prior research has shown that pictures of faces elicit emotions that are readily misattributed to other stimuli. Thus, the picture of a face that someone is shown right before rating a neutral image (i.e., an image that does not itself trigger an emotion) is likely to influence how favorably he or she rates that image. Having people rate neutral images immediately after being exposed to pictures of the faces of Black and of White people is, then, a way to measure their unconscious, or implicit, attitudes toward race. People who rate neutral images more negatively after seeing Black faces are considered to have negative attitudes toward African Americans. Fifty-six percent of the respondents to the 2012 Associated Press survey showed negative attitudes toward African Americans on the implicit attitudes test just described (Pasek, Krosnick, and Tompson 2012).

Take a Break

- Listen to an NPR broadcast about people's unconscious attitudes about race and how they are measured at the following web address: http://www.npr.org/templates/story/story.php?storyId=93137786.
  This July 31, 2008, radio broadcast can also be accessed from the NPR website (npr.org) by selecting *Talk of the Nation,* under programs, and All Dates. In the search box, type **implicit attitudes**.
- Go to the following Harvard University website: https://implicit.harvard.edu/implicit/. Take the Implicit Association Test (IAT) for race (Black-White). Choose a second IAT (e.g., on gender, age, disability, sexuality, etc.) and complete that test.

In addition, 51% of the Associated Press poll participants showed explicitly negative attitudes toward Blacks (Agiesta and Ross 2012). These attitudes were measured using questions like the following items, from Henry and Sears's (2002) symbolic racism scale (response options are "strongly disagree" to "strongly agree").

> It's really a matter of some people just not trying hard enough; if Blacks would only try harder, they could be just as well off as whites.

> Irish, Italians, Jews, and other minorities overcame prejudice and worked their way up. Blacks should do the same without special favors (as cited in Pasek, Krosnick, and Thompson 2012).

Symbolic racism is manifest in the belief that Blacks' disadvantaged status stems from internal dispositions (e.g., an unwillingness to take responsibility for their lives) rather than structural inequalities. Thus, symbolic racism is associated with the perception that Blacks' desire for better treatment is unjustified and is intertwined with conservative values, the belief that individual will is the main factor that determines the course of people's lives, and negative emotions directed toward racial/ethnic minorities. This type of racism is called symbolic because its foundation is an abstract value system acquired in childhood, rather than actual social experiences, and because it applies to Blacks as a general category rather than to any particular individual (Henry and Sears 2002). Note that this form of (symbolic) racism is different from the more overt racism common among Whites in the 1950s (Bobo and Charles 2009), which had its roots in White support for racial segregation.

Status, Conflict, and Changes in Racial Attitudes

Negative attitudes toward African Americans (implicit or unconscious and explicit or conscious, in the form of symbolic racism) increased substantially between 2008 and 2012, presumably due to backlash resulting from the election of an African

American president. Although the Associated Press does not have nationally representative data pertaining specifically to this issue, many Black Americans have spoken publicly about the increased antagonism they have experienced on the part of Whites since Obama was elected (Agiesta and Ross 2012).

The U.S. presidency is a highly prestigious position. Thus, many people view its occupation by an African American as significant evidence that Blacks have advanced in terms of their standing within this society. This opinion, in turn, may be seen as evidence of a decline in the relative status of Whites.

This view may be exacerbated by current economic conditions (the housing crisis and the economic recession). Negative racial attitudes are often rooted in material concerns—in particular, conflict over scarce resources (e.g., jobs and housing). Thus, negative racial attitudes tend to be the most prevalent among Whites who have experienced, or are experiencing, declines in economic status.

Racial and ethnic minorities also serve as scapegoats for the frustration Whites experience during times of economic hardship (Hovland and Sears 1940). **Scapegoating** occurs when people misattribute their misfortunes to others, typically members of groups that lack status and power within the larger society (or, sometimes, groups that are perceived as having too much money or status, as in the case of Jews) (Allport 1954).

Negative racial attitudes and scapegoating tend to be especially prevalent in geographic regions in which there is a substantial minority population because this increases the perception on the part of Whites that they are in competition with other groups for scarce economic and political resources (Blalock 1967). This may explain White voting patterns in the 2012 presidential election. Obama received the smallest percentage of the White vote in Mississippi, the state with the largest percentage of Black voters, whereas he won the White vote in those states with the smallest percentage of minority voters (Maine, Iowa, New Hampshire, Oregon, Connecticut, and Washington State) (Blow 2012).

Beliefs About Racial Inequality

The perception that the Obama presidency is evidence that Blacks' relative status within U.S. society has increased may also reinforce the belief that achievement reflects individual, and not societal, factors. Rather than focusing on probabilities and patterns (Blacks as a group are significantly disadvantaged relative to Whites), people in this country may use Obama's success as an indicator of an equal playing field.

Data from the General Social Survey (2010), based on a nationally representative sample, indicate that the majority of White adults (52%) believe that a lack of motivation among racial/ethnic minorities is a major contributor to race differences in achievement in this society. Less than one third of White adults in this country (30%) recognize discrimination as a significant contributor to racial/ethnic stratification. From their perspective, race doesn't matter, and racial/ethnic inequality in socioeconomic standing is due to individual, not structural, factors. Blacks and Latinos (the two minority groups for which there are sufficient GSS data for analysis) are significantly more likely than

Whites to favor a structural (discrimination) over an individual (motivation) explanation for racial stratification (Smith, Marsden, and Hout 2011).

Whites' beliefs about the causes of racial inequality reflect what sociologist Eduardo Bonilla-Silva (Bonilla-Silva and Lewis 1999; Bonilla-Silva 2003) calls color-blind racism. **Color-blind racism** has two aspects: (1) the belief that everyone should be, and is, treated equally and (2) the failure to recognize the structural roots of prevailing patterns of racial/ethnic stratification. Color-blind racism does not acknowledge the persistence of racial/ethnic discrimination within this society and how it affects individuals' opportunities for social mobility.

This orientation can be measured with the Color-Blind Racial Attitudes Scale (CoBRAS). This index, presented in Box 12.1, has three dimensions: racial privilege (questions 1–7), institutional discrimination (questions 8–14), and blatant racial issues (questions 15–20). Low scores on each of these subscales indicate the acknowledgment of the structural roots of race differences in achievement, whereas high scores are indicative of color-blind racism (Neville et al. 2000).

Mean scores on the CoBRAS by race/ethnicity and by gender from a college sample are included in Box 12.1 for comparative purposes. Latinos and African Americans are less likely than Whites to exhibit color-blind racial attitudes because racial and ethnic minorities are more aware of the pervasiveness of discrimination within contemporary society (Bonilla-Silva and Embrick 2001).

Women tend to have lower CoBRAS scores than men. This may reflect gender differences in perspective taking. As you may recall from Chapter 6, among college students, women are more likely than men to try to see things from the perspectives of other people across social settings. Thus, they may be more sensitive to the fact that individuals who occupy different positions within society (e.g., individuals from different racial/ethnic groups and different class backgrounds) are likely to have social experiences that vary substantially from their own. Although there are no large-scale surveys assessing perspective taking and racial attitudes, experimental manipulations that increase perspective taking have been shown to reduce individual-level prejudice among both men and women (Todd et al. 2011).

Color-blind racial attitudes give rise to symbolic racism, described earlier. They serve as a cognitive schema, which people use to interpret information they encounter relevant to race in their day-to-day encounters. People who exhibit color-blind racism tend to harbor negative racial attitudes and view as unfair government policies that give preference to any group. Because they believe that race-based discrimination is no longer a problem within this society, they question the legitimacy of giving some groups (racial/ethnic minorities) an advantage over another group (Whites) through programs like affirmative action (Neville et al. 2002).

Affirmative action includes antidiscrimination policies that address current patterns of exclusion by increasing racial/ethnic minorities' and women's access to selective colleges and universities and to high-status, high-paying jobs. The college slots and jobs subject to affirmative action are those in which minorities and women are underrepresented, or would be underrepresented, without this policy (Darity,

Box 12.1   Measuring Color-Blind Racial Attitudes

The Color-Blind Racial Attitudes Scale consists of the following 20 items that respondents rate on a scale of 1 (strongly agree) to 6 (strongly disagree). There are three subscales, assessing different dimensions of color-blind racial attitudes: racial privilege, institutional discrimination, and blatant racial issues. Higher scores represent a greater level of support for a color-blind racial ideology.

Racial privilege: Items reflect blindness to the existence of White privilege.

1. White people in the United States have certain advantages because of the color of their skin.*
2. Race is very important in determining who is successful and who is not.*
3. Race plays an important role in who gets sent to prison.*
4. Race plays a major role in the type of social services (e.g., type of health care or day care) that people receive in the United States.*
5. Racial and ethnic minorities do not have the same opportunities as White people in the United States.*
6. Everyone who works hard, no matter what race they are, has an equal chance to become rich.
7. White people are more to blame for racial discrimination than racial and ethnic minorities.*

Institutional discrimination: Items represent a limited awareness of the implications of institutional forms of racism.

8. Social policies, such as affirmative action, discriminate unfairly against White people.
9. White people in the United States are discriminated against because of the color of their skin.
10. English should be the only official language in the United States.
11. Due to racial discrimination, programs such as affirmative action are necessary to help create equality.*
12. Racial and ethnic minorities in the United States have certain advantages because of the color of their skin.
13. It is important that people begin to think of themselves as American and not African American, Mexican American, or Italian American.
14. Immigrants should try to fit into the culture and values of the United States.

Blatant racial issues: Items represent a general unawareness of pervasive racial discrimination.

15. Racial problems in the United States are rare, isolated situations.
16. Talking about racial issues causes unnecessary tension.
17. Racism is a major problem in the United States.*
18. It is important for public schools to teach about the history and contributions of racial and ethnic minorities.*
19. It is important for political leaders to talk about racism to help work through or solve society problems.*
20. Racism may have been a problem in the past, but it is not an important problem today.

*These items should be coded in reverse so that high scores reflect greater adherence to a color-blind racist ideology.

SAMPLE MEANS AND STANDARD DEVIATIONS ON THE COBRAS (ALL 20 ITEMS)*		
	MEAN	SD
White (n = 397)	68.44	11.76
Black (n = 114)	65.52	11.97
Latino (n = 32)	62.25	11.95
Men (n = 285)	70.65	12.07
Women (n = 300)	64.12	11.49
Total (n = 592)	67.30	11.83

*Sample sizes vary slightly due to missing data.
Note: Neville et al. (2000).

Deshpande, and Weisskopf 2011). Whites are substantially less likely than racial/ethnic minorities to be in favor of affirmative action (Wilson 2006).

In general, whites tend to oppose government policies that would change the balance of power within society by providing more opportunities to racial/ethnic minorities. Color-blind racism, which underlies this mind set, facilitates the reproduction of structurally based racial inequalities, despite its explicit egalitarian basis (the belief that everyone should be treated equally). Thus, Bonilla-Silva (2003) defines color-blind racism as racism without racists (Bonilla-Silva 2003).

Applying a similar line of reasoning, sociologist Lawrence Bobo (Bobo, Kleugel, and Smith 1997) uses the term **laissez-faire racism** to describe the mismatch, common among Whites, in expressed racial attitudes (everyone is equal) and the lack of support for public policies that would lead to greater racial equality. Laissez-faire means "no government involvement." By failing to support the kinds of government policies necessary to significantly impact the economic and social standing of racial/ethnic minorities at the aggregate level, laissez-faire racial attitudes perpetuate racial inequality and make widespread social change unlikely. For those who believe in laissez-faire racism, racial discrimination with its resultant perpetuation of racial stratification is justified by the notion that racial and ethnic minorities do not work hard enough and are not deserving of special treatment (Bobo et al. 1997).

Application: College Students' Race Journals

In order to assess how current perceptions about race and public policy influence people's everyday social interactions, 60 college students taking a sociology course

PHOTO 12.2

Although interracial interactions are certainly more common than in the past, people's social networks tend to be racially homogeneous.

at a university in the western part of the United States completed journals in which they described how they encountered race in their everyday lives. Of these 60 students, 82% were White, and 18% were racial/ethnic minorities. Racial events that involved explicitly negative racial attitudes or blatant discrimination were coded as indicative of either **"traditional" racism** (overt racism, involving racial slurs and blatant discrimination, presumed to be more common in the pre-civil rights era) or as **"liberal" racism** (the more subtle symbolic racism, color-blind racism, and laissez-faire racism described earlier in this chapter).

Over half (51%) of the 951 journal entries described instances of traditional racism. In these accounts, students reported that their friends or parents made racist statements (e.g., one White woman's father expressed gratitude that her new boyfriend was White); that they felt a certain way about someone, usually a Black male, solely because of that individual's race (e.g., one woman felt afraid that a Black male in the computer lab would steal her backpack); or that they witnessed a minority individual being treated poorly in a public setting, such as a restaurant or pharmacy, or were themselves treated poorly if they were a minority.

Other accounts described blatantly racist behaviors, but the students were hesitant to interpret them in that manner. For instance, a woman who heard the grandmother of a friend ask how the "little nigger boys down the street were" rationalized this statement by noting that the grandmother was old and been raised in the South.

The remaining journal entries were coded as instances of the newer, more subtle forms of "liberal racism" because they documented instances in which Whites presented themselves as the victims of liberal racial policies. These entries described conversations among Whites about how difficult it was to get into medical school in the era of affirmative action, how Blacks have it easy because they are good athletes, and how unfair it is that school isn't held on Black but not on White holidays (this was in reference to Martin Luther King Day). Overall, students' journal entries suggest that both blatant and the more subtle forms of racism, reflected in the denial of White privilege, are daily occurrences (Zamudio and Rios 2006).

What Do You Think?

- Are the students' responses just described consistent with your experiences?
- Consider keeping a race journal for a week or two. If you do, record your observations of the situations you encounter in which race is relevant (because the setting is mixed-race or because people are talking about race). Don't analyze your data. Just document what you see and hear. After the time frame for making journal entries has passed, go back and analyze your observations. You should begin by placing each of your entries into one of three categories: (1) "traditional" (blatant) racism, (2) "liberal" (symbolic, color-blind, and laissez-faire) racism, or (3) no racism. Then look for themes across your entries.

SOCIAL STRUCTURE AND SOCIAL COGNITION

Working within the social structure and personality (SSP) face of sociological social psychology, Feagin (2010) puts people's racial experiences into a broader structural context in his discussion of racial framing. **Frames** are cognitive representations that enable people to make sense of situations and events by directing their attention to certain aspects of reality and away from others (Goffman 1974).

The White Racial Frame

According to Feagin (2010), the White racial frame plays a critical role in shaping people's understandings of race in this country. The **White racial frame** is composed of negative stereotypes of racial/ethnic minorities, especially African Americans; cultural narratives extolling "White virtues," such as hard work, achievement, superiority, and the ability to overcome adversity and resistance from others; visual and auditory imagery (notions of racial/ethnic differences in appearance and accents); and emotions (e.g., the association of negative feelings, including fear, with racial/ethnic minorities).

The White racial frame is like a cognitive schema in that Whites (and non-Whites seeking to adhere to White norms) use it to interpret situations and to construct courses of action. However, it also has external manifestations that transcend any given individual, including collective memories and histories about race relations within this society. It is through continuous repetition, both in micro-level interactions and at the societal level in the operation of social institutions and media representations, that the White racial frame becomes entrenched within people's brains.

The White racial frame can be traced back to colonial America. It emerged with the formation of this country as a rationalization for the exploitation of racial/ethnic minorities (both Native Americans and African Americans) by Whites. Thus, White racism is rooted in the foundation of American society. We often forget that the United States has been characterized by legal segregation and slavery for the majority (about 85%) of its history (Feagin 2010).

In his discussion of White racism, Feagin (2010) emphasizes the manner in which wealth begets wealth and how this has resulted in an accumulation of disadvantage experienced by African Americans over generations. In particular, he points to the source of much White wealth today—namely, the federal laws (the Homestead Acts) that gave 246 million acres of land to White families between the 1860s and 1930. The White racial frame does not acknowledge the advantages Whites gained from these programs, which is, in part, why color-blind racial attitudes are so prevalent within our society.

African Americans still serve as a primary target of White racism in this country. Similarly, racist views of Native Americans have changed little over the years and include the belief that they are lazy, criminal, animalistic, and (inhumanly) fierce warriors. This warrior imagery is still prevalent in sports at the high school, college, and professional level (See Box 12.2).

As noted in Chapter 1, Latinos are the fastest-growing minority group within the United States. Thus, the dominant racial framing of Latinos is about invasion. Prevailing stereotypes misportray members of this ethnic group as lazy and prone to crime (Feagin 2010), making immigrants seem especially threatening.

Cultural stereotypes about racial and ethnic minorities underlie Whites' negative feelings about members of these groups, which often exist at a subconscious level, and support the status quo. That is, they lead Whites to reject policies, like affirmative action, that could change the structure of society. This results in a self-fulfilling prophecy at the macro level.

Remember the Thomas theorem, presented in the section on Chicago school symbolic interactionism in Chapter 3: situations defined as real are real in their consequences, even when the initial assessment is inaccurate (Thomas and Thomas 1928). As you may recall, this theorem serves as the basis for the self-fulfilling prophecy at the individual level, demonstrated in research on the effects of labeling on people's self-concepts and subsequent behaviors.

In his classic paper on racial/ethnic prejudice, Merton (1948) discusses how Whites' racist beliefs and negative feelings about members of racial/ethnic minority groups create a set of circumstances at the aggregate level that are then used (through

Box 12.2   Native American Imagery in Sports

The Atlanta Braves (baseball), The Chicago Blackhawks (hockey, logo above), The Cincinnati Chiefs (baseball), The Kansas City Chiefs (football), The Washington Redskins (football).

These and other professional sports teams still have mascots and other team paraphernalia (e.g., cups or jackets with the team logo) that portray Native Americans in stereotypical and derogatory ways, like the caricature of the Native American shown here.

Many colleges and universities have eliminated or changed their mascot, most in response to a 2005 decision by the National College Athletic Association (NCAA) to ban schools with hostile Native American imagery from hosting championship games or from displaying their mascots during championship events (Staurowsky 2007). Administrators at colleges and universities that have kept Native American associated team names and mascots (some schools have dropped their mascot, while keeping their name) have argued that they are not hostile or derogatory. Alumni, as well as current students, identify with their sports teams and their symbols. Thus, there is often a concern that donations to the school will decrease if they are changed. This is the main reason why many schools continue to use Native American imagery and names.

Does your school have a Native American name and mascot for its sports team? How do you feel about the use of Native American imagery in sports? Would people's reactions be the same if someone used religious (e.g., Christian) imagery in this manner?

If you're interested, go to the following website for a thoughtful commentary on this issue by ESPN columnist Paul Lukas: http://espn.go.com/blog/playbook/fandom/post/_/id/12057/time-to-rethink-native-american-imagery.

PHOTO 12.3

Flag with the Chicago Blackhawks team logo

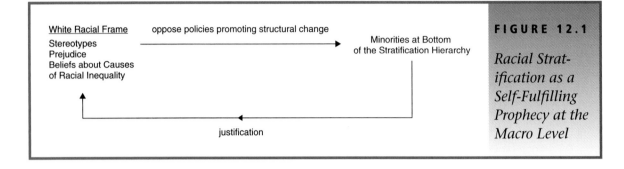

FIGURE 12.1

Racial Stratification as a Self-Fulfilling Prophecy at the Macro Level

faulty reasoning or logic) to justify the collective mind-set that created them. This **self-fulfilling prophecy at the societal level** is depicted in Figure 12.1. Although Merton didn't use this language, the beliefs and feelings he is talking about are similar to what Feagin (2010) calls the White racial frame.

The White racial frame continues to limit the opportunities given to Blacks and other disadvantaged minorities, even though discrimination based upon race is no longer legal. As a result, collectively, Blacks remain at the bottom of the stratification hierarchy. Whites see African Americans' location in the stratification hierarchy and assume that their beliefs about the inferiority of this group are justified. However, it is beliefs about the abilities of African Americans (and the negative emotions they generate) that lead to the rejection of the kinds of public policies necessary for these groups to experience widespread social mobility.

Counter-frames

Some Whites and members of racial/ethnic minority groups resist this orientation by adopting an alternative (counter) racial frame. In particular, the **antioppression counter-frame**, common among African Americans, has cognitive aspects concerning the structural basis of oppression, emotions such as moral outrage and the desire for change, and scripts for dealing with discrimination. However, African Americans who reject the White racial frame in favor of this antiracist frame are often denied the minimal socioeconomic resources available to African Americans who adhere to the views of the dominant culture. For this reason, there is strong pressure among African Americans to conform to the White racial frame (Feagin 2010).

Among African Americans, younger individuals are more likely than other age groups to hold beliefs consistent with the White racial frame. This pattern is shown in Figure 12.2, based on nationally representative data from the 2010 General Social Survey. As shown in the top half of Figure 12.2, among African Americans, members of the Millennial Generation are more likely than older age cohorts to attribute racial inequality to a lack of will and motivation, and less likely to believe it results from discrimination. Social attitudes and beliefs are usually more liberal among younger generations. The relationship between generation and beliefs about racial inequality among African Americans is the exception to this pattern. Among

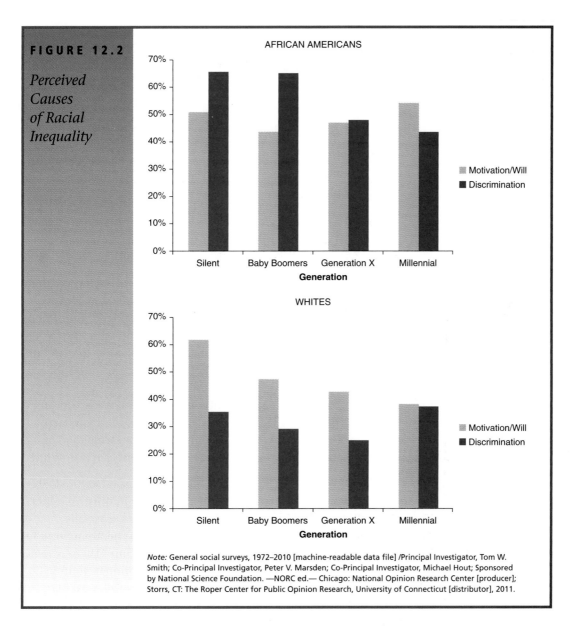

FIGURE 12.2

Perceived Causes of Racial Inequality

Note: General social surveys, 1972–2010 [machine-readable data file] /Principal Investigator, Tom W. Smith; Co-Principal Investigator, Peter V. Marsden; Co-Principal Investigator, Michael Hout; Sponsored by National Science Foundation. —NORC ed.— Chicago: National Opinion Research Center [producer]; Storrs, CT: The Roper Center for Public Opinion Research, University of Connecticut [distributor], 2011.

Whites, younger individuals have more liberal beliefs about race than older cohorts (Figure 12.2, bottom panel).

Q: What is the source of generational differences in African Americans' beliefs about the causes of racial inequality?

A: Bobo and associates (2012) suggest that generational differences in African Americans' beliefs about the roots of racial inequality may be due to:

- decreases in discrimination;
- decreases in young Blacks' sensitivity to discrimination;

- increases in the amount of time that has elapsed since the civil rights movement, which mobilized Blacks and increased their solidarity; or
- increases in the degree of variation in socioeconomic resources among the Black population.

In support of a socioeconomic resources explanation, the trend shown in Figure 12.2 is most evident among young Blacks who are highly educated (Bobo et al. 2012). However, it is important to note that, even among the Millennial Generation, on average, Whites (37%) are substantially less likely than Blacks (44%) to acknowledge the structural roots of racial inequality. This is because Whites are more likely to have internalized the White racial frame.

HOW RACIAL FRAMES ARE LEARNED

Racial frames are acquired in childhood, with other aspects of society's culture (Feagin 2010). Thus, parents play an important role in this socialization process.

Much of the empirical research on racial/ethnic socialization within the family has focused on racial/ethnic minorities. According to Hughes and associates' (2006) comprehensive review of this literature, the messages parents convey to their children about race/ethnicity fall into the following four categories:

1. *Egalitarianism.* Although there is variability across families, many African American parents emphasize racial equality and the importance of hard work and virtue. This pattern has also been noted among Latinos and other racial/ethnic minority groups, but it is rarely as prominent as it is in White households.

2. *Preparation for bias.* Discrimination is a theme in some minority parents' discussions with their children. These conversations are especially common in African American households and serve as the foundation for alternatives to the culturally dominant White racial frame. There is some evidence that parents' personal experiences with discrimination influence how much they invest in preparing their children for racial bias. In general, research suggests that being prepared for racial bias enhances children's well-being as they progress into adolescence and adulthood.

3. *Mistrust.* Minority parents may also warn their children about members of other racial groups and how members of these groups might impede the children's success. However, these conversations do not occur as regularly as those geared toward preparing children for discrimination.

4. *Cultural socialization.* **Cultural socialization**, the process through which parents teach children about their heritage, promote racial/ethnic pride, and expose them to cultural traditions, is common in minority families. Parents often regard the transmission of this type of knowledge as one of

the most important parts of the socialization process, as it serves as the basis for the formation of children's racial and ethnic identities (Hughes et al. 2006). Racial/ethnic identities, acquired during primary socialization within the family, may buffer the impact of negative messages on minorities' self-concepts encountered at school, in interaction with peers, or in the media (see Box 12.3).

Box 12.3   Race and Ethnicity on Primetime Television

In 1994, ABC aired one of the first sitcoms about an Asian American family, called *All American Girl,* staring comedienne Margaret Cho, who is of Korean descent. At one point, Cho was told by network executive that the show was "too Asian" to have widespread appeal. Then she was told that the show was not Asian enough. According to Cho, it was the shows blatant emphasis on race that limited the development of its characters and resulted in its cancellation after only one season (Caswell, Asia Society Website). Since then, no other sitcom emphasizing family relationships has featured primarily Asian characters. Although the 2010 show *Outsourced* (also cancelled after one season), set a customer service call center in India, had a predominantly Indian cast, the main character was White.

Northern Exposure, a popular show that aired on CBS from 1990 to 1995, focused on a Jewish male physician from New York City who was practicing medicine in a small community in Alaska. Some of the secondary cast members were Native American, but this show has been the exception. Few primetime television programs feature Native American actors or focus on Native American culture.

African and Latinos are also underrepresented in primetime programing. Moreover, they are often portrayed in derogatory ways. Blacks and Latinos are depicted as less intelligent and less moral than Whites, and Black and Latino males are portrayed as hot tempered more frequently than other

---

PHOTO 12.4

Comedienne Margaret Cho often focuses on her experiences as a Korean-American female in her comedy routines.

groups. Thus, the content of primetime television programs reinforces cultural stereotypes about race/ethnicity and ability, character, and violence (Mastro and Behm-Morawitz 2005; Monk-Turner et al. 2010).

Have you noticed differences in how different racial and ethnic groups are portrayed on television? Think about your favorite programs. What messages do they convey?

RACIAL AND ETHNIC IDENTITIES

Much of the research on race/ethnicity and identity had been guided by social identity theory (Phinney 1990), within the group processes and structures tradition. Because adolescence is the time frame characterized by identity development, most of these studies have focused on individuals within this age range and emerging adults (individuals in their late teens and early twenties who are transitioning into adulthood).

Race/Ethnicity as a Social Identity

The Multigroup Ethnic Identity Measure (MEIM) is frequently used by social identity theorists to assess the strength of adolescents' and young adults' ethnic identities. This index, appropriate for inclusion on a survey, measures three components of ethnic identity that pertain to everyone, regardless of their ethnicity: ethnic self-identification, ethnic behaviors (i.e., social interaction and participation in cultural traditions with other members of one's ethnic group), and ethnic group attachment and belonging (Phinney 1992). Box 12.4 includes the 14 items from the MEIM.

The MEIM is a measure of ethnic (vs. racial) identity because it focuses on cultural factors. Thus, the MEIM emphasizes the cultural basis of race, as well as ethnicity. Some social psychologists favor the term "ethnicity" over "race" because racial differences are really culturally, not biologically, based (i.e., they are socially constructed). However, it is important to note that the concepts of race and ethnicity are not always clearly distinguished and are often used interchangeably within the social psychological literature (Phinney and Alipuria 2006).

Among racial/ethnic minorities, having a clearly formed ethnic identity is associated with high levels of self-esteem and psychological well-being (Mossakowski 2003; Roberts et al. 1999). A strong sense of ethnic identity may be especially beneficial for members of disadvantaged groups within school settings (Baysu, Phalet, and Brown 2011).

An ethic identity may by singular or it may reflect an individual's membership in more than one racial/ethnic group. According to the 2010 U.S. Census, over nine million individuals in this society are multiracial (Humes, Jones, and Ramirez 2011). Research suggests that multiracial or ethnic individuals (multiracial, vs. multiethnic, is the census designation) typically engage in one of the following strategies when defining themselves in relation to other groups within society:

- They adopt a monoracial identity (e.g., a person who has one White and one Black parent who self-identifies as African American).

Box 12.4   Measuring Multigroup Ethnic Identity

The Multigroup Measure of Ethnic Identity (MEIM) measures three aspects of ethnic identity: positive ethnic attitudes and sense of belonging, ethnic identity achievement, and ethnic behaviors (Phinney 1992).

My ethnicity is
_____ Asian, Asian American, or Oriental
_____ Black or African American
_____ Hispanic or Latino
_____ White, Caucasian, European, not Hispanic
_____ American Indian
_____ Mixed, parents are from two different groups
_____ Other (write in): _____

Please indicate the extent to which you agree or disagree with each of the following items using the response options indicated:
   1 = strong disagree, 2 = disagree, 3 = agree, 4 = strongly agree

Item	Response
1. I have spent time trying to find out more about my own ethnic group, such as its history, traditions, and customs.	_____
2. I am active in organizations or social groups that include mostly members of my own ethnic group.	_____
3. I have a clear sense of my ethnic background and what it means for me.	_____
4. I think a lot about how my life will be affected by my ethnic group membership.	_____
5. I am happy that I am a member of the group that I belong to.	_____
6. I am not very clear about the role of my ethnicity in my life.*	_____
7. I really have not spent much time trying to learn more about the culture and history of my ethnic group.*	_____
8. I have a strong sense of belonging to my own ethnic group.	_____
9. I understand pretty well what my ethnic group membership means to me, in terms of how to relate to my own group and other groups.	_____
10. In order to learn more about my ethnic background, I have often talked to other people about my ethnic group.	_____
11. I have a lot of pride in my ethnic group and its accomplishments.	_____

12. I participate in cultural practices of my own group, such as special food, music, or customs. _____

13. I feel a strong attachment toward my own ethnic group. _____

14. I feel good about my cultural or ethnic background. _____

Total Score _____

*These items should be reverse coded (1 = 4; 2 = 3; 3 = 2; 4 = 1) before calculating your total score on the index.

Note:
Total score = Sum of scores on all 14 items.
Affirmation and belonging subscale score = Sum of scores on items 5, 8, 11, 13, and 14.
Ethnic identity achievement subscale score = Sum of scores on items 1, 3, 4, 6 (reverse), 7 (reverse), 9, and 10.

Ethnic behavior subscale score = Sum of scores on items 2 and 12.

- They opt for a dual identification, where self-definitions favoring one racial/ethnic identity over another vary with the social setting (e.g., home vs. work) (Phinney and Alipuria 2006) or the person with whom they are conversing (Khanna and Johnson 2010).

- They take on a new, hybrid identity specific to their unique heritage.

- They reject race/ethnicity in favor of other sources of identity (e.g., work roles or group affiliations). Individuals who adopt this strategy typically do so in situations within which race/ethnicity is not salient.

The identities multiracial individuals choose vary in accordance with their personal preferences, their proximity to various racial/ethnic communities, and the characteristics of the immediate social setting. Thus, they may change over time as individuals experience changes in their social environments, roles, and relationships (Phinney and Alipuria 2006).

How did you score on the MEIM (Box 12.4)? Mean scores on this index among middle school, high school, and college samples range between 2.7 (low) and 3.5 (high). On average, White students (including Jewish Americans, Irish Americans, and Italian Americans) tend to score lower than individuals who self-identify as African American, Latino, Asian, or multiethnic. Among college undergraduates, African Americans have the highest MEIM scores (average = 3.5) (Phinney 1992; Ponterroto et al. 2003; Roberts et al. 1999).

Although the understanding that one is a member of a particular racial/ethnic group is common to everyone (Phinney 1992), Whites often have less of a sense of ethnic identity than racial/ethnic minorities. This is because White culture is the norm upon which people are judged within this society (Perry 2001). We discussed this earlier when we talked about the American = White bias.

Keep in mind that it is power, and nothing inherent to Whiteness itself, that makes this the case. Those groups that control the majority of society's resources (money, political power, and social prestige) make and enforce the rules. If a group other than Whites were in power, they would be the norm-setting group. However, given this country's history, Whites have always been at the top of the stratification hierarchy. Thus, making the rules has been their prerogative, and White culture (appearance, style of speech, food, etc.) is the standard applied to everyone.

As a result, Whites are less cognizant than racial/ethnic minorities of the uniqueness of their group's experiences. Their assumption is often that everyone in society shares a similar background. Thus, they don't always recognize that White is a racial group (Rowe, Bennett, and Atkinson 1994). Members of nondominant groups tend to be more aware of the distinctiveness of their history and cultural traditions, as well as of their position relative to other groups within the stratification hierarchy.

Structural Perspectives

Structural symbolic interactionists argue that social identities (self-categorizations based on group memberships) become personal insofar as people view themselves in terms of the statuses upon which they are based (Stryker 1980). This is likely to happen when a particular status influences how people are perceived and treated across social situations. Positions within society like race/ethnicity and gender, as well as deviant statuses (e.g., drug user, mental patient, or criminal), often shape people's experiences in this manner. Thus, they are considered master statuses.

A **master status** is a status that overshadows all of the other statuses that an individual occupies in its effects on social interaction and the self-concept (Allport 1954; Becker 1963). According to structural symbolic interactionists (i.e., identity, vs. social identity, theorists), the "social" (my group) and the "personal" (who I am) become fused as people come to see themselves in terms of those statuses that have the greatest impact on their social relationships. The synthesis of the group and the personal is evidenced when people list their race or ethnicity in response to the Twenty Statements Test (TST), as racial/ethnic minorities, but not Whites, tend to do. Racial/ethnic differences in responses to the TST suggest that minorities are more likely than Whites to recognize that race/ethnicity affects how they are perceived and treated across social encounters.

Tokenism

Minority group members' greater consciousness than Whites of how race/ethnicity influences their interactions with others may also reflect contextual factors, including what structural social psychologists call tokenism. A **token** is a person who is a numerical minority (Kanter 1977), such as the sole African American working in a particular office or the only female player on an otherwise-male hockey team. **Tokenism** refers to the fact that being a numerical minority draws attention to one's race (or gender). Everyone, including the token, is aware of his or her uniqueness. Thus, being a token because of one's race/ethnicity is likely to make that individual's racial/ethnic identity salient to everyone present in the social setting, including the token him- or herself (McGuire et al. 1978; Niemann and Dovidio 1998; Pollak and Niemann 1998).

This argument pertains to any numerical minority, and not just non-Whites. However, being a token is a more common occurrence among racial and ethnic minorities than among Whites because minorities are more likely than Whites to be numerical minorities in everyday settings (Yip 2008), including schools and the workplace. Within these environments, tokens' behaviors are often taken as indicative of the character or characteristics of the groups to which they belong. Moreover, because they stand out, the performance of tokens usually receives more attention than the performance of individuals who belong to the numerical majority (Kanter 1977).

Whether this has positive or negative consequences depends largely upon the relative status of a token's in-group. The public performances, at work and in other settings, of racial/ethnic minorities are negatively affected by tokenism when they are in the presence of members of a higher status group (Whites). Tokenism has less of a negative impact on the behaviors of Whites, presumably because positive stereotypes lead to positive performance expectations and evaluations for members of this (dominant) group (Thompson and Sekaquaptewa 2002).

Similarly, men (especially White men) in predominantly female occupations (e.g., nursing, social work, or elementary education) have higher salaries than their female peers and are often on the fast track to promotion. The term "the glass escalator" refers to this latter effect. Women in predominantly male jobs, on the other hand, often encounter negative attitudes and discriminatory behaviors that thwart their advancement (the "glass ceiling") and result in an unfriendly and threatening workplace (Williams 1992; Wingfield 2009). Thus, once again, context matters. Even when it's about numbers (tokenism is numerically defined), it's not only about numbers. It's also about power and group relations at the macro level.

What Do You Think?

When was the last time you were the only individual with a particular characteristic in a public or semipublic setting? The characteristic can be anything, including race/ethnicity, but it should be something that was notable to others. If you're a racial/ethnic minority, you probably experience the conspicuousness associated with tokenism regularly. If you're White, you might have to think a bit to come up with an example. How did being a numerical minority make you feel? If this was a short-term encounter, how might you feel if the experience was longer in duration, as would be the case in school or in a job?

Symbolic Interactionist Research on Identity Construction

Focusing on the micro level, (Chicago school) symbolic interactionists have studied the processes through which racial/ethnic identities are constructed through face-to-face interaction, typically with peers. The article by Kurien (2005) on identity construction among second-generation immigrant college students of Indian descent, used as an example of symbolic interactionist research in Chapter 1, is a good illustration of this type of analysis. Recall that the Indian American college students Kurien studied constructed racial/ethnic identities that were consistent with their personal histories—in particular, their prior experiences with discrimination and their knowledge of the Hindu religion.

Many studies on identity construction within the symbolic interactionist tradition emphasize the intersection of identities (e.g., racial/ethnicity, religion, gender, class, or sexual orientation) and how they shape people's day-to-day experiences. Most of these analyses are qualitative in orientation and focus on two minority statuses (Howard 2000). Frequently one of the minority statuses pertains to individuals' sexual orientation.

For example, Schnoor (2006) discusses how gay Jews living in an urban area negotiated two identities that often conflict (gay and Jewish), given traditional gender roles and the emphasis on the nuclear family in the Jewish community. Drawing on results obtained from 30 in-depth interviews, he details the alternative strategies the individuals he studied used to manage their contradictory identities.

Some study participants (who Schnoor calls "Jewish Lifestylers") became highly religious and attempted to drop what they perceived as the undesirable gay identity. On the other hand, other study participants embraced their gay identity. These latter individuals ("Gay Lifestylers") made their gay identity the focal point of their lives by moving into a "gay neighborhood," by participating in social activities in which their sexual orientation was salient, and by downplaying or dropping their religious identity.

A third group of study participants ("Gay-Jewish Commuters") operated in both gay-oriented and religious settings, but kept these sets of interactions separate. As one participant put it:

> Like many people, I compartmentalize, and being gay is one thing, it's an integral part of me, and I enjoy it to its fullest extent. Being an observant Jew is something that I also enjoy and get satisfaction from, for a number of reasons. The two separately are both things that make me feel good about myself, so I want to participate in them. Bringing the two together gets a bit more problematic. And so that's why you'll see when I'm at the [Orthodox synagogue], I'm not really "out" at all. I want to enjoy the feelings that I get out of the observant experience, the prayer and that communal experience, and so I sort of put the other on hold and enjoy that. (Schnoor 2006: 51)

In contrast, a number of study participants ("Gay-Jewish Integrators") sought to synthesize their two identities. They did so by participating in gay Jewish organizations, by questioning Jewish teachings on homosexuality, or by emphasizing similarities in the experiences of gays and Jews, such as their shared oppression. Some Gay-Jewish Integrators also reported using Jewish values as a means to avoid potentially harmful behaviors associated the urban gay subculture (e.g., promiscuity and substance abuse).

Thus, the individuals Schnoor (2006) interviewed managed conflicting identities in varying and unique ways. Recent symbolic interactionist analyses of identity construction among other groups include studies of gay Mexican immigrants (Thing 2010) and gay Asian men (Han 2009), as well as African American single fathers (Coles 2002), Blaxican individuals (multiethnic individuals with Black and Mexican backgrounds) (Romo 2011), and African American college students who belong to fraternities and sororities (Hughey 2008). These studies draw our attention to the diverse ways in which people react to social situations, competing sets of normative expectations, and others' negative attitudes and discriminatory behaviors.

Across social settings, racial and ethnic minorities fight oppression by using the self as a guide for action. This may involve managing multiple identities, which conflict with other's conceptions of who that individual should be (e.g., being a racial/ethnic minority and gay or bisexual, a middle-class Black, or a Black law enforcement officer stopped by the police). By assessing situations and anticipating others' reactions, racial and ethnic minorities maintain boundaries, and thus a sense of an authentic or real self, while responding to situations that are threatening to their well-being.

Emotion management (controlling or changing one's emotions so that they are consistent with prevailing social norms) is often an important part of this process. Through the management of their emotions, racial/ethnic minorities maintain a sense of dignity and avoid the kinds of social encounters that are likely to result in negative outcomes (e.g., openly expressing anger in public settings or in response to biased treatment by the police, as in the case racial profiling) (el-Khoury 2011). In the following section, we discuss what might be done to reduce the societal patterns that necessitate this kind of response.

CREATING A MORE EGALITARIAN SOCIETY

When discussing strategies for social change, we make a distinction between micro-level (individual) and macro-level (structural) interventions designed to improve race relations within the United States. **Micro-level interventions** focus on the reduction of negative racial attitudes (prejudice at the individual level) or on the disruption of the micro-level social processes through which macro-level racial inequalities are reproduced in specific group settings. **Macro-level interventions**, on the other hand, are broader in focus and target discrimination across social contexts.

Micro-Level Interventions

As you know, people's proximate environments (e.g., their neighborhoods, schools, and jobs) are highly segregated by race and ethnicity. Thus, their social networks tend to exhibit substantial racial homophily (they tend to be racially homogenous). Most interventions designed to reduce negative racial attitudes involve increased contact between individuals from different racial and ethnic groups. A review of over 350 published studies on this topic (controlled experiments) suggests that contact does reduce racial/ethnic prejudice. However, the size of this effect is relatively small. On average, contact reduced negative racial attitudes by about 7% across studies.

Contact is the most effective in improving intergroup relations when it is combined with **interdependent cooperation** (work toward a common goal) among groups of equal status (Pettigrew and Tropp 2006). This is because this facilitates the redefinition of in- versus out-groups.

We discussed the process of self-categorization when we introduced social identity theory and talked about the eye color exercise in Chapter 5. Iowa teacher Jane Elliott made eye color a dividing characteristic in her elementary school classroom to show students what prejudice and discrimination was like. Making eye color salient readily initiated the construction of in-groups versus out-groups based on this characteristic. Going a step beyond the eye color exercise, the interventions discussed in the following section involve the manipulation of social settings in

PHOTO 12.5

Team sports are a common activity among summer campers.

order to facilitate the creation of common (inclusive) identities, which supersede in-group/out-group divisions.

Creating a Common Identity Through Interdependent Cooperation

Sherif's (1966) famous camp studies were some of the first **common identity interventions** (Gaertner and Dovidio 2000). The subjects in these field experiments (recall that a field experiment is an experiment that occurs outside of the laboratory) were White, Christian, middle-class, preadolescent boys attending summer camps in the late 1940s and early 1950s. In these controlled settings, the researchers altered the characteristics of the social environment and assessed the effects of their manipulations on intergroup relations.

Upon their arrival, the boys were assigned to one of two cabins. Camp activities were then structured to stimulate intergroup conflict so that the cabin in which the boys resided became a highly salient feature of the environment (e.g., the cabin of residence served as the basis for teams that competed in various sporting events). Not surprisingly, group identification was strong and conflict between boys from the rival cabins escalated as the studies progressed. The boys also believed that the members of their cabin (the in-group) had more desirable characteristics than the individuals from in the other cabin (the out-group). Thus, the competitive environment gave rise to attitudes and behaviors similar to those associated with conflict between racial/ethnic groups in other settings.

Rather than improving relations, increased contact between boys from the two cabins increased intergroup tensions and the frequency of physical aggression. However, when boys from different cabins were placed in situations in which they had to work together toward a common goal—repairing a broken-down truck (their transportation back to the camp for dinner), pooling money to rent a film, or determining the source of a problem with the camp's water supply—intergroup relations improved drastically. The boys also had more favorable attitudes toward residents of the other cabin. Contact in combination with interdependent cooperation reduced negative feelings and behaviors directed toward out-group members by facilitating the redefinition of group boundaries from "us versus them" to "we." Sherif's (1966) protocol has served as a model for interventions seeking to improve relations between individuals from different racial/ethnic groups in other social contexts.

The **jigsaw technique** (Aronson et al. 1978) is an application of this approach in elementary school classrooms that has received a fair amount of attention within the social psychological literature. Schools, in general, are environments in which individuals compete with one another for rewards such as teacher attention and good grades. Within this social context, racial/ethnic divisions are often magnified.

Teachers who use the jigsaw technique place students from different racial/ethnic groups into equal-status task groups. Each task group is given the assignment of preparing a report on a particular topic. Although each group member has a specific task to complete, the success of the group depends upon the integration of everyone's information. Thus, the task is like a jigsaw puzzle, in which various pieces come together to make the whole. The children are of equal status within the groups in that each individual has a piece of information of equal import to that of other group members.

The jigsaw technique has been especially useful in reducing prejudice and discrimination directed toward Mexican American students for whom English is a second language. Difficulties with communication in the school setting often make these children the targets of negative evaluations on the part of White peers. By encouraging self-categorization on a characteristic other than ethnicity, the jigsaw technique reduces negative racial attitudes and discrimination within this context. It's no longer Whites versus Latinos. The in-group and out-groups are one's own versus the other jigsaw groups (Aronson and Gonzalez 1988).

Interdependent cooperation, the occupation of equal statuses, interaction, and support for egalitarian social norms have also been shown to reduce negative racial attitudes in high schools by increasing individuals' likelihoods of cognitively representing the student body as a single group. This, in turn, results in more positive feelings toward nonmembership groups. Thus, a collective, common identity mediates the effects of situational characteristics (cooperation, equal status, etc.) on attitudes toward out-groups (Gaertner et al. 1994).

Gaertner and associates refer to the set of relationships just described as the **common in-group identity model** (Gaertner et al. 1993). The common in-group identity model is depicted in Figure 12.3.

Cognitive manipulations that facilitate the readiness with which individuals represent two or more groups as a single superordinate group may also be used to increase positive attributions about nonmembership groups (Gaertner and Dovidio 2000). Social identity theorists argue that inclusive identities can be primed. Thus, intergroup cooperation may not be required for individuals to shift their perceptions from "us versus them" to a shared collective identity.

As you may recall from our discussion of social identity theory in Chapter 5, situational manipulations that make inclusive identities salient reduce the negative impact of stereotypes on individuals' assessments of members of out-groups. For example, making the British, versus the Scottish identity, salient made Scottish participants' evaluations of a neighboring English community more positive (Hopkins and Moore 2001).

Environmental manipulations that make superordinate identities salient (e.g., shared team membership or support for a particular sports team) affect college students' attitudes toward individuals from other racial/ethnic groups in a similar manner. Moreover, research suggests that it is White students' attitudes toward racial/ethnic minorities that show the most improvement in situations that prime an inclusive group identity (Nier et al. 2001).

Whether these kinds of interventions would yield the desired outcomes in the face of intergroup conflict over one or more rewards (e.g., money, status, or prestige)

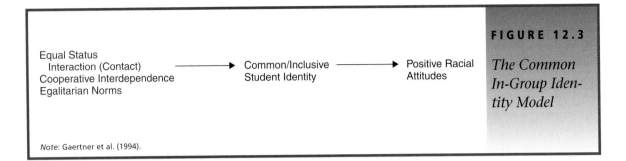

FIGURE 12.3

The Common In-Group Identity Model

Equal Status
  Interaction (Contact) —————▶ Common/Inclusive —————▶ Positive Racial
Cooperative Interdependence   Student Identity   Attitudes
Egalitarian Norms

Note: Gaertner et al. (1994).

is open to question. As discussed earlier, negative racial attitudes among Whites increase when they believe that they are in competition with racial and ethnic minorities for jobs or other economic or political resources. The research reviewed at the beginning of this section, in particular Sherif's camp studies, suggests that interdependent cooperation may be especially beneficial when there is direct competition between groups.

What Do You Think?

Can you think of at least one social situation in which each of the following identities would be salient (for a total of three situations, one for each identity)?

- College student
- Student at _____ (your college or university)
- _____ (one of your school-based group affiliations that serves as a basis for social identification; e.g., a Greek organization, a sports team, an academic or service club, a particular residence hall or hall floor, a particular school within the university, or a major).

How might the way in which you view the people around you differ across these three settings?

Challenging Status Beliefs

The interventions described in the previous section emphasize cognitions that emerge within the context of particular interactive encounters (e.g., at camp, in schools, or at athletic events). Thus, although they are of interest to sociological social psychologists, they are within the domain of psychological social psychology. Given their more macro focus, sociological social psychologists have directed their

PHOTO 12.6

Team uniforms help to solidify team-based social identities. In this setting, it is likely that team membership supersedes race/ethnicity as the basis for self-identification.

attention to mitigating the effects of societal beliefs that exist beyond any particular interactive setting.

Focusing on the hierarchical components of prevailing cultural stereotypes, status characteristics theorists have developed interventions that challenge prevailing status beliefs. As you know, status beliefs pertaining to race suggest that Whites are more able than racial/ethnic minorities, including African Americans. We have also discussed research (Goar and Sell 2005) showing that race differences in task-related behaviors among college students can be eliminated by altering the instructions provided to subjects so that the group task seems too complex and eclectic for anyone to perform at a higher level than others (the incompatible complexity manipulation). Similar **multiability interventions** have been shown to be equally effective in elementary school settings (Cohen 1982).

Other interventions designed to reduce racial/ethnic bias in small group encounters involve manipulations that enhance group members' expectations of racial/ethnic minorities. In **expectations training interventions**, for example, group members perceived as low status within society at large (racial/ethnic minorities) show their skills in a particular area by serving as teachers to members of groups regarded as high status (Whites). Thus, a specific status characteristic on which minorities are high ability is introduced into the interactive situation (Cohen 1982).

In a famous study by Cohen and Roper (1972), Black male middle school students were taught how to build a transistor radio (the MP3 player of the era). Then, in mixed-raced groups, these students showed their White male peers how to complete this task. This reduced racial bias in subsequent interactions during which groups of study participants (each group had two White and two Black students) played a game requiring them to make decisions about what to do in order to maximize their number of points. During this game, Blacks in the expert/teacher condition were as active and as influential as the White students. This was not the case in the condition in which no expert training was given. Whites were dominant within these groups (Cohen and Roper 1972). Similar interactive strategies have been used successfully with other racial/ethnic groups (e.g., Native Americans and Whites) (Cohen 1982).

Although interventions disrupting status hierarchies within small groups have been tested mainly within schools, they could readily be applied in work settings (Bianchi, Kang, and Stewart 2012). Research suggests that expectations training manipulations affect subjects' performance with different partners in other (similar) settings. Thus, they are likely to have effects that last beyond the experimental encounter (Markovsky, Smith, and Berger 1984; Pugh and Wahrman 1983).

Still, expectations training interventions are limited by their scope. The same is true of the multiability interventions, described earlier. Scope is an issue with virtually all micro-level interventions. They must be widely implemented, with many individuals in many different setting, in order to realize any large-scale changes in the population's attitudes or behaviors.

Macro-Level Structural Changes

One advantage of macro-level interventions is the extent of their reach (all, or the majority, of society's members). There were, for example, substantial changes in Whites' racial attitudes following the onset of the civil rights movement and the enactment of the Civil Rights Act of 1964, which made discrimination based on race illegal (Bobo et al. 2012). Changing behaviors appears to have changed attitudes in the manner specified by psychological social psychologists (Bem 1970). Cohorts of Whites born after the civil rights movement tend to have substantially more liberal views about race than individuals who came of age in the pre-civil rights era (Keeter and Taylor 2009).

Sociological social psychologists have argued that the primary way to reduce discrimination, and ultimately change the population's attitudes about race, is through the enforcement of antidiscrimination legislation and policies like affirmative action. Affirmative action is a way to level the playing field by combating the pressures toward similarity, identified by Kanter (1977). Although many

Whites oppose affirmative action because it gives preferential treatment to racial/ethnic minorities, the system as it currently functions gives preferential treatment to Whites. It always has. This is itself a type of affirmative action—one that maintains the advantaged status of the dominant racial/ethnic group within society (Pitts 2003).

Moving toward a more level playing field by giving preference to qualified minority (and female) candidates, affirmative action has the potential to reduce the self-fulfilling prophecy described in the preceding section (see Figure 12.1). The disproportional representation of Blacks and other disadvantaged racial/ethnic minorities at the bottom of the stratification hierarchy is taken as evidence of their inferiority. Thus, providing members of these groups with opportunities for advancement would necessarily disrupt this negative cycle.

Some sociological social psychologists (e.g., Feagin 2010) have also argued in support of reparations. **Reparations** involve admission by the U.S. government that it committed crimes against Blacks and restitution to the descendants of slaves. This restitution might come in the form of educational scholarships or monetary compensation (Dawson and Popoff 2004). By redressing the historical roots of contemporary racial stratification, reparations would counterbalance some of the wealth Whites have accumulated over generations due to government policies, such as the Homestead Acts, and slavery (Feagin 2010).

Most (96%) of White Americans are opposed to reparations (Dawson and Popoff 2004), as this type of policy runs counter to the notion that race shouldn't matter. Because they minimize racial disparities and attribute racial inequality to individual attributes, most Whites believe that racial equality has already been achieved. Thus, they do not see the need to alleviate past injustices which they view as irrelevant to contemporary society (Mazzocco et al. 2006).

Emphasizing current racial inequalities and their historical roots in school curricula may sensitize Whites to the contemporary significance of race in a color-blind society. But as sociological social psychologists, we know that the structure of society, in particular the distribution of resources across groups, shapes people's perceptions, emotions, and actions. Thus, without significantly altering the position of racial and ethnic minorities, in particular African Americans, within the stratification hierarchy, we are not likely to see a significant change in race relations within this society.

Regarding this, it is important to recognize that some minority groups (e.g., Jews) have been denigrated because of their economic success. Economic disenfranchisement among lower-class Whites often fuels this kind of prejudice (Blazak 2001), as well as negative attitudes toward other racial/ethnic groups, including, in recent years, immigrants. These latter macro-level patterns, associated with a growing gap between the rich and poor within this society, and declining economic opportunities for those at the bottom of the stratification hierarchy, must also be addressed through changes in public policy.

CHAPTER SUMMARY

Sociological social psychologists offer a unique approach to the study of race relations. Focusing on both macro- and micro-level social processes, they emphasize the manner in which prevailing societal patterns shape the attitudes, behaviors, and opportunities of individuals. Contemporary society is highly segregated by race/ethnicity, and prevailing patterns of prejudice and discrimination severely limit the achievements of racial and ethnic minorities. Interventions that change the feelings and actions of individuals may be useful in improving race relations within particular settings (e.g., a school or a business). However, widespread reductions in prejudice and discrimination, and the patterns of racial/ethnic inequality they both reflect and reproduce, require alterations to the structure of society best attained through changes in public policy.

Key Points to Know

- **Sociological social psychologists define prejudice as the shared feeling of superiority among Whites, the dominant racial/ethnic group within this society.** They have studied intergroup relations at the macro level, including patterns of institutional discrimination, as well as racial attitudes and discrimination at the micro level, and how cultural stereotypes influence individuals' behaviors.

- **Status beliefs are the hierarchical component of stereotypes.** Status beliefs result in biased performance expectations and discrimination in small group encounters and hinder the performance of racial and ethnic minorities in settings in which they are salient (stereotype threat).

- **Prejudice does not always result in discrimination at the individual level.** This is because people tend to behave in manner consistent with social norms, even if it is in opposition to the way in which they feel. There is also substantial evidence that behavior precedes, rather than follows, attitudes.

- **Discrimination based on race/ethnicity is pervasive within this society, at both the individual and institutional level. Many Whites also hold negative implicit and explicit attitudes about African Americans and other racial and ethnic minority groups.** Whites' attitudes toward African Americans, in particular, have become more negative in recent years, presumably due to backlash in response to the Obama presidency and the economic recession.

- **Social conditions that increase conflict, or perceived conflict, over scarce resources often result in an increase in negative racial attitudes among Whites.** When Whites misattribute their declining economic status to racial/ethnic minorities, they are engaging in scapegoating. Negative racial attitudes and scapegoating among Whites occur more readily in geographic regions where there is a high proportion of racial and ethnic minorities.

- **Most White Americans fail to recognize the pervasiveness of racial/ethnic prejudice and discrimination within this society. Thus, they attribute racial/ethnic inequality to individual attributes, such as a lack of motivation or will on the part of minorities, and deny its structural roots.** As a result, most Whites do not support the kinds of social policies required for the movement toward a more egalitarian society.

- **The pervasiveness of the White racial frame explains why this is the case. The White racial frame is like a cognitive schema, supported by collective memories and cultural myths about this country's racial history. It is composed, in particular, of stereotypes, prejudice, and beliefs about the causes of racial inequality, which shape people's interpretation of current social arrangements.** The White racial frame is rooted in this society's history, in particular slavery, and perpetuates racial inequality by serving as the foundation for a self-fulfilling prophecy at the macro level. Stereotypes, negative racial attitudes, and Whites' resistance to structural change continue to limit the opportunities of racial and ethnic minorities. The fact minorities remain low in the stratification hierarchy is then taken as evidence of their inferiority.

- **Some racial and ethnic minorities acquire counter-frames during the primary socialization process that challenge the White racial frame**. Cultural socialization is the process through which minority parents teach their children about their heritage and cultural traditions. Research within social identity theory indicates that having a strong ethnic identity is beneficial for minority youth.

- **Analyses within social structure and personality suggest that the kind of visibility that results from being a numerical minority (a token) has negative outcomes for members of disadvantaged groups. Conversely, micro-level symbolic interactionist analyses emphasize the creative and unique ways that racial and ethnic minorities construct identities that meet their needs within the constraints of the larger society**.

- **The social psychological literature on race relations has important policy implications.** Although micro-level interventions (e.g., contact with cooperative interdependence or expert training) can be used to improve race relations in specific settings, they are unlikely to significantly alter the structure of society. Macro-level interventions, including the enforcement of antidiscrimination laws and reparations, are broader in their reach and have the potential to reduce patterns of racial stratification rooted in this society's history.

Terms and Concepts for Review

Affirmative Action	Micro-level intervention
American = White bias	Minority
Antioppression counter-frame	Moral alchemy
Color-blind racism	Multiability interventions
Common identity interventions	Negative racial attitudes
Common in-group identity model	Prejudice
Cultural socialization	Proportional representation
Discrimination	Racial profiling
Expectations training interventions	Racism
Frames	Reparations
Implicit associations	Scapegoating
Institutional discrimination	Self-fulfilling prophecy (societal level)
Interdependent cooperation	Self-perception theory
Internal attribution	Stereotype threat
Jigsaw technique	Symbolic racism
Laissez-faire racism	Token
Liberal racism	Tokenism
Macro-level intervention	Traditional racism
Master status	White racial frame

Questions for Review and Reflection

1. Why is the relationship between prejudice and discrimination at the individual level so weak? Given an example of a situation where a White person is likely to discriminate against a racial/ethnic minority. Give an example of a social setting where this kind of discrimination is unlikely to occur.
2. What environmental factors increase negative racial attitudes on the part of Whites? How does this apply to the United States today?
3. Imagine that you have been asked to explain to a young child what race is and how it affects people's lives in the United States. What would you say? Discuss the White racial frame and use this concept to explain the prevalence of color-blind racial attitudes.

4. Suppose that you were elected to public office in the city or town where your school is located and your primary charge is to reduce racial/ethnic prejudice and discrimination in the local community. Describe race relations in your community (focus on your hometown, if you would prefer to do so). What would you do to improve things? Why would you expect these programs or policies to be effective?

CHAPTER 13

Social Influence, Social Constraint, and Collective Behavior

PHOTO 13.1A

Flashmob on Bourbon Street in New Orleans imitating a television commercial for pistachio nuts (February 1, 2013).

Flash mobs take breaching (norm violation) experiments to a new level, as participants collectively act in manner that makes it difficult for people to maintain their sense of a coherent and meaningful reality. Flash mobs are typically organized using electronic communications, including email, social media, and cell phones. Participants arrive at the designated scene and engage in preplanned behaviors that disrupt the normative order and leave people surprised and, in many cases, amused.

The first flash mob was organized in Manhattan in 2003 by Bill Wasik, an editor at *Harper's Magazine*. Approximately two hundred participants were notified of the event in advance via email. They were instructed to meet at various locations

PHOTO 13.1B

Teenagers participating in pillow-fighting flash mob in in St. Petersburg, Russia (June 10, 2012).

near the target site, where they received slips of paper with their destination—the rug department at a Macy's department store. Participants entered the store and surrounded a carpet in the far left corner. At that point, per their instructions, they told the store clerks that they were from a Long Island City commune and wanted to purchase a "love rug." Then the mob dispersed (Wasik 2006).

The concept of the flash mob caught on and has become an international phenomenon. In 2012, flash mobs in 115 cities across the globe participated in International Pillow Fight Day (Brennan 2012). Footage of these events has been widely circulated over the Internet.

Similar mass events have been staged for the purpose of proposing marriage or marketing universities. Both Ohio State and UCLA have sponsored collective "mob" events designed to attract potential students. Flash mobs have also been executed as political protests in the United States and internationally. For example, in the United States and England, groups of women have simultaneously nursed their babies in stores and restaurants in protest of the stigmatization of nursing in public. In 2012, in Saudi Arabia, where protests are illegal, family members of political detainees staged a flash mob-like event at a mall in order to get the attention of the media. Video footage was posted on YouTube, which increased awareness of this issue internationally (Alami 2012).

Mass protests, or marketing events, organized in the manner of a flash mob are called **smart mobs** because they are orchestrated for a political or economic purpose. This is in contrast to flash mobs, which are defined by their lack of a designated goal, other than to take people by surprise and disrupt the routine nature of commonplace social encounters. According to Rheingold (2002), who coined the term "smart mob," a flash mob is a specific type of smart mob—one that is designed to surprise, shock, or entertain.

The name "flash mob" comes from a short story about the negative aspects of a teleportation technology that allows people seeking thrills to beam into various public settings (Wasik 2006). Are flash mobs a negative consequence of modern technology, as this label implies? Are they really trivial or purposeless, as some people have charged? Why have they become so popular? That is, why are people so willing to engage in this behavior? We address these issues throughout the chapter, as we discuss social influence, social constraint, and collective behavior.

SOCIAL INFLUENCE

Social influence occurs when people's perceptions and behaviors are shaped by others (Cialdini and Goldstein 2004). Social psychologists trained as psychologists often study social influence. Many of these studies focus on compliance.

Research on Compliance

People exhibit **compliance** when they acquiesce to a request (Cialdini and Goldman 2004). Experiments on compliance focus on identifying when individuals are the most likely to do what someone asks of them. Some studies emphasize the cognitive basis of compliance. For example, research has shown that how a request is phrased affects compliance when it activates psychological processes, such as a desire for consistency. Other studies on compliance focus on social factors, such as the nature of the social setting in which behavior occurs. It is the latter kind of research that is of primary interest to sociological social psychologists.

Obedience to Authority

Milgram's obedience experiments are the most famous studies on compliance that emphasize situational factors. We mentioned these studies in Chapter 2, in the section on ethics in research. This research is considered ethically questionable because Milgram led his subjects to believe that they were shocking someone when this was not really the case. Although Milgram's experiments wouldn't be done today for ethical reasons, his findings tell us something important about human behavior and people's capacity for harming others. In particular, Milgram wanted to understand the behavior of Germans during the Holocaust. How could so many people have willingly participated in such heinous acts against other human beings (Meyer 1970)?

In his initial experiment, Milgram (1963) found that a large proportion of the study subjects (65%) were willing to provide the maximum level of shock to someone just because the experimenter told them to do so. He replicated these findings in a number of subsequent studies (Milram 1965). In those instances when subjects resisted the experimenter's order to continue giving shocks, the assurance that they would not be responsible should any harm come to the person receiving the shocks was often enough to ensure their continued participation.

The fact that the experiments took place at Yale University, and a researcher (Milgram, in his lab coat) was the one telling subjects what to do, presumably contributed to the study results. Yale is a highly respected institution, and subjects were likely to have believed that the experimenter knew what he was doing. Thus, he would have been regarded as a legitimate authority figure by most individuals within this society.

Obedience did drop some when the experiment was moved off campus into a warehouse in a nearby community (48% of the subjects were willing to give the highest level of shock in this setting). Obedience also decreased when the instructions to continue giving shocks occurred via tape rather than by the researcher in person. Less than a fourth of the subjects gave the highest level of shock in this condition.

In addition, the proximity between the subject and the person he or she was shocking had a large effect on subjects' willingness to harm someone simply because of instructions by the experimenter to do so. When subjects had contact with the victim, and were required to put his hand on a shock pad, obedience was substantially lower than when the victim was in another room (Milgram 1965).

It is often more difficult to harm someone when you can see the consequences of your actions firsthand. Imagine if you were a manager firing employees or a property owner evicting tenants for not paying their rent. It is easier to do this when you don't know these individuals, and even easier still if you can do the deed indirectly via a letter or a personal representative.

In thinking about Milgram's findings, you might be wondering whether everyone is equally susceptible to influence by people in positions of authority. In particular, one might expect gender to affect people's willingness to shock someone when asked to do so by an authority figure. Women might be more obedient than men because they are socialized to be more passive. Alternatively, men might be more likely than women to shock someone because they are socialized to be more aggressive, or because women tend to be more likely to take the perspective of the person getting the shocks and recognize the harm they are causing.

Q: What do you think? Do you think there are gender differences in levels of obedience within this context?

A: Research suggests that males and females are equally likely to give what they believe are harmful shocks to a confederate of an experimenter (Blass 1999; Burger 2009). This speaks to the power of the situation in shaping behavior. Factors such as aggression or empathy, acquired during socialization, are less important that the perceived legitimacy of the setting and the authority of the experimenter in shaping subjects' responses to an order to harm someone. The gender of the experimenter also appears to be unrelated to levels of obedience in experiments similar in design to those conducted by Milgram (Eagly 1978).

Research on Conformity in Groups

Conformity, another type of social influence, pertains to group encounters and is exhibited when an individual changes his or her behavior to match that of other group members. Psychological social psychologists who study this topic seek to identify the social conditions under which conformity is likely to occur (Cialdini and Goldstein 2004). These studies are of interest to sociological social psychologists because they explain when, and why, people's behaviors and perceptions are affected by others.

There are two forms of social influence that give rise to conformity in group settings.

1. **Normative influence** occurs when people's behaviors are shaped by others' expectations. People readily conform to individual or group expectations in order avoid negative evaluations from others.

2. **Informational influence** occurs when others serve as a source of information about the nature of reality. The motivation underlying this type of social influence is a desire to understand the social environment (Deutsch and Gerard 1955).

Whereas normative influence tends to yield public compliance, informational influence is associated with private acceptance. **Public compliance** occurs when people adopt behaviors that match those of other group members, but their actions don't necessarily reflect their perceptions of reality. People exhibit **private acceptance**, a deeper type of conformity, when both their perceptions and their behaviors reflect group norms (Israel 1964).

Asch's (1956) classic line-matching experiment provides an excellent illustration of normative influence and public compliance. Subjects in this study were asked to indicate which of three lines varying in length matched in length a fourth target line (see Figure 13.1). Subjects (college males) were placed in groups with other similar individuals who were really confederates of the experimenter. Per the experimenter's instructions, the confederates of the experimenter consistently gave false answers on the line-matching task. The naive subject sometimes gave a similar (inaccurate) response, which matched that of his group members. Given the nonambiguous nature of the task (it was obvious which lines were of the same length), the degree of conformity among the study subjects was fairly high. However, many of the subjects perceived a discrepancy between their answers and their perceptions.

FIGURE 13.1

In Asch's (1956) experiment on conformity, subjects were asked to indicate which of the lines on the right matched the target line

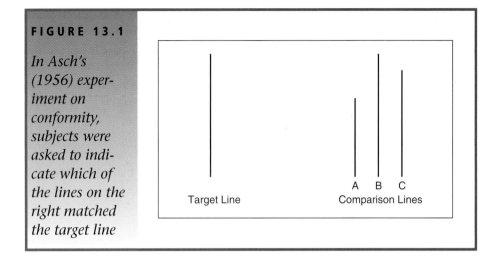

Target Line

A   B   C
Comparison Lines

That is, they gave answers that were inconsistent with what they actually saw (Asch 1956). They did so in order to avoid standing out from the group. Thus, they were exhibiting public compliance.

Not surprisingly, how readily individuals conform to group norms is influenced by broader societal factors. In their analysis of 133 studies similar to Asch's classic experiment, Bond and Smith (1996) found substantial variability in levels of conformity across 17 different cultures. Conformity was notably higher in cultures that are collectivist (group), versus individualist, in orientation. People in collectivist societies (e.g., Japan) tend to define themselves and their goals in relation to groups, such as the family or the community. Thus, they are more likely than people living in individualistic cultures (e.g., the United States and other Western societies) to value conformity (Bond and Smith 1996).

The results of Bond and Smith's (1996) analysis serve as a reminder that research findings based on studies conducted within the United States may not generalize to other countries. Many of the study results discussed in earlier chapters, on topics like the content of people's self-concepts and moral reasoning, appear to be specific to Western societies. It is unlikely that there are any perceptions or behaviors that generalize to all of the human species (Henrich, Heine, and Norenzayan 2010).

Asch's findings on conformity in groups within the United States are often contrasted with those from another set of famous studies, conducted by Sherif (1935). In Sherif's experiments, subjects were asked to estimate the distance a light beam moved on a wall. It really wasn't moving at all, although it appeared to be doing so. This optical illusion is called the autokinetic effect. Given the highly subjective nature of this task (everyone was likely to be seeing something slightly different), subjects' perceptions were shaped by their group members' estimates of how far the light beam moved. They used this information about the nature of the reality in question to determine what they were seeing. Thus, they exhibited the deeper type of conformity associated with private acceptance (Allen 1965).

Both normative and informational forms of social influence may operate simultaneously, or one form of influence may predominate over the other, depending upon the nature of the interactive encounter. In general, normative influence and public compliance occur when there is some objective point of reference, as was the case in Asch's study. On the other hand, information-based influence and private acceptance tend to occur when the nature of reality is more subjective, as in the case of a perception (Sherif's study) or an attitude (Israel 1964).

However, in the case of an attitude, the strength of people's initial feelings about something may affect their susceptibility to social influence. Holding a strong attitude may make people less readily influenced by the behaviors and perceptions of others (Allen 1965).

Think about the last time you saw a movie you really liked. Imagine that you were with a group of individuals whose opinions you respected, and they all stated a strong dislike for the movie ("The worst they've ever seen."). You might agree in order to fit in, but it is not likely that you would change your view about the film because you enjoyed it so much. In this situation, you would be demonstrating public compliance.

On the other hand, if you saw a movie and had mixed feelings about its quality, you would be more open to the deeper kind of influence that characterizes private acceptance. If a number of individuals you respect all said they hated this movie, you might state your agreement and believe it. That is, your perception may actually change as the result of others' responses. Private acceptance is likely to occur in this instance because you were uncertain as to how you felt about the movie to begin with.

What Do You Think?

Can you think of a situation in which you exhibited public compliance? What about private acceptance? Can you identify a setting in which your perceptions (or feelings) about something or someone were shaped by the reactions of others? What made you susceptible to this type of social influence? Do you think your gender made you more, or less, susceptible to the influence of others within this social setting?

Gender and Conformity

Neither Asch (1956) nor Sherif (1935) reported results for female subjects. However, a review of the results of subsequent experiments indicates that women may be somewhat more likely than men to exhibit conformity in group settings (Eagly 1978). Additional studies suggest that gender difference in conformity in groups is due to prevailing gender roles and the belief that men should behave in an independent fashion, and not to women's greater sensitivity to social cues or to the perspectives of other group members.

The fact that high-status individuals are less likely to be sanctioned by others than their low-status counterparts when they challenge group norms may also explain males' low levels of conformity relative to women in experimental task groups. This latter explanation is consistent with the main premises of status characteristics theory (Eagly and Chrvala 1986; Eagly, Wood, and Fishbaugh 1981).

Status Characteristics and Conformity

Recall that status characteristics theory, within the group processes and structures face of sociological social psychology, focuses on the effects of gender and other status characteristics on group dynamics, including people's susceptibility to social influence. In the standard status characteristics experiment, social influence is reflected in subjects' willingness to yield to an interaction partner when there is a disagreement about the nature of reality (e.g., whether a picture is predominantly white or black).

We discussed status characteristics theory in detail in Chapters 1 and 5. Our purpose here is to clarify how this model is used to estimate an individual's likelihood of being influenced by another person.

Imagine that you were matched with a partner and asked to complete a task requiring you to reach a judgment about the dominant color in each of a series of slides or computer images. Would you yield to your partner if the two of you gave different answers? Would you exhibit conformity by changing your answer, or would you stay with your original response? That is, would you be susceptible to social influence within this context?

Status characteristics theorists argue that being a member of one or more dominant groups (e.g., being male, highly educated, or White) makes it less likely that an individual will be influenced by others when this type of disagreement occurs (Berger et al. 1977). Thus, in order to answer our question (Would you yield to your partner?), you would need to know some more about that person. Assuming that you have no reason to believe that you or your partner has specific task-relevant knowledge or skills, your susceptibility to influence will be affected by your diffuse status characteristics (e.g., your gender, education, and race/ethnicity), relative to those of your partner.

The performance expectation you hold for yourself relative to your partner will determine how likely you are to change your answers when the two of you disagree. If you have the status advantage associated with being male (vs. female), highly educated, or White (vs. non-White), you will be less likely to change your answer to match that of your partner because both you and your partner will assume that you are more likely to know the right answer. If, on the other hand, your partner has the status advantage associated with being male (vs. female), highly educated, or White (vs. non-White), you will be more susceptible to social influence than that individual within this setting. This is because both you and your partner will assume that your partner is more likely to have the correct answer whenever the two of you give different responses.

Note that you and your partner should have the same performance expectation for you (vs. your partner) and for your partner (vs. you). This is because the process of status generalization just described is a reflection of status beliefs about the relative competence of various groups that are shared among society's members.

Status characteristics theorists argue that the effects of status characteristics on social influence generalize across social settings. Thus, in any group encounter oriented toward a common goal, your status characteristics, relative to those of the individuals with whom you're interacting, should affect the extent to which you will be susceptible to their influence.

Social Contagion Within Social Networks

Research also suggests that your perceptions and behaviors are likely to be shaped by the members of your social network. **Social contagion** occurs when attitudes, beliefs, or behaviors are transmitted form one group member to another. For example, if one of your friends buys a new high-end cell phone, and then another friend who really likes the way it works buys the same phone, then a third friend buys the phone so that she too has access to its various features, and then you buy one, and so forth, social contagion has occurred within your friendship network.

Studies show that happiness, loneliness, depression, taste in music and movies, divorce, smoking, drinking, drug use, and obesity are contagious in that they readily spread through people's social networks. As a result, these feelings, attitudes, and behaviors tend to cluster (i.e., they are common) in particular social networks (Christakis and Fowler 2013; VanderWeele 2011).

Application: Identifying the Social Processes That Lead to the Spread of Obesity

Because obesity is a current health concern, this characteristic has received a lot of attention within the research literature on social contagion effects. The researchers who initially studied obesity in social networks (Christakis and Fowler 2007) assumed that group norms concerning the acceptability of obesity would explain why people tended to be within the same weight range (measured using the body mass index, or BMI, which takes height into account) as their family members and friends. That is, they argued that, through regular social interaction, members of a social network construct a shared definition of what is an acceptable body weight, which then makes it more, or less, likely that they will become obese (Harmon 2011).

In order to determine whether this is the case, another group of researchers (Hruschka et al. 2011) conducted a study of women (n = 101) and members of their social networks. Each woman in the sample was asked to identify 20 individuals (women or men) with whom she regularly interacted. These network members, as well as the initial study participants, were given a series of questions designed to

PHOTO 13.2

Members of a friendship network at an outdoor dinner party.

measure their attitudes toward obesity and their ideal body size. These questions served as measures of network norms pertaining to weight.

The study results indicate that these norms explained only about 20% of the relationship between a woman's weight (BMI) and the weight of her network members. This suggests that factors other than social norms pertaining to the acceptability of obesity account for most (about 80%) of the homogeneity in body weight within social networks (Hruschka et al. 2011). These factors might include common activities among network members, like patterns of eating, dieting, or exercise (Christakis and Fowler 207; Hruschka et al. 2011).

What people eat and how much they exercise are also likely to be shaped by group norms. Thus, whereas research indicates that shared perceptions regarding the acceptability of obesity among members of a social network do not fully explain the fact that obesity clusters within social networks, other kinds of group norms (e.g., pertaining to diet, the frequency that people exercise, or what kind of exercises they engage in) may explain this pattern. Additional research is needed to determine why obesity, and other characteristics (e.g., divorce, loneliness, alcohol or drug use, and happiness), so readily spread through people's social networks.

Gossip

Gossip is information exchanged among individuals that focuses on other people's personal affairs and tends to be negative or scandalous in its content. Gossip typically occurs at the micro level and, like the characteristics discussed in the preceding section, it spreads within social networks. The exception to this is gossip presented within the media, in the tabloids, and on television. Gossip is the main focus of magazines like the *National Enquirer* and television programs like *Entertainment Tonight*. This type of gossip is similar in nature to rumor (Rosnow and Fine 1976), which we discuss later in the chapter.

Within people's social networks, gossip serves as a source of empowerment for individuals who lack status in other arenas (e.g., lower-level clerical staff in a large corporation) (Kanter 1977). Moreover, it promotes unity among group members (Gluckman 1963). Like sharing a common enemy, a common target of ridicule often makes people feel more similar, and closer, to one another.

Gossip may also be initiated for protective reasons. Disclosing information about another person's prior bad behavior, thereby reducing his or her likelihood of causing harm to another individual, makes people feel better. Thus, individuals are willing to pass on this kind of information, even when there is a personal cost associated with doing so (Feinberg et al. 2012).

Finally, gossip facilitates the maintenance of social norms (Gluckman 1963). Individuals fearing that they will be the target of gossip if they behave badly may be less likely to act in socially inappropriate ways. Thus, gossip may serve as a source of informal social control.

What Do You Think?

What was the last piece of gossip you encountered? Who provided this information? What, if any, functions might this behavior have served for the information giver and for the information receiver(s)?

SOCIAL CONSTRAINT

Social constraint is the term used by sociological social psychologists when talking about the effects of social norms on people's behaviors. It is distinct from social influence, which implies behavioral change. Within any social setting, there is a tension between constraint and agency, defined earlier as individuals' capacity to act in a self-directed manner. People's behaviors both reflect and, at the aggregate level, create society. Whereas social psychologists working within social structure and personality view social norms as social facts that shape behavior, symbolic interactionists focus on the processes through which people construct, modify, or reproduce social norms within the context of their social encounters.

Much of the literature on the emergence of social norms suggests that people construct norms that meet the needs of the group, given the challenges posed by the broader environment in which they are located (Horne 2001). We illustrated this earlier when we discussed the experiences of the survivors of the plane crash in the Andes Mountains. The crash survivors had to eat human flesh in order to survive, so they constructed a new set of social norms that enabled them to do so, while maintaining positive self-concepts. Once a new normative order was created, this set of expectations shaped the crash survivors' subsequent actions (Henslin 2007).

People behave in a manner consistent with prevailing social norms in most situations in order to avoid negative responses from others. Failure to act appropriately in public settings results in embarrassment, a negative emotion that people seek to avoid. We also regulate our private behaviors in order to avoid experiencing guilt or, in those cases when a particular action would result in a perceived self-deficiency, shame.

Nonetheless, it is not uncommon for groups of individuals to act in ways that are outside of what is perceived as normative in everyday settings. Sociological social psychologists have studied when and why this occurs, as well as its consequences.

COLLECTIVE BEHAVIOR

Collective behavior refers to behavior at the aggregate level that is distinct from, or in opposition to, routine societal patterns (Turner and Killian 1987). Collective behavior is of particular interest to sociological social psychologists because it is the root of social change.

Fashions and Fads

Fashions and fads are forms of collective behavior that have been studied by sociological social psychologists since the early 1900s (e.g., Blumer 1939; Park and Burgess 1924; Simmel 1904). **Fashions** involve a rapid increase, and then decrease, in the popularity of a particular style or product, usually clothing or music. Fashions are structured by businesses within particular industries (e.g., the clothing or music industry) and they are cyclical or systematic in nature, in that one style or item routinely replaces the current model. For example, in the music industry, disco was replaced by punk and New Wave music, which was replaced by grunge, rap, and then hip-hop.

Fads are less systematic than fashions and are defined by their episodic nature. Something, often a toy or novelty item, rapidly becomes popular, but this popularity is short-lived. Unlike a fashion, once it has run its course, the fad is over.

Two good examples of fads are the hula hoop, which peaked in popularity in the late 1950s (Best 2006), and the pet rock in the 1970s, pictured in the following photo. Streaking also became a fad in the 1970s and was a common occurrence on many college campuses (Aguirre, Quarantelli, and Mendoza 1988). See Box 13.1 for a list of fads by the decade within in which they occurred. Can you think of any other recent fads?

Box 13.1   Fads by Decade

1950s	1980s
Hula Hoop	Pop Rocks
Gumby (a rubber children's toy)	Rubik's Cube
Droodle (a cartoon)	Breakdancing
1960s	**1990s**
Black lights	Beanie Babies
Twister (game)	The Macarena (dance)
Buttons with slogans	Pokéman cards
1970s	**2000s**
Streaking	Speed dating
Pet rock	Sudoku puzzles
Mood rings	Bratz dolls

Note: http://www.crazyfads.com.

Flash mobs, discussed at the beginning of the chapter, might well fall into the category of fad, depending on their longevity. As is typical of a fad, they caught on fast (Wasik 2006). If flash mobs all but disappear once their novelty wears off, like streaking in the 1970s, then they can be considered a fad.

However, if the popularity of flash mobs reflects an underlying tension resulting from the structure of modern society (e.g., the perception that behavior is overly regulated), they may not be as frivolous as some individuals have suggested. Insofar as they are rooted in a collective tension or concern, flash mobs may persist and become a permanent part of this and other cultures. **Diffusion** occurs when something that initially appears to be a fad remains popular and becomes a common item or activity within society. The men's wristwatch, which first appeared around 1915 and was presumed at that time to be a fad, illustrates this type of pattern (Best 2006).

Note that the name "flash mob" emerged shortly after the initial events were staged (Wasik 2006). Language, and specifically the naming of an item or behavior, plays a key role in the birth of fad. There are no fads without names because the name itself is what makes the trend stand out as distinct (Meyersohn and Katz 1957). There would have been no pet rocks, mood rings, or Beanie Babies without these (or some other) labels (e.g., "pet stone" would have served just as well as "pet rock").

Presumably these items became so popular because they were initially perceived as unique and neat or funny. Once an item catches on and becomes the thing to have, ownership provides people with a sense of status or acceptance within their social networks. Within this context, participation in a fad is also likely to be perceived as exciting and fun (Best 2006).

Institutional Fads

However, not all fads are trivial, like those in Box 13.1. Institutional fads, common in medicine and education, often have significant effects on people's well-being. **Institutional fads** result in shifts in the ways professionals practice that are regarded as pseudoscientific and controversial because they are not based on sound evidence of their effectiveness or superiority over other methods (Vyse 2005). These patterns are of particular interest to sociological social psychologists working within the social structure and personality tradition. Examples of institutional fads include the use of lethal injections in executions (Dever, Best, and Haas 2008), low-carb dieting (Best 2006), genetic explanations for alcohol and drug addiction (Anderson, Swann, and Lane 2010), and measurement-free (i.e., test-free) special education curricula (Heward and Silvesri 2005).

According to Best (2006), institutional fads are common within this society for three reasons:

1. People are socialized to believe in rationality, progress, and perfectibility. Thus, we are open to new ways of doing things.

2. Institutions within this society usually operate as autonomous units. This means that people in positions of power within these settings (e.g., school principals or hospital administrators) have a fair degree of latitude in the decisions they make. This, in turn, means that there are many social settings in which new approaches might be adopted.

3. Both individuals and organizations have dense social networks. At the individual level, a social network is dense when everyone in the network knows one another. At the institutional level, a social network is dense when people belong to multiple organizations. Dense social networks composed of many links between individuals (e.g., teachers) and organizations (e.g., school and national or regional teachers' associations) facilitate the spread of new techniques and ways of handling routine tasks or problems, even when there is little evidence to support their effectiveness.

People can combat this tendency (i.e., they can make themselves more "fad proof") by remaining skeptical of claims that seem too good to be true and by making decisions based on evidence, rather than a fear that they or their organization will be left behind if they don't readily adopt the latest trend (Best 2006). Theories, techniques, styles of practice, and interventions should become standard practice only after they have been subjected to, and supported by, rigorous scientific testing (Favell 2005).

Rumors and Urban Legends

Rumors are another episodic collective phenomena (i.e., they come and then go) studied by sociological social psychologists. **Rumors**, like gossip, may focus on individuals' personal lives. However, rumors often pertain to broader and potentially important issues (e.g., the harmfulness of a product or the health of high-profile politician) and they tend to be more widespread than gossip (Rosnow and Fine 1976). Thus rumors are considered a type of public opinion.

Public opinion refers to the ephemeral beliefs and attitudes constructed on a mass scale as people continually seek to define new situations, events, and issues. Rumors differ from other forms of public opinion in that they have not been verified by individuals or organizations regarded within society as legitimate authorities (Peterson and Gist 1951). In this respect, rumors are similar to legends (Rosnow and Fine 1976).

Legends are narratives presented as though they are to be believed, although they may not be accepted as factual by either the audience or the storyteller. Whereas legends traditionally have magical or religious themes, **urban legends** focus on institutions and behaviors that are part of life in urban areas. Urban legends have largely replaced more traditional legends within this society (Fine 1987). Urban legends, as well as rumors, can be considered a type of collective behavior because they involve the exchange of information that differs in content from commonly held beliefs about objects, activities, and events within society.

The following three urban legends have been systematically analyzed by sociological social psychologists.

1. The Kentucky Fried Rat

The story about the Kentucky Fried rat was an urban legend that circulated in the 1970s. Although it had multiple versions, the gist of the story was that someone purchased a meal from the Kentucky Fried Chicken restaurant chain and received rat, rather than chicken, meat. This was evident when the person eating the rat (or, in some cases, a mouse) noticed a strange taste or bones unlike those of a chicken. In one version of the urban legend, the person who consumed the rat suffered a heart attack and died as a result. Allegedly her family was suing the restaurant chain (Fine 1980).

2. Tainted Halloween Treats

You may remember hearing about razor blades in Halloween treats when you were a child. Apples were said to be the prime candidates for this type of tampering. The urban legend purporting that apples with razor blades and poisoned candy are commonly given to children trick-or-treating on Halloween, and thus a cause for serious concern, started circulating in the early 1970s. The alleged instances of adulterated treats attained a high profile and were the subject of a number of newspaper articles on Halloween sadism during the 1970s and 1980s. At that time, people were highly concerned about the risk of tainted Halloween candy, despite the fact that there is little evidence that this was ever a widespread problem (Best and Horiuchi 1985). Tainted Halloween treats are still perceived as a threat. In fact, in one recent poll focusing on Halloween safety, one fourth of the parents surveyed indicated that they were worried that their children would be poisoned by the candy they received from trick-or-treating (Safe Kids World Wide 2011).

3. Pop Rocks and Coca-Cola: A Fatal Combination

Another well-known urban legend in the 1970s and 1980s focused on deaths resulting from mixing Pop Rocks (a sodium bicarbonate candy that pops in people's mouths when it mixes with their saliva) and Coca-Cola. As is often the case, this urban legend was especially popular among youths. In one version of the story, the person who died from this combination was Mikey, the child who appeared in a well-known commercial for Life Cereal, popular during the same era. This urban legend was prominent for many years and was probably still in circulation at the beginning of the new millennium (Noymer 2001).

Q: What do the three urban legends just summarized have in common, and what purpose do they serve?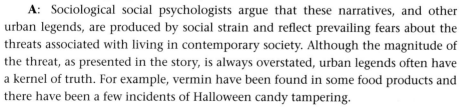

A: Sociological social psychologists argue that these narratives, and other urban legends, are produced by social strain and reflect prevailing fears about the threats associated with living in contemporary society. Although the magnitude of the threat, as presented in the story, is always overstated, urban legends often have a kernel of truth. For example, vermin have been found in some food products and there have been a few incidents of Halloween candy tampering.

Urban legends about contaminated food are common and reflect concerns about consuming food prepared outside of the home, with unknown ingredients and handlers. The Kentucky fried rat is certainly consistent with this theme (Fine 1987). Similarly, the urban legend about razor blades or poison in Halloween candy reflects this theme, as well as prevailing concerns about the safety of children and fear of crime (Best and Horiuchi 1985).

Stories about people dying from mixing Pop Rocks and Coca-Cola may reflect an underlying concern about the unknown contents of the things we eat. Although Pop Rocks were popular because the sounds they made were so unusual, it is unlikely that few people understood why they did this. Both Pop Rocks and Coke cause a similar sensation in one's mouth, which was probably why they were linked in the legend. The root of the association between Pop Rock deaths and Mikey is unknown, other than the fact that both the Life Cereal commercial and Pop Rocks were popular around the same time. Whatever its source, the Pop Rocks story was certainly one that grabbed people's attention. Urban legends like this are perceived as entertaining because they are so shocking. Someone died because they combined two popular food products! The shock value of this kind of story facilitates its social transmission.

Interestingly, experimental studies suggest that people are the most likely to pass on urban legends that are disgusting. Many stories about food fall into this category. The systematic analysis of the content of urban legend websites shows a similar pattern. Stories that evoke the most disgust are the most widely circulated on the Internet (Heath, Bell, and Sternberg 2001).

Urban legends often have relatively long lives, sometimes lasting for over a decade (e.g., the Halloween candy and the Pop Rocks legends). This is because they persist well beyond the belief of their original adherents.

Belief in urban legends at the individual level is usually short-lived because a review of available evidence reveals them to be untrue. Thus, urban legends spread in a manner similar to nonfatal infectious diseases, passed on by individuals to members of their social networks. Individuals catch a nonfatal infectious disease and then get better, while others with whom they have contact contract the disease, so the rate of disease within society remains at a constant level even though the individuals who have the disease continuously change. Showing a similar pattern, urban legends spread, not because the number of believers increases, but because legend adherents who transition to nonbelievers are replaced by new (typically young) believers.

Paradoxically, attempts to refute an urban legend may increase its life-span. Actively discouraging people from believing an urban legend may make it last longer, as the age at which new believers are recruited tends to decrease within this context. That is, when an urban legend's validity is openly challenged, people start passing it on to even younger recruits, the only individuals likely to believe the story, which is likely to increase its popularity (Noymer 2001).

> ## What Do You Think?
>
> Get together with two or three of your classmates and identify three or four urban legends that you've encountered recently. Analyze their content. What themes, or concerns, do they reflect? Where did you hear or read about these alleged incidents?

Mass Hysteria

Mass hysteria is a form of collective behavior that occurs when people behave in ways that are perceived by others within society to be unconventional, emotional, and irrational. It includes panics and somatoform epidemics.

Panics

A **panic** results from unfounded and irrational beliefs that lead people to misperceive a situation as threatening. When a panic occurs, people quickly diverge from common interactional patterns in an attempt to save themselves and their property (Smelser 1962).

Panic in response to rapidly decreasing stock prices precipitated the Great Depression. Trading on Wall Street became frantic, with people shouting, "Sell, Sell, Sell" so loudly on the floor of the stock exchange on the morning of Black Tuesday (October 29, 1929) that the opening bell couldn't be heard. As trading progressed at a wild pace, rumors about investors jumping out windows due to large losses circulated and resulted in even lower stock prices (Suddath 2008).

In response to financial concerns resulting from the stock market crash, there was a run on banks across the country. A large number of individuals, afraid that they would lose their savings if their bank went under, withdrew their money. This, in turn, resulted in a self-fulfilling prophecy. Due to the large number of cash withdrawals, many banks failed in the 1930s (Merton 1948), which further hindered the country's economic recovery. Financial panics are relatively common and often have long-term consequences (Sobel 1988).

A 1938 a radio broadcast by Orson Wells of an adaption of H. G. Wells's classic science fiction novel *War of the Worlds* created a national panic rooted in another kind of perceived threat: alien invasion. Thousands of people across the country believed that the radio program was a news broadcast and that malevolent Martians had landed on Earth. As a result, they cried, prayed, and sought out family members in order to say their final farewells. However, many people did not react in this manner. Some individuals were skeptical and investigated the story, calling police to ask about the broadcast or seeking to verify its authenticity through some other source. Presumably, the information received eased any initial concerns they might have had about the program's content.

Level of education was one personal characteristic associated with the belief that the program was a news broadcast. Individuals who had completed college were much less likely to have believed that the story was real than individuals with less formal schooling.

People's responses to the radio program were also shaped by the time when they tuned into the show. Those individuals who tuned in late were the most likely to believe that the invasion was real. Only 4% of the people who listened to the program from its onset believed that it was an actual news broadcast.

Another situational factor that influenced individuals' responses to the broadcast included the reactions of members of their social networks. Those individuals who panicked often reported that they had talked to family members who were highly upset by the program and believed that it referred to a real event.

Finally, structural factors may have played a role in creating a context conducive to panic. In 1938, social norms were changing rapidly; the country had not yet recovered from the depression of 1929; and there had recently been a war scare, which was broadcast in a manner similar to the *War of the Worlds* program. This chain of events may have increased people's readiness to believe that the dramatic presentation of *War of the Worlds* pertained to a real event (Cantril 1940).

Panics may also occur within the context of a crisis situation (e.g., when a building collapses or there is a fire, or during the onset of a natural disaster), as large numbers of people seek to exit the area (Smelser 1962). Although panics are commonly depicted in movies, research suggests that crisis situations don't often generate this type of response. Instead, people often help others before trying to save themselves (Clarke 2002). This appears to have been the case in a number of recent school shootings, events that could easily have initiated a panic as people sought to escape the shooter. There have been many media accounts of people helping, or protecting others, in these situations, often resulting in their own deaths. Due to a lack of empirical evidence, the utility of the concept of panic for understanding behavior in crisis situations has been questioned within the social psychological literature (Clarke 2002).

Somatoform Epidemics

Somatoform epidemics, another form of mass hysteria, occur when a group of individuals exhibit physical symptoms that are social and psychological, rather than physical, in origin. These syndromes are also called conversion disorders.

The symptoms of the disorder, often similar to those associated with known physical illnesses, are transmitted through people's social networks in schools, in the workplace, or in the larger community. Thus, they do not exhibit a pattern typical of physical contagion. Rather than spreading through physical contact, they spread among individuals who are connected socially (Eaton 1999). That is, they spread much like actions and feelings that are relatively common within society, such as divorce, obesity, happiness, and loneliness. The symptoms of a somatoform epidemic differ from the latter behaviors and emotions only in that their content is clearly outside of what is considered normative, without the presence of an underlying physical disease.

The **june bug epidemic** is one of the most well-known cases of a somatoform epidemic. Sixty-two workers at a textile factory in a small Southern city (mostly women) reported symptoms including nausea, feeling faint, numbness in the extremities, and body rashes. The symptoms were attributed to bites from insects contained within a shipment of cloth from England.

The epidemic persisted for 11 days, during which almost all of the affected individuals received medical care. Doctors from the U.S. Public Health Service, as well as local health officials, tried to determine the cause of the illness. Despite widespread acceptance of the link between insect bites and the symptoms among the affected individuals and others who worked in the factory, no medical cause for the epidemic was ever found. Thus, it was attributed to hysterical contagion (Kerckhoff and Back 1968).

Somatoform epidemics, like the case just described, occur across cultures and are more common than one might think. For example, Boss (1997) found 70 somatoform epidemics documented within the research literature within a 20-year time frame (1973–1993). Of the reported cases, 34 (almost 50%) occurred within the United States. Schools and factories appear to be the most common locations of somatoform outbreaks, and women are more likely to exhibit these kinds of symptoms than men. This may be due to women's greater exposure to the triggers presumed to be the cause of the illnesses (Boss 1997). In the case of the june bug epidemic, for instance, it was primarily women who were exposed to the cloth that contained the insects believed to be the cause of the illness.

Somatoform epidemics often appear bizarre to those outside of the afflicted group and serve as a reminder of the power individuals exert in constructing their realities. Within the social psychological literature, it has been suggested that somatoform epidemics exhibit many of the emergent characteristics of crowd behavior (Eaton 1999).

TAKE A BREAK

Listen to a news story about a potential somatoform epidemic among adolescent females in a small town in upstate New York. The families of the girls who are ill with what appear to be neurological symptoms have resisted this label and are demanding further medical evaluation and treatment. Go to http://www. npr.org/2012/03/10/148372536/the-curious-case-of-teen-tics-in-le-roy-n-y.

This March 10, 2012, radio broadcast can also be accessed from the NPR website (npr.org) by selecting *All Things Considered*, under programs, and All Dates. In the Search box, type either "somatoform disorder" or "conversion disorder."

Behavior in Crowds

Social psychological theories of behavior in crowds have focused on the social contagion of emotion and behavior, the consequences of anonymity, and the social construction of norms.

Social Contagion

Early theories of crowd behavior (LeBon 1896; Blumer 1939) emphasized the transformative aspects of this interactive context. Crowds were presumed to take hold of individuals through a process of social contagion and transform them so that they acted in ways contrary to normal conduct. From this perspective, collective behavior emerges as the result of a sequence of circular reactions, in which individuals' respond to and reinforce one another's actions (McPhail 1991). The outcome of this process was believed to be behavior that is unrestrained, irrational, and potentially harmful. When a crowd gets out of hand and engages in behavior deemed problematic, it is usually referred to as a mob.

Deindividuation

Mob behavior is characterized by a process psychological social psychologists call deindividuation. **Deindividuation** occurs when the anonymity provided by a

PHOTO 13.4

Black Friday shoppers looking for bargains on electronic items at a Best Buy store in San Diego, CA (November 25, 2011).

group reduces people's social inhibitions. When deindividuation occurs, formal and informal mechanisms of social control are suspended, and people do things that they would not do in other situations (Festinger, Pepitone, and Newcomb 1952).

Although flash mobs are organized events, it is the anonymity of the crowd that makes people so willing to publically violate social norms (Wasik 2006). Arguably, there are few individuals who would do this on their own.

Mobs of holiday shoppers seeking bargains at stores like Walmart during the early morning hours on Black Friday (the day after Thanksgiving) also illustrate the phenomenon of deindividuation. In 2008, over 2,000 individuals at a Walmart store in Valley Stream, New York, broke through glass doors and entered the store, trampling store employees. One worker died at the scene, and four shoppers were injured in the stampede (McFadden and Macropoulos 2008). Similar events, some resulting in deaths, have occurred at other stores offering a limited number of items, typically televisions and other electronic devices, at highly discounted prices.

Although the shoppers involved in these events may not have behaved in a similar manner without the cover of the crowd, it is unlikely that anonymity, and subsequent deindividuation, alone gave rise to this behavior. The emotionally charged nature of these events, and the tension that arises out of people's fear that they will lose the competition for the coveted items, facilitates this kind of behavior. Expectations cultivated by the media, through advertising, and the value placed on material goods and getting a good deal within this culture may also contribute store stampedes.

In an attempt to limit the potential for injury and death during the 2012 holiday season, some stores ran their sales in intervals, so that only one bargain item was available during a set (often two-hour) period. This limited the size of the crowd at any given time. Since the 2008 stampede, stores have also increased their numbers of security personnel. Nonetheless, critics have argued that retailers are creating dangerous situations when they advertise bargains but have very few of these items in stock. This competitive shopping environment, designed to maximize profits, is highly conducive to the formation of mobs like the one at the Valley Stream Walmart.

Emergent Norms

At its onset, crowd behavior involves what sociological social psychologists call milling. **Milling** occurs when individuals peruse a particular location (e.g., the storefront during the early morning hours of Black Friday). Milling is common in settings where large numbers of people have congregated. However, the nature of milling has been heavily debated within the social psychological literature. Whereas contagion theorists view milling as the equivalent to the movement one observes among a herd of cattle, working within the symbolic interactionist tradition, Turner and Killian (1987) emphasize the verbal and cognitive aspects of this process. They argue that milling individuals seek to construct a definition of the situation by getting verbal feedback from others about what is happening and what is likely to happen.

They also ask others what the group should do (e.g., "Should we storm the store doors?") and who should act first.

Turner and Killian (1987) argue that norms governing individuals' behaviors in crowds emerge through a process of keynoting. **Keynoting** occurs when individuals present suggestions as to how people should respond in an ambiguous situation. The keynote (suggestion) accepted by the crowd will be the one that best matches the motives of the majority of its members.

As the situation becomes defined as one that demands a particular type of response, it becomes increasingly difficult for the individuals present to resist this interpretation. Thus, the acceptance of any particular course of action by members of the crowd reduces uncertainty, and the hesitancy to act, among others who are present. It is through this process that a norm emerges (cited in McPhail 1991).

Turner and Killian's (1987) **emergent norm theory** is a very different approach to the study of behavior in crowds than earlier models. From this perspective, behavior in crowds is not spontaneous or irrational, as suggested by social contagion theories. Nor is it the result of a process of deindividuation, as suggested by psychological social psychologists. Rather, it is the product of social norms, constructed by the individuals who are present within the social encounter.

It is likely that emergent norms provide the foundation for somatoform epidemics, discussed in the previous section. Members of a group construct a definition of the situation through their social interactions, which develops into group norms that support their psychosomatic symptoms (Stahl and Lebedon 1974).

SOCIAL MOVEMENTS

Sociological social psychologists who study collective behavior are especially interested in social movements. A **social movement** is a collectivity of individuals acting together to promote or resist change within the group or society to which they belong (Turner and Killian 1987).

Social movements are a topic of interest to sociological social psychologists because their initiation, and their success, reflects both structural and individual-level factors and because they illustrate the ways individuals affect society. Social movements often result in widespread social change. There is power in numbers. At the individual level, it is often difficult to resist broader social forces. However, by acting collectively, people have the capacity to change the structure of society (Mills 1959).

Early Theories

Early theories of social protest focused on behavior in crowds and viewed action within this context as irrational and uncontrolled. This was the lens through which social movements were viewed until the 1960s.

Value-Added Theory

Smelser's (1962) **value-added theory** is broader in focus than the latter models and emphasizes the structural roots of collective behavior. According to Smelser, people are likely to engage in social movements and other forms of collective behavior when society has certain characteristics. Each characteristic, or condition, adds value by building on those that preceded it. Thus, the order in which the conditions emerge is important in providing the foundation for collective action.

In Smelser's model, the conditions that give rise to collective behavior, including social movements, are as follows:

1. *Structural conduciveness*. The structure of society must allow for collective behavior. In a society that limits communication between individuals, for example, protest will be unlikely. On the other hand, within a society such as the United States, social media and other forms of technologically mediated communication facilitate the dissemination of information and the organization of protests (including smart mobs).

2. *Structural strain*. Structural strain may result from a variety of sources, including the isolation and alienation associated with life in an industrial society (Kornhauser 1959). However, according to Smelser (1962), strain is often economic in origin. Thus, actual or perceived economic deprivation is viewed as an important precursor to social movements, but only within societies that are structured to allow for this type of response (condition 1).

3. *Growth and spread of a generalized belief*. Beliefs about the source of, and the appropriate response to, strain are important precursors of collective behavior. Note that Smelser's emphasis on generalized belief, as is relates to structural strain, is consistent with the focus of research within the social structure and personality camp.

4. *Precipitating factors*. There is usually some kind of dramatic event (e.g., a Black family moving into a White neighborhood during the pre-civil rights era) that provides a specific reference point for collective action. (Smelser 1962)

5. *Mobilization for action*. Smelser (1962) argues that leaders (like Martin Luther King Jr. prior to the civil rights movement) play an important role in mobilizing people once the previous four conditions have been met.

6. *The operation of social control*. How agents of social control, including the police, the courts, the media, religious groups, and community leaders respond to collective behavior determines its course. Agents of social control may not take a side, or they may actively facilitate or thwart a social movement. Sometimes they unintentionally increase public support for a social movement when they respond to protesters in a way that is perceived as excessively harsh or violent (Smelser 1962). This was the case in

PHOTO 13.5

Civil Rights March on Washington DC (August 28, 1963)

Birmingham, Alabama, in 1963, when the police used dogs and high-pressure water hoses to control Black children participating in a protest march. This action was shown on news broadcasts across the country. The brutality of the police response drew attention to race relations in the South and increased support for the civil rights movement among Whites.

Smelser's (1962) model is wider in its scope than earlier theories of social movements, which focused primarily on behavior in crowds. However, critics have argued that Smelser's perspective has a conservative bias given its roots in the structural functionalist perspective within sociology. Structural functionalism views collective behavior as disruptive to the social system. Thus, rather than seeing collective behavior as positive because it gives rise to social change, collective behavior is viewed as a potential social problem. Most contemporary sociological social psychologists who study collective behavior do not share structural functionalists' orientation. Rather, they tend to see social movements as a response to legitimate concerns about how society operates and view social change in a more positive light (Porta and Dani 2006).

Other Models Within Social Structure and Personality

Focusing on the link between societal conditions and social protest, social structure and personality researchers have emphasized the relationship between perceived injustice and the desire for social change. In particular, they have suggested that participation in social movements is associated with the following psychological characteristics:

- Relative deprivation, resulting from the perception that one is less well-off than members of one or more reference groups (Geschwender and Geschwender 1973; Gurr 1970) or from downward social mobility. It was assumed that people who were downwardly mobile would experience relative deprivation when they compared themselves to individuals in their previous position.

- Rising expectations associated with prolonged periods of economic growth that are not accompanied by widespread upward social mobility.

- The unfilled expectations that occur when a period of increased well-being is followed by a downturn in the economy (as cited in Melucci 1988).

- Frustration resulting from conflicting role expectations associated with inconsistent statuses (e.g., having a high level of education and a low-prestige job) (Lenski 1954).

Despite the popularity of these models in the 1960s and 1970s, they were not consistently supported by the results of empirical studies. Thus, by the end of the 1970s, the resource mobilization approach had supplanted the latter models.

Resource Mobilization

The resource mobilization perspective (McAdam 1982; McCarthy and Zald 1973; Oberschall 1973) is an economic model of collective behavior that highlights the importance of resources, in particular money and labor, at the aggregate level (McCarthy and Zald 1977). This theoretical framework, which views actors as highly rational, has had a tremendous influence on the focus of research on social movements conducted within the United States since the 1970s (Jenkins 1983). Its central tenets are as follows:

- There is usually enough discontent within society at any given time to give rise to a social movement. However, social movements occur only when the resources required for their execution are present.

- Organizations are necessary to aggregate and manage resources. Thus, social movements necessarily have a structure composed of grassroots, regional, or national organizations that focus on attaining the movement's goals (McCarthy and Zald 1977). Examples of **social movement organizations** in the United States include the American Civil Liberties Union (ACLU), the American Federation of Labor and Congress of Industrial Organizations (AFL-CIO), the National Association for the Advancement of Color People (NAACP), the

National Organization for Women (NOW), Greenpeace, and the Gay and Lesbian Activists Alliance (GLAA).

- The success of a social movement is based on the involvement of individuals and organizations from outside, as well as within, the movement. Thus, the nature of the strategies used to mobilize support for a movement is an important topic of study.

- Social movement organizations use the infrastructure of society, including the media and people's social networks, to mobilize support for the movement.

- Individuals and organizations become involved in a social movement when the benefits exceed the costs of doing so (McCarthy and Zald 1977).

As you can see, the resource mobilization perspective is more of a macro-level structural than a social psychological model of collective behavior. It focuses largely on social movement organizations and does not fully consider variations in individuals' social experiences or perspectives (Klandermans 1984). In fact, from this perspective, all people are viewed as equivalent.

However, not all individuals who hold a similar structural position and share a similar **ideology** (beliefs, values, and understandings of the world) will participate in a social movement (Stryker, Owens, and White 2000). The question is, why? This is the issue pertaining to social movements of primary interest to sociological social psychologists (Klandermans 1997).

Why Individuals Participate in Social Movements

Sociological social psychologists have explained different levels of movement participation among similar kinds of individuals by focusing on the processes through which people construct meanings and define situations (Klandermans 1991).

Framing

Symbolic interactionists have studied the ways social movement organizations mobilize participants through the process of frame alignment. As you know from our discussion of the White racial frame, frames serve as schemata within which individuals interpret their experiences and plan patterns of action. **Frame alignment** refers to the link between social movement organizations' and individuals' interpretive schemata, so that their goals, activities, and ideologies are consistent. Frame alignment is accomplished through four processes: frame bridging, frame amplification, frame extension, and frame transformation. Through these processes, the movement is pitched, or marketed, in a way that makes people more likely to join it.

Frame bridging is a relatively common strategy for mobilizing potential movement participants. It involves linking ideologically similar frames pertaining to a particular issue. Social movement organizations appeal to members of organizations or groups, often via mail or email, with similar orientations in order to conjure additional participation and support. For example, in order to gain support for their cause, a prolife organization might send informational literature to members of a group that supports traditional family values.

Frame amplification is used by social movement organizations to make a particular value or belief that is presumed to be important to a pool of individuals not yet involved in the movement salient in their campaign. For example, neighborhood organizers opposed to the location of a homeless shelter in their immediate area might emphasize family values and how transients likely to use the shelter might pose a threat to local women and children.

Frame extension is used by social movement organizations to capture interests or views that are not part of their primary objectives but are likely to resonate with those of potential participants. Hosting rock and punk bands at peace rallies is a good example of this strategy. This increases the likelihood that individuals who are otherwise uninterested will attend these events. Social movement organizations might also expand their message to appeal to others demographic groups. For example, a peace movement with a predominantly White, middle-class membership might mobilize racial/ethnic minorities by expanding its scope to include an opposition to racism.

Frame transformation is used by social movement organizations to get people to change the way they view something. Something that is taken for granted or viewed as normative is transformed into something problematic, unjust, and in need of remediation (Snow et al. 1986). This frame alignment strategy has been central to the Occupy Wall Street movement, which seeks to get people to recognize and reject as problematic an economic structure in which 1% of the population controls the much of society's wealth (see Box 13.2).

Box 13.2   The Occupy Wall Street Movement

The Occupy Wall Street movement, which began in September 2011 with the Occupy Wall Street protest in New York City, focuses on reducing inequality in the United States and globally. Occupy protests have occurred in many U.S. cities and countries. On May Day 2012, as part of a general strike, the 99% (as distinct from the top 1%, who control most of the wealth in this society and internationally) were asked to boycott work, school, stores, and banks in a show of solidarity.

Unlike in traditional labor movements, many Occupy participants are from middle-class backgrounds. Moreover, the Occupy movement lacks a formal organizational structure and is not hierarchical (top down). Within the Occupy movement, decisions about the direction the movement takes and how actions will be executed are made through consensus (unanimous agreement) in general assemblies, rather than by individuals at the top of a bureaucratic hierarchy or through majority rule, as has typically been the case in social movements within the United States.

Because consensus decision making is new to many movement participants, there is likely to be a learning curve. As a result, the political culture of the city in which Occupy participants reside, including the number of local activists who have used consensus decision making in other contexts, may shape the efficiency with which they are able to use this strategy. Individuals experienced with consensus decision making may serve as models for, or instruct, other Occupy participants who are not accustomed to making group decisions in this manner (Leach, Morris and Yerkey 2012).

Think about how the groups to which you belong (e.g., a fraternity or sorority, clubs, your family, and your friendship groups) usually make decisions.

- When are you the most likely to adopt a consensus decision-making strategy?
- In what situations are you most likely to experience top-down decision making or majority rule?

PHOTO 13.6

Occupy Wall Street encampment in Zuccotti Park in New York City (November 5, 2011)

Frame alignment processes are critical for cultivating situational definitions that give rise to collective action. By increasing movement participation, frame alignment may be instrumental in the success of a social movement (Benford and Snow 2000).

Framing also refers to the more general process through which individuals interpret their position within society and its causes. In particular, the adoption of an injustice frame, which leads one to view the position of one's group as more disadvantaged than it should be, is an important precursor to participation in a social movement (Gamson 1992).

Symbolic interactionists who have applied the emergent norm approach (Turner and Killian 1987) to social movements have focused on *how* existing structural conditions become defined as unjust. Often this process is facilitated by an event that dramatizes or personalizes a social issue. This increases the salience of the issue and draws attention to its problematic nature, which gives rise to new situational definitions and the emergence of norms concerning the appropriate course of action (Turner 1996). For example, recent incidents of gun violence in schools have shifted people's perspectives on the ready availability of guns within this society and resulted in increased activism among individuals on both sides of the issue (those for and those opposed to increasing gun control).

THE FREE RIDER PROBLEM

However, not everyone who desires social change (or who wants to prevent change, as in the case of pro-gun activists) will get involved in a relevant social movement. This is because people can benefit from a social movement even when they don't actively participate in it. This gives rise to what is commonly referred to as the free rider problem. The **free rider problem** refers to the fact that many individuals will opt not to participate in a social movement that they recognize as good for society because the movement's success is not regarded as dependent upon their individual actions (Olson 1965).

What Do You Think?

The free rider problem is also relevant to group tasks where all members receive the same outcome (e.g., a grade) based on the group's final output. Have you ever experienced the free rider problem within this context? What can students do to reduce their likelihoods of encountering free riders when they work with others on a class project? What can professors do to limit the occurrence of this pattern?

Social Movement Participation as a Self-Fulfilling Prophecy

In recent years, as well as serving as an organizational tool, the Internet has been used to broadcast footage from protests, including smart mobs, to increase awareness of perceived injustices and to show that there is widespread support for the cause. This kind of exposure may increase support for a social movement. It may also increase individuals' willingness to get involved in the movement themselves.

Research shows that people's expectations about others' behaviors are instrumental in shaping their likelihood of participating in a social movement. Estimating others' participation in a social movement enables individuals to evaluate a movement's probability of success in providing a benefit to society and how they might contribute to this outcome. Thus, at the aggregate level, the expectation that others will participate in a social movement results in a self-fulfilling prophecy. People who think others will participate in a movement are more likely to participate in the movement because they regard the movement as likely to be successful. This, in turn, results in higher participation and increases the likelihood of movement success (Klandermans 1984).

Participation itself also tends to increase people's commitment to a social movement (Klandermans 2002). Psychological social psychologists have shown that people tend to infer that they hold beliefs and feelings that are consistent with their actions across social settings. Given this, involvement in social movement activities and actions (e.g., work on behalf of a social movement organization or participation in a protest) is likely give rise to a pro-movement mind-set, which increases individuals' likelihood of subsequent participation in the movement (Ferree and Miller 1985).

Socially Based Identities and Participation in Social Movements

People may also participate in social movements for identity reasons. According to identity theorists, working within the Iowa/Indiana school of symbolic interactionism, social movement organizations and events serve as social contexts within which individuals interact with others and have the opportunity to form new relationships. Thus, involvement in a social movement may be a way for people to cultivate new (socially based) identities.

However, changes in the content of individuals' self-concepts resulting from social movement participation are often gradual. Typically, the identities social movement participants develop are extensions of the way they viewed themselves prior to joining the movement. When the change in the self-concept of movement participants is more drastic, it is usually rooted in two processes: (1) the reinterpretation of the past within the context of their new self-view and (2) the verification of new identities through group activities with other movement participants.

New identities that can be readily integrated into people's exiting self-concepts are the most likely to result in sustained participation in a social movement. New identities that are highly discrepant with prior self-views, on the other hand, may lead people to leave the movement (Pinel and Swann 2000).

People's non-movement-related identities also influence the trajectory of their involvement in social movements. The extent to which movement and nonmovement relations overlap is an important determinant of behavior for identity theorists. Overlap is high when the majority of a movement participant's friends and family members are also active in the social movement. When this is the case, the extent that the individual identifies with the movement, and participates in movement-related activities, is likely to be high (Stryker 2000).

Competing, nonoverlapping, social relations are also of relevance to participants' investment in a social movement. A movement participant with few competing role involvements (e.g., marital, parental, school, work, friendship-based, etc.) is more likely to become heavily involved in movement-related activities (e.g., protests and activities directed toward getting others involved in the movement) than

PHOTO 13.7

These Tunisians are rallying (with Tunisian soldiers standing guard) in commemoration of a fruit seller whose actions sparked the Tunisian revolution (December 17, 2011). This revolution is considered to be the beginning of the Arab Spring.

someone who has many other role-based commitments. Moreover, because participation in a social movement is a function of roles and social relationships outside of, as well as within, the movement, it is likely to change as individuals experience role transitions (e.g., marriage or parenthood) or other changes in their lives (Hardnack 2011; Stryker 2000).

Social Networks, Social Support, and High-Risk Activism

Research has shown that social movement participants often share membership in preexisting groups, and social networks play an important role in the recruitment of new participants (Turner 1996). Relationships among activists may also influence individuals' trajectories of involvement in a social movement. Agents of social control often respond to protestors with violence. Hence, being on the forefront of a social movement can be risky. The 2011 Arab Spring, when protests simultaneously occurred in many Arab nations, has resulted in many deaths. The numbers of lives lost is especially high in Libya, Syria, and Egypt.

Activism that is likely to have negative personal consequences is highly stressful, and social relationships among social movement participants often serve as an important source of social support in this context. Moreover, the sense of community cultivated among activists, rooted in mutually supportive social relationships, increases feelings of solidarity and reinforces their shared social identity, making sustained participation in a social movement more likely (Gamson 1992).

Collective Identity and Participation in Social Movements

Collective (i.e., social) identity is also an important precursor to participation in a social movement. Unlike socially based (personal) identities, which are rooted in social relationships and face-to-face interaction, social identities emerge through the process of self-categorization (us vs. them). This occurs when the way society is organized makes membership in a particular social category (e.g., African American, woman, or immigrant) salient, so that it serves as the basis for the formation of cognitive in- versus out-group divisions (Klandermans 2002).

The formation of a collective identity minimizes the distinction between individual and group interests. Thus, it increases people's likelihoods of participating in a social movement, even when they know that they may benefit from the movement even if they don't get involved themselves. Thus, collective identity is a potential solution to the free rider problem (Gamson 1992).

As evidenced in the preceding sections, it is through the application of multiple perspectives that social psychologists have enhanced their understanding of who is likely to join a social movement. The micro-level determinants of participation in

PERCEPTION/PROCESS/ CHARACTERISTIC	THEORETICAL FRAMEWORK	FACE OF SOCIAL PSYCHOLOGY
Injustice frame, situational definitions and emergent norms supportive of collective action	Symbolic interactionism	Symbolic interactionism
Perception that movement has many participants	Consistent with symbolic interactionism (situational definitions shape behavior)	Symbolic interactionism
Involvement in movement (increases commitment to movement)	Cognitive dissonance/ self-perception theory (behavior shapes attitudes)	Psychological
Desire for new (socially based) identities or need to verify existing (socially based) identities	Structural symbolic interactionism (Identity theory)	Symbolic Interactionism/ Social structure and personality
Social support from fellow activists	Not applicable*	Social structure and personality
Collective (i.e., social) identity (synthesis of individual and group interests)	Social identity theory	Group processes and structures

*Research in the social structure and personality tradition is rarely governed by a particular theoretical framework.

TABLE 13.1

Summary of the Micro-Level Perceptions, Processes, and Characteristics that Increase Social Movement Participation

social movements, and the faces of social psychology within which relevant concepts and are located, are summarized in Table 13.1.

NEW SOCIAL MOVEMENTS

Collective identity is especially important within the context of new social movements. **New social movements** (Melucci 1980) emerge in postindustrial societies (societies where the main economic products are information and services, rather than manufactured goods) and are distinct from the working-class labor movements that characterized the industrial era (Pichardo 1997). New social movements emphasize attitudes toward work, nature, and consumption that differ from traditional values in support of capitalism (hierarchical relationships, economic inequality, and little concern for the environment). Participants in new social movements are reacting to industrialization, bureaucratization, and a loss of identity, and they are usually middle (versus working) class (Klandermans 1991).

Sociological social psychologists who study this form of collective behavior argue that the participants in new social movements are seeking recognition for their new lifestyles and identities (Polletta and Jasper 2001). From this perspective, the construction of a collective (social) identity among social movement participants is important because it increases commitment to the movement and challenges prevailing views about how society should be (Gamson 1992). According to new social movement theory, movement participants' social identities and the culture of a social movement (the norms, values, and beliefs of its participants) serve as the basis for the transformation of society's culture.

The Arab Spring and the Occupy Wall Street movement (Box 13.2) are new social movements (Langman 2013). The gay rights movement, the environmental movement, the animal rights movement, and the peace movement are some other examples of new social movements.

COALITIONS

A **coalition** involves cooperation between two or more actors in order to increase the rewards received in a social exchange (Thibaut and Kelley 1959). As you know, sociological social psychologists working within the social exchange framework are especially interested in power within exchange relations, based on resources and exchange alternatives. In Chapter 5 we introduced Nora, who planned to expand her number of potential exchange partners so that she would be in a better position to bargain with Mr. Gutierrez, the owner of the business she sells for.

Nora might also enhance her power relative to Mr. Gutierrez by forming a coalition with other salespeople in the area who also work for him. If they too desire to increase the amount of money they receive for selling Mr. Gutierrez's jewelry, they might collectively agree upon some basic business terms that are in their favor. For example, they might agree not to contract with Mr. Gutierrez unless they all get some set rate of commission that is higher than what they are currently earning. Mr. Gutierrez will not be in a position to resist this if doing so would leave him without any sales representatives. Thus, this strategy could potentially increase the revenues of all of the sales people who contract with Mr. Gutierrez's company. When actors in an exchange network act collectively in this manner, they are able to maximize the rewards they receive from an exchange partner by (1) combining their resources (in this case, sales ability) and (2) reducing their partner's exchange options (sales personnel).

A sense of collective identity facilitates the formation of coalitions for the same reason that it increases individuals' likelihoods of joining a social movement. Actors who lack power within an exchange relation are the most likely to participate in a coalition when they have a collective (social) identity because they will view their personal and group interests as one and the same. When actors perceive their individual interests as apart from those of the group, they may seek to benefit from the coalition without actually joining it. That is, they may become free riders. Without widespread participation, a coalition loses its power to increase the rewards received within the exchange. Thus, the formation of a collective identity among actors in the subordinate position within an exchange relation may be critical to their success in increasing the rewards obtained (Simpson and Macy 2004).

Coalition formation regularly occurs in power-imbalanced exchange relations, where actors may be individuals, as in the case of Nora and other sales representatives within her industry, or members of a labor union; companies, such as small businesses working together to more effectively compete with a larger corporation; or countries, joining forces in an attempt to control the actions of a nation perceived as a risk for unwarranted aggression, as in the recent case of the Iranian nuclear crisis. Coalitions are also common within social movements (Meyer and Corrigall-Brown 2005), and social movement organizations often form alliances with local governments and the courts in order to attain particular goals (e.g., the gay and lesbian movement seeking marriage rights) (Stearns and Almedia 2004). Moreover, social movements themselves sometimes form coalitions (e.g., the labor, antiwar, environmental, and women's movements within the United States have formed strategic alliances in the past) in order to increase their likelihood of bringing about social change (Van Dyke and McCammon 2010).

SOCIAL MOVEMENT OUTCOMES

A review of the research literature on social movement outcomes (Guigni 1998) shows that social movements can influence society either directly, by radically transforming society's economic and political structures, or indirectly, through incorporation. **Incorporation** is the process through which social movements are absorbed into the existing structure of society and affect legislation or the nature of the political process (cited in Oliver, Cadena-Roa, and Strawn 2003).

Social movements frequently make social issues (e.g., abortion, the use of nuclear power, war, or gun control) a part of public discourse and pressure politicians to respond to the concerns of their participants. Moreover, they affect how policies are made within social organizations and in the larger society. For example, diversity and sexual harassment workshops common in colleges and universities are largely a response to collective action in the 1960s and 1970s, and crime victims are allowed to make statements to the jury before sentencing due largely to the victims' rights movement (Meyer 2003).

Even when a social movement fails in attaining its political goals, it may be considered successful if it heightens people's awareness of particular issues, and injustices, within society. By challenging dominant cultural beliefs, social movements lead people to question the way society operates and to consider alternative forms of social organization as possibilities (Melucci 1989).

Social movements also influence the psychological states and behaviors of their participants (Meyer 2003). Sociological social psychologists working within the social structure and personality tradition are especially interested in these outcomes (Kiecolt 2000).

Social structure and personality (SSP) researchers studying the effects of social movements on their participants have focused on individuals who came of age during the late 1960s and early 1970s, the era of the civil rights, student, antiwar, and women's movements. An examination of these individuals' attitudes and experiences suggests that participation in protest has long-term effects. In particular, relative to their nonactivist peers, individuals who were involved in protests during the late 1960s had liberal political, religious, and familial orientations that persisted into their adult years. Presumably, this is because social movement organizations and protests serve as proximal environments within which socialization occurs. Through social interaction within these contexts, people develop cognitive schemata within which subsequent experiences are interpreted and acted upon.

Social networks may also contribute to the long-term effects of social movements on their participants. Movement participants and nonparticipants associate with different kinds of people. Insofar as these relationships are maintained, or relationships with other like-minded individuals are cultivated in new environments, values, norms, and orientations toward the world that distinguish between movement participants and nonparticipants will be reinforced (Sherkat and Blocker 1997). As a result, movement-based identities, verified through social interaction within the context of people's social networks, may persist for decades.

Often, individuals with salient activist identities participate in multiple social movements as they move throughout the life course. Among these individuals, the reciprocal relationship between the group and the individual may be especially strong. Involvement in a social movement shapes identity, which leads to subsequent participation in the movement, which in turn provides reinforcement for the activist identity (Kiecolt 2000).

CHAPTER SUMMARY

People's perceptions and behaviors are shaped by other individuals and the society in which they participate. At the micro level, psychological social psychologists have studied the ways situational factors shape people's susceptibility to social influence. Focusing on the interplay between structure and agency, sociological social psychologists have emphasized the ways people are constrained by, and construct, social norms. Although individuals are sometimes powerless in the face of broader social forces, through collective action, in the form of social movements, people can change the way society operates. Sociological social psychologists have identified factors that increase people's likelihood of participating in a social movement and the ways social movements affect their participants.

Key Points to Know

- **Research on social influence within psychological social psychology has identified the factors that make people prone to obedience and specified how and when conformity is likely to occur in group settings.** Public compliance involves normative influence and is evidenced when people change their behaviors but not their perceptions. Private acceptance is rooted in informational influence. People exhibit this type of conformity when they aren't really sure what they see, feel, or believe.

- **Within the group processes and structures tradition within sociological social psychology, status characteristic theory makes predictions about individuals' susceptibility to social influence based upon their status characteristics relative to those of other actors. Sociological social psychologists have also focused on social contagion within social networks.** In particular, they have studied divorce, alcohol and drug use, emotions (happiness and loneliness), obesity, and gossip. Additional research is needed to determine whether changing group norms explain the spread of characteristics like obesity among network members.

- **Much of the time, people behave in ways that are consistent with prevailing social norms. When a group of individuals acts in a manner that is outside of routine societal patterns, they are engaging in collective behavior.** Collective behavior is of interest to sociological social psychologists because it is a precursor to social change. Collective behavior includes fashions and fads, rumors and urban legends, mass hysteria, action in crowds, and social movements.

- **Although many fads are relatively harmless, at the institutional level they can have serious consequences.** Institutional fads are common within this society because progress and perfectability are dominant culture beliefs; our institutions and organizations are decentralized, giving administrative staff a fair degree of latitude when deciding what instruments, practices, or interventions to use; and both people and organizations have dense social networks, which facilitates the spread of information.

- **Urban legends are popular within this culture because they reflect strains and concerns about modern life.** They are also entertaining. The more disgusting the story, the more likely it is to be passed on to others.

- **Mass hysteria includes panics and somatoform epidemics. Whereas panics may not be as common as they were once thought to be, somatoform epidemics occur with a fair degree of regularity.** The symptoms people experience, without any identifiable underlying disease, tend to mirror those of physical illnesses.

- **Early theories depicted crowd behavior as unrestrained and irrational. Emergent norm theory, a more contemporary model of behavior in crowds within the symbolic interaction face of social psychology, emphasizes the ways individuals in crowds construct norms, which govern their subsequent actions**. From this perspective, the situational definition that best matches the motives of the majority of those individuals present will serve as the basis for the emerging norms.

- **Prominent theories of social movements went from (1) emphasizing the contagious and irrational nature of collective behavior to (2) viewing social movements as structurally based, but disruptive to the social order, to 3) focusing on frustration resulting from existing structural conditions as a precursor to collective action. When the latter theories weren't supported by research, the resource mobilization approach gained in popularity.** The research mobilization perspective is more of a structural than a social psychological model of collective behavior because it focuses on social movement organizations rather than individuals.

- **Why individuals choose to participate in social movements is the key issue of interest to sociological social psychologists who study this form of collective behavior.** Symbolic interactionists have specified the framing strategies that social movement organizations use to get people involved in the movement. Framing also explains why some people, but not others, perceive existing structural conditions as problematic.

- **The recognition that they can benefit from a social movement even if they don't participate, called the free rider problem, may**

prevent people from joining a social movement even when they are unhappy with the way society operates. Individuals experiencing discontent with the structure of society are more likely to become involved in a social movement when they think a lot of other people have joined the movement, when participation enables them to construct or maintain positive socially based identities, when they receive social support from other activists, and when they have a collective (i.e., social) identity that fuses individual and group interests.

- **In new social movements, collective identity and the culture of the movement itself serve as catalysts for social change. Collective identity is also instrumental in the formation of coalitions, which affect social change by empowering actors in an exchange relation.**

- **Social movements often result in social change and affect the lives of their participants.** Their consequences for society can be direct (widespread political change) or indirect (e.g., changes in legislation and political processes). At the micro level, participation in a social movement frequently leads to shifts in individuals' social relationships and self-concepts. These effects tend to be long lasting.

Terms and Concepts for Review

Coalition	June bug epidemic
Collective behavior	Keynoting
Compliance	Legends
Conformity	Mass hysteria
Deindividuation	Milling
Diffusion	New social movements
Emergent norm theory	Normative influence
Fads	Panic
Fashions	Private acceptance
Flash mobs	Public compliance
Frame alignment	Public opinion
Frame amplification	Rumors
Frame bridging	Smart mobs
Frame extension	Social constraint
Frame transformation	Social contagion
Free rider problem	Social influence
Gossip	Social movements
Ideology	Social movement organizations
Incorporation	Somatoform epidemics
Informational influence	Urban legends
Institutional fads	Value-added theory

Questions for Review and Reflection

1. Contrast research on social influence conducted by sociological social psychologists working within the status characteristics framework, in the group processes and structures face of sociological social psychology, with research on conformity conducted by psychological social psychologists.

2. How do sociological social psychologists define collective behavior? What do fads, urban legends, mass hysteria, crowd behavior, and social movements have in common?

3. What is the free rider problem? Describe the characteristics and social experiences that make individuals likely to join a social movement.

4. Suppose that you wanted to make your college or university more environmentally friendly by adopting a campus-wide recycling and waste reduction program (e.g., by having various offices replace paper with email communications). Why is it important to have the support of other students at your school? How might you get other students on campus to share your concerns and join you in your quest for relevant changes in school policy?

REFERENCES

Aber, J. Lawrence., Neil G. Bennett, Dalton C. Conley, and Jiali Li. 1997. "The Effects of Poverty on Child Health and Development." *Annual Review of Public Health* 18:463–483.

Acevedo, Bianca P. and Arthur Aron. 2009. "Does a Long-Term Relationship Kill Romantic Love?" *Review of General Psychology* 13:59–65.

Acosta, Yesenia D. and G. Patricia de la Cruz. 2011. "The Foreign-Born From Latin American and the Caribbean: 2010." *American Community Survey Brief,*. Retrieved September 4, 2012 (http://www.census.gov/prod/2011pubs/acsbr10–15.pdf).

Adams, Josh. 2009. "Marked Difference: Tattooing and Its Associations With Deviance in the United States." *Deviant Behavior* 30:266–292.

Adams, Natalie and Pamela Bettis. 2003. "Commanding the Room in Short Skirts: Cheering as the Embodiment of Ideal Girlhood." *Gender & Society* 17:73–91.

Adelman, Robert M. 2004. "Neighborhood Opportunities, Race, and Class: The Black Middle Class and Residential Segregation." *City and Community* 3:43–63.

Adler, Patricia A. and Peter Adler. 1998. *Peer Power: Preadolescent Culture and Identity*. New Brunswick, NJ: Rutgers University Press.

Adler, Patricia A. and Peter Adler. 2011. *Constructions of Deviance: Social Power, Context, and Interaction*. Belmont, CA: Wadsworth Publishing.

Agiesta, Jennifer and Sonya Ross. 2012. "Racial Attitudes Have Not Improved in the Four Years Since Obama Took Office." *The Christian Science Monitor*, October 27. Retrieved September 4, 2012. (http://www.csmonitor.com/USA/Latest-News-Wires/2012/1027/Racial-attitudes-have-not-improved-in-the-four-years-since-Obama-took-office).

Agnew, Robert. 1992. "Foundations for a General Strain Theory of Crime and Delinquency." *Criminology* 30:47–87.

Agnew, Robert. 2000. "Sources of Criminality: Strain and Subcultural Theories." Pp. 349–371 in *Criminology: A Contemporary Handbook,* edited by Joseph F. Sheley. Belmont, CA: Wadsworth.

Agnew, Robert and Helene White. 1992. "An Empirical Test of General Strain Theory." *Criminology* 30:475–499.

Agrawal, Rakesh K. and Jagriti Sadhana. 2010. "Emotional Labour and Employee Engagement in Call Centres: A Study in Indian Context." *International Journal of Work Organization and Emotion* 3:351–367.

Aguirre, Benigo G., E. L. Quarantelli, and Jorge L. Mendoza. 1988. "The Collective Behavior of Fads: The Characteristics, Effects, and Career of Streaking." *American Sociological Review* 53:569–584.

Ajrouch, Kristine J. and Abdi M. Kusow. 2007. "Racial and Religious Contexts: Situational Identities Among Lebanese and Somali Muslim Immigrants." *Ethnic & Racial Studies* 30:72–94.

Ajzen, Icek and Martin Fishbein. 2005. "The Influence of Attitudes on Behavior." Pp. 173–221 in *The Handbook of Attitudes,* edited by D. Albarracin, B. T. Johnson, and M. P. Zanna. Mahwah, NJ: Erlbaum.

Akers, Ronald L. 1998. *Social Learning and Social Structure: A General Theory of Crime and Deviance*. Boston, MA: Northeastern University Press.

Alami, Mona. 2012. "Rare Protests Break Out in Saudi Arabia." *USA Today* via pressconnects.com, September. Retrieved September 4, 2012 (http://kiaoragaza.wordpress.com/2012/10/09/rare-protests-breaking-out-in-saudi-arabia/).

Alba, Joseph W. and Lynn Hasher. 1983. "Is Memory Schematic?" *Psychological Bulletin* 93:203–231.

Albas, Daniel and Cheryl Albas. 1988. "Aces and Bombers: The Post-Exam Impression Management Strategies of Students." *Symbolic Interaction* 11:289–302.

Alger, Janet M. and Steven F. Alger. 2003. *Cat Culture: The Social World of a Cat Shelter*. Philadelphia, PA: Temple University Press.

Allen, Vernon L. 1965. "Situational Factors in Conformity." Pp. 133–170 in *Advances in Experimental Social Psychology*, vol. 2, edited by L. Berkowitz. New York, NY: Academic Press.

Allport, Gordon W. 1954. *The Nature of Prejudice*. Reading, MA: Addison-Wesley.

Alwin. Duane F. and Ryan. J. McCammon. 2004. "Generations, Cohorts, and Social Change." Pp. 23–50 in *Handbook of the Life Course*, edited by J. T. Mortimer and M. J. Shanahan. New York, NY: Springer.

Amato, Paul R. 2000. "The Consequences of Divorce for Adults and Children." *Journal of Marriage and Family* 62:1269–1287.

Amato, Paul R. 2003. "Reconciling Divergent Perspectives: Judith Wallerstein, Quantitative Family Research, and Children of Divorce." *Family Relations: An Interdisciplinary Journal of Applied Family Studies* 52:332–339.

Amato, Paul R. and Alan Booth. 1991. "The Consequences of Divorce for Attitudes Toward Divorce and Gender Roles." *Journal of Family Issues* 12:306–322.

Amato, Paul R. and Danielle D. DeBoer. 2001. "The Transmission of Marital Instability Across Generations: Relationship Skills or Commitment to Marriage." *Journal of Marriage and Family* 63:1038–1051.

Amato, Paul R. and Bryndl Hohmann-Marriott. 2007. "A Comparison of High- and Low-Distress Marriages That End in Divorce." *Journal of Marriage and Family* 69:621–638.

Amato, Paul R. and Denise Previti. 2003. "People's Reasons for Divorcing: Gender, Social Class, the Life Course, and Adjustment." *Journal of Family Issues* 24:602–626.

Amato, Paul R. and Stacy J. Rogers. 1999. "Do Attitudes Toward Divorce Affect Marital Quality." *Journal of Family Issues* 20:69–86.

Ambady, Nalini and Robert Rosenthal. 1993. "Half a Minute: Predicting Teacher Evaluations From Think Slices of Nonverbal Behavior and Physical Attractiveness." *Journal of Personality and Social Psychology* 64:431–441.

American Psychiatric Association. 2013. *Diagnostic and Statistical Manual of Mental Disorders,* 5th ed. (DSM 5). Washington, DC: American Psychiatric Publishing.

Amichai-Hamburger, Yair, Mila Kingsbury, and Barry H. Schneider. 2012. "Friendship: An Old Concept With New Meaning?" *Computers in Human Behavior* 29:33–39.

Anderson, C.A., A. Shibuya, N. Ihori, E.L. Swing, B.J. Busham, A. Sakamoto, H.R. Rothstein, and M. Saleem. 2010. "Violent Video Game Effects on Aggression, Empathy, and Prosocial Behavior in Eastern and Western Countries: A Meta-Analytic Review." *Psychological Bulletin* 136:251–173.

Anderson, Tammy, Holly Swan, and David C. Lane. 2010. "Institutional Fads and the Medicalization of Drug Addiction." *Sociological Compass* 4:476–494.

Aneshensel, Carol S. 2009. "Toward Explaining Mental Health Disparities." *Journal of Health and Social Behavior* 50:377–94.

Aneshensel, Carol S. and Jo E. Phelan. 1999. "The Sociology of Mental Health: Surveying the Field." Pp. 3–17 in *Handbook of Sociology of Mental Health*, edited by Carol S. Aneshensel and Jo Phelan. Dordrecht, Netherlands: Kluwer Academic Publishers.

Ansalone, George. 2001. "Schooling, Tracking and Inequality." *Journal of Children and Poverty* 7:33–47.

Aoki, Kumiko and Edward J. Downs. 2002. "An Analysis of Young People's Use of and Attitudes Toward Cell Phones." *Telematics and Informatics* 20:349–364.

Armstrong, Elizabeth, Laura Hamilton, and Paula England. 2010. "Is Hooking Up Bad for Young Women?" *Contexts* 9:22–27.

Arnett, Jeffrey Jensen. 2000. "Emerging Adulthood: A Theory of Development From the Late Teens Through the Twenties." *American Psychologist* 55:469–480.

Arnett, Jeffrey Jensen. 2005. "The Developmental Context of Substance Use in Emerging Adulthood." *Journal of Drug Issues* 35:235–254.

Arnett, Jeffrey Jensen and Susan Taber. 1994. "Adolescence Terminable and Interminable: When Does Adolescence End." *Journal of Youth and Adolescence* 23:517–537.

Aronson, Elliot and Alex Gonzalez. 1988. "Desegregation, Jigsaw, and the Mexican-American Experiment." Pp. 301–314 in *Eliminating Racism: Profiles in Controversy,* edited by Phyllis A. Katz and Dalmas A. Taylor. New York, NY: Plenum Press.

Aronson, Elliot and Judson Mills. 1959. "The Effect of Severity of Initiation on Liking for a Group." *Journal of Abnormal and Social Psychology* 59:177–181.

Aronson, Elliot, C. Stephan, J. Sikes, N. Blaney, and M. Snapp. 1978. *The Jigsaw Classroom.* Beverly Hills, CA: Sage Publications.

Asch, Solomon E. 1956. "Studies of Independence and Conformity: A Minority of One Against a Unanimous Majority." *Psychological Monographs: General and Applied* 70:1–70.

Associated Press. 2009. "Center Tries to Treat Addicts." *New York Times*, September 6, P. A18.

Associated Press. 2012. "Racial Attitudes Survey," Conducted by GfK. October 29. Retrieved March 21, 2013 (http://surveys.ap.org/data/GfK/AP_Racial_Attitudes_Topline_09182012.pdf.).

Aukett, Richard, Jane Ritchie, and Kathryn Mill. 1988. "Gender Differences in Friendship Patterns." *Sex Roles* 19:57–66.

Avison, William R. and Jinette Comeau. 2013. "The Impact of Mental Illness on the Family." Pp. 543–561 in *Handbook of the Sociology of Mental Health,* edited by Carol S. Aneshensel, Jo C. Phelan, and Alex Beirman. New York, NY: Springer.

Babbitt, Charles E. and Harold J. Burbach. 1990. "A Comparison in Self Orientation Among College Students Across the 1960s, 1970s, and 1980s." *Youth and Society* 21:472–482.

Bachman, Jerald G., Patrick M. O'Malley, Peter Freedman-Doan, Kali H. Trzesniewski, and M. Breant Donnellan. 2011. "Adolescent Self-Esteem: Differences by Race/Ethnicity, Gender and Age." *Self and Identity* 104:445–473.

Bachman, Jerald G., Katherine N. Wadsworth, Patrick M. O'Malley, Lloyd D. Johnston, and John E. Schulenberg. 1997. *Smoking, Drinking and Drug Use in Young Adulthood: The Impacts of New Freedoms and New Responsibilities.* Mahwah, NJ: Erlbaum.

Back, Mitja, Albrecht Kufner, and Boris Egloff. 2010. "The Emotional Timeline of September 11, 2001." *Psychological Science* 21:1417-1419.

Backman, Carl W. 1981. "Attraction in Interpersonal Relationships." Pp. 253–268 in *Social Psychology: Sociological Perspectives,* edited by M. Rosenberg and R. H. Turner. New York, NY: Basic Books.

Balliet, Danie, Norman P. Li, Shane J. Macfarlan, and Mark VanVugt. 2011. "Sex Differences in Cooperation: A Meta-Analytic Review of Social Dilemmas." *Psychological Bulletin* 137:881-909.

Bandura, Albert. 1977. *Social Learning Theory.* Englewood Cliffs, NJ: Prentice Hall.

Bandura, Albert, Dorothea Ross, and Sheila A. Ross. 1961. "Transmission of Aggression Through Imitation of Aggressive Models." *Journal of Abnormal and Social Psychology* 63:575–582.

Baysu, Gulseli, Karen Phalet, and Rupert Brown. 2011. "Dual Identity as a Two-Edged Sword: Identity Threat and Minority School Performance." *Social Psychology Quarterly* 74:121–143.

Becker, Howard S. 1963. *Outsiders: Studies in the Sociology of Deviance.* New York, NY: Free Press.

Becker, Howard S. and Blanch Geer. 1957. "Participant Observation and Interviewing: A Comparison." *Human Organization* 16:28–32.

Bem, Daryl J. 1967. "Self-Perception: The Dependent Variable of Human Performance." *Organizational Behavior and Human Performance* 2:105–121.

Bem, Daryl J. 1970. *Beliefs, Attitudes, and Human Affairs.* Belmont, CA: Brooks/Cole.

Bem, Daryl J. 1972. "Self-Perception Theory." Pp. 1–62 in *Advances in Experimental Social Psychology,* vol. 6, edited by L. Berkowitz. New York, NY: Academic Press.

Benford, Robert D. and David A. Snow. 2000. "Framing Processes and Social Movements: An Overview and Assessment." *Annual Review of Sociology* 26:611–639.

Benson, Michael L. 1985. "Denying the Guilty Mind: Accounting for Involvement in a White-Collar Crime." *Criminology* 23:590–599.

Berg, Justin Allen. 2009. "Core Networks and Whites' Attitudes Toward Immigrants and Immigration Policy." *Public Opinion Quarterly* 73:7–31.

Berger, Joseph. 1992. "Expectations, Theory, and Group Processes." *Social Psychology Quarterly* 55:3–11.

Berger, Joseph, Thomas L. Conner, and M. Hamit Fisek (eds.). 1974. *Expectations States Theory: A Theoretical Research Paradigm*. Cambridge, MA: Winthrop.

Berger, Joseph, M. Hamit Fisek, Robert Z. Norman, and Morris Zelditch Jr. 1977. *Status Characteristics and Social Interaction*. New York, NY: Elsevier

Berger, Joseph, Robert Z. Norman, James Balkwell, and Roy F. Smith. 1992. "Status Inconsistency in Task Situations: A Test of Four Status Processing Principles." *American Sociological Review* 57:843–855.

Berger, Joseph, Susan J. Rosenholtz, and Morris Zelditch. 1980. "Status Organizing Processes." *Annual Review of Sociology* 6:479–508.

Berger, Joseph, David G. Wagner, and Morris Zelditch Jr. 1985. "Expectations States Theory Review and Assessment." Pp. 1–72 in *Status, Rewards and Influence: How Expectations Organize Behavior*, edited by J. Berger and M. Zelditch. San Francisco, CA: Jossey-Bass.

Berger, Joseph and Murray Webster Jr. 2006. "Expectations, Status, and Behavior." Pp. 268–300 in *Contemporary Social Psychological Theories*, edited by P.J. Burke. Stanford, CA: Stanford University Press.

Bernstein, Basil. 1972. "A Sociolinguistic Approach to Socialization, With Some Reference to Educability." Pp. 465–497 in *The Ethnography of Communication*, edited by John Joseph Gumperz and Dell H. Hymes. New York, NY: Holt, Rinehart and Winston.

Berscheid, Ellen, Karen Dion, Elaine Walster, and G. William Walster. 1971. "Physical Attractiveness and Dating Choice: A Test of the Matching Hypothesis." *Journal of Experimental Social Psychology* 7:173–189.

Berscheid, Ellen and Harry T. Reis. 1998. "Attraction and Close Relationships." Pp. 193–281 in *The Handbook of Social Psychology*, 4th ed, edited by S. Fiske, D. Gilbert, G. Lindzey, and E. Aronson. New York, NY: Random House.

Berscheid, Ellen and Elaine H. Walster. 1974. "Physical Attractiveness." Pp. 157–215 in *Advances in Experimental Social Psychology*, vol. 7, edited by L. Berkowitz. New York, NY: Academic Press.

Berscheid, Ellen and Elaine H. Walster. 1978. *Interpersonal Attraction*. Reading, MA: Addison Wesley.

Besen, Yasmine. 2006. "Exploitation or Fun? The Lived Experiences of Teenage Employment in Suburban America" *Journal of Contemporary Ethnography* 35:319–340.

Best, Joel. 2006. *Flavor of the Month: Why Smart People Fall for Fads*. Berkeley, CA: University of California Press.

Best, Joel and Gerald T. Horiuchi. 1985. "The Razor Blade in the Apple: The Social Construction of Urban Legends." *Social Problems* 32:488–499.

Bettencourt, B. Ann and Norman Miller. 1996. "Gender Differences in Aggression as a Function of Provocation: A Meta-Analysis." *Psychological Bulletin* 119:422–447.

Beyer, Sylvia. 2002. "The Effects of Gender, Dysphoria, and Performance Feedback on the Accuracy of Self-Evaluations." *Sex Roles* 47:453–464.

Bhave, Devasheesh P. and Theresa M. Glomb. 2009. "Emotional Labour Demands, Wages and Gender: A Within-Person, Between-Jobs Study." *Journal of Occupational and Organizational Psychology* 82:683–707

Bianchi, Alison J., Soong Moon Kang, and Daniel Stewart. 2012. "The Organizational Selection of Status Characteristics: Status Evaluations in an Open Source Community." *Organization Science* 23:299–307.

Bianchi, Suzanne M., John P. Robinson, and Melissa A. Milkie. 2006. *Changing Rhythms of American Family Life*. New York, NY: Russel Sage Foundations.

Biddle, Bruce J. 1979. *Role Theory: Expectations, Identities and Behaviors*. New York, NY: Academic Press.

Blakemore, Judith E. Owen, and Renee E. Centers. 2005. "Characteristics of Boys' and Girls' Toys." *Sex Roles* 53:619–633.

Blalock, Hubert M. 1967. *Toward a Theory of Minority-Group Relations*. New York, NY: Wiley.

Blass, Thomas. 1999. "The Milgram Paradigm After 35 Years: Some Things We Now Know About Obedience to Authority." *Journal of Applied Social Psychology* 29:955–978.

Blau, Peter M. 1964. *Exchange and Power in Social Life*. New York, NY: John Wiley and Sons.

Blau, Peter M. and Otis Duncan. 1967. *The American Occupational Structure*. New York, NY: Wiley.

Blauner, Robert. 1964. *Alienation and Freedom: The Factory Worker and His Industry*. Chicago, IL: University of Chicago Press.

Blazak, Randy. 2001. White Boys to Terrorists Men: Target Recruitment of Nazi Skinheads." *American Behavioral Scientist* 44:982–1000.

Blinn-Pike, Lynn, Sheri Worthy, Lokken Jonkman, and Jeffrey N. Smith. 2008. "Emerging Adult Versus Adult Status Among College Students: Examination of Explanatory Variables." *Adolescence* 43: 577–591.

Block, Jeanne H. 1983. "Differential Premises Arising from Differential Socialization of the Sexes." *Child Development* 54:1335–1354.

Blow, Charles M. 2012. "Election Data Drive." *The New York Times, The* Opinion Pages. November 9. Retrieved September 4, 2012. (http://www.nytimes.com/2012/11/10/opinion/blow-election-data-dive.html?_r=1&).

Blumberg, Paul. 1968. *Industrial Democracy*. New York, NY: Schocken Books.

Blumer, Herbert. 1939. "Collective Behavior." Pp. 219–288 in *Principles of Sociology,* edited by Robert E. Park. New York, NY: Barnes and Noble.

Blumer, Herbert. 1958. "Race Prejudice as a Sense of Group Position." *The Pacific Sociological Review* 1:3–7.

Blumer, Herbert. 1969. *Symbolic Interactionism: Perspective and Method*. Englewood Cliffs, NJ: Prentice-Hall.

Blumstein, Philip W. 1975. "Identity Bargaining and Self-Conception." *Social Forces* 53:476–485.

Blumstein, Philip and Peter Kollock. 1988. "Personal Relationships." *Annual Review of Sociology* 14:467–490.

Boase, Jeffrey, John B. Horrigan, Barry Wellman, and Lee Rainie. 2006. "The Strength of Internet Ties." Pew Internet and American Life Project. Washington, DC. Retrieved September 4, 2013 (http://www.pewinternet.org/~/media/Files/Reports/2006/PIP_Internet_ties.pdf.pdf).

Bobo, Lawrence D. 1999. "Prejudice as Group Position: Micro-Foundations of a Sociological Approach to Racism and Racial Relations." *Journal of Social Issues* 55:445–472.

Bobo, Lawrence D. and Camille Z. Charles. 2009. "Race in the American Mind: From the Moynihan Report to the Obama Candidacy." *Annals of the American Academy of Political and Social Science* 621:243–259.

Bobo, Lawarence D., Camille Z. Charles, Maria Krysan, and Alicia Simmons. 2012. "The Real Record on Racial Attitudes." Pp.38–83 in *Social Trends in the United States, 1972–2006: Evidence from the General Social Survey,* edited by Peter V. Marsden. Princeton, NJ: Princeton University Press.

Bobo, Lawrence, James R. Kluegel, and Ryan A. Smith. 1997. "Laissez-Faire Racism: The Crystallization of a Kinder, Gentler Anti-Black Ideology." Pp. 15–44 in *Racial Attitudes in the 1990s: Continuity and Change,* edited by S. A. Tuch and J. K. Martin. Westport, CT: Praeger.

Bodenhausen, Galen V. and Jennifer A. Richeson. 2010. "Prejudice, Stereotyping, and Discrimination." Pp. 341–383 in *Advanced Social Psychology,* edited by Roy F. Baumeister and Eli J. Finkel. New York, NY: Oxford University Press.

Bogle, Kathleen A. 2008. *Hooking Up: Sex, Dating and Relationships on Campus*. New York, NY: New York University Press.

Bond, Rod and Peter B. Smith. 1996. "Culture and Conformity: A Meta-Analysis of Studies Using Asch's (1952b, 1956) Line Judgment Task." *Psychological Bulletin* 119:111–137.

Bonikowski, Bart. 2005. "Flying While Arab (Or Was It Muslim? Or Middle Eastern): Theoretical Analysis of Racial Profiling After 9/11." *The Discourse of Sociological Practice* 7. Retrieved September 4, 2013 (http://omega.cc.umb.edu/~sociology/journal/dsp_index.htm)

Bonilla-Silva, Eduardo. 2003. "Racial Attitudes or Racial Ideology? An Alternative Paradigm for Examining Actors' Racial Views." *Journal of Political Ideologies* 8:63–83.

Bonilla-Silva, Eduardo and David G. Embrick. 2001. "Are Blacks Color Blind Too? An Interview-Based Analysis of Black Detroiters' Racial Views." *Race and Society* 4:47–67.

Bonilla-Silva, Eduardo and Amanda Lewis. 1999. "The New Racism: Racial Structure in the United States, 1960s–1990s." Pp. 55–101 in *Race, Ethnicity, and Nationality in the United States,* edited by P. Wong. Boulder, CO: Westview Press.

Boss, Leslie R. 1997. "Epidemic Hysteria: A Review of the Published Literature." *Epidemiologic Reviews* 19:233–243.

Brandt, Allan M. 2000. "Racism and Research: The Case of the Tuskegee Syphilis Experiment." *Hastings Center Report* 8:21–29.

Branscombe, Nyla R. and Daniel L. Wann. 1994. "Collective Self-Esteem Consequences of Outgroup Derogation when a Valued Social Identity is on Trial." *European Journal of Social Psychology* 24:641–657.

Bransford, John D. and Marcia K. Johnson. 1972. "Contextual Prerequisites for Understanding: Some Investigations of Comprehension and Recall." *Journal of Verbal Learning and Verbal Behavior* 11:717–726.

Brennan, Lyle. 2012. "All-out War: 115 Cities Explode in a Flurry of Feathers for International Pillow Fight Day." *The Daily Mail,* April. Retrieved September 4, 2013 (http://www.dailymail.co.uk/news/article-2126610/International-Pillow-Fight-Day-2012–115-cities-explode-flurry-feathers.html).

Brewer, Dominic J., Daniel I. Rees, and Laura M. Argys. 1995. "Detracking America's Schools: The Reform Without the Cost?" *Phi Delta Kappan* 77:210–215.

Brooks, Clem and Catherine Bolzendahl. 2004. "The Transformation of US Gender Role Attitudes: Cohort Replacement, Social-Structural Change, and Ideological Learning." *Social Science Research* 33:106–133.

Brooks-Gunn, Jeanne and Greg J. Duncan. 1997. "The Effects of Poverty on Children." *The Future of Children* 7:55–71.

Bruce, Darryl, Angela Dolan, and Kimberly Phillips-Grant. 2000. "On the Transition From Childhood Amnesia to the Recall off Personal Memories." *Psychological Science* 11:360–364.

Brunson, Rod K. and Jody Miller. 2006. "Young Black Men and Urban Policing in the United States." *British Journal of Criminology* 46:613–640.

Bucher, Jacob. 2011. "General Issue (G.I.) Strain: Applying Strain Theory to Military Offending." *Deviant Behavior* 32:846–875.

Buchmann, Claudia, Thomas A. Diprete, and Anne McDaniel. 2008. "Gender Inequalities in Education." *Annual Review of Sociology* 34:319–337.

Bui, Hoan N. 2009. "Parent-Child Conflicts, School Troubles, and Differences in Delinquency Across Immigrant Generations." *Crime and Delinquency* 55:412–441.

Burdette, Amy M., Christopher G. Ellison, Terrence D. Hill, and Norval Glenn. 2009. "Hooking Up at College: Does Religion Make a Difference." *Journal for the Scientific Study of Religion* 48: 535–551.

Bureau of Labor Statistics. 2011. "Employed Persons by Age, Sex, and Race". Current Population Survey. Retrieved on January 19, 2012 (http://www.bls.gov/cps/tables.htm#charemp)

Burger, Jerry M. 2009. "Replicating Milgram: Would People Still Obey Today?" *American Psychologist* 64:1–11.

Burgess, Robert L. and Ronald L. Akers. 1966. "A Differential Association-Reinforcement Theory of Criminal Behavior." *Social Problems* 14:128–147.

Burke, Peter J. 1991. "Identity Processes and Social Stress." *American Sociological Review.* 56:836–849.

Burke, Peter J. 2006. "Identity Change." *Social Psychology Quarterly* 69:81–96.

Burke, Peter J. and Alicia D. Cast. 1997. "Stability and Change in the Gender Identities of Newly Married Couples." *Social Psychology Quarterly* 60:277–290.

Burke, Peter J. and Michael M. Harrod. 2005. "Too Much of a Good Thing?" *Social Psychology* 68:359–374.

Burke, Peter J. and David Reitzes. 1981. "The Link Between Identity and Role Performance." *Social Psychology Quarterly* 44:83–92.

Burke, Peter J. and Jan E. Stets. 2009. *Identity Theory.* New York, NY: Oxford University Press.

Burt, Ronald S. 2005. *Brokerage and Closure: An Introduction to Social Capital.* New York, NY: Oxford University Press.

Buss, Arnold H. 1980. *Self-Consciousness and Social Anxiety.* San Francisco, CA: W. H. Freeman.

Buss, Arnold H. and Stephen R. Briggs. 1984. "Drama and the Self in Social Interaction." *Journal of Personality and Social Psychology* 47:1310–1324.

Butler, Edward G. 1993. "Alcohol Use by College Students: A Rites of Passage Ritual." *NASPA Journal* 31:48–55.

Byrne, Don, Oliver London, and Keith Reeves. 1968. "The Effects of Physical Attractiveness, Sex, and Attitude Similarity on Interpersonal Attraction." *Journal of Personality* 36:259–271.

Byun, Sookeun, Ruffini B. Celestino, Juline E. Mills, Alecia C. Douglas, Mamadou Niang, Svetlana Stepchenkova, Seul Ki Lee, Jihad Loutfi, Jung-Kook

Lee, Mikhail Atallah, and Mariana Blanton. 2009. "Internet Addiction: Metasynthesis of 1996–2006 Quantitative Research." *CyberPsychology and Behavior* 12:203–207.

Cahill, Spencer E. 1983. "Re-Examining the Acquisition of Sex Roles: A Symbolic Interactionist Approach." *Sex Roles* 9:1–15.

Cahill, Spencer E. 1986. "Language Practices and Self Definition: The Case of Gender Identity Acquisition." *The Sociological Quarterly* 27:295–311.

Cahill, Spencer E. 2003. "Childhood." Pp. 857–874 in *Handbook of Symbolic Interactionism,* edited by L. T. Reynolds and N. J. Herman-Kinney. Lanham, MD: Rowman and Littlefield.

Cahill, Spencer E., William Distler, and Cynthia Lachowetz. 1985. "Meanwhile Backstage: Public Bathrooms and the Interaction Order." *Urban Life* 14:33–58.

Caldwell, Mayta A. and Letitia Anne Peplau. 1982. "Sex Differences in Same-Sex Friendship." *Sex Roles* 8:721–732.

Campbell, Douglas T. 1958. "Common Fate, Similarity, and Other Indices of Aggregates of Persons as Social Entities." *Behavioral Science* 3:14–25.

Cancian, Francesca M. 1987. *Love in America: Gender and Self-Development.* Cambridge, England: Cambridge University Press.

Cantor, Joanne R., Dolf Zillman, and Jennings Bryant. 1975. "Enhancement of Experienced Sexual Arousal in Response to Erotic Stimuli Through Misattribution of Unrelated Residual Excitation." *Journal of Personality and Social Psychology* 32:69–75.

Cantril, Hadley. 1940. *The Invasion From Mars: A Study in the Psychology of Panic.* Brunswick, NJ: Transaction Publishers.

Cast, Alicia D. 2003. "Power and the Ability to Define the Situation." *Social Psychology Quarterly* 66:185–201.

Caswell, Michelle. "Margret Cho: She's The One That She Wants." Asia Society. Retrieved December 14, 2012 (http://asiasociety.org/arts/film/margaret-cho-shes-one-she-wants)

Center for Disease Control. 2009. "Number and Rate of Discharges From Short-stay Hospitals and of Days of Care, with Average Length of Stay. Retrieved on November 30, 2012 (http://www.cdc.gov/nchs/data/nhds/2average/2009ave2_firstlist.pdf).

Chambliss, Daniel F. 1996. *Beyond Caring: Hospitals, Nurses, and the Social Organization of Ethics.* Chicago, IL: University of Chicago Press.

Chambliss, William J. 1973. "The Saints and the Roughnecks." *Society* 11:24–31.

Chapple, Constance L., Julia A. McQuillan, and Terceira A. Berdahl. 2005. "Gender, Social Bonds, and Delinquency: A Comparison of Boys' and Girls' Models." *Social Science Research* 34:357–383.

Cheung, Chau-Kiu and Kwan-Kwok Leung. 2002. "Postmodern and Modern Value Orientations and Life Satisfaction Among Hong Kong Chinese." *Social Behavior and Personality* 30:697–708.

Chou, Hui-Tzu Grace and Nicolas Edge. 2012. "'They Are Happier and Having Better Lives Than I Am': The Impact of Using Facebook on Perceptions of Others' Lives." *Cyberpsychology, Behavior and Social Networking* 15:117–121.

Christakis, Nicholas A. and James H. Fowler. 2013. "Social Contagion Theory: Examining Dynamic Social Networks and Human Behavior." *Statistics in Medicine* 32:556–577.

Christie-Mizell, C. Andre and Robert L. Peralta. 2009. "The Gender Gap in Alcohol Consumption During Late Adolescence and Young Adulthood: Gendered Attitudes and Adult Roles." *Journal of Health and Social Behavior* 50:410–426.

Cialdini, Robert B. 1988. *Influence: Science and Practice.* Boston, MA: Longman Higher Education.

Cialdini, Robert B. and Noah. J. Goldstein. 2004. "Social Influence: Compliance and Conformity." *Annual Review of Psychology* 55:591–622.

Cicourel, Aaron V. 1973. *Cognitive Sociology: Language and Meaning in Social Interaction.* London, UK: Penguin.

Cicourel Aaron V. and John I. Kitsuse. 1963. *The Educational Decision Makers.* New York, NY: Free Press.

Clark, Candace. 1987. "Sympathy Biography and Sympathy Margin." *American Journal of Sociology* 93:290–321.

Clarke, Lee. 2002. "Panic: Myth or Reality?" *Contexts* 1:21–26.

Clopton, Nancy A. and Gwendolyn T. Sorell. 1993. "Gender Differences in Moral Reasoning." *Psychology of Women Quarterly* 17:85–101.

Cobb, Sydney. 1976. "Social Support as a Moderator of Life Stress." *Psychosomatic Medicine* 38:300–14.

Cochran, C.D. and W. Daniel Hale. 1985. "College Student Norms on the Brief Symptom Inventory." *Journal of Clinical Psychology* 41(6):777–779.

Cohen, Elizabeth G. 1982. "A Multi-Ability Approach to the Integrated Classroom." *Journal of Reading Behavior* 14:439–460.

Cohen, Elizabeth G. and Susan S. Roper. 1972. "Modification of Interracial Interaction Disability: An Application of Status Characteristics Theory." *American Sociological Review* 37:643–657.

Cohen, Sheldon, Tom Karmark, and Robin Mermelstein. 1983. "A Global Measure of Perceived Stress." *Journal of Health and Social Behavior* 24: 385–396.

Coles, Roberta. 2002. "Black Single Fathers: Choosing to Parent Full-Time." *Journal of Contemporary Ethnography* 31:411–439.

Collins, Randall. 1981. "On the Microfoundations of Macrosociology." *American Journal of Sociology* 86:984–1014.

Collins, Randall. 1990. "Stratification, Emotional Energy and Transient Emotions." Pp. 27–57 in *Research Agendas in the Sociology of Emotions,* edited by T. Kempner. Albany, NY: State University of New York

Condry, John and Sandra Condry. 1976. "Sex Differences: A Study of the Eye of the Beholder." *Child Development* 47:812–819.

Cook, Karen S. and Richard M. Emerson. 1978. "Power, Equity and Commitment in Exchange Networks." *American Sociological Review* 43:721–739.

Cook, Karen S., Russell Hardin, and Margaret Levi. 2007. *Cooperation Without Trust?* New York, NY: Russell Sage Foundation.

Cooley, Charles Horton. 1902. *Human Nature and the Social Order.* New York, NY: Charles Scribner's Sons.

Cooley, Charles Horton. 1909. *Social Organization: A Study of the Larger Social Mind.* New York, NY: Charles Scribner's Sons.

Coontz, Stephanie. 1997. *The Way We Really Are: Coming to Terms with America's Changing Families.* New York, NY: Basic Books.

Coontz, Stephanie. 2005. *Marriage, A History: How Love Conquered Marriage.* New York, NY: Viking Press.

Cooper, Joel. 2007. *Cognitive Dissonance: Fifty Years of Classic Theory.* Thousand Oaks, CA: Sage Publications.

Correll, Shelly J. and Cecilia L. Ridgeway. 2006. "Expectations State Theory." Pp. 29–51 in *Handbook of Social Psychology,* edited by John Delamater. New York, NY: Springer.

Corrigan Patrick W. and David L. Penn. 1999. "Lessons from Social Psychology on Discrediting Psychiatric Stigma." *American Psychologist* 54:765–776.

Corsaro, William A. 1985. *Friendship and Peer Culture in the Early Years.* Norwood, NJ: Albex.

Corsaro, William A. 1997. *The Sociology of Childhood.* Thousand Oaks, CA: Pine Forge Press.

Corsaro, William A. and Donna Eder. 1990. "Children's Peer Cultures." *Annual Review of Sociology* 16:197–220.

Corsaro, William A. and Laura Fingerson. 2006. "Development and Socialization in Childhood." Pp. 125–156 in *Handbook of Social Psychology,* edited by J. Delameter. New York, NY: Springer.

Cosgrove, Lisa, Sheldon Krimsky, Manisha Vijayaraghaven, and Lisa Schneider. 2006. "Financial Ties Between DSM-IV Panel Members and the Pharmaceutical Industry." *Psychotherapy and Psychosomatics* 75:154–160.

Costa, Paul T., Jr., Antonio Terracciano, and Robert R. McCrae. 2001. "Gender Differences in Personality Traits Across Cultures: Robust and Surprising Findings." *Journal of Personality and Social Psychology* 81:322–331.

Cottle, Michelle. 1999. "Selling Shyness." *The New Republic,* August 2 Issue24-29

Couch, Carl J. 1962. "Family Role Specialization and Self-Attitudes in Children." *Sociological Quarterly* 3:115–121.

Coverman, Shelley. 1989. "Role Overload, Role Conflict and Stress: Addressing Consequences of Multiple Role Demands." *Social Forces* 67:965–982.

Crawford, Duane W., Du Feng, Judith L. Fischer, and Lisa K. Diana. 2003. "The Influence of Love, Equity, and Alternatives on Commitment in Romantic Relationships." *Family and Consumer Sciences Research Journal* 31:253–271.

Crawford, Lizabeth A. and Katherine B. Novak. 2002. "Parental and Peer Influences on Adolescent

Drinking: The Relative Impact of Attachment and Opportunity." *Journal of Child and Adolescent Substance Abuse* 12:1–26.

Crawford, Lizabeth A. and Katherine B. Novak. 2006. "Alcohol Abuse as a Rite of Passage: The Effect of Beliefs About Alcohol and the College Experience on Undergraduates' Drinking Behaviors." *Journal of Drug Education* 36:193–212.

Crawford, Lizabeth A. and Katherine B. Novak. 2008. "Parent-Child Relations and Peer Associations as Mediators of the Family Structure-Substance Use Relationship." *Journal of Family Issues* 29:155–184.

Crawford, Lizabeth A. and Katherine B. Novak. 2011. "Beliefs About Alcohol and the College Experience, Locus of Self, and College Undergraduates' Drinking Patterns." *Sociological Inquiry* 81:477–494.

Crosnoe, Robert. 2000. "Friendships in Childhood and Adolescence: The Lifecourse and New Directions." *Social Psychology Quarterly* 63:377–391.

Cunnien, Keith A., Nicole MartinRogers, and Jeylan T. Mortimer. 2009. "Adolescent Work Experience and Self-Efficacy." *International Journal of Sociology and Social Policy* 29:164–175.

Currah, Paisley and Lisa Jean Moore. 2009. "We Won't Know Who You Are:" Contesting Sex Designations in New York City Birth Certificates." *Hypatia* 24:113–135.

Darity Jr., William, Ashwini Deshpande, and Thomas Weisskopf. 2011. "Who Is Eligible? Should Affirmative Action Be Group- or Class-Based?" *American Journal of Economics and Sociology* 70:238–268.

Darley John M. and Bibb Latane. 1968a. "Bystander Intervention in Emergencies: Diffusion of Responsibility." *Journal of Personality and Social Psychology* 8:377–383.

Darley, John M. and Bibb Latane. 1968b. "Group Inhibition of Bystander Intervention in Emergencies." *Journal of Personality and Social Psychology* 10:215–221.

Dasgupta, Nilanjana, Debbie E. McGhee, Anthony G. Greenwald, and Mahzarin R. Banaji. 2000. "Automatic Preference for White Americans: Eliminating the Familiarity Explanation." *Journal of Experimental Social Psychology* 36:316–328.

Davis, Joshua Ian, Ann Senghas, Fredric Brandt, and Kevin N. Ochsner. 2010. "The Effects of BOTOX Injections on Emotional Experience." *Emotion* 10:433–440.

Davis, Kingsley. 1940. "Extreme Social Isolation of a Child." *American Journal of Sociology* 45:554–565.

Davis, Kingsley. 1947. "A Final Note on a Case of Extreme Isolation." *American Journal of Sociology* 52:432–437.

Davis, Mark H. 1980. "A Multidimensional Approach to Individual Differences in Empathy." *Dissertation Abstracts International* 40:3480.

Davis, Mark H. 1983. "Measuring Individual Differences in Empathy: Evidence for a Multidimensional Approach." *Journal of Personality and Social Psychology* 44:113–126.

Daw, Jennifer. 2002. "Researchers, Physicians and Psychologists Fall on Various Sides of the Debate over Premenstrual Dysphoric Disorder." *Monitor on Psychology, American Psychological Association* 33(9): 58

Dawson, Michael C. and Rovana Popoff. 2004. "Reparations: Justice and Greed in Black and White." *The Du Bois Review* 1:47–92.

de Boinod, Adam Jacot. 2005. *The Meaning of Tingo and Other Extraordinary Words from Around the World.* New York, NY: Penguin Books.

DeCoster, Vaughn. 2002. "Predicting Emotions in Everyday Social Interactions." *Journal of Human Behavior in the Social Environment* 6:53–73.

Deitch, Elizabeth A., Adam Barsky, Rebecca M. Butz, Suzanne Chan, Arthur P. Brief, and Jill C. Bradley. 2003. "Subtle yet Significant: The Existence and Impact of Everyday Racial Discrimination in the Workplace." *Human Relations* 56:1299–1324.

deLara, Ellen W. 2008. "Bullying and Aggression on the School Bus: School Bus Drivers' Observations and Suggestions." *Journal of School Violence* 7:48–70.

DeMello, M, 1995. "'Not Just for Bikers Anymore': Popular Representations of American Tattooing." *Journal of Popular Culture* 29:37–52.

Denzin, Norman K. 1975. "Play, Games and Interaction: The Contexts of Childhood Socialization." *The Sociological Quarterly* 16:458–478.

Derogatis, Leonard R. 1975. *Brief Symptom Inventory.* Baltimore, MD: Clinical Psychometric Research.

Derogatis, Leonard R. 1993. *Brief Symptom Inventory: Administration, Scoring and Procedures Manual,* 4th ed. Minneapolis, MN: NCS, Pearson.

Deutsch, Morton and Harold B. Gerard. 1955. "A Study of Normative and Informational Social Influences Upon Individual Judgment." *The Journal of Abnormal and Social Psychology* 51:629–636.

Dever, Mega, Joel Best, and Kenneth C. Haas. 2008. "Methods of Executions as Institutional Fads." *Punishment and Society* 10:227–252.

Devos, Thierry and Mahzarin R. Banaji. 2005. "American = White?" *Journal of Personality and Social Psychology* 88:447–466.

Diehl, Michael. 1990. "The Minimal Group Paradigm: Theoretical Explanations and Empirical Findings." *European Review of Social Psychology* 1:263–292.

Diener, Ed and Marissa Diener. 1995. "Cross-Cultural Correlates of Life Satisfaction and Self-Esteem." *Journal of Personality and Social Psychology* 68: 653–663.

Diener, Ed, Ed Sandvik, Larry Seidtiz, and Marissa Diener. 1993. "The Relationship Between Income and Subjective Well-Being: Relative or Absolute?" *Social Indicators Research* 28:195–223.

Dillard, Courtney., Larry D. Browning, Sim B. Sitkin, and Kathleen M. Sutcliffe. 2000. "Impression Management and the Use of Procedures at the Ritz-Carlton: Moral Standards and Dramaturgical Discipline." *Communication Studies* 51:404–4414.

Dinovitzer, Ronit, John Hagan, and Ron Levi. 2009. "Immigration and Youthful Illegalities in a Global Edge City." *Social Forces* 88:337–372.

Dion, Karen, Ellen Berscheid, and Ellen Walster. 1972. "What Is Beautiful Is Good." *Journal of Personality and Social Psychology* 24:285–290.

Dipietro, Stephanie M. and Jean Marie McGloin. 2012. "Differential Susceptibility? Immigrant Youth and Peer Influence" *Criminology* 50:711–742.

Dobson, Keith and Renee-Louise Franche. 1989. "A Conceptual and Empirical Review of the Depressive Realism Hypothesis." *Canadian Journal of Behavioural Science* 21:419–433.

Dohrenwend, Bruce P., J. Blake Turner, Nicholas A. Turse, Roberto Lewis-Fernandez, and Thomas J. Yager. 2008. "War-Related Post-Traumatic Stress Disorder in Black, Hispanic, and Majority White Vietnam Veterans: The Roles of Exposure and Vulnerability." *Journal of Traumatic Stress* 21:133–141.

Domhoff, William. 1974. *Bohemian Grove and Other Retreats: A Study in Ruling Class Cohesiveness.* New York, NY: Harper Colophon Books.

Dovidio, John F., Steve L. Ellyson, Caroline F. Keating, Karen Heltman, and Clifford E. Brown. 1988. "The Relationship of Social Power to Visual Displays of Dominance Between Men and Women." *Journal of Personality and Social Psychology* 54:233–242.

Dowdall, George W. 1999. "Mental Hospitals and Deinstitutionalization." PP. 519-537 In *Handbook of the Sociology of Mental Health,* edited by Carol S. Aneshensel and Jo C. Phelan. New York, NY: Kluwer Academic/Plenum Publishers.

Downey, Douglas B. and Shana Pribesh. 2004. "When Race Matters: Teachers' Evaluations of Students' Classroom Behavior." *Sociology of Education* 77: 267–282.

Driskell, James E. and Brian Mullen. 2006. "Status Expectations and Behavior: A Meta-Analytic Review and Test of the Theory." Pp. 73–81 in *Small Groups,* edited by John M. Levine and Richard L. Moreland. New York, NY: Psychology Press.

Durkheim, Emile. 1895. *Rules of the Sociological Method.* New York, NY: Free Press.

Durkheim, Emile. 1897. *Suicide.* New York, NY: Free Press.

Dutton, Donald G. and Arthur P. Aron. 1974. "Some Evidence for Heightened Attraction Under Conditions of High Anxiety." *Journal of Personality and Social Psychology* 17:208–213.

Eagly, Alice H. 1978. "Sex Differences in Influenceability." *Psychological Bulletin* 85:86–116.

Eagly, Alice H. and Carole Chrvala. 1986. "Sex Differences in Conformity: Status and Gender Role Interpretations." *Psychology of Women Quarterly* 10:203–220.

Eagly, Alice H., Wendy Wood, and Lisa Fishbaugh. 1981. "Sex Differences in Conformity: Surveillance by the Group as a Determinant of Male Nonconformity." *Journal of Personality and Social Psychology* 40:384–394.

Easterlin, Richard A. 2001. "Income and Happiness: Towards a Unified Theory." *The Economic Journal* 3:465–485.

Eaton, Asia A. and Suzanna Rose. 2011. "Had Dating Become More Egalitarian? A 35 Year Review Using Sex Roles." *Sex Roles* 64:843–862.

Eaton, William W. 1999. "Social Transmission in Acute Somatoform Epidemics." Pp. 417–438 in *Handbook of the Sociology of Mental Health,* edited by Carol S. Aneshensel and Jo C. Phelan. New York, NY: Springer.

Edelmann, Robert J. 1985. "Individual Differences in Embarassment: Self-Consciousness, Self-Monitoring and Embarrassability." *Personality and Individual Differences* 6:223–230.

Edelmann, Robert J. 1987. *The Psychology of Embarrassment.* Chichester, UK: Wiley.

Eder, Donna. 1985. "The Cycle of Popularity: Interpersonal Relations Among Female Adolescents." *Sociology of Education* 58:154–165.

Eder, Donna and Maureen T. Hallinan. 1978. "Sex Differences in Children's Friendships." *American Sociological Review* 43:237–250.

Eder, Donna and Stephen Parker. 1987. "The Cultural Reproduction of Gender: The Effect of Extracurricular Activities on Peer-Group Culture." *Sociology of Education* 60:200–213.

Einstadter, Werner J. and Stuart Henry. 2006. *Criminological Theory: An Analysis of its Underlying Assumptions.* Lanham, MD: Rowman & Littlefield Publishers.

Eitle, David and John Taylor. 2011. "General Strain Theory, BIS/BAS Levels and Gambling Behavior." *Deviant Behavior* 32:1–27.

Elder, Todd E. 2010. "The Importance of Relative Standards in ADHD Diagnoses: Evidence Based on Child's Date of Birth." *Journal of Health Economics* 29:641–656.

Elhoweris, Halo, Kagendo Mutua, Negmeldin Alsheikh, and Pauline Holloway. 2005. "The Effect of Children's Ethnicity on Teacher's Referral and Recommendation Decisions in Gifted and Talented Programs." *Remedial and Special Education* 26:25–31.

el-Khoury, Laura J. 2011. "Being While Black: Resistance and the Management of the Self." *Social Identities* 18:85–100.

Ellison, Nicole B., Charles Steinfield, and Cliff Lampe. 2007. "The Benefits of Facebook 'Friends': Social Capital and College Students' Use of Online Social Network Sites." *Journal of Computer-Mediated Communication* 12:1143–1168.

Else-Quest, Nicole M., Janet Shibley Hyde, and Marcia C. Linn. 2010. "Cross-National Patterns of Gender Differences in Mathematics: A Meta-Analysis." *Psychological Bulletin* 136:103–127.

Emerson, Richard M. 1962. "Power-Dependence Relations." *American Sociological Review* 27:31–41.

Emerson, Richard M. 1981. "Social Exchange Theory." Pp. 30–65 in *Social Psychology: Sociological Perspectives,* edited by M. Rosenberg and R. Turner. New York, NY: Academic Press.

Erickson, Kai. 1986. "On Work and Alienation." *American Sociological Review* 51:1–8.

Erickson, Kristan, Robert Crosnoe, and Sanford M. Dornbusch. 2000. "A Social Process Model of Adolescent Deviance: Combining Social Control and Differential Association Perspectives." *Journal of Youth and Adolescence* 29:395–425.

Erol, Ruth Yasemin and Ulrich Orth. 2011. "Self-Esteem Development From Age 14 to 30 Years: A Longitudinal Study." *Journal of Personality and Social Psychology* 101:607–619.

Essex, Marilyn, Sue Estroff, Steven Kane, Sara McLanahan, Jim Robbins, Rebecca Dresser, and Ronald Diamond. 1980. "On Weinstein's 'Patient Attitudes Toward Mental Hospitalization': A Review of Quantitative Research." *Journal of Health and Social Behavior* 21:393–396.

Evans, Louwanda and Joe R. Feagin. 2012. "Middle-Class African American Pilots: The Continuing Significance of Racism." *American Behavioral Scientist* 56:650–665.

Farnworth. Margaret and Michael J. Leiber. 1989. "Strain Theory Revisited: Economic Goals, Educational Means, and Delinquency." *American Sociological Review* 54:263–274.

Favell, Judith E. 2005. "Sifting Sound Practice From Snake Oil." Pp. 19–30 in *Controversial Therapies in Developmental Disabilities: Fads, Fashion, and Science in Professional Practice,* edited by John W. Jacobson, Richard M. Foxx, and James A. Mulick. Mahwah, NJ: Lawrence Erlbaum Associates.

Fazio, Russell H., Mark P. Zanna, and Joel Cooper. 1977. "Dissonance and Self-Perception: An Integrative View of Each Theory's Proper Domain of Application." *Journal of Experimental Social Psychology* 13:464–479.

Feagin, Joe R. 2010. *Racist America: Roots, Current Realities and Future Reparations*. New York, NY: Routledge.

Feinberg, Matthew, Robb Willer, Jennifer Stellar, and Dacher Keltner. 2012. "The Virtues of Gossip: Reputational Information Sharing as Prosocial Behavior." *Journal of Personality and Social Psychology* 102:1015–1030.

Felmlee, Diane H. 2006. "Interaction in Social Networks." Pp. 389–410 in *Handbook of Social Psychology,* edited by J.D. Delameter. New York, NY: Springer.

Felmlee, Diane H. and Susan Sprecher. 2006. "Love." Pp. 389–409 in *Handbook of the Sociology of Emotions,* edited by J. Stets and J. Turner. New York, NY: Springer.

Felmlee, Diane, Susan Sprecher, and Edward Bassin. 1990. "The Dissolution of Intimate Relationships: A Hazard Model." *Social Psychology Quarterly* 53:13–30.

Fenigstein, Allan, Michael F. Scheier, and Arnold H. Buss. 1975. "Public and Private Self-Consciousness: Assessment and Theory." *Journal of Consulting and Clinical Psychology* 43:522–527.

Ferree, Myra Marx and Frederick D. Miller. 1985. "Mobilization and Meaning: Toward an Integration of Social Psychological and Resource Perspectives on Social Movements." *Sociological Inquiry* 55:38–61.

Ferris, Kerry O. 2001. "Through a Glass, Darkly: The Dynamics of Fan-Celebrity Encounters." *Symbolic Interaction* 24:25–47.

Festinger, Leon. 1957. *A Theory of Cognitive Dissonance.* Stanford, CA: Stanford University Press.

Festinger, Leon, Anthony Pepitone, and Theodore Newcomb. 1952. "Some Consequence of Deindividuation in a Group." *Journal of Abnormal and Social Psychology* 47:382–389.

Figert, Anne E. 2010. "Premenstrual Syndrome as Scientific and Cultural Artifact." Pp. 132-141 in *Women Worldwide: Transnational Feminists Perspectives on Women,* edited by Janet Lee and Susan M. Shaw. New York, NY: McGraw-Hill.

Fine, Cordelia. 2010. *Delusions of Gender: How Our Minds, Society, and Neurosexism Create Difference.* New York, NY: W. W. Norton & Company.

Fine, Gary Alan. 1980. "The Kentucky Fried Rat: Legends in Modern Mass Society." *Journal of the Folklore Institute* 17:222–243.

Fine, Gary Alan. 1987. "The City as Folklore Generator: Legends in the Metropolis." *Urban Resources* 4:61.

Fine, Gary Alan. 1987. *With the Boys.* Chicago, IL: University of Chicago Press.

Fischer, Claude S. 2011. *Still Connected: Family and Friends in American Since 1970.* New York, NY: Russell Sage Foundation.

Fiske, Susan T. 1998. "Stereotyping, Prejudice, and Discrimination." Pp. 357–411 in *Handbook of Social Psychology,* vol. 2, edited by D. T. Gilbert, S. T. Fiske, and G. Lindzey. New York, NY: McGraw-Hill.

Fiske, Susan T. and Shelley E. Taylor. 2008. *Social Cognition: From Brains to Culture.* Boston, MA: McGraw-Hill.

Flippen, Chenoa and Marta Tienda. 2000. "Pathways to Retirement: Patterns of Labor Force Participation and Labor Market Exit Among Pre-Retirement Population by Race, Hispanic Origin, and Sex." *The Journals of Gerontology* 55B: 514–527.

Floyd, Frank J. and Guenter H. Wasner. 1994. "Social Exchange, Equity, and Commitment: Structural Equation Modeling of Dating Relationships." *Journal of Family Psychology* 8:55–73.

Folkes, Valerie S. 1982. "Forming Relationships and the Matching Hypothesis." *Personality and Social Psychology Bulletin* 8:631–636.

Forest, Amanda L. and Joanne V. Wood. 2012. "When Social Networking Is Not Working: Individuals with Low Self-Esteem Recognize but Do Not Reap the Benefits of Self-Disclosure on Facebook." *Psychological Science* 23:295–302.

Foster, Eric K. 2004. "Research on Gossip: Taxonomy, Methods and Future Directions." *Review of General Psychology* 8:78–99.

Fox, Kathleen A., Matthew R. Nobles, and Ronald L. Akers. 2011. "Is Stalking a Learned Phenomenon? An Empirical Test of Social Learning Theory." *Journal of Criminal Justice* 39:48–59.

Franko, Debra L. and James P. Roehrig. 2011. "African American Body Images." Pp. 221–228 in *Body Image: A Handbook of Science, Practice and Prevention,* 2nd ed., edited by Thomas F. Cash. New York, NY: Guilford Press.

Freud, Sigmund. [1923] 1990. *The Ego and the Id.* New York, NY: WW. Norton & Company

Freud, Sigmund. 1949. *An Outline of Psychoanalysis.* New York, NY: W. W. Norton & Company.

Froming, William J., Eric B. Corley, and Laurie Rinker. 1990. "The Influence of Public Self-Consciousness and the Audience's Characteristics on Withdrawal from Embarrassing Situations." *Journal of Personality* 58:603–621.

Fulco, Carolyn E., Catharyn T. Liverman, and Harold C. Sox (eds.). 2000. *Gulf War and Health*, vol. 6, *Physiologic, Psychologic, and Psychosocial Effects of Deployment-Related Stress*. Washington, DC: National Academy Press.

Furnham, Adrian and Helen Cheng. 2000. "Lay Theories of Happiness." *Journal of Happiness Studies* 1:227–246.

Furstenberg, Frank F. 2008. "The Intersections of Social Class and the Transition to Adulthood." *New Directions for Child and Adolescent Development*. Special Issue, Social Class and Transition to Adulthood, edited by Jalen T. Mortimer. 119:1-10.

Gaertner, Samuel L. and John F, Dovidio 1986. "The Aversive Form of Racism." Pp. 61–89 in *Prejudice, Discrimination, and Racism*, edited by John F. Dovidio and Samuel L. Gaertner. Orlando, FL: Academic Press.

Gaertner, Samuel L. and John F. Dovidio. 2000. *Reducing Intergroup Bias: The Common Ingroup Identity Model*. Philadelphia, PA: The Psychology Press.

Gaertener, Samuel L., John F. Dovidio, Phyllis A. Anastasio, Betty A. Bachman, and Mary C. Rust. 1993. "The Common Group Identity Model: Recatergorization and the Reduction of Intergroup Bias." *European Review of Social Psychology* 4:1–26.

Gaertener, Samuel L., Mary C. Rust, John F. Dovidio, Betty A. Bachman, and Phyllis A. Anastasio. 1994. "The Contact Hypothesis: The Role of Common Ingroup Identity in Reducing Intergroup Bias." *Small Groups Research* 25:224–249.

Galambos, Nancy, Erin T. Barker, and Harvey H. Krahn. 2006. "Depression, Self-Esteem, and Anger in Emerging Adulthood: Seven-Year Trajectories." *Developmental Psychology* 42:350–365.

Galician, Mary-Lou. 2004. *Sex, Love and Romance in the Mass Media: Analysis and Criticism of Unrealistic Portrayals and Their Influence*. New York, NY: Routledge.

Gallant, Mary J. and Sherryl Kleinman. 1983. "Symbolic Interactionism vs. Ethnomethodology." *Symbolic Interaction* 6:1–18.

Gallup. 2001. "Black-White Relations in the United States, 2001 Update." Gallup Poll Social Audit. Retrieved on June 14, 2013 (http://iws2.collin.edu/lstern/GALLUP-RACE-AUDIT.pdf).

Gamson, W.A. 1992. "The Social Psychology of Collective Action." Pp. 53–76 in *Frontiers in Social Movement Theory*, edited by A.D. Morris and C.M. Mueller. New Haven, CT: Yale University Press.

Garfinkel, Harold. 1956. "Conditions of Successful Degradation Ceremonies." *American Journal of Sociology* 61:240–244.

Garfinkel, Harold. 1964. "Studies of the Routine Grounds of Everyday Activities." *Social Problems* 11:225–250.

Garfinkel, Harold. 1967. *Studies in Ethnomethodology*. Cambridge, MA: Polity Press.

Gates, Gary J. 2007. "Geographic Trends Among Same-Sex Couples in the U.S. Census and the American Community Survey." The Williams Institute, UCLA School of Law. Retrieved on March 15, 2013 (http://www.policyarchive.org/handle/10207/bitstreams/18110.pdf).

Gentile, Britanny, Jean M. Twenge, and W. Keith Campbell. 2010. "Birth Cohort Differences in Self-Esteem, 1988–2008: A Cross-Temporal Meta-Analysis." *Review of General Psychology* 14:261–268.

George, Linda K. 1999. "Life Course Perspectives on Mental Health." Pp. 565–583 in *Handbook of Sociology of Mental Health*, edited by Carol S. Aneshensel and Jo Phelan. Dordrecht, Netherlands: Kluwer Academic Publishers.

Gergen, Kenneth J. 1991. *The Saturated Self: Dilemmas of Identity in Contemporary Life*. New York, NY: Basic Books.

Geschwender, Barbara A. and James A. Geschwender. 1973. "Relative Deprivation and Participation in the Civil Rights Movement." *Social Science Quarterly* 54:405–417.

GfK Group. 2012. "The Associated Press Racial Attitudes Survey." Retrieved on June 15, 2013 (http://surveys.ap.org/data/GfK/AP_Racial_Attitudes_Topline_09182012.pdf).

Gibbs, Jack P. 1981. *Norms, Deviance, and Social Control*. New York, NY: Elsevier.

Gibbs, Larry and Krista K. Payne 2011. *First Divorce Rate, 2010* (FP-11–09). National Center for Family and Marriage Research. Retrieved March 12, 2013 (http://ncfmr.bgsu.edu/pdf/family_profiles/file101821.pdf).

Giddens, Anthony. 1984. *The Constitution of Society: Outline of the Theory of Structuration*. Berkeley, CA: University of California Press.

Giddens, Anthony. 1991. *Modernity and Self-Identity: Self and Society in the Late Modern Age.* Stanford University Press.

Giddens, Anthony. 1992. *The Transformation of Intimacy: Sexuality, Love and Modern Societies.* Stanford, CA: Stanford University Press.

Gilens, Martin. 1996. "Race and Poverty in America: Public Misperceptions and the American News Media." *Public Opinion Quarterly* 60:515–541.

Gilligan, Carol. 1982. *In a Different Voice: Psychological Theory and Women's Development.* Cambridge, MA: Harvard University Press.

Glaser, Barney G. and Anselm L. Strauss. 1967. *The Discovery of Grounded Theory*: Strategies For Qualitative Research. Hawthorne, NY: Aldine Transaction.

Glenn, Norval and Elizabeth Marquardt. 2001. "Hooking Up, Hanging Out, and Hoping for Mr. Right: College Women on Dating an Mating Today." New York, NY: Institute of American Values. Retrieved September 4, 2013 (http://www.americanvalues.org/Hooking_Up.pdf)

Gluckman, M. 1963. "Gossip and Scandal." *Current Anthropology* 4:307–316.

Goar, Carla and Jane Sell. 2005. "Using Task Definition to Modify Racial Inequality Within Task Groups." *Sociological Quarterly* 46:525–543.

Godwyn, Mary. 2006. "Using Emotional Labor to Create and Maintain Relationships in Service Interactions." *Symbolic Interaction* 29:487–506.

Goffman, Erving. 1956. "Embarrassment and Social Organization." *American Journal of Sociology* 62:264–271.

Goffman, Erving. 1959. *The Presentation of Self in Everyday Life.* Garden City, NY: Doubleday.

Goffman, Erving. 1961. *Asylums: Essays on the Social Situation of Mental Patients and Other Inmates.* Garden City, NY: Anchor Books.

Goffman, Erving. 1963. *Stigma: Notes on the Management of Spoiled Identity.* Englewood Cliffs, NJ: Prentice Hall.

Goffman, Erving. 1974. *Frame Analysis: An Essay on the Organization of Experience.* New York, NY: Harper and Row.

Gold, Steven J. 1989. "Differential Adjustment Among New Immigrant Family Members." *Journal of Contemporary Ethnography* 17:408–434.

Goldberg, Wendy A., Erin Kelly, Nicole L. Matthews, Hannah Kang, Weilin Li, and Mariya Sumaroka. 2012. "The More Things Change, the More They Stay the Same: Gender, Culture, and College Students' Views About Work and Family." *Journal of Social Issues* 68:814–837.

Goode, William J. 1960. "A Theory of Role Strain." *American Sociological Review* 25:483–496.

Gordon, Steven L. 1981. "The Sociology of Sentiment and Emotion." Pp. 562–592 in *Social Psychology: Sociological Perspectives,* edited by Morris Rosenberg and Ralph H. Turner. New York, NY: Basic Books.

Gordon, Steven L. 1989. "Institutional and Impulsive Orientations in Selectively Appropriating Emotions to Self." Pp. 115–135 in *The Sociology of Emotions: Original Essays and Research Papers,* edited by David D. Franks and E. Doyle McCarthy. Greenwich, CT: JAI Press.

Gove, Walter and Terry Fain. 1973. "The Stigma of Mental Hospitalization: An Attempt to Evaluate its Consequences." *Archives of General Psychiatry* 28:494–500.

Grace, Sherry L. and Kenneth L. Cramer. 2002. "Sense of Self in the New Millennium: Male and Female Student Responses to the TST." *Social Behavior and Personality* 30:271–280.

Graff, Amy. 2012. "Canadian Couple Won't Reveal Child's Gender." The Mommy Chronicles Blog. *The San Francisco Chronicle,* May 24. Retrieved on October 8, 2012 (http://blog.sfgate.com/sfmoms/2011/05/24/canadian-couple-wont-reveal-childs-gender/).

Graham, James M. 2011. "Measuring Love in Romantic Relationships: A Meta-Analysis." *Journal of Social and Personal Relationships* 28:748–771.

Grattet, Ryken. 2011. "Societal Reactions to Deviance." *Annual Review of Sociology* 37:185–204.

Grauerholz, Elizabeth. 1987. "Balancing Power in Dating Relationships." *Sex Roles* 17:563–571.

Gray-Little, Bernadette and Adam R. Hafdahl. 2000. "Factors Influencing Racial Comparisons of Self-Esteem: A Quantitative Review." *Psychological Bulletin* 126:26–54.

Greene, Steven. 2004. "Social Identity Theory and Party Identification." *Social Science Quarterly* 85:136–153.

Greenberg, Edward S. and Leon Grunberg. 1995. "Work Alienation and Problem Alcohol Behavior." *Journal of Health and Social Behavior* 36:83–102.

Griffin, Em and Glenn G. Sparks. 1990. "Friends Forever: A Longitudinal Exploration of Intimacy in Same-Sex Friends and Platonic Pairs." *Journal of Social and Personal Relationships* 7:29–46.

Griffitt, William. 1970. "Environmental Effects on Interpersonal Affective Behavior." *Journal of Personality and Social Psychology* 15:240–244.

Gruzd, Anatoliy, Barry Wellman, and Yuri Takhteyev. 2011. "Imagining Twitter as an Imagined Community" *American Behavioral Scientist* 55:1294–1318.

Guigni, Marco 1998. "Was It Worth the Effort?" *Annual Review of Sociology* 24:293–371.

Gurr, Ted Robert. 1970. *Why Men Rebel.* Princeton, NJ: Princeton University Press.

Hall, Jeffrey A. and Nancy K. Baym. 2011. "Calling and Texting (Too Much): Mobile Maintenance, Expectations, (Over)dependence, Entrapment, and Friendship Satisfaction." *New Media and Society* 14:316–331.

Halpern, Diane F. 2004. "A Cognitive-Process Taxonomy for Sex Differences in Cognitive Abilities." *Current Directions in Psychological Science* 13:135–139.

Han, Chong-suk. 2009. "Asian Girls are Prettier: Gendered Presentations as Stigma Management Among Gay Asian Men." *Symbolic Interaction* 32:106–122.

Harber, Kent D., Reshma Stafford, and Kathleen A. Kennedy. 2010. "The Positive Feedback Bias as a Response to Self-Image Threat." *British Journal of Social Psychology* 49:207–218.

Hardnack, Chris. 2011. "More Than an Activist: Identity Competition and Participation in a Revolutionary Socialist Organization." *Qualitative Sociology Review* 7:64–84.

Harlow, Roxanna. 2003. " 'Race Doesn't Matter, But…': The Effect of Race on Professors' Experiences and Emotion Management in the Undergraduate Classroom." *Social Psychology Quarterly* 66: 348–363.

Harmon, Katherine. 2011. "How Obesity Spreads in Social Networks." *Scientific American,* May. Retrieved September 4, 2013 (http://www.scientificamerican.com/article.cfm?id=social-spread-obesity).

Harris, Kathleen Mullan. 2009. "The National Longitudinal Study of Adolescent Health (Add Health), Wves I & II, 1994–1996; Waves III, 2001–2002; Wave IV, 2007–2009 [machine-readable data file and documentation]." Chapel Hill, NC: Carolina Population Center, University of North Carolina at Chapel Hill.

Harrod, Wendy, Bridget K. Welch, and Jeff Kushhowski. 2009. "Thirty-One Years of Group Research in Social Psychology Quarterly (1975–2005)." *Current Research in Social Psychology* 14:75–103.

Hartley, Wynona G. 1968. "Self-Conception and Organizational Adaptation." Paper presented at the Annual Meeting of the Midwest Sociological Society, Omaha, NE.

Harvey, Kate, Tom Burns, Tom Fahy, Chatherine Manley, and Theresa Tattan. 2001. "Relatives of Patients With Severe Psychotic Illness: Factors That Influence Appraisal of Caregiving and Psychological Distress." *Social Psychiatry and Psychiatric Epidemiology* 36:456–461.

Hatfield, Elaine C. 1988. "Passionate and Companionate Love." Pp. 191–217 in *The Psychology of Love,* edited by R.J. Sternberg and M.L. Barnes. New Haven, CT: Yale University Press.

Hatfield, Elaine C., Lisamarie Bensman, and Richard L. Rapson. 2012. "A Brief History of Social Scientists' Attempts to Measure Passionate Love." *Journal of Social and Personal Relationships* 29:143–164.

Hatfield, Elaine C., David Greenberger, Jane Traupmann, and Philip Lambert. 1982. "Equity and Sexual Satisfaction in Recently Married Couples." *Journal of Sex Research* 18:18–32

Hatfield, Elaine C. and Susan Sprecher. 1986. "Measuring Passionate Love in Intimate Relationships." *Journal of Adolescence* 9:383–410.

Hatfield, Elaine C. and G. William Walster. 1978. *A New Look at Love.* Lanham, MD: University Press of America.

Hawdon, James E. 2005. *Drug and Alcohol Consumption as Functions of Social Structures: A Cross-Cultural Sociology.* Lewiston, NY: The Edwin Mellen Press Ltd.

Hayes, Jeffrey A. 1997. "What Does the Brief Symptom Inventory Measure in College and University Counseling Center Clients?" *Journal of Counseling Psychology* 44(4):360–367.

Haynie, Dana L., Harry E. Weiss, and Alex R. Piquero. 2008. "Race, the Economic Maturity Gap, and Criminal Offending in Young Adulthood." *Justice Quarterly* 25:595–622.

Heath, Chip, Chris Bell, and Emily Sternberg. 2001. "Emotional Selection Memes: The Case of Urban

Legends." *Interpersonal Relations and Group Processes* 81:1028–1041.

Hegtvedt, K.A. 1990. "The Effects of Relationship Structure on Emotional Responses to Inequity." *Social Psychology Quarterly* 53:214–228.

Heise, David R. 1977. "Social Action as the Control of Affect." *Behavioral Science* 22:163–177.

Heise, David R. 1999. "Controlling Affective Experience Interpersonally." *Social Psychology Quarterly* 62:4–16.

Heise, David R. and Elsa Lewis. 1988. *Programs Interact and Attitude: Software and Documentation.* Dubuqu, IA: Wm. C. Brown Publishers.

Heiss, J. 1981. "Social Roles." Pp. 94–129 in *Social Psychology: Sociological Perspectives,* edited by Morris Rosenberg and Robert H. Turner. New Brunswick, NJ: Transaction.

Hendrick, Susan S. and Clyde Hendrick. 1986. "A Theory and Method of Love." *Journal of Personality and Social Psychology* 50:392–402.

Hendrick, Susan S. and Clyde Hendrick. 2006. "Measuring Respect in Close Relationships." *Journal of Personal Relationships* 23:881–899.

Hendrick, Susan S., Clyde Hendrick, and Amy Dicke 1998 "The Love Attitude Scale: Short Form." *Journal of Social and Personal Relationships* 15:147–159.

Hendrick, Clyde, Susan S. Hendrick, Franklin H. Foote, and Michelle J. Slapion-Foote. 1984. "Do Men and Women Love Differently?" *Journal of Social and Personal Relationships* 1:177–195.

Hendrix, Katherine G. 1997. "Student Perceptions of Verbal and Nonverbal Cues Leading to Images of Black and White Professor Credibility." *The Howard Journal of Communication* 8:251–273.

Henrich, Joseph, Steven J. Heine, and Ara Norenzayan. 2010. "The Weirdest People in the World?" *Behavioral and Brain Sciences* 33:61–83, 111–135.

Henry, P.J. and David O. Sears. 2002. "The Symbolic Racism 2000 Scale." *Political Psychology* 23:253–283.

Henslin, James M. 2007. "The Survivors of the F-227." Pp. 237–245 in *Down to Earth Sociology,* 14th ed., edited by James M. Henslin. New York, NY: Free Press.

Heritage, John. 1984. *Garfinkle and Enthomethodology.* New York, NY: Polity Press.

Herman, Nancy J. 1995. *Deviance: A Symbolic Interactionist Approach.* Walnut Creek, CA: AltaMira Press.

Hermens, Daniel F., Jim Lagopoulos, Juliette Tobias-Webb, Tamara De Regt, Gleyns Dore, Lisa Jukes, Noline Latt, and Ian B. Hickie. 2013. "Pathways to Alcohol-Induced Brain Impairment in Young People: A Review." *Corex* 49:3–17.

Hernandez, Donald J. 1993. "When Households Continue, Discontinue and Form." Washington, DC: United States Bureau of the Census.

Hertlein, Katherine M. and Fred P. Piercy. 2006. "Internet Infidelity: A Critical Review of the Literature." *The Family Journal* 14:366–371.

Hess, Elizabeth. 2008. *Nim Chimpsky: The Chimp Who Would Be Human.* New York, NY: Bantam.

Heward, William L. and Susan M. Silvesri 2005 "The Neutralization of Special Education." Pp. 193–214 in *Controversial Therapies in Developmental Disabilities: Fads, Fashion, and Science in Professional Practice,* edited by John W. Jacobson, Richard M. Foxx, and James A. Mulick. Mahwah, NJ: Lawrence Erlbaum Associates.

Hingson, Ralph W., Wenxing Zha, and Elissa R. Weitzman. 2009. "Magnitude of and Trends in Alcohol-Related Mortality and Morbidity Among U.S. College Students Ages 18–24, 1998–2005." *Journal of Studies on Alcohol and Drugs,* supplement no. 16:12–20. Retrieved September 4, 2013. (http://www.ncbi.nlm.nih.gov/pmc/articles/PMC2701090/?tool=pubmed).

Hirschi, Travis. 1969. *Causes of Delinquency.* Berkeley, CA: University of California Press.

Hitsch, Gunter J., Ali Hortacsu, and Dan Ariely. 2010. "What Makes You Click? Mate Preferences in Online Dating." *Quantitative Marking and Economics* 8:393–427.

Hochschild, Arlie Russell. 1979. "Emotion Work, Feeling Rules, and Social Structure." *Journal of Sociology* 85:551–575.

Hochschild, Arlie Russell. 1983. *The Managed Heart: Commercialization of Human Feeling.* Berkeley, CA: University of California Press.

Hochschild, Arlie. 1989. *The Second Shift: Working Parents and the Revolution at Home.* New York, NY: Penguin Books.

Hodson, Randy. 2007. "Alienation." Pp. 119–121 in *The Blackwell Encyclopedia of Sociology,* edited by G. Ritzer. Oxford, UK: Blackwell.

Hoffman, Moshe, Uri Gneezy, and John A. List. 2011. "Nurture Affects Gender Differences in Spatial Abilities." *Proceedings of the National Academy of Sciences of the United States of America* 108:14786–14788.

Hogan, Richard and Carolyn C. Perrucci. 1998. "Producing and Reproducing Class and Status Differences: Racial and Gender Gaps in Employment and Retirement Income." *Social Problems* 45:528–549.

Hogg, Michael A. 2006a. "Social Identity Theory." Pp. 111–136 in *Contemporary Social Psychological Theories*, edited by Peter J. Burke. Palo Alto, CA: Stanford University Press.

Hogg, Michael A. 2006b. "Intergroup Relations." Pp. 479–502 in *Handbook of Social Psychology*, edited by John Delameter. New York, NY: Springer.

Hogg, Michael A. and Scott A. Reid. 2006. "Social Identity, Self-Categorization, and the Communication of Group Norms." *Communication Theory* 16:7–30.

Hogg, Michael A., Deborah J. Terry, and Katherine M. White. 1995. "A Tale of Two Theories: A Critical Comparison of Identity Theory with Social Identity Theory." *Social Psychology Quarterly* 58:255–269.

Hoijer, Harry. 1954. *Language in Culture: Conference on the Interrelations of Language and Other Aspects of Culture*. Chicago, IL: University of Chicago Press.

Holstein, James A. and Jaber F. Gubrium. 2000. *The Self We Live By: Identity in a Postmodern World*. New York, NY: Oxford University Press.

Homans, George. 1961. *Social Behavior*. New York, NY: Harcourt, Brace & World.

Homans, George. 1974. *Social Behavior: Its Elementary Forms*. New York, NY: Harcourt, Brace, Jonanovich.

Honderich, Ted. 2005. *On Determinism and Freedom*. Edinburgh, UK: Edinburgh University Press.

Hopkins, Nick and Christopher Moore. 2001. "Categorizing the Neighbors: Identity, Distance and Stereotyping." *Social Psychology Quarterly* 64:239–252.

Horne, Christine. 2001. "The Enforcement of Norms: Group Cohesion and Meta-Norms." *Social Psychology Quarterly* 64:253–266.

Hornsey, Matthew J. 2008. "Social Identity Theory and Self-Categorization Theory: A Historical Review." *Social and Personality Psychology Compass* 2:204–222.

Horwitz, Alan V. and Susan C. Reinhard. 1995. "Ethnic Differences in Caregiving Duties and Burden Among Parents and Siblings of the Seriously Mentally Ill." *Journal of Health and Social Behavior* 36:138–150.

House, James S. 1977. "The Three Faces of Social Psychology." *Sociometry* 40:161–177.

House, James S. 1981. "Social Structure and Personality." Pp. 525–561 in *Social Psychology: Sociological Perspectives*, edited by M. Rosenberg and R. H. Turner. New York, NY: Basic Books.

Hovland, Carl I. and Robert R. Sears. 1940. "Minor Studies on Aggression: VI. Correlation of Lynchings with Economic Indices." *Journal of Psychology: Interdisciplinary and Applied* 9:301–310.

Howard, Jay R. 2002. "Do College Students Participate More in Discussion in Traditional Delivery Courses or Interactive Telecourses? A Preliminary Comparison." *The Journal of Higher Education* 73:764–780.

Howard, Judith A. 2000. "Social Psychology of Identities." *Annual Review of Sociology* 26:367–393.

Hruschka, Daniel, Alexandra Brewis, Amber Wutich, and Benjamin Morin. 2011. "Shared Norms Provide Limited Explanation for the Social Clustering of Obesity." *American Journal of Public Health* 101:S295–S300.

Huang, Bu White, Helene R. Kosterman, Rick Catalano, Richard F. Hawkins, and J. David. 2001. "Developmental Associations Between Alcohol and Interpersonal Aggression During Adolescence." *Journal of Research in Crime and Delinquency* 38:64–83.

Huesmann, L. Rowell, Jessica Moise-Titus, Cheryl-Lynn Podolski, and Leonard D. Eron. 2003. "Longitudinal Relations Between Children's Exposure to TV Violence and Their Aggressive and Violent Behavior in Young Adulthood: 1977–1992." *Child Development* 39:201–221.

Hughes, Diane, James Rodriguez, Emilie P. Smith, Deborah J. Johnson, Howard C. Stevenson, and Paul Spicer. 2006. "Parents' Ethnic-Racial Socialization Practices: A Review of Research and Directions for Future Study." *Developmental Psychology* 42:747–770.

Hughes, Mikayla, Kelly Morrison, and Kelli Jean K. Asada. 2005. "What's Love Got to Do With It? Exploring the Impact of Maintenance Rules, Love Attitudes, and Network Support on Friends With Benefits Relationships." *Western Journal of Communication* 69:49–66.

Hughey, Matthew W. 2008. "Virtual (Br)others and (Re)sisters: Authentic Black Fraternity and Sorority Identity on the Internet." *Journal of Contemporary Ethnography* 37:528–560.

Humes, Karen R., Nicholas A. Jones, and Roberto R. Ramirez. 2011. "Overview of Race and Hispanic Origin." 2010 Census Briefs, U.S. Bureau of the Census. Retrieved September 4, 2013 (http://www.census.gov/prod/cen2010/briefs/c2010br-02.pdf).

Humphrey, Laud. 1970. *Tearoom Trade: Impersonal Sex in Public Places*. Chicago, IL: Aldine.

Hurst, Allison L. 2007. "Telling Tales of Oppression and Dysfunction: Narratives of Class Identity Reformation." *Qualitative Sociology Review* 3:82–104.

Hyde, Janet Shibley. 1990. "Meta-Analysis and the Psychology of Gender Differences." *Signs: Journal of Women in Culture and Society* 16:55–73.

Hyde, Janet Shibley. 2007. "New Directions in the Study of Gender Similarities and Differences." *Current Directions in Psychological Science* 16:259–263.

Inglehart, Ronald and Christian Welzel. 2005. *Modernization, Cultural Change, and Democracy: The Human Development Sequence*. New York, NY: Cambridge University Press.

Irvine, Leslie. 2004. "A Model of Animal Selfhood: Expanding Interactionist Possibilities." *Symbolic Interaction* 27:3–21.

Israel, Joachim. 1964. "Experimental Change of Attitudes Using the Asch-Effect." *Acta Sociologica* 7:95–104.

Jackson, Pamela Braboy. 1997. "Role Occupancy and Minority Health." *Journal of Health and Social Behavior* 38:237–255.

Jackson, Pamela Braboy. 2004. "Role Sequencing: Does Order Matter for Mental Health." *Journal of Health and Social Behavior* 45:132–154.

Jadva, Vasanti, Melissa Hines, and Susan Golombok. 2010. "Infants Preferences for Toys, Colors and Shapes: Sex Differences and Similarities." *Archives of Sexual Behavior* 39:1261–1273.

Jaffee, Sara and Janet Shibley Hyde. 2000. "Gender Differences in Moral Orientation: A Meta-Analysis." *Psychological Bulletin* 126:703–726.

Jahoda, Gustav. 2007. A *History of Social Psychology: From the Eighteenth-Century Enlightenment to the Second World War*. New York, NY: Cambridge University Press.

James, William. 1884. "What Is an Emotion?" *Mind* 9:188–205.

James, William. 1890. *The Principles of Psychology*. New York, NY: Henry Holt.

Jamieson, Amie, Andrea Curry, and Gladys Martinez. 1999. "School Enrollment in the United States: Social and Economic Characteristics of Students." *Current Population Reports*. July. Washington, DC: U.S. Census Bureau.

Jaret, Charles, Donald Reitzes, and Nadezda Shapkina. 2005. "Reflected Appraisals and Self-Esteem." *Sociological Perspectives* 48:403–419.

Jencks, Christopher, James Crouse, and Peter Mueser. 1983. "The Wisconsin Model of Status Attainment: A National Replication with Improved Measures of Ability and Aspiration." *Sociology of Education* 56:3–19.

Jenkins, J. Craig. 1983. "Resource Mobilization Theory and the Study of Social Movements." *Annual Review of Sociology* 9:527–553.

Jensen, Gary F. and Raymond Eve. 1976. "Sex Differences in Delinquency: An Examination of Popular Sociological Explanations." *Criminology* 13:427–448.

Jepsen, Lisa K. and Christopher A. Jepsen. 2002. "An Empirical Analysis of the Matching Patterns of Same-Sex and Opposite-Sex Couples." *Demography* 39:435–452.

Johnson, Monica K. 2004. "Further Evidence on Adolescent Employment and Substance Use: Differences by Race and Ethnicity." *Journal of Health and Social Behavior* 45:187–197.

Johnson, Monica K., Robert Crosnoe, and Glen H. Elder Jr. 2011. "Insights on Adolescence From a Life Course Perspective." *Journal of Research on Adolescence* 21:273–280.

Jones, Susan R. 2009. "Constructing Identities at the Intersections: An Autoethnographic Exploration of Multiple Dimensions of Identity." *Journal of College Student Development* 50:287–304.

Jussim, Lee and Kent D. Harber. 2005. "Teacher Expectations and Self-Fulfilling Prophecies: Knowns and Unknowns, Resolved and Unresolved Controversies." *Personality and Social Psychology Review* 9:131–155.

Kahn, Joan R. and Elena M. Fazio. 2005. "Economic Status Over the Life Course and Racial Disparities in Health." *The Journals of Gerontology* 60B:76–84.

Kahneman, Daniel and Angus Deaton. 2010. "High Income Improves Evaluation of Life but Not Emotional Well-Being." *Proceedings of the National Academy of Sciences* 107:16494–16499

Kaiser, Ann P. and Elizabeth M. Delaney. 1996. "The Effects of Poverty on Parenting Young Children." *The Peabody Journal of Education.* 71:66–85.

Kamir, Orit. 2001. *Every Breath You Take: Stalking Narratives and the Law.* Ann Arbor, MI: University of Michigan Press.

Kane, Emily W. 2006. " 'No Way My Boys Are Going to Be Like That!': Parents' Reponses to Children's Gender Nonconformity." *Gender & Society* 20:149–176.

Kanter, Rosabeth Moss. 1977. *Men and Women of the Corporation.* New York, NY: Basic Books.

Kaplan, Howard B. 2006. "Social Psychological Perspectives on Deviance." Pp. 451–478 in *Handbook of Social Psychology,* edited by J. Delameter.: New York, NY: Springer.

Karp, David A. 1996. *Speaking of Sadness: Depression, Disconnection, and the Meanings of Illness.* New York, NY: Oxford University Press.

Karp, David A., Lynda Lytle Holstrom, and Paul S. Gray. 1998. "Leaving Home for College: Expectations for Selective Reconstruction of Self." *Symbolic Interaction* 21:253–276.

Karp, David A. and William C. Yoels. 1976. "The College Classroom: Some Observations on the Meanings of Student Participation." *Sociology and Social Research* 60:421–438.

Kaufman. Joanne M. 2005. "Explaining the Race/Ethnicity-Violence Relationship: Neighborhood Context and Social Psychological Processes." *Justice Quarterly* 22:224–251.

Keeter, Scott and Paul Taylor. 2009. "The Millennials." Pew Research Center. Retrieved September 4, 2013 (http://www.pewresearch.org/2009/12/10/the-millennials/).

Kemper, Theodore D. 1978. *A Social Interactional Theory of Emotion.* New York, NY: Wiley.

Kemper, Theodore D. 1987. "How Many Emotions Are There? Wedding the Social and the Autonomic Component." *American Journal of Sociology* 93:263–289.

Kemper, Theodore D. 1990. *Research Agendas in the Sociology of Emotion.* Albany, NY: State University of New York Press.

Kemper, Theodore D. 2002. "Predicting Emotions in Groups: Some Lessons from 9/11." Pp. 53–68 in *Emotions and Sociology,* edited by Jack Barbalet. Oxford, UK: Blackwell.

Kendall, Todd D. 2011. "The Relationship Between Internet Access and Divorce." *Journal of Family and Economic Issues* 32:449–460.

Kennedy, Sheela and Larry Bumpass. 2008. "Cohabitation and Children's Living Arrangements: New Estimates From the United States." *Demographic Research* 19:1663–1692. Retrieved on March 15, 2013 (http://www.demographic-research.org/volumes/vol19/47/19–47.pdf).

Kerckhoff, Alan C. and Kurt W. Back. 1968. *The June Bug: A Study of Hysterical Contagion.* New York, NY: Appleton-Century-Crofts.

Kessler, Ronald C. 2010. "The Prevalence of Mental Illness." Pp. 46–63 in A *Handbook for the Study of Mental Illness,* edited by Teresa L. Scheid and Tony N. Brown. New York, NY: Cambridge University Press.

Kessler, Ronald C. and Marilyn Essex. 1982. "Marital Status and Depression: The Importance of Coping Resources." *Social Forces* 61:484–507.

Ketrow, Sandra M. 1999. "Nonverbal Aspects of Group Communication." Pp. 251–287 in *The Handbook of Group Communication Theory and Research,* edited by Lawrence R. Frey, Dennis Gouran, and M. Scott Pull. Thousand Oaks, CA: Sage Publications.

Khanna, Nikki and Cathryn Johnson. 2010. "Passing as Black: Racial Identity Work Among Biracial Americans." *Social Psychology Quarterly* 73:380–397.

Kiecolt, K. Jill. 2000. "Self-Concept Change in Social Movements." Pp. 110–131 in *Self, Identity, and Social Movements,* edited by Sheldon Stryker, Timothy J. Owens, and Robert W. White. Minneapolis, MN: University of Minneapolis Press.

Kim, Junghyun Roselyn and Jong-Eun Lee. 2011. "The Facebook Paths to Happiness: Effect of the Number of Facebook Friends and Self-Presentation on Subjective Well-Being." *Cyberpsychology, Behavior, and Social Networking* 14:359–364.

Kinch, John W. 1967. "A Formalized Theory of Self-Concept." Pp. 245–261 in *Symbolic Interaction: A Reader in Social Psychology,* edited by Jerome G. Manis and Bernard N. Meltzer. Boston, MA: Allyn and Bacon.

Kinney, David. 1993. "From Nerds to Normals: The Recovery of Identity Among Adolescents From

Middle School to High School." *Sociology of Education* 6:21–40.

Kirk, Stuart A. and Herb Kutchins. 1992. *The Selling of DSM: The Rhetoric of Science in Psychiatry.* Hawthorne, NY: Aldine de Gruyter.

Kituse, John. 1962. "Societal Reaction to Deviance: Problems of Theory and Method." *Social Problems* 9:247–256.

Klandermans, Bert. 1984. "Mobilization and Participation in a Social Movement: Social Psychological Expansions of Resource Mobilization Theory." *American Sociological Review* 48:583–600.

Klandersman, Bert. 1991. "New Social Movements and Resource Mobilization: The European and the American Approach Revisted." *Politics and the Individual: International Journal of Political Specialization and Political Psychology* 1:89–11.

Klandermans, Bert. 1997. *The Social Psychology of Protest.* Oxford, UK: Blackwell.

Klandermans, Bert. 2002. "How Group Identification Helps Overcome the Dilemma of Collective Action." *American Behavioral Scientist* 45:887–900.

Klein, Helen A., Nancy M. Levenburg, Marie McKendall, and William Mothersell. 2007. "Cheating During the College Years: How Do Business School Students Compare." *Journal of Business Ethics* 72:197–206.

Kling, Kristen C., Janet Shibley Hyde, Carolin Showers, and Brenda N. Buswell. 1999. "Gender Differences in Self-Esteem: A Meta-Analysis." *Psychological Bulletin* 124:470–500.

Kohlberg, Lawrence. 1969. "Stage and Sequence: The Cognitive-Developmental Approach to Socialization." Pp. 347–480 in *Handbook of Socialization Theory and Research,* edited by D. Goslin. Chicago, IL: Rand McNally.

Kohlberg, Lawrence. 1976. "Moral Stages and Moralization: The Cognitive-Developmental Approach." Pp. 170–205 in *The Psychology of Moral Development,* vol. 2, edited by L. Kohlberg. San Francisco, CA: Harper and Row.

Kohn, Melvin L. 1969. *Class and Conformity: A Study in Values.* Homewood, IL: The Dorsey Press.

Kohn, Melvin L. and Carmi Schooler, 1969. "Class, Occupation, and Orientation." *American Sociological Review* 34:659–678.

Kohn, Melvin L. and Carmi Schooler. 1982. "Job Conditions and Personality: A Longitudinal Assessment of Their Reciprocal Effects." *American Journal of Sociology* 87:1257–1286.

Konrath, Sara H., Edward H. O'Brien, and Courtney Hsing. 2011. "Changes in Dispositional Empathy in American College Students Over Time: A Meta-Analysis." *Personality and Social Psychology Review* 15:180–198.

Kornhauser, William. 1959. *The Politics of Mass Society.* New York, NY: Simon & Schuster.

Kozol, Jonathan. 2005. *Shame of the Nation: The Restoration of Apartheid Schooling in America.* New York, NY: Three Rivers Press.

Krahe, Barbara, Ingrid Moller, L. Rowell Huesmann, Lucyna Kirwil, Juliane Ferber, and Anja Berger. 2011. "Desensitization to Media Violence: Links with Habitual Media Violence, Exposure, Aggressive Cognitions, and Aggressive Behavior." *Journal of Personality and Social Psychology* 100:630–646.

Kraut, Robert, Michael Patterson, Vicki Lundmark, Sara Kiesler, Tridas Mukophadhyay, and William Scherlis. 1998. "Internet Paradox: A Social Technology that Reduces Social Involvement and Psychological Well-Being?" *American Psychologist* 53:1017–1031.

Kuhn, Manford S. and Thomas S. McPartland. 1954. "An Empirical Investigation of Self-Attitudes." *American Sociological Review* 19:69–85.

Kurdek, Lawrence A. 2004. "Are Gay and Lesbian Cohabitating Couples Really Different From Heterosexual Married Couples?" *Journal of Marriage and Family* 66:880–900.

Kurdek, Lawrence A. 2006. "Differences Between Partners from Heterosexual, Gay, and Lesbian Cohabitating Couples." *Journal of Marriage and Family* 68:509–528.

Kurdek, Lawrence A. 2008. "A General Model of Relationship Commitment: Evidence from Same-Sex Partners." *Personal Relationships* 15:391–405.

Kurien, Prema. 2005. "Being Young, Brown, and Hindu." *Journal of Contemporary Ethnography* 34:434–469.

Labeff, Emily E., Robert E. Clark, Valerie J. Haines, and George M. Diekhoff. 1990. "Situational Ethics and College Student Cheating." *Sociological Inquiry* 60:190–197.

Landy, David and Harold Sigall. 1974. "Beauty Is Talent: Task Evaluation as a Function of the Performer's

Physical Attractiveness." *Journal of Personality and Social Psychology* 29:299–304.

Lange, Carl G. 1885/1912. "The Mechanism of the Emotions" (translated by B. Rand). Pp. 672–684 in *The Classical Psychologists,* edited by B. Rand. Boston, MA: Houghton.

Langer, Gary and Peyton M. Craighill. 2009. "Fewer Call Racism a Major Problem Though Discrimination Remains." *ABC News.* Retrieved May 5, 2013 (http://abcnews.go.com/PollingUnit/Politics/story?id=6674407#.UbyDtmzD-cy).

Langman, Lauren. 2013. "Occupy: A New New Social Movement." *Current Sociology* 61:510–524.

LaPiere, Richard T. 1934. "Attitudes vs. Actions." *Social Forces* 13:230–237.

Lareau, Annette. 2002. "Invisible Inequality: Social Class and Childrearing in Black and White Families." *American Sociological Review* 67:747–776.

Lash, Scott. 1990. *The Sociology of Postmodernism.* New York, NY: Routledge.

Lawler, Edward J. 2001. "An Affect Theory of Social Exchange." *American Journal of Sociology* 107:321–352.

Lawler, Edward J. and Jeongkoo Yoon. 1996. "Commitment in Exchange Relations: Test of a Theory of Relational Cohesion." *American Sociological Review* 61:89–108.

Lawson, Erma Jean and Aaron Thompson. 1999. *Black Men and Divorce.* Thousand Oaks, CA: Sage Publications.

Leach, Darcy K., Jessica Morris, and Sean Yerkey. 2012. "Decision-Making in 'Leaderless' Movements: Occupy Wall Street and the Resurgence of Participatory Democracy in the U.S." Paper presented at the Annual Meeting of the Midwest Sociological Society. March 31. Minneapolis, MN

LeBon, Gustave. 1896. *The Crowd: Study of the Popular Mind.* London, UK: T. Fisher Unwin.

Lee, James D. 2002. "More Than Ability: Gender and Personal Relationships Influence Science and Technology Involvement." *Sociology of Education* 75:349–373.

Lee, Jennifer and Jeremy Staff. 2007. "When Work Matters: The Varying Impact of Work Intensity on High School Dropout." *Sociology of Education* 80:158–178.

Lee, John Alan 1973. *The Colors of Love: An Exploration of the Ways of Loving* Toronto, Canada: New Press.

Leeb, Rebecca T. and F. Gillian. Rejskind. 2004. "Here's Looking at You Kid: A Longitudinal study of Perceived Differences in Mutual Gaze Behavior in Young Infants." *Sex Roles* 50:1–14.

Lefley, Harriet P. 2010. "Mental Health Systems in a Cross-Cultural Context." Pp. 135–161 in *A Handbook for the Study of Mental Health: Social Contexts, Theories and Systems,* 2nd ed., edited by Teresa L. Scheid and Tony N. Brown. New York, NY: Cambridge University Press.

Legerski, Elizabeth M. and Marie Cornwall. 2010. "Working-Class Job Loss, Gender, and the Negotiation of Household Labor." *Gender and Society* 24:447–474.

Lehmiller, Justin J. and Christopher R. Agnew. 2011. "May-December Paradoxes: An Exploration of Age-Gap Relationships in Western Society." Pp. 39–61 in *The Dark Side of Close Relationships II,* edited by William R. Cupach and Brian H. Spitzberg. New York, NY: Routledge/Taylor & Francis Group.

Leippe, Michael R. and Donna Eisenstadt. 1994. "Generalization of Dissonance Reduction: Decreasing Prejudice Through Induced Compliance." *Journal of Personality and Social Psychology* 67:395–413.

Lemert, Edwin M. 1972. *Human Deviance: Social Problems and Social Control.* Englewood Cliffs, NJ: Prentice Hall.

Lenhart, Amanda, Rich Ling, Scott Campbell, and Kristen Purcell. 2010. "Teens and Mobile Phones." Pew Internet and American Life Project. Washington, DC. Retrieved on March 16, 2013 (http://www.pewinternet.org/).

Lenneberg, Eric H. 1967. *Biological Foundations of Language.* New York, NY: Wiley.

Lennon, Mary C. 1998. "Domestic Arrangements and Depression: An Examination of Household Labor." Pp. 409–421 in *Adversity, Stress, and Psychopathology,* edited by B. P. Dohrenwend. New York, NY: Oxford University Press.

Lenski, Gerhard. 1954. "Status Crystalization: A Non-Vertical Dimension of Social Status." *American Sociological Review* 19:405–413.

Lepianka, Dorota, John Gelissen, and Wim van Oorschot. 2010. "Popular Explanations of Poverty in Europe: Effects of Contextual and Individual Characteristics Across 28 European Countries." *Acta Sociologica* 1:53–72.

Lever, Janet. 1976. "Sex Differences in the Games Children Play." *Social Problems* 23:478–487.

Lever, Janet. 1978. "Sex Differences in the Complexity of Children's Play and Games." *American Sociological Review* 43:471–483.

Levinger, George. 1974. "A Three-level Approach to Attraction; Toward an Understanding of Pair Relatedness." Pp. 99–120 in *Foundations of Interpersonal Attraction*, edited by Theodore L. Huston. New York, NY: Academic Press.

Levinger, George. 1982. "A Social Exchange View on the Dissolution of Pair Relationships." Pp. 97–122 in *Family Relations: Rewards and Costs*, edited by F. I. Nye. Beverly Hills, CA: Sage Publications.

Lickel, Brian, David L. Hamilton, Grazyna Wieczorkowska, Amy Lewis, Steven J. Sherman, and A. Neville Uhles. 2000. "Varieties of Groups and the Perception of Group Entitativity." *Journal of Personality and Social Psychology* 78:223–246.

Link, Bruce G. and Francis T. Cullen. 1990. "The Labeling Theory of Mental Disorder: A Review of the Evidence." *Research in Community and Mental Health* 6:75–105.

Link, Bruce G. and Jo C. Phelan. 1999. "The Labeling Theory of Mental Disorder: The Consequences of Labeling." Pp. 361–376 in *A Handbook for the Study of Mental Health,* edited by Allan V. Horwitz and Teresa L. Scheid. New York, NY: Cambridge.

Link, Bruce G., Elmer Struening, Francis T. Cullen, Patrick E. Shrout, and Bruce P. Dohrenwend. 1989. "A Modified Labeling Theory Approach to Mental Disorder: An Empirical Assessment." *American Sociological Review* 54:400–423.

Linville, Patricia W. 1985. "Self-Complexity and Affective Extremity: Don't Put All Your Eggs in One Cognitive Basket." *Social Cognition* 3:94–120.

Linville, Patricia W. 1987. "Self-Complexity as a Cognitive Buffer Against Stress-Related Illness and Depression." *Journal of Personality and Social Psychology* 52:663–676.

Liptak, Adam. April 10, 2011. "Judges See Sentencing Injustice, but the Calendar Disagrees." *The New York Times,* p. A10.

Livingston, Robert W. 2002. "The Role of Perceived Negativity in the Moderation of African Americans' Implicit and Explicit Racial Attitudes." *Journal of Experimental Social Psychology* 38:405–413.

Long, Karen and Russell Spears. 1997. "The Self-Esteem Hypothesis Revisited: Differentiation and the Disaffected." Pp. 296–317 in *The Social Psychology of Stereotyping and Group Life,* edited by Russell Spears, Penelope Oakes, Naomi Ellemers, and S. Alexander Haslam. Malden, MA: Blackwell Publishing.

Longest, Kyle C. and Michael J. Shanahan. 2007. "Adolescent Work Intensity and Substance Abuse: The Mediational and Moderational Roles of Parenting." *Journal of Marriage and the Family* 69:703–720.

Looker, E. Dianne and Peter C. Pineo. 1983. "Social Psychological Variables and Their Relevance to the Status Attainment of Teenagers." *American Journal of Sociology* 88:1195–1219.

Lovaglia, Michael J. and Jeffrey A. Houser. 1996. "Emotional Reactions and Status in Groups." *American Sociological Review* 61:867–883.

Lucas, Samuel R. 1999. *Tracking Inequality: Stratification and Mobility in American High Schools*. New York, NY: Teachers College Press.

Lucas, Samuel R. and Mark Berends. 2002. "Sociodemographic Diversity, Correlated Achievement, and De Facto Tracking." *Sociology of Education* 75:328–348.

Luftey, Karen and Jalen T. Mortimer. 2006. "Development and Socialization Through the Adult Life Course." Pp. 183–202 in *Handbook of Social Psychology,* edited by J. Delameter. New York, NY: Springer.

Lujansky, Harald and Gerold Mikula. 1983. "Can Equity Theory Explain the Quality and the Stability of Romantic Relationships?" *British Journal of Social Psychology* 22:101–112.

Maccoby, Eleanor E. and Carol Nagy Jacklin. 1974. *The Psychology of Sex Differences*. Stanford, CA: Stanford University Press.

MacKinnon, Sean P., Christian H. Jordan, and Anne E. Wilson. 2011. "Birds of a Feather Sit Together: Physical Similarity Predicts Seating Choice." *Personality and Social Psychology Bulletin* 37:879–892.

MacLeod, Jay. 1995. *Ain't No Makin' It: Aspirations and Attainment in a Low-Income Neighborhood*. Boulder, CO: Westview Press.

Madon, Stephanie, Max Guyll, Ashley A. Buller, Kyle C. Scherr, Jennifer Willard, and Richard Spoth. 2008. "The Mediation of Mothers' Self-Fulfilling Effects on Their Children's Alcohol Use: Self-Verification, Informational Conformity, and Modeling Processes." *Journal of Personality and Social Psychology* 38:499–520.

Madon, Stephanie, Max Guyll, Richard Spoth, and Jennifer Willard. 2004. "Self-Fulfilling Prophecies:

The Synergistic Accumulative Effect of Parents' Beliefs on Children's Drinking Behavior." *Psychological Science* 15:837–845.

Maines, David. 1996. "On Postmodernism, Pragmatism, and Plasterers: Some Interactionist Thoughts and Queries." *Symbolic Interaction* 19:323–340.

Mandell, Nancy. 1986. "Peer Interaction in Daycare Settings: Implications for Social Cognition." Pp. 55–79 in *Sociological Studies of Child Development,* vol. 1, edited by Patricia Adler and Peter Adler. Greenwich, CT: JAI Press.

Mannheim, Karl. 1952. *Essays on the Sociology of Knowledge.* Edited by Paul Kecskemeti. London, UK: Routledge and Kegan Paul.

Manning, Wendy D. and Jessica Cohen. 2012. "Cohabitation and Marital Dissolution: An Examination of Recent Marriages." *Journal of Marriage and Family* 74:377–387.

Markovsky, Barry, LeRoy F. Smith, and Joseph Berger. 1984. "Do Status Interventions Persist?" *American Sociological Review* 49:373–382.

Markus, Hazel R. 1980. "The Self in Thought and Memory." Pp. 102–130 in *The Self in Social Psychology,* edited by Daniel M. Wegner and Robin R. Vallacher. Hillsdale, NJ: Erlbaum.

Martin, Kathleen. A. and Mark R. Leary. 2001. "Self-Presentational Determinants of Health Risk Behavior Among College Freshmen." *Psychology and Health* 16:1–11.

Mascolo, Michael F. and Kurt W. Fisher. 1995. "Developmental Transformations in Appraisals for Pride, Shame and Guilt." Pp. 64–113 in *Self-Conscious Emotions the Psychology of Shame, Guilt, Embarrassment and Pride,* edited by June Price Tangney and Kurt W. Fischer. New York, NY: Guilford Press.

Massey, Douglas S. and Mary J. Fischer. 2005. "Stereotype Threat and the Academic Performance of Students at Selective Colleges and Universities." *DuBois Review* 2:45–67.

Mastro, Dana and Elizabeth Behm-Morawitz. 2005. "Latino Representation on Primetime Television." *Journalism and Mass Communication Quarterly* 82:110–130.

Matsueda, Ross L. and Kathleen Anderson. 1998. "The Dynamics of Delinquent Peers and Delinquent Behavior." *Criminology* 36:269–308

Matsueda, Ross L. and Karen Heimer. 1987. "Race, Family Structure, and Delinquency: A Test of Differential Association and Social Control Theories." *American Sociological Review* 52:826–840.

Matthews, Lisa S., K. A. S. Wickrama, and Rand D. Conger. 1996. "Predicting Marital Instability from Spouse and Observer Reports of Marital Interaction." *Journal of Marriage and Family* 58:641–655.

Mauer, Marc. 2009. "The Changing Racial Dynamics of the War on Drugs." The Sentencing Project. Washington, DC: Retrieved September 4, 2013 (http://www.sentencingproject.org/doc/dp_raceanddrugs.pdf)

Mazur, Allan. 1985. "A Biosocial Model of Status in Face-to-Face Primate Groups." *Social Forces* 64:377–402.

Mazzoco, Philip J., Timothy C. Brock, Gregory J. Brock, Kristina R. Olson, and Mahzarin Banaji. 2006. "The Cost of Being Black: White Americans' Perceptions and the Question of Reparations." *Du Bois Review* 3:261–297.

McAdam, Doug. 1982. *Political Processes and the Development of Black Insurgency 1930–1970.* Chicago, IL: The University of Chicago Press.

McCabe, Donald L. 1992. "The Influence of Situational Ethics on Cheating Among College Students." *Sociological Inquiry* 62:365–374.

McCarthy, John D. and Mayer N. Zald. 1973. *The Trends of Social Movements in America: Professionalization and Resource Mobilization.* Morristown, NJ: General Learning Press.

McCarthy, John D. and Mayer N. Zald. 1977. "Resource Mobilization and Social Movements: A Partial Theory." *The American Journal of Sociology* 82:1212–1241.

McCleary, Richard and Richard A. Tewksbury. 2010. "Female Patrons of Porn." *Deviant Behavior* 31:208–223.

McClendon, McKee J. 1976. "The Occupational Status Attainment Processes of Males and Females." *American Sociological Review* 41:52–64.

McDonough, Peggy, and Vivienne Walters. 2001. "Gender and Health: Reassessing Patterns and Explanations." *Social Science and Medicine* 52(4):547–559.

McDougall, Patricia and Shelley Hymel. 2007. "Same-Gender Versus Cross-Gender Friendship Conceptions: Similar or Different?" *Merrill-Palmer Quarterly* 53(3):Article 4. Retrieved September 4, 2013 (http://digitalcommons.wayne.edu/mpq/vol53/iss3/4/).

McFadden, Roger D. and Angela Macropoulos. 2008. "Wal-Mart Employee Trampled to Death." *The New*

York Times, November 29. Retrieved February 8, 2013 (http://www.nytimes.com/2008/11/29/business/29walmart.html?_r=2&scp=1&sq=walmart%20employee%20trampled%20to%20death&st=cse&).

McGuire, William J., Claire V. McGuire, Pamela Child, and Terry Fujioka. 1978. "Salience of Ethnicity in the Spontaneous Self-Concept as a Function of One's Ethnic Distinctiveness in the Social Environment." *Journal of Personality and Social Psychology* 36:511–520.

McKelvie, Stuart J. and Sharon J. Matthews. 1976. "Effects of Physical Attractiveness and Favourableness of Character on Liking." *Psychological Reports* 38:1223–1230.

McLanahan, Sara S. and Christine Percheski. 2008. "Family Structure and the Reproduction of Inequality." *Annual Review of Sociology* 34:257–276.

McLeod, Jane D. and Kathryn J. Lively. 2006. "Social Structure and Personality." Pp. 77–102 in *Handbook of Social Psychology*, edited by J. D. Delameter. New York, NY: Springer.

McLoyd, Vonnie C. and Leon Wilson. 1991. "The Strain of Living Poor: Parenting, Social Support, and Child Mental Health." Pp. 105–135 in *Children in Poverty: Child Development and Public Policy*, edited by A. C. Huston. New York, NY: Cambridge University Press.

McMullin, Julie Ann and John Cairney. 2004. "Self-Esteem and the Intersection of Age, Class, and Gender. *Journal of Aging Studies* 18:75–90.

McPartland, Thomas S. 1965. *Manual for the Twenty Statements Problem (revised)*. Kansas City, MO: Greater Kansas City Mental Health Foundation, Department Research.

McPhail, Clark. 1991. *The Myth of the Madding Crowd*. New York, NY: Aldine De Gruyter.

McPherson, Miller, Lynn Smith-Lovin, and James M. Cook. 2001. "Birds of a Feather: Homophily in Social Networks." *Annual Review of Sociology* 27:415–444.

Mead, George Herbert. 1934. *Mind Self and Society*. Chicago, IL: Chicago University Press.

Mead, George Herbert. 1964. *Selected Writings*. Edited by Andrew J. Reck. Chicago, IL: University of Chicago Press.

Mead, Margret. 1935/2001. *Sex and Temperament in Three Primitive Societies*. New York, NY: Perennial, HarperCollins.

Meeker, Barbara F. 1981. "Expectations States and Interpersonal Behavior." Pp. 290–319 in *Social Psychology: Sociological Perspectives*, edited by M. Rosenberg and R. H. Turner. New York, NY: Basic Books.

Mehen, Mehan Hugh and Houston V. Wood. 1975. "The Morality of Ethnomethodology." *Theory and Society* 2:509–530.

Meltzer, Bernard N. and John W. Petras. 1970. "The Chicago and Iowa Schools of Symbolic Interactionism." Pp. 3–17 in *Human Nature and Collective Behavior*, edited by T. Shibutani. Englewood Cliffs, NJ: Prentice-Hall.

Melucci, Alberto. 1980. "The New Social Movements: A Theoretical Approach." *Social Science Information* 19:199–226.

Melucci, Alberto. 1988. "Getting Involved: Identity and Mobilization in Social Movements." *Research in Social Movements, Conflicts and Change* 1:329–348.

Melucci, Alberto. 1989. *Nomads of the Present: Social Movements and Individual Needs in Contemporary Society*. Philadelphia, PA: Temple University Press.

Menne, Cadiz Joy M. and Robert E. Sinnett. 1971. "Proximity and Social Interaction in Residence Halls." *Journal of College Student Personnel* 12:26–31.

Merten, Don. 1997. "The Meaning of Meanness: Popularity, Competition, and Conflict Among Junior High School Girls." *Sociology of Education* 70:175–191.

Merton, Robert K. 1938. "Social Structure and Anomie." *American Sociological Review* 3:672–682

Merton, Robert K. 1948. "The Self-Fulfilling Prophecy." *Antioch Review* 8:193–201.

Merton, Robert K. 1957. "The Role-Set: Problems in Sociological Theory." *British Journal of Sociology* 8:106–120.

Merton, Robert K. 1968. *Social Theory and Social Structure*. New York, NY: Free Press.

Merton, Robert K. and Alice S. Rossi. 1968. "Contributions to the Theory of Reference Group Behavior." Pp. 279–334 in *Social Theory and Social Structure*. New York, NY: Free Press.

Meyer, David S. 2003. "How Social Movements Matter." *Contexts* 2:30–45.

Meyer, David S. and Catherine Corrigall-Brown. 2005. "Coalitions and Political Context: U.S. Movements Against Wars in Iraq." *Mobilization* 10:327–344.

Meyer, Philip. 1970. "If Hitler Asked You to Electrocute a Stranger Would You? *Esquire,* February, pp. 73, 128, 130 and 132.

Meyers, Stephenie. 2005. *Twilight.* New York, NY: Little, Brown and Company.

Meyersohn, Rolf and Elihu Katz. 1957. "Notes on a Natural History of Fads." *The American Journal of Sociology* 62:594–601.

Michaels, James W., Alan C. Acock, and John N. Edwards. 1986. "Social Exchange and Equity Determinants of Relationship Commitment." *Journal of Social and Personal Relationships* 3:161–175.

Milgram, Stanley. 1963. "Behavioral Study of Obedience." *Journal of Abnormal and Social Psychology* 64:371–378.

Milgram, Stanley. 1965. "Some Conditions of Obedience and Disobedience to Authority." *Human Relations* 18:57–76.

Milgram, Stanley. 1974. *Obedience to Authority: An Experimental View.* London, UK: Tavistock.

Milkie, Melissa A. 1994. "A Social World Approach to Cultural Studies: Mass Media and Gender in the Adolescent Peer Group." *Journal of Contemporary Ethnography* 23:354–380.

Miller, Joan G. 1984. "Culture and the Development of Everyday Social Explanation." *Journal of Personality and Social Psychology* 46:961–978.

Miller, Joanne, Carmi Schooler, Melvin Kohn, and Karen A. Miller. 1979. "Women and Work: The Psychological Effects of Occupational Conditions." *American Journal of Sociology* 85:66–94.

Miller, Rowland S. 2009. "Shyness, Social Anxiety, and Embarrassability." Pp. 176–191 in *Handbook of Individual Differences in Social Behavior,* edited by M.R. Leary and R.H. Hoyle. New York, NY: Guilford Press.

Miller, Rowland S. and June Price Tangney. 1994. "Differentiating Embarrassment and Shame." *Journal of Social and Clinical Psychology* 13:273–287.

Miller-Tutzauer, Carol, Kenneth E. Leonard, and Michael Windle. 1991. "Marriage and Alcohol Use: A Longitudinal Study of 'Maturing Out'." *Journal of Studies of Alcohol* 52:434–440.

Millon, Theodore. 1975. "Reflections on Rosenhan's 'On Being Sane in Insane Places.'" *Journal of Abnormal Psychology* 84:456–461.

Mills, C. Wright. 1959. *The Sociological Imagination.* New York, NY: Oxford University Press.

Mirowsky, John and Catherine E. Ross. 1989. *Social Causes of Psychological Distress.* New York, NY: Aldine de Gruyter.

Mirowsky, John and Catherine E. Ross. 2010. "Well-Being Across the Life Course." Pp. 361–383 in *The Handbook for the Study of Mental Health,* 2nd ed., edited by Teresa L. Scheid and Tony N. Brown. New York, NY: Cambridge University Press.

Modigliani, Andre. 1966. "Embarrassment and Social Influence." *Dissertation Abstracts International* 28:294–295A.

Modigliani, Andre. 1968. "Embarrassment and Embarrassability." *Sociometry* 31:313–326.

Molm, Linda D. 1987. "Linking Power Structure and Power Use." Pp. 101–129 in *Social Exchange Theory,* edited by Karen S. Cook. Beverly Hills, CA: Sage Publication.

Molm, Linda D. 1990. "Structure, Action and Outcomes: The Dynamics of Power in Exchange Relations." *American Sociological Review* 55:427–447.

Molm, Linda D. 1994. "Is Punishment Effective? Coercive Strategies in Social Exchange." *Social Psychology Quarterly* 57:75–94.

Molm, Linda D. 1997. "Risk and Power Use: Constraints on the Use of Coercion in Exchange." *American Sociological Review* 62:113–133.

Molm, Linda D. 2003. "Power, Trust and Fairness: Comparisons of Negotiated and Reciprocal Exchange." Pp. 31–65 in *Advances in Group Processes: Power and Status,* vol. 20, edited by Shane R. Thye and John Skvoretz. New York, NY: Elsevier Press.

Molm, Linda D. and Karen S. Cook. 1995. "Social Exchange and Exchange Networks." Pp. 209–35 in *Sociological Perspectives on Social Psychology,* edited by Karen S. Cook, Gary Alan Fine, and James S. House. Boston, MA: Allyn and Bacon.

Molm, Linda D., David R. Schaefer, and Jessica L. Collet. 2007. "The Value of Reciprocity." *Social Psychology Quarterly* 70:199–217.

Molm, Linda D., Nobuyuki Takahashi, and Gretchen Peterson. 2000. "Risk and Trust in Social Exchange: An Experimental Test of a Classical Proposition." *American Journal of Sociology* 105:1396–1427.

Monk-Turner, Elizabeth, Mary Heiserman, Crystle Johnson, Vanity Cotton, and Manny Jackson. 2010. "The Portrayal of Racial Minorities on Prime Time Television: A Replication of the Mastro and Greenberg Study a Decade Later." *Studies in Popular Culture* 32:101–114.

Monsour, Michael. 1992. "Meanings of Intimacy in Cross- and Same-Sex Friendships." *Journal of Social and Personal Relationships* 9:277–295.

Moore, James C. 1968. "Status and Influence in Small Group Interactions." *Sociometry* 31:47–63.

Moore, Kristin A., Zakia Redd, Mary Burkhauser, Kassim Mbwana, and Ashleigh Colins. 2009. "Children in Poverty: Trends, Consequences, and Policy Options." Research brief no. 2009–11. Washington, DC: Child Trends. Retrieved September 4, 2013 (http://www.childtrends.org/files/child_trends-2009_04_07_rb_childreninpoverty.pdf).

Moreland, Richard and Sascha Topolnski. 2010. "The Mere Exposure Phenomenon: A Lingering Melody by Robert Zajonc." *Emotion Review* 2:329–339.

Moretti, Marlene M., Z.V. Segal, C.D. McCann, B.F. Shaw, D.T. Miller, and D. Vella. 1996. "Self-Referent Versus Other-Referent Information Processing in Dysphoric, Clinically Depressed, and Remitted Depressed Subjects." *Personality and Social Psychology Bulletin* 22:68–80.

Morris, Edward W. 2005. "Tuck in That Shirt!" Race, Class, Gender, and Discipline in an Urban School." *Sociological Perspectives* 48:25–48.

Morris, Michael W. and Kaiping Peng. 1994. "Culture and Cause: American and Chinese Attributions for Social and Physical Events." *Journal of Personality and Social Psychology* 67:949–971.

Mortimer, Jeylan T. and Jon Lorence. 1995. "Social Psychology of Work." Pp. 497–523 in *Sociological Perspectives on Social Psychology*, edited by K.S. Cook, G.A. Fine, and J.S. House. Boston, MA: Allyn and Bacon.

Mortimer, Jeylan T. and Roberta G. Simmons. 1978. "Adult Socialization." *Annual Review of Sociology* 4:421–454.

Mossakowski, Krysia N. 2003. "Coping With Perceived Discrimination: Does Ethnic Identity Protect Mental Health?" *Journal of Health and Social Behavior* 44:318–331.

Mossakowski, Krysia N. 2007. "Are Immigrants Healthier? The Case of Depression Among Filipino Americans." *Social Psychology Quarterly* 70:290–304.

Mossakowski, Krysia N. 2012. "Racial/Ethnic Inequality in Wealth During Young Adulthood and Midlife: A Social Psychological Perspective of the Middle Class." *American Behavioral Scientist* 56:728–746.

Mottaz, Clifford M. 1981. "Some Determinants of Work Alienation." *Sociological Quarterly* 22:515–529.

Murstein, Bernard I. 1972. "Physical Attractiveness and Marital Choice." *Journal of Personality and Social Psychology* 22:8–12.

Musolf, Gil Richard. 1996. "Interactionism and the Child: Cahill, Corsaro and Denzin on Childhood Socialization." *Symbolic Interactionism* 19:303–321.

Nadler, Arie, Gal Harpaz-Gorodeisky, and Yael Ben-David. 2009. "Defensive Helping: Threat to Group Identity, Ingroup Identification, Status Stability, and Common Group Identity as Determinants of Intergroup Help-Giving." *Journal of Personality and Social Psychology* 97:823–834.

Nanda, Serena. 1999. *Gender Diversity: Crosscultural Variations*. New York, NY: Waveland Press.

National Institute of Mental Health (NIMH). 2011. "Survey Assesses Trends in Psychiatric Hospitalization Rates." Science News from 2011. Retrieved June 17, 2013 (http://www.nimh.nih.gov/news/science-news/2011/survey-assesses-trends-in-psychiatric-hospitalization-rates.shtml).

Neff, Joan L. and Dennis E. Waite. 2007. "Male Versus Female Substance Abuse Patterns Among Incarcerated Juvenile Offenders: Comparing Strain and Social Learning Variables." *Justice Quarterly* 24:106–132.

Neimeyer, Robert A. and Kelly A. Mitchell. 1988. "Similarity and Attraction: A Longitudinal Study." *Journal of Social and Personal Relationships* 5:131–148.

Nelson, Anders. 2005. "Children's Toy Collections in Sweden-A less Gender-Typed Country." *Sex Roles* 52:93–102.

Nelson, Steven M. 2007. "Offender Crime Perspectives: A Study in Affect Control Theory." PhD dissertation, Department of Sociology, The University of Arizona, Tucson, AZ.

Neville, Helen A., Roderick L. Lilly, Georgia Duran, Richard M. Lee, and LaVonne Browne. 2000. "Construction and Initial Validation of the Color-Blind Racial Attitudes Scale (CoBRAS)." *Journal of Counseling Psychology* 47:59–70.

Newport, Frank. 2008. "Wives Still Do Laundry, Men Do Yard Work." Gallup Poll. Retrieved on July 22, 2011 (http://www.gallup.com/poll/106249/Wives-Still-Laundry-Men-Yard-Work.aspx).

Newport, Frank. 2012. "Half of Americans Support Legal Gay Marriage." Gallup Poll. Retrieved on March 15, 2013 (http://www.gallup.com/poll/154529/half-americans-support-legal-gay-marriage.aspx).

Nguyen, A., J. Taylor, and Steven. Bradley. 2002. "Relative Pay and Job Satisfaction: Some New Evidence." Working paper no. 045. Department of Economics, Lancaster University Management School. Retrieved November 8, 2012 (http://www.lums.lancs.ac.uk/publications/viewpdf/000192).

Niemann, Yolanda Flores, and John E. Dovidio. 1998. "Relationship of Solo Status, Academic Rank, and Perceived Distinctiveness to Job Satisfaction of Racial/Ethnic Minorities." *Journal of Applied Psychology* 83:55–71.

Nier, Jason A., Samuel L. Gaertner, John F. Dovidio, Brenda S. Banker, Christine Mary Ward. 2001. "Changing Interracial Evaluations and Behavior: The Benefits of Common Group Identity." *Group Processes and Intergroup Relations* 4:299–316.

Norton, Michael I., Jeanna H. Frost, and Dan Ariely. 2007. "Less Is More: The Lure of Ambiguity, or Why Familiarity Breeds Contempt." *Journal of Personality and Social Psychology* 92:97–105.

Noymer, Andrew. 2001. "The Transmission and Persistence of 'Urban Legends': Sociological Application of Age-Structured Epidemic Models." *Journal of Mathematical Sociology* 25:299–323.

Oakes, Jeannie. 2005. *Keeping Track: How Schools Structure Inequality,* 2nd ed. New Haven, CT: Yale University Press.

Oberschall, Anthony. 1973. *Social Conflict and Social Movements.* Englewood Cliffs, NJ: Prentice Hall.

O'Brien, Ed, Sara H. Konrath, Daniel Gruhn, and Anna Linda Hagen. 2013. "Empathic Concern and Perspective Taking: Linear and Quadratic Effects of Age Across the Adult Life Span." *The Journals of Gerontology Series B: Psychological Science and Social Sciences* 68:168–175.

O'Brien, Laurie T., Christian S. Crandall, April Horstman-Reser, Ruth Warner, AnGelica Alsbrooks, and Alison Blordorn. 2010. "But I'm No Bigot: How Prejudiced White Americans Maintain Unprejudiced Self-Images." *Journal of Applied Social Psychology* 40:917–946.

O'Brien, Robert M. 1999. "Measuring the Convergence/Divergence of Serious Crime Arrests for Males and Females: 1960–1995." *Journal of Quantitative Criminology* 15:97–114.

O'Connell, Martin and Sarah Feliz. 2011. "Same-Sex Couple Household Statistics From the 2010 Census." SEHSD working paper no. 2011–26. U.S. Census Bureau. Retrieved on March 15, 2013 (http://www.census.gov/hhes/samesex/).

O'Dea, Jennifer A. and Suzanne Abraham. 1999. "Association Between Self-Concept and Body Weight, Gender, and Pubertal Development Among Male and Females Adolescents." *Adolescence* 34:69–79.

Offer, Shira and Barbara Schneider. 2011. "Revisiting the Gender Gap in Time-Use Patterns: Multitasking and Well-Being among Mothers and Fathers in Dual-Earner Families." *American Sociological Review* 76:809–833.

Olafsdottir, Sigrun. 2011. "Medicalization and Mental Health: The Critique of Medical Epansion and a Consideration of How National States, Markets and Citizens Matter." Pp. 230–260 in *The SAGE Handbook of Mental Health and Illness,* edited by David Pilgrim, Anne Rogers, and Bernice A. Pescosolido. London, UK: Sage Publications.

Oliver, Pamela E., Jorge Cadena-Roa, and Kelley D. Strawn. 2003. "Emerging Trends in the Study of Social Movements and Collective Behavior." Pp. 213–244 in *Political Sociology for the 21st Century: Research in Political Sociology,* vol. 12, edited by Betty A. Dobratz, Lisa K. Waldner, and Timothy Buzzell. Stanford, CT: JAI Press.

Olson, Mancur. 1965. *The Logic of Collective Action: Public Goods and the Theory of Groups.* Cambridge, MA: Harvard University Press.

Ophir, Eyal, Clifford Nass and Anthony D. Wagner. 2009. "Cognitive Control in Media Multitaskers." *Proceedings of the National Academy of Sciences of the United States of America* 106:15583-15587.

Orbuch, Terri L., Joseph Veroff, Halimah Hassan, and Julie Horricks. 2002. "Who Will Divorce: A 14-Year Longitudinal Study of Black Couples and White Couples." *Journal of Social and Personal Relationships* 19:179–202.

Organization for Economic Cooperation and Development (OECD). 2012. *Closing the Gender Gap: Act Now* Paris, France: OECD Publishing.

Osgood, Charles E., William H. May, and Murray S. Miron. 1975. *Cross-Cultural Universals of Affective Meaning*. Urbana, IL: University of Illinois Press.

Osgood, Charles, George J. Suci, and Percy Tannenbaum. 1957. *The Measurement of Meaning*. Urbana, IL: University of Illinois Press.

Otto, Luther B. and Archibald O. Haller. 1979. "Evidence for a Social Psychological View of the Status Attainment Process: Four Studies Compared." *Social Forces* 57:887–914.

Owen, Jesse J., Galena K. Rhoades, Scott M. Stanley, and Frank D. Fincham. 2010. "Hooking Up Among College Students: Demographic and Psychosocial Correlates." *Archives of Sexual Behavior* 39:653–663.

Owens, Timothy J. 2006. "Self and Identity." Pp. 205–232 in *Handbook of Social Psychology,* edited by John Delamater. New York, NY: Springer.

Pager, Devah and Bruce Western. 2012. "Identifying Discrimination at Work: The Use of Field Experiments." *Journal of Social Issues* 68:221–237.

Pagliaro, Stefano, Francesca Romana Alparone, Maria Giuseppina Pacilli, and Angelica Mucci-Faina. 2012. "Managing a Social Identity Threat: Ambivalence Toward the Ingroup as Psychological Disengagement." *Social Psychology* 43:41–46.

Paik, Haejung and George Comstock. 1994. "The Effects of Television Violence on Antisocial Behavior: A Meta-Analysis." *Communication Research* 21:516–546.

Painter II, Matthew A. 2010. "Get a Job and Keep It! High School Employment and Adult Wealth Accumulation." *Research in Social Stratification and Mobility* 28:233–249.

Park, Robert E. and Ernest W. Burgess. 1924. "Assimilation, Social." Pp. 734–783 in *Encyclopedia of the Social Sciences,* vol 2, edited by Edwin R. A. Seligman and Alvin Johnson New York, NY: MacMillan.

Parker, Douglas A. and Jacob A. Brody. 1982. "Risk Factors for Alcoholism and Alcohol Problems Among Employed Men and Women." Pp. 99–127 in *Occupational Alcoholism: A Review of Research Issues.* NIAAA research monograph no. 8. Washington, DC: U.S. Government Printing Office.

Pascale, Celine-Marie. 2008. "The Specter of Whiteness." *Studies in Symbolic Interaction* 30:167–182.

Pascoe, C.J. 2007. *Dude, You're a Fag: Masculinity and Sexuality in High School*. Berkeley, CA: University of California Press.

Pasek Josh, Jon A. Krosnick, and Trevor Thompson. 2012. "The Impact of Anti-Black Racism on Approval of Barack Obama's Job Performance on Voting in the 2012 Presidential Election." Retrieved November 11, 2012 (http://www.stanford.edu/dept/communication/faculty/krosnick/docs/2012/2012%20Voting%20and%20Racism.pdf

Passas, Nikos. 1990. "Anomie and Corporate Deviance." *Contemporary Crises* 14:157–178.

Patchin, Justin W. and Sameer Hinduja. 2011. "Traditional and Nontraditional Bullying Among Youth: A Test of General Strain Theory." *Youth and Society* 43:727–751

Pavalko, Eliza K., Courtenay M. Harding, and Bernice A. Pescosolido. 2007. "Mental Illness Careers in an Era of Change." *Social Problems* 54:504–522.

Pavitt, Charles. 1999. "Theorizing About the Communication/Leadership Relationship: Causal and Functional Forms" Pp. 313–334 in *Handbook of Group Communication Theory and Research,* edited by L. R. Frey, D. S. Gouran, and M. S. Poole. Thousand Oaks, CA: Sage Publications.

Payne, Krista. K. 2011. "On the Road to Adulthood: Sequencing of Family Experiences." National Center for Family and Marriage Research. Retrieved September 4, 2013 (http://ncfmr.bgsu.edu/pdf/family_profiles/file102409.pdf)

Pearlin, Leonard I. 1989. "The Sociological Study of Stress." *Journal of Health and Social Behavior* 30:241–256.

Pearlin, Leonard I. 1999. "Stress and Mental Health: A Conceptual Overview." Pp. 161-175 in *A Handbook for the Study of Mental Health,* edited by Allan V. Horwitz and Theresa L. Scheid. New York, NY: Cambridge University Press.

Pearlin, Leonard. I., Elizabeth Menaghan, Morton A. Lieberman, and Joseph T. Mullan. 1981. "The Stress Process." *Journal of Health and Social Behavior* 22: 337–356.

Pearlin, Leonard I. and Carmi Schooler. 1978. "The Structure of Coping." *Journal of Health and Social Behavior* 19:2–21.

Penhollow, Tina, Michael Young, and William Bailey. 2007. "Relationship Between Religiosity and 'Hooking Up' Behavior." *American Journal of Health Education* 38:338–345.

Perry, Pamela. 2001. "White Means Never Having to Say You're Ethnic: White Youth and the Construction of 'Cultureless' Identity." *Journal of Contemporary Ethnography* 30:56–91.

Pescosolido, Bernice A. and Carol A. Boyer. 1999. "How Do People Come to Use Mental Health Services? Current Knowledge and Changing Perspectives." Pp. 392–411 in A *Handbook for the Study of Mental Health*, edited by Allan V. Horwitz and Teresa L. Scheid. New York, NY: Cambridge University Press.

Pescosolido, Bernice A., J.K. Martin, J.S. Long, T.R. Medina, Jo C. Phelan, and Bruce G. Link. 2010. "A Disease Like Any Other? A Decade of Change in Public Reactions to Schizophrenia, Depression and Alcohol Dependence." *American Journal of Psychiatry* 167:1321–1330.

Pescosolido, Bernice, B.L. Perry, J.K. Martin, Jane D. McLeod, and P.S. Jenson. 2007. "Stigmatizing Attitudes and Beliefs About Treatment and Psychiatric Medications for Children with Mental Illness." *Psychiatric Service* 58:613–618.

Peterson, Warren A. and Noel Gist. 1951. "Rumor and Public Opinion." *The American Journal of Sociology* 57:159–167.

Petras, John W. and Bernard N. Meltzer. 1973. "Theoretical and Ideological Variations in Symbolic Interactionism." *Catalyst* 7:1–8.

Pettigrew, Thomas F. and Linda R. Tropp. 2006. "A Meta-Analytic Test of Intergroup Contact Theory." *Journal of Personality and Social Psychology* 90:751–783.

Pettit, Michele L. and Kathy A. DeBarr. 2011. "Perceived Stress, Energy Drink Consumption, and Academic Performance Among College Students. *Journal of American College Student Health* 59: 335–341.

Phinney, Jean S. 1990. "Ethnic Identity in Adolescents and Adults: Review of Research." *Psychological Bulletin* 108:499–514.

Phinney, Jean S. 1992. "The Multigroup Ethnic Identity Measure: A New Scale for Use With Diverse Groups." *Journal of Adolescent Research* 7:156–176.

Phinney, Jean S. and Linda L. Alipuria. 2006. "Multiple Social Categorization and Identity Among Multiracial, Multiethnic, and Multicultural Individuals: Processes and Implications." Pp. 211–238 in *Multiple Categorization: Processes, Models and Applications*, edited by Richard J. Crisp and Miles Hewstone. New York, NY: Psychology Press.

Piaget, Jean. 1926. *The Language and Thought of the Child*. London, UK: Paul Kegan.

Pichardo, Nelson A. 1997. "New Social Movements: A Critical Review." *Annual Review of Sociology* 23:411–430.

Pietromonaco, Paula R. and Hazel Markus. 1985. "The Nature of Negative Thoughts in Depression." *Journal of Personality and Social Psychology* 48:799–807.

Pillemer, Jane, Elaine Hatfield, and Susan Sprecher. 2008. "The Importance of Fairness and Equity for the Marital Satisfaction of Older Women." *Journal of Women and Aging* 20:215–230.

Pinel, Elizabeth C. and William B. Swann Jr. 2000. "Finding the Self Through Others: Self-Verification and Social Movement Participation." Pp. 132–152 in *Self, Identity, and Social Movements: Social Movements, Protest, and Contention*, vol. 13, edited by Timothy Owens and Sheldon Stryker. Minneapolis, MN: University of Minnesota Press.

Pitts, Leonard. 2003. "Affirmative Action's Big Winners: White Males." Chicago Tribune News, October 21. Retrieved on Jan. 10, 2013 (http://articles.chicagotribune.com/2003-10-21/news/0310210293_1_affirmative-action-racial-preference-white-men)

Plant, E. Ashby, Janet Shibley Hyde, Dacher Keltner, and Patricia G. Devine. 2000. "The Gender Stereotyping of Emotions." *Psychology of Women Quarterly* 24:81–92.

Pollak, Kathryn I. and Yolanda Flores Niemann. 1998. "Black and White Tokens in Academia: A Difference of Chronic Versus Acute Distinctiveness." *Journal of Applied Social Psychology* 28:954–972.

Polletta, Francesca and James M. Jasper. 2001. "Collective Identity and Social Movements." *Annual Review of Sociology* 27:283–305.

Pollner, Melvin. 1987. *Mundane Reason: Reality in Everyday and Sociological Discourse*. Cambridge, UK: Cambridge University Press.

Pomerleau, Andree Bolduc, Daniel Malcuit, and Louise Gerard Cosette. 1990. "Pink or Blue: Environmental Gender Stereotypes in the First Two Years of Life." *Sex Roles* 22:359–367.

Ponterroto, Joseph G., Denise Gretchen, Shawn O. Utsey, Thomas Stratcuzzi, and Robert Saya Jr. 2003. "The Multigroup Ethnic Identity Measure (MEIM): Psychometric Review and Further Validity Testing." *Educational and Psychological Measurement* 63:502–515.

Porta, Donatella Della and Mario Diani. 2006. *Social Movements: An Introduction.* Malden, MA: Wiley-Blackwell.

Portes, Alejandro and Kenneth L. Wilson. 1976. "Black-White Differences in Educational Attainment." *American Sociological Review* 41:414–431.

Pratt, Travis C., Francis T. Cullen, Christine Sellers, L. Thomas Winfree Jr., Tamara D. Madensen, Leah E. Daigle, Noelle E. Fearn, and Jacinta M. Gau. 2010. "The Empirical Status of Social Learning Theory: A Meta Analysis." *Justice Quarterly* 27:765–802.

Press, Julie E. and Eleanor Townsley. 1998. "Wives' and Husbands' Housework Reporting." *Gender and Society* 12:188–218.

Previti, Denise and Paul R. Amato. 2003. "Why Stay Married? Rewards, Barriers, and Marital Stability." *Journal of Marriage and Family* 65:561–573.

Pugh, M.D. and Ralph Wahrman. 1983. "Neutralizing Sexism in Mixed-Sex Groups: Do Women Have to Be Better Than Men?" *Journal of Sociology* 88:746–762.

Pugliesi, Karen. 1987. "Deviation in Emotion and the Labeling of Mental Illness." *Deviant Behavior* 8:79–102.

Purcell, Kristen. 2011. "Search and Email Still Top the List of Most Popular Online Services: Two Activities Nearly Universal Among Internet Users." Pew Research Center Internet and Life Project. Washington, DC. Retrieved September 4, 2013 (http://pewinternet.org/Reports/2011/Search-and-email.aspx)

Purser, Gretchen. 2009. "The Dignity of Job-Seeking Men: Border Work Among Immigrant Day Laborers." *Journal of Contemporary Ethnography* 38:117–139.

Putney, Norella and Vern L. Bengston. 2002. "Socialization and the Family: A Broader Perspective." Pp. 165–194 in *Advances in Life-Course Research: New Frontiers in Socialization,* edited by R.A. Settersten Jr. and T.J. Owens. London, UK: Elsevier.

Putney, Norella M. and Vern L. Bengtson. 2005. "Family Relations in Changing Times: A Longitudinal Study of Five Cohorts of Women." *International Journal of Sociology and Social Policy* 25:92–119.

Rafaeli, Anat and Robert I. Sutton. 1989. "The Expression of Emotion in Organizational Life." *Research in Organizational Behavior* 11:1–43.

Raskin, Robert and Howard Terry. 1988. "A Principle-Components Analysis of the Narcissistic Personality Inventory and Further Evidence of its Construct Validity." *Journal of Personality and Social Psychology* 54:890–902.

Reber, Rolf, Norbert Schwarz, and Piotr Winkielman. 2004. "Processing Fluency and Aesthetic Pleasure: Is Beauty in the Perceiver's Processing Experience?" *Personality and Social Psychology Review* 8:364–382.

Regnerus, Mark and Jeremy Uecker. 2011. *Premarital Sex in America: How Young Americans Meet, Mate, and Think About Marrying.* New York, NY: Oxford University Press.

Reid, Landon D. 2010. "The Role of Perceived Race and Gender in the Evaluation of College Teaching on RateMyProfessors.com." *Journal of Diversity in Higher Education* 3:137–152.

Regier, Darrel A., William E. Narrow, Emily A. Kuhl, and David J. Kupfer. 2011. "Introduction." Pg. xxi in The Conceptual Evolution of DSM-5, edited by Darrel A. Regier, William E. Narrow, Emily A. Kuhl, and David J. Kupfer. Arlington, VA: American Psychiatric Publishing, Inc.

Reynolds, Larry T. 1993. *Interactionism: Exposition and Critique.* Walnut Creek, CA: Altamira Press.

Rheingold, Howard. 2002. *Smart Mobs: The Next Social Revolution.* New York, NY: Basic Books.

Rideout, Victoria, J., Ulla G. Foehr, and Donald F. Roberts. 2010. "Generation M^2: Media in the Lives of 8- to 18-Year-Olds." A Kaiser Family Foundation Study. Retrieved December 15, 2012 (http://www.kff.org/entmedia/upload/8010.pdf).

Ridge, Damien and Sue Ziebland. 2012. "Understanding Depression Through a 'Coming Out' Framework." *Sociology of Health and Illness* 34:730–745.

Ridgeway, Cecilia L. 1984. "Dominance, Performance, and Status in Groups: A Theoretical Analysis." Pp. 59–93 in *Advances in Group Processes: Theory and Research,* vol. 1, edited by E. Lawler. Greenwich, CT: JAI Press.

Ridgeway, Cecilia L. 2001. "Gender, Status and Leadership." *The Journal of Social Issues* 57:637–655.

Ridgeway, Cecilia L. and Cathryn Johnson. 1990. "What Is the Relationship Between Socioemotional

Behavior and Status in Task Groups?" *American Journal of Sociology* 95:1189–1212.

Ridgeway, Cecilia L. and Henry A. Walker. 1995. "Status Structures." Pp. 281–310 in *Sociological Perspectives on Social Psychology,* edited by K. S. Cook, G. A. Fine, and J. S. House. Boston, MA: Allyn and Bacon.

Ritzer, George. 1996. *Modern Sociological Theory,* 4th ed. New York: McGraw Hill.

Ritzer, George and Douglas J. Goodman 2004. *Sociological Theory,* 6th ed. New York: McGraw Hill

Rivas, Esteban. 2005. "Recent Use of Signs by Chimpanzees (*Pan troglodytes*) in Interactions with Humans." *Journal of Comparative Psychology* 119:404–417.

Roberts, Andrea L., Steven E. Gilman, J. Breslau, N. Breslau, and K. C. Koenen. 2011. "Race/Ethnic Differences in Exposure to Traumatic Events, Development of Post-Traumatic Stress Disorder, and Treatment-Seeking for Post-Traumatic Stress Disorder in the United States." *Psychosomatic Medicine* 41:71–83.

Roberts, Robert E., Jean S. Phinney, Louise C. Masse, Y. Richard Chen, Catherine R. Roberts, and Andrea Romero. 1999. "The Structure of Ethnic Identity of Young Adolescents From Diverse Ethnocultural Groups." *The Journal of Early Adolescence* 19:310–322.

Robinson, Dawn T. and Lynn Smith-Lovin. 1992. "Selective Interaction as a Strategy for Identity Maintenance: An Affect Control Model." *Social Psychology Quarterly* 55:12–28.

Robinson, Dawn T. and Lynn Smith-Lovin. 2006. "Affect Control Theory." Pp. 137–164 in *Contemporary Social Psychological Theories,* edited by Peter Burke. Stanford, CA: Stanford University Press.

Robinson, Dawn T., Lynn Smith-Lovin, and Allison K. Wisecup. 2006. "Affect Control Theory." Pp. 179–02 in *Handbook of the Sociology of Emotions,* edited by Jan E. Stets and Jonathan H. Turner. New York, NY: Springer.

Romo, Rebecca. 2011. "Between Black and Brown: Blaxican (Black-Mexican) Multiracial Identity in California." *Journal of Black Studies* 42:402–426.

Roscoe, Bruce and Karen L. Peterson. 1983. "The TST for Assessing the Self-Concepts Of College Students: Comparisons With Earlier Years." *College Student Journal* 17:134–136.

Rosenbaum, Jill and Lorraine Prinsky. 1991. "The Presumption of Influence: Recent Reponses to Popular Music Subcultures." *Crime and Delinquency* 7:528–535.

Rosenberg, Morris. 1965. *Society and the Adolescent Self-Image.* Princeton, NJ: University Press.

Rosenberg, Morris. 1979. *Conceiving the Self.* New York, NY: Basic Books.

Rosenberg, Morris and Leonard I. Pearlin. 1978. "Social Class and Self Esteem Among Children and Adults." *American Journal of Sociology* 84:53–78.

Rosenberg, Morris and Ralph H. Turner (eds.). 2004. *Social Psychology: Sociological Perspectives on Social Psychology*: Piscataway, NJ: Transaction Publishers.

Rosenfeld, Michael J. 2008. "Racial, Educational and Religious Endogamy in the United States: A Comparative Historical Perspective." *Social Forces* 87:1–33.

Rosenfeld, Michael J. and Rueben J. Thomas. 2012. "Searching for a Mate: The Rise of the Internet as a Social Intermediary." *American Sociological Review* 77:523–547.

Rosenhan, David L. 1973. "On Being Sane in Insane Places." *Science* 179:250–258.

Rosenthal, Robert and Lenore Jacobson. 1966. "Teachers' Expectancies: Determinants of Pupils' IQ Gains." *Psychological Reports* 19:115–118.

Rosenthal, Robert and Lenore Jacobson. 1968. *Pygmalion in the Classroom: Teacher Expectations and Pupils' Intellectual Development.* New York, NY: Holt, Rinehart and Winston.

Rosnow, Ralph L. and Gary A. Fine. 1976. *Rumor and Gossip: The Social Psychology of Hearsay.* New York, NY: Elsevier

Rosoff, Stephen M., Henry N. Pontell, and Robert Tillman. 2004. *Profit Without Honor: White-Collar Crime and the Looting of America.* Upper Saddle River, NJ: Prentice Hall.

Ross, Catherine E. and John Mirowsky. 2006. "Social Structure and Psychological Functioning: Distress, Perceived Control, and Trust." Pp. 411–450 in *Handbook of Social Psychology,* edited by John Delamater. New York, NY: Springer.

Ross, Lee. 1977. "The Intuitive Psychologist and His Shortcomings: Distortions in the Attribution Process." Pp. 172–214 in *Advances in Experimental Social Psychology,* vol 10, edited by L. Berkowitz. San Diego, CA: Academic Press.

Rowe, Wayne, Sandra K. Bennett, and Donald R. Atkinson. 1994. "White Racial Identity Models: A Critique and Alternative Proposal." *The Counseling Psychologist* 22:129–146.

Rubin, Jeffrey, Z., Frank J. Provenzano, and Zella Luria. 1974. "The Eye of the Beholder: Parents Views on Sex of Newborns." *American Journal of Orthopsychiatry* 44:512–519.

Rymer, Russ. 1993. *Genie: An Abused Child's Flight From Science*. New York, NY: HarperCollins.

Sachs-Ericsson, Natalie and James A. Ciarlo. 2000. "Gender, Social Roles and Mental Health: An Epidemiological Perspective." *Sex Roles A Journal of Research* 43:339–362.

Sadker, David, Myra Sadker, and Laura Zittleman. 2009. *Still Failing at Fairness: How Gender Bias Cheats Girls and Boys in School and What We Can Do About It*. New York, NY: Scribner.

Safe Kids World Wide. 2011. "Halloween Safety: A National Survey of Parents' Knowledge, Attitudes and Behaviors." Retrieved March 10, 2013 (http://www.safekids.org/research-report/halloween-safety-national-survey-parents-knowledge-attitudes-and-behaviors-october).

Saltz, Robert F. 2004/2005. "Preventing Alcohol-Related Problems on College Campuses: Summary of the Final Repot of the NIAAA Task Force on College Drinking." *Alcohol Research and Health* 28: 249–251.

Sampson, Robert J. and John H. Laub. 1993. *Crime in the Making: Pathways and Turning Points Through Life*. Cambridge, MA: Harvard University Press.

Sanders, C. and A. Arluke. 1993. "If Lions Could Speak: Investigating the Animal-Human Relationship and the Perspective of Nonhuman Others." *Sociological Quarterly* 34:377–390.

Sandstrom, Kent L. and Gary Alan Fine. 2003. "Triumphs, Emerging Voices, and the Future." Pp. 1041–1057 in *Handbook of Symbolic Interactionism*, edited by Nancy J. Herman-Kinney. Walnut Creek, CA: AltaMira Press.

Sarason, Irwin G., James H. Johnson, and Judith M. Siegal. 1978. "Assessing the Impact of Life Changes: Development of the Life Experiences Survey." *Journal of Counseling and Clinical Psychology* 46(5):932–946.

Sarbin, Theodore R. and Victor L. Allen. 1968. "Role Theory." Pp. 488–567 in *Handbook of Social Psychology,* vol. 1, 2nd ed., edited by G. Lindzey and E. Aronson. Reading, MA: Addison-Wesley.

Savage-Rumbaugh, Sue, Stuart G. Shanker, and Talbot J. Taylor. 1998. *Apes, Language and the Human Mind*. Oxford, UK: Oxford University Press.

Schachter, Stanley and Jerome E. Singer. 1962. "Cognitive, Social, and Physiological Determinants of Emotional State." *Psychological Review* 69:379–399.

Scheff, Thomas J. 1963. "The Role of the Mentally Ill and the Dynamics of Mental Disorder." *Sociometry* 26:436–453.

Scheff, Thomas J. 1966. *Being Mentally Ill: A Sociological Theory*. Chicago, IL: Aldine Publishing Company.

Scheff, Thomas J. 1985. "The Primacy of Affect." *American Psychologist* 40:849–850.

Scheff, Thomas J. 1990. "Socialization of Emotions: Pride and Shame as Causal Agents." Pp. 281-304 in *Research Agendas in the Socialization of Emotions*, edited by Theodore D. Kemper. Albany, NY: State University of New York.

Scheid, Teresa and Tony N. Brown. 2010. *Handbook for the Sociology of Mental Health*, 2nd ed. New York, NY: Cambridge University Press.

Scherr, Kyle C., Stephanie Madon, Max Guyll, Jennifer Willard, and Richard Spoth. 2011. "Self-Verification as a Mediator of Mothers' Self-Fulfilling Effects on Adolescents' Educational Attainment." *Personality and Social Psychology Bulletin* 37:587–600.

Schippers, Mimi. 2008. "Doing Difference/Doing Power: Negotiations of Race and Gender in a Mentoring Program." *Symbolic Interactionism* 31: 77–98.

Schnoor, Randal F. 2006. "Being Gay and Jewish: Negotiating Intersecting Identities." *Sociology of Religion* 67:43–60

Schoen, Robert and Vladimir Canudas-Romo. 2006. "Timing Effects on Divorce: 20th Century Experience in the United States." *Journal of Marriage and Family* 68:749–758.

Schoenfeld, Elizabeth A., Carrie A. Bredow, and Ted L. Huston. 2012. "Do Men and Women Show Love Differently in Marriage?" *Personality and Social Psychology Bulletin* 38:1396–1409.

Schoenhals, Mark, Marta Tienda, and Barbara Schneider. 1998. "The Educational and Personal Consequences of Adolescent Employment." *Social Forces* 77:723–762.

Schooler, Carmi. 1996. "Cultural and Social-Structural Explanations of Cross-National Psychological Differences." *Annual Review of Sociology* 22:323–349.

Schooler, Carmi, Mesfin S. Mulatu, and Gary Oates. 2004. "Occupational Self-Direction, Intellectual Functioning, and Self-Directed Orientation in

Older Workers: Findings and Implications for Individuals and Societies." *American Journal of Sociology* 110:161–197.

Schulman, Kevin A., Jesse A. Berlin, William Harless, Jon F. Kerner, Shyrl Sistrunk, Bernard J. Gersh., Ross Dube, Christopher K. Taleghani, Jennifer E. Burke, Sankey Williams, John, M. Eisenberg, William Ayers and Jose J. Escarce.l. 2009. "The Effect of Race and Sex on Physician's Recommendation for Cardiac Catheterization." *The New England Journal of Medicine* 340:618–626.

Schutz, Alfred. 1953. "Common-Sense and Scientific Interpretation of Human Action." *Philosophy and Phenomenological Research* 14:1–38.

Schutz, Alfred. 1955. "Symbol, Reality and Society." Pp. 135-203 in *Symbols and Society,* edited by Lyman Bryson, L. Finkelstein, H, Hoagland and R. M. MacIver New York, NY: Harper and Brothers.

Schutz, Heidi and Bernard Six. 1996. "How Strong Is the Relationship Between Prejudice and Discrimination? A Meta-Analytic Answer." *International Journal of Intercultural Relations* 20:441–462.

Schwalbe, Michael L. 1988. "Role Taking Reconsidered: Linking Competence and Performance to the Social Structure." *Journal for the Theory of Social Behavior* 18:411–436.

Schwalbe, Michael L. 1991a. "Role Taking, Self-Monitoring, and the Alignment of Conduct with Others." *Personality and Social Psychology Bulletin* 17:51–57.

Schwalbe, Michael L. 1991b. "Social Structure and the Moral Self." Pp. 281–303 in *The Self-Society Dynamic: Cognition, Emotion and Action,* edited by Judith A. Howard and Peter L. Callero. New York, NY: Cambridge University Press.

Scott, Marvin B. and Stanford Lyman. 1968. "Accounts." *American Sociological Review* 33:46–62.

Scott, Mindy E., Erin Schelar, Jennifer Manlove, and Carol Cui. 2009. "Young Adult Attitudes About Relationship and Marriage: Times May Have Changed, but Expectations Remain High." Child Trends. Publication no. 2009–30. Retrieved September 4, 2013 (http://www.childtrends.org/Files//Child_Trends-2009_07_08_RB_YoungAdultAttitudes.pdfRetrieved 2/27/2013).

Scull, Andrew. 2011. *Madness: A Very Short Introduction.* Oxford, England: Oxford University Press.

Seeman, Melvin and Carolyn S. Anderson. 1983. "Alienation and Alcohol-the Role of Work, Mastery and Community in Drinking Behavior." *American Sociological Review* 48:60–77.

Seeman, Melvin, Alice Z. Seeman, and Art Budros. 1988. "Powerlessness, Work, and Community: A Longitudinal Study of Alienation and Alcohol Use." *Journal of Health and Social Behavior* 29:185–198.

Segal, Mady W. 1974. "Alphabet and Attraction: An Unobtrusive Measure of the Effect of Propinquity in a Field Setting." *Journal of Personality and Social Psychology* 30:654–657.

Seng, Julia. S., Laura P. Kohn-Wood, and Lillian A. Odera. 2005. "Exploring Racial Disparity in Posttraumatic Stress Disorder Diagnosis: Implications for Care of African American Women." *Journal of Obstetric, Gynecologic and Neonatal Nursing* 34:521–530.

Serpe, Richard T. 1987. "Stability and Change in Self: A Structural Symbolic Interactionist Explanation." *Social Psychology Quarterly* 50:44–55.

Serpe, Richard T. and Sheldon Stryker. 1987. "The Construction and Reconstruction of Social Relationships." Pp. 41–66 in *Advances in Group Processes,* edited by Edward Lawler and Barry Markovsky. Greenwich, CT: JAI Press.

Sewell, William H. and Robert M. Hauser. 1980. "The Wisconsin Longitudinal Study of Social and Psychological Factors in Aspirations and Achievements." *Research in Sociology of Education and Socialization* 1:59–99.

Shanahan, Michael J., Michael Finch, Jeylan T. Mortimer, and Seongryeol Ryu. 1991. "Adolescent Work Experience and Depressive Affect." *Social Psychology Quarterly* 54:299–317.

Shepard, Roger N. and Jacqueline Metzler. 1971. "Mental Rotation of Three-Dimensional Objects." *Science* 171:701–703.

Sherif, Muzafer. 1935. "A Study of Some Social Factors in Perception." *Archives of Psychology* 27:60.

Sherif, Muzafer. 1966. *Group Conflict and Cooperation.* London, UK: Routledge and Kegan Paul.

Sherkat, Darren E. and T. Jean Blocker. 1997. "Explaining the Political and Personal Consequences of Protest." *Social Forces* 75:1049–1070.

Shott, Susan. 1979. "Emotion and Social Life: A Symbolic Interactionist Perspective." *American Journal of Sociology* 84:1317–1334.

Shrauger, J. Sidney, Eric Mariano, and Todd H. Walter. 1998. "Depressive Symptoms and Accuracy in the Prediction of Future Events." *Personality and Psychology Bulletin* 24:880–892.

Simcock, Gabrielle and Harlene Hayne. 2002. "Breaking the Barrier? Children Fail to Translate Their Preverbal Memories Into Language." *Psychological Science* 13:225–231.

Simmel, Georg. 1904. "Fashion." *International Quarterly* 10:130–155.

Simon, Robin W. 1992. "Parental Role Strains, Salience of Parental Identity, and Gender Differences in Psychological Distress." *Journal of Health and Social Behavior* 33:25–35.

Simpson, Brent and Michael W. Macy. 2004. "Power, Identity, and Collective Action in Exchange." *Social Forces* 82:1373–1409.

Simpson, Jeffry A. 1987. "The Dissolution of Romantic Relationships: Factors Involved in Relationship Stability and Emotional Distress." *Journal of Personality and Social Psychology* 53:683–692.

Simpson, Ruth. 2005. "Men in Non-Traditional Occupations: Career Entry, Career Orientation and Experience of Role Strain." *Gender, Work and Organization* 12:363–380.

Singer, Eleanor. 1981. "Reference Groups and Social Evaluations." Pp. 66–93 in *Social Psychology: Sociological Perspectives,* edited by M. Rosenberg and R. H. Turnder. New York, NY: Basic Books.

Smelser, Neil J. 1962. *Theory of Collective Behavior.* New York, NY: The Free Press.

Smith, Edward E. and David A. Swinney. 1992. "The Role of Schemas in Reading Text: A Real-Time Examination." *Discourse Processes* 15:303–316.

Smith, M. Brewster. 1994. "Selfhoood at Risk: Postmodern Perils and the Perils of Postmodernism." *American Psychologist* 49: 401–411.

Smith, Tom W. 2007. "Job Satisfaction in the United States." NORC/University of Chicago. Retrieved on July 27, 2011 (http://www-news.uchicago.edu/releases/07/pdf/070417.jobs.pdf).

Smith, Tom W., Peter V. Marsden, and Michael Hout. 2011. General Social Surveys, 1972–2010 [machine-readable data file] / Sponsored by National Science Foundation.—NORC ed.—Chicago, IL: National Opinion Research Center [producer]; Storrs, CT: The Roper Center for Public Opinion Research, University of Connecticut [distributor].

Snow, David A. 2001. "Extending and Broadening Blumer's Conceptualization of Symbolic Interactionism." *Symbolic Interaction* 24:367–377.

Snow, David. A. and Cynthia L. Phillips. 1982. "The Changing Self-Orientations of College Students: From Institution to Impulse." *Social Science Quarterly* 63:462–476.

Snow, David, Cherylon Robinson, and Patti McCall. 1991. "Cooling Out Men in Singles Bars and Night Clubs: Observations on the Interpersonal Survival Strategies of Women in Public Places." *Journal of Contemporary Ethnography* 19:423–449.

Snow, David A., E. Burke Rochford Jr., Steven K. Worden, and Robert D. Benford. 1986. "Frame Alignment Processes, Micromobilization, and Movement Participation." *American Sociological Review* 51:464–481.

Sobel, Robert. 1988. *Panic on Wall Street: A History of America's Financial Disasters With a New Exploration of the Crash of 1987.* New York, NY: E. P. Dutton.

Spenner, Kenneth I. 1988. "Social Stratification, Work and Personality." *Annual Review of Sociology* 14: 69–97.

Spitzer, Robert L. 1981. "The Diagnostic Status of Homosexuality in DSM-III: A Reformulation of the Issues." *American Journal of Psychiatry* 138:210–215.

Sporer, Siegfried L. and Jane Goodman-Delahunty. 2009. "Disparities in Sentencing Decisions." Pp. 379–401 in *Social Psychology of the Punishment of Crime,* edited by Margit Oswald, Steffen Bieneck, and Jorg Hupfeld-Heinemann. New York, NY: John Wiley & Sons.

Sprecher, Susan. 1986. "The Relation Between Inequity and Emotions in Close Relationships." *Social Psychology Quarterly* 49:309–321.

Sprecher, Susan. 1988. "Investment Model, Equity, and Social Support Determinants of Relationship Commitment." *Social Psychology Quarterly* 51:318–328.

Sprecher, Susan. 2001. "Equity and Social Exchange in Dating Couples: Associations with Satisfaction, Commitment, and Stability." *Journal of Marriage and Family* 63:599–613.

Sprecher, Susan. 2009. "Relationship Initiation and Formation on the Internet." *Marriage and Family Review* 45:761–782.

Sprecher, Susan, Diane Felmlee, Sandra Metts, Beverly Fehr, and Debra Vanni. 1998. "Factors Associated With Distress Following the Breakup of a Close Relationship." *Journal of Social and Personal Relationships* 15:791–809.

Sprecher, Susan and Susan S. Hendrick. 2004. "Self-Disclosure in Intimate Relationships: Associations With Individual and Relationship Characteristics Over Time." *Journal of Social and Clinical Psychology* 23:857–877.

Sprecher, Susan and Pamela C. Regan. 2002. "Liking Some Things (in Some People) More than Others: Partner Preferences in Romantic Relationships and Friendships." *Journal of Social and Personal Relationships* 19:436–481.

Sprecher, Susan, Maria Schmeeckle, and Diane Felmlee. D. 2006. "The Principle of Least Interest: Inequality in Emotional Involvement in Romantic Relationships." *Journal of Family Issues* 27:1255–1280.

Stahl, Sidney M. and Morty Lebedun. 1974. "Mystery Gas: An Analysis of Mass Hysteria." *Journal of Health and Social Behavior* 15:44–50.

Stanley, Scott M., Galena K. Rhoades, Paul R. Amato, Howard J. Markman, and Christine A. Johnson. 2010. 'The Timing of Cohabitation and Engagement: Impact on First and Second Marriages." *Journal of Marriage and Family* 72:906–918.

Staurowsky, Ellen J. 2007. "'You Know, We Are All Indian': Exploring White Power and Privilege in Reactions to the NCAA Native American Mascot Policy." *Journal of Sport and Social Issues* 31:61–76.

Stearns, Linda B. and Paul D. Almedia. 2004. "The Formation of State Actor Social Movement Coalitions and Favorable Policy Outcomes." *Social Problems* 51:478–504.

Steele, Claude M. and Joshua Aronson. 1995. "Stereotype Threat and the Intellectual Test Performance of African Americans." *Journal of Personality and Social Psychology* 69:797–811.

Sternberg, Robert J. 1996. "Love Stories." *Personal Relationships* 3:1359–1379.

Stets, Jan E. 2003. "Emotions and Sentiments." Pp. 309–335 in *Handbook of Social Psychology*, edited by John DeLamater. New York, NY: Kluwer Academic/Plenum.

Stokoe, Elizabeth. 2006. "On Ethnomethodology, Feminism and the Analysis of Categorical Reference to Gender in Talk-In-Interaction." *Sociological Review* 54:467–494.

Storms, Michael D. 1973. "Videotape and the Attribution Process: Reversing Actors' and Observers' Points of View." *Journal of Personal and Social Psychology* 27:165–175.

Stouffer, Samuel A., Edward A. Schuman, Leland C. DeVinney, Shirley A. Star, and Robin M. Williams Jr. 1949. *Studies in Social Psychology in World War II: The American Soldier,* vol. 1, *Adjustment During Army Life.* Princeton, NJ: Princeton University Press.

Strack, Fritz, Leonard L. Martin, and Sabine Stepper. 1988. "Inhibiting and Facilitating Conditions of the Human Smile: A Nonobtrusive Test of the Facial Feedback Hypothesis." *Journal of Personality and Social Psychology* 54:768–777.

Stryker, Sheldon. 1980. *Symbolic Interactionism: A Social Structural Version.* Menlo Park, CA: Benjamin Cummings.

Stryker, Sheldon. 2000. "The Past Present and Future of Identity Theory." *Social Psychology Quarterly* 63:284–297.

Stryker, Sheldon. 2000. "Identity Competition: Key to Differential Social Movements Participants." Pp. in 21–40 in *Self, Identity, and Social Movements,* edited by Sheldon Stryker, Timothy Joseph Owens, and Robert White. Minneapolis, MN: University of Minnesota Press.

Stryker, Sheldon, Timothy Joseph Owens, and Robert White. 2000. *Self, Identity, and Social Movements.* Minneapolis, MN: University of Minnesota Press.

Stryker, Sheldon and Richard T. Serpe. 1994. "Identity Salience and Psychological Centrality: Equivalent, Overlapping, or Complementary Concepts?" *Social Psychology Quarterly* 57:16–35.

Stryker, Sheldon and Anne Statham. 1985. "Symbolic Interactionism and Role Theory." Pp. 311–378 in *The Handbook of Social Psychology,* 3rd ed., edited by Lindzey Gardner and Eliot Aronsen. New York, NY: Random House.

Stryker, Sheldon and Kevin D. Vryan. 2006. "The Symbolic Interactionist Frame." Pp. 3–28 in *Handbook of Social Psychology,* edited by John Delameter. New York, NY: Springer.

Stueve, Anne, Phyllis Vine and Elmer L. Struening. 1997. "Perceived Burden Among Caregivers of Adults with Serious Mental Illness: Comparison of Black, Hispanic, and White Families." *American Journal of Orthopsychiatry* 67:199–209

Suddath, Claire. October 2008. "Brief History of the Crash of 1929." *Time*. Retrieved From http://www.time.com/time/nation/article/0,8599,1854569,00.html

Sullivan, Harry Stack. 1940. "Some Conceptions of Modern Psychiatry." *Psychiatry* 3:1–117.

Sum, Andrew, Ishwar Khatiwada and Sheila Palma. 2011. "The Continued Collapse of the Nation's Teen Summer Job Market: Who Worked in the Summer of 2011." Center for Labor Market Studies, Northeastern University.

Summers-Effler, Erika. 2006. "Ritual Theory." In *The Handbook of the Sociology of Emotions*, edited by Jan E. Stets and Jonathon H. Turnder. New York, NY: Springer.

Sumner, William G. 1906. *Folkways*. Boston: Ginn

Sutherland, Edwin H. 1937. *The Professional Thief*. Chicago: University of Chicago Press

Sutherland, Edwin H. 1939. *Principles of Criminality*, 4th Edition. Philadelphia: Lippincott

Sutherland, Edwin H. 1940. "White-Collar Criminality." *American Sociological Review* 5:1–12

Suttles, Gerald D. 1970. "Friendship as a Social Institution." Pp.95–135 in *Social Relationships*, edited by George J. McCall, Michal M. McCall, Norman K. Denzin, Gerald D. Suttles and Suzanne B. Kurth. Chicago: Aldine.

Swann, William B., Christine Larsen Chang-Schneider and Katie McClarty. 2007. "Do People's Self-Views Mater? Self-Concept and Self-Esteem in Everyday Life." *American Psychologist* 62:84–94.

Swann, William B. and Brett Pelham. 2002. "Who Wants Out When the Going Gets Good? Psychological Investment and Preference for Self-Verifying College Roommates." *Self and Identity* 1:219–233.

Swann, William B., Alan Stein-Seroussi and R. Brian Giesler. 1992. "Why People Self-Verify." *Journal of Personality and Social Psychology* 62:392–401.

Swann, William B., Richard M. Wenzlaff, Douglas S. Krull and Brett W. Pelham. 1992. "Allure of Negative Feedback: Self-Verification Strivings Among Depressed Persons." *Journal of Abnormal Psychology* 101:293–306.

Swann, William B., Richard M. Wenzlaff and Romin W. Tafarodi. 1992. "Depression and the Search for Negative Evaluations: More Evidence of the Role of Self-Verification Strivings." *Journal of Abnormal Psychology* 101:314–317.

Swidler, Ann. 2001. *Talk of Love: How Culture Matters*. Chicago, IL: University of Chicago Press.

Sykes, Gresham and David Matza. 1957. "Techniques of Neutralization: A Theory of Delinquency." *American Sociological Review*. 22: 664–670.

Szasz, Thomas. 1970. *The Manufacture of Madness: A Comparative Study of the Inquisition and the Mental Health Movement*. Syracuse University Press.

Tajfel, Henri. 1970. "Experiments in Intergroup Discrimination." *Scientific American* 223:96–102.

Tajfel, Henri. 1978. *Differentiation Between Social Groups: Studies in the Social Psychology of Intergroup Relations*. London: Academic Press.

Tajfel, Henri. 1982. "Social Psychology of Intergroup Relations." *Annual Review of Psychology* 33:1–39

Tangney, June Price and Ronda L. Dearing. 2002. *Shame and Guilt*. New York: Guildord.

Tangney, June Price, Kerstin Youman and Jeff Stuewig. 2009. "Proneness to Shame and Proneness to Guilt." Pp. 192–209 in *Handbook of Individual Differences in Social Behavior*, edited by M.R. Leary and R.H. Hoyle. New York, NY: Guilford Press.

Tapia, Mike. 2011. "U.S. Juvenile Arrests: Gang Membership, Social Class, and Labeling Effects." *Youth and Society* 43:1407–1432,

Taylor, Lindsay Shaw, Andrew T. Fiore, G.A. Mendelsohn and Coye Cheshire. 2011. "Out of My League: A Real-World Test of the Matching Hypothesis." *Personality and Social Psychology Bulletin* 37:942–954.

Taylor Paul and Scott Keeter. 2010. *Millennials: A Portrait of Generation Next*. PEW Research Center. Retrieved July 21, 2011. (http://pewresearch.org/millennials/)

Tenney, Elizabeth R., Erick Turkheimer and Thomas F. Oltmanns. 2009. "Being Liked is More than Having a Good Personality: The Role of Matching." *Journal of Research in Personality* 43:579–585.

Terrace, Herbert. 1980. *NIM, A Chimpanzee Who Learned Sign Language*. Eyre Methuen

Thibaut, John W. and Harold H. Kelley. 1959. *The Social Psychology of Groups*. New York: Wiley.

Thing, James. 2010. "Gay, Mexican and Immigrant: Intersecting Identities Among Gay Men in Los

Angeles." *Social Identities: Journal for the Study of Race, Nation and Culture* 16:809–831.

Thoits, Peggy A. 1983. "Multiple Identities and Psychological Well-Being: A Reformulation and Test of the Social Isolation Hypothesis." *American Sociological Review* 48:174–187.

Thoits, Peggy A. 1985. "Self-Labeling Processes and Mental Illness: The Role of Emotional Deviance." *American Journal of Sociology* 92:221–249.

Thoits, Peggy A. 1989. "The Sociology of Emotions." *Annual Review of Sociology*. 15:317–342.

Thoits, Peggy A. 1995. "Social Psychology: The Interplay between Sociology and Psychology." *Social Forces* 73:1231–1245.

Thoits, Peggy A. 2003. "Personal Agency in the Accumulation of Multiple Role-Identities. Pp. 179–194 in *Advances in Identity Theory and Research*, edited by Peter J. Burke, Timothy J. Owens, Richard Serpe, and Peggy A. Thoits. New York: Kluwer Academic/Plenum.

Thoits, Peggy A. 2010. "Stress and Health: Major Findings and Policy Implications." *Journal of Health and Social Behavior* 51 (Special Issue):S41-S53.

Thomas, William I. and Dorothy Swaine Thomas. 1928. *The Child in America: Behavior Problems and Programs*. New York: Knopf.

Thompson, Mischa and Denise Sekaquaptewa. 2002. "When Being Different is Detrimental: Solo Status and the Performance of Women and Racial Minorities." *Analyses of Social Issues and Public Policy* 2:183–203.

Thornberry, Terence P., Alan J. Lizotte, Marvin D. Krohn, Margaret Farnworth and Sung Joon Jang. 1994. "Delinquent Peers, Beliefs, and Delinquent Behavior: A Longitudinal Test of Interactional Theory." *Criminology* 32:47–83.

Thorndike, Edward L. 1920. "A Constant Error in Psychological Ratings." *Journal of Applied Psychology* 4:25–29.

Thorne, Barrie. 1993. *Gender Play: Boys and Girls in School*. Rutgers University Press.

Thorne, Barrie and Zella Luria. 1986. "Sexuality and Gender in Children's Daily Worlds." *Social Problems*. 33: 176–190.

Timimi, Sami. 2004. "ADHD is Best Understood as a Cultural Construct." *British Journal of Psychiatry* 184:8–9.

Timimi, Sami and Jonathon Leo. 2009. *Rethinking ADHD: From Brain to Culture*. Palgrave Macmillan.

Tittle, Charles R., Wayne J. Villemez and Douglas A. Smith. 1978. "The Myth of Social Class and Criminality: An Empirical Assessment of the Empirical Evidence." *American Sociological Review* 43:643–656.

Todd, Andrew R., Galen V. Bodenhausen, Jennifer A. Richeson and Adam D. Galinsky. 2011. "Perspective Taking Combats Automatic Expressions of Racial Bias." *Journal of Personality and Social Psychology* 100:1027–1042.

Travis, Russell and Steven C. Velasco. 1994. "Social Structure and Psychological Distress Among Blacks and Whites in America." *The Social Science Journal* 31: 197–201.

Triplett, Ruth A. and Roger Jarjoura. 1997. "Specifying the Gender-Class-Crime Relationship: Exploring the Effects of Educational Expectation." *Sociological Perspectives* 40:293–323.

Trujillo, Carla M. 1986. "A Comparative Examination of Classroom Interactions Between Professors and Minority and Non-Minority College Students." *American Educational Research Journal* 23:629–642.

Trzesniewski, Kali H. and M. Brent Donnellan. 2009. "How Should We Study Generational 'Changes'- Or Should We? A Critical Examination of the Evidence for Generation Me." *Social and Personality Compass*. 3:775–784.

Trzesniewski, Kali H., M. Brent Donnellan, Terrie E Robins, Richard W. Poulton and Richie Caspi. 2006. "Low Self-Esteem During Adolescence Predicts Poor Health, Criminal Behavior, and Limited Economic Prospects During Adulthood." *Developmental Psychology* 42:381–390.

Turkle, Sherry. 2011. *Alone Together: Why We Expect More From Technology and Less from Each Other*. New York, NY: Basic Books.

Turner, Heather A. and R. Jay Turner. 2005. "Understanding Variations in Exposure to Social Stress." *Health: An Interdisciplinary Journal for the Social Study of Health, Illness and Medicine*. 9:209–240.

Turner, R. Jay. 1981. "Social Support as a Contingency in Psychological Well-Being." *Journal of Health and Social Behavior* 22:357–67.

Turner, Jay C. 1985. "Social Categorization and the Self-Concept: A Social Cognitive Theory of Group Behavior." Pp. 77–121 in *Advances in Group*

Processes: Theory and Research. vol. 2, edited by E.J. Lawler. Greenwich, CT: JAI Press

Turner, Jay C. 2003. "The Pursuit of Socially Modifiable Contingencies in Mental Health." *Journal of Health and Social Behavior* 44:1–17.

Turner, Jonathan H. and Jan E Stets. 2005. *The Sociology of Emotions.* New York: Cambridge University Press.

Turner, Jonathon H. and Jan E. Stets. 2006. "Sociological Theories of Human Emotions." *Annual Review of Sociology* 32:25–52.

Turner, R. Jay. 1999. "Social Support and Coping." Pp. 198–211 in *The Sociology of Mental Illness.* Edited by Alan V. Horwitz and Teresa L. Scheid. New York, NY: Cambridge University Press.

Turner, R. Jay and William R. Avison. 2003. "Status Variations in Stress Exposure Among Young Adults: Implications for the Interpretation of Prior Research." *Journal of Health and Social Behavior* 44:488–505.

Turner, R. Jay and Donald A. Lloyd. 1999. "The Stress Process and the Social Distribution of Depression." *Journal of Health and Social Behavior* 40:374–404.

Turner, R. Jay and Franco Marino. 1994. "Social Support and. Social Structure: A Descriptive Epidemiology." *Journal of Health and Social Behavior* 25: 193–212.

Turner, R. Jay, Blair Wheaton, and Donald A. Lloyd. 1995. "The Epidemiology of Social Stress." *American Sociological Review* 60:104–125.

Turner, Ralph H. 1976. "The Real Self: From Institution to Impulse." *American Journal of Sociology* 81:989–1016.

Turner, Robert H. 1978. "The Role and the Person." *American Journal of Sociology* 84:2–23.

Turner, Robert H. 1996. "The Moral Issue in Collective Behavior and Collective Action." *Mobilization* 1:1–16.

Turner, Ralph H. and Lewis M. Killian. 1987. *Collective Behavior, 3rd Edition.* Englewood Cliffs, NJ: Prentice-Hall.

Turner, Victor W. 1969. *The Ritual Process: Structure and Anti-Structure.* Ithaca: Cornell University Press.

Twenge Jean M. 2006. *Generation Me: Why Today's Young Americans Are More Confident, Assertive, Entitled—and More Miserable Than Ever Before.* New York, NY: Free Press.

Twenge, Jean M. and Joshua D. Foster. 2010. "Birth Cohort Increases in Narcissistic Personality Traits Among American College Students, 1982–2009." *Social Psychological and Personality Science* 1:99–106.

Twenge, Jean M., Sara Konrath, Joshua D. Foster, W. Keith Campbell, and Brad J. Bushman. 2008. "Further Evidence of an Increase in Narcissism Among College Students." *Journal of Personality* 76:919–928.

Uecker, Jeremy E. 2008. "Religion, Pledging, and the Premarital Sexual Behavior of Married Young Adults." *Journal of Marriage and Family* 70:728–744.

University of Michigan Institute for Social Research. 2007. "Time, Money and Who Does the Laundry." *Research Update.* January 4. Retrieved from http://www.isr.umich.edu/home/news/research-update/2007–01.pdf

U.S. Bureau of the Census. October 2010. "School Enrollments, Table 7." Current Population Survey. Retrieved September 4 (http://www.census.gov/hhes/school/data/cps/2010/tables.html)

U.S. Census Bureau, November 2011 Internet Release Date, "Estimated Median Age at First Marriage, by Sex: 1890 to the Present." Current Population Survey, March and Annual Social and Economic Supplement, 2011 and Earlier. Retrieved June 4, 2013 (www.census.gov/population/socdemo/hh-fam/ms2.xls)).

U.S. Census Bureau. 2011. *Current Population Survey, March* and *Annual Social and Economic Supplements,* 2011. Retried July 12, 2013 (www.census.gov/population/socdemo/hh-fam/ms2.xls).

U.S. Census Bureau. 2012. *Statistical Abstract of the United States: 2012* (131st Edition) Washington, DC, 2011. Retrieved September 4, 2013 (http://www.census.gov/compendia/statab/>).

U.S. Department of Housing and Urban Development. 2010. "Report to Congress on the Root Causes of the Foreclosure Crises." Office of Policy Development and Research. Retrieved February 8, 2013 (http://www.huduser.org/portal/publications/foreclosure_09.pdf)

U.S. Department of Justice. 2009. "Stalking Victimization in the United States." Retrieved December 29, 2012 (http://www.ovw.usdoj.gov/docs/stalking-victimization.pdf).

Usher, JoNell A. and Ulric Neisser. 1993. "Childhood Amnesia and the Beginnings of Memory for Four Early Life Events." *Journal of Experimental Psychology* 122:155–165.

Valkenburg, Patti M. and Jochen Peter. 2009. "Social Consequences of the Internet for Adolescents: A Decade of Research." *Current Directions in Psychological Science* 18:1–5.

Valkenburg, Patti M., Jochen Peter and Alexander P. Schouten. 2006. "Friend Networking Sites and Their Relationship to Adolescent's Well-Being and Social Self-Esteem." *CyberPsychology & Behavior* 9:584–590.

Valkenburg, Patti M., Alexander P. Schouten and Jochen Peter. 2005. "Adolescents' Internet-Based Identity Experiments: An Exploratory Survey." *New Media and Society* 7:383–402.

Vandenburgh, Henry. 1999. *Feeding Frenzy: Organizational Deviance in the Texas Psychiatric Industry.* University Press of America.

VanderWeele, Tyler J. 2011. "Sensitivity Analysis for Contagion Effects in

Van Dyke, Nella and Holly McCammon. 2010. "Introduction." In *Strategic Alliances: New Studies of Social Movement Coalitions*, edited by Nella Van Dyke and Holly McCammon. Minneapolis, MN: University of Minnesota Press.

Van Eeden-Moorefield, Brad, Christopher R. Martell, Mark Williams and Marilyn Preston. 2011. "Same-Sex Relationships and Dissolution: The Connection between Heteronormativity and Homonormativity." *Family Relations: An Interdisciplinary Journal of Applied Family Studies* 60:562–571.

Van Gennep, A. 1960. *The Rite of Passage.* London: Routledge and Kegan Paul.

Vogt Yuan, Anastasia S. 2010. "Body Perceptions, Weight Control Behavior, and Changes in Adolescents' Psychological Well-Being Over Time: A Longitudinal Examination of Gender." *Journal of Youth and Adolescence* 39:927–939.

Vowell, Powell R. and Jieming Chen. 2004. "Predicting Academic Misconduct: A Comparative Test of Four Sociological Explanations." *Sociological Inquiry* 74:226–249.

Vowell, Powell R. and David C. May. 2007. "Another Look at Classic Strain Theory: Poverty Status, Perceived Blocked Opportunity, and Gang Membership as Predictors of Adolescent Violent Behavior." *Sociological Inquiry* 70:42–60.

Vyse, Stuart. 2005. "Where do Fads Come From." Pp. 3–18 in *Controversial Therapies in Developmental Disabilities: Fads, Fashion, and Science in Professional Practice*, edited by John W. Jacobson, Richard M. Foxx and James A. Mulick. Mahwah, NJ: Lawrence Erlbaum Associates.

Wadeson, Harriet and William T. Carpenter Jr. 1976. "Subjective Experiences of Schizophrenia." *Schizophrenia Bulletin* 2:302–316.

Wagner, David G. 1988. "Status Violations: Toward and Expectations States Theory of the Social Control of Status Deviance." Pp. 110–122 in *Status Generalizations: New Theory and Research*, edited by M. Webster Jr. and M Foschi. Stanford, CA: Stanford University Press.

Wagner, David G. 2007. "Symbolic Interactionism and Expectations States Theory: Similarities and Differences." *Sociological Focus* 40:121–137.

Wagner, David G. and Joseph Berger. 1997. "Gender and Interpersonal Task Behaviors." *Sociological Perspectives* 40:1–32.

Waller, Willard, 1938. *The Family: A Dynamic Interpretation.* New York: The Cordon Company.

Waller, Willard, and Reuben Hill. 1951. *The Family: A Dynamic Interpretation.* New York: Hold, Rinehart & Wilson.

Walster, Elaine. 1971. "Passionate Love." Pp. 85–99 in *Theories of Attraction and Love*, edited by B.I. Murstein. New York: Springer.

Walster, Elaine, Vera Aronson, Darcy Abrahams and Leon Rottman. 1966. "Importance of Physical Attractiveness in Dating Behavior." *Journal of Personality and Social Psychology* 4:508–516.

Walster, Elaine, G. William Walster and Ellen Berscheid. 1978. *Equity: Theory and Research.* Boston, MA: Allyn and Bacon.

Walters, Nathan P. and Edward N. Trevelyan 2011. "The Newly Arrived Foreign-Born Population of the United States: 2010." *American Community Survey Brief*, November. http://www.census.gov/prod/2011pubs/acsbr10–16.pdf

Warr, Mark. 2002. *Companions in Crime: The Social Aspects of Criminal Conduct.* New York: Cambridge University Press.

Warren, John R. and Jennifer C. Lee. 2003. "The Impact of Adolescent Employment on High School Dropout: Differences by Individual and Labor-Market Characteristics." *Social Science Research* 32:98–128.

Warren, Patricia and Amy Farrell. 2009. "The Environmental Context of Racial Profiling." *Annals of the American Academy of Political and Social Science* 623:52–63.

Warren, Patricia, Donald Tomaskovic-Devey, William R. Smith, Matthew Zingraff and Marcinda Mason. 2006. "Driving While Black: Bias Processes and Racial Disparity in Police Stops." *Criminology* 44:709–738.

Wasik, Bill. March 2006. "My Crowd Or, Phase F: A Report From the Inventor of the Flash Mob." *Harper's Magazine*. Retrieved from http://harpers.org/archive/2006/03/my-crowd/

Watkins, Phillip, C., Karen Vache, Steven P. Verney and Andrew Matthews. 1996. "Unconscious Mood-Congruent Memory Bias in Depression." *Journal of Abnormal Psychology* 105:34–41.

Waxler, Nancy E. 1979. "Is Outcome from Schizophrenia Better in Nonindustrial Societies? The Case of Sri Lanka." *The Journal of Nervous and Mental Disease* 167:144–157.

Weber, Max. 1968. *Economy and Society: An Outline of Interpretive Sociology*. New York: Bedminster Press.

Webster. Murray, Jr. and James E. Driskell. 1978. "Status Generalization: A Review and Some New Data." *American Sociological Review* 43:220–236.

Wechsler, Henry Nelson and F. Toben. 2001. "Binge Drinking and the American College Student: What's Five Drinks?" *Psychology of Addictive Behaviors*. 15: 287–291.

Weigert, Andrew J. and Viktor Gecas. 2003. "Self." Pp. 267–288 in *Handbook of Symbolic Interactionism*, edited by Larry T. Reynolds and Nancy J. Herman-Kinney. Lanham, MD: Altamira Press.

Weigert, Andrew J. and Viktor Gecas. 2005. "Symbolic Interactionist Reflections on Erikson, Identity, and Postmodernism." *Identity: An International Journal of Theory and Research* 5:161–174.

Weinstein, Eugene A. and Paul Deutschberger. 1963. "Some Dimensions of Altercasting." *Sociometry* 26:454–466.

Weinstein, Raymond M. 1979. Patient Attitudes Toward Mental Hospitalization: A Review of Quantitative Research." *Journal of Health and Social Behavior* 20:237–258.

Weitzer, Ronald and Steven A. Tuch. 2004. "Racial Perceptions of Police Misconduct." *Social Problems* 51:305–325.

Weitzman, Elissa R., and Ying-Yeh Chen. 2005. "Risk Modifying Effect of Social Capital on Measures of Heavy Alcohol Consumption, Alcohol Abuse, Harms, and Secondhand Effects: National Survey Findings." *Journal of Epidemiology and Community Health*. 59: 303–309.

Weitzman, Elissa and Ichiro Kawachi. 2000. "Giving Means Receiving: The Protective Effect of Social Capital on Binge Drinking on College Campuses." *American Journal of Public Health* 90:1936–1939.

Weller, Elizabeth B., S.C. Cook, Robert L. Hendren and Joseph L. Woolston. 1995. *On the Use of Mental Health Services by Minors: Report of the American Psychiatric Associations Task Force*. Washington DC: American Psychiatric Association.

West, Candace and Don H. Zimmerman. 1987. "Doing Gender." *Gender and Society* 1:125–151.

Wethington, Elaine. and Ronald C. Kessler. 1986. "Perceived Support, Received Support, and Ajdustment to Stressful Life Events." *Journal of Health and Social Behavior* 27:78–89.

Wharton, Amy S. 2009. "The Sociology of Emotional Labor." *Annual Review of Sociology*. 35:147–165.

Wheaton, Blair. 1999. "The Nature of Stressors." In A *Handbook for the Study of Mental Health*, edited by Allan V. Horwitz and Theresa L. Scheid. New York: Cambridge University Press.

White, Gregory L., Sanford Fishbein and Jeffrey Rutstein. 1981. "Passionate Love and the Misattribution of Arousal. *Journal of Personality and Social Behavior* 1981:56–62.

White, Helene R and Randy L. LaGrange. 1987. "An Assessment of Gender Effects in Self-Report Delinquency." *Sociological Focus* 20:195–213.

Whitehead, Kevin A. 2009. "Categorizing the Categorizer": The Management of Racial Common Sense in Interaction." *Social Psychology Quarterly* 72:325–342.

Whitely, Bernard E. 1998. "Factors Associated with Cheating Among College Students: A Review." *Research in Higher Education* 39:235–274.

Widyanto, Laura and Mark Griffiths. 2006. "'Internet Addiction:' A Critical Review." *International Journal of Mental Health and Addiction* 4:31–51.

Wieder D. Lawrence. 1974. *Language and Social Reality: The Case of Telling the Convict Code*. The Hague:

Mouton (reprinted, 1988, by University Press of America.

Wierzbicka, Anna. 1999. *Emotions Across Languages and Cultures: Diversities and Universals*. New York, NY: Cambridge University Press.

Williams, Amanda L. and Michael J. Merten. 2008. "A Review of Online Social Networking Profiles by Adolescents: Implications for Future Research and Intervention." *Adolescence* 43:253–274.

Williams, Christine L. 1992. "The Glass Escalator: Hidden Advantages for Men in the "Female" Professions." *Social Problems* 39:253–267.

Williams, David R., Yan, Yu, James S. Jackson and Norman B. Anderson. 1997. "Racial Differences in Physical and Mental Health: Socio-economic Status, Stress and Discrimination." *Journal of Health Psychology* 2:335–351.

Willis, Paul. 1977. *Learning to Labor: How Working Class Kids Get Working Class Jobs*. Columbia University Press.

Willoughby, Brian J. and Judi Dworkin. 2009. "The Relationship Between Emerging Adults' Expressed Desire to Mary and Frequency of Participating in Risk-Taking Behaviors." *Youth and Society* 40: 426–450.

Wilson, Thomas C. 2006. "Whites' Opposition to Affirmative Action: Rejection of Group-based Preferences as Well as Rejection of Blacks." *Social Forces* 85:111–120.

Wiltfang, Gregory L. and Mark Scarbecz. 1990. "Social Class and Adolescents' Self-Esteem: Another Look." *Social Psychology Quarterly* 53:174–183.

Wingfield, Adia Harvey. 2009. "Racializing the Glass Escalator: Reconsidering Men's Experiences with Women's Work." *Gender and Society* 23:5–26

Winograd, Morley and Michael D. Hais. 2011. *Millennial Momentum: How a New Generation is Remaking America*. Rutgers University Press.

Wolburg, Joyce M. 2001. "The 'Risky Business' of Binge Drinking Among College Students: Using Risk Models for PSAs and Anti-drinking Campaigns." *Journal of Advertising* 30:23–39.

Wolfinger, Nicholas H. 2003. "Family Structure Homogamy: The Effects of Parental Divorce on Partner Selection and Marital Stability." *Social Science Research* 32:80–97.

Wood, Eileen, Serge Desmarais, and Sara Gugula. 2002. "The Impact of Parenting Experience on Gender Stereotypes Toy Play of Children." *Sex Roles* 47:39–49.

Wood, Wendy, Frank Y. Wong and J. Gregory Chachere. 1991. "Effects of Media Violence on Viewer's Aggression in Unconstrained Social Interaction." *Psychological Bulletin*. 109: 371–383.

Wright, Eric R., William P. Gronfein, and Timothy J. Owens. 2000. "Deinstitutionalization, Social Rejection and the Self-Esteem of Former Mental Patients." *Journal of Health and Social Behavior* 41:68–90.

Yip, Tifffany. 2008. "Everyday Experiences of Ethnic and Racial Identity Among Adolescents and Young Adults." Pp. 182–202 in *Handbook of Race, Racism, and the Developing Child*, edited by S.M. Quintana and C. McKown. New Jersey: John Wiley & Sons.

Young, Kimberly S. 1998. *Caught in the Net: How to Recognize the Signs of Internet Addiction and a Winning Strategy for Recovery*. New York: John Wiley & Sons, Inc.

Young, Kimberly S. 2004. "Internet Addiction: A New Clinical Phenomenon and Its Consequences." *American Behavioral Scientist* 48:402–415.

Youngreen, Reef and Christopher D. Moore. 2008. "The Effects of Status Violations on Hierarchy and Influence in Groups." *Small Group Research* 38:569–587.

Zajonc, Robert B. 1968. "Attitudinal Effects of Mere Exposure." *Journal of Personality and Social Behavior, Monograph Supplement* 9:1–27.

Zajonc, Robert B. 1989. "Facial Efference and the Experience of Emotion." *Annual Review of Psychology* 40:249–280

Zajonc, Robert B., Sheila T. Murphy and Marita Inglehart. 1989. "Feelings and Facial Efference: Implications for a Vascular Theory of Emotion." *Psychological Review* 96:395–416.

Zamudio, Margaret M. and Francisco Rios. 2006. "From Traditional to Liberal Racism: Living Racism in the Everyday." *Sociological Perspectives* 49:483–501.

Zarbatany, Lynne, Patricia McDougall and Shelley Hymel. 2000. "Gender-Differentiated Experience in the Peer Culture: Links to Intimacy in Preadolescence." *Social Development* 9:62–79.

Zhang, Yuanting and Jennifer Van Hook. 2009. "Marital Dissolution among Interracial Couples." *Journal of Marriage and Family* 71:95–107.

Ziller, Robert C. 1990. *Photographing the Self: Methods for Observing Personal Orientations*. Thousand Oaks, CA: Sage Publications.

Zimbardo, Phillip C. 1974. "On the Ethics of Intervention in Human Psychological Research: With Special Reference to the Stanford Prison Experiment." *Cognition* 2:243–256.

Zimbardo, Philip C. 2004. "Researcher: It's Not Bad Apples, It's the Barrel." *CNNACCESS*. May 21. (www.CNN.com/2004/US/05/21/zimbardo.access.)

Zosuls, Kristina M., Diane N. Ruble, Catherine S. Tamis-LeMonda, Partick E. Shrout, Marc H. Bornstein and Faith K. Gruelich. 2009. "The Acquisition of Gender Labels In Infancy: Implications for Gender-Typed Play." *Developmental Psychology* 45: 688–701.

Zurcher, Louis. 1972. "The Mutable Self: An Adaptation to Sociocultural Change." *Et Al* 3:3–15.

Zurcher, Louis. 1977. *The Mutable Self: A Self-Concept for Social Change*. Beverly Hills: Sage Publications.

CREDIT LINES

Photo 6.1: Tooga / The Image Bank / Getty Images

Photo 6.2a: Ebby May / Taxi / Getty Images

Photo 6.2b: VisionsofAmerica / Joe Sohm / Getty Images

Photo 6.3a: Brand X Pictures / Brand X Pictures / Getty Images

Photo 6.3b: Jay Reilly / Workbook Stock / Getty Images

Photo 6.3c: Jon Feingersh / Blend Images / Getty Images

Box 6.4: San Francisco chronicle by HEARST CORPO-RATION. Reproduced with permission of HEARST CORPORATION in the format Republish in a book via Copyright Clearance Center.

Box 6.5: Reprinted with permission from Mark Davis.

Photo 6.4: Daniel Pangbourne / Digital Vision / Getty Images

Figure 6.1: Shepard, Roger N. and Jacqueline Metzler "Mental Rotation of Three-Dimensional Objects" Science, New Series, Vol. 171, No. 3972 (Feb. 19, 1971), pp. 701–703. Reprinted with permission from AAAS.

Photo 7.1a: BSIP / Universal Images Group / Getty Images

Photo 7.1b: BSIP / Universal Images Group / Getty Images

Building a Snowman: Reprinted with permission from Taylor and Francis from Smith, Edward E. and David A. Swinney, 1992, "The Role of Schemas in Reading Text: Real Time Examination," *Discourse Processes* 15:303–316

Box 7.2: Copyright © 1975 by the American Psychological Association. Reproduced with permission. The official citation that should be used in referencing this material is Table 1, p. 524, from Public and private self-consciousness; Assessment and theory. Fenigstein, Allan; Scheier, Michael F.; Buss, Arnold H. Journal of Consulting and Clinical Psychology, Vol 43(4), Aug. 1975; 522–527, doi: 10.1037/h0076760. No further reproduction or distribution is permitted without written permission from the American Psychological Association.

Photo 7.2: David De Lossy / Photodisc / Getty Images

Photo 7.3: Yellow Dog Productions / Lifesize / Getty Images

Photo 8.1: Brendan O'Sullivan / Photolibrary / Getty Images

Figure 8.1: Strack, Martin and Stepper 1988. Strack, Fritz, Leonard L. Martin and Sabine Stepper. 1988. "Inhibiting and Facilitating Conditions of the Human Smile: A Nonobtrusive Test of the Facial Feedback Hypothesis." *Journal of Personality and Social Psychology.* 54:768–777.

Photo 8.2: Digital Vision / Digital Vision / Getty Images

Photo 8.3: Joel Sartore / National Geographic / Getty Images

Box 8.2: Reprinted with permission from the estate of Andre Modigliani, proceeded over by his wife, Carol Novak: Modigliani, Andre. 1966. "Embarrassment and Social Influence." *Dissertation Abstracts International.* 28:294–295A.

Photo 8.4: Juan Silva / The Image Bank / Getty Images

Photo 8.5: Stewart Cohen / Photolibrary / Getty Images

Table 8.3: *Reprinted with permission from Wiley*: Kemper, Theodore D. 2002. "Predicting Emotions in Groups: Some Lessons from September 11. In Emotions and Sociology, edited by Jack Barbalet. Sociological Review Monograph, 50(1):53–68.

Photos 9.1a & 9.1b: Photo credit: Elizabeth Crawford

Photo 9.2a: craftvision / Vetta / Getty Images

Photo 9.2b: Purestock / Purestock / Getty Images

Photo 9.2c: Mike Kemp / Tetra images / Getty Images

Photo 9.3: New York Daily News Archive / New York Daily News / Getty Images

The Perceived Stress Scale: Journal of health & social behavior by AMERICAN SOCIOLOGICAL ASSOCIATION Copyright 1983 Reproduced with permission of SAGE PUBLICATIONS INC. JOURNALS in the format Republish in a textbook via Copyright Clearance Center.

Photo 10.1: Frank Rossoto Stocktreck / Digital Vision / Getty Images

Photo 10.2: Catherine Ledner / Stone+ / Getty Images

Photo 10.3: Jerry Cooke / Time & Life Pictures / Getty Images

Photo 10.4: Nick David / Photonica World / Getty Images

Box 10.2: Heather A. & R. Jay Turner. "Understanding variations in exposure to social stress." Health (Vol. 9 Issue 2) pp. 32© 2005 by SAGE Publications, Reprinted by Permission of SAGE Publications.

Photo 11.1: Bill Aron / PhotoEdit

Photo 11.2: CBS Photo Archive / CBS / Getty Images

Photo 11.3a: Novastock / Photolibrary /Getty Images

Photo 11.3b: Martin Knight / Britain on View / Getty Images

Photo 11.4: David Joel / Stone / Getty Images

Photo 11.5: Laurence Mouton / PhotoAlto Agency RF Collections / Getty Images

Box 11.1: Reprinted from "Passionate and Companionate Love." *Journal of Adolescence*, 9/4, Author(s), Elaine Hatfield, Susan Sprecher, 383–410, 1986, with permission from Elsevier.

Box 11.2: Hendrick, Clyde, Susan S. Hendrick and Amy Dick. "The Love Attitudes Scale: Short Form." *Journal of Social and Personal Relationships* (Vol. 15 Issue 2) pp. 147–159. © 1998 by SAGE Publications, Reprinted by Permission of SAGE Publications.

Box 11.3: Social psychology quarterly by AMERICAN SOCIOLOGICAL ASSOCIATION Copyright 1988 Reproduced with permission of SAGE PUBLICATIONS INC. JOURNALS in the format Republish in a textbook via Copyright Clearance Center.

Box 11.4: Amato, Paul R. and Stacy J. Rogers. "Do Attitudes Toward Divorce Affect Marital Quality." *Journal of Family Issues* (20), pp. 69–86. © 1999 by SAGE Publications, Reprinted by Permission of SAGE Publications.

Photo 12.1: Image of Oblio and Arrow from the motion picture *The Point*. Image Copyright Fred Wolf Films, Inc. and Estate of Harry Nilsson. Used by permission. All rights reserved.

Photo 12.2: kali9 / E+ / Getty Images

Photo 12.3: Chicago Tribune / McClatchy-Tribune / Getty Images

Photo 12.4: Tom Briglia / FilmMagic / Getty Images

Photo 12.5: Yellow Dog Productions / The Image Bank / Getty Images

Photo 12.6: Fuse / Fuse / Getty Images

Box 12.1: Copyright © 200 by the American Psychological Association. Reproduced with permission. The official citation that should be used in referencing this material is Table 1, p. 62, from Neville, H.A., Lilly, R.L., Duran, G., Lee, R.M., & Browne, L. (2000). Construction and Initial Validation of the Color-Blind Racial Attitudes Scale (CoBRAS). *Journal of Counseling Psychology,* 47(1), 59–70. Doi: 10.1037/0022–0167.47.1.59. No further reproduction or distribution is permitted without written permission from the American Psychological Association.

Box 12.2: Phinney, Jean S. "The Multigroup Ethnic Identity Measure: A New Scale for Use with Diverse Groups" *Journal of Adolescent Research* (Vol. 7 Issue 2), pp. 21 © 1992 by SAGE Publications, Reprinted by Permission of SAGE Publications.

Photo 13.1a: Tasos Katopodis / Getty Images Entertainment / Getty Images

Photo 13.1b: AFP / AFP / Getty Images

Photo 13.2: Blend Images / Ariel Skelley / the Agency Collection / Getty Images

Photo 13.3: This undated 1975 photo shows a Pet Rock with its pet carrier, complete with air holes, and care manual, Houston, Texas. (AP Photo/Houston Chronicle, Dan Hardy) © 2014 Associated Press

Photo 13.4: Sandy Huffaker / Getty Images News / Getty Images

Photo 13.6: DON EMMERT / AFP / Getty Images

Photo 13.7: FETHI BELAID / AFP / Getty Images

GLOSSARY

Accounts: Explanations people create to give meaning to their experiences (Chapter 3) or to reduce guilt and shame associated with the violation of society's rules. (Chapter 9)

Affect: Refers to positive and negative evaluative states (e.g., like or dislike). (Chapter 8)

Affect control theory (ACT): A model of the identity-behavior relationship within the symbolic interactionist tradition based on the assumption that emotions signal the manner in which an individual is experiencing a situation. Negative emotions indicate a discrepancy between cultural definitions of how someone with a particular identity should act and his or her behavior. (Chapter 8)

Affirmative action: Antidiscrimination policies designed to combat patterns of exclusion by increasing racial/ethnic minorities' and women's access to selective colleges and universities and to high-status, high-paying jobs in which they would otherwise be underrepresented; a macro-level intervention strategy. (Chapter 12)

Agape: A love style evidenced in sacrifice and putting the needs of one's partner above one's own. (Chapter 11)

Agency: The capacity of individuals to resist broader social forces and to act in unique and creative ways and in a self-directed manner. (Chapter 1)

Agents of socialization: Individuals, groups, organizations, and social institutions that play a role in shaping people's perceptions and behaviors throughout one's life. (Chapter 6)

Alienation: A concept developed by Marx to refer to the separation of the self and experience. Alienation occurs when people lack control over their work and thus become estranged from the work process and from their basic human nature. (Chapter 4)

Altercasting: Occurs when someone projects an identity consistent with his or her own personal goals onto another individual. (Chapter 11)

American = White bias: The association of central aspects of the American identity with Whiteness. (Chapter 12)

Anomie: State that occurs when societal norms are unclear and people aren't sure how to behave. (Chapter 9)

Anticipatory socialization: The process of thinking about and acting like someone who occupies a role that one is planning to transition into. (Chapter 6)

Antioppression counter-frame: An alternative (counter) frame to the White racial frame that emphasizes the structural roots of racial inequality, moral outrage, and the desire for change. (Chapter 12)

Appeal to higher loyalties: A technique of neutralization in which the individual sacrifices the demands or rules of the larger society for those of smaller groups to which he or she belongs. (Chapter 9)

Attachment: An aspect of the social bond referring to individuals' emotional ties to important people in their life, such as parents, peers, and school personnel. See social control theory. (Chapter 9)

Autonomy: Refers to the level of control employees have over how and when they complete their jobs. (Chapter 4)

Back region: Dramaturgical concept referring to settings where people are not highly self-conscious and concerned with managing impressions. (Chapter 3)

Balanced relation: An exchange relation in which the individuals involved have equal power. (Chapter 5)

Behaviorist psychology: An approach within psychological social psychology that focuses on the effect of rewards and punishments on behavior. (Chapter 5)

Belief: An aspect of the social bond referring to the degree to which individuals accept and believe in societal values and rules, including the law. See social control theory. (Chapter 9)

Breaching experiment: An exercise in which social norms are intentionally violated in order to assess how individuals construct and maintain a coherent sense of reality. (Chapter 3)

Buffering effect: When a variable works to decrease the effect of an independent variable on a dependent variable. For example, social support buffers (minimizes) the effect of stressors on distress. (Chapter 10)

Causal relationship: When variation in one variable leads to or causes variation in another variable. (Chapter 2)

Chicago school symbolic interactionism: A variant of symbolic interactionism that focuses on understanding the construction and negotiation of meanings through interactions in specific social contexts using qualitative research methods. (Chapter 3)

Chronic strains: Ongoing problems, like conflict at work, conflict with one's spouse, or role strain, that increase individuals' risk for psychological distress. (Chapter 10)

Coalition: An alliance that involves cooperation between two or more actors in order to increase the rewards received in a social exchange. (Chapter 13)

Coercive power: Imposing one's will on another through the use of punishments in a social exchange relationship. (Chapter 5)

Cognitive dissonance: A negative tension resulting from an inconsistency in one's beliefs or between one's beliefs and behavior. (Chapter 10)

Cognitive schema: A mental representation containing information about objects, people, and events that is organized in such a way that the whole is greater than the individual pieces of information on which it is based. (Chapter 4)

Cohabitation effect: The research finding that cohabitation (living together without being married) increases the risk for divorce only when the couple lives together before becoming engaged. (Chapter 11)

Cohort: A group of individuals born at the same time who share a common set of experiences. (Chapter 4)

Collective behavior: Behavior at the aggregate level (in groups or crowds) that is distinct from, or in opposition to, routine societal patterns. (Chapter 13)

Color-blind racism: A form of racism that is rooted in the belief that everyone should be, and is, treated equally combined with a failure to recognize the structural roots of prevailing patterns of racial/ethnic stratification. (Chapter 12)

Commitment: Investment in; within social exchange theory, continuing to exchange resources with a particular partner even when there are better options. (Chapter 5); within identity theory, the number of role relationships an individual has with other people based on a particular identity. (Chapter 7); within control theory, an aspect of social bonding based on the level of investment individuals have in conventional activities and goals, such as education and work. See social control theory. (Chapter 9)

Common identity intervention: A micro-level strategy of intervention that involves manipulating the social setting to facilitate the creation of common (inclusive) identities that supersede in-group/out-group divisions based on race/ethnicity. (Chapter 12)

Common in-group identity model: A model of race relations developed within social identity theory. Common in-group identities (in contrast to an us vs. them mentality) emerge in response to interdependence among members of different racial/ethnic groups, equal status between groups, contact, and support for egalitarian norms among group members. (Chapter 12)

Companionate love: A form of love that is focused on the affection we feel for individuals with whom we share our lives; it involves feelings of closeness, emotional intimacy, comfort, and friendship. (Chapter 11)

Compliance: Refers to individuals agreeing to a request made by someone. (Chapter 13)

Components principle: Within the social structure and personality perspective, the identification of the specific structural aspects of society that are the most relevant for understanding the aspect of personality or behavior under investigation. (Chapter 4)

Condemnation of condemners: A technique of neutralization in which individuals shift the focus away from their own acts to the motives and behaviors of the people who disapprove of the rule violation. (Chapter 9)

Conformity: When an individual changes his or her behavior so that it matches the behavior of others. (Chapter 13)

Consolidation of responsibility: When the responsibility for action, such as classroom discussion, becomes concentrated in the hands of a few individuals within a group context. (Chapter 3)

Constraint: When individuals' perceptions, feelings, and behaviors are shaped by society. (Chapter 1)

Control principle: The notion that people strive to keep transient impressions in line with fundamental sentiments, a key principle of affect control. (Chapter 8)

Convenience sample: A sample in which participants for a study are selected based on convenience or availability rather than at random. (Chapter 2)

Conventional morality: Kohlberg's second stage of moral development in which moral reasoning is based on meeting the expectations of others and on the social consequences of an action. (Chapter 6)

Coping resources: Social and psychological resources that people can draw on to help them deal with the stressors they experience; includes social support, self-esteem, and a sense of mastery. (Chapter 10)

Coping strategies: Refers to things people do to minimize the negative effects of stressors. (Chapter 10)

Core ties: Network connections characterized as close, personal relationships. (Chapter 11)

Correlation: When an increase in scores of one variable is associated with an increase or decrease of scores in another variable. (Chapter 2)

Covering: Using self-presentational strategies to keep a stigmatized aspect of the self from being the focal point of interactions with others. (Chapter 9)

Covert nonparticipant observation: A method of data collection where the researcher observes the activities of individuals without interacting with them and without their knowledge. (Chapter 2)

Covert participant observation: A method of data collection where the researcher participates in the activities of the individuals being studied without them being aware that he or she is a researcher. (Chapter 2)

Crime: A violation of the criminal law; a subcategory of deviance. (Chapter 9)

Cross-sectional data: Data collected by a research at only one point in time. (Chapter 2)

Cultural socialization: The process through which parents teach children about their heritage, promote racial/ethnic pride, and expose them to cultural traditions; common in minority families. (Chapter 12)

Cybernetic model: A model in which there is a feedback loop such that outputs are used as benchmarks for the control of inputs, like a thermostat. (Chapter 8)

Debriefing: When the researcher tells subjects at the end of an experiment about the real purpose of a study and addresses any negative feelings or concerns they have about their experience as subjects. (Chapter 2)

Deceit: Used within the dramaturgical framework to refer to attempts to mislead others through the use of language in order to manage the impressions conveyed to others. (Chapter 7)

Deductive reasoning: The type of logic that underlies the quantitative research process, which goes from the general (theory) to the specific (observation). (Chapter 2)

Deep acting: A form of emotion management that involves conscious attempts to change the way one feels so that it is consistent with one's behaviors and prevailing feeling rules. (Chapter 8)

Deflections: Within affect control theory, discrepancies between transient impressions and fundamental sentiments. (Chapter 8)

Degradation ceremonies: Rituals designed to transform the identity of an individual and to expel him or her from membership in the group; response to deviant behavior. (Chapter 9)

Deindividuation: The process whereby the anonymity provided by a group reduces people's social inhibitions and leads to behaviors that would not occur in other situations. (Chapter 13)

Deinstitutionalization: The large-scale movement of individuals with mental illness from inpatients in mental hospitals to outpatients treated within the community. (Chapter 10)

Delinquency: Deviant behavior engaged in by adolescents (youths ages 12–18). (Chapter 1)

Denial of injury: A technique of neutralization in which individuals argue that no one was hurt by their behavior. (Chapter 9)

Denial of responsibility: A technique of neutralization in which individuals deny any responsibility for their deviant behavior or its consequences by arguing that it wasn't their fault, that it was unintentional, it was an accident, etc. (Chapter 9)

Denial of victim: A technique of neutralization in which individuals transform the victim of their actions into the one who was responsible for what happened or into the wrongdoer. (Chapter 9)

Dependent variable: A variable that is affected by another variable; the outcome or effect in a cause-and-effect relationship. (Chapter 2)

Depersonalization: The stripping away of personal identity and the treatment of individuals more like objects than as humans. (Chapter 10)

Desocialization: The process of erasing the past identities and selves of an individual so that that person can be reprogrammed; the first phase of the resocialization process. (Chapter 10)

Deviance: Behavior that violates a social norm. (Chapter 9)

Deviance disavowal: A technique in which individuals openly acknowledge their stigmatized characteristics or identities and work to present themselves in a positive light. (Chapter 9)

Deviant behavior: A recognized violation of prevailing group or societal norms, which may or may not be illegal. (Chapter 1)

Deviant subculture: A group based on members' shared deviance, within which behaviors regarded as deviant by outsiders are considered normative. (Chapter 9)

Diagnostic and Statistical Manual (DSM): A manual produced by the American Psychiatric Association (APA) that defines and classifies psychiatric disorders. (Chapter 10)

Differential association theory: A theory stating that deviance is learned through interaction with others as part of a socialization process. (Chapter 9)

Differential exposure model: A model used to explain group differences in psychological distress that states that disadvantaged groups within society have higher levels of distress than advantage groups because the members of disadvantaged groups are exposed to more stressors than members of advantaged groups. (Chapter 10)

Differential reinforcement theory: Extension of differential association theory that specifies the mechanisms through which deviance is learned (patterns of reinforcement). (Chapter 9)

Differential vulnerability model: A model used to explain group differences in levels of psychological distress that argues that members of disadvantaged groups have higher levels of distress than member of advantaged groups because economic and social disadvantage reduces people's coping resources, which makes them more vulnerable to stressors. (Chapter 10)

Diffuse status characteristics: Attributes of individuals, including gender, race/ethnicity, and class (education), that shape performance expectations in task groups, even when they are not related to the task at hand. *See status characteristics theory.* (Chapter 5)

Diffusion: Occurs when something that initially appears to be a fad remains popular and becomes a common item or activity within society. (Chapter 13)

Diffusion of responsibility: A situation in which the responsibility for helping in an emergency situation is spread across all the observers of the event. (Chapter 1)

Disclosure: Sharing one's deviant identity with others in the hope that they will accept one anyway. (Chapter 9)

Discrimination: Differential treatment based on group membership; a behavior. (Chapter 12)

Display rules: Social norms that tell us how we should express our emotions. (Chapter 8)

Dissolution stage: The final stage of personal relationships, in which the relationship ends. (Chapter 11)

Distributive justice: Within social exchange theory, the perceived fairness of a relationship and the underlying expectation that inputs into a relationship should equal outputs. (Chapter 8)

Documentary method: The search for meaningful patterns commonly employed by lay people, as well as professional sociologists; qualitative method used by sociological social psychologists when studying behavior in natural settings. (Chapter 3)

Doing gender: When an individual in a social encounter acts in a way that is consistent with the societal expectations placed on members of his or her sex category (male or female). (Chapter 1)

Domains of self: Cognitive schemata that reflect the different aspects of one's self, which include identities and distinct sets of relationships or behaviors that may be associated with more than one identity (e.g., "social" or "friendly"). (Chapter 10)

Dramaturgical perspective: A perspective within the symbolic interactionist tradition associated with the work of Goffman that emphasizes how we present ourselves and manage impressions in our interactions with others. (Chapter 3)

Dyad: A two-person group. (Chapter 5)

Ego: Within Freud's theory of personality, rational thought processes. (Chapter 6)

Embarrassability: A transsituational susceptibility to the experience of embarrassment. (Chapter 8)

Embarrassment: A physiological arousal that arises when social norms are violated in public encounters either by oneself or by others. (Chapter 8)

Emergent norm theory: A theory of collective behavior that emphasizes the ways individuals construct norms, which govern their subsequent actions. (Chapter 13)

Emerging adulthood: A period that spans from the end of high school into the mid-twenties, during which individuals straddle adolescence and mature adulthood. (Chapter 6)

Emotion: Affective states or feelings that have a physiological, cognitive, cultural, and behavioral component. (Chapter 8)

Emotional energy: Within Collin's interaction ritual theory, long-term positive feelings and group solidarity that emerge with the escalation of the emotional tone of a group encounter. (Chapter 8)

Emotional labor: Refers to emotion management at or in relation to one's occupation. (Chapter 8)

Emotion management (emotion work): Refers to conscious attempts by individuals to control or change their feelings. (Chapter 8)

Emotion norms: Societal expectations (rules or guidelines) about how individuals should experience and express emotions. (Chapter 8)

Endogamous marriage: Marriage between individuals of the same group (e.g., same race/ethnicity, social class, or religion). (Chapter 11)

Equity: An exchange relationship in which there is a balance of rewards between relationship partners; in an equitable relationship, each partner gives rewards proportional to those received. (Chapter 5)

Eros: A love style characterized by strong physical attraction and intense emotion; this love style is often associated with passionate love. (Chapter 11)

Ethnic group: A category of individuals perceived as distinct due to cultural characteristics, including customs, language, and a shared heritage. (Chapter 1)

Ethnographic research: A qualitative method of data collection that involves the collection of descriptive and detailed information about a group; also called participant observation. (Chapter 2)

Ethnomethodology: A theoretical framework related to symbolic interactionism that emphasizes the ways individuals construct or maintain a coherent sense of reality. (Chapter 3)

Exchange network: Two or more interconnected exchange relations, where power reflects an actor in the network's exchange options versus those of other actors in the network. (Chapter 5)

Expectation states theory: A theory that focuses on the relationship between performance expectations and behaviors in task groups and how the status structures of task groups, once they emerge, are reproduced through subsequent social interactions; theory out of which status characteristics theory was developed. (Chapter 1, Chapter 5)

Expectations training interventions: A micro-level intervention in which group members perceived as low status within society at large show their skills in a particular area by serving as teachers to members of groups regarded as high status. (Chapter 12)

Experiment: A quantitative method of data collection in which the researcher randomly assigns subjects to different groups, exposes each group to a different level of an independent variable, and then compares scores on the dependent variable across groups to assess the effects of the independent variable. (Chapter 2)

External validity: When study results can be generalized to the population from which the study sample was selected. (Chapter 2)

Fads: A form of collective behavior that is defined by its episodic nature whereby something, often a toy or novelty item, rapidly becomes popular, but the popularity is short-lived. (Chapter 13)

"Fag" talk: The use of terms like "fag" and "homo" by young children who may not know what these words mean (other than the fact that they are derogatory) as verbal taunts directed toward marginalized individuals. (Chapter 11)

Fashions: A form of collective behavior that involves a rapid increase and then decrease in the popularity of a particular style or product (e.g., type of clothing or music), at which time it is replace by a new model. (Chapter 13)

Feeling: An individual's subjective experience of an emotion. (Chapter 8)

Feeling rules: Social norms that tell us how we should and should not feel in particular situations. (Chapter 8)

Feigning: A term used by Goffman to describe nonverbal strategies (e.g., dress, posture, and demeanor) used by people to manage the impressions they convey to others. (Chapter 7)

Feral children: Children raised in the wild without human interaction who are thus completely unsocialized. (Chapter 6)

Flash mobs: A collective activity organized through electronic communications or social media in which participants arrive at a designated location and engage in preplanned behaviors that disrupt the normative order. (Chapter 13)

Folkways: A type of social norm that is not a moral imperative; social conventions, like norms prescribing that people eat three meals a day or that they buy their good friends birthday gifts. (Chapter 9)

Formal control: Encouragement of conformity to social norms through sanctions imposed by authorized individuals. (Chapter 9)

Frames: Cognitive representations that enable people to make sense of situations and events by directing their attention to certain aspects of reality and away from other aspects. (Chapter 12)

Frame alignment: The link between social movement organizations and individuals' interpretative schemata, so that their goals, activities, and ideologies are consistent. (Chapter 13)

Frame amplification: A strategy used by social movement organizations to make particular values or beliefs salient when they are presumed to be important to a pool of individuals that are not yet involved in the movement. (Chapter 13)

Frame bridging: A relatively common strategy for mobilizing potential movement participants that involves linking ideologically similar, but structurally unrelated, frames pertaining to a particular issue. (Chapter 13)

Frame extension: A strategy used by social movement organizations to capture interests or views that are not part of their primary objectives but are likely to resonate with those of potential participants. (Chapter 13)

Frame transformation: A strategy used by social movement organizations to change the way people view something, so that it is no longer taken for granted or viewed as normative but regarded as problematic, unjust, and in need of remediation. (Chapter 13)

Free rider problem: The fact that many individuals will opt not to participate in a social movement that they recognize as good for society because they know that the movement's success is not dependent upon their personal contributions. (Chapter 13)

Friendship: Nonrelated, nonromantic personal relationships that are voluntary and relatively flexible in their trajectory. (Chapter 11)

Friends with benefits: A label used to refer to an ongoing sexual, but not romantic relationship, between two friends. (Chapter 11)

Front region: Within the dramaturgical framework, the settings where we present ourselves to others, similar to the stage where a performance occurs in front of an audience. (Chapter 2)

Fundamental attribution error: The tendency to misattribute situation-specific behaviors by others to their personal characteristics. (Chapter 11)

Fundamental sentiments: Within affect control theory, this refers to the affective meanings about identities and behaviors that are shared by societal members and thus transcend any given situation. (Chapter 8)

Game stage: The final stage in Mead's theory of the development of the self, in which children learn how to take the role of another at the cognitive level, manage and understand multiple social roles, and negotiate tiers of societal expectation (individuals and the larger group). (Chapter 6)

Gender: The preferences, abilities, and behaviors associated with being male or female in a given society. (Chapter 1, Chapter 6)

Gender roles: The expected behaviors of males or females within a given society. (Chapter 4, Chapter 6)

General strain theory: Theory linking delinquency to strain resulting from multiple sources (e.g., the failure to achieve economic or noneconomic goals, racial discrimination, or negative events) and negative emotions. (Chapter 9)

Generalizability: When findings from a research study apply to a population of interest or to other people in other settings. (Chapter 2)

Generalized other: An understanding of broader societal values and norms, as well as the recognition that one is an individual member of a larger group. (Chapter 6)

Gossip: Information exchanged among individuals that focuses on other people's personal affairs and tends to be negative or scandalous in its content. (Chapter 13)

Grounded theory: A theory developed based on data using inductive reasoning. (Chapter 2)

Group processes and structures (GPS): A sociological social psychology perspective that examines how the social structure influences group processes. (Chapter 1)

Guilt: An emotion that emerges when an individual feels he or she has acted immorally or in a way that is against his or her beliefs and values. (Chapter 8)

Halo effect: The tendency to associate other valued traits with someone once we have a positive view of them or have already attributed a positive trait to them. (Chapter 1)

Hiding behaviors: Behaviors individuals engage to distance themselves from the scrutiny of others after they have engaged in a behavior regarded as deviant. (Chapter 8)

Homophily: A characteristic of social networks; when the individuals in a social network are similar to one another in their demographic and social characteristics. (Chapter 11)

Homosocial-homosexual reproduction of the managerial ranks: The process through which middle-class White male managers in the company Kanter (1997) studied selected other middle-class White males for promotion into upper management. (Chapter 4)

Hooking up: The practice among college students and young adults of connecting with partners for casual sex; the term may be used to refer to kissing, sexual intercourse, or something in between. (Chapter 11)

Hookup culture: A term used to refer to the social settings and groups where prevailing norms support casual sex. (Chapter 11)

Hypothesis: A statement specifying an expected relationship between two or more variables that can be tested. (Chapter 2)

I: According to Mead, the subject phase of the self; it is our spontaneous reactions to people, events, and situations that is largely unconditioned and never fully within our control. (Chapter 3)

Id: Within Freud's theory of personality, the innate, irrational, and unconscious drives that affect people's behaviors; biologically based. (Chapter 6)

Ideology: Beliefs, values, and understandings of the world. (Chapter 13)

Identity: The socially based part of the self-concept that serves as the basis on which individuals categorize and present themselves. (Chapter 7)

Identity control system: The model of the identity-behavior relationship specified by identity control theory, in which negative feelings serve as a signal that an identity is not being verified; when this happens, people either adjust their behavior or change their identity. (Chapter 8)

Identity control theory (ICT): An extension of identity theory that emphasizes individuals' tendency to seek confirmation for their sense of self and the role of emotion in this self-verification process. (Chapter 8)

Identity salience: Within identity theory, this refers to the readiness with which people enact roles associated with a particular status. (Chapter 7)

Identity standard: The way an individual defines a particular identity, which influences his or her behavior. (Chapter 7)

Identity theory: A theory within the Indiana/Iowa school of symbolic interactionism that focuses on the impact of social structure on the content of people's self-concepts and the effect of the self-concept on behaviors. (Chapter3, Chapter 7)

Identity threat: Occurs when people receive negative information about in-group members or anticipate structural changes that will make their groups' status precarious. (Chapter 7)

Implicit associations: Unconscious beliefs and attitudes about members of various groups within society. (Chapter 12)

Impression management: Self-presentational strategies that enable individuals to claim identities, avoid embarrassment, and gain the approval or positive regard of others. (Chapter 3)

Incompatible complexity: Tasks that are complex and require a variety of different abilities so that no individual or group can be expected to outperform others; a type of multiability intervention within the status characteristics tradition. (Chapter 5)

Incorporation: The process through which social movements are absorbed into the existing structure of society and affect legislation or the nature of the political process. (Chapter 13)

Independent variable: A variable that affects another variable. The cause in a cause-and-effect relationship. (Chapter 2)

In-depth interview: A qualitative data-collection method in which the researcher asks individuals open-ended questions with the goal of obtaining detailed information about their social experiences. (Chapter 2)

Index: A set of questions designed to measure the same underlying concept (variable); the scores on each question are typically summed to get an overall score or measure of the concept (variable) of interest. (Chapter 2)

Inductive reasoning: The type of logic that underlies the qualitative research process, which goes from specific observations (e.g., data collection) to general conclusions and interpretation (theory). (Chapter 2)

Informal control: Encouragement of conformity to social norms through interpersonal feedback. (Chapter 9)

In-group: A group we identify with and see ourselves as a member of. (Chapter 5)

Initiation stage: A stage of relationships in which individuals get to know one another. (Chapter 11)

Informational influence: A type of social influence that occurs when others serve as a source of information about the nature of reality. (Chapter 13)

Institutional discrimination: Discrimination that occurs at the societal level (macro level) and results from the way social institutions (e.g., education, the criminal justice system, and the political system) operate on a day-to-day basis. (Chapter 12)

Institutional fad: A fad that results in shifts in the ways professionals (e.g., doctors, teachers) practice that is not based on sound (scientific) evidence of its effectiveness or superiority over other methods. (Chapter 13)

Institutional review board (IRB): A group of university or organizational representatives that oversees and evaluates studies proposed by researchers to make sure that subjects' rights will not be violated. (Chapter 2)

Interaction ritual theories: Theories of emotion that focus on the energy that emerges in interactions. (Chapter 8)

Interdependent cooperation: When two or more groups work collaboratively toward a common goal. (Chapter 12)

Intergenerational mobility: Social mobility that occurs when an individual's location in the social structure changes relative to his or her parents' location. (Chapter 4)

Internal attribution: Locating the cause of a behavior within the individual and his or her attributes, characteristics, or attitudes. (Chapter 12)

Internal control: Encouragement of conformity to social norms through guilt (and sometimes through shame). (Chapter 9)

Internal validity: A situation in which the independent variable is known to be the cause of the dependent variable. (Chapter 2)

Interrole conflict: A type of role strain that occurs when the roles (behavioral expectations) attached to two or more different statuses are in opposition to, or in conflict with, one another. (Chapter 4)

Interpretive approach: An approach to studying primary socialization that synthesizes elements of symbolic interactionism and Piaget's cognitive development model. (Chapter 6)

Interpretive reproduction: Creative productions within peer groups that reshape information from the larger (adult) society to fit the concerns of the peer group. (Chapter 6)

Intimacy: Feelings of closeness that emerge with the disclosure of highly personal information. (Chapter 11)

Intragenerational mobility: Social mobility (movement within the class structure) that occurs over the course of one's lifetime. (Chapter 4)

Intrarole conflict: A type of role strain that occurs when the roles (behavioral expectations) attached to a particular status are in opposition to, or in conflict with, one another. (Chapter 4)

Involvement: An aspect of the social bond that reflects the time and energy spent participating in conventional activities, such as sports, school clubs, studying, and youth groups. *See social control theory*. (Chapter 9)

Iowa/Indiana school of symbolic interactionism: A variant of symbolic interactionism that emphasizes social structure and its effect on the self-concept and behavior; also called structural symbolic interactionism. (Chapter 3)

James-Lange theory of emotion: A theory of emotion that links different types of physiological arousal to distinct emotions. (Chapter 8)

Jigsaw technique: An intervention used in elementary school classrooms to change the basis of in-group/out-group division from race/ethnicity to assigned task groups; students with information of equal value to the task at hand work toward a common goal in mixed-race or mixed-ethnicity task groups in order to facilitate the construction of a common task-group identity. (Chapter 12)

June bug epidemic: A well-known somatoform epidemic in which workers at a textile factory in a small Southern city reported symptoms including nausea, feeling faint, numbness in the extremities, and body rashes; despite widespread acceptance of the link between insects contained within a shipment of cloth from England and the symptoms affecting the individuals, no medical cause for the epidemic was ever found; thus, the epidemic was attributed to hysterical contagion. (Chapter 13)

Keynoting: Making suggestions as to how individuals in a crowd should respond to ambiguous situation. (Chapter 13)

Labeling theory: A symbolic interactionist perspective of deviance that focuses on the social and psychological consequences of being defined by others as deviant and the mechanisms through which the reactions of others facilitate the development of a deviant identity. (Chapter 9)

Laissez-faire racism: A term used to describe the mismatch in expressed racial attitudes (everyone is equal) and the lack of support for public policies that would lead to greater racial equality. (Chapter 12)

Laws: A type of social norm (rule or guideline for behavior) that is formally codified and enforced by the state through the criminal justice system. (Chapter 9)

Legends: Narratives presented as though they are to be believed although they may not be considered factual by either the audience or the storyteller. (Chapter 13)

"Liberal" racism: A subtle form of racism (e.g., symbolic racism, color-blind racism, and laissez-faire racism). (Chapter 12)

Life course perspective: A theoretical framework within social structure and personality that guides' researchers attention to role transitions and variations in social relationships across the age spectrum. (Chapter 4)

Life events: Discrete events that require adjustment on the part of individuals (e.g., marriage, death of a loved one); type of stressor. (Chapter 10)

Liminal status: A transitory status (between two developmental stages) in which individuals are separated from and perceived as distinct from the broader society and thus have more freedom from societal constraints. (Chapter 6)

Locus of self: The source of the experiences people view as indicative of a true or real self, institutions (social roles), or more spontaneous impulsive experiences. (Chapter 7)

Longitudinal data: Data collected by the researcher at two or more different points in time. (Chapter 2)

Looking-glass self: A term coined by Cooley to describe how our understanding of ourselves is shaped by the feedback we receive from others. (Chapter 7)

Love styles: Psychological orientations or approaches to love composed of sets of attitudes and beliefs about love and lead to particular types of romantic behavior; the six love styles are eros, mania, storage, pragma, agape, and ludus. (Chapter 11)

Ludus: A love style reflected in manipulation, dishonesty, a lack of intimacy, and a large number of sexual partners. (Chapter 11)

Macro-level analysis: An analysis focused on data collected on aggregate units such as groups, organizations, countries, cities, states, and large-scale social processes (e.g., industrialization). (Chapter 1)

Macro-level intervention: Interventions designed to reduce discrimination across social contexts by focusing on the level of social structure. (Chapter 12)

Maintenance stage: The third stage of relationships in which the relationship, once established, is maintained or continued over a period of time. (Chapter 11)

Major traumas: Events that are perceived as extremely disturbing (e.g., childhood sexual abuse) and often have long-term consequences for an individual; type of stressor. (Chapter 10)

Mania: A love style that reflects the obsessive component of passionate love that fluctuates between pain and ecstasy. (Chapter 11)

Mass hysteria: A form of collective behavior that occurs when people act in ways that are perceived by others within society to be unconventional, emotional, and irrational; includes panics and somatoform epidemics. (Chapter 13)

Master status: A status that overshadows all of the other statuses that an individual occupies in its effect on interaction and the self-concept. (Chapter 12)

Mastery: Refers to the degree to which individuals believe they have control over the forces that shape their lives. (Chapter 10)

Matching hypothesis: The tendency to consider individuals similar to oneself in physical attractiveness and other desirable characteristics as potential mates. (Chapter 11)

Material culture: Tangible objects created by humans (e.g., a house, clothes, television, makeup). (Chapter 6)

Me: According to Mead, the object phase of the self that allows for self-reflection and evaluation through the process of taking the role of the other or society in general. (Chapter 3)

Mean: The average of a set of numbers determined by adding up all of the scores and dividing by the total number of scores. (Chapter 2)

Mediating variable: A variable that occurs between an independent and dependent variable and explains why the variation in the independent variable results in variation in the dependent variable. Sometimes referred to as an intervening variable. (Chapter 4)

Medicalization: The process through which a behavior, set of behaviors, or perceptions is defined as a disease. (Chapter 10)

Medical model of mental illness: A model of mental illness that is based on the assumption that mental disorders are biologically based diseases. (Chapter 10)

Mere exposure effect: The process whereby repeated exposure to an individual results in familiarity and thus increased liking. (Chapter 11)

Meso level: The unit of analysis that exists in between the macro (social structure) and the micro level (individual). (Chapter 4)

Methodological empathy: Viewing the world through the eyes of those who are being studied and providing detailed accounts of how they interpret relationships, situations, and events. (Chapter 2)

Micro-level analysis: An analysis focused on data collected at the level of individuals. (Chapter 1)

Micro-level interventions: Interventions that focus on the reduction of negative racial (or other) attitudes or on the disruption of the micro-level social processes through which macro-level racial

(or other) inequalities are reproduced in specific group settings. (Chapter 12)

Microsociology: Sociological analyses with a micro-level unit of analysis, typically the individual. (Chapter 3)

`Minimal groups: The social identities formed through the process of self-categorization in laboratory experiments when a characteristic that distinguishes between groups that is usually considered insignificant is made salient. (Chapter 5)

Minority: A group that lacks access to important societal resources and thus is disadvantaged and toward the bottom of society's stratification hierarchy. (Chapter 12)

Modified labeling theory: A theory that focuses on how being diagnosed with a mental illness (receiving a formal label) affects individuals' self-concepts and social relationships; posits that stigma associated with mental illness within the larger society, and the fact that individuals with mental illness recognize and react to this stigma, often results in negative outcomes. (Chapter 10)

Mood: A chronic affective state that is typically less intense than an emotion. (Chapter 8)

Moral alchemy: The perceptual process through which the same behavior is seen as positive when it is exhibited by members of one group and negative when it is exhibited by members of another group (typically a group that is the target of prejudice and discrimination within society). (Chapter 12)

Morality: Ideas about what is good or right and bad or wrong. (Chapter 6)

Morality of caring: A style of moral reasoning that emphasizes the social consequences of action and situational factors when evaluating the morality of a course of action. (Chapter 6)

Morality of justice: A style of moral reasoning that involves the application of general rules and standards without regard for specific situational factors when evaluating the morality of a course of action. (Chapter 6)

Moral reasoning: The ability to determine right from wrong and to evaluate actions and their likely consequences. (Chapter 6)

Mores: A type of social norm that pertains to what people in a society perceive as serious matters (e.g., don't commit murder, don't commit incest, or don't engage in cannibalism). (Chapter 9)

Mortification of self: The death of, or eradication of, people's self-concepts that occurs when they are not able to receive verification for who they are from others in social interaction. (Chapter 10)

Motivated deviance: Situations in which (a) an individual can, but chooses not to, behave in accordance with prevailing group norms or (b) an individual belongs to a group with norms that others within society consider to be deviant. (Chapter 9)

Multiability interventions: Strategies used by status characteristic theorists to reduce bias in task groups. Group members are led to believe that no one will have all of the abilities necessary to excel at the task at hand, which disrupts the status generalization process. (Chapter 12)

n: A lowercase n is a symbol that is commonly used to denote the sample size, as in n = sample size. Note: A capital N is used to denote the size of a population. (Chapter 2)

Nature-nurture question: The question (debate) as to what extent individuals' attitudes, preferences, and behaviors are products of biological factors (e.g., genetics) or the social environment they experience (nurture). (Chapter 6)

Negative racial attitudes: Individual-level (or micro-level) prejudice; a negative attitude about a member of a group based on an overgeneralization without regard for individual variation within the group. (Chapter 12)

Negative relationship: Exists when increases in scores on one variable are associated with decreases on scores in another variable. (Chapter 2)

Negatively connected exchange network: An exchange network in which the exchange in one relation reduces exchanges in another. (Chapter 5)

Negotiated exchange: An exchange in which actors bargain over resources. (Chapter 5)

Negotiation stage: The second stage of relationships in which the individuals involved establish patterns of behaviors and expectations concerning the role each will play in the relationship. (Chapter 11)

Network-episode model (NEM): A model addressing the issue of psychiatric treatment, which argues that the characteristics of people's ties to others (e.g., number of people in their network) and beliefs about the effectiveness of mental health care shape individuals' treatment trajectories. (Chapter 10)

Network expansion: Increasing the size of your exchange network; a mechanism for increasing one's structurally based power. (Chapter 5)

New social movements: A form of social movement that emerges in postindustrial societies and emphasizes attitudes toward work, nature, and consumption that differ from traditional values in support of capitalism. (Chapter 13)

Noncoercive (or reward) power: The ability to impose one's will on another through the control of rewards. (Chapter 5)

Nonmaterial culture: Aspects of culture that we cannot see or touch, including values, beliefs, and knowledge. (Chapter 6)

Nonmutual alternatives: A state prior to the dissolution of a relationship in which one's partner becomes interested in someone else when one has no similar (competing) interest in an alternative partner. (Chapter 11)

Normative influence: A form of social influence that occurs when people's behaviors are shaped by others' expectations. (Chapter 13)

Occupational self-direction: A characteristic of occupations reflected in the complexity of the work, the level of supervision, and employees' ability to make decisions. (Chapter 4)

Operational definition: The specification of how a particular variable will be operationalized or measured (quantified) in a study. (Chapter 2)

Operationalization: The process of specifying how a particular variable will be measured. (Chapter 2)

Opportunity costs: In social exchange theory, the potential rewards that are lost when an actor chooses one exchange partner over others. (Chapter 5)

Out-group: A group we perceive ourselves as not belonging to. (Chapter 5)

Overt participant observation: A participant research study in which the researcher has identified him- or herself as a researcher to those being studied. (Chapter 2)

Panic: Unfounded and irrational beliefs that lead people to misperceive a situation as threatening and thus encourage them to quickly diverge from common interactional patterns in an attempt to save themselves and their property. (Chapter 13)

Participant observation: A qualitative method of gathering data that involves interacting with individuals and observing their behaviors in their natural environment. (Chapter 2)

Passing: Involves deliberately concealing or hiding a stigmatized characteristic and acting as a "normal" individual (someone who does not possess a stigmatized characteristic). (Chapter 9)

Passionate love: A form of love that is reflected in an intense longing for another person. (Chapter 11)

Path model: A figure that shows the direct and indirect effect of independent variables on a dependent variable. (Chapter 4)

Peer culture: A subculture characterized by shared activities, values, and concerns that emerge in children's face-to-face interactions and reflect, but rarely mimic, adult culture. (Chapter 6) contribute

Performance expectations: Assessments of one's own and other group members' likely contribution to the completion of a groups assigned task. *See expectations states theory.* (Chapter 5)

Personality: Within psychology, ways of perceiving and responding to the world that are stable across social settings. (Chapter 6); within the social structure and personality perspective, relatively stable psychological attributes, which include attitudes, values, beliefs, motives, perceptions, and feelings. (Chapter 4)

Personal relationships: Relationships defined by the interdependence that exists between the interaction partners; in such relationships, one person's behavior is shaped by the actions of the other person in the relationship. (Chapter 10)

Physical intimacy: Involves touching and sexual activity, as in the case of romantic relationships, especially marriage. (Chapter 11)

Play stage: The second stage in Mead's theory of the development of the self in which children learn to take the role of another person behaviorally by participating in role-playing activities. (Chapter 6)

Population: The entire set of individuals or cases (e.g., countries, schools, couples, etc.) to which a study is to be generalized. (Chapter 2)

Positive relationship: Exists when increases in scores on one variable are associated with increases in scores on another variable. (Chapter 2)

Postconventional morality: The third stage in Kohlberg's theory of moral development in which moral decisions are made based on the recognition of individual rights and conformity to shared understandings of standards and duties. (Chapter 6)

Postmodern: A label applied to late-stage capitalist societies, in which technologically mediated representations become reality; in such a society, identities are idiosyncratic and temporary and presumed to be rooted in consumption. (Chapter 7)

Power: The ability to impose one's will on another person. (Chapter 5)

Power and status theory of emotions: Kemper's theory that emphasizes the effects of power (authority) and status (prestige or honor) on people's emotive experiences; from this perspective, gains in power increase positive emotions, declines in power result in negative emotions, and the abuse of power gives rise to guilt. (Chapter 8)

Power-dependence relation: A social exchange relationship in which an actor's ability to secure desired rewards from other sources serves as a structural basis of power. (Chapter 5)

Pragma: A love style manifested as a "shopping around" approach to love. (Chapter 11)

Preconventional morality: The first stage in Kohlberg's theory of moral development in which decisions are made based on the desire to avoid punishment from someone in a position of authority. (Chapter 6)

Prejudice: A collective sentiment that emerges from the relationship between groups within society and the shared perception of superiority among members of the dominant group that transcends the feelings of any one individual. (Chapter 12)

Preparatory stage: The first stage in Mead's theory of the development of the self in which children recognize that there are other roles in society than their own and imitate the behaviors of significant others. (Chapter 6)

Primary deviance: Within labeling theory, behavior in violation of social norms that goes unnoticed (or unlabeled) by others and as a result has no long-term consequences for the individual. (Chapter 9)

Primary emotions: Emotions that occur in all humans and are presumed to be physiological in origin and physiologically distinct from one another. (Chapter 8)

Primary group: A small, relatively long-lasting group in which there is regular interaction and strong emotional ties among members. (Chapter 5)

Primary socialization: The acquisition of language and the learning of the core norms and values of society that occurs during childhood. (Chapter 6)

Primary stressor: Stressors that give rise to other (secondary) stressors. (Chapter 10)

Priming: Occurs when people are exposed to something that makes certain information more readily accessible in memory. (Chapter 5)

Principle of least interest: A principle that states that the individual with the greater ability to reward (or punish) another has the least to lose should the relationship end. (Chapter 5)

Private acceptance: A type of conformity in which both individuals' perceptions and behaviors reflect group norms. (Chapter 13)

Private self-consciousness: The tendency to be highly aware of one's internal states, including one's thoughts and emotions. (Chapter

Probabilistic: An effect that is likely but not guaranteed. (Chapter 4)

Propinquity: Physical proximity; an important factor in the initiation of most relationships. (Chapter 11)

Proportional representation: When the percentage of people from a particular racial/ethnic (or other group, e.g., gender) in a particular context matches the percentage of people from that group that live in the United States; a method for assessing racial fairness at the macro level. (Chapter 12)

Props: Objects used by individuals to convey a particular impression to others in a social interaction. *See dramaturgical approach.* (Chapter 3)

Proximity principle: Within the social structural and personality perspective, emphasis on identifying how the social structure affects individuals through their immediate social environment (meso level). (Chapter 4)

Psychological distress: The psychological manifestation of stress; feelings of depression, anxiety, or hostility that, although bothersome, are often not sever enough to result in a clinical diagnosis. (Chapter 4, Chapter 10)

Psychological social psychology (PSP): A social psychological perspective rooted within the discipline of psychology that focuses on the effect of the immediate situation on the perceptions, feelings, and behaviors of individuals. (Chapter 1)

Psychology: A social science that focuses on cognitive factors and social relationships at the micro level. (Chapter 1)

Psychology principle: Within the social structure a personality perspective, directs the researcher's attention to how macro-level structures (the components principle) are processed by individuals at the micro level. (Chapter 4)

Public compliance: A type of conformity that occurs when people adopt behaviors that match those of other group members but their actions don't necessarily reflect their perceptions. (Chapter 13)

Public opinion: Beliefs and attitudes constructed on a mass scale as people continually seek to define new situations, events, and issues. (Chapter 13)

Public self-consciousness: Individuals' tendency to focus on the self-evaluative nature of their public performances. (Chapter 3)

Punishment: A negative consequence (e.g., fines, withdrawal of affection) for a behavior or action. (Chapter 5)

Pygmalion effect: Occurs when an initial assessment that is false results in a shift in self-expectations and behavior that ultimately lead to its confirmation: a self-fulfilling prophecy. (Chapter 7)

Qualitative research: A method of data collection that relies on inductive reasoning and involves the observation and analysis of participants' social interactions in natural settings or the analysis of detailed personal accounts of participants' social experiences. (Chapter 2)

Quantitative research: A method of data collection that relies on deductive reasoning and involves testing theories through the collection of numerical (quantified) data. (Chapter 2)

Race: A group perceived as having distinct biological or genetic traits; socially constructed because group boundaries and their significance change with the societal and historical context. (Chapter 1)

Racial profiling: A police practice in which individuals are targeted based on their race or ethnicity. (Chapter 12)

Racism: Negative racial attitudes and discriminatory behaviors that are consistent with broader institutional patterns. (Chapter 12)

Random assignment: A procedure for assigning subjects to the groups of an experiment (levels of the independent variable) based on chance. (Chapter 2)

Random sampling: A procedure for selecting participants for a study from the population of interest in a random manner so that the study results will generalize to that population. (Chapter 2)

Range: The difference between the highest and lowest score on a measure; a measure of variability. (Chapter 2)

Real self: An authentic or core self that we believe represents our true nature. (Chapter 7)

Reciprocal exchange: An exchange that usually takes place over a lengthy period of time during which an individual assumes that favors or rewards will be returned but there is no guarantee that this will be the case. (Chapter 5)

Reconstruction principle: Within affect control theory, the idea that people redefine situations by altering the characteristics of people present in the encounter whenever deflections are too large to repair. (Chapter 8)

Reference group: A group that serves as a basis for comparison when evaluating our own characteristics and experiences. (Chapter 4)

Reflected appraisals: Our perceptions of how we believe others view us. (Chapter 7)

Relational bases of power: Power within relationships that is based in aspects of the relationship such as the relative love or liking (who loves their partner more) and an individual's opportunities for other relationships that are equally or more beneficial relative to those of the current partner. (Chapter 11)

Relative deprivation: Feelings of discontent or unfairness that result from the perception that one is less well-off than members one's reference group. (Chapter 4)

Reliability: When the findings from a study can be replicated or reproduced. (Chapter 2)

Reparations: A macro-level strategy that involves the admission by the U.S. government that it committed crimes against Blacks and restitution to the descendants of slaves.

Representative sample: A sample that is similar to and accurately reflects the characteristics of the population from which it was drawn. (Chapter 2)

Residual deviance: A catchall category of deviance that includes those behaviors that violate social norms for which we have no specified label. (Chapter 10)

Resocialization: The process through which people are reprogrammed with new values and norms following one or more serious transgressions. (Chapter 10)

Response rate: The percentage of individuals selected into a sample who actually participate in the study. (Chapter 2)

Retrospective labeling: When people reflect back on the past behaviors of an individual and interpret them in a manner that is consistent with the new (deviant) label. (Chapter 9)

Reward: A positive consequence (e.g., money, social acceptance) for a behavior or action. (Chapter 5)

Role: A set of normative expectations or rules about how one should behave, think, and feel that is attached to a status. (Chapter 1, Chapter 4)

Role modeling: Occurs when people acquire behaviors by observing others. (Chapter 6)

Role overload: A type of role strain in which an individual does not have enough time or resources to fulfill the role expectations associated with two or more statuses. (Chapter 4)

Role-person merger: When an identity is so entrenched within an individual's self-concept that he or she engages in role behaviors associated with that identity even when it is not appropriate to do so. (Chapter 7)

Role set: The various roles (behavioral expectations) that are attached to a particular status. (Chapter 4)

Role strain: Difficulties experienced when an individual is unable to meet his or her role obligations or fulfill the expectations associated with a status. (Chapter 4)

Role taking Involves viewing oneself as an object from the perspective of another individual, group, or society at large and planning patterns of action that meet the expectations of others and broader societal norms. Also called perspective taking. (Chapter 3, Chapter 6)

Role-taking propensity: The readiness with which people use their role-taking skills. (Chapter 6)

Role transition: When an individual either exits a role he or she has occupied for some time or enters a new role. (Chapter 6)

Romantic relationship: Dating relationships, marriage, and marriage-like relationships. (Chapter 11)

Rumors: A type of public opinion that is episodic and often pertains to broader and potentially more important issues than gossip. (Chapter 13)

Sample: A subset of a population from which data is collected. (Chapter 2)

Sapir-Whorf hypothesis: The idea that language shapes perception; also called the linguistic relativity hypothesis. (Chapter 6)

Saving face: Recovering from, or avoiding, public disgrace. (Chapter 3)

Scapegoating: When people misattribute their misfortunes to others, typically to members of groups that lack status and power within society. (Chapter 12)

Schizophrenia: A type of psychosis, meaning that the individual experiencing these symptoms has a break with reality. (Chapter 10)

Secondary data analysis: Survey data previously collected that is used and analyzed in a new (different) study. (Chapter 2)

Secondary deviance: Deviant behavior that occurs after a person has been labeled and is a response to the fact that the deviant label has been applied. (Chapter 9)

Secondary emotions: Socially constructed emotions that are acquired through the socialization process as people learn to pair physiological arousal that emerges in different situations with culturally defined labels. (Chapter 8)

Secondary group: A group in which members have few emotional ties with one another and interact to achieve a common goal or meet a common need. (Chapter 5)

Secondary socialization: The learning that occurs during adulthood and often builds upon what was learned in childhood. (Chapter 6)

Secondary stressors: Stressors caused by other stressors. (Chapter 10)

Self: According to Mead, the process of interaction between the "I" and the "me"; predominantly social in origin. (Chapter 3, Chapter 6)

Self-categorization theory: The cognitive dimension of social identity theory that focuses on the construction of group-based social identities. (Chapter 5)

Self-complexity: The number of domains of self that people have and the degree to which they overlap; an individual with a complex self-structure holds multiple self-domains with little overlap. (Chapter 10)

Self-concept: The characteristics, thoughts, and feelings people attribute to themselves; how you see yourself. (Chapter 3)

Self-directed orientation: A concept used within social structure and personality to refer to a person's sense of personal responsibility, trustfulness, and openness to change. (Chapter 4)

Self-enhancement: The desire for positive feedback from others so that one's self-image is maintained or improved; the motivation behind conscious and strategic impression management.

Self-esteem: An individual's overall, or global, positive or negative self-evaluation. (Chapter 7)

Self-fulfilling prophecy: A process in which an initial assessment or definition of a situation (whether correct or not) generates subsequent perceptions and behaviors that result in the confirmation of the initial assessment (i.e., it makes it come true). (Chapter 5)

Self-fulfilling prophecy at the societal level: The process by which societal beliefs and negative feelings about members of a particular group create a set of circumstances at the aggregate level that are then used (through faulty reasoning or logic) to justify the collective mind-set that created them. (Chapter 12)

Self-perception theory: A theory that states that people observe their own behaviors, much like they observe the behaviors of others, and assume that they hold attitudes that are consistent with their actions; the idea that people infer their attitudes from their behavior. (Chapter 12)

Self-presentation: How people act when they are around others; may be honest or deceptive (Chapter 7)

Self-schemata: Information stored in memory about one's personal attributes, which facilitates the processing of information of relevance to the self. (Chapter 7)

Self-verification: The desire to have one's identities or self-conceptions confirmed by others. (Chapter 7)

Sentiments: Socially constructed patterns of sensations, cultural meanings, and expressive gestures that pertain to a social object, most often another individual; includes love, loyalty, friendship, grief, patriotism, sorrow, and nostalgia. (Chapter 8)

Sex: Biological differences between men and women. (Chapter 1, Chapter 6)

Sexual double standard: The cultural belief that it is OK for men, but not for women, to have multiple sex partners. (Chapter 11)

Shame: An emotion that arises when an individual realizes that another individual, a group to which they belong, or society at large views him or her as deficient in some way. (Chapter 8

Significant other: A term used to refer to anyone important to a child, including parents, siblings, and peers. (Chapter 6)

Significant symbol: A gesture that brings out the same meaning in oneself as it does in others. (Chapter 3)

Significant ties: Network connections that are characterized by people's relationships that are less close, or intimate, than close ties but where individuals are more than acquaintances. (Chapter 11)

Situational definition: An individual's (or group's) perception or interpretation of a particular situation, event, or person. (Chapter 3)

Small groups: Groups of relatively small size characterized by three criteria: (1) physical proximity of members to one another, (2) perceived similarity among members, and (3) a shared fate among members. (Chapter 5)

Smart mob: Mass protests or marketing events organized using modern technologies for a political or economic purpose. (Chapter 13)

Snowball sampling: A nonrandom sampling technique in which participants for a study are selected by identifying individuals who meets the study criteria and then asking them to introduce the researcher to people they know, who then introduce them to people they know, and so forth. (Chapter 2)

Social class: A group that shares the same position within the stratification system. (Chapter 1)

Social constraint: A concept used by sociological social psychologists when talking about the effects of social norms on people's behaviors. (Chapter 13)

Social constraint: A term used by sociological social psychologists to refer to the effects of social norms on people's behaviors. (Chapter 13)

Social contagion: Occurs when attitudes, beliefs, or behaviors are transmitted from one group member to another. (Chapter 13)

Social cognition: The study of how individuals store, process, and retrieve information about themselves and others. (Chapter 4)

Social control theory: Theory that deviance occurs when an individual's bond to conventional society is weakened. (Chapter 9)

Social exchange theory: A theoretical framework within the group process and structure face of sociological social psychology that focuses on the exchange of resources and emphasizes power in social relationships. (Chapter 5)

Social facts: A term coined by sociologist Emile Durkheim to refer to collective properties of societies that are exterior to any one individual and constrain people's behavior by leading them to act or think in particular ways. (Chapter 1, Chapter 2)

Social identity: Within social identity theory, a cognitive construct constructed through a process of self-categorization (us vs. them) that reflects people's perceived group memberships. (Chapter 5)

Social identity theory: A theoretical framework within the group process and structure orientation that emphasizes the ways that our identification with groups affects how we view ourselves and others. (Chapter 5)

Social influence: When people's perceptions and behaviors are shaped by others. (Chapter 13)

Social institution: A cluster of patterned status-role relationships that have developed over time to meet basic societal needs. Some examples of social institutions include the family, the economy, and schools. (Chapter 4)

Socialization: The process through which people develop the ability to communicate through language and gain an understanding of their culture, including social values, norms, and the knowledge and skills required for participation in society. (Chapter 6)

Social learning theory: A theory within psychological social psychology that emphasizes the effects of patterns of reinforcement (reward) and punishment on people's acquisition of behaviors, beliefs, and attitudes. (Chapter 6)

Socially based identity: An internalized status; also called an identity (vs. a social identity). (Chapter 7)

Social movement: A collectivity of individuals acting together to promote or resist change within the group or society to which they belong. (Chapter 13)

Social movement organizations: Grassroots, regional, or national organizations that focus on attaining the goals of a social movement. (Chapter 13)

Social network: The links or connections that exist between individuals and among groups. (Chapter 4)

Social norms: Shared rules and expectations for social behavior within a specific context. (Chapter 1)

Social psychology: A field of study that bridges the disciplines of psychology and sociology and focuses on the impact of the social context and groups on the perceptions, feelings, and behaviors of individuals. (Chapter 1)

Social stratification: A system of ranking groups in a hierarchy from low to high based on their access to and possession of important societal resources, including money, power, and prestige. (Chapter 1)

Social structure and personality (SSP): A research orientation in sociological social psychology that focuses on the effects of society on individuals' perceptions and behaviors. (Chapter 1)

Social support: A coping resource that is rooted in peoples' ties to others and includes information received from others that leads them to believe they are "esteemed and valued" and "cared for and loved." (Chapter 10)

Socioeconomic status (SES): A measure of an individual's position in the stratification system as reflected by education, occupational prestige, and income. (Chapter 1)

Sociological perspective: A way of viewing the world that places people's experiences within the larger social and historical context. (Chapter 1)

Sociological social psychology: A subfield of sociology that focuses on how the social context in which social interaction occurs influences individuals' thoughts, feelings, and behavior. (Chapter 1)

Sociology: A social science that focuses on the study of society. (Chapter 1)

Socioemotive behavior: The ways that individuals express emotions within groups; includes both positive (e.g., acting friendly) and negative (e.g., disagreeing with someone) behaviors. (Chapter 8)

Somatoform epidemic: A form of mass hysteria in which a group of individuals exhibit physical symptoms that are social and psychological, rather than physical, in origin. (Chapter 13)

Specific status characteristics: Attributes and abilities relevant to specific tasks that affect performance expectations in task groups. *See status characteristics theory.* (Chapter 5)

Spurious relationship: A relationship between two variables that is the result of variation in a third variable. (Chapter 2)

Standard deviation: A statistical measure of variation that indicates the average deviation of a score from the mean (average) in a distribution of scores. (Chapter 2)

Status: A recognized social position within society. (Chapter 1, Chapter 4)

Status beliefs: Sets of assumptions about a particular group within society relative to another (e.g., men vs. women); the hierarchical component of stereotypes. (Chapter 5)

Status characteristics: Attributes such as race, ethnicity, and gender, which are associated with societal beliefs about worthiness and competence and thus affect the way people are perceived and treated. *See diffuse status characteristics* (Chapter 1, Chapter 5)

Status characteristics theory (SCT): A subtheory within the expectations states tradition that explains how beliefs about the relative competence of groups within society (e.g., men and women; Whites and racial/ethnic minorities) influence the creation and maintenance of status structures (stratification) within task-oriented groups. (Chapter 5)

Status generalization: The process through which diffuse status characteristics are associated with task-relevant abilities and thus influence performance expectations and subsequent behaviors in group settings. *See status characteristics theory.* (Chapter 5)

Status structures: The hierarchy within a group, based on *subjective rankings of group* members given their perceived likelihood of moving the group toward the successful completion of its goals. *See expectations states theory.* (Chapter 5)

Status violation theory: An expansion of status characteristics theory that focuses on how members of task-oriented groups respond to behaviors deemed inappropriate given an actor's status characteristics. (Chapter 9)

Stereotype: An unfounded belief about members of a particular group that is believed to make them distinct from other groups within society. (Chapter 5)

Stereotype threat: The recognition on the part of individuals that anything they do has the potential to confirm a negative stereotype about their group. (Chapter 12)

Stigma: A trait or characteristic that causes one to lose prestige and social status in the eyes of others. (Chapter 9)

Storage: A love style that is reflected in a companionate or "best friends" approach to love. (Chapter 11)

Strain theory: A theory linking a disjuncture between societal goals and the legitimate means of attaining these ends to strain that is presumed to result in deviance and crime. (Chapter 9)

Stress: The body's reaction to threatening situations and events; a biological state. (Chapter 10)

Stress proliferation: When something bad happens (a primary stressor) and this leads to one or more other (secondary) stressors. (Chapter 10)

Stressors: External conditions that cause stress. (Chapter 10)

Structural basis of power: Power within relationships that is based in or reflects patterns of inequality at the macro (or societal) level. The two structural bases of power in romantic relationships are gender and socioeconomic resources (education, occupational standing, and personal earnings). (Chapter 11)

Structural role theory: A theoretical perspective that explains the impact of social structure on individuals in terms of the role expectations that are attached to the statuses they occupy. (Chapter 4)

Structural symbolic interactionism: Another name for Iowa/Indiana school symbolic interactionism, given its focus on the effects of the structure of society on the self-concept. (Chapter 1)

Subculture: A group of individuals with values and norms that differ from those of the mainstream or dominant culture. (Chapter 2

Superego: Within Freud's theory of personality, a person's conscience; a reflection of parental or societal values and norms. (Chapter 6)

Surface acting: A form of emotion management that involves displaying emotions in a manner that is socially appropriate for the social setting. (Chapter 8)

Survey: A quantitative method of data collection in which information is gathered from individuals through their responses to a fixed set of questions asked in a predetermined order. (Chapter 2)

Symbolic interactionism (SI): An orientation in sociological social psychology that emphasizes the ways in which meanings are negotiated and constructed through face-to-face interactions at the micro level. (Chapter 1)

Symbolic racism: The belief that Blacks' disadvantaged status within society stems from internal dispositions (e.g., an unwillingness to take responsibility for their lives) rather than from structural inequalities. (Chapter 12)

Sympathy: A role-taking emotion that involves empathy and sharing in the feelings of another individual. (Chapter 8)

Sympathy margin: An account that accrues credits and debits as a function of the merit of an individual's claim to sympathy in the eyes of others. (Chapter 8)

Techniques of neutralization: Accounts or explanations for behavior designed to neutralize the negative affect associated with violating social norms. (Chapter 9)

Theoretical framework: A broad perspective or viewpoint based on a set of assumptions about how the world works; frameworks provide researchers with a set of concepts and specify how these are related. (Chapter 3)

Theory: A set of interrelated cause-and-effect statements about the way societies operate and influence behavior that can be tested. (Chapter 2)

Token: A person who is a numerical minority. (Chapter 12)

Tokenism: The fact that being a numerical minority draws attention to one's race (or gender) and is likely to make the individual's race/ethnicity (or gender) identity salient to themselves, as well as others. (Chapter 12)

Total institution: An agent of resocialization in which individuals are separated from the larger society and attempts are made to alter their behaviors through a process of retraining or reprogramming. (Chapter 10)

Tracking: The placement of students into different classes or courses of study based on their perceived ability. (Chapter 4)

"Traditional" racism: Overt racism involving racial slurs and blatant discrimination. (Chapter 12)

Transient impressions: Within affect control theory, the affective meanings that are tied to specific events or situations. (Chapter 8)

Triad: A three-person group. (Chapter 5)

Triangulation: The use of multiple methods to validate study findings. (Chapter 2)

Trust: When people believe that another person or group will act in their interest, either because they have an incentive to do so, or because they care about them. (Chapter 5)

Two-factor theory of emotion: A theory of emotion that states that emotions have two components: physiological arousal and a cognitive label. (Chapter 8)

Unbalanced relation: An exchange relation in which one individual has more power than the other due to the possession of valued rewards and the presence of other exchange options. (Chapter 5)

Unit of analysis: What is being studied (e.g., individuals, groups, societies). (Chapter 1)

Unmotivated deviance: A violation of social norms that occurs when people recognize that an individual is failing to meet others' expectations because he or she is unable to do so. (Chapter 9)

Urban legend: A legend that focuses on institutions and behaviors that are part of life in urban areas. (Chapter 13)

Validity: The accuracy of findings from a study. (Chapter 2)

Value-added theory: An early theory of social movements that posits that people are likely to engage in social movements and other forms of collective behavior when certain societal conditions exist; the necessary conditions for collective behavior are hierarchical in that particular conditions emerge only when other condition exist. (Chapter 13)

Variable: Something that can take on different attributes (or vary). (Chapter 2)

Vicarious, or indirect, reinforcement and punishment: Occurs when someone observes another individual being rewarded or punished for engaging in a particular behavior and that experience shapes their own behavior. (Chapter 6)

White-collar crime: Crimes committed by people of relatively high status at work. (Chapter 9)

White racial frame: A frame composed of negative stereotypes of racial/ethnic minorities, especially African Americans; cultural narratives extolling White virtues such as hard work, achievement, superiority, and conquest; visual imagery (notions or racial/ethnic differences in appearances and accents); and emotions (negative feelings, e.g., fear). (Chapter 12)

Wisconsin model of status attainment: A model developed by researchers at the University of Wisconsin that identifies the social psychological processes through which parents' social class influences individuals' education and occupational achievement. (Chapter 4)

INDEX

accounts: in ethnomethodology 90

activism, high-risk 463

adolescents: and internet relationships 379–80; research on work experience of 11–15; self-esteem in 220; treatment of for mental illness 336–7

adrenalin 247

adulthood, emerging 206–7, 209

affect 212–19, 244

affect control theory (ACT) 262–4

affirmative action 403, 405, 426–7

African Americans: attitudes on racism of 410–11; attitudes toward 400–2; as college professors 102; cultural stereotypes of 394; discrimination against 391–2, 394, 397, 398–402 (*see also* racism); disproportionate representation in prison population 398; divorce rate of 373; generational differences in beliefs about racial inequality 410–12; MEIM score of 416; as a minority 389; in mixed marriages 373; and passing 299; portrayal on television 413; and PTSD 324, 325; self-esteem in 215; and the stratification hierarchy 410; and teenage employment 13–14; and the White racial frame 410

age cohort *see* cohort

agency 7; vs. structure in symbolic interactionism 93, 98; vs. structure in group processes and structures 167; vs. structure in social structure and personality 112–13

agents of socialization 176

Agnew, Robert 286–7

Akers, Ronald 291

Albas, Cheryl 87

Albas, Daniel 87

alcohol, and arousal 349; *see also* substance abuse

alienation 119–20

altercasting 368–9

American = White bias 399

American Sociological Association Code of Ethics 59

American Soldier, The (Stouffer et al.) 104

Andes flight disaster (1972) 73–4, 443

animals, communication and cognition in 69–70

Annie's Mailbox 3–4

anomie 284, 286

anticipatory socialization 204

Anti-Drug Abuse act (1986) 391

antioppression counter-frame 410

appeal to higher loyalties 303

Arab Spring (2011) 463

arousal: alcohol and attraction 349; misattribution of and passionate love 348–9; in boys peer groups 354

Asch, Solomon 436–7

Asian Americans: as college professors 102; divorce rate of 373; MEIM score of 416; portrayal on television 413

attachment (social control theory) 287

attention-deficit/hyperactivity disorder (ADHD) 327–8

attitudes, implicit and explicit 400; negative racial 391

autonomy 120

back region 85

balanced relation 152–3

Bandura, Albert 178

Becker, Howard S. 65–6, 79, 80, 84, 288–9

behavior: and identity 222–4; and self-concept 219–28; and self-esteem 219–20; self-regulation of 255–9, 272

behaviorist psychology 151

belief (social control theory) 287

Berger, Joseph 144–50

Besen, Yasmine 11–12, 49–52, 54, 66

best friends 354; *see also* friendship

biased samples 35

binge drinking 206–7, 209; *see also* substance abuse

Blacks *see* African Americans

Blumer, Herbert 72

Bohemian Grove and Other Retreats: A Study in Ruling Class Cohesiveness (Domhoff) 364

Botox 245–6

breaching experiments 90–2

breaking up, relationships 372–3

Brief Symptom Inventory (BSI) 313–14

buffering effect 316

Burke, Peter 222–4, 261–2

bystander effect 9–10